James Clarence Mangan

Selected Writings

Edited with an introduction
by SEAN RYDER

UNIVERSITY COLLEGE DUBLIN PRESS
PREAS CHOLÁISTE OLLSCOILE
BHAILE ÁTHA CLIATH

In memory of Evelyn Leamy

For ever, for ever, you have my heart,
O, Elleen a-Ruin!

First published 2004
by University College Dublin Press
Newman House
86 St Stephen's Green
Dublin 2, Ireland

www.ucdpress.ie

Introduction and notes © Sean Ryder 2004

ISBN 1 904558 09 7 hb
ISBN 1 900621 92 4 pb

CIP data available from the British Library

Typeset in Ireland
in Adobe Caslon and Walbaum Book
by Elaine Shiels, Bantry, County Cork
Text design by Lyn Davies
Printed in England on acid-free paper
by MPG Books Ltd, Bodmin, Cornwall

Contents

PROSE

Acknowledgements

I am very grateful to the following individuals, who in different ways have helped bring this edition to completion: Adrienne Anifant, Kevin Barry, Tadhg Foley, James McCabe, J.C.C. Mays and especially Áine Ní Léime. Michael, Tristan, Rebecca and Éanna deserve thanks for being patient and impatient at appropriate moments.

Many thanks are also due to the remarkable patience and support of Barbara Mennell at UCD Press. The staff of the James Hardiman Library of NUI, Galway, the National Library of Ireland, the Royal Irish Academy and the British Library have all been most helpful.

The edition would not have been possible without the financial support provided by the following: the Irish Research Council for the Humanities and Social Sciences; the Millennium Research Fund of NUI, Galway; the travel bursary scheme of the Royal Irish Academy; and the publication funds of the National University of Ireland and of NUI, Galway.

SEAN RYDER
Galway, January 2004

Introduction

I

James Clarence Mangan was born in Dublin just before Robert Emmet's failed rebellion in 1803, and died in destitution in 1849, as the Great Famine drew to a close. It is tempting to link Mangan's life and work with such events, as John Mitchel did when he decided that Mangan's 'history and fate were indeed a type and shadow of the land he loved so well . . . Like Ireland's, his light flickered upward for a moment, and went out in the blackness of darkness.'[1] Accounts of Mangan's impoverishment, his reclusive behaviour, his addiction to alcohol (and perhaps opium), combined with the darkness of late poems like 'The Nameless One', have encouraged readers to see Mangan as the epitome of pathos, and a mirror of the degraded colonial condition of nineteenth-century Ireland itself. In a similar but less political spirit, some critics have labelled Mangan Ireland's *'poète maudit'*, chronically alienated not just from inhospitable Irish conditions but also from society in general.[2]

But there are other Mangans too, whose identities are as varied as the poet's many *noms-de-plume*: Mr James Mangan; M.; J. M.; J. C. M.; C.; C. M.; B. A. M.; Z.; Clarence; Drechsler; Selber; Terrae Filius; Hi-Hum; Whang-Hum; Mark Anthony; Vacuus; The Man in the Cloak; The Out-and Outer; Peter Puff Secundus; Monos; A Yankee; Lageniensis; A Mourne-r; Herr Hoppandgoön Baugtrauter; Herr Popandgoön Tutchemupp; Solomon Dryasdust; Dr Berri Abel Hummer; and, appropriately for a man who seems never to have travelled more than a few miles from Dublin—'A Constant Reader, Clarence-street, Liverpool'. Mangan's pseudonyms even included the names of many real poets, especially Turkish and Persian ones, whom he credits with the authorship of poems that are actually his own; or, as he claimed in the case of the Persian poet Hafiz, at least '*Half-his*'.[3] Similarly, a survey of Mangan's work reveals an astonishing range of styles, genres and subject-matter. Mangan could turn in a controlled and convincing performance in bardic mode, as in his majestic 'Elegy on the

1 John Mitchel, *Poems by James Clarence Mangan*, ed. John Mitchel (New York: Haverty, 1859), 15.
2 See, for example, Anthony Cronin in the foreword to *Selected Poems of James Clarence Mangan*, ed. Michael Smith (Dublin: Gallery, 1974), 11.
3 See p. 411, below.

Tironian and Tirconnellian Princes', but he could also supply ingenious doggerel and jingles that rivalled Fr Prout. He could write chilling accounts of psychic disintegration, as in 'Moreen: a Love-Lament', but also wistful, reflective medi-tations, as in 'Twenty Golden Years Ago'. His Gothic fantasies rival Poe's. He is equally accomplished at orientalist extravaganzas, sonnets, epigrams, marches, anthems and imitation *aisling*s. In a poem like 'Eighteen Hundred Fifty' he is not content merely to create a fake translation from a non-existent German poet, but feels compelled to provide it with crazed annotations by a humourless imaginary German scholar as well. He could never resist a pun, however painful, and his manic wordplay in a letter like one to Gavan Duffy reprinted in this edition foreshadows the linguistic hyperactivity of *Finnegans Wake*.[4]

The material details behind this remarkable imaginative life are known only through scattered and sketchy records. Mangan was born into the Dublin Catholic petit-bourgeoisie. His mother, Catherine Smith, had come from a family of 'strong farmers' in Co. Meath, with business interests in Dublin. When, in 1798, she married James Mangan, a hedge schoolmaster from Co. Limerick, she was running one of her family's businesses, a grocery at 3 Fishamble Steet, near Christchurch. The young James (the name 'Clarence' was a pen-name adopted much later) was educated in Jesuit schools in the Liberties of Dublin, where he learned classics, mathematics, French, Italian and Spanish. The grocery trade was successful enough that James Mangan senior began to speculate in property, with apparently catastrophic results: John McCall vividly paints a picture of the poet's father, 'addicted to pomp and show, . . . in the habit of giving costly balls and parties, and when he had not room enough in his own house to entertain his numerous guests he often invited them to hotels in the city, or to pic-nics on the green sward of county Wicklow. In consequence of this extravagance, as may be foreseen, he very soon ran through most of his worldly effects.'[5] The family's financial decline seems to have necessitated several changes of address, and in 1818 led to the 15-year-old poet being apprenticed to a scrivener. Mangan thereafter became the chief breadwinner for his mother, his improvi-dent father, his two younger brothers and (perhaps) a sister. He appears to have continued supporting his parents until their deaths in the 1840s. The career of professional copyist was one that Mangan found demeaning and soul-destroying, but it was his main occupation for most of the rest of his life—he worked as a legal scrivener until 1838, then as a copyist for the Ordnance Survey until 1843, then as a cataloguer for the Trinity College Library until 1846. The poet's last three or four years were desperate and unsettled; he lived mainly from his writing and from the generosity of friends. He cultivated an eccentric appearance: Charles

4   See pp. 439–41, below.
5   John McCall, *Life of James Clarence Mangan* (Dublin: T. D. Sullivan, [1883]), 4.

Gavan Duffy remembered him 'dressed in a blue cloak (mid-summer or mid-winter), and a hat of fantastic shape, under which golden hair as fine and as silky as a woman's hung in unkempt tangles, and deep blue eyes lighted a face as colourless as parchment'.[6] Sometimes this attire was supplemented by two voluminous umbrellas and green goggles. For the most part he seems to have avoided close personal relationships. Little is known of his romantic life. He told Gavan Duffy that he had made a proposal of marriage to a Margaret Stackpoole in 1834, but that she had rejected him. Respectable friends like Duffy, John O'Donovan and Fr C. P. Meehan viewed Mangan with a combination of sympathy, frustration and distaste as he delivered his poems for immediate payment, or borrowed money, then disappeared into the world of 'tap-rooms and low public houses'.[7] Mangan's final years saw him producing some of his most powerful work, even though he was living in alcoholic squalor with an equally dysfunctional brother. In May 1849 Mangan was admitted to the cholera sheds at Kilmainham. Shortly after his release he was found by friends in a destitute state and brought to the Meath Hospital, where he died on 20 June 1849. Although Mangan had become a well-known figure in Dublin literary circles, no more than five people attended his funeral at Glasnevin.

II

Assessing Mangan's literary achievement means reckoning with a writing career that spanned over thirty years. In that period he produced, astonishingly, nearly a thousand poems as well as critical prose, short fiction and a brief autobiography. His earliest published works were faddish puzzle poems that he contributed to popular Dublin almanacs between 1818 to 1826. By the early 1830s, he had become associated with the writers of the iconoclastic Comet Club, contributing playful poems and prose pieces to the liberal *Comet* newspaper and the *Dublin Satirist*. In the early 1830s also he made the acquaintance of scholars like John O'Donovan, George Petrie and Owen Connellan, who were to inspire his interest in Irish-language material and supply him with raw translations to versify. Sometime in the 1820s or early 1830s he learned or taught himself enough German to translate some of the great German romantic poets, including Goethe, Schiller and Rückert. From 1834 to 1846 he published 22 lengthy articles containing translations of German poetry in the liberal unionist *Dublin University Magazine*. It was mainly these 'Anthologia Germanica' articles, along with a series of Turkish, Persian and Arabian translations entitled 'Literae Orientales', that brought him

6   Charles Gavan Duffy, *Young Ireland: A Fragment of Irish History 1840–1845* (Dublin: Gill, 1884), 109–10.
7   John Keegan's phrase, quoted in D. J. O'Donoghue, *The Life and Writings of James Clarence Mangan* (Edinburgh: Geddes; Dublin: Gill, 1897), 178.

to the attention of Samuel Ferguson, William Carleton, Charles Lever, John Anster and others of the Dublin literary elite. Mangan's oriental translations were in fact derived from pre-existing German and French translations, although many were not actually translations but inventions of his own. He did translate Italian and Spanish poetry from the original, but certainly not the Serbian, Polish, Chinese, 'Hindostanee', 'Chippewawian', 'Tartarian' or several other languages that he claimed to translate for the *DUM*. From 1846 to 1849 Mangan published his poems chiefly in nationalist newspapers, with some contributions to James Duffy's *Irish Catholic Magazine*. Since 1836 he had been a friend of Charles Gavan Duffy, co-founder of the *Nation*, and in his last years he became close to John Mitchel and Joseph Brenan, who published him in the radical *United Irishman* and *Irishman* papers. It was these years that produced his most famous and oft-anthologised poems like 'Dark Rosaleen', 'A Vision of Connaught in the Thirteenth Century', and 'The Nameless One'. The late 1840s also saw Mangan working as a versifier for the scholar and publisher John O'Daly, turning O'Daly's literal translations of Munster poetry into English verse, often at impromptu sessions across the counter of O'Daly's shop in Anglesea Street.

From the 1830s on, Mangan was essentially a professional poet, and his writing habits were always conditioned by financial need, practical opportunity, and his difficult domestic circumstances. He appears to have written a great deal in public houses, where he was able to get ink and paper for free; we also know from his correspondence that he sometimes composed in libraries and that he wrote with great speed and little revision. A fellow employee at the Ordnance Survey in the late 1830s remembered Mangan composing his famous Irish translation 'Woman of the Three Cows' in half an hour in the Survey's back office. In 1847 the poet told Gavan Duffy he normally translated at a rate of 80 lines a day (for which he would have earned nearly £1).[8]

Mangan's reputation as a major figure was established even during his lifetime. When John Mitchel first spotted him perched on a ladder in Trinity College Library in 1845, he was already famous enough that Mitchel's companion identified the poet with a certain hushed respect. Not all his contemporaries felt he deserved the reputation he had acquired by the 1840s. The poet John Keegan regarded him as 'a madman and a drunkard and without a spark of religion',[9] while John de Jean Frazer remarked 'For the life of me I cannot see where is Mangan's merit at all.'[10] However, editions of Mangan's poetry by Mitchel and C. P. Meehan kept Mangan in print throughout the late nineteenth century, and

---

8   *Collected Works of James Clarence Mangan*, ed. Jacques Chuto et al. (Dublin and Portland, Or.: Irish Academic Press, 1996–2002), VI, 270, 263.
9   Quoted in O'Donoghue, 177.
10 Ibid., 177.

Yeats's championing of Mangan as one of his poetic forefathers helped secure his reputation as a canonical figure.

In some ways Yeats's and Joyce's views of Mangan reveal more about the two great modernists than they do about Mangan. Yeats's opinions of the poet fluctuated according to his own changing preoccupations. As a young aspiring nationalist, Yeats described Mangan as a model to be emulated. Later, disillusioned with that literary heritage, he wrote more critically of Mangan's poetic immaturity: 'He had not thought out or felt out a way of looking at the world peculiar to himself.'[11] Later again, in the *Autobiographies*, where he claims personal responsibility for preserving the memory of the best nineteenth-century Irish writers, including Mangan, he is willing to praise Mangan as 'our one poet raised to the first rank by intensity'.[12] Joyce's views of Mangan are also determined by his own literary ambitions and anxieties. Although admiring of Mangan's technical skills—'one of the most inspired singers that ever used the lyric form in any country'—Joyce also argued that Mangan was 'the type of his race', a position that inevitably inhibited his artistic freedom. Joyce ultimately sees Mangan as a victim of oppressive conditions in a way that leaves him twisted and stultified— a 'feeble' figure in whom 'a hysteric nationalism receives its final justification'.[13] He becomes, in fact, an image of the writer Joyce was determined not to become.

In spite of this, Mangan is much closer to Joyce than the latter seems to have acknowledged. Mangan's work is littered with Joycean neologisms, for instance, from simple compounds like 'verysad' (from 'The Wail and the Warning of the Three Khalenders') to more spectacular efforts like 'transmagnificanbandancial' (which was almostly certainly the source of Joyce's neologism 'contransmagnificandjewbangtantiality' in *Ulysses*).[14] So too, there are shared forms of political attitude. The cosmopolitanism in a late poem like 'Consolation and Counsel' is closer to the spirit of Stephen Dedelus than it is to the 'hysteric nationalism' Joyce associates with Mangan:

My countrymen! you have much to learn and see;
You have yet to know yourselves, and what you are,
And what you are *not*, and cannot hope to be,
    Till Fate shall break the severing bar
That insulates you now from Europe's Mind

11 W. B. Yeats, *Letters*, ed. Allan Wade (London: Rupert Hart-Davis, 1954), 447.

12 W. B. Yeats, *Autobiographies* (London: Macmillan, 1959), 396.

13 James Joyce, *Occasional, Critical and Political Writing*, ed. Kevin Barry (Oxford: Oxford University Press, 2000), 136.

14 See p. 456, below.

In fact, of all subsequent Irish writers, it is perhaps the novelist Flann O'Brien who echoes Mangan most thoroughly, although there is no clear evidence of conscious influence. Both are writers who make a virtue of the absurd, both are masters of erudite parody, and both have an unnerving tendency to slide almost instantly from hilarity to chilling blackness. A Mangan text like 'An Extraordinary Adventure in the Shades' invites the reader into an O'Brienesque state of hallucination that is at once comic and disturbing, a vista of psychological disintegration beneath a humorous veneer. And what other writer, apart from Flann O'Brien, might imagine a world in which the great philosopher Socrates is to be found wandering through the Athenian marketplace 'whistling *Planxty Kelly*, with variations'?[15]

III

Mangan is in many ways the antithesis of the romantic poet, at least in its Wordsworthian guise. For one thing, lacking the luxury of leisure time, and experiencing little tranquillity in which to recollect emotion, Mangan wrote always for financial gain, and he wrote rapidly and opportunistically. This is not to say that his poetry is mere hack work. In one of his critical commentaries, Mangan puts forward a view of artistic responsibility that demands nothing less than a 'heroic tone, that elevation of spirit, without which Poetry is but a name, and its life nothing better than mere artificiality and appearance'.[16] Poetry, in other words, has a deep moral purpose, one that has little to do with personal expression or mere craft. It is a reader-centred aesthetic, in which the power of the poem to 'elevate the spirit' of the reader is paramount, rather than the poem's origin, its novelty, or the sincerity of its author. 'We should never judge of authors from their works', Mangan reminds us.[17] In fact it is because of this principle that Mangan's autobiography reads more like a parable than a biographical narrative— he himself imagined the work to be primarily a 'warning to the uneducated votary of Vice' rather than a piece of detailed self-revelation.

Such a utilitarian aesthetic allows the poet to assume a range of voices and personae, on the basis that whatever style achieves the required effect is the appropriate one. The *Dublin Review* in 1845 was right to call him 'a complete literary Proteus', his poetry becoming 'pious and didactic with Hölty or Klopstock— humorous and burlesque with Dunkel—it plunges into the depths of mysticism with de la Motte Fouqué—and laughs with the world with Kotzebue or Bürger'.[18]

15   See p. 100, below.
16   See p. 238, below.
17   *Dublin University Magazine* (April 1839), 494.
18   *Dublin Review* (December 1845), 313.

Inspiration comes not in a 'spontaneous overflow' from his own imagination, but as an imitative reaction to the poetry of others. Creative imitation, or translation, is just one symptom of a very fundamental aspect of Mangan's practice, that is, his attraction to pre-existing literary structures or rules from which to work. From the beginning, Mangan seems to have relished the challenge posed by technical constraints, whether those constraints were generic conventions, elaborate rhythms or strict rhyming schemes. His juvenile puzzle poems show this appetite for rules, as does the early poem 'To the Memory of the Late Lamented Mr. John Kenchinow, Butcher, of Patrick Street' where, to win a bet, Mangan succeeded in writing a 60-line poem in which every line rhymed with either 'Kenchinow' or his 'stall'. Later in his career he produced astonishing studies in sound and rhythm by using long lines and complicated rhyming patterns, as in his version of Rückert's 'The Ride round the Parapet' or in his vivid 'O'Hussey's Ode to the Maguire'. A curiosity piece like 'A Railway of Rhyme' shows Mangan's fascination with form extending even to typography. One positive result of this practice is that there is hardly a poet in English with the mastery of so many styles, and what Mangan's *œuvre* lacks in consistency and coherence of voice, it perhaps compensates for in technical virtuosity. In fact this virtuosity in some ways becomes a signature of its own. The Young Irelander John O'Hagan, noting the difference between Mangan's quirky genius and that of other poets who attempted similar verbal tricks, remarked that it was 'a great mistake in trying to ride Mangan's phooca. In the original himself there is a curious felicity which prevent us from being annoyed at his forced rhymes, but in any one else it does not do at all.'[19]

Thus Mangan's use of multiple masks and styles follows logically from his aesthetic principles, and is not solely a result of eccentricity or insecurity. It is not merely a regrettable failure of taste, or discipline, or lack of artistic stimulation, as critics have sometimes argued. Many of Mangan's contemporaries used pseudonyms; in fact it was practically the norm for poets publishing in Irish periodicals. The difference is that no one—except perhaps Mangan's contemporary Fr Prout, who published what he insisted were the Latin 'originals' of *Moore's Melodies*—fully understood and exploited the radical aesthetic possibilities of pseudonymity. Mangan's determination to test the limits of authorial deception led him to invent poets and poems just so that he could appear to be translating them, a process he himself calls 'the antithesis of plagiarism'.[20] In fact this refusal to be 'authentic' in the conventional sense makes the poet seem unexpectedly contemporary, almost a prototype of the postmodern writer, who has recognised the intertextuality of all writing, knows that the illusion of the 'author-god' is

---

19 Charles Gavan Duffy, *My Life in Two Hemispheres* (London: Fisher Unwin, 1898), II, 138.
20 See p. 413, below.

dead, and understands that literary sincerity is a rhetorical effect. Like a good postmodernist, Mangan aims to demonstrate that the derivative and the creative are not mutually exclusive.

David Lloyd gives a useful political gloss to this phenomenon, seeing in Mangan's evasions of identity a resistance to the ideology of Irish bourgeois nationalism. Such an ideology demands that individuals submerge their identities into the collective self of the Irish nation. The true poet is one whose voice is assimilated to the authentic 'national voice'—a demand that cannot be easily reconciled with Mangan's waywardness, either at the level of his writing or his life. Nor did Mangan find it easy to share in the kind of bourgeois earnestness that accompanied this nationalist discourse in the 1840s (hence perhaps his curious silence about Thomas Davis, the most earnest of them all). In his plurality and opacity, and his refusal to be representative of anything other than his own idiosyncratic self, Mangan actually poses a potential threat to bourgeois nationalism. That did not, ironically, prevent Irish nationalists from claiming Mangan as one of their own right through the nineteenth century, largely on the basis of three or four poems that seemed to embody the national spirit. Nor is this to say that nationalism was not a regular preoccupation of Mangan's. As with many of his class, education and religion, nationalism was inevitably part of the cultural air Mangan breathed, and his poems are an interesting reflection of the changing emphases and issues within Irish nationalism over the course of twenty years. One of his earliest poems is a rebus on the name of Robert Emmet, and we know that he was on the fringes of the Repeal movement from the early 1830s, later publicly pledging his support for John Mitchel's militant brand of nationalism. Yet one of his last poems, written in the aftermath of the failed 1848 rebellion and the worst years of the Famine, repudiates the apocalyptic war-flames of 'Dark Rosaleen' in favour of a different kind of struggle:

> Knowledge is Power, not Powder. That man strikes
> A blow for Ireland worth a hundred guns
> Who trains one reasoner. Smash your heads of Pikes,
>   And form the heads of Men, my sons!
> ('Consolation and Counsel')

Like other aspects of his work, Mangan's political views evolved in response to the circumstances in which he wrote, worked and published, and it is not always possible to judge the 'sincerity' any of the political sentiments expressed in his poems. In 'Anthologia Germanica No. XIX', Mangan appears to mock Ferdinand Freiligrath's 'Young Germanism', yet elsewhere is happy to publish nationalist poems by Young Germanists such as Heine without disapproval.

Often the original politics of a translated poem are undermined by the surrounding prose commentary. Mangan's oriental poems allow him to perform similar evasions whereby he both is, and is not, commenting on Irish political affairs. The East is often a cipher for Ireland, the latter being a place where the eastern Khan and the Irish *ceann* are indistinguishable, according to Mangan's 'A Vision of Connaught in the Thirteenth Century'. And in 'To the Ingleezee Khafir, Calling Himself Djaun Bool Djenkinzun', Mangan dons an anonymous oriental mask in order to attack the smugness of the English abroad, in the process making a political link between the Irish and Asian experiences of British expansion. The publication context of many of these oriental poems also gives them a political edge—the *Nation* newspaper, for example, gave extensive coverage to the British military campaigns in Afghanistan and China in the 1840s, and made much of the analogy between British tyranny in the orient and imperial rule at home. At other times, of course, Mangan simply uses orientalism as a vehicle for the indulgence of his surreal humour and technical skill. Poems like 'Song for Coffee-Drinkers' and 'The Ruby Mug' play on the reader's stereotyped expectations about the exotic orient, but subvert the stereotypes through their mock-heroic narratives or witty wordplay.

A consideration of Mangan's politics reminds us that like Thomas Moore before him and James Joyce after him, Mangan came from petit-bourgeois Catholic Dublin at a time when the city was a curious mixture of cosmopolitanism and provinciality, poised uneasily between an imperial centre in London and a colonial and largely Gaelic hinterland. Dublin's cosmopolitanism meant that Mangan learned modern continental languages, that he trained for a profession, that he inhabited a literate culture that was well informed about the wider world, and that his earliest cultural reference points were primarily British and European rather than Gaelic. But Dublin's provinciality, so memorably delineated by James Joyce some years later, gave a particular cast to the Irish writer's relation with the English language, as Stephen Dedalus recognises in *A Portrait of the Artist as a Young Man* (1916). The Irish writer using English was in a provincial condition, where he or she was shaped culturally by an imperial power while being simultaneously alienated from the centre of that power, even when speaking its language. As a Dubliner, Mangan spoke English as his native tongue, but as an Irishman, English was also in a certain sense a foreign language, with which he had an instrumental but not historical or cultural relationship. In one critical passage, Mangan expresses his love for 'our own mother tongue', by which he means English; yet his obsessive verbal play, his incessant punning, are all symptomatic of an insecure relation to English, albeit one which, like Joyce, he exploits as a kind of linguistic freedom. Interestingly, towards the end of his life, most of Mangan's poetic efforts involved translating from Irish. A similar paradoxical relation exists here, insofar as the Gaelic tradition is part of his heritage (his father in fact would almost certainly have been an Irish speaker), yet Irish for Mangan is a foreign tongue that he can only encounter indirectly through the literal translations of his friends. In such circumstances, it is difficult for a writer not to recognise the relativity of language, and to feel a fascination with its malleability.

Of course, while it may be tempting to read Mangan as the blissful practitioner of verbal play and subversive wit, it is also necessary to remember, as Terry Eagleton would have it, the 'oppressive as well as emancipatory aspect of colonial identities which are unstable, self-fashioning, intertextual'.[21] Mangan's proto-postmodernity can be read as a sign of trauma as well as *jouissance*: to be a 'nameless one' is not just a sign of a kind of freedom, it is also a condition of loss. Mangan's work, particularly in his last years, constantly reminds us of the price that may be have to be paid for creative eccentricity in a culture that is itself deeply fractured and uncertain of its past or future.

IV

This edition is the only one to reprint an extensive selection of Mangan's critical prose, fiction, letters and autobiography along with his poetry. Where possible, the edition restores poems to their original format, that is, embedded in Mangan's illuminating and sometimes whimsical prose commentaries. The restored commentaries, musical accompaniments and headnotes (even those which may be by Mangan's editors rather than the poet himself) allow us some insight into how Mangan's first readers would have encountered his work—as part of a critical essay, say, or a song collection. By placing these materials in the body of the edition, rather than relegating them to footnotes, the present edition tries to avoid introducing artificial hierarchies between poems and prose where such hierarchies did not exist in the design of original. It may also allow the reader to sense some kind of continuity among the diversity of poems; up to now, the connecting threads supplied by the prose have been missing from most people's reading experience of Mangan. The voice of Mangan as critic, when restored to its original prominence, does in fact provide a kind of 'centre' to his writing identity, a controlling consciousness around the multiple voices of the poetry.

The selection in this volume attempts to include all of the well-known poems, but also tries to suggest the breadth of Mangan's interests and skills. The sections are arranged chronologically, with examples drawn from all phases of the poet's career. Readers may find areas of Mangan's work that have not always received

---

21 Terry Eagleton, 'Prout and Plagiarism' in *Ideology and Ireland in the Nineteenth Century*, ed. Tadhg Foley and Sean Ryder (Dublin: Four Courts Press, 1998), 22.

the attention they have deserved, such as his religious poetry, which ranges from the daringly sceptical 'Neither One Nor T'other' to powerful renderings of early Irish hymns like 'Holy are the Works of Mary's Blessed Son'. It is also possible to trace certain recurrent issues and themes—even at the age of 17, for instance, Mangan could turn out a poem as gloomy as the famous lyrics he wrote at the end of his life, a fact that suggests the possibility of a technical fascination with the genre as well as the existence of a depressive personality.

The selection of stand-alone prose in the edition challenges the erroneous view of Mangan as an impractical and otherworldly figure. In his prose he emerges as an inventive and inquisitive mind, engaged with political and philosophical issues of his time, albeit with a compulsion for wordplay. The critical writings have been selected chiefly to illustrate some of Mangan's opinions on subjects such as translation, oriental literature and contemporary authors. An item like the *Anthologia Germanica* extract about the poet Ludwig Tieck is included for its witty exuberance, and because it is a useful illustration of Mangan's argumentative method. He rarely conducts an argument in a linear or logical fashion; instead he works by reiteration. Thus the critique of Tieck is not a reasoned analysis but a progressive accumulation of outrageous jibes. This does not make for complex literary analysis, but it does provide a kind of entertaining illumination.

One turns to Mangan's letters in the hope of finding glimpses into the more private psychological or emotional world of the poet, but most of the surviving handful of letters are essentially business letters, concerned with arranging publication, or seeking a loan. One exception is the peculiar unsent letter to 'Tynan', in which Mangan ventilates some of his political opinions at greater length than elsewhere. Another is the miserable letter Mangan wrote from his relatives' house in Kiltale, Co. Meath in the summer of 1847, which gives an insight not only into Mangan's discomfort when displaced from his native urban haunts, but also into his bristly personality which must have made him a difficult companion, even for sympathetic friends. The more familiar Mangan of pathos and distress is encountered in a brief late letter to Gavan Duffy, begging for assistance. Even the shaky handwriting of the original manuscript of this letter suggests pathos, as if it represented a cruel unravelling of the elegant scrivener's hand of Mangan's earlier life.

Choosing copy-texts for the edition has been relatively straightforward, and each copy-text is identified in brackets at the end of each poem or article. There are very few Mangan manuscripts in existence, and his texts have uncomplicated publication histories that only rarely involve authorial revision. Very occasionally Mangan republished poems, altering them to suit the demands of the new periodical or the changed political scene (as in his satirical poem 'Asses', which changed its cast of characters each time it reappeared in 1832, 1840 and 1843).

Sometimes, of course, even small alterations can be significant: when 'Our First Number' was first published in the *Nation* in October 1842, line 47 imagined the newspaper's readership extending from 'the Suir to the Tweed, from the Boyne to the Humber'. When reprinted in the anthology *Spirit of the Nation* in 1843, the 'Tweed' had become the 'Rhine', a revealing indication of the paper's spiralling confidence. But the intention of the present edition has not been to demonstrate the textual evolution of any poem. I have instead merely reproduced a single version of each selected poem, not necessarily because it represents Mangan's original or final intentions, but because it seems particularly interesting in its own right, or interesting because of the place or occasion of its publication. The date and location of each text's publication are given in brackets at its end.

In keeping with the style of their first publication, Mangan's own original footnotes are given at the foot of the relevant page in the body of the edition, while my 'Explanatory Notes' are given in a separate section at the end of the volume. Spellings and misspellings found in the original texts have been retained, except for obvious misprints which have been noted in the list of emendations. All words and phrases enclosed in square brackets are editorial interpolations, including some titles for poems untitled in the original.

Further reading

Jacques Chuto's *James Clarence Mangan: A Bibliography* (Dublin and Portland, Or.: Irish Academic Press, 1999) is an essential resource. It itemises all of Mangan's extensive publications, identifies many of his literary sources, and lists most of the nineteenth and twentieth-century secondary literature on Mangan. An impressive six-volume *Collected Works of James Clarence Mangan* (Dublin and Portland, Or.: Irish Academic Press, 1996–2002) has been edited by Chuto and others and contains the complete canon of poetry and prose. Unlike the present edition, however, it separates the poems from their original prose contexts, and divides Mangan's prose between endnotes and two separate prose volumes. The following critical and biographical works are other useful starting points for further reading:

Jacques Chuto, 'Mangan, Petrie, O'Donovan, and a Few Others: The Poet and the Scholars', *Irish University Review*, VI, 2 (Autumn 1976), 169–87.
Patricia Coughlan, 'Fold over Fold, Inveterately Convolv'd: Some Aspects of Mangan's Intertextuality' in *Anglo-Irish and Irish Literature*, ed. B. A. Bramsbäck and M. Croghan (Uppsala: Studia Anglistica, 1988), II, 191–200.

Seamus Deane, *Strange Country: Modernity and Nationhood in Irish Writing since 1790* (Oxford: Clarendon Press, 1996).

Henry J. Donaghy, *James Clarence Mangan* (New York: Twayne, 1974).

James Joyce, 'James Clarence Mangan (1902)' and 'James Clarence Mangan (1907)' in *Occasional, Critical and Political Writing*, ed. Kevin Barry (Oxford: Oxford University Press, 2000), 53–60, 127–36.

James Kilroy, *James Clarence Mangan* (Lewisburg: Bucknell University Press, 1970).

David Lloyd, *Nationalism and Minor Literature: James Clarence Mangan and the Emergence of Irish Cultural Nationalism* (Berkeley: University of California Press, 1987).

Peter MacMahon, 'James Clarence Mangan, the Irish Language, and the Strange Case of *The Tribes of Ireland*', *Irish University Review*, VIII, 2 (Autumn 1978), 209–22.

C.P. Meehan, 'Preface' to *Poets and Poetry of Munster*, 3rd ed. (Dublin: Duffy, [1883]), iii–xxx.

John Mitchel, 'James Clarence Mangan: His Life, Poetry, and Death' in *Poems by James Clarence Mangan*, ed. John Mitchel (New York: Haverty, 1859), 7–31.

D. J. O'Donoghue, *The Life and Writings of James Clarence Mangan* (Edinburgh: Geddes; Dublin: Gill, 1897).

Sean Ryder, 'Male Autobiography and Cultural Nationalism: John Mitchel and James Clarence Mangan', *Irish Review* 13 (1992/1993), 70–7.

Ellen Shannon-Mangan, *James Clarence Mangan: A Biography* (Dublin and Portland, Or.: Irish Academic Press, 1996).

Francis J. Thompson, 'Mangan in America, 1850–1860: Mitchel, Maryland and Melville', *Dublin Magazine*, XXVII, 3 (1952), 30-41.

Robert Welch, *A History of Verse Translation from the Irish, 1789–1897* (Gerrards Cross: Colin Smythe, 1988).

——, *Irish Poetry from Moore to Yeats* (Gerrards Cross: Colin Smythe, 1980).

W. B. Yeats, 'Clarence Mangan' in *Uncollected Prose*, vol. 1, ed. John P. Frayne (London: Macmillan, 1970), 114–19.

Chronology

1803
James Mangan born 1 May, Fishamble Street, Dublin.
Robert Emmet's rebellion in Dublin (23 July).

1810–17
Attends Jesuit school in Saul's Court, followed by Courtney's Academy in Derby
Square and schools in Arran Quay and Chancery Lane. Learns elements of Latin,
French, Italian and Spanish.

1818
Apprenticed to Kenrick's scrivenery in York Street; publishes first poems in *Grant's*
and *New Ladies'* almanacs.

1825
End of apprenticeship; works as scrivener for solicitor Matthew Frank's office,
Merrion Square.

1829
Befriends Hayes family of Dolphin's Barn, Dublin, tutors Catherine Hayes in
German; works in solicitor Thomas Leland's office in Fitzwilliam Square (prob-
ably until 1838).
Catholic Emancipation Act passed.

1830
Revolution in France. Start of 'tithe war' in Ireland.

1831
Signs petition of Dublin law clerks in favour of repeal of the Union.

1832
Contributes to anti-tithe newspaper *The Comet* and to the *Dublin Penny Journal*;
adopts pen-name 'Clarence'. Death of Catherine Hayes.
First Reform Bill passed by British parliament.

1834

First contribution to *Dublin University Magazine*; meets Stackpoole family and may have proposed to Margaret Stackpoole.

1835

Death of younger brother John.

1836

Meets Charles Gavan Duffy.

1838

Employed by George Petrie and John O'Donovan as copyist for Ordnance Survey. Fr Theobald Mathew begins national temperance campaign.

1840

First translation from Irish ('The Woman of the Three Cows'). Contributes to Belfast *Vindicator* under Duffy's editorship. Contributes to Petrie's *Irish Penny Journal*.

1841

Ordnance Survey funding reduced; Petrie secures employment for Mangan as cataloguer in library of Trinity College Dublin.

1842

Establishment of *Nation* newspaper, chief organ of 'Young Ireland'; Mangan contributes several poems to early issues.

1843

Death of father (26 September).
Mass meetings throughout Ireland in support of O'Connell's Repeal movement.

1844

Employment in Trinity College Library reduced to half time.

1845

Curry publishes Mangan's two-volume *German Anthology*, partly financed by Gavan Duffy. Meets Fr C. P. Meehan.
Death of Thomas Davis; appearance of potato blight.

1846
Death of mother (6 August). Contributes extensively to the *Nation*.
Young Ireland faction, including Duffy and John Mitchel, separates from main-
stream Repeal movement.

1847
Spends some weeks during summer with mother's family in Kiltale, Co. Meath.
Contributes to *Duffy's Irish Catholic Magazine*.
Intensification of famine; death of O'Connell.

1848
Mangan hospitalised (May–June).
Mitchel breaks with Gavan Duffy, establishes radical *United Irishman* newspaper,
later sentenced to transportation for sedition. Revolution in France. Unsuccessful
insurrection in Ireland (July).

1849
Mangan contributes to *Irishman* newspaper; works on *Poets and Poetry of Ireland*
and *Tribes of Ireland* translations with John O'Daly; contracts cholera but recovers
(May), found in destitute state (13 June), dies in Meath Hospital (20 June).

POETICAL WORKS

Lines, written at 17

How sleepless and slowly the night passes over
With him, the poor wretch, of misfortune the sport
Who wanders, a homeless & fortuneless rover,
O'er the waste of that world, which denies him support!
How bitter the tear through his eyelash that gushes   5
As haply some thought of the joys that are flown
Through the vista of memory unconsciously rushes,
And he feels that his heart is with sorrow alone!

Oh! slowly, oh! sleepless his night passes over,
But with morn is the close of his wretchedness near?   10
Ah! no, for the spectres that evermore hover
Around his low couch still resound in his ear,
That he never shall know what it is to be griefless
That his woe-bringing pilgrimage ne'er shall be o'er,
Till exhausted by agony—wretched, reliefless,   15
He sinks to the bed he shall rise from no more.

[unpublished manuscript]

Enigma [The Enchanted Earl of Kildare]

'Who is it that rides through the forest so fast,
While night howls around him—while shrill roars the blast?'   LEWIS

Who is he? yon huntsman, all clad in dark green—
How wild his appearance! how noble his mien!
  His mantle it waves to the wind;
His silver shod courser with eyes dashing fire,
Scarce breathing a moment the air to respire,   5
  Leaves hill, dale and valley behind.

Alone, unaccompanied, onward he flies,
When straight at a distance a village he spies;—
  Will that terminate his long chase?
Ah! no, the abodes of mankind he must flee,   10
And woe to that mortal whoever he be,
  That looks on the wanderer's face.

When rises each morning the sun in the east,
Then wakes the wild Huntsman, and starts from his rest,
   Which lasts but the space of an hour;   15
Sometimes with dogs, and at others alone,
Sometimes with firearms, but mostly with none,
   All o'er the green sward he must scour.

Compelled thus to wander alone and forlorn,
In youth from his friends and his family torn,   20
   By those he's enforced to obey;
The green fields of Erin, their place of abode,
The mortal who falls in the track of their road
   Ne'er more sees the sunshine of day.

Well known to Hibernia in field as in state,   25
Well worthy the title of 'Humane and Great.'
   While yet his career was his own;
He mourned that his country her wrongs should endure,
In silence, in sorrow, regardless of cure—
   That aught should have caused her to groan.   30

Now Bards of Hibernia, whose geniuses bright
Bring forth the bright rays of effulgence from night,
   Declare me his title revered;
Whose past fate the public have long ceased to mourn,
Yet why drop the tear of regret on his urn?   35
   The knowledge of future is spared!
             [James Mangan, *Grant's Almanack*, 1820]

Enigma [A Vampire]

Bleak was the night, the winds were high.
   The lightning streamed along the wold,
And through the black and moonless sky
   Was many a burst of thunder rolled.

Within his tower the warrior sate,   5
   And oft-times as he gazed about him,
'He will not come! why should I wait?'
   He cried, ''twere well to go without him!'

And once, and even while he spoke,
  He rose and turned to view the night,   10
And grasped his claymore, and his cloak,
  And eke his helmet plumed and bright.

'Say, shall a nightstorm on a moor
  Me from my vengeful purpose win?'
He said; when slowly oped the door,   15
  And lo! a *stranger* stood within.

Of stature more than man's was he,
  All clad in robes of deepest black,
Save where the shrinking eye might see
  A *blood-red ribbon* round his neck.   20

Not further than the door he came,
  Nor spake a word—nor moved a limb—
Cold, dark, and mute, the night might claim
  Her clouds, but not her storms from him.

'Who may'st thou be?' the warrior said;   25
  The Stranger raised and waved his arm,
'Twas like the movement of the dead;
  It held no wand, yet owned a charm,

For whiter grew the warrior's cheek,
  And ever used to high command,   30
His sword refused to aid a weak,
  And quitted quick a nerveless hand.

The Stranger glanced his eye around;
  'Twas fixed and dull and leaden-grey,
While from his lips with tomb-like sound,   35
  The words that follow found their way:

'The dark intentions of thy heart,
  Proud warrior! stay a little time;
Remain tonight even where thou art,
  The morrow best befits the crime.   40

'For thou and I ere night be o'er
  Have much to say and more to do;
Things never said or done before,
  Which mortal never heard nor knew.

'Nay, cease, all words were doubly vain.   45
  Once more I tell thee, where thou art,
Even there this night thou shalt remain;
  Till morn we cannot, must not, part.

'And think thee, warrior, as thou wilt,
  Thou canst not gain relief from men;   50
He—the accomplice of thy guilt—
  Lies lifeless in the nearmost glen!'

What more he said may not be told
  To aught that bears the name of man;
For in a book it lies enrolled,   55
  Which mortals have no power to scan.

A mystery overhangs that night,
  Profound and dark as waters deep;
Passed shrieks—vain struggles—bootless might—
  The warrior slept a death-like sleep.   60

*   *   *   *

Away was fled *the Stranger wight,*
  When night and storm had passed away,
But in his tower by morning's light,
  A bloodless *corpse* the warrior lay.
            [James Mangan, *Grant's Almanack*, 1822]

Rebus [Emmet]

The land that we love, and the sway that we own,
  (May the land by the sway never ceased to be blessed),
The Ruler himself, and the seat of his throne,
  And the rod that our souls shall forever detest:

Connect the initials, his name they will show,   5
Ever loved of Ierna, and sacred to woe:
An oak, which though firm to each tempest that passed it,
Was doomed by a flash, bright and false, to be blasted.

For long o'er his darksome and pillowless bed,
  Have the sorrowing winds of the evening been sighing;   10
Full often alas! hath the passenger's tread
  Pressed on the sad spot where his remains are lying.

Ierna, the man who thy slavery mourned,
Whose bosom for ever and hopelessly burned
To behold thee a nation, and happy, and free,   15
Must ever be dear to thy children and thee.

And is there a heart that refuses to cherish
  His image within it? or is there a breast
That could think on the fate which condemned him to perish,
  With all its best feelings unroused from their rest?   20

Oh! no, for till life and its sorrows be past,
His name in our memory unsullied shall last;
While each tear to the woes of his country he gave,
Her sons shall repay o'er the patriot's grave.

[James Mangan, *Grant's Almanack*, 1822]

Enigma—To the Memory of the Late Lamented
Mr. John Kenchinow, Butcher, of Patrick Street

Come, get the black, the mourning pall,
  (The reason I will mention now),
And with it, Blockheads, Bards and all,
Assist to cover Dia's hall
  For the loss of Johnny Kenchinow.   5

'And is he gone!' cry one and all.
  To keep you in suspension now,
Is not my wish; yes, at the call
Of Death was lately doomed to fall
  Lamented Johnny Kenchinow.   10

If any one refuse to yawl,
  Ye Bards, I will convince ye now,
That, though at first a stubborn Saul
Ye be, ere long, repentant Paul
  Shall weep for Johnny Kenchinow.   15

Alas! this world's a slippery ball
  And do I reprehension now
Deserve, for saying that a straw'll
At times compel a man to sprawl
  Like peerless Johnny Kenchinow?   20

Messina's Cobbler, him of Gaul,
  Nay, he whose home Valentia now
Is, never pierced with shining awl
A shoe more sure than Death's sharp claw'll
  Pierce us like Johnny Kenchinow.   25

Great man! to see thy empty stall—
  (A stall there's not a bench in now)—
Unnerves me quite. I scarce can scrawl
A word, while tears more sour than gall
  Flow for thee, Johnny Kenchinow.   30

What though thy legs were long and tall,
  Them is the wet clay drenching now;
And eke those hands, so wont to haul
The mutton from the well-soiled wall
  By thee built, Johnny Kenchinow.   35

Thy Widow's purse, of course, is small,
  So may the State a pension now
Allow her, as a threadbare shawl
And sieve-like shoes for respite call
  In vain from Johnny Kenchinow.   40

Her name, howe'er, no man dare maul;
  She is an upright wench, (and now,
I talk of wenches) none could squall
So loud by half, or rather bawl,
  At the wake of Johnny Kenchinow.   45

But Judy's praises here to drawl
  Is none of my intention now.
In sooth 'twere needless, and withal,
My Muse is ill disposed to brawl
  Of aught, save Johnny Kenchinow.   50

Ye far-famed wits whom rhymes enthrall,
  I pray you pay attention now:
Say, will ye come? Oh! yes, ye shall,
To view the worms that slowly crawl
  O'er the bed of Johnny Kenchinow.   55

And if the sight your souls appal,
  Pray tell me what must fence ye now
Against that grief, which doubtless all
Who read this woe-creating scrawl
  Must feel for Johnny Kenchinow.   60
        [James Mangan, *New Ladies' Almanack*, 1822]

The Young Parson's Dream

In the lone stillness of the new-year's night,
  A Bishop at his window stood, and turned
His dim eyes to the firmament, where bright
  And pure a million rolling planets burned,
And then upon the earth all cold and white,—   5
  And felt that moment that, of all who mourned
And groaned upon its bosom, none there were
With his hypocrisy and great despair.

For near him lay his grave; concealed from view,
  Not by the flowers of youth, but by the snows   10
Of age alone: in torturing thought he flew
  Over the past, and on his memory rose
That picture of his life which memory drew
  With all its fruits, diseases, sins, and woes:
A ruined frame, a blighted soul, dark years   15
Of agony, remorse, and withering fears!

Like spectres now his days of youth came back,
  And that cross-road of life where, when a boy,
His father placed him first; its right hand track
  Leads to a land of glory, peace and joy,   20
Its left to wilderness, waste and black,
  Where snakes and plagues and poisonous blasts destroy.
Where was he now? alas! the serpents hung
Coiled round his heart, their venom on his tongue.

Choaked with unutterable grief, he cried—   25
  'Restore to me my youth! oh Heaven! restore
'My morn of life! oh father! be my guide,
  'And let me, let me choose my path once more!'
But on the wide waste air his ravings died
  Away, and all was silent as before.   30
His youth had glided by, swift as the wave;
His father came not; he was in his grave.

Wild lights went flickering by; a star was falling;
  Down to the miry marsh he saw it rush.
'Myself,' he said, and oh! the thought was galling,   35
  And hot and heart-wrung tears began to gush:
Sleepwalkers crossed his glance in shapes appalling,
  Huge windmills lifted up their arms to crush,
And death-like faces started from the dim
Depths of the charnel-house and glared on him.   40

Amid these overboiling bursts of feeling,
  Rich music, heralding the young year's birth,
Flowed from a distant STEEPLE, like the pealing
  Of some celestial organ o'er the earth.
Milder emotions over him came stealing;   45
  He felt the spirit's awful, priceless worth—
'Return'—again he cried imploringly,
'Oh my lost youth! return, return to me!'

And youth returned, and age withdrew his terrors,
  Still was he young, for he had dreamed the whole: 50
But faithful is the picture conscience mirrors,
  Whenever PARSON avarice gluts the soul.

Alas! too real were his sins and errors.
  Too truly had he made the earth his goal:
He wept and blessed his God that with the will   55
He had the power to choose the right path still.

Here, youthful curate, ponder—and if thou,
  Like him, art reeling over the abyss
Of church hypocrisy and mammon, now,
  This ghastly dream may be thy guide to bliss.   60
But should age once bring MITRES to thy brow,
  Its wrinkles will not leave a dream like this—
Thy tears may then flow vainly o'er the urn
Of innocence, that never can return!

      [Unsigned, *The Parson's Horn-Book, Part II*, 1831]

To My Native Land

Awake! arise! shake off thy dreams!
  Thou art not what thou wert of yore:
Of all those rich, those dazzling beams,
  That once illum'd thine aspect o'er,
Show me a solitary one   5
Whose glory is not quenched and gone.

The harp remaineth where it fell,
  With mouldering frame and broken chord;
Around the song there hangs no spell—
  No laurel wreath entwines the sword;   10
And startlingly the footstep falls
Along thy dim and dreary halls.

When other men, in future years,
  In wonder ask, how this could be?
Then answer only by thy tears,   15
  That ruin fell on thine and thee,
Because thyself wouldst have it so—
Because thou welcomedst the blow!

To stamp dishonour on thy brow
  Was not within the power of earth;   20
And art thou agonised, when now
  The hour that lost thee all thy worth,
And turned thee to the thing thou art,
Rushes upon thy bleeding heart?

Weep, weep, degraded one—the deed,   25
  The desperate deed was all thine own:
Thou madest more than maniac speed
  To hurl thine honours from their throne.
Thine honours fell, and when they fell
The nations rang thy funeral knell.   30

Well may thy sons be seared in soul,
  Their groans be deep by night and day;
Till day and night forget to roll,
  Their noblest hopes shall morn decay—
Their freshest flowers shall die by blight—   35
Their brightest suns shall set in night.

The stranger, as he treads thy sod,
  And views thine universal wreck,
May execrate the foot that trod
  Triumphant on a prostrate neck.   40
But what is that to thee? Thy woes
May hope in vain for pause or close.

Awake! arise! shake off thy dreams!
  'Tis idle all to talk of power,
And fame, and glory—these are themes   45
  Befitting ill so dark an hour:
Till miracles be wrought for thee,
Nor fame, nor glory, shalt thou see.

Thou art forsaken by the earth,
  Which makes a by-word of thy name: 50
Nations, and thrones, and powers, whose birth
  As yet is not, shall rise to fame,
Shall flourish, and may fall—but thou
Shalt linger as thou lingerest now.

And till all earthly powers shall wane,   55
  And Time's grey pillars, groaning, fall;
Thus shall it be, and still in vain
  Thou shalt essay to burst the thrall
Which binds, in fetters forged by fate,
The wreck and ruin of WHAT ONCE WAS GREAT!   60
                     [J. C. M., *Comet*, 15 July 1832]

The Dying Enthusiast to his Friend
FOR THE DUBLIN PENNY JOURNAL

Life—like a dome of many-colored glass—
Stains the white radiance of Eternity,
Until Death tramples it to fragments.   SHELLY [*sic*]

Speak no more of life—
  What can life bestow
In this amphitheatre of strife,
  All times dark with tragedy and woe?
Knowest thou not how care and pain   5
Build their lampless dwelling in the brain,
Ever as the stern intrusion
  Of our teachers, Time and Truth,
Turns to gloom the bright illusion
  Rainbowed on the soul of youth?   10
Wouldst thou have me live when this is so?
    Oh! no—no!

As the flood of Time
  Sluggishly doth flow,
Look how all of beaming and sublime   15
  Sinks into the black abysm below!
Yea, the loftiest intellect
Earliest on the strand of life is wrecked,
Nought of lovely—nothing glorious
  Lives to triumph o'er decay;   20
Desolation reigns victorious—
  Mind is dungeon-walled by clay.
Could I bear to feel mine own laid low?
    Oh! no—no!

O'er the troubled earth   25
  Thronging millions go—
But, behold how Genius, Love, and Worth,
  Move like lonely phantoms, to and fro.
Suns are quenched, and kingdoms fall,
But the doom of these outdarkens all!   30
Die they, then? Yes, Love's devotion,
  Stricken, withers in its bloom;
Fond affections, deep as ocean,
  In their cradle find their tomb.
Shall I linger but to count each throe?   35
    Oh! no—no!

Prison-bursting Death!
  Welcome, then, thy blow!
Thine is but the forfeit of my breath,
  Not the Spirit—not the Spirit's glow!   40
Spheres of Beauty! hallowed Spheres,
Undefaced by time, undimmed by tears,
Henceforth hail! Oh! who would grovel
  In a world impure as this,
Who would dwell in cell or hovel   45
  When a palace might be his?
Dare I longer the bright lot forego?
    Oh! no—no!
      [M., *Dublin Penny Journal*, 5 January 1833]

Elegiac Verses on the Early Death of a Beloved Friend

I stood aloof—I dared not to behold
Thy relics covered over with the mould;
I shed no tear—I uttered not a groan—
But yet I felt heart-broken and alone.

How feel I now? The bitterness of grief   5
Has passed; for all which is intense is brief.
A softer sadness overshades my mind,
But there thy memory ever lies enshrined.

And if I mourn, for this is human too,
I mourn no longer that thy days were few;   10
Nor that thou hast escaped the tears and woe,
And deaths on deaths the living undergo.

Thou diedst in the spring-time of thine years;
Life's juggling hopes and spirit-wasting fears,
Thou knewest but in romance; and to thine eyes   15
Man shone a god—the earth a Paradise.

Thou diedst ere the icy breath of scorn
Froze the warm feelings of thine youthful morn;
Ere thou couldst learn that man is but a slave,
And this blank world a prison and a grave.   20

Weep not for me, but for yourselves,—was said
By HIM who bore the cross on which HE bled;—
And if I drop a solitary tear,
It is that thou art gone, while I am here.

Thy spirit is at *peace*:—oh, blessed word!   25
Forgotten by the million, or unheard;
While mine still struggles down this vale of death,
And courts the favor of a little breath.

Through every stage of life's consuming fever
The soul is proud to be her own deceiver;   30
And revels,—aye!—in such a world as this,
In golden dreams of never-palling bliss.

But he who, looking on the naked chart
Of life, feels nature sinking at his heart,—
He who is drugged with sorrows,—he for whom   35
Affliction carves a pathway to the tomb,

He will unite with me to bless that Power
Who gathers and transplants the fragile flower,
Ere yet the spirit of the whirlwind storm
Comes forth in wrath to ravage or deform.   40

And if it be that GOD himself removes
From peril and contagion those HE loves,

Weep such no more, but strew with freshest roses
The hallowed mound where Innocence reposes.

The world is round me now; but sad and single   45
I stand amid the throng with whom I mingle,
Not one of all of whom can be to me
The bosom treasure I have lost in thee.

Pure as the lamp that burned in Tullia's tomb,
Friendship's first rays will yield as dense a gloom,   50
But when such friendship,—death-extinguished,—dies,
No Phoenix from its ashes can arise.

The poetry of young existence lives
But in the gorgeous light her dawning gives:
Alas! her Heaven is overcast too soon—   55
The sun is darkened, and goes down at noon.

Oh! fairy visions of my childhood's fancy!
The mind's young mysteries! Nature's necromancy!
Haunt not my memory now—she can but borrow
From your lost glories aliment for sorrow.   60

Mock not—oh! torture not the aching glance
Of one who never more shall breathe romance.
Ah! why have you existed but to render
All future gloom the blacker by your splendor?

But wherefore should our feelings overflow,   65
Where but to feel is to be choked with woe?
And all with me merge in this one emotion,
As seas are lost in the eternal ocean.

Enough:—I go to join the hollow crowd—
Mirth rings among us, and the laugh is loud;   70
For here society exacts her task,
And each assumes his own peculiar mask.

I go—but still to see, where'er I turn,
The ever-present phantom of thine urn;
And feel that in my bosom's inmost cell   75
Thy sainted image evermore shall dwell.

[Clarence, *Comet*, 10 February 1833]

The One Mystery
FOR THE DUBLIN PENNY JOURNAL

'Tis idle: —we exhaust and squander
  The glittering mine of thought in vain:
All-baffled reason cannot wander
  Beyond her chain.
The flood of life runs dark—dark clouds   5
  Make lampless night around its shore:
The dead, where are they? In their shrouds—
  Man knows no more!

Evoke the Ancient and the Past:
  Will one illuming star arise?   10
Or must the film from first to last
  O'erspread thine eyes?
When life, love, glory, beauty, wither,
  Will wisdom's page, or science' chart
Map out for thee the region whither   15
  Their shades depart?

Supposest thou the wondrous powers
  To high imaginations given,
Pale types of what shall yet be ours
  When earth is heaven?   20
When this decaying shell is cold,
  O! sayest thou the soul shall climb
That magic mount she trod of old,
  Ere childhood's time?

And shall the sacred pulse that thrilled,   25
  Thrill once again to Glory's name?
And shall the conquering Love that filled
  All earth with flame,
Reborn, revived, renewed, immortal,
  Resume his reign in prouder might,   30
A sun beyond the ebon portal
  Of death and night?

No more, no more;—With aching brow,
 And restless heart, and burning brain,
We ask the When, the Where, the How,   35
 And ask in vain.
And all philosophy, all faith,
 All earthly, all celestial lore,
Have but ONE voice, which only saith,
 Endure,—adore!   40

  [Clarence, *Dublin Penny Journal*, 11 May 1833]

'Life is the Desert and the Solitude'
YOUNG

It is the joyous time of June,
 And fresh from nature's liberal hand,
Is richly lavished every boon
 The laughing earth and skies demand;
 How shines the variegated land—   5
How swell the many sparkling streams!
 All is as gorgeous and as grand
As the creation wherewith teems
The poet's haunted brain, amid his noonday dreams.

Falls now the golden veil of even—   10
 The vault on high, the intense profound,
Breaks into all the hues of heaven;
 I see far off the mountains crowned
 With glory—I behold around
Enough of summer's power to mould   15
 The breast not altogether bound
By grief to thoughts whose uncontrolled
Fervour leaves feeling dumb and human utterance cold.

Yet I am far—oh! far from feeling
 The life—the thrilling glow—the power   20
Which have their dwelling in the healing
 And holy influence of the hour,
 Affliction is my doom and dower,

And cares, in many a darkening throng,
　Like nightclouds round a ruin, lour   25
Over a soul which (never strong
To stem the tide of ill) will not resist them long.

And all that glances on my vision,
　Inanimate or breathing:—rife
With voiceless beauty half Elysian,   30
　Or youthful and exuberant life,
　Serves but to nurse the sleepless strife
Within,—arousing the keen thought,
　Quickborn, which stabbeth like a knife,
And wakes anticipations fraught   35
With heaviest hues of gloom, from memory's pictures wrought.

What slakeless fire is still consuming
　This martyred heart from day to day?
Lies not the bower where love was blooming
　Time-trampled into long decay?   40
　Alas! when hope's illusive ray
Plays round our paths, the bright deceiver
　Allures us only to betray,
Leaving us thenceforth wanderers ever
Forlorn along the shores of life's all-troubled river.   45

Had I but dreamed in younger years
　That time should paralyse and bow
Me thus—thus fill mine eyes with tears—
　Thus chill my soul and cloud my brow,
　No! I had not been breathing now—   50
This heart had long ago been broken;
　I had not lived to witness how
Deeply and bitterly each token
Of by-gone joy will yield which misery hath bespoken.

Alas! for those who stand alone—   55
　The shrouded few who feel and know
What none beside have felt and known;
　To all of such a mould below
　Is born an undeparting woe,

Beheld by none and shared with none,   60
  A cankering worm whose work is slow,
And gnaws the heartstrings one by one,
And drains the bosom's blood, till the last drop be gone.

[Clarence, *Comet*, 21 July 1833]

The Philosopher and the Child

Clarence was mad (*drunk*, dare we say) when he wrote the following; the five
lines, at the conclusion, marked in Italics are sufficient proof of our assertion.—

I met a venerable man, with looks
Of grand and meek benignity: he wore
Deep written on his brow the midnight lore
Accumulated from the wealth of books.
Wisdom and mildness from his features beamed   5
And by his side there moved a little child
With auburn locks, who pleasantly beguiled
The listening ear of that old man, who seemed
To be her sire, with playful words, which from
The heart of childhood, innocence, fresh fountain,   10
Spring brightly bubbling upward, till they come
To lose themselves on manhood's desert mountain.
So spake that lovely little child; and as
I gazed on her and on that aged man
With eye so thoughtful and with cheek so wan   15
I mused on Plato and Pythagoras,
But most I thought of Socrates, and of
The guardian-angel whose undying love
Never forsook the hoary sage of Greece
Until she closed his eyes in holy peace,   20
When tyrants, awed, acknowledged with a sigh
How nobly a philosopher can die!
And as these thoughts flashed flitting through my brain
I heard that venerable man so mild
Thus mutter to the sweet and blessed child,   25
'Bad luck to dat owl' rap from Mary's lane,
Dat come and axed me for to sky de copper!

Bad luck to him, de vagabone! to rob
An' swindle me wid pitch and toss, an' fob
De penny dat I wanted for de cropper!'   30

Oh Clarence! Clarence! oh! oh!! oh!!! order a Jarvey forthwith, and drive off to Sir Arthur Clarke's—odds, shower-baths, and stomach-pumps; you are in a raging fever, man—absolute *delirium tremens*—make your will and leave Pelthers Paisley the Coroner—a lock of your wig for the trouble he'll have on your inquest.

[Clarence, *Comet*, 4 August 1833]

Curiosity
FROM THE GERMAN OF SCHILLER

From this dim dell, which gloom and cloud,
And death-black mists for ever shroud,
Could I but wander, dared I flee,
How gladsome should my spirit be!
O! who will lend me wings to fly   5
To yon tall hills that kiss the sky,
And rise majestic and eternal,
The bright, the young, the ever-vernal!

Soft seraph-lutes from thence I hear,
Divinest lyres enchant mine ear—   10
I feel the warm young wind that brings
Me balsalm on his fanning wings—
I see the gold-red fruits that bloom,
And twinkle far through leafy gloom,
And flowers whose never-waning dyes   15
Dread not the blight of winter skies.

How lovely all must be where shines
A sun whose glory ne'er declines!
What richly-odorous airs must wander
Around the immortal mountains yonder!   20
But hark! that low funeral sound
Of waters gathering darkly round!
In sullen gloom the surges roll
That seem to drown my fainting soul.

A bark, a bark appears!—it nears!   25
But where is he who guides or steers?
In waverer! in, and unalarmed—
In, trembling fool! the sails are charmed!
Thou must believe—thou shalt not falter,
The gods disown the doubter's altar.   30
Nought but a wonder like to this
Can waft thee to the land of wonders and of bliss.

[Clarence, DUM, August 1834]

from *Anthologia Germanica–No. I*
The Lyrical and Smaller Poems of Schiller

[These Lyrics'] great hallowing charm is the captivating, rather than faithful resemblance they bear with the realities they profess to be images of. Schiller has judiciously forborne from carrying into them any portion of that stormy vehemence, and blasting invective, for which his tragedies are sometimes remarkable. This is precisely as it should be. Schiller was aware that if the might of Tragedy lies in the fervour of its appeal to our passions, Poetry has won its distinguishing triumph when it succeeds in interesting our affections. His poetry, therefore, will be found to be of a majestical and mild order, occasionally philosophical, but more generally pathetic, and at all times attempering ardour with meekness, like the enthusiasm of a woman. [...]

The last specimen I shall here hazard from this great poet is remarkable as being the only piece in which he speaks at length of himself, the sunshine and clouds of his life, his early expectations, his harsh disappointments in after years, and the solace that yet remained for him. The picture is a painful one to contemplate, and were it not from the hand of a master one would feel reluctant to obtrude it upon public notice.

The Unrealities
'So willst du treulos von mir scheiden'

And dost thou faithlessly abandon me?
Must thy cameleon phantasies depart?
Thy griefs, thy gladnesses take wing and flee
The bower they built in this lonely heart?

O, Summer of Existence, golden, glowing!   5
Can nought avail to curb thine onward motion?
In vain! The river of my years is flowing
And soon shall mingle with the eternal ocean.

Extinguished in dead darkness lies the sun
That lighted up my shivered world of wonder;   10
Those fairy bands Imagination spun
Around my heart have long been rent asunder.
Gone, gone for ever is the fine belief
The all-too-generous trust in the Ideal;
All my Divinities have died of grief,   15
And left me wedded to the Rude and Real.

As clasped the enthusiastic Prince* of old
The lovely statue, stricken by its charms,
Until the marble, late so dead and cold,
Glowed into throbbing life beneath his arms,   20
So fondly round enchanting Nature's form
I too entwined my passionate arms, till, pressed
In my embraces, she began to warm
And breathe and revel in my bounding breast.

And, sympathising with my virgin bliss,   25
The speechless things of Earth received a tongue:
They gave me back Affection's burning kiss,
And loved the Melody my bosom sung:
Then sparkled hues of Life on tree and flower,
Sweet music from the silver fountain flowed;   30
All soulless images in that brief hour
The Echo of my Life divinely glowed!

How struggled all my feelings to extend
Themselves afar beyond their prisoning bounds!
O! how I longed to enter Life and blend   35
Me with its words and deeds, its shapes and sounds!
This human theatre, how fair it beamed
While yet the curtain hung before the scene!
Uprolled, how little then the arena seemed!
That little how contemptible and mean!   40

* Pygmalion.

How roamed, imparadised in blest illusion,
With soul to which upsoaring Hope lent pinions,
And heart as yet unchilled by Care's intrusion,
How roamed the stripling-lord through his dominions!
The Fancy bore him to the palest star   45
Pinnacled in the lofty æther dim:
Was nought so elevated, nought so far,
But thither the Enchantress guided him!

With what rich reveries his brain was rife!
What adversary might withstand him long?   50
How glanced and danced before the Car of Life
The visions of his thought, a dazzling throng!
For there was FORTUNE with her golden crown,
There flitted LOVE with heartbewitching boon,
There glittered starrydiademed RENOWN,   55
And TRUTH, with radiance like the sun of noon!

But ah! ere half the journey yet was over,
That gorgeous escort wended separate ways;
All faithlessly forsook the pilgrim-rover,
And one by one evanished from his gaze.   60
Away inconstant-handed FORTUNE flew;
And while the thirst of Knowledge burned alway,
The dreary mists of Doubt arose and threw
Their shadow over TRUTH's resplendent ray.

I saw the sacred garlandcrown of FAME   65
Around the common brow its glory shed:
The rapid Summer died, the Autumn came,
And LOVE, with all his necromancies, fled,
And ever lonelier and silenter
Grew the dark images of Life's poor dream,   70
Till scarcely o'er the dusky scenery there
The lamp of HOPE itself could cast a gleam.

And now, of all, Who, in my day of dolor,
Alone survives to clasp my willing hand?
Who stands beside me still, my best consoler,   75
And lights my pathway to the Phantomstrand?

Thou, FRIENDSHIP! stancher of our wounds and sorrows,
From whom this lifelong pilgrimage of pain
A balsam for its worst afflications borrows;
Thou whom I early sought, nor sought in vain!   80

And thou whose labours by her light are wrought,
Soother and soberer of the spirit's fever,
Who, shaping all things, ne'er destroyest aught,
Calm OCCUPATION! thou that weariest never!
Whose efforts rear at last the mighty Mount   85
Of Life, though merely grain on grain they lay,
And, slowly toiling, from the vast account
Of Time strike minutes, days and years away!

[Unsigned, *DUM*, January 1835]

A Railway of Rhyme

'Order is Heaven's first law.'   POPE

Now I will try a most Hercule-	An
Achievement, which I guess I sha'n't a-	Ban-
don till I finish it, for if I	Can
Succeed, I'll count myself as great as	Dan
O'Connell, or that reverend wag, D-	E-an
Swift; and there never yet was such a	Fan-
tastical rhymer since the world be-	Gan,
From Cork to Rome, and thence to Ispa-	Han,
In Persian, Irish, or Ital-	Ian,
As Jonathan, which name in Dutch is	Jan.
My fame will far exceed that of Mar-	K An-
tony, of Homer, Caesar, Corio-	Lan-
us, or, in short, of any mortal	Man,
Even Mendez Pinto, also called Fer-	Nan,
Whose book I'll read on getting a l-	O-an
Thereof, because I'm told it will ex-	Pan-
d my mind, and stuff and store it with a	Quan-
tity of facts true as the Alco-	Ran.
But first I calculate I'll munch a	San-
dwich, which I'll nobly wash down with a	Tan-

Line numbers in right margin: 5 (line 5), 10 (line 10), 15 (line 15), 20 (line 20)

kard of stout ale, then dress like Don J	U-an,
And stroll to COHEN's neat Cigar Di-	Van,
(Though smoking overmuch has made me	Wan,)
And there I'll hear folks talk much more like	Xan-
tippe than Socrates or John Bun-	Yan, 25
Of whom, however, I'm no parti-	Zan.

[Clarence, *Weekly Dublin Satirist*, 10 January 1835]

from *Anthologia Germanica–No. III*
Miscellaneous Poems and Metrical Tales

Mignon's Song
BY GOETHE

O! dost thou know the clime where citron fruits are blooming fair?
The gold-hued orange burns among the dusky greenery there;
From skies of speckless blue are wafted airlets warm and soft;
There sleepy myrtles grow; there trees of laurel stand aloft.
    That bright land dost thou know?   5
    Thither with thee, my love, I long to go.

And dost thou know the Pile, with roof on colonnades reclining?
The broad saloon is bright; the chambers there are darkly shining,
And alabaster forms look down upon me pityingly.
Alas, unhappy child! what ill the world has done to thee!   10
    That dwelling dost thou know?
    Thither, protector mine, with thee I'll go.

Knowest thou the mountain's brow? Its pathway clouds and shadows cover:
Amid the darkling mist the mule pursues his blind way over.
The dragon and his brood lurk in its thousand cavern-hollows;   15
The rent rock topples down; the headlong sweep of waters follows.
    That mountain dost thou know?
    Thither our way lies. Father, let us go.

[Unsigned, *DUM*, April 1835]

Sonnet

Bird, that discoursest from yon poplar bough,
  Outweeping night, and in thy eloquent tears
  Holding sweet converse with the thousand spheres
That glow and listen from Night's glorious brow,
Oh, may thy lot be mine! that, lonely now,   5
  And doom'd to mourn the remnant of my years,
  My song may swell to more than mortal ears,
  And sweet as is thy strain be poured my vow.

Bird of the poet's paradise! by thee
  Taught where the tides of feeling deepest tremble,   10
Playful in gloom, like some sequestered sea,
  I too amidst my anguish would dissemble,
And tune misfortune to such melody,
  That my despair thy transports should resemble.

                              [Unsigned, *DUM*, June 1835]

from *Anthologia Germanica–No. V*
Faust, and the Minor Poems of Goethe

[...] From the smaller pieces of Goethe we shall first select two of the Ballads—
Das Lied des gefangnen Grafen, and *Erlkönig*. [. . .] The second Ballad has
been translated, we believe, by Sir Walter Scott, and by others. We give it in
a novel dress.

The Alder-King

Who is it rides across the dun
  And desolate wolds?
It is the father—and his son
  In his arms he holds:
He rides through Night, he rides through storm,   5
  And from wild to wild,
But in his mantle, wrapped up warm,
  He carries the child.

(The Father)   'My son, my son, why dost thou bow
              Thy head, as in fear?'   10

  (The Son)   'O, father! father! seest not thou
              The Alder-King near?
          The Alder-King!—he glares on me
              With his crown and trail!'

(The Father)   'Hush! hush! my child—I only see   15
              The mist from the vale.'

(The Spectre)   'O, come with me, dear little boy!
              Come with me, O, come!
          I've many a pretty play and toy
              For thee at my home: 20
         Pied flowers are springing on the strand;
              My mother, she, too,
         Shall weave thee dresses gay and grand
              Of a gold-bright hue.'

  (The Son)   'List! father, list!—the Alder-King's   25
              Words creep on mine ear—
         He whispers me such wileful things!
              O! dost thou not hear?'

(The Father)   'Peace, peace, my darling child!—be still!
              Thy hearing deceives: 30
         The wind at midnight whistles shrill
              Through the shrunken leaves.'

(The Spectre)   'My charming babe! dost hear me call?
              Come hither to me!
         Come! and my pretty daughters all   35
              Shall wait upon thee;
         And they and thou so merrily
              Shall dance and shall leap;
         They'll play with thee, and sing for thee,
              And rock thee asleep.'   40

  (The Son)   'O, father, look!—O, father mine!
              Descriest thou not

His daughters? Look!—their garments shine
  From yon gloomy spot!'

(The Father) 'My son! my son! thou dost but rave;   45
    All night in that way
  One sees the one-armed willows wave
    So ancient and grey.'

(The Spectre) 'Sweet child! I love thy comely shape
    So come! come away!   50
  Nay! nay! thou shalt not thus escape;
    I'll make thee obey.'

(The Son) 'Ha, father! ha!—the Alder-King—
    He grasps me so tight!
  Father! I've suffered some bad thing   55
    From his hand tonight.'

The father, shuddering, swiftly rides
  O'er the lightless wild,
And closelier in his mantle hides
  The terrified child.
With toil and pain he nears the gate,   60
  And reins in his horse—
Unhappy father!—'tis too late!
  In thine arms is a corse.

But Goethe, though he rambled at times into the fields of the Marvellous, never looked for his happiest harvest in them. He felt himself on strange ground, for he loved the domains of Nature and Reality; and the statues which these twain had set up in the gallery of Time, were the gods before whom, from first to last, his idolatry—if we may so speak without irreverence—exhausted the greater portion of its fervour. Goethe appears to have been skilled in the languages of the East. But his acquaintance with these was not made available in administering to the popular appetite for those monstrous fictions with which the stores of Oriental literature abound. He has transferred to his own pages perhaps just as much of the minds of other men as was worthy of being made immortal. Everywhere he gives us the *tableaux vivans* of Man and Man's world—if not exactly as they are, at all events exactly as his eye took their dimensions. Some odd pages, indeed, smell so much more suspiciously of the Weimar, than of the

Wonderful Lamp, that we read them twice over before our doubts are altogether dissipated. But all are alike genuine—we would not even except the *Köptishce Lieder;* and yet these run very much in this fashion—

A Song from the Coptic

Quarrels have long been in vogue among sages;
  Still, though in many things wranglers and rancorous,
All the philosopher-scribes of all ages
  Join, *una voce*, on one point to anchor us.
Here is the gist of their mystified pages,   5
Here is the wisdom we purchase with gold—
𝔠𝔥𝔦𝔩𝔡𝔯𝔢𝔫 𝔬𝔣 𝔏𝔦𝔤𝔥𝔱, 𝔩𝔢𝔞𝔳𝔢 𝔱𝔥𝔢 𝔴𝔬𝔯𝔩𝔡 𝔱𝔬 𝔦𝔱𝔰 𝔪𝔲𝔩𝔦𝔰𝔥𝔫𝔢𝔰𝔰,
𝔗𝔥𝔦𝔫𝔤𝔰 𝔱𝔬 𝔱𝔥𝔢𝔦𝔯 𝔫𝔞𝔱𝔲𝔯𝔢𝔰, 𝔞𝔫𝔡 𝔣𝔬𝔬𝔩𝔰 𝔱𝔬 𝔱𝔥𝔢𝔦𝔯 𝔣𝔬𝔬𝔩𝔦𝔰𝔥𝔫𝔢𝔰𝔰;
𝔅𝔢𝔯𝔯𝔦𝔢𝔰 𝔴𝔢𝔯𝔢 𝔟𝔦𝔱𝔱𝔢𝔯 𝔦𝔫 𝔣𝔬𝔯𝔢𝔰𝔱𝔰 𝔬𝔣 𝔬𝔩𝔡.

Hoary old Merlin, that great necromancer,   10
Made me, a student, a similar answer,
When I besought him for light and for lore:
𝔗𝔬𝔦𝔩𝔢𝔯 𝔦𝔫 𝔳𝔞𝔦𝔫! 𝔩𝔢𝔞𝔳𝔢 𝔱𝔥𝔢 𝔴𝔬𝔯𝔩𝔡 𝔱𝔬 𝔦𝔱𝔰 𝔪𝔲𝔩𝔦𝔰𝔥𝔫𝔢𝔰𝔰,
𝔗𝔥𝔦𝔫𝔤𝔰 𝔱𝔬 𝔱𝔥𝔢𝔦𝔯 𝔫𝔞𝔱𝔲𝔯𝔢𝔰 𝔞𝔫𝔡 𝔣𝔬𝔬𝔩𝔰 𝔱𝔬 𝔱𝔥𝔢𝔦𝔯 𝔣𝔬𝔬𝔩𝔦𝔰𝔥𝔫𝔢𝔰𝔰;
𝔊𝔯𝔞𝔫𝔦𝔱𝔢 𝔴𝔞𝔰 𝔥𝔞𝔯𝔡 𝔦𝔫 𝔱𝔥𝔢 𝔮𝔲𝔞𝔯𝔯𝔦𝔢𝔰 𝔬𝔣 𝔶𝔬𝔯𝔢.   15

And on the ice-crested heights of Armenia,
And in the valleys of broad Abyssinia,
Still spake the Oracle just as before:
𝔚𝔬𝔲𝔩𝔡𝔰𝔱 𝔱𝔥𝔬𝔲 𝔥𝔞𝔳𝔢 𝔭𝔢𝔞𝔠𝔢, 𝔩𝔢𝔞𝔳𝔢 𝔱𝔥𝔢 𝔴𝔬𝔯𝔩𝔡 𝔱𝔬 𝔦𝔱𝔰 𝔪𝔲𝔩𝔦𝔰𝔥𝔫𝔢𝔰𝔰,
𝔗𝔥𝔦𝔫𝔤𝔰 𝔱𝔬 𝔱𝔥𝔢𝔦𝔯 𝔫𝔞𝔱𝔲𝔯𝔢𝔰, 𝔞𝔫𝔡 𝔣𝔬𝔬𝔩𝔰 𝔱𝔬 𝔱𝔥𝔢𝔦𝔯 𝔣𝔬𝔬𝔩𝔦𝔰𝔥𝔫𝔢𝔰𝔰;
𝔅𝔢𝔢𝔱𝔩𝔢𝔰 𝔴𝔢𝔯𝔢 𝔟𝔩𝔦𝔫𝔡 𝔦𝔫 𝔱𝔥𝔢 𝔞𝔤𝔢𝔰 𝔬𝔣 𝔶𝔬𝔯𝔢.   20

Another Song, from the same Coptic

Go!—but heed and understand
This my last and best command:
Turn thine Youth to such advantage
As that no reverse shall daunt Age.
Learn the serpent's wisdom early;   5
And contemn what Time destroys;

Also, wouldst thou creep or climb,
Chuse thy rôle, and chuse in time,
Since the scales of Fortune rarely
Show a liberal equipoise.   10
𝕿𝖍𝖔𝖚 𝖒𝖚𝖘𝖙 𝖊𝖎𝖙𝖍𝖊𝖗 𝖘𝖔𝖆𝖗 𝖔𝖗 𝖘𝖙𝖔𝖔𝖕,
𝕱𝖆𝖑𝖑 𝖔𝖗 𝖙𝖗𝖎𝖚𝖒𝖕𝖍, 𝖘𝖙𝖆𝖓𝖉 𝖔𝖗 𝖉𝖗𝖔𝖔𝖕;
𝕿𝖍𝖔𝖚 𝖒𝖚𝖘𝖙 𝖊𝖎𝖙𝖍𝖊𝖗 𝖘𝖊𝖗𝖛𝖊 𝖔𝖗 𝖌𝖔𝖛𝖊𝖗𝖓,
𝕸𝖚𝖘𝖙 𝖇𝖊 𝖘𝖑𝖆𝖛𝖊, 𝖔𝖗 𝖒𝖚𝖘𝖙 𝖇𝖊 𝖘𝖔𝖛𝖊𝖗𝖊𝖎𝖌𝖓,
𝕸𝖚𝖘𝖙, 𝖎𝖓 𝖋𝖎𝖓𝖊, 𝖇𝖊 𝖇𝖑𝖔𝖈𝖐 𝖔𝖗 𝖜𝖊𝖉𝖌𝖊,   15
𝕸𝖚𝖘𝖙 𝖇𝖊 𝖆𝖓𝖛𝖎𝖑 𝖔𝖗 𝖇𝖊 𝖘𝖑𝖊𝖉𝖌𝖊.

[Unsigned, *DUM*, March 1836]

from *Stray Leaflets from the German Oak*

Ichabod! the glory hath departed
LUDWIG UHLAND

I ride through a dark, dark Land by night,
Where moon is none and no stars lend light,
   And rueful winds are blowing;
Yet oft have I trodden this way ere now
With Summer zephyrs a-fanning my brow   5
   And the gold of the sunshine glowing.

I roam by a gloomy Garden-wall;
The deathstricken leaves around me fall,
   And the nightblast wails its dolors;
How oft with my love I have hitherward strayed   10
When the roses flowered, and all I surveyed
   Was radiant with Hope's own colors!

But the gold of the sunshine is shed and gone,
And the once bright roses are dead and wan,
   And my love in her low grave moulders,   15
And I ride through a dark, dark Land by night
With never a star to bless me with light,
   And the Mantle of Age on my shoulders.

[Unsigned, *DUM*, August 1836]

from *Anthologia Germanica–No. X*
Tieck and the Other Song-Singers of Germany

[. . .] *The King of Thule* proffers us what we take for his gem-adorned crown—
but this being pompously placed on our head, turns out to be a Zany's cap hung
round with bells. [. . .]

The King of Thule

Oh! true was his heart while he breathèd,
  That King over Thulé of old,
So she that adored him bequeathèd
  Him, dying, a beaker of gold.

At banquet and supper for years has   5
  He brimmingly filled it up,
His eyes overflowing with tears as
  He drank from that beaker-cup.

When Death came to wither his pleasures
  He parcelled his cities wide,   10
His castles, his lands, and his treasures,
  But the beaker he laid aside.

They drank the red wine from the chalice,
  His barons and marshals brave;
The monarch sat in his rock-palace   15
  Above the white foam of the wave.

And now, growing weaker and weaker,
  He quaffed his last Welcome to Death,
And hurled the golden beaker
  Down into the flood beneath.   20

He saw it winking and sinking,
  And drinking the foam so hoar;
The light from his eyes was shrinking,
  Nor drop did he ever drink more.

'It is the speaker's last argument that weighs with me,' said Byron. It is to the last word of a song that our ears tingle. There is a vibration from the last word that we miss in every other word; mirthful, if the song be mirthful; melancholy, if the song be melancholy. We always look down at the end of the ballad, and if the last word be pretty, we fall at once in love with the entire, as the Prince in the fairy-tale fell in love with Cinderella directly he cast eyes on her slipper. The last word

Comes o'er our ear like the sweet South,

(not Dr. South, the preacher,)

Breathing upon a bank of violets,

(a leaf-bank, if not a branch-bank,) and

Stealing, and giving odour,

(like a pickpocket abstracting a scented handkerchief.)

It so happens that the last word of each of our last two ballads is *more*. Talismanic word! which puzzled Horne Tooke, and which the world so well understands, the sound of which in England is Life, and in France is Death. It calls upon us for other songs. Long let it so continue to call. Let the echo of that call visit the cells of our brain oft in the deep midnight for months to come. We will yet hear and answer. But now, and for a season, our lips are sealed. Unless we alter our mind. A contingency which may occur. Nobody knows. At present, however, our resolution is firm.

The torch shall be extinguished, which hath lit
Our midnight lamp—and what is writ is writ.
Would it were worthier!

We close this Anthology by a poem from Kerner.

'Reading and writing,' says honest Dogberry, 'comes by nature.' There is a good deal of truth in this remark; more by half than Shakespeare imagined. A poet takes to ink as a duckling takes to water: 'he lisps in numbers, for the numbers come.' It is all instinct. The individual is passive in this matter. He is like a voyager at sea, without power to leave the vessel he is in, or arrest its progress. He follows the Will-o'-the-Wisp of Rhyme, 'a weary chase, a wasted hour,' because he must follow it, and for no other reason. So rushes the iron towards the loadstone, the moth towards the flame, the earth towards the sun.

At the same time it is to be noted, that as to 'reading and writing,' the poet uniformly reads and writes just as much and as well as, and no more and no better than Nature ordains. This is the age of wonders; but still every body cannot excel everybody, even in poetry. It is a result of the natural, no less than of the canon law, that there shall be many Priors and few Popes. The eloquence of one man will shake thrones, where that of twenty other men cannot interfere with the equilibrium of a three-legged stool.

With these irrefragable truths we have been familiar from childhood. It would, therefore, be quite impossible that we should ever censure anybody for his or her intellectual deficiencies. We have never presumed to censure our particular friend Kerner. We have expressed some pity for him generally, because, in despite of etiquette and education, we now and then express what we feel, but we have never threatened him with the tomahawk.

He is unfortunate, poor fellow. Nature has, as yet, only half taught him to read and write. His *Reading-made-Difficult* is still in his venerable hands, and when we ask for a specimen of his calligraphy we are invited to contemplate a blurred copy-book, full of pot-hooks and hangers. What then?—His brains were not of his own constructing. The worst that can be said of him is, that he has made indifferent poetry because he was unable to make different. We are not irrational enough to condemn, or even to contemn him. On the contrary, we have doled out, to the fraction of a pennyweight, the precise avoirdupois quantum of panegyric that his deserts called for. Surely, therefore, he ought to be contented.

But if, as we suspect, he remain still as dissatisfied as ever, we would just request his attention to the following translation, and ask him whether he be not, after all, our debtor to a very serious extent.

My Adieu to the Muse
1830

Winter is nearing my dark threshold fast:
  Already in low knells and broken wailings,
Ever austerer, menaces the blast
  Which, soon a tempest, with its fierce assailings
Will swoop down on its unresistant prey.   5
  The Iris-coloured firmament, whereto
Imagination turned, weeps day by day,
  For some lost fragment of its gold and blue,
And the dun clouds are mustering thick, that soon
  Will overdark the little of the beams   10
Of that unfaithful and most wasted Moon

Of Hope, that yet with pallid face (as gleams
A dying lamp amid grey ruins,) wins
  The cozened spirit o'er its flowerless path.
So be it! When the wanderer's night begins,   15
  And the hoarse winds are heard afar in wrath,
He gazes on the curtained West with tears,
  And lists disturbedly each sound, nor sees
Aught but dismay in the vague Night, nor hears
  Aught but funereal voices on the breeze,   20
But when—his hour of gloom and slumber done—
  He looks forth on the re-awakened globe,
  Freshly apparelled in her virgin robe
Of morning light and crownèd with the sun,
His heart bounds like the light roe from its lair.   25
  And shall it not be thus with me—the trance
  Of death once conquered and o'erpast?—Perchance:
I know not, but I cannot all despair.
I have grieved enough to bid Man's world farewell
  Without one pang—and let not this be turned   30
  To my disparagement what time my unurned
Ashes lie trodden in the churchyard dell;
For, is not Grief the deepest, purest, love?
  Were not the tears that I have wept alone
Beside the midnight river, in the grove,   35
  Under the yew, or o'er the burial-stone,
The outpourings of a heart that overflowed
  With an affection worlds beyond control,
The pleasurable anguish of a soul
  That, while it suffered, fondly loved and glowed?   40
  It may be that my love was foolishness,
And yet it was not wholly objectless
In mine own fancy, which, in soulless things,
  Fountains and wildwood blossoms, rills and bowers,
  Read words of mystic lore, and found in flowers   45
And birds, and clouds, and winds, and gushing springs
Histories from ancient spheres like the dim wanderers
  Whose path is in the great Inane of Blue,
  And which, though voiceless, utter to the few
Of Earth whom Heaven and Poesy make ponderers   50
  Apocalyptic oracles and true.

My Fatherland! my Mother-Earth! I owe
  Ye much, and would not seem ungrateful now;
  And if the laurel decorate my brow,
Be that a set-off against so much woe   55
  As Man's applause hath power to mitigate:
If I have won, but may not wear it yet,
  The wreath is but unculled, and soon or late
Will constitute my vernal coronet,
  Fadeless—at least till some unlooked-for blight fall—   60
For, thanks to Knowledge, fair Desert, though sometimes
  Repulsed and baffled, wins its meed at last,
And the reveil-call which on Fame's deep drum Time's
  Hands beat for some lost hero of the Past,
  If mute at morn and noon, will sound ere nightfall,   65
Hard though the struggle oft be which is made,
  Not against Power throned in its proud pavilions,
Not against Wealth in trumpery sheen arrayed,
  But against those who speed as the Postillions
Of Mind before the world, and, in their grade   70
  Of teachers, can exalt or prostrate millions.
I have said I would not be an ingrate—No!
  'Twere unavailing now to examine whence
The tide of my calamities may flow—
  Enough that in my heart its residence   75
Is permanent and bitter:—let me not
Perhaps rebelliously arraign my lot.
If I have looked for nobleness and truth,
  In souls where Treachery's brood of scorpions dwelt,
  And felt the awakening shock as few have felt,   80
And found, alas! no anodyne to soothe,
  I murmur not; to me was overdealt,
No doubt, the strong and wrong romance of Youth.
Less blame I for each lacerating error,
  For all the javelin memories that pierce   85
Me now, that world wherein I willed to mirror
  The visions of my boyhood, than the fierce
Impulses of a breast that scarce would curb
  One ardent feeling, even when all was gone
  Which makes Life dear, and ever frowned upon   90
Such monitors as ventured to disturb

Its baleful happiness. Of this no more.
My benison be on my native hills!
  And when the sun shall shine upon the tomb
Where I and the remembrance of mine ills   95
Alike shall slumber, may his beams illume
  Scenes happy as they oft illumed before,
Scenes happier than these feet have ever trod!
May the green Earth glow in the smile of God!
May the unwearying stars as mildly twinkle   100
  As now—the rose and jessamine exhale
    Their frankincense—the moon be still as pale—
The pebbled rivulets as lightly tinkle—
  The singing-birds in Summer fill the vale
With lays whose diapasons never cloy!   105
  May Love still garland his young votaries' brows!
  May the fond husband and his faithful spouse
List to the pleasant nightingale with joy!
May radiant Hope for the soft souls that dream
  Of golden hours long, long continue brightening 110
An alas! traitorous Future with her beam,
  When in forgotten dust my bones lie whitening!
And, for myself, all I would care to claim
  Is kindness to my memory—and to those
  Whom I have tried, and trusted to the close,   115
Would I speak thus: Let Truth but give to Fame
My virtues with my failings; if this be,
Not all may weep but none will blush for me;
And—whatsoever chronicle of Good,
  Attempted or achieved, may stand to speak   120
  For what I was, when kindred souls shall seek
To unveil a life but darkly understood,—
Men will not, cannot write it on my grave
  That I, like myriads, was a mindless clod,
  And trod with fettered will the course they trod, 125
Crouched to a world whose habitudes deprave
And sink the loftiest nature to a slave,
  Slunk from my standard and renounced my God.
They will not, cannot tell, when I am cold,
  That I betrayed even once a plighted trust,   130
  Wrote but a single vow in Summer dust,

Or, weakly blinded by the glitter, sold
The best affections of my heart for gold,
And died as fickle as the wind or wave;
No! they will not write this upon my grave.   135
                    [Unsigned, *DUM*, March 1837]

from *Literæ Orientales–No. I*
Persian and Turkish Poetry

[. . .] It is our policy, roamers as we are through the Enchanted Caverns of
Oriental Poetry, to commence our scheme of operations, like the pupil of the
Dervish Noureddin in the tale, by picking up from the ground a few stray jewels
of slight weight and no very brilliant water, before we proceed to ransack the
coffers and carry off the ponderous golden vases that lie piled about us. So opens
an Indian juggler his exhibition by tossing two or three small brass balls into the
air, yet by and by brings down more stars than pave the visible heaven to play in
dazzling dance around his head. It is in harmony with order to preface great
achievements by little: thus the Russian Gastronomer, Alexis Ruganoff, when
about to devour a hog, a sheep, and an ovenful of loaves, regularly introduced his
three courses by one horn of brandy. We need not therefore, we hope, offer any
formal apology for confining ourselves in this leading, but we trust, not leaden,
article of ours, to those terse and laconic pieces of poetry whose brevity, when it
fails to display the soul of wit, will at least make dulness more endurable.

     To resume, then, with an epigram or two.

EPIGRAM
To a friend who had invited the author to supper and
*read to him a book of his Ghazels**
FROM THE POEMS OF DJESERI KASIM-PASHA, SURNAMED SAFI,
OR THE SPECKLESS
OB. 1518

Thine entertainment, honest friend, had one insufferable fault;
  Too little salt was in thy songs, too much about thy meats and sallads;
In future shew a better taste; take from thy table half the salt;
  And put it where 'tis wanted more, in thine insipid batch of ballads.

* A Ghazel is a short piece of Oriental poetry, rarely consisting of more than twenty lines, and
usually limited to ten. It is distinguished by the recurrence of one particular rhyme from beginning
to end; in most instances also the name of the poet is introduced into it.

EPIGRAM
To Yusuf Ben Ali Ben Yacoob
FROM THE POEMS OF SCHEICHI II. SURNAMED DJAGHIDSHURDSHI
OB. 1526

I wrote, Y**** is a wretched proser,
Though tolerable verse-composer;
But 'twas not *thee* I satirised;
And I confess I feel surprised
To see thee thus take fire like nitre;   5
  For thou art wrong, and thou should'st know it;
Thou *art*, indeed, a poor prose-writer,
  But *not* a tolerable poet.

A TRIPLET
On the reign of the great Sultan
BY NEDSCHATI

Such are the stillness and peace that prevail through the Sultan's dominions
That the dread Angel of Death, when he startles thy couch with his pinions
Can bring thee no stillier peace than is found in the Sultan's dominions.

To 'make a solitude and call it peace' is so frequent a mistake with sovereigns
that we were at first inclined to scrawl the word *Epigram* over this too. But the
Sultan alluded to was Bajazet, who had conferred many favors on the poet, and
repeatedly entertained him at dinners; and so the thing, we take it, must have
passed in its day for a compliment.

No. XVI [the following poem] is in the true spirit of Oriental hyperbole.

To Miriam, on her Hair
BY SELMAN
OB. 1530. FROM THE AKAD* OF KINALISADE

Ethiopians are thy locks;
  In each hair
  Lurks a snare

* String of Pearls.

Worse than Afric's gulfs and rocks;
  They who swear   5
  By that hair
Swear the Koran's oath aright:
By the black Abyss of Night!

This is even more heinous than Shelley's couplet—

  Roses such as maidens wear
  In the deep midnight of their hair.

[...] We propose in our next article giving some account of the *Iskander Nameh*, or Book of Alexander, by the celebrated Ottoman poet AHMEDI, *viz.* Most Praiseworthy. From his poems in Nasmi's anthology we at present extract the Ghazel beginning,

  Shoile alem tab olur ruchsari djanan her gedji.

Ghazel

FROM THE POEMS OF AHMEDI
OB. 1412

Red are her cheeks like rubies, so red that every night,
Despairing to outglow them, the sun withdraws from sight.
All day I drink this ruby wine, those rubies rich and bright,
But these distil in pearls that fill my dim eyes every night.
The nightingale rebukes me; he says my song is trite;*   5
But can I sing when tortures wring my bosom night by night?
While others woo her in their dreams and slumbers of delight,
I groan and weep, I cannot sleep, I weep the livelong night.
Oh! I am slain with deadly pain—slain, slain with pain outright,
That on her breast her locks should rest so softly all the night.   10
Of AHMED's tears and torments, and love's unhappy blight
The lamp will tell that in his cell† burns lower night by night.

---

* *I.e.* The song of the nightingale makes mine seem trite by comparison.
† His dwelling was a cave at the foot of Mount Olympus.

[...] 'My adversary,' says Scaliger, in one of his controversial folios, *'ought to blush when he sees the lengthiness and tediousness of my work, which he hath in some sort necessitated me to write, that I might put him down.'* Now, we are anti-Scaligerian, take us generally, and by the mustachios of Mohammed himself we swear that with the brevity and beauty of this article the public must be enchanted to a degree rather, to say the truth, too painful to be dwelt on; and with respect to which, therefore, propriety dictates to us the preservation of a dignified, we will not add, a stern, silence. They, the said public, shall not feel otherwise, on penalty of being fiercely cut, every anti-human soul of them, wherever we encounter them, at home and abroad, in street and square, north, south, east, west, at church, mart, levee, and theatre. Let them, and they may abide by the consequence. We know how to 'shame the fools.' Our native city shall be in our eyes as a City of the Dead, and WE, agreeably to the Fichtean philosophy, the only existent individual in town. We shall pace the *trottoirs*, perceiving nobody, astounded at our own solitariness, and musing, with Baconian profundity, over that instability of human affairs which in the space of thirty days has removed from the metropolis a population so celebrated for its singular dissensions, to substitute in its stead a type of plural unity—to wit, Ourself. Like Alexander Selkirk, we shall be 'out of humanity's reach, and must finish our journey (to the suburbs) alone.' WE in short, shall be everything and the public nothing, after the manner of the Second and Third Estates of the Abbé Sieyés. Till, upon some bland morning in October, weary of wandering hither and thither in this astounded, musing, and misty-eyed state, we shall at once halt, and proceed, with a majesty of manner worthy of the world's wonder, to appropriate to our own use all such cash and portable valuables as may have been thoughtfully left in our way throughout the wilderness around us; chanting, the while, sundry snatches of songs and songs of snatches by the Arab Robbers of the Desert.

In the meantime we think that after all we have sung we are entitled to a call; and so we call for a series of rounds of applause, to be repeated and renewed until our further pleasure be signified, for our concluding ditty.

The Time of the Roses
FROM THE TURKISH OF MESIHI
OB. 1512

Morning is blushing; the gay nightingales
Warble their exquisite songs in the vales;
Spring, like a spirit, floats everywhere,
Shaking sweet spice-showers loose from her hair:
Murmurs half-musical sounds from the stream,   5
Breathes in the valley and shines in the beam.
  In, in at the portals that Youth uncloses,
  It hastes, it wastes, the Time of the Roses!

Meadows, and gardens, and sun-lighted glades,
Palaces, terraces, grottoes, and shades   10
Woo thee; a fairy-bird sings in thine ear,
Come and be happy!—an Eden is here!
Knowest thou whether for thee there be any
Years in the Future? Ah! think on how many
  A young heart under the mould reposes,   15
  Nor feels how wheels the Time of the Roses!

In the red light of the many-leaved rose,
Mahomet's wonderful mantle re-glows.*
Gaudier far, but as blooming and tender,
Tulips and martagons revel in splendour.   20
Drink from the Chalice of Joy, ye who may!
Youth is a flower of early decay,
  And Pleasure a monarch that Age deposes,
  When past, at last, the Time of the Roses!

See the young lilies, their scymitar-petals   25
Glancing like silver 'mid earthier metals:
Dews of the brightest in life-giving showers
Fall all the night on these luminous flowers.
Each of them sparkles afar like a gem.
Wouldst thou be smiling and happy like them?   30
  O, follow all counsel that Pleasure proposes;
  It dies, it flies, the Time of the Roses!

---

* When Mohammed, says tradition, covered his head with the hood of his mantle, the covering
shone like bright crimson wool steeped in oil.

Pity the roses! Each rose is a maiden,
Prankt, and with jewels of dew overladen:
Pity the maidens! The moon of their bloom   35
Rises, to set in the cells of the tomb.
Life has its Winter:—When Summer is gone,
Maidens, like roses, lie stricken and wan.
  Though bright as the Burning Bush of Moses,
  Soon fades, fair maids, the Time of your Roses!   40

Lustre and odours and blossoms and flowers,
All that is richest in gardens and bowers,
Teach us morality, speak of Mortality,
Whisper that Life is a swift Unreality!
Death is the end of that lustre, those odours;   45
Brilliance and Beauty are gloomy foreboders
  To him who knows what this world of woes is,
  And sees how flees the Time of the Roses!

Heed them not, hear them not! Morning is blushing,
Perfumes are wandering, fountains are gushing.   50
What though the rose, like a virgin forbidden,
Long under leafy pavilion lay hidden;
Now far around as the vision can stretch,
Wreaths for the pencils of angels to sketch,
  Festoon the tall hills the landscape discloses.   55
  O! sweet, though fleet, is the Time of the Roses!

Now the air—drunk from the breath of the flowers—
Faints like a bride whom her bliss overpowers;
Such and so rich is the fragrance that fills
Æther and cloud that its essence distils,   60
As through thin lily-leaves earthward again,
Sprinkling with rose-water garden and plain.
  O! joyously after the Winter closes,
  Returns and burns* the Time of the Roses!

O! for some magical vase to imprison   65
All the sweet incense that yet has not risen!
And the swift pearls that, radiant and rare,
Glisten and drop through the hollows of Air!

* And still when the merry date-season is *burning.—Lalla Rookh.*

Vain! they depart, both the Beaming and Fragrant!
So, too, Hope leaves us, and Love proves a vagrant.   70
   Too soon their entrancing illusion closes,
   It cheats, it fleets, the Time of the Roses!

Tempest, and Thunder, and War were abroad;
Riot and Turbulence triumphed unawed;
SOLIMAN rose, and the thunders were hushed,   75
Faction was prostrate, and Turbulence crushed;
Once again Peace in her gloriousness rallies;
Once again shine the glad skies on our valleys;
   And sweetly anew the poet composes
   His lays in praise of the Time of the Roses!   80

*I, TOO, MESIHI, ALREADY RENOWNED,
CENTURIES HENCE BY MY SONGS SHALL BE CROWNED;
FAR AS THE STARS OF THE WIDE HEAVEN SHINE,
MEN SHALL REJOICE IN THIS CAROL OF MINE.
LEILA! THOU ART AS A ROSE UNTO ME: 85
THINK ON THE NIGHTINGALE SINGING FOR THEE;
   FOR HE WHO ON LOVE LIKE THINE REPOSES,
   LEAST HEEDS HOW SPEEDS THE TIME OF THE ROSES!
            [Unsigned, *DUM*, September 1837]

from *Anthologia Germanica–No. XI*
Miscellaneous Poems

[... A young poet] whose name (DRECHSLER) we have seen only in periodicals, has written several excellent songs of this class [drinking-songs]. One of these in particular we should like to attempt but for its preposterous length: we give, however, the concluding stanzas.

Our matchless countryman, Sam Lover, would perhaps do us the favor of setting them to music. Meanwhile, we recommend them to every other psalm-lover generally.

---

* In the MS. of Nasmi's Anthology this stanza is written in large and gorgeous characters.

Fragment of Another [Drinking Song]

XI
Albeit we smile
When we behold
A beerless pot
Or a punchless bowl,
Yet that is bile;   5
Such smile is cold;
It brightens not
The sunken soul!

XII
Ah, no! to illume
Both souls and brows   10
Go, fill the toom,
Both bowl and quart;
And troll a song,
And toast your *frows*,
For nights are long   15
And Life is short!

XIII
And Love is sweet,
And Song is gay,
And punch is strong,
And wine is bright,   20
And Time is fleet,
And joys decay,
Nor wine nor song
Outlives the night!

XIV
And, friends of mine!   25
Long nights above
Our mould the wind
Will wail and rave,
And punch and wine
And songs of love   30
Shall no man find
Inside his grave.

The last stanza is perhaps more thoroughly German than any we have ever quoted.

[Unsigned, *DUM*, December 1837]

from *Literæ Orientales–No. II*
Turkish Poetry

[. . .] Turkish poetry abounds in short pieces, intended for epigrams, and chiefly complimentary of beauty. We give a few samples, though their wit may not, we admit, be readily understood or sympathised with.

The apostrophised maiden, for example, is sometimes entreated to veil and sometimes to unveil; to veil lest the world should be dazzled, and again to unveil that it may not be left altogether too dark. Let us hear RAHIKI.

To Mihrí

My starlight, my moonlight, my midnight, my noonlight,
Unveil not, unveil not, or millions must pine.
Ah! didst thou lay bare
Those dark tresses of thine,
Even Night would seem bright   5
To the hue of thy hair, which is black as Despair.
My starlight, my moonlight, my midnight, my noonlight,
Unveil not, unveil not, or millions must pine:
Ah! didst thou disclose
Those bright features of thine,   10
The Red Vale* would look pale
By thy cheek, which so glows that it shames the rich rose.
My starlight, my moonlight, my midnight, my noonlight,
Unveil not, unveil not, or millions must pine:
Ah! didst thou lay bare   15
That white bosom of thine,
The bright sun would grow dun
Nigh a rival so rare and so radiantly fair!
My starlight, my moonlight, my midnight, my noonlight,
Unveil not, unveil not!   20

* Kuzzil Ragh, the Red Valley; in all probability the Valley of Roses at Edreen.

[. . .] A refined conceit in its way was that of THALIB, whom illness had so completely wasted, that he was —invisible!

Genuine Ethereality
FROM THALIB. BORN AT MECCA. OB. 1590.

Mine eyes, of old the beamiest of the beamy,
    Are now, alas! the filmiest of the filmy;
        So meagre am I, too, *no* lath is like me;
Death for my shadowy thinness cannot see me,
    And when he enters my sad cell to kill me,   5
        His lance will not know how or where to strike me!

The expression, rather than the sentiment, of the following couplet by the same writer, strikes us as poetical:—

Double Trouble

I am blinded by thy hair and by my tears together;
The dark night and the rain come down on me together.

[My heart is a monk]

[. . .] But a mere simile is always poetry with an Oriental: thus RAHIKI writes, 'My heart is a monk, and thy bosom his cloister: so sleeps the bright pearl in the shell of the oyster,' and the thought is extolled; [. . .]

YAKINI left a Divan for after-ages; a *melange*, like most Divans, of admirable, tolerable and execrable. The most characteristic of his compositions, and that by which he most deserves to be remembered, is his *Kahveh Kassidet*, or Coffee-ditty. Our version of it does not quite satisfy ourself, but, as it may amuse others, we shall hazard it:

Song for Coffee-Drinkers

Pour Mocha Coffee as a flood
    Into my coffee tea-cup,
And give me—if I may intrude—
    A strong cup—not a weak cup.
I once liked * əuᴉM and thought it good,   5
    But now it makes me—hiccup!
And I get drunk—and mighty rude—
    And raise the devil's kick-up!

The əuᴉM my youth soaked in like sand,
    Has not (quite) left my head since;   10
My sins were great, you understand,
    And I soon, (for my said sins)
Was visited by fever and—
    A hakim† with his med'cines,
So, juggler-like, my cup in hand,   15
    I drink this drink instead since.

My curse on ıʞɐɹ and its mates,
    The suck-bloods! Here I say to
The beardless booby that awaits
    His time to shine a Plato,   20
That if he wants to bribe the Fates,
    He must drain ev'ry day two
Full coffee-pots—as Avɪ‡ states—
    And I, YAKINI, state too!

The man who, in his prime, and long   25
    Ere guzzling makes him sick, quits
The Chian flask as overstrong
    Displays most poli-tic wits;

---

* *Badeh*, wine, and *Raki*, arrack, are written with reversed letters in this poem, as the word Satan was formerly written by German divines, *uvʇvȿ*. We may remark here, *en passant*, for the especial illumination of such 'country gentlemen' as might otherwise be inclined to suspect the authenticity of these poems, that nineteen twentieths of those allusions to *wine* and *winebibbing* which startle us in the writings of Mohammedan poets are regarded by Sir William Jones and other competent authorities as susceptible of a figurative interpretation.

† Physician.

‡ A Physician of Yakini's era.

But if he'd live *in* or *by* song,
    He must bow out *all* liquids   30
Save coffee, ere he'll swell the throng
    Of geniuses and quick wits.

This drink, for which I own a right
    Especial predilection,
I take to be both morn and night   35
    An excellent refection:
It cheers the midriff, clears the sight,
    Acuminates reflection,
And last, not least, bestows a bright
    Mahogany complexion.*   40

Should any jackass take this still
    In snuff, and be too scoffy,
May he, left coffeeless, fall ill,
    And perish of a-tròphy!
Great Islambol† will ever swill,   45
    Despite of Shiekh and Sofi,‡
The drink that rules the roast, (until
    You boil it) that is—Coffee!

[…] Sentiments like the following are rare in Eastern poetry:—

Lament
BY MULHEED. BORN IN ADIRANOPLE. OB. 1538, AT CONSTANTINOPLE.

My drooping heart, well mayest thou mourn
  That Liberty is dead, and Courage!
That both are gone without return,
  That Hope exists no more for *our* age!

---

* 'He was a Turk, the color of mahogany.'—*Beppo.*
† 'Les Turcs nomment Constantinople *Islambol* par une corruption affectée, au lieu d'*Istambol*, mot formé lui-même par corruption des mot grecs εἰς τὴυ πόλιν. Ce mot *Islambol* presente en turc l'idée d'une ville où l'*islamisme* est florissant; de *islam*, la religion musulmane, et *bol*, abondant.'—DE SACY.
‡ The Sheiks and the Sofis, it is well-known, laboured strenuously, but ineffectually, to prevent the introduction of coffee into Constantinople.

The magazines wherein of old   5
  The Great and Good piled up their storage
Of gallant feats, ensamples bold,
  Have crumbled down to dust in *our* age!
The stately Tree of Liberty,
  Which, when the storms of tyrant Power rage,   10
Might yet lend shelter to the Free,
  Is shrunken and decayed in *our* age!*
The fakir begs on every road;†
  The heartwealth grows a worthless dowerage,
Because the mighty souls that glowed   15
  In ages past glow not in *our* age!
Hope thou no more of Man, MULHEED!
  The stars forfend, the Fates discourage
Heroic scheme and glorious deed
  Among the sluggish souls of *our* age!   20

We venture an indifferent, but an exact version of a few lines by the unfortunate Prince BAYAZEED SHAHI, son of Suleiman, who was put to death by Selim, the Shah of Persia, in 1561. He is said to have written them the night before his execution.

Relic

OF PRINCE BAYAZEED, SON OF SULEIMAN. *OB. 1561.*

Slow through my bosom's veins their last cold blood is flowing,
Above my heart even now I feel the rank grass growing.
Hence to the Land of Nought! The caravan is starting—
Its bell already tolls the signal for departing.

* It flourished elsewhere in other times, yet may be remembered hereafter for little better than giving occasion to an epigrammatic couplet by Marmontel—

  Ah, Liberté cherie! en vain on te poursuit;
  Partout on voit ton arbre et nulle part tes fruits.

  Ah, well-belovèd Liberty! in vain we seek thee, go where
  We may; thy Tree is everywhere, thy fruits, alas, are nowhere.

† Man is now but a fakir (a beggar) on the highways of the world.

Rejoice, my soul! Poor bird, thou art at last delivered!   5
Thy cage is crumbling fast; its bars will soon be shivered.
Farewell, thou troubled world, where Sin and Crime run riot,
For SHAHI henceforth rests in GOD's own House of Quiet.

These are certainly impressive and pathetic lines, because one feels that, under the circumstances, they could not have been penned for effect. [...]

Our next article will probably terminate our review of Ottoman Poetry. It will depend on circumstances whether we shall afterwards enter upon Persian and Arabic. At present we have no great inclination to either. To acknowledge the truth, at the close of our paper, *we dislike Eastern poetry*. Its great pervading character is mysticism—and mysticism and stupidity are synonymous terms in our vocabulary. No luxuriance of imagination can atone for the absence of perspicuity. A poet above all men should endeavour to make words the images of things. He should not disdain to graduate in the school of the logician. The shadow on the wall can as easily strike a blow as the poet can produce an impression without lucidness both of conception and language. It is the error of poets that they consider themselves bound to be at all hazards original. They are ignorant that the value of originality is to be tested by the character of the originality, and that the Dull is something totally different from even a remote modification of the Entertaining. They may be assured that every thought worth expressing has already been expressed forty thousand times over. Ideas resemble all other things; there is but a certain useable number of them in the world; and though that number may be vast, it is not infinite. The very phrase, 'march of mind,' indicates the existence of a goal, or it follows that we are all in the monstrous condition of travelling without a prospect of terminating our journey. The stock in trade of the mind—an embargo being first laid on all commodities, the sale of which were a fraud on the purchaser—(and really a poet should have as much conscience as a pedler) is soon catalogued. 'The thing that hath been is that which shall be,' only into another shape transmuted. To repudiate all that is antiquated, merely because it is antiquated, as the Hindoos drive the aged of their kindred into the Hoogly, is fashionable, but wrong. Poets do not stand the higher in the estimation of the rational for writing insufferable nonsense about embalmed reminiscences, and sunny tresses, and spirit-voices. Instead of creating nondescript forms out of new materials they should rather endeavour to mould existing materials into new and more beautiful forms. In doing this they would be rendering service to the world and to themselves. Mysticism would disappear from literature, and poetry for the first time stand a reasonable chance of becoming in reality what hitherto it has been only in name—popular for its intrinsic excellence.

[Unsigned, *DUM*, March 1838]

from *Anthologia Germanica–No. XII*
The Less Translatable Poems of Schiller

[. . .] Now for a tremendous attempt to knock down an armed Goliah with a
penny-hammer—to batter the walls of Jericho by the aid of pop-gun ordnance.
Bitter must have been the beer and bad the tobacco to whose workings we owe
the growlings of Great Frederick against

Philosophy and Philosophers
Der Satz, durch welchen alles Ding.

The Talisman by means whereof
  All things have shape and being,
Which licenses our globe to move,
Which framed and guides the orbs above,
  And keeps from disagreeing   5
The heterogenous parts that make
Up all known bodies is, you take,
  A principle—and this is
  Its name—*Whatever is, is:*

Ice is a cold thing, fire a hot,   10
  Most men are two-legged creatures;
Such truths as these of course are what
Even those may know who never got
  Logicians for their teachers;
But he who learns Philosophy   15
Can tell that one and two—make three,
  That rules are—categoric,
  And fire emits—caloric.

Before old Homer sang his song
  Great heroes met disasters;   20
So, good men did their duty long
Ere even this age, with all its throng
  Of lecturers, our masters;
But not a soul knew *how,* or *why,*
Until Descartes explained it by   25
  Causation and Vibration,
  And their concatenation.

Weak things must yield to strong, we wiss,
  As china breaks ere granite;
Who lacks the skill to hit must miss;   30
'Tis trite that Might is Right on this
  Our orbèd, morbid planet.
But how the case would stand had Earth
Known Ethics and all that from birth,
  You'll find set forth at large in   35
  Our folios, text and margin.

'𝕿𝖍𝖆𝖙 𝖒𝖊𝖓 𝖉𝖔 𝖇𝖊𝖘𝖙𝖊 𝖎𝖓 𝖈𝖔𝖒𝖕𝖆𝖓𝖎𝖊,
  𝕴𝖘 𝖕𝖗𝖔𝖛𝖊𝖉 𝖋𝖗𝖔𝖒 𝖈𝖆𝖑𝖈𝖚𝖑𝖆𝖙𝖎𝖔𝖓,
𝕬 𝖋𝖆𝖈𝖙𝖊 𝖆𝖘 𝖈𝖑𝖊𝖆𝖗𝖊 𝖆𝖘 𝖈𝖑𝖊𝖆𝖗𝖊 𝖈𝖆𝖓 𝖇𝖊:
𝕬𝖘 𝖉𝖗𝖔𝖕𝖘 𝖈𝖔𝖒𝖇𝖎𝖓𝖊𝖉 𝖈𝖔𝖒𝖕𝖔𝖘𝖊 𝖆 𝖘𝖊𝖆   40
  𝕸𝖊𝖓 𝖏𝖔𝖞𝖓𝖊𝖉 𝖈𝖔𝖒𝖕𝖔𝖘𝖊 𝖆 𝖓𝖆𝖙𝖎𝖔𝖓.
𝕿𝖍𝖊𝖓 𝕷𝖆𝖜𝖊 𝖆𝖘𝖘𝖚𝖒𝖊𝖘 𝖙𝖍𝖊 𝖕𝖑𝖆𝖈𝖊 𝖔𝖋 𝕱𝖔𝖗𝖈𝖊,
𝕬𝖓𝖉𝖊 𝖊𝖖𝖚𝖆𝖑 𝖗𝖎𝖌𝖍𝖙𝖊𝖘 𝖆𝖗𝖊 𝖙𝖍𝖎𝖓𝖌𝖊𝖘 𝖔𝖋 𝖈𝖔𝖚𝖗𝖘𝖊.'
  So teach and preach together in
  Their books Vattel and brethren.   45

But Mighty Nature teaches too—
  The Universal Mother
Still moulds the Many or the Few
To meet the ends She keeps in view;
  And wisdom knows no other.   50
While dolts and dreamers moot the case
She still maintains the human race
  And balks each system-monger
  By means of Love and Hunger.
           [Unsigned, *DUM*, July 1838]

from *Literæ Orientales–No. III*
Turkish Poetry

[...] *The Martyrdom of Houssain* is a poem of great beauty. It is a sort of Elegiac Epic, after the Persian models. Its principal and most striking feature is the singular liberality of its sentiments. This was so remarkable immediately upon its appearance that an outcry was raised against the writer, and he was accused of promulgating heretical opinions. But LAMII had anticipated the attack, and was prepared to meet it. He publicly summoned the leading Imams, the Cadi, all the Khodjas and the principal nobility and gentry of Brusa to appear before him on an appointed day in the Great Mosque and hear him recite the poem; and he pledged himself to answer all objections. The step was bold, but successful. All Brusa crowded to the Mosque, predetermined to anathematise, but Nature had gifted Lamii with a voice of marvellous power and compass; and where one cannot edify, it is no contemptible advantage to be able to electrify. The result was the still higher elevation of his character in the minds of his audience as a Musselman and a poet. [...] The episodical conceit of the *Hundred-leafèd Rose*, which occurs in this poem, must, we imagine, have also had some effect in winning over public judgment in his favour,—though KINALIZADE omits any allusion to its instrumentality on the occasion. It runs thus:—that is, if we may venture to claim for our version any participation in the eloquence, ease and beauty of the original lay.

The Hundred-leafed Rose

I AM, saith the Rose, as the Voice from the Bush
     That spake upon HOREB to MOSE:*
Hence hangs, like MANSZUR,† her head with a blush
     The Hundred-leafèd Rose.

* *Tzsun ena Elhakk szirren atzdi nari Musa gul*; literally,—I am God, says the Rose, like the fire of Moses. The Rose is here supposed to adopt the language of the Arabian Mystics, who professed themselves partakers of the Divine Nature.
† Manszur, surnamed *al Halladj*, and called by his biographers Abou-Moghit Houssain Ben Manszur Akbar Halladj, was an Arabian and a celebrated Doctor of the Law in the reign of the Khalif Moktader. His character is not well understood at the present day; some writers think him a saint, others a magician, others an imposter, and others a blasphemer. The last class accuse him of having once cried out to the multitude, *Ana Alhakk!* I am God!—and they assert that he was put to death for this exclamation. That he was executed is certain, but what the grounds of his condemnation were must remain matter of doubt. Some biographers say that he had an enemy in the Grand Vizier Ahmed, and that Ahmed, finding a passage in one of his treatises which stated that if a Musselman could not perform the Pilgrimage to Mecca he should do something equivalent in merit at home, put him to death for the heresy of assuming that there could be anything equivalent in merit with the Pilgrimage to Mecca. Others assert it to have been matter of notoriety that Manszur was wont to make the trees bear fruit in Winter and to bring down showers of silver drachms among the people by lifting up his hands—and that, being a magician, he met the just requital of his crimes. All agree, however, that he was scourged, tortured and burned for impiety or heterodoxy of some kind in the 309th year of the Hejira, and that he died declaring that he was unjustly condemned and that God would avenge his death. The allusion in the line

    Hence hangs, like Manszur, her head with a blush, the Hundred-leafèd Rose,

is to his presumed confusion at the place of execution.

Like crispèd gold, laid fold over fold,　　　　　　　　　5
　　Like the sun that at Eventide glows,
Like the furnace-bed of AL-KHALILL*
　　Is the Hundred-leafèd 𝕽𝖔𝖘𝖊.
Her cloak is green, with a gloomy sheen,
　　Like the garment of beauteous JOSE,†　　　　　　10
And prisoned round by a sentinelled wall
　　Is the Hundred-leafèd 𝕽𝖔𝖘𝖊.
Like ISSA,‡ whose breath first woke from Death
　　The souls in this world of woes,
She vivifies all the fainting air,　　　　　　　　　15
　　The Hundred-leafèd 𝕽𝖔𝖘𝖊.
Profound as the wells where HARUT and MARUT
　　Of BABEL are hung by the toes,§
Are the damask deeps where the odour sleeps
　　Of the Hundred-leafèd 𝕽𝖔𝖘𝖊.　　　　　　　　　20
As the Prophet's° word in the Solitudes
　　Made the doors of the rock unclose,
The Summer's voice unrolls the buds
　　Of the Hundred-leafèd 𝕽𝖔𝖘𝖊.
Like SOLOMON's throne in olden years　　　　　　25
　　Her crimson richness shews;
And the Dives protect with a ring of spears
　　The seal of the sacred 𝕽𝖔𝖘𝖊.**
The Flower of Flowers as a convent towers
　　Where Virtue and Truth repose;　　　　　　　30
The leaves are the halls, and the convent-walls
　　Are the thorns that fence the 𝕽𝖔𝖘𝖊.

---

* *Al-Khalill*, The Friend, elliptically for *Al-Khalill Allah*, The Friend of God, *viz*: Abraham. One of the Mohammedan traditions concerning Abraham is, that he was cast into a fiery furnace by Nimrod, King of Chaldea, for refusing to pay divine honors to that monarch: the tradition adds that as soon as he was thrown in the furnace became converted into a bed of roses.

† The Egyptian Joseph.

‡ Jesus.

§ Two fallen angels, teachers of sorcery, who are condemned for their crimes to remain suspended by the feet in separate wells of Babylon to the Day of Judgment.

° The prophet Saleh, who was called on by the Themudites, an idolatrous Arabian tribe, to prove the existence of his God by miracle, and accordingly made a camel come forth from the centre of a solid rock in the sight of all.—See D'HERBELOT, *vol*. iii. *p*. 172.

** A metaphoric allusion, by no means of the lucidest, to the seal-ring of Suleiman Djared, who by means of it exercised unlimited power over the Dives and Genii. This Suleiman (or Solomon) is said to have been the fifth monarch of the world after Adam.

Like BALKIS* Queen for her queenly mien,
    Like BALKIS for queenly clothes,
Is the bride of the bowers, the pride of the flowers,   35
    The Hundred-leafèd Rose.
Like DAOUD† King on the psaltery playing,
    Each wooing Zephyr that goes
At will from flower to flower a-Maying
    Hath sweetest airs for the Rose.   40
Who sees the sun set round and red
    Over LEBANON's brow of snows,
May dream how burns in a lily-bed
    The Hundred-leafèd Rose.
The sun is an archer swift and strong,   45
    With a myriad silver bows,
And each beam is a barb to pierce the garb
    Of the Hundred-leafèd Rose.
While the moon all the long, long, spectral night
    Her light o'er the garden throws,   50
Like a beauty shrinking away from sight
    Is the Hundred-leafèd Rose.
Like the tears of a maiden, whose heart, ever laden
    With sorrowful thought, overflows
At her weeping eye, are the dews that lie   55
    On the feminine cheek of the Rose.
As Man after Fame, as the moth round the flame,
    As the steer when his partner lows,
Is the Nightingale, when his fruitless wail
    Is poured to the silent Rose.   60
A Princess tranced by a talisman's power,
    Who bloomingly slumbers, nor knows
That the sorcerer's spell encircles her bower,
    Is the Hundred-leafèd Rose.
Alas! that her kiosk‡ of emerald rare   65
    Should be powerless all to oppose
The venom of Serpent Envy's glare§
    When its eye is fixed on the Rose.

---

* The Queen of Sheba, who came from the South to admire the splendor and be edified by the wisdom of Solomon.
† David.
‡ Pavilion.
§ An allusion to the popular Oriental belief that there are jewels which possess the power of blinding serpents and rendering their venom innoxious.

A virgin alone in an alien land,
  Whose friends are but smiling foes,   70
A palace plundered by every hand
  Is the Hundred-leafèd 𝕽𝖔𝖘𝖊.
O! why should she dwell in a desert dell
  With the darnel and mandrake?—Those
Were never meet mates for her, the proud,   75
  The Hundred-leafèd 𝕽𝖔𝖘𝖊.
In an Eden which Heat hath never consumed,
  Where Winter-night never froze,
Should only bloom, should ever have bloomed,
  The Hundred-leafèd 𝕽𝖔𝖘𝖊.   80
O! give her the gardens of PERISTAN,*
  Where only the musk-wind blows,
And where she need fear nor Storm nor Man,
  The Hundred-leafèd 𝕽𝖔𝖘𝖊.
For the Summer's hand of love and light   85
  In the luminous flowers it strows
Earth's valleys withal, drops none so bright
  As the Hundred-leafèd 𝕽𝖔𝖘𝖊.

Hail, SULEIMAN Sultan! Shadow of GOD!
  Great Prince, whose bounty bestows   90
And scatters jewels like dust abroad,
  As the Wind the leaves of the 𝕽𝖔𝖘𝖊.
The pining world felt sick and sad,
  And laboured with troubles and throes,
Till thine avatar bade all be glad.   95
  Like the young Spring's earliest 𝕽𝖔𝖘𝖊.
Now light is in Heaven and health upon Earth,
  June joyously comes and goes;
Rich Plenty has drowned the remembrance of Dearth,
  And the Thistle gives way to the 𝕽𝖔𝖘𝖊.   100
The shepherd is piping a tune of delight,
  The husbandman reaps as he sows;
The gardens forget the black seasons of blight,
  And Summer is vain of the 𝕽𝖔𝖘𝖊.

* Fairy-land.

Reign, Sultan, for ever! and this be thy praise,   105
     Though Eulogy overflows
With the marvels thy marvellous era displays,
     That *thou raisedst the perishing* 𝕽𝖔𝖘𝖊.*

    Both AASHIK and KINALIZADE concur in representing LAMII as extremely
successful in his Ghazels and epigrammatic verses. We have glanced over both;
and we confess, with all respect for both the poet and his commentators, that we
can say but little in behalf of the former. The latter please us more; and from
among them we select the few that follow.

What is Love?

What is Love? I asked a lover—
  Liken it, he answered, weeping,
  To a flood unchained and sweeping
Over shellstrewn grottoes, over
  Beds of roses, lilies, tulips,   5
O'er all flowers that most enrich the
  Garden, in one headlong torrent,
Till they shew a wreck from which the
  Eye and mind recoil abhorrent.
    Hearts may woo hearts, lips may woo lips,   10
And gay days be spent in gladness,
  Dancing, feasting, lilting, luting,
But the end of all is Sadness,
  Desolation, Devastation,
    Spoliation and Uprooting!   15

Volto Sciolto e Pensieri Stretti

Lock up thy heart within thy breast alway,
  And wear it not as bait upon thy face,
For there be more devouring beasts of prey
  Than haunt the woods, among the human race.

---

* Thou causedst a decaying empire to flourish anew.

Haroun Al-Rashid and the Dust

I am but dust, said Hassan, as he bowed
  His face to earth abashèd;
And in my Khalif's glance I flourish or I wither;
Since you are only dust, replied aloud
  The great Haroun-Al-Rashid,   5
Be good enough to tell me what wind has blown you hither.

Description of Morning

  Another night is fled
  Another morning rises red
  The silver stars that twinkle
    Through saffron curtains here and there
  Gleam like the pearls that sprinkle   5
    A virgin's golden hair.
  New beams and brighter smile
  Along the skies, and while
  Aurora's colors clamber
    The mountains of the dawn   10
  The sun, a globe of amber,
    In silentness has drawn
Within his own warm sphere, as morn by morn he draws,
Each glistening straw that strews the Way of Straws.*

A New Moon

Darksome though the Night of Separation
  Unto two fond hearts must ever prove,
Those twin sorcerers, Hope, Imagination,
  Raise a moon up from the Well of Love.†

* The Turks call the Milky Way *Saaman Yoli*, the Straw-way.
† [Mangan refers the reader to an earlier note in the article, which reads:] The Veiled Prophet, Mokanna, is said to have had the power of raising up lights and voices from the Well of Naksheb. See *D'Herbelot*, and Moore's *Lalla Rookh*. Other Eastern imposters, since his era, have also made themselves famous by causing moons and stars to come up from other wells.

Lamii's Apology for his Nonsense

I was parrot, mute and happy, till,
    Once on a time,
  The fowlers pierced my woods and caught me;
Then blame me not; for I but echo still
    In wayward rhyme   5
  The melancholy wit they taught me.
           [Unsigned, *DUM*, September 1838]

from *Anthologia Germanica–No. XIV*
Gellert's Tales and Fables

The Ghost and the Poet
*A Tale of the Pig and the Poke**

The Pig and Poke was haunted by a Ghost
Night after night for weeks. In vain mine host,
Driven to the uttermost extremity,
Had tried to sink him into the Red Sea,
Or blow him to the Coast of Coromandel,   5
In vain had cursed him by bell, book, and candle,
And lavished charm and conjuration,
  And exorcism and spell to banish
The spectre from his tavern-station:
  His visitor declined to vanish,   10
And came to him each night at Twelve o'clock,
  Not cased, like Hamlet's father's ghost, in steel,
But wrapped up in a great white smock, or frock,
  Or graveshroud, if you will, from head to heel.

At length one of the *genus irritabile*,   15
  Which I don't like to render, Snappish race,
A Poet, whom the world had handled shabbily,
  Took up his quarters in the Pig and Poke;

---

* *Die Katze im Sack*, The Cat in the Bag—an inn so called.

And, as our poor ghost-ridden Boniface
  Of late had found it a lugubrious joke 20
To sit alone o'nights, he sent a card
Of invitation to the ill-used bard,
Entreating him to come and crack a flask,
And, if it were not overmuch to ask,
To read him a few passages, or stanzas, 25
From one of his divine extravaganzas.

Accordingly the Poet went, and read
Some fifty frosty strophés, which, he said,
He meant should serve him as the base or proem
Whereon to rear the fabric of a poem 30
Sublime as that old Castle called Otranto's;
The whole to be built up in seventy cantos:
Then, dropping this thing like a hot potato,
  He fixed himself in attitude to read
A drama to be called *The Modern Cato*, 35
A dull, convulsive play—all starts! and breaks—
Which, though his landlord thought it no great shakes,
  Himself admired remarkably indeed.

In sailed the Ghost. The Poet, who saw nothing
  Except his own MS., went on inflicting; 40
  But oh! my goosequill fails me in depicting
The blending puzzlement, amaze, and loathing
Of the grave Gentleman in Calico.
He stood, and having heard a scene or so,
And scratched, as Milton says, 'what seemed his head,'* 45
And turned all colors, buff, snuff, slate, and red,
'By Jing,' said he to himself, 'I find I have reckoned
  For once without my host. This curst First Act
  Sweats my dry bones like winking!'—and in fact
He flitted ere the opening of the Second. 50

* 'What seemed his head
The likeness of a kingly crown had on.'
                  Paradise Lost.

The vintner was rejoiced; and the night following
He begged his lodger would resume Apollo-ing.
'Ah,' smiled the Poet, and took up his drama.
  He read. In came the Ghost, as usual, soon.
   'What! singing to the same infernal tune   55
Again?' thought he. 'The curse of Puck and Bramah
Be on you for a bore of magnitude!
  I cannot stand this!'—and he turned and travelled
Back slowly to the church-yard, growling. 'Good!'
  Chuckled mine host. 'So, Fee-Faw-Fum, you are gravelled!   60
Egad, since Poetry is such a dose to you
We'll henceforth serve it up instead of Prose to you.'

But, p'rhaps the Poet had begun to smoke
  What sort of handle had been made of him,
   For Boniface next night was left alone.   65
The clock struck Twelve!—and with the twelfth dead stroke
  The apparition came—and looked *so* grim!
   'Sam!' cried the landlord in a trumpet-tone,
'Search every rat-hole of the Pig and Poke,
But fetch the Poet and his drama here!'   70
'O, no! no! no!' exclaimed the Ghost—his fear
Supplying him for once with human speech,—
'Let me not see, not hear *him*, I beseech!
That fellow re-assassinates the Dead;
  And blow me if I brook a second killing!   75
Good bye, Rum codger! Snore in peace!' He said,
  And vanished in the twinkling of a shilling.

The satire here happens to be ineffective, because it is misapplied. In our opinion the author of *The Modern Cato* was a poet of some promise. We lately purchased several of his posthumous MSS. in Germany, at the rate of twopence halfpenny the pound weight; and really we are burning them rather slowly. With the help of punch and patience we find almost every five and fortieth page readable. His allusion to his own grave, for example, taken from his *Troglodyte Anthology, Vol. I. Book II. Part III. Chap. IV. Sec. V. Page* 666, is affecting enough to draw tears from the eyes of a wig-block.

[When men behold old mould rolled cold]

When men behold old mould rolled cold
Around my mound of ground, found crowned
  Alas! with grass,
Mankind, though blind, will find my mind
Was kind, refined, resigned, but shrined   5
  Like gas in glass!

[. . .] Our friend [Gellert] is somewhat partial to the hauling of moribunds by head, neck, and shoulders into his fables. We have already had two samples, and here is a third:

The Dying Father

A father had two sons,—the one called Will,
  The other Christy,—*this* a bright young lad
And *that* a humdrum. The good man fell ill,
  And, finding himself getting very bad,
Stretched on the bed of death, he glanced with misty   5
Regards about the room in quest of Christy.
'My son,' he said, 'sad thoughts begin to darken
  My mind. You are a genius. What a task it
Will be for you to face the world! But, hearken!
  Inside my desk there lies a little casket   10
Of jewels. Take them all, my son,
And lock them up, and give your brother none.'

The youth was wonderstruck. He thought this droll,
  And, looking in his father's face, he said,
'But, bless me, father!—if I take the whole   15
  What is poor Will to do? I greatly dread—'
'Dread nothing, Christy,' interrupted t'other;
  'There's not the slightest ground for this timidity;
I'll warrant you your booby of a brother
  Will make his way through life by sheer stupidity!'   20

  Just, for instance, as We have done. Into what corner of the globe have not our paraphrases penetrated?

'Like Psaphon's birds, speaking their master's name
In every language syllabled by fame.'

Yet it is solely our stupidity which, like steam, has impelled us onward. People have often talked of 'the stupidest man alive.' They little dreamt that they were then talking of Us. Yes; it is time for us to proclaim it; we are that identical individual, and no mistake. Our stupidity has been growing upon us from our boyhood; and, enormous as our stock at present is, we are proud to state that we are perpetually receiving additions to it. We are stupider to-day than we were yesterday, and there is not a shadow of a doubt upon our mind that we shall be stupider to-morrow than we are to-day. The man whose vanity leads him to imagine that he can by any human exertion become as stupid as we, labours under a deplorable infatuation—a delusion of rare magnitude—an hallucination afflicting even unto tears. Such a man may indeed deserve success in his endeavours; but he cannot command it: his dream is brilliant, but deceptive; and he must soon awaken from it to all the bitter agony of disappointed hope. We say it without vaunting, our stupidity is a result *sui generis*—a phenomenon to be contemplated with wonder—not to be discussed without a certain awe—to be analysed only by intellects of the first order—obscurely to be comprehended even by them—and never to be paralleled by any. Many persons are called by courtesy stupid, when in point of fact they are only smoky, or perhaps in a degree muzzy; but, for us, we are not only decidedly stupid, but we are sunken, lost, buried, immeasurable toises down in the nethermost depths of the lowest gulf of the last vortex of stupidity. Not one solitary ray of intelligence relieves the dense gloom that enwraps our faculties. Friends and foes alike acknowledge that our state is one to excite the deepest sympathies of the philanthropist, as well as the unbounded amazement of the psychologist and pathognomist. Hence it is that we are spared the necessity of all that exertion and solicitude which break the hearts of thousands. Our stupidity is our sheet-anchor; the bulwark of our strength; the pioneer that levels all impediments before us; the talisman whose touch converts ideas into gold. By means of our stupidity we flourish; we prosper; we laugh and grow fat; we are monthly winning greener laurels, and hourly getting on at an ever-accelerated pace, towards the Goal of Fame. Would that all mankind could imitate us!—could be as stupid and triumphant as we! But this may not be: some must be wise and others otherwise; what is one man's meat is another man's poison; that which is bred in the bone will not come out of the flesh; we cannot put old heads on young shoulders; and one man is born with a silver spoon in his mouth, and another with a wooden ladle.

[Unsigned, *DUM*, January 1839]

from *Anthologia Germanica–No. XV*
Wetzel's Poems

My Home
Kennt ihr das schöne Eiland.

Morn and Eve a star invites me,
  One imploring silver star,
Woos me, calls me, lures me, lights me,
  O'er the desert Deep afar
To a lovely Orient land,   5
  Where the sun at morning early
Rises fresh, and young, and glowing,
Where the air is light and bland,
  And the raindrops fall so pearly—
Therefore am I going, going   10
  HOME to this my lovely land,
Where the sun at morning early
  Rises fresh, and young, and glowing,
Where the airs are light and bland,
  And the rain is warm and pearly!   15
All unheeding, all unknowing,
I am speeding, I am going,
Going home to my—to *my* land,
To my only, lonely island
  In the desert Deep afar,   20
Yet, unknowing and undreaming
  Why I go, or How, or Whither,*
  Save that one imploring star,
Ever burning, ever beaming,
  Woos me, lures me, lights me thither!   25

Some German poets are singularly fond of trying to pass themselves off as persons who ought to be shut up in deserts and transported to desolate islands. Scattered through their books we encounter occasional mysterious allusions to certain dark incidents in their lives—much meeting the eye and more being

---

* *Weisz nicht auch Wohin und Wie:* I know neither *whither* nor how: the *wohin* here is of course used in reference to the geographical position of the island.

meant for the mind. Now this is disgusting affectation. It is a claptrap unworthy
of intellectual men. Byron tried it and got credit for sincerity from some half
dozen persons, of whom Goethe, poor old man, was one. Yet Byron's was a wild
life, and he *might* have done something to 'plunge his years in fatal penitence.'
Where he failed to pass for worse than he could be, who is likely to succeed? [...]
Our friend Wetzel does not pretend to be a very *mauvais sujet:* he has nothing to
confess; he 'sleeps in spite of thunder.' He is in fact, 'more sinned against than
sinning'—wretched only, not guilty—he weeps blood, but has drawn none—
writes daggers,* but never brandishes them. His characteristic fault is that of
talking *à la* Jacob Bœhmen—

> 'His thoughts are theorems—his words a problem—
> As if he deemed that mystery would enoble 'em.'

[Unsigned, *DUM*, July 1839]

from *Literæ Orientales–No. IV*
Arabian, Persian and Turkish Poetry

The Howling Song of Al-Mohara
ARABIAN
'Ahēēm sheerăree kildee tsharkēēn dilinee pir tab.'

My heart is as a House of Groans
  From dusky eve to dawning grey;
     Allah, Allah hu!
The glazed flesh on my staring bones
  Grows black and blacker with decay;   5
     Allah, Allah hu!
  Yet am I none whom Death may slay;
I am spared to suffer and to warn;
     Allah, Allah hu!
My lashless eyes are parched to horn   10
  With weeping for my sin alway;
     Allah, Allah hu!

---

* Noted weapons, *en passant*, with 'all the tribe.'

For blood, hot blood that no man sees,
　The blood of one I slew
Burns on my hands—I cry therefóre,   15
All night long, on my knees,
　　Evermore,
　　Allah, Allah hu!

Because I slew him over wine,
　Because I struck him down at night,   20
　　Allah, Allah hu!
Because he died and made no sign,
　His blood is always in my sight;
　　Allah, Allah hu!
　Because I raised my arm to smite   25
While the foul cup was at his lips,
　　Allah, Allah hu!
Because *I* wrought *his* soul's eclipse
　He comes between me and the Light;
　　Allah, Allah hu!   30
　His is the form my terror sees,
　　The sinner that I slew;
　My rending cry is still therefóre,
　All night long, on my knees,
　　Evermore,   35
　　Allah, Allah hu!

Under the all-just Heaven's expanse
　There is for me no resting-spot;
　　Allah, Allah hu!
I dread Man's vengeful countenance,   40
　The smiles of Woman win me not;
　　Allah, Allah hu!
　I wander among graves where rot
The carcases of leprous men;
　　Allah, Allah hu!   45
I house me in the dragon's den
　Till Evening darkens grove and grot;
　　Allah, Allah hu!
　But bootless all!—Who penance drees
　Must dree it his life through;   50

My heartwrung cry is still therefóre,
All night long, on my knees,
    Evermore,
    Allah, Allah hu!

The silks that swathe my hall deewân*   55
Are damaskeened with moons of gold:
    Allah, Allah hu!
Musk-roses from my Gulistân†
  Fill vases of Egyptian mould;
    Allah, Allah hu!   60
  The Koran's treasures lie unrolled
Near where my radiant night-lamp burns;
    Allah, Allah hu!
Around me rows of silver urns
  Perfume the air with odours old;   65
    Allah, Allah hu!
  But what avail these luxuries?
   The blood of him I slew
  Burns red on all—I cry therefóre,
  All night long, on my knees,   70
    Evermore,
    Allah, Allah hu!

Can Sultans, can the Guilty Rich
  Purchase with mines and thrones a draught,
    Allah, Allah hu!   75
From that Nutulian‡ fount of which
  The Conscience-tortured whilome quaffed?
    Allah, Allah hu!
  Vain dream! Power, Glory, Riches, Craft,
Prove magnets for the Sword of Wrath;   80
    Allah, Allah hu!
Thornplant Man's last and lampless path,
  And barb the Slaying Angel's shaft;
    Allah, Allah hu!

* Sofa.
† Rose-garden.
‡ Lethean.

O! the Bloodguilty ever sees   85
  But sights that make him rue,
As I do now, and cry therefóre,
All night long, on my knees,
    Evermore,
    Allah, Allah hu!   90

[. . .] *The Time of the Barmecides* [. . .] we published some months back, but in such suspicious company that it probably remained unread, except by the few— very few—persons who have always believed us too honorable to attempt imposing on or mystifying the public. We now therefore take the liberty to re-introduce the poem to general notice, embellished with improvements, merely premising that if any lady or gentleman wish to have a copy of the original—or indeed of any original of any of our oversettings—we are quite ready to come forward and treat:—terms cash, except to young ladies.

The Time of the Barmecides*

ARABIAN
'Hudukabar dakkish, deelabar peerish.'

My eyes are filmed, my beard is grey,
  I am bowed with the weight of years;
I would I were stretched in my bed of clay,
  With my long-lost youth's compeers!
For back to the Past, though the thought brings woe,   5
  My memory ever glides,—
To the old, old time, long, long ago,
  The Time of the Barmecides!
To the old, old time, long, long ago,
  The Time of the Barmecides.   10

Then Youth was mine, and a fierce wild will,
  And an iron arm in war,
And a fleet foot high upon ISHKAR's hill,
  When the watch-lights glimmered afar,

---

* The Baramekee, or Barmecides, were the most illustrious of the Arabian nobles for hospitality, intelligence and valor. Their downfal, which was effected by court intrigues, occurred in the reign of the celebrated Haroun Al-Rasheed, about the beginning of the ninth century.

And a barb as fiery as any I know,   15
  That Khoord* or Beddaween rides,
Ere my friends lay low,—long, long ago,
  In the Time of the Barmecides,
Ere my friends lay low,—long, long ago,
  In the Time of the Barmecides.   20

One golden djam† illumed my board,
  One silver zhaun‡ was there;
At hand my tried Karamanian sword
  Lay always bright and bare,
For those were the days when the angry blow   25
  Supplanted the word that chides,—
When hearts could glow—long, long ago,
  In the Time of the Barmecides,
When hearts could glow—long, long ago,
  In the Time of the Barmecides.   30

Through city and desert my mates and I
  Were free to rove and roam,
Our diapered canopy the deep of the sky,
  Or the roof of the palace-dome—
O! ours was that vivid life to and fro   35
  Which only Sloth derides—§
Men spent Life so, long, long ago,
  In the Time of the Barmecides,
MEN spent Life so, long, long ago,
  In the Time of the Barmecides.   40

I see rich Bagdad once agen,
  With its turrets of Moorish mould,
And the Khalif's twice five hundred men,°
  Whose binishes** flamed with gold;

---

* Syrian.
† Goblet.
‡ Dish.
§ Though sluggards deem it but a foolish chace,
  And marvel men should quit their easy chair.—*Byron*.
° His body-guard.
** Cavalry-cloaks.

I call up many a gorgeous show   45
  Which the Pall of Oblivion hides—
All passed like snow, long, long ago,
  With the Time of the Barmecides;
All passed like snow, long, long ago,
  With the time of the Barmecides!   50

But mine eye is dim, and my beard is grey,
  And I bend with the weight of years;—
May I soon go down to the House of Clay
  Where slumber my Youth's compeers!
For with them and the Past, though the thought wakes woe,   55
  My memory ever abides;
And I mourn for the times gone long ago,
  For the Times of the Barmecides!
I mourn for the times gone long ago,
  For the Times of the Barmecides!   60

To Sultan Murad II

  Earth sees in thee
  Her Destiny:*
Thou standest as the Pole—and she
  Resembles
The Needle, for she turns to thee,   5
  And trembles.

[. . .] Before encasing our pen we cannot avoid adverting with regret to the apathy of our contemporaries, English and Irish, on the subject of foreign literature, Eastern and Western. Is it not shameful that we should have been left to fight our Oriental battle single-handed? According to Vallencey every Irishman is an Arab. Yet, what Irishman has come forward to second our exertions? The whole of the reviewing press has nobly sustained us—indeed has lauded us beyond our deserts; and we thankfully acknowledge the obligation. But what we want and demand is active cooperation. We have looked for that in vain; and why we cannot understand. What is the reason that no voice has issued from any

* *Murad* signifies Destiny.

of our academies or colleges? What spell has paralysed among us that spirit of enterprise which led Bowring to the farthest shores of the Danube in search of pentameters, and gave Anster power to penetrate the darkest recesses—the masonic crypts—of Goethe's dædal mind? Where is such enthusiasm witnessable to-day?—

[Where art thou, Soul of Per-Version?]

Where art thou, Soul of Per-Version?
  Where be thy fantasies jinglish?
Why lies intact so much Prussian and Persian,
  And whither has fled the phrase, 'Done into English?'

Up from thy sofa, Lord EGERTON!   5
  Marshal the BLACKIES and GILLIESES!
Bravo, VON BROCKHAUS!*—give gold by the wedge or ton!
  Pay, till all Europe cry out, 'What a till is his!'

O! when Translation's so feasible,
  Where is the scamp would be scheming off?   10
BOWRING, you sponge! have you ceased to be squeezable?
  ANSTER the Bland! what the deuce *are* you dreaming of?
                         [Unsigned, *DUM*, April 1840]

---

*The great European publisher, of Leipsic, who keeps a legion of translators in pay. By the way, we are glad to see that one of these, our esteemed friend Baron Mac Guckin, is bringing out Ibn Khallahan in monthly parts, *à l'anglaise*. This is jolly. Mac could not have put his thumb on a work more wanted than that of Khallahan, nor could the Arabian biographer be in hands better able to take his likeness to a wrinkle than Mac's.

from *Stray Leaflets from the German Oak–Second Drift*

The Erl-King's Daughter, a Danish Ballad
HERDER

Sir Olf rode fast towards Thurlston's walls,
To meet his bride in his father's halls.

He saw blue lights flit over the graves;
The Elves came forth from their forest-caves.

They danced anear on the glossy strand,   5
And the Erl-King's daughter held out her hand.

'O, welcome, Sir Olf, to our jubilee!
Step into the circle and dance with me.'

'I dare not dance, I dare not stay;
To-morrow will be my nuptial-day.'   10

'Two golden spurs will I give unto thee,
And I pray thee, Sir Olf, to tarry with me.'

'I dare not tarry, I dare not delay,
To-morrow is fixed for my nuptial-day.'

'Will give thee a shirt so white and fine,   15
Was bleached yestreen in the new moonshine.'

'I dare not hearken to Elf or Fay,
To-morrow is fixed for my nuptial-day.'

'A measure of gold will I give unto thee,
And I pray thee, Sir Olf, to dance with me.'   20

'The measure of gold I will carry away,
But I dare not dance, and I dare not stay.'

'Then, since thou wilt go, even go with a blight;
A true-lover's token I leave thee, Sir Knight.'

She lightly struck with her wand on his heart,   25
And he swooned and swooned from the deadly smart.

She lifted him up on his coal-black steed;
'Now hie thee away with a fatal speed!'

The shone the moon, and howled the wolf,
And the sheen and the howl awoke Sir Olf.   30

He rode over mead, he rode over moor,
He rode till he rode to his own house-door.

Within sate, white as the marble, his bride,
But his greyhaired mother stood watching outside.

'My son, my son, thou art haggard and wan;   35
Thy brow is the brow of a dying man.'

'And haggard and wan I well may be,
For the Erl-King's Daughter hath wounded me.'

'I pray thee, my son, dismount and bide;
There is mist on the eyes of thy pining bride.'   40

'O, mother, I should but drop dead from my steed;
I will wander abroad for the strength I need.'

'And what shall I tell thy bride, my son,
When the morning dawns and the tiring is done?'

'O, tell my bride that I rode to the wood,   45
With my hound in leash and my hawk in hood.'

When morning dawned with crimson and grey,
The bride came forth in her wedding array.

They poured out mead, they poured out wine;
'Now where is thy son, O, goldmother mine?'   50

'My son, golddaughter, rode into the wood,
With his hounds in leash and his hawk in hood.'

Then the bride grew sick with an ominous dread.
'O, woe is my heart, Sir Olf is dead.'

She drooped like a lily that feels the blast,   55
She drooped, and drooped, till she died at last.

They rest in the charnel side by side,
The stricken Sir Olf and his faithful bride.

But the Erl-King's Daughter dances still,
When the moonlight sleeps on the frosted hill.   60

Twenty Golden Years Ago
SELBER

O, the rain, the weary, dreary rain,
   How it plashes on the window-sill!
Night, I guess too, must be on the wane,
   Strass and Gass* around are grown so still.
Here I sit, with coffee in my cup—   5
   Ah! 'twas rarely I beheld it flow
In the taverns where I loved to sup
      Twenty golden years ago!

Twenty years ago, alas!—but stay—
   On my life, 'tis half-past twelve o'clock!   10
After all, the hours *do* slip away—
   Come, here goes to burn another block!
For the night, or morn, is wet and cold,
   And my fire is dwindling rather low:—
I had fire enough, when young and bold,   15
      Twenty golden years ago!

Dear! I don't feel well at all, somehow:
   Few in Weimar dream how bad I am;
Floods of tears grow common with me now,
   High-Dutch floods, that Reason cannot dam.   20

* Street and lane.

Doctors think I'll neither live nor thrive
  If I mope at home so—I don't know—
Am I living *now*? I *was* alive
    Twenty golden years ago.

Wifeless, friendless, flaggonless, alone,   25
  Not quite bookless, though, unless I chuse,
Left with nought to do, except to groan,
  Not a soul to woo, except the Muse—
O! this, this is hard for *me* to bear,
  Me, who whilome lived so much *en haut*,   30
Me, who broke all hearts like chinaware
    Twenty golden years ago!

P'rhaps 'tis better;—Time's defacing waves
  Long have quenched the radiance of my brow—
They who curse me nightly from their graves   35
  Scarce could love me were they living now;
But my loneliness hath darker ills—
  Such dun duns as Conscience, Thought and Co.,
Awful Gorgons! worse than tailors' bills
    Twenty golden years ago!   40

Did I paint a fifth of what I feel,
  O, how plaintive you would ween I was!
But I won't, albeit I have a deal
  More to wail about than Kerner has!
Kerner's tears are wept for withered flowers,   45
  Mine for withered hopes; my Scroll of Woe
Dates, alas! from Youth's deserted bowers,
    Twenty golden years ago!

Yet may Deutschland's bardlings flourish long!
  Me, I tweak no beak among them;—hawks   50
Must not pounce on hawks; besides, in song
  I could once beat all of them by chalks.
Though you find me, as I near my goal,
  Sentimentalizing like Rousseau,
O! I had a grand Byronian soul   55
    Twenty golden years ago!

Tick-tick, tick-tick!—Not a sound save Time's,
  And the windgust, as it drives the rain—
Tortured torturer of reluctant rhymes,
  Go to bed, and rest thine aching brain!   60
Sleep!—no more the dupe of hopes or schemes;
  Soon thou sleepest where the thistles blow—
Curious anticlimax to thy dreams
    Twenty golden years ago!
                    [J. C. M., *DUM*, June 1840]

Alexander and the Tree

"From this tree it was that the Voice came which spake of old to Ishkander (Alexander the Great), saying, as an oracle, 'Ishkander indeed cometh into India, but goeth from hence into the Land of Darkness.'"—Apocryphal History of Alexander the Great.

The sun is bright, the air is bland,
  The heavens wear that stainless blue
Which only in an Orient land
  The eye of man may view;
And lo! around, and all abroad,   5
  A glittering host, a mighty horde—
And at their head a demigod
  Who slays with lightning-sword!

The bright noon burns, but idly now
  Those warriors rest by copse and hill,   10
And shadows on their Leader's brow
  Seem ominous of ill:
Spell-bound, he stands beside a tree,
  And well he may, for through its leaves
Unstirred by wind, come brokenly   15
  Moans, as of one that grieves!

How strange! he thought;—Life is a boon
  Given, and resumed—but *how*? and *when*?
But now I asked myself how soon
  I should go home agen!   20

How soon I might once more behold
　My mourning mother's tearful face;
How soon my kindred might enfold
　Me in their dear embrace!

There was an Indian Magian there—   25
　And, stepping forth, he bent his knee:
'Oh, king!' he said, 'be wise!—beware
　This too prophetic tree!'
'Ha!' cried the king, 'thou knowest, then, Seer,
　What yon strange oracle reveals?'   30
'Alas!' the Magian said, 'I hear
　Deep words, like thunder-peals!

'I hear the groans of more than Man,
　Hear tones that warn, denounce, beseech:
Hear—woe is me!—how darkly ran   35
　That stream of thrilling speech!
"Oh, king," it spake, "all-trampling king!
　Thou leadest legions from afar—
But Battle droops his clotted wing!
　Night menaces thy star!   40

'"Fond visions of thy boyhood's years
　Dawn like dim light upon thy soul;
Thou seest again thy mother's tears
　Which Love could not control!
Ah! thy career in sooth is run!   45
　Ah! thou indeed returnest home!
The Mother waits to clasp her son
　Low in her lampless dome!

'"Yet go, rejoicing! He who reigns
　O'er Earth alone leaves worlds unscanned;   50
Life binds the spirit as with chains;
　Seek thou the Phantom-Land!
Leave Conquest all it looks for here—
　Leave willing slaves a bloody throne—
Thine henceforth is another sphere,   55
　Death's realm, the dark Unknown!"'

The Magian paused; the leaves were hushed,
  But wailings broke from all around,
Until the Chief, whose red blood flushed
  His cheek with hotter bound,   60
Asked, in the tones of one with whom
  Fear never yet had been a guest—
'And when doth Fate achieve my doom?
  And where shall be my rest?'

'Oh, noble heart!' the Magian said,   65
  And tears unbidden filled his eyes,
'We should not weep for thee!—the Dead
  Change but their home and skies:
The moon shall beam, the myrtles bloom
  For thee no more—yet sorrow not!   70
The immortal pomp of Hades' gloom
  Best consecrates thy lot.

'In June, in June, in laughing June,
  And where the dells show deepest green,
Pavilioned overhead, at noon,   75
  With gold and silken sheen—
These be for thee—the place, the time;
  Trust not thy heart, trust not thine eyes,
Behind the Mount thy warm hopes climb,
  The Land of Darkness lies!'   80

Unblenching at the fateful words,
  The Hero turned around in haste—
'On! on!' he cried, 'ye million swords,
  Your course, like mine, is traced;
Let me but close Life's narrow span   85
  Where weapons clash and banners wave;
I would not live to mourn that Man
  But conquers for a grave!'
            [M., *Irish Penny Journal*, 25 July 1840]

The Editor's Room–Second Conclave

'And politics, and policy, and piety,
  Are topics which I sometimes introduce,
Not only for the sake of their variety,
  But as subservient to a moral use.'—BYRON

COLLOQUII PERSONÆ.—*Editor himself, Popandgoön Tutchemupp, Count Klaapptraapp, In-Cog, Henry MacManus, R.H.A., Non Compos, the Man in the Cloak, the Poker, &c., &c., &c.*

(*Time, Evening*)

Editor—Count, will you draw that curtain? Thank you: we can see what we are about now. What book's that, Non Compos? Brown,—if I should judge from your abstract metaphysical air.

Non Compos—Not Brown, but Gray.

Count—Ah! dat ish de poet:—ish Gray read now?

In-Cog—My dear Klaapptraapp, why will you ask—pardon me—such silly questions? How can grey possibly be red, now or at any other time? Evidently you have not gone deep into Sir William Hamilton's theory of colours. MacManus, what do you say? As an artist, you should be capable of delivering a categorical judgment on a question to which, perhaps, your meditations may have been often dedicated, at that witching time of night when mankind are wrapt in slumber, the moon in clouds, and my cloaked friend yonder in his eternal toga, or toggery.

MacManus—No nonsense in conclave! I wish Twiddle were here to draw your teeth with his etymology, orthography, syntax, and prosody. *Quid rides*, Non Compos—eh? Anything *outré* there?

Non Compos—Why, I'll tell you:—when our worthy Editor bade the Count draw the window-curtain, my eye fell on a line in Gray, which, upon reflection, I now think must have been written with a prospective notion of the window-tax:

'*Dear* as the *light* that visits these sad eyes.'

In-Cog—And, for my part, I thought of Milton's 'Hail, holy light!'—Didn't you, too, Mac?

MacManus—I? *No*—for I don't admire 'wholly light,' or light wholly—I prefer the judicious admixture of light and shade.

Count—Ah, yesh; de light in de Shades ish ver fine—ver bright: I vosh be dere hundred time at night, in Dublin, in de street of Grafton, and I vosh hab read tree—four—five newshpaper—full of, ah!—de magnifique tours de phrase, and—vat you call de—ah—ah—six-squib-a-dealing vords—in de leaden article.

MacManus—Leaden enough, Count; but I suppose you mean sesquipedalian words. By the way, friend Editor, is there anything this evening?

Editor—Interrogate the Cloak thereanent, for I don't feel at all myself just now; probably because I was reading M'Nish's tale of the 'Metempsychosis' before dinner.

Man in the Cloak—Where's the *Morning Herald*?

Editor—Under the *Standard* there, at your elbow, I imagine.

Man in the Cloak—My dear friend, they are every one—*Herald, Times, Post,* and all—deplorably under the standard. I can't find it; but no matter: shall I read you my last from the *Far-away-down-in-the-South Gazette*—my safety valve when I am desirous of letting out my redundant poetical steam?

Omnes—Read—read—read!

Non Compos—If you don't read, we'll forthwith break so many bottles of ginger-beer against your wigged sconce, that, withersoever you go in future for the next thirty years, it shall be conjectured, from the scent of your saturated cloak, that you have but just bolted from a teetotaller's shop.

The Man in the Cloak—(*affecting to read*)—

Asses

*'In truth,' said Martinus, 'every mother's son of us is
in the same predicament.'*—POPE's Martinus Scriblerus.

Buffon divides men into classes,
  But this his druggist-shop conception
Is humbug;—all alike are asses—
  I make myself even no exception.
In fact I'll prove myself an ass-   5
  ertor of truth—the more's the pity—
And then make you besides an ass-
  entor to my dis-ass-trous ditty.

There's Brougham and Vaux (Lord!)—what an ass-
  ailant he is of poor Lord Melbourne!   10
While Melbourne is himself an ass-
  ociate of glum-faced England's well-born;
Then, as Premier, he's quite an ass-
  afœtida pill to Londonderry,
Who is, by jing, a humdrum ass-   15
  everating twaddler, dull and dreary!

O'Connell's a tremendous ass-
  aulter of tyranny and Tories:
The LIBERAL PRESS, too, is his ass-
  istant, and shares—hurrah!—his glories.   20
Ned Bulwer has been long an ass-
  pirant for fame and foolscap laurels,
But Bowring makes himself an ass-
  iduous refreshener of stale morals.*

Trash Gregg's a genuine assish ass-   25
  inine ass—only hear him braying!
Each Orange ruffian is an ass-
  assin at heart, athirst for slaying!
My friend Non Compos here's an ass-
  tonishing dab at quizzing quizzes;   30
And Hal MacManus is an ass-
  ured brush at catching gemmen's phizzes.

In short the world is one great ass-
  semblage of hoaxed and hoaxing ninnies,
'Mong which even I myself *am–ass*   35
  More bran than grist—more jokes than guineas;
Still I don't mind—nor care to ass-
  uage my distresses like your sobbers;
Wrapped in this cloak, my grand cuir-ass,
  I laugh at all,—Rads, Whigs and Robbers!†   40

---

* See, O, reader! his 'Deontology,' in the which he endeavours to make some remote approach
towards rendering Bentham in a slight degree intelligible.
† In Irish parlance *Tory* familiarly means *Robber*.

Editor—I protest, my friend, you don't extemporise worse than your cotempo-
raries—I say extemporise, for I perceive you hold in your daddle the advertisement
sheet of the *Times*. Here's the *Herald* for you now.

Man in the Cloak—Commit it unto the Poker, I pray thee, cousin, for he hath
a fruitful wit, and will assuredly find something in it to tickle thine editorial ear,
and the ear of thy lieges.

Poker—(*glancing over the Herald*)—Upon my word, that's not so bad! Here's
a comparison of O'Connell with Punch—and a chuckle of exultation over the
superior antics of the latter personage. Suppose I throw my comments on it
into rhyme?

Omnes—Capital!—capital!

Tutchemupp—Now, O, Cloak! thou mayest hang thyself up for a season.

Poker—(*Extemporising, save in his text*)—

[Let England's Old Womanhood tremble no more]

'On this head we have no apprehension: Mr. O'Connell may be
a diverting mob-actor, but he is not, after all, half so diverting
as Punch.'—Morning Herald, July 16.

Let England's Old Womanhood tremble no more,
   Let the Peelites securely dine, breakfast, and lunch;
Though O'Connell makes burning harangues by the score,
   Still he can't, or he *will* not,—cut capers like Punch!

Though the wrongs of the people in number exceed   5
   The potatoes that Irishmen saltlessly munch,
Let the cock-a-hoop Tories ne'er stop to take heed,
   For—O'Connell's not half such a grinner as Punch!

There were mighty strange things done by Merlin of yore,
   And queer tales are narrated of old Mother Bunch,   10
But a wonder like this was ne'er heard of before,
   That injustice shall rule, since—O'Connell's not Punch!

How the Mayor (our *Lower'd* Mayor) when he hears it, will grasp
   His thick truncheon!—for rhyme's sake we'll call it his trunch—
And the Guilds, who were thought to have gasped their last gasp,   15
   How they'll roar with delight! for—O'Connell's not Punch!

And thou, Ireland, who stoodest so straight t'other day,
  Thou stoopest anew like a man with a hunch,
Since the ass of the *Herald* came out with his bray,
  That—in short that—O'Connell's no puppet, like Punch!   20

O! there's only one chance that can save us from wreck,
  And help Dan to get rid of his foes in a bunch,—
That the puppet may break, by good fortune, his neck,
  As the showman some night makes a *tumbler* of Punch!

Man in the Cloak—Bravo, my friend! Suffer me to pat you on the back: I like to encourage indisputable talent.—(*Going over and gravely patting the Poker between the shoulders.*)—At the same time I do think that these rapscallion Tories should be left to wallow in their own filth: where their object is to try which shall fling most dirt at the other, neither party is likely to 'withdraw from the contest' covered with glory—on the contrary, both parties are likely to withdraw, covered with mud. You remember, or forget, what Socrates said to a friend of his once. He was peripatetically recreating himself by a lounge through the market-place of Athens, when a fellow without, or *with*, sixpence worth of rags on his person, came up to him and proceeded to vituperate him like thirty fishwomen. To the astonishment of the market people, Socrates merely began whistling *Planxty Kelly*, with variations. The rag-stack thereupon redoubled his abuse—it grew 'a louder yet and yet a louder strain.' Socrates replied by going through '*Thady, you gander*,' in the spirit of an amateur. Just then a friend of his happened to be passing, and the hubbub compelled him to stop and listen. 'Why, Socky,' said he, 'this is non-comprehensible: how *can* you stand such a tongue without retorting?' 'My dear commonplace friend,' was the philosopher's reply—and he helped himself to a minute dose of Lundy Foot's Royal—'I have made it a rule, whenever a jack-ass kicks me, to refrain from kicking *him*. There is a moral degradation in touching such an animal with one's toe. Moreover, from the force of the kick, one may have to lament a repeal of the union between the sole and the upper leather of one's boot. But this last is a trifle,' added he with dignity, as he rattled two-pence halfpenny in his trowsers' pocket. Such, my friend, was the equanimity uniformly exhibited by that great man—an equanimity that I would recommend you to imitate in dealing with your adversaries, both private and political.

(Here the Man in the Cloak surceases, and looks out from the eylet-holes of his garment for applause, when he discovers that the apartment has been vacated by the rest of the conclave. Marvelling much what such a general desertion may mean, he flings himself into an arm-chair, and in another minute is as fast as an anchor.)

[Unsigned, *Vindicator*, 25 July 1840]

Ancient Irish Literature–No. I

THE ancient literature of Ireland is as yet but little known to the world, or even to ourselves. Existing for the most part only in its original Celtic form, and in manuscripts accessible only to the Irish scholar resident in our metropolis, but few even of those capable of understanding it have the opportunity to become acquainted with it, and from all others it is necessarily hidden. We therefore propose to ourselves, as a pleasing task, to make our literature more familiar, not only to the Irish scholar, but to our readers generally who do not possess this species of knowledge, by presenting them from time to time with such short poems or prose articles, accompanied with translations, as from their brevity, or the nature of their subjects, will render themselves suitable to our limited and necessarily varied pages—our selections being made without regard to chronological order as to the ages of their composition, but rather with a view to give a general idea of the several kinds of literature in which our ancestors of various classes found entertainment.

The specimen which we have chosen to commence with is of a homely cast, and was intended as a rebuke to the saucy pride of a woman in humble life, who assumed airs of consequence from being the possessor of three cows. Its author's name is unknown, but its age may be determined, from its language, as belonging to the early part of the seventeenth century; and that it was formerly very popular in Munster, may be concluded from the fact, that the phrase, Easy, oh, woman of the three cows! (ʒo ʀeɪóh a bhean na ττʀí mbó) has become a saying in that province, on any occasion upon which it is desirable to lower the pretensions of proud or boastful persons.   P.

The Woman of Three Cows

O, Woman of Three Cows, agragh! don't let your tongue thus rattle!
O, don't be saucy, don't be stiff, because you may have cattle.
I have seen—and, here's my hand to you, I only say what's true—
A many a one with twice your stock not half so proud as you.

Good luck to you, don't scorn the poor, and don't be their despiser,   5
For worldly wealth soon melts away, and cheats the very miser,
And Death soon strips the proudest wreath from haughty human brows;
Then don't be stiff, and don't be proud, good Woman of Three Cows!

See where Momonia's heroes lie, proud Owen More's descendants,
'Tis they that won the glorious name, and had the grand attendants!   10
If *they* were forced to bow to Fate, as every mortal bows,
Can *you* be proud, can *you* be stiff, my Woman of Three Cows!

The brave sons of the Lord of Clare, they left the land to mourning;
Movrone! for they were banished, with no hope of their returning—
Who knows in what abodes of want those youths were driven to house?   15
Yet *you* can give yourself these airs, O, Woman of Three Cows!

O, think of Donnell of the Ships, the Chief whom nothing daunted—
See how he fell in distant Spain, unchronicled, unchanted!
He sleeps, the great O'Sullivan, where thunder cannot rouse—
Then, ask yourself, should *you* be proud, good Woman of Three Cows!   20

O'Ruark, Maguire, those souls of fire, whose names are shrined in story—
Think how their high achievements once made Erin's greatest glory—
Yet now their bones lie mouldering under weeds and cypress boughs,
And so, for all your pride, will yours, O, Woman of Three Cows!

The O'Carrolls also, famed when Fame was only for the boldest,   25
Rest in forgotten sepulchres with Erin's best and oldest;
Yet who so great as they of yore in battle or carouse?
Just think of that, and hide your head, good Woman of Three Cows!

Your neighbour's poor, and you it seems are big with vain ideas,
Because, *inagh!** you've got three cows, one more, I see, than *she* has.   30
That tongue of yours wags more at times than Charity allows,
But, if you are strong, be merciful, great Woman of Three Cows!

THE SUMMING UP
Now, there you go! You still, of course, keep up your scornful bearing,
And I'm too poor to hinder you; but, by the cloak I'm wearing,
If I had but *four* cows myself, even though you were my spouse,   35
I'd thwack you well to cure your pride, my Woman of Three Cows!
                             [M., *Irish Penny Journal*, 29 August 1840]

* Forsooth.

Ancient Irish Literature–No. II

In a preceding paper under this heading we lately gave a sample from the lighter class of native Irish poetry of the seventeenth century, namely, 'The Woman of Three Cows.' We have now to present our readers with a specimen of a more serious character, belonging to the same age—an Elegy on the death of the Tironian and Tirconnellian princes, who having fled with others from Ireland in the year 1607, and afterwards dying at Rome, were there interred on St Peter's Hill, in one grave.

The poem is the production of O'Donnell's bard, Owen Roe Mac an Bhaird, or Ward, who accompanied the family in their flight, and is addressed to Nuala, O'Donnell's sister, who was also one of the fugitives. As the circumstances connected with the flight of the Northern Earls, and which led to the subsequent confiscation of the six Ulster Counties by James I, may not be immediately in the recollection of many of our readers, it may be proper briefly to state, that their departure from this country was caused by the discovery of a letter directed to Sir William Ussher, Clerk of the Council, which was dropped in the Council-chamber on the 7th of May, and which accused the Northern chieftains generally of a conspiracy to overthrow the government. Whether this charge was founded in truth or not, it is not necessary for us to express any opinion; but as in some degree necessary to the illustration of the poem, and as an interesting piece of hitherto unpublished literature in itself, we shall here, as a preface to the poem, extract the following account of the flight of the Northern Earls, as recorded in the Annals of the Four Masters, and translated by Mr O'Donovan:—

'Maguire (Cuconnaught) and Donogh, son of Mahon, who was son of the Bishop O'Brien, sailed in a ship to Ireland, and put in at the harbour of Swilly. They then took with them from Ireland the Earl O'Neill (Hugh, son of Ferdoragh) and the Earl O'Donnell (Rory, son of Hugh, who was son of Magnus) and many others of the nobles of the province of Ulster. These are the persons who went with O'Neill, namely, his Countess, Catherina, daughter of Magennis, and her three sons; Hugh, the Baron, John and Brian; Art Oge, son of Cormac, who was son of the Baron; Ferdoragh, son of Con, who was son of O'Neill; Hugh Oge, son of Brian, who was son of Art O'Neill; and many others of his most intimate friends. These were they who went with the Earl O'Donnell, namely, Caffer, his brother, with his sister Nuala; Hugh, the Earl's child, wanting three weeks of being one year old; Rose, daughter of O'Doherty and wife of Caffer, with her son Hugh, aged two years and three months; his (Rory's) brother son Donnell Oge, son of Donnell, Naghtan son of Calvach, who was son of Donogh Cairbreach O'Donnell, and many others of his intimate friends. They embarked on the Festival of the Holy Cross in Autumn.

'This was a distinguished company; and it is certain that the sea has not borne and the wind has not wafted in modern times a number of persons in one ship more eminent, illustrious, or noble, in point of genealogy, heroic deeds, valour, feats of arms, and brave achievements, than they. Would that God had but permitted them to remain in their patrimonial inheritances until the children should arrive at the age of manhood! Woe to the heart that meditated, woe to the mind that conceived, woe to the council that recommended the project of this expedition, without knowing whether they should, to the end of their lives, be able to return to their native principalities or patrimonies.'

An Elegy on the Tironian and Tirconnellian Princes Buried at Rome
'a bhean ꜰuaiꞃ ꜰaill aiꞃ an ꝼꝼeaꞃꞇ!'

O, Woman of the Piercing Wail,
  Who mournest o'er yon mound of clay
    With sigh and groan,
Would God thou wert among the Gael!
  Thou wouldst not then from day to day   5
    Weep thus alone.
'Twere long before, around a grave
  In green Tirconnell, one could find
    This loneliness;
Near where Beann-Boirche's banners wave   10
  Such grief as thine could ne'er have pined
    Companionless.

Beside the wave, in Donegall,
  In Antrim's glens, or fair Dromore,
    Or Killilee,   15
Or where the sunny waters fall,
  At Assaroe, near Erna's shore,
    This could not be.
On Derry's plains—in rich Drumclieff—
  Throughout Armagh the Great, renowned   20
    In olden years,
No day could pass but Woman's grief
  Would rain upon the burial-ground
    Fresh floods of tears!

O, no!—from Shannon, Boyne, and Suir,   25
  From high Dunluce's castle-walls,
    From Lissadill,
Would flock alike both rich and poor,
  One wail would rise from Cruachan's halls
    To Tara's hill;   30
And some would come from Barrow-side,
  And many a maid would leave her home
    On Leitrim's plains,
And by melodious Banna's tide,
  And by the Mourne and Erne, to come   35
    And swell thy strains!

O, horses' hoofs would trample down
  The Mount whereon the martyr-saint*
    Was crucified.
From glen and hill, from plain and town,   40
  One loud lament, one thrilling plaint,
    Would echo wide.
There would not soon be found, I ween,
  One foot of ground among those bands
    For museful thought,   45
So many shriekers of the *keen*†
  Would cry aloud, and clap their hands,
    All woe-distraught!

Two princes of the line of Conn
  Sleep in their cells of clay beside   50
    O'Donnell Roe:
Three royal youths, alas! are gone,
  Who lived for Erin's weal, but died
    For Erin's woe!
Ah! could the men of Ireland read   55
  The names these noteless burial-stones
    Display to view,
Their wounded hearts afresh would bleed,
  Their tears gush forth again, their groans
    Resound anew!   60

---

* St Peter. This passage is not exactly a blunder, though at first it may seem one: the poet supposes the grave itself transferred to Ireland, and he naturally includes in the transference the whole of the immediate locality around the grave.—Tr.

† *Caoine*, the funeral-wail.

The youths whose relics moulder here
  Were sprung from Hugh, high Prince and Lord
    Of Aileach's lands;
Thy noble brothers, justly dear,
Thy nephew, long to be deplored   65
    By Ulster's bands.
Theirs were not souls wherein dull Time
  Could domicile Decay or house
    Decrepitude!
They passed from Earth ere Manhood's prime,   70
  Ere years had power to dim their brows
    Or chill their blood.

And who can marvel o'er thy grief,
  Or who can blame thy flowing tears,
    That knows their source?   75
O'Donnell, Dunnasava's chief,
  Cut off amid his vernal years,
    Lies here a corse
Beside his brother Cathbar, whom
  Tirconnell of the Helmets mourns   80
    In deep despair—
For valour, truth, and comely bloom,
  For all that greatens and adorns,
    A peerless pair.

O, had these twain, and he, the third,   85
  The Lord of Mourne, O'Niall's son,
    Their mate in death—
A prince in look, in deed, and word—
  Had these three heroes yielded on
    The field their breath,   90
O, had they fallen on Criffan's plain,
  There would not be a town or clan
    From shore to sea
But would with shrieks bewail the Slain,
  Or chant aloud the exulting *rann**   95
    Of jubilee!

* Song.

When high the shout of battle rose,
　On fields where Freedom's torch still burned
　　Through Erin's gloom,
If one, if barely one of those　　　　　　　　　　　　　　100
　Were slain, all Ulster would have mourned
　　The hero's doom!
If at Athboy, where hosts of brave
　Ulidian horsemen sank beneath
　　The shock of spears,　　　　　　　　　　　　　　　　105
Young Hugh O'Neill had found a grave,
　Long must the North have wept his death
　　With heart-wrung tears!

If on the day of Ballach-myre
　The Lord of Mourne had met, thus young,　　　　　　　110
　　A warrior's fate,
In vain would such as thou desire
　To mourn, alone, the champion sprung
　　From Niall the Great!
No marvel this—for all the Dead,　　　　　　　　　　　115
　Heaped on the field, pile over pile,
　　At Mullach-brack,
Were scarce an *eric** for his head,
　If Death had stayed his footsteps while
　　On victory's track!　　　　　　　　　　　　　　　　120

If on the Day of Hostages
　The fruit had from the parent bough
　　Been rudely torn
In sight of Munster's bands—Mac-Nee's—
　Such blow the blood of Conn, I trow,　　　　　　　　125
　　Could ill have borne.
If on the day of Ballach-boy
　Some arm had laid, by foul surprise,
　　The chieftain low,
Even our victorious shout of joy　　　　　　　　　　　130
　Would soon give place to rueful cries
　　And groans of woe!

* A compensation or fine.

If on the day the Saxon host
  Were forced to fly—a day so great
    For Ashanee*—   135
The Chief had been untimely lost,
  Our conquering troops should moderate
    Their mirthful glee.
There would not lack on Lifford's day,
  From Galway, from the glens of Boyle,   140
    From Limerick's towers,
A marshalled file, a long array
  Of mourners to bedew the soil
    With tears in showers!

If on the day a sterner fate   145
  Compelled his flight from Athenree,
    His blood had flowed,
What numbers all disconsolate
  Would come unasked, and share with thee
    Affliction's load!   150
If Derry's crimson field had seen
  His life-blood offered up, though 'twere
    On Victory's shrine,
A thousand cries would swell the *keen*,
  A thousand voices in despair   155
    Would echo thine!

O, had the fierce Dalcassian swarm
  That bloody night on Fergus' banks,
    But slain our Chief,
When rose his camp in wild alarm—   160
  How would the triumph of his ranks
    Be dashed with grief!
How would the troops of Murbach mourn
  If on the Curlew Mountains' day,
    Which England rued,   165
Some Saxon hand had left them lorn,
  By shedding there, amid the fray,
    Their prince's blood!

* Ballyshannon.

Red would have been our warriors' eyes
  Had Roderick found on Sligo's field   170
    A gory grave,
No Northern Chief would soon arise
  So sage to guide, so strong to shield,
    So swift to save.
Long would Leith-Cuinn have wept if Hugh   175
  Had met the death he oft had dealt
    Among the foe;
But, had our Roderick fallen too,
  All Erin must, alas! have felt
    The deadly blow!   180

What do I say? Ah, woe is me!
  Already we bewail in vain
    Their fatal fall!
And Erin, once the Great and Free,
  Now vainly mourns her breakless chain,   185
    And iron thrall!
Then, daughter of O'Donnell! dry
  Thine overflowing eyes, and turn
    Thy heart aside!
For Adam's race is born to die,   190
  And sternly the sepulchral urn
    Mocks human pride!

Look not, nor sigh, for earthly throne,
  Nor place thy trust in arm of clay—
    But on thy knees   195
Uplift thy soul to GOD alone,
  For all things go their destined way
    As He decrees.
Embrace the faithful Crucifix,
  And seek the path of pain and prayer   200
    Thy Saviour trod;
Nor let thy spirit intermix
  With earthly hope and worldly care
    Its groans to GOD!

And Thou, O mighty Lord! whose ways   205
  Are far above our feeble minds
    To understand,
Sustain us in these doleful days,
  And render light the chain that binds
    Our fallen land!   210
Look down upon our dreary state,
  And through the ages that may still
    Roll sadly on,
Watch Thou o'er hapless Erin's fate,
  And shield at least from darker ill   215
    The blood of Conn!
      [M., *Irish Penny Journal*, 17 October 1840]

Ancient Irish Literature–No. IV

THE composition we have selected as our fourth specimen of the ancient literature of Ireland, is a poem, more remarkable, perhaps, for its antiquity and historical interest, than for its poetic merits, though we do not think it altogether deficient in those. It is ascribed, apparently with truth, to the celebrated poet Mac Liag, the secretary of the renowned monarch Brian Boru, who, as our readers are aware, fell at the battle of Clontarf in 1014; and the subject of it is a lamentation for the fallen condition of Kincora, the palace of that monarch, consequent on his death.

The decease of Mac Liag, whose proper name was Muircheartach, is thus recorded in the Annals of the Four Masters, at the year 1015:—

'Mac Liag, i.e. Muirkeartach, son of Conkeartach, at this time laureate of Ireland, died.'

A great number of his productions are still in existence; but none of them have obtained a popularity so widely extended as the poem before us.

Of the palace of Kincora, which was situated on the banks of the Shannon, near Killaloe, there are at present no vestiges.

Lamentation of Mac Liag for Kincora
a Chinn-coraòh caiòhi brian?

Oh, where, Kincora! is Brian the Great?
And where is the beauty that once was thine?

Oh, where are the princes and nobles that sate
At the feast in thy halls, and drank the red wine?
    Where, oh, Kincora?   5

Oh, where, Kincora! are thy valorous lords?
Oh, whither, thou Hospitable! are they gone?
Oh, where are the Dalcassians of the Golden Swords?*
And where are the warriors Brian led on?
    Where, oh, Kincora?   10

And where is Murogh, the descendant of kings—
The defeater of a hundred—the daringly brave—
Who set but slight store by jewels and rings—
Who swam down the torrent and laughed at its wave?
    Where, oh, Kincora?   15

And where is Donogh, King Brian's worthy son?
And where is Conaing, the Beautiful Chief?
And Kian, and Corc? Alas! they are gone—
They have left me this night alone with my grief!
    Left me, Kincora!   20

And where are the chiefs with whom Brian went forth,
The never-vanquished son of Evin the Brave,
The great King of Onaght, renowned for his worth,
And the hosts of Baskinn, from the western wave?
    Where, oh, Kincora?   25

Oh, where is Duvlann of the Swiftfooted Steeds?
And where is Kian, who was son of Molloy?
And where is King Lonergan, the fame of whose deeds
In the red battle-field no time can destroy?
    Where, oh, Kincora?   30

And where is that youth of majestic height,
The faith-keeping Prince of the Scots?—Even he,
As wide as his fame was, as great as was his might,
Was tributary, oh, Kincora, to me!
    Me, oh, Kincora!   35

* *Ccolg n-or*, of the swords *of gold*, i.e. of the *gold-hilted* swords.

They are gone, those heroes of royal birth,
Who plundered no churches, and broke no trust,
'Tis weary for me to be living on earth
When they, oh, Kincora, lie low in the dust!
    Low, oh, Kincora!   40

Oh, never again will Princes appear,
To rival the Dalcassians of the Cleaving Swords!
I can never dream of meeting afar or anear,
In the east or the west, such heroes and lords!
    Never, Kincora!   45

Oh, dear are the images my memory calls up
Of Brian Boru!—how he never would miss
To give me at the banquet the first bright cup!
Ah! why did he heap on me honour like this?
    Why, oh, Kincora?   50

I am Mac Liag, and my home is on the Lake;
Thither often, to that palace whose beauty is fled,
Came Brian to ask me, and I went for his sake.
Oh, my grief! that I should live, and Brian be dead!
    Dead, oh, Kincora!   55

        [M., *Irish Penny Journal*, 9 January 1841]

The Jacobite Relics of Ireland–No. I

The Jacobite relics of England, and to a still greater extent those of Scotland, have been given to the world, and are well deserving of such preservation; for they reflect no small light on the character and temperament of the English and Scottish people during the last century. But until the appearance of Mr Hardiman's Irish Minstrelsy it was hardly known that in their political enthusiasm for the fate of a decaying family the Irish people participated with so large a portion of those of the sister islands, and that it gave birth to an equal number of poetical effusions in our own country—but with this difference, that their sentiments are usually veiled an allegorical form, and always in the Irish language. To Mr Hardiman we are indebted for the preservation of the originals of many of those productions, and also for translations of them. These translations are however too free to enable the English reader to form any very accurate idea of the Irish originals, and we are therefore tempted to present a series of these relics to our readers, with translations of a more literal and faithful description; not limiting ourselves to those which have already appeared in Mr Hardiman's work—as in the specimen which we have selected to commence with, which is still popularly sung in Ireland to the old melody called 'Kathaleen Ny-Houlahan.'

We may observe, that the name of the author of this song, if ever known, is no longer remembered; but there seems to be no doubt that the song itself is of Munster origin.

Kathaleen Ny-Houlahan

Long they pine in weary woe, the nobles of our land,
Long they wander to and fro, proscribed, alas! and banned;
Feastless, houseless, altarless, they bear the exile's brand,
　But their hope is in the coming-to of Kathaleen Ny-Houlahan!

Think her not a ghastly hag, too hideous to be seen,　　　　　　　5
Call her not unseemly names, our matchless Kathaleen:
Young she is, and fair she is, and would be crowned a queen,
　Were the king's son at home here with Kathaleen Ny-Houlahan!

Sweet and mild would look her face, O none so sweet and mild,
Could she crush the foes by whom her beauty is reviled;　　　　　10
Woollen plaids would grace herself and robes of silk her child,
　If the king's son were living here with Kathaleen Ny-Houlahan!

Sore disgrace it is to see the Arbitress of thrones,
Vassal to a *Saxoneen* of cold and sapless bones!
Bitter anguish wrings our souls—with heavy sighs and groans　　15
　We wait the Young Deliverer of Kathaleen Ny-Houlahan!

Let us pray to Him who holds Life's issues in His hands—
Him who formed the mighty globe, with all its thousand lands;
Girdling them with seas and mountains, rivers deep, and strands,
　To cast a look of pity upon Kathaleen Ny-Houlahan!　　　　　　20

He, who over sands and waves led Israël along—
He, who fed, with heavenly bread, that chosen tribe and throng—
He, who stood by Moses, when his foes were fierce and strong—
　May He show forth His might in saving Kathaleen Ny-Houlahan!
　　　　　　　　　　　　　　[M., *Irish Penny Journal*, 16 January 1841]

from *Anthologia Germanica–No. XVII*
Ballads and Romances

[...] And now for a spirited and *ritterlich* romance from one of the most original-minded of modern German poets—Frederic Rückert.

The Ride round the Parapet
'*Sie sprach: ich will nicht sitzen im stillen Kämmerlein.*'

SHE said, I was not born to mope at home in loneliness,—
    The Lady Eleanora von Alleyne.
She said, I was not born to mope at home in loneliness,
When the heart is throbbing sorest, there is balsam in the forest,
    There is balsam in the forest for its pain,   5
        Said the Lady Eleanora,
    Said the Lady Eleanora von Alleyne.

She doffed her silks and pearls, and donned instead her hunting-gear,
    The Lady Eleanora von Alleyne.
She doffed her silks and pearls, and donned instead her hunting-gear,   10
And, till Summertime was over, as a huntress and a rover,
    Did she couch upon the mountain and the plain,
        She, the Lady Eleanora,
    Noble Lady Eleanora von Alleyne.

Returning home agen, she viewed with scorn the tournaments,—   15
    The Lady Eleanora von Alleyne.
Returning home agen, she viewed with scorn the tournaments;
She saw the morions cloven and the crowning chaplets woven,
    And the sight awakened only the disdain
        Of the Lady Eleanora,   20
    Of the Lady Eleanora von Alleyne.

My feeling towards Man is one of utter scornfulness,
    Said Lady Eleanora von Alleyne.
My feeling towards Man is one of utter scornfulness,
And he that would o'ercome it, let him ride around the summit   25
    Of my battlemented Castle by the Maine,
        Said the Lady Eleanora,
    Said the Lady Eleanora von Alleyne.

So came a knight anon to ride around the parapet,
    For Lady Eleanora von Alleyne.   30
So came a knight anon to ride around the parapet,
Man and horse were hurled together o'er the crags that beetled nether.
    Said the Lady, There, I fancy, they'll remain!
      Said the Lady Eleanora,
    Queenly Lady Eleanora von Alleyne!   35

Then came another knight to ride around the parapet,
    For Lady Eleanora von Alleyne.
Then came another knight to ride around the parapet,
Man and horse fell down, asunder, o'er the crags that beetled under.
    Said the Lady, They'll not leap the leap again!   40
      Said the Lady Eleanora,
    Lovely Lady Eleanora von Alleyne!

Came other knights anon to ride around the parapet,
    For Lady Eleanora von Alleyne.
Came other knights anon to ride around the parapet,   45
Till six and thirty corses of both mangled men and horses
    Had been sacrificed as victims at the fane
      Of the Lady Eleanora,
    Stately Lady Eleanora von Alleyne!

That woeful year was by, and Ritter none came afterwards   50
    To Lady Eleanora von Alleyne.
That woeful year was by, and Ritter none came afterwards.
The castle's lonely basscourt looked a wild o'ergrown-with-grasscourt;
    'Twas abandoned by the Ritters and their train
      To the Lady Eleanora,   55
    Haughty Lady Eleanora von Alleyne!

She clomb the silent wall, she gazed around her sovranlike,
    The Lady Eleanora von Alleyne.
She clomb the silent wall, she gazed around her sovranlike;
And wherefore have departed all the Brave, the Lionhearted,   60
    Who have left me here to play the Castellain?
      Said the Lady Eleanora,
    Said the Lady Eleanora von Alleyne.

And is it fled for aye, the palmy time of Chivalry?
   Cried Lady Eleanora von Alleyne.   65
And is it fled for aye, the palmy time of Chivalry?
Shame light upon the cravens! May their corpses gorge the ravens,
   Since they tremble thus to wear a woman's chain!
     Said the Lady Eleanora,
   Said the Lady Eleanora von Alleyne.   70

The story reached at Gratz the gallant Margrave Gondibert
   Of Lady Eleanora von Alleyne.
The story reached at Gratz the gallant Margrave Gondibert.
Quoth he, I trow the woman must be more or less than human;
   She is worth a little peaceable campaign,   75
     Is the Lady Eleanora,
   Is the Lady Eleanora von Alleyne!

He trained a horse to pace round narrow stones laid merlonwise,
   For Lady Eleanora von Alleyne.
He trained a horse to pace round narrow stones laid merlonwise.   80
Good Grey! do thou thy duty, and this rocky-bosomed beauty
   Shall be taught that all the vauntings are in vain
     Of the Lady Eleanora,
   Of the Lady Eleanora von Alleyne!

He left his castle-halls, he came to Lady Eleanor's,   85
   The Lady Eleanora von Alleyne.
He left his castle-halls, he came to Lady Eleanor's.
O, lady, best and fairest! here am I,—and, if thou carest,
   I will gallop round the parapet amain,
     Noble Lady Eleanora,   90
   Noble Lady Eleanora von Alleyne!

She saw him spring to horse, that gallant Margrave Gondibert,
   The Lady Eleanora von Alleyne.
She saw him spring to horse, that gallant Margrave Gondibert.
O, bitter, bitter sorrow! I shall weep for this to-morrow!   95
   It were better that in battle he were slain,
     Said the Lady Eleanora,
   Said the Lady Eleanora von Alleyne.

Then rode he round and round the battlemented parapet,
For Lady Eleanora von Alleyne.   100
Then rode he round and round the battlemented parapet.
The Lady wept and trembled, and her paly face resembled,
   As she looked away, a lily wet with rain;
     Hapless Lady Eleanora!
   Hapless Lady Eleanora von Alleyne!   105

So rode he round and round the battlemented parapet,
   For Lady Eleanora von Alleyne!
So rode he round and round the battlemented parapet,
Accurst be my ambition! He but rideth to perdition,
   He but rideth to perdition without rein!   110
     Wept the Lady Eleanora,
   Wept the Lady Eleanora von Alleyne.

Yet rode he round and round the battlemented parapet,
   For Lady Eleanora von Alleyne.
Yet rode he round and round the battlemented parapet.   115
Meanwhile her terror shook her,—yea, her breath well nigh forsook her,
   Fire was burning in the bosom and the brain
     Of the Lady Eleanora,
   Of the Lady Eleanora von Alleyne!

Then rode he round and off the battlemented parapet   120
   To Lady Eleanora von Alleyne.
Then rode he round and off the battlemented parapet,
Now blest be GOD for ever! This is marvellous! I never
   Cherished hope of laying eyes on thee agayne,
     Cried the Lady Eleanora,   125
   Joyous Lady Eleanora von Alleyne!

The Man of Men thou art, for thou hast fairly conquered me,
   The Lady Eleanora von Alleyne!
The Man of Men thou art, for thou hast fairly conquered me.
I greet thee as my lover, and, ere many days be over,   130
   Thou shalt wed me and be Lord of my domain,
     Said the Lady Eleanora,
   Said the Lady Eleanora von Alleyne.

Then bowed the graceful knight, the gallant Margrave Gondibert,
  To Lady Eleanora von Alleyne.   135
Then bowed that graceful knight, the gallant Margrave Gondibert,
And thus he answered coldly, There be many who as boldly
    Will adventure an achievement they disdain,
      For the Lady Eleanora,
    For the Lady Eleanora von Alleyne.   140

Mayest bide until they come, O, stately Lady Eleanor!
  O, Lady Eleanora von Alleyne!
Mayest bide until they come, O stately Lady Eleanor!
And thou and they may marry, but, for me, I must not tarry,
    I have won a wife already out of Spain,   145
      Virgin Lady Eleanora,
    Virgin Lady Eleanora von Alleyne!

Thereon he rode away, the gallant Margrave Gondibert,
  From Lady Eleanora von Alleyne.
Thereon he rode away, the gallant Margrave Gondibert,   150
And long in shame and anguish did that haughty Lady languish,
    Did she languish without pity for her pain,
      She the Lady Eleanora,
    She the Lady Eleanora von Alleyne.

And year went after year, and still in barren maidenhood   155
  Lived Lady Eleanora von Alleyne.
And wrinkled Eld crept on, and still her lot was maidenhood,
And, woe! her end was tragic; she was changed, at length, by magic,
    To an ugly wooden image, they maintain;
      She, the Lady Eleanora,   160
    She, the Lady Eleanora von Alleyne!

And now, before the Gate, in sight of all, transmogrified,
  Stands Lady Eleanora von Alleyne.
Before her castle-gate, in sight of all, transmogrified,
And he that won't salute her must be fined in foaming pewter,   165
    If a boor,—but if a burgher, in champagne,
      For the Lady Eleanora,
    Wooden Lady Eleanora von Alleyne!
                                        [Unsigned, *DUM*, February 1842]

from *Stray Leaflets from the German Oak–Third Drift*

O, Maria, Regina Misericordiæ!
KARL SIMROCK

There lived a Knight long years ago,
Proud, carnal, vain, devotionless.
  Of GOD above, or Hell below,
    He took no thought, but, undismayed,
Pursued his course of wickedness.   5
    His heart was rock; he never prayed
  To be forgiven for all his treasons;
  He only said, at certain seasons,
    'O, MARY, Queen of Mercy!'

Years rolled, and found him still the same,   10
Still draining Pleasure's poison-bowl;
  Yet felt he now and then some shame;
    The torment of the Undying Worm
At whiles woke in his trembling soul;
    And then, though powerless to reform,   15
  Would he, in hope to appease that sternest
  Avenger, cry, and more in earnest,
    'O, MARY, Queen of Mercy!'

At last Youth's riotous time was gone,
And Loathing now came after Sin.   20
  With locks yet brown, he felt as one
    Grown grey at heart; and oft, with tears,
He tried, but all in vain, to win
    From the dark desert of his years
  One flower of hope; yet, morn and e'ening,   25
  He still cried, but with deeper meaning,
    'O, MARY, Queen of Mercy!'

A happier mind, a holier mood,
A purer spirit, ruled him now:
　No more in thrall to flesh and blood,   30
　　He took a pilgrim-staff in hand,
And, under a religious vow,
　　Travailed his way to Pommerland.
　There entered he an humble cloister,
　Exclaiming, while his eyes grew moister,   35
　　'O, MARY, Queen of Mercy!'

Here, shorn and cowled, he laid his cares
Aside, and wrought for GOD alone.
　Albeit, he sang no choral prayers,
　　Nor matin hymn nor laud could learn,   40
He mortified his flesh to stone;
　　For him no penance was too stern;
　And often prayed he on his lonely
　Cell-couch at night, but still said only,
　　'O, MARY, Queen of Mercy!'   45

And thus he lived, long, long; and, when
GOD's angels called him, thus he died.
　Confession made he none to men,
　　Yet, when they anointed him with oil,
He seemed already glorified.   50
　　His penances, his tears, his toil,
　Were past; and now, with passionate sighing,
　Praise thus broke from his lips while dying,
　　'O, MARY, Queen of Mercy!'

They buried him with mass and song   55
Aneath a little knoll so green;
　But, lo! a wonder-sight!—Ere long
　　Rose, blooming, from that verdant mound,
The fairest lily ever seen;
　　And, on its petal-edges round,   60
　Relieving their translucent whiteness,
　Did shine these words in gold-hued brightness,
　　'O, MARY, Queen of Mercy!'

And, would God's angels give thee power,
Thou, dearest reader, might'st behold   65
  The fibres of this holy flower,
    Upspringing from the dead man's heart
In tremulous threads of light and gold:
    Then wouldst thou choose the better part!*
  And thenceforth flee Sin's foul suggestions;   70
  Thy sole response to mocking questions,
    'O, Mary, Queen of Mercy!'

Gone in the Wind
FRIEDRICH RÜCKERT
(From the Persian)

Solomon! where is thy throne? It is gone in the wind.
Babylon! where is thy might? It is gone in the wind.
Like the swift shadows of Noon, like the dreams of the Blind,
Vanish the glories and pomps of the earth in the wind.

Man! canst thou build upon aught in the pride of thy mind?   5
Wisdom will teach thee that nothing can tarry behind;
Though there be thousand bright actions embalmed and enshrined,
Myriads and millions of brighter are snow in the wind.

Solomon! where is thy throne? It is gone in the wind.
Babylon! where is thy might? It is gone in the wind.   10
All that the genius of Man hath achieved or designed
Waits but its hour to be dealt with as dust by the wind.

Say, what is Pleasure? A phantom, a mask undefined;
Science? An almond, whereof we can pierce but the rind;
Honour and Affluence? Firmans that Fortune hath signed   15
Only to glitter and pass on the wings of the wind.

* Luke x. 42.

Solomon! where is thy throne? It is gone in the wind.
Babylon! where is thy might? It is gone in the wind.
Who is the Fortunate? He who in anguish hath pined!
He shall rejoice when his relics are dust in the wind! 20

Mortal! be careful with what thy best hopes are entwined;
Woe to the miners for Truth—where the Lampless have mined!
Woe to the seekers on earth for—what none ever find!
They and their trust shall be scattered like leaves on the wind.

Solomon! where is thy throne? It is gone in the wind. 25
Babylon! where is thy might? It is gone in the wind.
Happy in death are they only whose hearts have consigned
All Earth's affections and longings and cares to the wind.

Pity, thou, reader! the madness of poor Humankind,
Raving of Knowledge,—and Satan so busy to blind! 30
Raving of Glory,—like me,—for the garlands I bind
(Garlands of song) are but gathered, and—strewn in the wind!

Solomon! where is thy throne? It is gone in the wind.
Babylon! where is thy might? It is gone in the wind.
I, Abul-Namez, must rest; for my fire hath declined, 35
And I hear voices from Hades like bells on the wind.

[J. C. M., *DUM*, June 1842]

Our First Number

I
'Tis a great day, and glorious, O Public! for you—
This October Fifteenth, Eighteen Forty and Two!
For on this day of days, lo! THE NATION comes forth,
To commence its career of Wit, Wisdom, and Worth—
To give Genius its due—to do battle with Wrong— 5
And achieve things undreamed of as yet, save in song.
Then arise! fling aside your dark mantle of slumber,
And welcome in chorus 𝕿𝖍𝖊 𝕹𝖆𝖙𝖎𝖔𝖓'𝖘 𝕱𝖎𝖗𝖘𝖙 𝕹𝖚𝖒𝖇𝖊𝖗.

II

Here we are, thanks to Heaven, in an epoch when Mind
Is unfettering our captives and couching our blind;   10
And the Press with its thunders keeps marring the mirth
Of those tyrants and bigots that still curse the earth.
Be it ours to stand forth and contend in the van
Of truth's legions for freedom, that birthright of man,
Shaking off the dull cobwebs that else might encumber   15
Our weapon—the pen—in 𝕿𝖍𝖊 𝕹𝖆𝖙𝖎𝖔𝖓'𝖘 𝕱𝖎𝖗𝖘𝖙 𝕹𝖚𝖒𝖇𝖊𝖗.

III

We announce a New Era—be this our first news—
When the serf-grinding Landlords shall shake in their shoes;
While the Ark of a bloodless yet mighty Reform
Shall emerge from the flood of the Popular Storm!   20
Well we know how the lickspittle panders to Power
Feel and fear the approach of that death-dealing hour;
But we toss these aside—such vile vagabond lumber
Are but just worth a groan from 𝕿𝖍𝖊 𝕹𝖆𝖙𝖎𝖔𝖓'𝖘 𝕱𝖎𝖗𝖘𝖙 𝕹𝖚𝖒𝖇𝖊𝖗.

IV

Though we take not for motto, *Nul n'a de l'esprit*,   25
(As they once did in Paris) *hors nos bons amis*,
We may boast that for first-rate endowments, our band
Form a phalanx unmatched *in*—or *out* of—the land.
Poets, Patriots, Linguists, with reading like Parr's—
Critics keener than sabres—Wits brighter than stars;   30
And Reasoners as cool as the coolest cu-cumber
Form the host that shine out in 𝕿𝖍𝖊 𝕹𝖆𝖙𝖎𝖔𝖓'𝖘 𝕱𝖎𝖗𝖘𝖙 𝕹𝖚𝖒𝖇𝖊𝖗.

V

We shall sketch living manners—and men—in a style
That will scarcely be sneezed at, we guess, for a while;
Build up stories as fast as of yore Mother Bunch,   35
And for Fun of all twists take the shine out of 'Punch;'
Thus our Wisdom and Quizdom will finely agree
Very much, Public dear, we conceive, as you see
Do the lights and the shades that illume and adumber
Each beautiful page in 𝕿𝖍𝖊 𝕹𝖆𝖙𝖎𝖔𝖓'𝖘 𝕱𝖎𝖗𝖘𝖙 𝕹𝖚𝖒𝖇𝖊𝖗.   40

VI

A word more:—To OLD IRELAND our first love is given;
Still, our friendship hath arms for all lands under Heaven.
We are Irish—we vaunt it—all o'er and all out;
But we wish not that England shall 'sneak up the spout!'
Then, O, Public! here, there, and elsewhere through the world,　　　45
Whereso'er TRUTH's and LIBERTY's flags are unfurl'd,
From the Suir to the Tweed, from the Boyne to the Humber,
Raise one Shout of Applause for 𝕿𝖍𝖊 𝕹𝖆𝖙𝖎𝖔𝖓'𝖘 𝕱𝖎𝖗𝖘𝖙 𝕹𝖚𝖒𝖇𝖊𝖗.

                  [Unsigned, *Nation*, 15 October 1842]

EPIGRAM *['Well, Pat, my boy']*

'Well, Pat, my boy,' said I, 'I've had some chat
  With the ground landlord of this wilderness.'
'The *grinding* one your Honor means,' grinned Pat;
  'It is the tenants that are *ground*, I guess.'

            [Terrae Filius, *Nation*, 22 October 1842]

Rayther Inconsistent

How queer to hear your Tory-journal readers
  Rail at the Chartist mobs in fishwife tones,
For *listening* only once to 'silly *leaders*,'
  When, day by day, themselves *read* sillier ones!

             [Vacuus, *Nation*, 22 October 1842]

Pleasant Prospects for the Land-Eaters

What stuff to talk of Rent as high!
  'Tis just all round my castor;—
Why, *Rent* is now the only *tie*
  Between the Slave and Master;
And, what's much worse, 'tis evident　　　5
  To those who raise this pother,
That all *ties* will ere long be *rent*
  That bind the one to t'other.

          [Terrae Filius, *Nation*, 29 October 1842]

from *The Three Half Crowns*

[. . .] The case of Giam-Battista Casti, maker of the book under our thumb, is a melancholy one in point. If ever man stood fair for becoming eminent, Casti was the individual. As a poet of great and varied powers he might have looked forward to an European celebrity. As a Roman citizen he was endowed with every requisite to assume a toploftical position in civil society. As a man of general genius, literary and scienstuffical, he distanced all his townspeople by a long chalk—shining among them like a dollar amid a bag of halfpence. But 'all that's bright must fade'—and so and soon did Casti's prospects. In a luckless hour he cast away from him, not knowing value, that 'pearl richer than all his tribe'—his independence of mind. He went into debt for Three Giulii—a matter somewhat less than eighteen-pence English—and dished himself for all the days of his years.

Poor Giam-Battista!—Ill-starred Casti! Yet there was one more excuse for him. He had for some weeks before the fatal act been quite out at elbows, and his plans to raise the wind had failed like so many bankers. Like Leigh Hunt at Pisa, he 'spent a gloomy time of it, walking about the stony alleys' in the suburbs of Rome, and meditating on the decided inferiority of two jugs of pump-water to one flask of Montefiascone. He had really no resource. He was in a 'fix' with Fortune. It may be matter for grief, but is surely none for wonder, that he should have made the most of an opportunity one day thrown in his way by a *rencontre* with his Evil Genius, in the shape of an icemonger from the city, who came up to him, took him by a button, and began a conversation with him on the nature and properties of Tin. It was natural that, feeling himself unable to stand alone, he should have requested another to stand a loan for him. This was the whole 'head and front of his offending.' He could not have dreamt at such a moment that, like 'the proud Count Palatine' in Byron's Mazeppa, he was destined 'to dearly pay in after days' for his folly—to come down with heavy compound interest of tears and rhymes for the cash he had thus transferred from his friend's pocket to his own. Repentence, however, soon reared her snaky crest amid his roses. Hear how he began piping in a few weeks after the transaction:

*(The poet bewaileth his ill luck in having
contracted the debt of Tre Giulii*)*
'Io non potrò dimenticar mai più.'

I weep as I recall the day my Dun
  Lent me those fatal 𝕿𝖍𝖗𝖊𝖊 𝕳𝖆𝖑𝖋-𝕮𝖗𝖔𝖜𝖓𝖘: he stood
  A full half-hour in shilly-shallying mood
Poising them in his hand, and—one by one—
Counting them o'er, as first he had begun.   5
  Even then I saw no human likelihood
Of my repaying them—and I still see none.
  Small wonder, therefore, if I sometimes brood
With bitter tears over my dismal fate,
  Besonnetizing and bewailing it,   10
    Loathing my food, which at such seasons I
Exert myself in vain to masticate,
  And suffering in such style as makes me fit
    For nothing but to—go to bed, and—die!

Poor Casti, in fact, became thoroughly wretched—his only resource was to keep disburthening his conscience in sonnets, and of these he threw off two hundred, filled with the overflowings of a wounded spirit. You perceive as you read him that it is all up with him. He can't get the least ease. The weight of the Tre Giulii Debt lies on him, as the weight of the National Debt lay on Cobbett. Turn whither he will, the chilling image of the dealer in ice is ever on his beat. It clings closelier to him than his very shadow—for (according to the German psychologists) a man's shadow doesn't accompany him into his dreams—whereas, even in his dreams, the poet still feels himself shuddering under the cold eye of the iceman. Nay, if he thinks that if, like Dædalus or Icarus, he could make himself a pair of pinions and mount into the firmament, his tormentor would get another pair, and in the twinkling of a sixpence be at his shoulder. Thus he discusses this cloudy topic:—

---

* In our translations we have taken the liberty of enlarging this debt to Three Half-Crowns. Things should always be made respectable. We applaud the taste of that painter, who, in representing Belshazzar's Feast, decorated the wrist of the Hand on the Wall with ruffles and sleeve-buttons.

(He is of the opinion that his Creditor would
pursue him unto the Isle of Sky)
'Se Dedalo ingegnoso ai fianchi uni.'

Yes!—doubtless 'twas delightful beyond measure
  To Dædalus to sail, as in a skiff,
  Through the blue seas of Æther, high o'er cliff
And tower! Worth more than all the golden treasure
Of Earth too, must have been the pleasure   5
  Astolfo felt, when, on his hippogriff,
  He went sky-scaling, to discover if
He might mount to the moon, and there make seizure
Of the poor Paladin's abstracted brains.*
  And yet I wish not to be wingèd, or   10
Thus raised above Earth's petty pains and plains.
And why? Because I know that if I were,
  The devil would dispatch my Creditor
Up after me, to dun me in the air!

[. . .] In Sonnet XVIII., seeing an eagle soaring over his head, he thinks how
happy it is for the birds that they can pass from one country to another without
being arrested on their way by a demand for 'Three Giulii.'
  In the next a novel thought strikes him, and—

(He proposes a plan of mutual accommodation to his Creditor)
'Tu mi chiedi danari, ed io non gli ho.'

You bother me for coin, and I've got none,
  And so, you see, my time and yours are lost:
  Well, then! I'll here propose t'ye, free of cost,
A plan, fair both for Debitor and Dun.
Attend—When one has got no money one   5
  Can pay no money—that's as plain's a post.
So, *you* shall cease to dun *me*, even in fun,
  And I, *de l'autre côté*, like a ghost—

* See the Orlando Furioso—Canto xxxiv.

Shall wait till *you* speak first. Thus, 'tis quite clear,
  Peace will subsist between us,—and what more   10
    Dare you desire? It is a horrid sin
Eternally to teaze and bait and bore
  A poor Pilgarlic of a Sonnetteer,
    Whose only crime is that he has no Tin!

  The advantage derivable from this plan, however, being, like the handle of a
teapot, all on one side, the Creditor, we suppose, objects to it; and so the Poet
goes on lamenting and lampooning. [. . .]
  In Sonnet XLI, the Poet apostrophises the happy days of the Golden Age,—
quand la Reine Berthe filait.

  'Felici tempi, in cui Berta filò!'
  O, primitive times, when good Queen Bertha span!

  There were then, he says, no I.O.U.'s, sheriff's officers, or Court-of-Conscience
summonses; such a coin as a Guilio could not be met with, and above all, his
Creditor was as yet a nonentity; so that the luxurious quiet enjoyed by people in
those days must have been truly delightful.
  In Sonnet XLVI. he discusses the question, Whether his Creditor be a greater
scoundrel than an Algerine pirate; and thinks that he is, because the Pirate is
satisfied with robbing a man of what he has, whereas his Creditor wants to rob
him of what he has not, and never can have, namely Three Giulii.
  He remarks (Sonnet L.) that earthquakes, hurricanes, &c., have been greatly
on the increase of late years, and that these and other signs of the times indicate
that the end of the world is not far off. This being the case, he wonders that his
Creditor hasn't something more serious to think about than dodging him all day
for three paltry pieces of money.
  A little further on—

(He compares his debt to a small pimple, which by
degrees grows to the magnitude of a cabbage–tumour)
'Se su le gambe, su la faccia, o su.'

Some fine May morn you 'wake, and find a small
  Pimple established on your neck—or nose—
Thereof at first you think nothing at all,
  But weeks pass, and your jolly pimple shows

Itself a tumour, the which grows and grows,   5
Till, waxing bigger than a cannon-ball,
   Like that, it lays you on your back—nor goes
Till you go with it—under plumes and pall.
Thus 'twas and 'tis with Me in this case. When
   I first incurred my Debt it seemed a trifle—   10
      A nothing—a mere pimple, so to say:
Now 'tis a tumour—an enormous wen—
   An incubus—a mountain—and will stifle
      My very life and soul, I think, some day!

One morning (so he relates) he goes to see an Exhibition of Sculptures, but is horrified by meeting among them a statue bearing a marked resemblance to his Creditor; whereupon he rushes down stairs with a vow on his lips never to enter such a place again.

   He says that his Creditor has so often asked him for the Three Giulii that, let him (the Poet) talk on what subject he will, his first answer to a question is always, 'I really haven't got them.'

   Being once alone in a place where there is an echo, he is surprised to hear a demand made on him for Three Giulii. He looks around, but seeing no one, he tries to recollect himself, and then finds that he has been unconsciously repeating aloud to himself the dunning-formulary of his Creditor.

   He says that he finds bark a good specific in a fever, and that when he has caught cold he derives great benefit from a cup of tea. His Creditor alone is a disease incurable by any remedy.

   The Ternary Number, he thinks, is a mysterious one. There were three Graces, three Furies, and three Fates; Cerberus had three heads; Apollo was distinguished by his Tripod, or three-legged stool; and Neptune by his Trident, or three-pronged fork. He wonders, therefore, whether any part of what he suffers be attibutable to the circumstances of his owing Three Giulii, and not two or four. [...]

   One thing puzzles Giam-Battista. He cannot comprehend why it is that whenever he steps out on the *pavé* for a little unfresh air, his Creditor should be always walking up the same side of the street which *he* is proceeding to walk down. This phenomenon sets him a-pondering, and after some time

*(His opinion is that he attracts his Creditor towards
him by a species of Animal Magnetism)*
'Dica chi vuol, l'Attrazzion si da.'

Let Doctors dissertate about Attraction,
  And preach long lectures upon Gravitation,
  Indulging thereanent in speculation
For which no human creature cares one fraction,
  'Tis all mere twaddle-talk and iteration: 5
Of these mysterious modes of Nature's action
  There never yet was any explanation
To anybody's perfect satisfaction.
However, this I stubbornly believe,
  And for the proof thereof see no great need   10
    To take down Isaac Newton from the shelf—
That, move whither I will—noon, morn, or eve,
  I manage to attract with awful speed
    My 𝕿𝖍𝖗𝖊𝖊 𝕳𝖆𝖑𝖋-𝕮𝖗𝖔𝖜𝖓𝖘' Tormentor tow'rds myself!

    Some people, who have no sympathy with suffering, may fancy they see something humorous in all this; and the worst of the matter is that we fear they are not quite in the wrong. As we get deeper into the poet's book we ourself begin to suspect that we have a wag to deal with. It is certainly very odd to find him pushing up every now and then to his Creditor, and, after treating the poor man to such a punch in the ribs as makes him stagger, turning about with his face to the public, and roaring as if not he, but the other, had been the assailant—*Ex. gr.*

*(He floors his Creditor in an argument
on the immortality of the soul)*
'Non già per impugnar la verita.'

My Creditor, who is upon the whole
  No shakes of a philosopher, one day
  Disputed with me—as an ass might bray—
Anent the nature of the human soul.
  'I guess,' quoth he, 'it must at length decay   5
And die: ten thousand centuries may roll,
But what begins must end; and 'twould be droll
  If things born yesterday should live alway.

Beginning, I repeat, implies an end.'
 Whereon I answered, with a deal of dignity,   10
'That's all mine eye, my heterodoxish friend!
  You once began to dun me, yet *that* bore
 Ends not and will not end; your base malignity
  Feeds fat upon my torments evermore!'

(He professes to know nothing about any thing
except the fact that he owes Three Giulii)
'Spesso al mio Creditor vien volontà.'

Anon, he'll call again, and, when he finds
 I don't 'come down,' he'll talk, as 'twere, with wonder
Of Nature's works—ask all about the winds,
 And clouds, and water-spouts—what causes thunder—
 How far the earth and moon may be asunder—   5
And fifty other queries of such kinds:
To all which I—aware that muddy minds
 Will stupidly misunderstand and blunder—
Content myself with answering, 'My good Creditor,
On these points you had best consult the Editor   10
Of the New Farthing-Rushlight Magazine.
 For my part, all I know is this, that I
Owe 𝕿𝖍𝖗𝖊𝖊 𝕳𝖆𝖑𝖋-𝕮𝖗𝖔𝖜𝖓𝖘 to you, for which I've been
 Dunned night and day, and shall be till I die.'

  For cool impudence this, we think, may be pronounced matchless. [...]
  He consoles himself, however, by reflecting that the ancient, sententious
knock-down phraseology of the Lacedemoniacs is, after all, the real thing; and

(He thinks his Creditor ought to admire even
a refusal, if given in proper Spartan fashion)
'La soverchia in parlar prolissità.'

Longwindedness in prose and eke in rhyme
 I horribly abominate: that short
 Sharp, *tranchant* style of speaking is my forte
In vogue through Sparta once upon a time.

Thus, when King Philip, thinking it no crime,   5
  Requested from the proud Byzantine Court
  A passage for his navy through their port,
Pour toute reponse they sent him one sublime,
Brief, thundering NO!* How far above all mean,
  Small, sneaking, shuffling, diplomatic art   10
    Such answer soars! Then, Creditor of mine,
When we twain meet, and you commence a scene,
  And ask, 'Pray, can you pay me even a part?'
    And I shout, 'NO!' count that intensely fine!

(He says that his Creditor is a more terrible sight than a comet,
because his movements cannot be calculated on before-hand)
'Cometa, che pel Ciel cinta sen va.'

The blood-red Comet, which, in fiery sweep,
  Burns round the welkin, threatening each beholder
  With War or Plague ere Time be greatly older,
Bids, I protest, no deadlier terrors creep
  Through my pale veins, nor makes my chilled heart colder   5
Than doth my Dun when, with a sly, bo-peep
Abord and aspect, stealthy as a sheep,
  He taps me, catchpole-fashion, on the shoulder.
Such Comet is, no doubt, a terrible sight;
  Still, staring at it from one's tenth-flat attic,   10
    One knows what time 'twill go, and come, and go;
But where, or when, at morn, eve, noon, or night,
  My Comet will flare up I never know—
  His movements are so desperately erratic!

At last, gathering courage from despair itself,

---

* To this the poet appends the following note:—Avendo Filippo il Macedone domandato ai
Bizantini il passaggio per gli stati loro, essi gli risposero colla sola particola negativa *Ου*.

(He tells his Creditor that the more he's dunned,
the more he won't pay one stiver!)
'Dunque mentre mi chiedi i Giulj tre.'

Since you've begun, O, teazingest of men,
  To dun me every quarter of an hour,
'Tis clear that in nine cases out of ten
  You act from habit—not Volition's power.
Your words my rattle out of you, but when   5
  They do I hear them as one would a shower
  Of pop-gun pellets levelled at some tower,
Whereof the guns know nothing there and then.
I lately read in some old Magazine
  Of some Automaton of German breed   10
    That used to speak by means of tubes and springs;
'Tis thus You speak to Me, you mere machine!
  So I'll not mind you further—and indeed
    At best your eloquence is no great things.

   We have now, as we think, indifferently well fulfilled our duty as *traduttore* by
our friend Giambattista. One other Sonnet, in that noble Alexandrine metre in
which all Sonnets ought to be written, and we close his book—yet not, we hope,
for the last time.

(He threatens finally to escape into some desert,
turn jack-ass, and live on thistles)
'O, inutile travaglio! o vanità.'

O, *mentis vanitas!* O, assishness of Man!
  What boots it me, alas! that with enormous toil
  I snore through Paracelsus, Plato, Bacon, Boyle,
And other humdrum humbugs? Chasing the πο Παν
Of Knowledge, I have trudged from Bershebah to Dan,   5
  And all is barren!—I have spent my midnight oil
  For nought, and sown my seeds upon a stony soil,
And now the Mills of Science yield me only bran!
There-fore Philosophy, I guess, is not the ticket;
  There-fore I'll cut and run from all my books, and seek   10
Some savage mountain-den or wild outlandish thicket,

And there keep cudgelling my brains from week to week,
Til I discover how, despite Miss Fortune's frowns,
I may, by hook of crook, make prize of Three Half-Crowns.

[Unsigned, *DUM*, December 1842]

from *Anthologia Germanica–No. XVIII*
Freiligrath's Poems

[. . .] Among the really first-rate things in this volume are the following stanzas
on the death of poor Grabbe—an enthusiastic young German poet, who closed
his brief but dazzling literary career in 1836, having been literally burned out of
life by the fire of his imagination.

Grabbe

There stood I in the Camp. 'Twas when the setting sun
Was crimsoning the tents of the Hussars.
The booming of the Evening-gun
Broke on mine ear. A few stray stars
Shone out, like silverblank medallions   5
Paving a sapphire floor. Then flowed in unison the tones
Of many hautboys, bugles, drums, trombones,
And fifes, from twenty-two battalions.

They played, 'Give glory unto GOD our Lord!'
A solemn strain of music and sublime,   10
That bade Imagination hail a coming time,
When universal Mind shall break the slaying sword,
And Sin and Wrong and Suffering shall depart
An Earth which Christian love shall turn to Heaven.
A dream!—yet still I listened, and my heart   15
Grew tranquil as that Summer-even.

But soon uprose pale Hecate—she who trances
The skies with deathly light. Her beams fell wan, but mild,
On the long lines of tents, on swords and lances,
And on the pyramids of musquets piled   20

Around. Then sped from rank to rank
The signal-order, '*Tzako ab!*' The music ceased to play.
The stillness of the grave ensued. I turned away.
Again my memory's tablets showed a saddening blank!

Meanwhile another sort of scene   25
Was acted at the Outposts. Carelessly I strolled,
In quest of certain faces, into the Canteen.
Here wine and brandy, hot or cold,
Passed round. At one long table Fredericks-d'or
Glittered *à qui mieux mieux* with epaulettes,   30
And, heedless of the constant call, '*Who sets?*'
Harpwomen played and sang old ballads by the score.

I sought an inner chamber. Here sat some
Dragoons and Yagers, who conversed, or gambled,
Or drank. The dice-box rattled on a drum.   35
I chose a seat apart. My speculations rambled.
Scarce even a passive listener or beholder,
I mused: 'Give glory————' '*Qui en veut?*'—The sound
Came from the drum-head. I had half turned round
When some one touched me on the shoulder.   40

'Ha!—is it you?' 'None other.' 'Well!—what news?
How goes it in Mulhausen?' Queries without end
Succeed, and I reply as briefly as I chuse.
An hour flies by. 'Now then, adieu, my friend!'—
'Stay!—tell me————' 'Quick! I am off to *Rouge et Noir.*'—   45
'Well—one short word, and then Good Night!—
Grabbe?'—'Grabbe? He is dead. Wait: let me see. Ay, right!
We buried him on Friday last. *Bon soir!*'

An icy thrill ran through my veins.
Dead! Buried! Friday last!—and here!—*His* grave   50
Profaned by vulgar feet! Oh, Noble, Gifted, Brave!
Bard of *The Hundred Days**—was this to be thy fate indeed?
I wept; yet not because Life's galling chains
No longer bound thy spirit to this barren earth;
I wept to think of thy transcendent worth   55
And genius—and of what had been their meed!

* A poem by Grabbe, thus entitled.

I wandered forth into the spacious Night,
Till the first feelings of my heart had spent
Their bitterness. Hours passed. There was an Uhlan tent
At hand. I entered. By the moon's blue light   60
I saw some arms and baggage and a heap
Of straw. Upon this last I threw
My weary limbs. In vain! The moanful night-winds blew
About my head and face, and Memory banished Sleep.

All night *he* stood, as I had seen him last,   65
Beside my couch. Had he indeed forsaken
The tomb? Or, did I dream, and should I waken?
My thoughts flowed like a river, dark and fast.
Again I gazed on that columnar brow:
'Deserted House! of late so bright with vividest flashes   70
Of Intellect and Passion, can it be that thou
Art now a mass of sparkless ashes?

'Those ashes once were watch-fires, by whose gleams
The glories of the Hohenstauffen race,*
And Italy's shrines,* and Greece's hallowed streams*   75
Stood variously revealed—now, softly, as the face
Of Night illumined by her silver Lamp—
Now, burning with a deep and living lustre,
Like the high beacon-lights that stud this Camp,
Here, far apart,—there, in a circular cluster.   80

'This Camp! Ah, yes! methinks it images well
What thou hast been, thou lonely Tower!—
Moonbeams and lamplight mingled—the deep choral swell
Of Music in her peals of proudest power,
And then—the tavern dice-box rattle!   85
The Grand and the Familiar fought
Within thee for the mastery; and thy depth of thought
And play of wit made every conflict a drawn battle!

'And, oh! that such a mind, so rich, so overflowing
With ancient lore and modern phantasy,   90
And prodigal of its treasures as a tree
Of golden leaves when Autumn-winds are blowing,

---

* The allusions are to Grabbe's historical and illustrative works.

That such a mind, made to illume and glad
All minds, all hearts, should have itself become
Affliction's chosen Sanctuary and Home!—   95
This is in truth most marvellous and sad!

'Alone the Poet lives—alone he dies.
Cain-like, he bears the isolating brand
Upon his brow of sorrow. True, his hand
Is pure from blood-guilt, but in human eyes   100
His is a darker crime than that of Cain,—
Rebellion against Social Wrong and Law!'
Groaning, at length I slept, and in my dreams I saw
The ruins of a Temple on a desolate plain.

Here perhaps it were best for us to conclude, leaving the fine cadences of this
remarkable poem fresh upon the reader's memory. [...]

[Unsigned, *DUM*, January 1843]

from *Stray Leaflets from the German Oak–Fifth Drift*

Schnapps
SELBER

I

The poet layeth a wager of a fourpenny-piece that he will concoct an intenser poem on Schnapps than any other garretteer extant.

I'm rather slow at extravaganzas,
   And what your poets call thunderclaps;
I'll therefore spin you some sober stanzas
   Concerning nothing at all but Schnapps.
And though my wisdom, like Sancho Panza's   5
   Consists entirely of bits and scraps,
I'll bet you fourpence that no man plans as
   Intense a poem as I on Schnapps.

II

He panegyriseth Schnapps, and quoteth a pronoun from Quintus Horatius Flaccus.

Schnapps is, you know, the genteelest liquid
   That any tapster in Potsdam taps;   10
When you've tobacco, and chew a thick quid,
   You've still to grin for your glass of Schnapps.

You then wax funny, and show your slick wit,
　　And smash to smithers with kicks and slaps
Whatever's next you—in Latin *quicquid*—   15
　　For I quote Horace when lauding Schnapps.

III

He describeth himself, nath-
less, as being a most mod-
erate Schnapper, excepting
when he happeneth to stag-
ger into bad company.

I've but one pocket for quids and coppers,
　　Which last moreover are mostly raps,
Yet, 'midst my ha'pence and pipes and stoppers
　　I still find room for a flask of Schnapps.   20
My daily quantum is twenty croppers,
　　Or ten half-naggins;—but, when with chaps
Who, though good Schappers, are no slipsloppers,
　　I help to empty a keg of Schnapps.

Magnus hiatus, lugubre
deflendus.

*　　*　　*　　*　　*　　*　　*　　*　　*
　*　　*　　*　　*　　*　　*　　*　　*

XXXVII

Being fifty, sixty, or therebetwixt, I   25
　　　Guess many midnights can't now elapse

He concludeth, in pathetic
strain, by anticipating for
himself a speedy demise
among—not hogsheads, but
hogs' heads.

Before the hour comes in which my fixt eye
　　　Must look its last upon Earth and Schnapps.
I'll kick the pail, too, in some dark pigstye,
　　　Imbibing hogwash, or whey perhaps,   30
Which, taken sep'rate, or even mixt, I
　　　Don't think superior at all to Schnapps!

The Coming Event
SELBER

Curtain the lamp, and bury the bowl—
　　The ban is on drinking!
Reason shall reign the queen of the soul
　　When the spirits are sinking.
Chained lies the demon that smote with blight   5
　　Men's morals and laurels;
So, hail to Health, and a long Good-night
　　To old wine and new quarrels!

Nights shall descend, and no taverns ring
  To the roar of our revels;   10
Mornings shall dawn, but none of them bring
  White lips and blue devils.
Riot and Frenzy sleep with Remorse
  In the obsolete potion,
And Mind grows calm as a ship on her course   15
  O'er the level of Ocean.

So should it be!—for Man's world of romance
  Is fast disappearing,
And shadows of CHANGES are seen in advance,
  Whose epochs are nearing;   20
And days are at hand when the Best will require
  All means of salvation,
And the souls of men shall be tried in the fire
  Of the Final Probation.

And the Witling no longer or sneers or smiles;   25
  And the Worldling dissembles;
And the blankminded Sceptic feels anxious at whiles,
  And wonders, and trembles;
And fear and defiance are blent in the jest
  Of the blind Self-deceiver;   30
And infinite hope is born in the breast
  Of the childlike Believer.

Darken the lamp, then, and bury the bowl,
  Ye Faithfullest-hearted!
And, as your swift years hasten on to the goal   35
  Whither worlds have departed,
Spend strength, sinew, soul, on your toil to atone
  For past idlesse and errors;
So best shall ye bear to encounter alone
  𝕿𝖍𝖊 𝕰𝖛𝖊𝖓𝖙 and its terrors.   40
                [J. C. M., *DUM*, February 1844]

from *Literæ Orientales–No. V*
Ottoman Poetry

The literature of the Ottomans can lay claim to an antiquity nearly coëval with that of their empire itself. Its origin may be dated from the commencement of the fourteenth century, soon after the downfall of the heroic but unfortunate Seldshukian or *Turkish* dynasty of Asia Minor, and when the formidable House of Osman, rising on the ruins of its rival, had browbeaten Europe into a recognition of its power.

At this period there flourished contemporaneously three eminent Persian poets—Djelal-ed-Deen Rûmeh, Alla-ed-Defflet, and the Sheikh Saadr-ed-Deen. Their works were for the most part of a deeply religious and mystic nature. As, however, to borrow the expression of a learned living philologist, 'Persian poetry has always been the sun to which the sunflower of Ottoman poetry has turned,' these works at once became the models to which Ottoman genius did homage, and which it regarded as worthiest of study and imitation. The earliest poet of the infant empire of whom we have any authentic account is Aasheek Pasha, who wrote a curious work, in ten books, on the nature of the inner life, and the mysterious power that dwells in the Septenary Number, especially as exhibited in the seven planets, the seven earths, the seven heavens, the seven metals, the seven ages of man, and the seven divine revelations, namely, the Book of Adam, the Book of Seth, the Book of Enoch, the Pentateuch, the Psalter, the Gospel, and the Korán. This work, however, does not find many readers at the present day, even in Turkey.

Aasheek-Pasha was followed by the Emeer Aalem Effendi, a teacher of the mystical Mevlevee, from whose poems we take the following philosophical

Stanza

See how the worlds that roll afar
    Serenely beam on one another!
There nowhere burns a sun or star
    But helps to cheer some darker brother.
Wouldst thou, O, Man! be good and wise,   5
    Share thus thy light among thy neighbours:
In giving, not in hoarding, lies
    The truest meed of Learning's labours!

Among the other poets of this era were the Sheikhs Mahmûd and Elwaan Sheerazi, Djelal-Arghun, Shah-Tchelebee, and Burhan-ed-Deen, another

Mevlevee Sheikh, from whose writings his biographer, Ghaleeb, extracts these rather dogmatical verses:—

Good Counsel

Tutor not thyself in science: go to masters for perfection;
        Also speak thy thoughts aloud:
Whoso in the glass beholdeth nought besides his own reflection
        Bides both ignorant and proud.

Study not in one book only: bee-like, rather, at a hundred   5
        Sources gather honeyed lore:
Thou art else that helpless bird which, when her nest has once been plundered,
        Ne'er can build another more.

[. . .] Another brilliant light of those times was Fahareyeh. He was a native of Caramania, that fine 'land of the mountain and the flood'—the Scotland in fact of the East for the bold picturesqueness of its natural scenery. Caramania was the last province of Asia Minor that submitted to the Ottoman yoke; and long and gallant and bloody was the resistance it first offered to the conquering arms of its invaders. A history of that memorable struggle, by the way, is much wanted. Why should not one of the first-rate men of our era,—Dr. Wilde, for instance,—undertake it? Let the doctor only speak on the hint we throw out, and we shall be ready, at a day's notice, to deposit in his hands a dozen or so of such poems as the following:—

The Caramanian Exile

I
I see thee ever in my dreams,
        Karaman!
Thy hundred hills, thy thousand streams,
        Karaman! O, Karaman!
As when thy goldbright Morning gleams,   5
As when the deepening Sunset seams
With lines of light thy hills and streams,
        Karaman!
So thou loomest on my dreams,
        Karaman!   10
Nightly loomest on my dreams,
        Karaman! O, Karaman!

II
The hot bright plains, the sun, the skies,
              Karaman!
Seem deathblack marble to mine eyes,   15
              Karaman! O, Karaman!
I turn from Summer's blooms and dyes;
Yet in my dreams Thou dost arise
In welcome glory on mine eyes,
              Karaman!   20
In thee my life of life yet lies,
              Karaman!
Thou still art holy in mine eyes,
              Karaman! O, Karaman!

III
Ere my fighting years were come,   25
              Karaman!
Troops were few in Erzerome,
              Karaman! O, Karaman!
Their fiercest came from Erzerome;
They came from Ukhbar's palace dome;   30
They dragged me forth from thee, my home,
              Karaman!
Thee, my own, my mountain home,
              Karaman!
In life and death my spirit's home,   35
              Karaman! O, Karaman!

IV
Oh, none of all my sisters ten,
              Karaman!
Loved like me my fellow-men,
              Karaman! O, Karaman!   40
I was mild as milk till then,
I was soft as silk till then;
Now my breast is as a den,
              Karaman!
Foul with blood and bones of men,   45
              Karaman!
With blood and bones of slaughtered men,
              Karaman! O, Karaman!

V
My boyhood's feelings, newly born,
   Karaman!   50
Withered, like young flowers uptorn,
   Karaman! O, Karaman!
And in their stead sprang weed and thorn:
What once I loved now moves my scorn;
My burning eyes are dried to horn,   55
   Karaman!
I hate the blessèd light of Morn,
   Karaman!
It maddens me the face of Morn,
   Karaman! O, Karaman!   60

VI
The Spahi wears a tyrant's chains,
   Karaman!
But bondage worse than this remains,
   Karaman! O, Karaman!
His heart is black with million stains: 65
Thereon, as on Kaf's blasted plains,
Shall never more fall dews and rains,
   Karaman!
Save poison-dews and bloody rains,
   Karaman!   70
Hell's poison-dews and bloody rains,
   Karaman! O, Karaman!

VII
But Life at worst must end ere long,
   Karaman!
Azreel* avengeth every wrong,   75
   Karaman! O, Karaman!
Of late my thoughts rove more among
Thy fields;—foreshadowing fancies throng
My mind, and texts of bodeful song,
   Karaman!   80
Azreel is terrible and strong,
   Karaman!
His lightning-sword smites all ere long,
   Karaman! O, Karaman!

*The Angel of Death.

VIII

There's care to-night in Ukhbar's halls,   85
        Karaman!
There's hope, too, for his trodden thralls,
        Karaman! O, Karaman!
What lights flash red along yon walls?
Hark! hark!—the muster-trumpet calls!—   90
I see the sheen of spears and shawls,
        Karaman!
The foe! the foe!—they scale the walls,
        Karaman!
To-night Murád or Ukhbar falls,   95
        Karaman! O, Karaman!

One is not often electrified by such bursts of passion and feeling in Ottoman poetry. The chief characteristics of that poetry consist rather of deep religious fervour and a certain tone of tender melancholy—the result of opium-eating and coffee-drinking,—or perhaps of the poetical temperament such as it works on the other side of the Caspian. Such a tone may be now and then detected even in the songs of the Khalenders—those Troubadours of the East, half minstrels, half mendicants, whose wild and wandering habits must have excited to the highest pitch of activity both their animal spirits and intellectual faculties. After all, it is not unpleasant. Sung to the vibratory music of the lute, especially, would not, for example, such a ballad as this thrill through the very soul of the listener?

The Wail and the Warning of the Three Khalenders

THE WAIL

I

    La' lahá il-Allah!*
Here we meet, we three, at length,
  Amrah, Osman, Perizad,
Shorn of all our grace and strength
  Poor, and old, and verysad!   5
We have lived, but live no more,
  Life has lost its gloss for us

---

*There is but the one God.

Since the days we spent of yore
  Boating down the Bosphorus.
    La' lahá il-Allah!   10
    The Bosphorus, the Bosphorus!
    For Life has lost its gloss for us
  Since the days we spent of yore
    Upon the pleasant Bosphorus!

II
    La' lahá il-Allah!   15
Days indeed! A shepherd's tent
  Served us then for house-and-fold;
All to whom we gave or lent
  Paid us back a thousandfold.
Troublous years, by myriads wailed,   20
  Rarely had a cross for us,
Never when we gaily sailed
  Singing down the Bosphorus.
    La' lahá il-Allah!
    The Bosphorus, the Bosphorus!   25
    There never came a cross for us
  While we daily, gaily sailed
    Adown the meadowy Bosphorus!

III
    La' lahá il-Allah!
Blithe as birds we flew along,   30
  Laughed, and quaffed, and stared-about;
Wine and roses, mirth and song,
  Were what most we cared-about.
Fame we left for quacks to seek,
  Gold was dust and dross for us,   35
While we lived, from week to week,
  Boating down the Bosphorus.
    La' lahá il-Allah!
    The Bosphorus, the Bosphorus,
    And gold was dust and dross for us,   40
  While we lived, from week to week,
    A-boating down the Bosphorus!

IV
  La' lahá il-Allah!
Friends we were, and would have shared
 Purses, had we twenty full.   45
If we spent, or if we spared,
 Still our funds were plentiful.
Save the hours we passed apart
 Time brought home no loss for us;
We felt full of hope and heart   50
 While we clove the Bosphorus.
  La' lahá il-Allah!
  The Bosphorus, the Bosphorus!
  Old Time brought home no loss for us.
We felt full of health and heart   55
 Upon the foamy Bosphorus!

V
  La' lahá il-Allah!
Ah! for Youth's delirious hours
 Man pays well in afterdays,
When quencht hopes and palsied powers   60
 Mock his love-and-laughterdays.
Thorns and thistles on our path
 Took the place of moss for us,
Till false Fortune's tempestwrath
 Drove us from the Bosphorus.   65
  La' lahá il-Allah!
  The Bosphorus, the Bosphorus!
  When thorns took place of moss for us
Gone was all! Our hearts were graves
 Deep, deeper than the Bosphorus.   70

VI
  La' lahá il-Allah!
Gone is all! In one abyss
 Lie Health, Youth, and Merriment.
All we've learned amounts to this—
 𝕷𝔦𝔣𝔢'𝔰 𝔞 𝔰𝔞𝔡 𝔢𝔵𝔭𝔢𝔯𝔦𝔪𝔢𝔫𝔱.   75
What it is we trebly feel
 Pondering what it was for us,
When our shallop's bounding keel
 Clove the joyous Bosphorus.

La' lahá il-Allah!   80
The Bosphorus, the Bosphorus!
We wail for what Life was for us
When our shallop's bounding keel
So clove the joyous Bosphorus!

THE WARNING
VII
    La' lahá il-Allah!   85
Pleasure tempts; yet Man has none
  Save himself t' accuse if her
Temptings prove, when all is done,
  Lures hung out by Lucifer.
GUARD YOUR FIRE IN YOUTH, O, FRIENDS!   90
  MANHOOD'S IS BUT PHOSPHORUS;
AND BAD LUCK ATTENDS AND ENDS
  BOATINGS DOWN THE BOSPHORUS!
    La' lahá il-Allah!
    The Bosphorus, the Bosphorus!   95
    Youth's fire soon wanes to phosphorus;
  And slight luck or grace attends
    Your boaters down the Bosphorus!

    The doleful jocularity of the first of the two following poems, and the spirit of
devout resignation to Providence that pervades the second, will be like admired:—

Love and Madness

Ilbabeeb! Thy heart's a rock;
  I must put my helm a-lee,
    Or my bark will soon be wrecked, if
Love refuse to stay the shock.
  Ah, relent! For thee and me   5
    Life's but a brief perspective!
Think how soon on Death's dark shore
  She who plagues and they who pine,
    Both Despoiler and Despoiled meet!
Why must Medjnûns evermore   10
  Drink their tears as wormwood wine,
    And devour their hearts as broiled-meat?

Thy fair face, whose light might guide
  Ships by night, is as a book
    Which Love's hand has writ at large in;   15
And thy locks on either side,
  In their inkblack lustre, look
    Like the glosses down its margin!
Such a face, with such a heart!—
  Oh, 'tis ghastly! We men may   20
    Mourn our nature when we scan it;
But let none take Woman's part!
  Man, at worst, is made of clay;
    Woman seems a block of granite!

All day long I sulk and sculk   25
  To and fro till night, and then
    Slumber flies mine eye and eyelid.
I must hire some cobler's bulk,
  Watchman's box, or jackal's den,
    Where I may remain a while hid!   30
I, once plump as Sheeraz' grape,
  Am, like Thalbh of thin renown,*
    Grown most chasmy, most phantasmy,
Yea, most razor-sharp in shape!—
  Fact! And if I'm—blown through town   35
    I'll—cut all the sumphs who pass me!

Heaven first of all within Ourselves

I stood where the home of my boyhood had been,
  In the Bellflower Vale, by the Lake of Bir-ból;
And I pensively gazed on the wreck of a scene
  Which the dreams of the Past made so dear to my soul.

For its light had grown dim while I wandered afar,   5
  And its glories had vanished, like the leaves on the gale,
And the frenzy of Man and the tempests of War
  Had laid prostrate the pride of my Bellflower Vale.

* See an epigram in our second article.

I thought how long years of disaster and woe
  Scarce woke in my bosom one sigh for the Past,   10
How my hopes, like the home of my childhood, lay low,
  While the spirit remained clam to the last.

Then I looked on the lake that lay deep in the dell
  As pellucidly fair as in summers gone by,
And amid the sad ruins of cottage and cell   15
  Still mirrored the beautiful face of the sky.

And I said, So may Ruin o'ertake all that we love,
  And our minds, like Bir-ból, abide bright evermore;
So the heart that in grief looks to ALLAH above,
  Still reflects the same heaven from its depths as before!   20

  [...] A song, supposed to be sung by a migratory gang of Thugs from India,
lies before us. Fortunately it is of questionable authenticity, as might indeed be
suspected from the unoriental *equivoque* in the opening line.

The Thugs' Ditty

We are *neck*-or-nought scamps—three-fourths of a dozen—
    That's nine, if you please.
We tipple and smoke; we hocus and cozen,
    And that sort of thing.
All night under sheds in Marzawán city   5
    We snooze at our ease.
We are slashers—that's truth. It's the tune of the ditty
    We constantly sing!

In vain the Kapeedjies* pursue us with sticks and
    Long hullabaloos;   10
They are fast in the mud, like ships on a quicksand,
    While *we*'re on the wing.
The Moolahs talk big—they meet in committee,
    And shake in their shoes.
We are strappers—that's truth. It's the tune of the ditty   15
    We rattlingly sing!

* Police.

All not of our clique are sneaks or suburbans.
    We settle their hash,
And sell to dellauls* their toggery and turbans
    For what they may bring.   20
Yet our gains from these handsome exploits—more's the pity—
    Scarce keep us in cash.
Never mind! We are wags. That's the tune of the ditty
    We laughingly sing!

We encounter, however, a refreshing contrast to this abominable song in:

The Soffees' Ditty

I

> Bismillah! Thou art warned, O, Soffee! that
> mere outward austerities, however excellent
> in themselves, will not make thee perfect.

Haircloth and vigils and fasts, and a vow against coffee,
Cleansers from sin though they be, will make no one a Soffee.
Much is essential besides the bare absence of sleekness,
Namely, Docility, Poverty, Courage, and Meekness,
Wisdom, and Silence, and Patience, and Prayer without ceasing:—   5
Such are the tone and the tune of the ditty that *we* sing.

II

> Bismillah! Beware lest thou live in the habitual
> commission of any single sin; for, though the
> sin itself may be slight, the constant repe-
> tition of it renders it most grievous.

Woe unto those who but banish one vice for another!
Far from thy thoughts be such damning delusion, O, brother!
Pluck thy heart out, and abjure all it loves and possesses
Rather than cherish one sin in its guilty recesses.   10
Donning new raiment is nobler than patching and piecing:—
Such are the tone and the tune of the ditty that *we* sing.

* Brokers.

III

> Bismillah! And, O, Soffee! whensoever the
> glitter of money meets thine eye, avert thy
> face! It were better for thee to lodge a
> serpent in thy bosom than a money-purse.

Money (saith Seyd Ul-ud-Deen) eats the soul as a cancer;
Whoso loves money has more than the guilt of Ben-Manser.*
Wouldst thou, O Soffee! keep clear of the snare that entangles   15
Those whom at night on their couches the Evil One strangles,
Ask not and task not, abstain from extortion and fleecing—
Such are the tone and the tune of the ditty that *we* sing.

IV

> Bismillah! There is no strength or wisdom but
> in GOD, the High, the Great! Thou, O
> Soffee, art but a creature of clay; therefore,
> indulge not in pride!

Cast away Pride as the bane of thy soul: the Disdainful
Swallow much mire in their day, and find everything painful.   20
Still in its cave shall the diamond beam on, because humble,
When the proud pillar, that stands as a giant, must crumble.
Stoop! and thy burden will keep, like the camel's, decreasing.
Such are the tone and the tune of the ditty that *we* sing.

V

> Bismillah! The devil, O, Soffee! will doubtless
> try to make thee very miserable. But be
> thou consoled; for the seven hells are closed
> hereafter against those who descend into
> them here.

Art thou made wretched by memories, and fears, and chimeras?   25
Grieve not! for so were the Soffees and saints of past eras.
All must abandon Life's lodgings, but none who depart take
Any invalider passport to Hell than the heart-ake.
Satan enslaveth, and Pain is GOD's mode of releasing—
Such are the tone and the tune of the ditty that *we* sing.   30

* Abou-Mogheedh-Huseyn-Ben-Manser-al-Halladj, a celebrated Arabian magician and mystic
of the ninth century. He suffered death under the reign of the Khalif Moktader, for promulgating
certain incomprehensible metaphysico-religious doctrines concerning the nature of the soul.

VI

> Bismillah! It is good for thee to be much
> afflicted. As Suleymán-Ben-Daood hath
> said, The heart is made better by the sad-
> ness of the countenance.

Like the lone lamp that illumines a Sheikh's mausoleum,
Like a rich calcedon shrined in some gloomy museum,
Like the bright moon before Midnight is blended with Morrow,
Shines the pure pearl of the soul in the Chalice of Sorrow!
Mourners on earth shall be solaced with pleasures unceasing—　　　35
Such are the tone and the tune of the ditty that *we* sing.

VII

> Bismillah! As Man soweth so doth he reap; his
> thoughts and deeds come back to him in
> another world; and as these are good or ill so
> is he for ever happy or miserable. Ponder this
> well; and let each fleeting hour impress thee
> deeplier with the awful truth, that Time
> is the purchase-money of Eternity.

Life is an outlay for infinite blessings or curses—
Evil or Good—which Eternity's Bank reimburses.
Thou, then, O, Soffee, look well to each moment expended!
So shall thy hands overflow, and thy guerdon be splendid,　　　40
When thy brow faces the wall,* and thy pangs are increasing—
These be the tone and the tune of the ditty that *we* sing.

　　The Soffees—so called from the Arabic word, *soof: i.e.*, wool, in allusion to the
coarseness of their garments, or, in the opinion of some, from σοφός, wise,—are
an order of Darveeshes who devote themselves to continual prayer, mortifi-
cation, and contemplation of the Divine Perfections, and often display a zeal and
constancy in the practice of their penitential austerities worthy the imitation of
Christians. A history of Mohammedan asceticism generally would, we have a
notion, greatly contribute to enlighten us with respect to much that is at present
mysterious in the nature of the human soul. [. . .]

　　　　　　　　　　　　　　　　　　　　　　　[Unsigned, *DUM*, May 1844]

* Viz., that wall of the death-chamber which is in the direction of Mekka.

Echoes of Foreign Song

Into the current poetry of Europe, mere English readers can have small insight. Translations are commonly made from authors of long standing; while of the active, present mind of their cotemporaries they are left ignorant. To some small extent we may be able to remedy this omission in THE NATION; and to that end we purpose giving, from time to time, a few specimens of the modern poetry of European nations. They will be selected, as far as possible, so as to reflect the public mind of each country, which is always to be gathered in some shape from its popular poetry.

'Der Freiheit eine Gasse' — A Lane for Freedom
(FROM THE GERMAN OF GEORGE HERWEGH) *1841*

'My suffering country SHALL be freed,
    And shine with tenfold glory!'
So spake the gallant Winkelreid,
    Renowned in German story.
'No tyrant, even of kingly grade,   5
    Shall cross or darken *my* way!'
Out flashed his blade, and so he made
    For Freedom's course a highway!

We want a man like this, with power
    To rouse the world by *one* word;   10
We want a Chief to meet the hour,
    And march the masses onward.
But Chief or none, through blood and fire,
    My Fatherland lies *thy* way!
Then men must fight who dare desire   15
    For Freedom's course a highway!

Alas! I can but idly gaze
    Around in grief and wonder;
The PEOPLE's will alone can raise
    The people's shout of thunder.   20
Too long, my friends, you faint for fear,
    In secret crypt and bye-way.
At last be Men! Stand forth, and clear
    For Freedom's course a highway!

You intersect wood, lea, and lawn,   25
  With roads for monster waggons,
Wherein you speed like lightning, drawn
  By fiery iron dragons.
So do! Such work is good, no doubt;
  But why not seek some nigh way   30
For *Mind* as well? Path also out
  For Freedom's course a highway!

Yes! up! and let your weapons be
  Sharp steel and self-reliance!
Why waste your burning energy   35
  In void and vain defiance,
And phrases fierce but fugitive?
  'Tis deeds, not words, that *I* weigh—
Your swords and guns alone can give
  To Freedom's course a highway!   40
        [J. C. M., *Nation*, 23 November 1844]

from *Anthologia Germanica–No. XIX*
Miscellaneous Poems

About five years back, as our readers may remember, Ferdinand Freiligrath published his first volume of poems. It was a rather wild and clever affair—all seas and sand-spouts, whales and buffaloes—Hottentots, Troglodytes,

  '—Anthropophagi, and men whose heads
  Did grow beneath their shoulders,'

and it produced, accordingly, an extensive sensation. The German people were electrified by it. The king of Prussia placed its author on the pension list. Most miraculous fact of any, even the reviewers praised it! A few transcendental cynics, alone, laughed in derision, but their mirth met no response, for there really were in the book,

  'Thoughts that did often lie too deep for sneers.'

In short, it succeeded. The originality of such an idea as that of poetising topo-graphy and natural history, took the public by surprise; and Ferdinand was in a fair way of making his fortune.

He had formerly been in trade: here was now a golden opportunity for him to regain the position he had forfeited. He might go back to the shop, and set up in the huckstery line under the brilliantest auspices. However, he did no such thing. He had other views than could be obtained from the inside of a butter-firkin. His grand ambition was to take the shine yet brightlier as an author. He would bring out another book, all wild-cats and hurricanes again, but still not quite the same as the former; and so he sat down, with half-a-hundred weight of paper before him, to think how *he* should manage *that* job.

The Westphalian tea-unions, meanwhile, were nearly as anxious as himself on the score, but they were more in the dark, for they couldn't tell what sort of book he intended to write. It was, of course, clear that he wouldn't repeat him-self—that he wouldn't mind catching any more Tartars. But what he *would* do was the question. Would he fall back on forms and conventionalities with Goethe, or ascend into the 'Ideal,' like Schiller? People shook their heads. Was he likely to try his hand at the construction of gingerbread gimcracks of castles, after the manner of Uhland? A universal horselaugh negatived the notion. Had he, then, a decided inclination to descend into Hades with Kerner, and study the mysteries of caco-magnetism among demons and incubi? This appeared an out-and-out improbability. In a word, all agreed that he was too much of a genius to copy.

'His soul was like a star, and dwelt apart'

from the cloudy tabernacles of the whole tribe of metrical push-pin-players. As Selber tersely observes,

'He had once beat all of them by chalks,'

and there seemed no valid reason why he shouldn't go on beating them to the end of all the chapters. *He*, at least, was not a bag of chaff, a make-believe, a wire-and-pulley get-up, but an unmistakeable specimen of muscle and sinew; and he would shew that he was.

Well, and did he shew that he was? We shall answer that query in, perhaps, our next anthology. At present all that we can say is that he came out in due season, armed to the teeth, and scowling like ten thunder-clouds. He had become a young Germanist! It was even so. He who, in 1841, had thus expressed himself in a poem on the execution of the unfortunate Don Diego Leon:

['He was the tool of tyrants.' Be it so!]

'He was the tool of tyrants.' Be it so!
Cares Poetry for Party? No!
The Poet gathers his perennial bays
  In all domains. Reign Kings of Earth who chuse!
Since Homer sang, since Illium's dazzling days,   5
  He owns no sovereign, save the Muse.
He reverences Napoleon's mighty mind,
  Yet weeps, too, when the Bourbon D'Enghien dies.*
He knows Man but as a Man: you cannot bind
  His catholic soul by party-ties!   10

placarded his principles as follows, in 1844—

[Be my goal, or not, a vain chimera]

Be my goal, or not, a vain chimera,
  By the People's Rights I take my stand;
  'March, O Poet, with thy land and era!'
  So *now* read I Schiller's high command.

    His book was entitled 'Ein Glaubensbekenntniss,' (A Confession of Faith,) and
was in two parts—one part containing some poems written while he was an old
German, and the other, those concocted by him after he had been ground Young
by the heartless tyranny of the aristocracy. We quote a portion of his preface:—

    'I have always been of a confiding and hopeful character; and the turn which
affairs have lately taken in Prussia has inflicted so much the more painful a shock
on my mind. It is to this that the reader owes the large number of poems in the
second part of my volume, as compared with those of the first. None of those
poems were "concocted," as the phrase is—(well, then, we beg his pardon)—
each of them arose out of some circumstances of the moment; and all were alike
the result of deep-rooted and thorough conviction on my part. Before I penned

---

*The original is much stronger, but its truth is questionable.
  'Er beugt sein Knie dem Helden Bonaparte,
  Und hört mit Zürnen D'Enghien's Todesschrei.'
A courtier, or a hypocrite, may act in this duplex way, but scarcely a poet.

them, I had resigned to the king all further claims on his bounty. My much-talked-of pension was bestowed on me in the beginning of 1842; and since the termination of 1843, I have ceased to receive it.

.   .   .   .

'In trustfully commending this volume to the hearts of the German people, I am certain that the reflective and candid will be able, from its contents, accurately to trace the progress of my faith and feelings. They will perceive that my conversion was not sudden, but gradual; not the product of levity, or wild enthusiasm, but the result of enquiry and enlightened persuasion. And it will come to this with the entire nation before long! We are all engaged in a blind struggle for the attainment of political consciousness: light will, by-and-by, break in upon us. In the mean time, the severest reproach that can be addressed to me, is, that I have suffered my "catholic soul" to be bound by "party-ties." I admit that I have! I have gone over, without shrinking or faltering, to the ranks of those brave men who are exerting themselves to stem the tide of tyranny with breast and brow. For me, henceforth, no existence without liberty! Whatever be the fate of this book—whatever be my own fate—as long as the system of oppression under which I behold my fatherland groaning shall endure, so long shall my voice and arm be raised in support of the efforts of all who are labouring for national regeneration. So help me, next to GOD, the confidence of my countrymen! My face is turned towards the Future.'

Noble fellow! How we should wish to have witnessed the interview between him and the king! 'Take back the remnant of your bribe-money!' we may suppose him to have exclaimed with the air of a hussar, as perhaps he handed three groschen—four pence halfpenny—in a piece of twisted paper to Frederick William, who probably fainted on the spot. Honour to such heroism! With what a lofty air of independence Ferdinand must that day have stalked into the humble ordinary at the corner of Hochstrasse, and demanded, for the first time in his life, a dinner of rolls and radishes on tick!

We purpose to extract at some length from his volume in a future article. For the present we shall confine ourself to a translation of one of its poems—a ballad on the 'Wei3ze Frau,' or White Lady, who,—as the petrel shews itself before the tempest,—has recently re-appeared in Prussia, by way of giving princes and people fair promise of the approach of troublous times. Our readers, we presume, have heard or read of

The White Lady

(She is popularly supposed to have been the princess Agnes of Meran, who married Otto, Count of Orlamund, and murdered her two children, from a notion that they stood in the way of her subsequent union with Albert the Fair, Burgrave of Nuremburg, with whom she had fallen in love. Her death occurred about the middle of the fourteenth century. Professor Stilling seems to doubt the identity of the 'Weiʒze Frau' with Lady Agnes, but he allows it to be 'an almost universally admitted fact,' that the 'Frau' has been, from time to time, seen in sundry castles throughout Prussia, Bavaria, and Bohemia. The Legations-councillor George Döring, editor of the Franfort *Iris*, has communicated some interesting anecdotes with respect to her to Dr. Kerner, for which we refer very German readers to Vol. VI. of that indefatigable demonologist's 'Blätter aus Prevorst.')

Once more the Phantom Countess, attired in white, appears,
With mourning and with wailing, with tremors and with tears,
Once more appears a-gliding forth from pictures and from walls,
In Prussia's gorgeous palaces and old baronial halls—
And the guards that pace the ramparts and the terrace-walks by night,   5
Are stricken with a speechlessness and swooning at the sight.
        O pray for Lady Agnes!
        Pray for the soul of Lady Agnes!

What bodes this resurrection upon our illumined stage?
Comes she perchance to warn and wake a ghostless, godless age?   10
Announces she the death of Kings and Kaisers as of yore—
A funeral and a crowning—a pageant, and no more?
I know not—but men whisper through the land, from south to north,
That a deeper grief, a wider woe, to-day has called her forth.
        O pray for Lady Agnes!   15
        Pray for the hapless Lady Agnes!

She nightly weeps—they say so!—o'er the beds of Young and Old,
O'er the infant's crimson cradle—o'er the couch of silk and gold.
For hours she stands, with clasped hands, lamenting by the side
Of the sleeping Prince and Princess—of the Landgrave and his bride;   20
And at whiles along the corridors is heard her thrilling cry—
'Awake, awake, my kindred!—the Time of Times is nigh!'
        O pray for Lady Agnes!
        Pray for the suffering Lady Agnes!

'Awake, awake my kindred! O saw ye what I see,   25
Sleep never more would seal your eyes this side eternity!
Through the hundred-vaulted cavern-crypts where I and mine abide,
Boom the thunders of the rising storm, the surgings of the tide—
You note them not: you blindly face the hosts of Hate and Fate!
Alas! your eyes will open soon—too soon, yet all too late!'   30
  O pray for Lady Agnes!
  Pray for the soul of Lady Agnes!

'Oh, God! Oh, God! the coming hour arouses even the Dead;
Yet the Living thus can slumber on, like things of stone or lead.
The dry bones rattle in their shrouds, but you, you make no sign!   35
I dare not hope to pierce your souls by those weak words of mine,
Else would I warn from night to morn, else cry, 'O Kings, be just!
Be just, if bold! Loose where you may: bind only where you must!'
  O pray for Lady Agnes!
  Pray for the wretched Lady Agnes!   40

'I, sinful one, in Orlamund I slew my children fair:
Thence evermore, till time be o'er, my dole and my despair,
Of that one crime in olden time was born my endless woe;
For that one crime I wander now in darkness to and fro.
Think *ye* of me, and what I dree, you whom no law controls,   45
Who slay your people's holiest hopes, their liberties, their souls!'
  O pray for Lady Agnes!
  Pray for the hapless Lady Agnes!

'Enough! I must not say *Good* night, or bid the doomed fare*well!*
Down to mine own dark home I go—my Hades' dungeon-cell.   50
Above my head lie brightly spread the flowers that Summer gives,
Free waters flow, fresh breezes blow, all nature laughs and lives;
But where *you* tread the flowers drop dead, the grass grows pale and sere,
And round you floats in clotted waves Hell's lurid atmosphere!'
  O pray for Lady Agnes!   55
  Pray for the wandering Lady Agnes!

She lifts on high her pallid arms—she rises from the floor,
Turns round and round without a sound, then passes through the door.
But through the open trellices the warden often sees
Her moonpale drapery floating down the long dim galleries;   60

And the guards that pace the ramparts and the terrace-walks by night
Are stricken with a speechlessness and swooning at the sight,
     O pray for Lady Agnes!
     And myriads more with Lady Agnes!

    In Wolff's *Hausschatz*—the repertory of an incredible quantity of middling poetry—we meet with a song by one Heyden, a name unfamiliar to our ears. Of course we do not pledge our honour that our version of it is at all a faithful one, in the translatorial sense of the word. About the term *Wechabite*, in the second stanza, we entertain some doubt: possibly it may not mean 'Wahabee.' The Wahabee fanatics, we believe, displayed rather too much than too little zeal in defence of the 'holy places.'

The Last Words of Al-Hassan

Farewell for ever to all I love!
  To river and rock farewell!
To Zoumlah's gloomful cypress-grove,
  And Shaarmal's tulipy dell!
To Deenween-Kúllaha's light blue bay,   5
  And Oreb's lonely strand!
My race is run—I am called away—
  I go to the Lampless Land.
      'Llah Hu!
I am called away from the light of day   10
  To my tent in the Dark Dark Land!

I have seen the standard of Ali stained
  With the blood of the Brave and Free,
And the Kaaba's Venerable Stone profaned
  By the truculent Wahabee.   15
O, Allah, for the light of another sun,
  With my Bazra sword in hand!—
But I rave in vain—my course is run—
  I go to the Lampless Land.
      'Llah Hu!   20
My course is run—my goal is won—
  I go to the Dark Dark Land!

Yet why should I live a day—an hour?
  The friends I valued lie low;
My sisters dance in the halls of the Giaour;*   25
  My brethren fight for the foe.
None stood by the banner this arm unfurled
  Save Khàrada's mountain-band.
'Tis well that I leave so base a world,
  Though to dwell in the Lampless Land—   30
      'Llah Hu!
'Tis well that I leave so false a world,
  Though to dwell in the Dark Dark Land!

Even she, my loved and lost Ameen,
  The moon-white pearl of my soul,   35
Could pawn her peace for the show and sheen
  Of silken Istambόl!
How little did I bode what a year would see,
  When we parted at Samarkhànd—
My bride in the harem of the Osmânlee,   40
  Myself in the Lampless Land!
      'Llah Hu!
My bride in the harem of the Osmânlee,
  Myself in the Dark Dark Land!

We weep for the Noble who perish young,   45
  Like flowers before their bloom—
The great-souled Few who, unseen and unsung,
  Go down to the charnel's gloom;
But, written on the brow of each, if Man
  Could read it and understand,   50
Is the changeless decree of Heaven's Deewàn—
  We are born for the Lampless Land!
      'Llah Hu!
By the dread firmàn of Heaven's Deewàn—
  All are born for the Dark Dark Land!   55

---

* Literally *dog*, (the Irish *Gadhar*), and figuratively *infidel*. It is a monosyllable.

The wasted moon has a marvellous look
  Amiddle of the starry hordes—
The heavens, too, shine like a mystic book,
  All bright with burning words.
The mists of the dawn begin to dislimn   60
  Zahàra's castles of sand.
Farewell!—farewell! Mine eyes feel dim—
  They turn to the Lampless Land.
      'Llah Hu!
My heart is weary—mine eyes are dim—   65
  I would rest in the Dark Dark Land!

[. . . An] earnest and energetic writer of the Gallician school is August Lamey, a native of Kohl, seventy three years old, whose early youth was passed amid the exciting scenes of the revolution of '89. He thinks in French though he writes in German, and appears to entertain rather a contempt for the Transrhenane character. 'Ihr,' he exclaims, addressing the Germans—'ihr seid der Ruhe froh, und brennt nicht für das höhere Gut der Freiheit! Uns (Frenchmen) war ein Phónix aufgestiegen, der fern von euch in Dunste kreiset: darum, ihr Enkel, reden wir euch nicht mit euren Zungen und denken nicht mit eurem Geiste.' We give the spirited verses in which this fine sentiment occurs.

Fuimus!

I am one of some half thousand from the millions of a reign
  Departed with the years before the flood—
A reign of Anarchy and Grandeur, Intellect and Crime,
    Which witnessed all of Ill or Good
The lifewhile of a world can shew—phenomena such as Time   5
    Shall never, never see again!

Then spread far forth, like billowy fire, the feelings that of old
  Had smouldered in the bosoms of the Few;
Immortal Freedom then was born, and dwelt with mortal men;
    And France, the thundress, rose, and threw   10
Her giant shadow o'er the quaking earth! Since then
    Hath half a stormy century rolled!

You, Germans, you are dead in soul! Your luxury is Repose;
    We hated that! The price of Liberty
We knew to be our hearts' best blood, and *that* we freely gave;   15
        We poured it forth in oceans, we!
Even till we saw the Night again close o'er us like a grave
        Where first our Sun of Glory rose!

We have learned all terrible truths that Revolution came to teach—
    We have known all marvellous changes Time could show—   20
We have seen the Phœnix of a world whose ashes on the winds
        Were scattered long and long ago!
Therefore, pale Youth of Germany, we think not with your minds,
        Nor can you understand our speech!

    Now for a song from Julien Mosen, a Voigtlander, and, albeit a lawyer by pro-
fession, a true poet in temperament.

The Death of Hofer

At Mantua long had lain in chains
    The gallant Hofer bound;
        But now his day of doom was come—
        At morn the deep roll of the drum
Resounded o'er the soldiered plains.   5
        O Heaven! with what a deed of dole
    The hundred thousand wrongs were crowned
        Of trodden down Tyról!*

With iron-fettered arms and hands
    The hero moved along.   10
        His heart was calm, his eye was clear—
        Death was for traitor slaves to fear!
He oft amid his mountain bands,
        Where Inn's dark wintry waters roll,
    Had faced it with his battle song,   15
        The Sandwirth of Tyról.

* We suppose we need scarcely remark that this word is properly accented on the second syllable.

Anon he passed the fortress wall,
  And heard the wail that broke
    From many a brother thrall within.
    'Farewell!' he cried. 'Soon may you win   20
Your liberty! GOD shield you all!
    Lament not me! I see my goal.
  Lament the land that wears the yoke,
    Your land and mine, Tyról!'

So through the files of musqueteers   25
  Undauntedly he passed,
    And stood within the hollow square.
    Well might he glance around him there,
And proudly think on by-gone years!
    Amid such serfs *his* bannerol,   30
  Thank GOD! had never braved the blast
    On thy green hills, Tyról!

They bade him kneel; but he with all
  A patriot's truth replied—
    'I kneel alone to GOD on high—   35
    As thus I stand so dare I die,
As oft I fought so let me fall!
    Farewell'—his breast a moment swoll
  With agony he strove to hide.—
    'My Kaiser and Tyról!'   40

No more emotion he betrayed.
  Again he bade farewell
    To Francis and the faithful men
    Who girt his throne. His hands were then
Unbound for prayer, and thus he prayed:—   45
    'God of the Free, receive my soul!
  And you, slaves, Fire!' So bravely fell
    Thy foremost man, Tyról!

We should very much like to elaborate an Anthology from Rückert. Like Wordsworth, Rückert has been eminently successful in his attempts to invest the every-day incidents of life, 'the common growth of Mother Earth,' with the graces of poetry; but he is wholly free from the stilted pedantry which one regrets to meet with occasionally in the Great Lakist. In his purely metaphysical poems he does not shine. A translator of these must either amplify them or cut them short—perhaps cut them altogether. Here is a thought borrowed from Neander, and is actually gasping for air.

Ein Wort Neander's. A saying of Neander

Den Schöpferischen, herrschend über seine Zeit
Erhabnen Geist, wie darfst du ihn aus seiner Zeit
Erklären? Aus ihm selbst erklare seine Zeit!

Ever must thy toil be frustrate
While thou strivest to illustrate
GOD from Human Soul and State:
These abide unvoiceful ever;
Shadow serves to *indicate*   5
Substance, but *contains* it never.
Whoso seeks the Unseen Eternal
In the Finite Visible
Is but groping for the Kernel
On the outside of the Shell.   10

'Aus ihm selbst erkläre seine Zeit!' advises Neander, but merely, as it would seem, for sake of the antithesis, for even the adviser himself, subtle a theologian as he is, could scarcely obey such a behest. As a suggestion to Hegel, (at whose 'absolute philosophy' the thought is obviously *visée*) it is sheer folly. We have left it where we found it.

The following is at once a happy *jeu d'esprit*, and a melancholy truth.

Memnon and Mammon

'Thine Eastern Lays, O friend! are dear
To my soul! I sing them, and in mine ear
   All Memnon's mythical dolors are tingling!'
So wrote to me recently One of Us.
I shewed the passage to Ludovic Huss;   5
And Ludovic read it precisely thus—
'Thine Eastern Lays, O friend! are dear

To my soul! I sing them, and in mine ear
All Mammon's musical dollars are jingling!'
The irony here is rather severe;   10
But the man *of* a MILLION, the modern Xerxes
(Of ducats) can hardly do other than sneer
   At the MAN *in* a million who coins but—verses!
The world prefers—thought he Poet imbues
   His pages with Fancy's brilliantest colors—   15
The 'gold itself' to the golden hues,
   And Mammon's dollars to Memnon's dolors!

   That Rückert's oriental translations deserve such praise we are not prepared
to admit; but we are perhaps blinded by our western prejudices. We submit a
specimen of those translations:—

And Then No More

I saw her once, one little while, and then no more:
'Twas Eden's light on Earth awhile, and then no more.
Amid the throng she passed along the meadow-floor:
Spring seemed to smile on Earth awhile, and then no more,
But whence she came, which way she went, what garb she wore,   5
I noted not; I gazed awhile, and then no more!

I saw her once, one little while, and then no more:
'Twas Paradise on Earth awhile, and then no more.
Ah! what avail my vigils pale, my magic lore?
She shone before mine eyes awhile, and then no more.   10
The shallop of my peace is wrecked on Beauty's shore.
Near Hope's fair isle it rode awhile, and then no more!

I saw her once, one little while, and then no more:
Earth looked like Heaven a little while, and then no more.
Her presence thrilled and lighted to its inner core   15
My desert breast a little while, and then no more.
So may, perchance, a meteor glance at midnight o'er
Some ruined pile a little while, and then no more!

I saw her once, one little while, and then no more:
The earth was Peri-land awhile, and then no more.   20
Oh, might I see but once again, as once before,
Through chance or wile, that shape awhile, and then no more!
Death soon would heal my griefs! This heart, now sad and sore,
Would beat anew a little while, and then no more.

We shall conclude our present paper by two poems from Selber. It is fortunate for us that we are not required to criticise as well as to translate, for we should scarcely know what judgment to pronounce on this eccentric writer. Selber is not a young Germanist, though, from certain passages in his works, he might pass for one—nay for one of the reddest-hot revolutionists. Perhaps we should describe him aptliest by representing him as a compound of supernaturalist, republican, moral philosopher, and utilitarian—the supernaturalist predominating. He appears to have 'begun the world' with a redundance of enthusiasm, and to have, accordingly, duly realised the saddening truth of the sentiment advanced by Moore—(if we misquote our friend Tom he will be good enough to send us a set of his works—)

Oh! life is a waste of wearisome hours,
   That seldom the rose of enjoyment adorns;
And the toes that are foremost to dance among flowers,
   Are also the first to be troubled with corns!

Nobody can translate Selber to advantage: his peculiar idiosyncrasy unfortunately betrays itself in every line he writes—and there exists, moreover, an evident wish on his part to show the world that he possesses

'A life within himself, to breathe without mankind.'

'What a happy fellow was Jacobi!' he observes. 'He could doubt his own identity, and that of every man!—but for me—"Ich bin ich, und leider bin kein Andrer!"' We beg our readers to cast their eyes over the following poem, and to note also the comments of Dr. Berri Abel Hummer thereon:—

Eighteen Hundred Fifty

I am I,—mineself, and none beside:
  That's a fact, in spite of Herr Jacobi.
Would it were not! for I cannot hide
  From my heart my growing autophoby.
Were metempsychosian figments true,   5
  I'd bequeath, good world, an ugly gift t'ye—
My sad soul to wit, which waits the new
  State of things in Eighteen Hundred Fifty!*
Will that epoch license me to see
Faith triumphant and the nations free—   10
Or but make a dismal dupe of me?
  Like De Quincey waking from some glowing
    Opium-dream to study Kant and groan—
      ... Hark! the winds, the rueful winds are blowing,
          And, alas! I dwell alone!   15

Sick to death of all I see, my thoughts
  Take a turn much like the last of Cato's.
I renounce for weeks mine old onslaughts
  On long lines of rashers and potatoes,
And, eschewing courses and dessert,   20
  Pic-nic off a lark with schnapps of stiff tea;
But though 'foul *is* fair,'† *such* fowl and fare
  Won't go down in Eighteen Hundred Fifty!
Truth to tell, I vowed a vow two-thirds
Of a year back not to munch small birds,   25
Yet I swallow (them and) mine own words!
  Which is shabby. But of late I'm growing
    Tired of polishing bone after bone.
      ... Hark! again the doleful winds are blowing,
          And, alas! I live alone!   30

* One of Selber's odd notions is that people make circles in time as well as in space. Hence he fancies that we shall come round again to the golden age about the middle of the present century. The poor crazed creature!—B. A. HUMMER

† These words are from an English tragedy, called *Shanksbare*, by William Maccabet. I mention this to illustrate the extensiveness of my acquaintance with foreign literature. I wrote to Professor Macwhopper of Glasgow, intimating my conviction that William Maccabet was the author of the tragedy; and the professor's reply was—'Will you mak' a bet he *was* the author?' My readers will mark his note of interrogation: it is beautifully symbolical of the Scotch propensity to question all things, even those about which there can be no question.—B.A.H.

Would you know my history rather well,
  Calculate how felt the Arabian glassman
Ere—and after—his one basket fell.
  That's the ticket! And what's worse, alas! Man
Rarely vaunts a marked advantage o'er   35
  Me herein. Perpend how shy a shift he
Makes to bag three halfpence at threescore!
  For myself, if Eighteen Hundred Fifty
Still shall find me sighing o'er a lack
Of rixdollars, Rhenish, and taback,   40
I shall drive to Paris and turn quack.
  Humbug seems the rifest science going
    Since the days of Dee's delightful stone.*
      ... Hark! again the midnight winds are blowing,
        And, alas! I mope alone!   45

O, ye rosy ghosts of buried hours,
  Haunters of a head which *they* made hoary,
How you mock one when Disaster lours
  With your shameless Tantalusian glory!
Memory draws upon her ill-got wealth   50
  All the more as Fancy waxes thrifty.
I want neither! Give me Hope and Health,
  Give me LIFE, O Eighteen Hundred Fifty!
Give me back, not Youth's imaginings,
But its feelings, which are truer things!   55
Helicon, thou should'st be dammed! One sings
  Only sadlier where thy stream is flowing:
    I drink water from the Rhine and Rhone.†
      ... Hark! again the rueful winds are blowing,
        And, alas! I drink alone!   60

---

* The sneer conveyed in the expression 'Dee's deelichtvoll Stein'—as though the Lucid Stone of Dr. *Dee* were merely *full* of his own *light*, in other words, were a humbug—was hardly to have been expected from my friend Selber. Dee might have been an enthusiast, but Selber is an imposter. Look to his oversettings! (*Uebersetzungen.*)—B.A.H.

† Then I commiserate his water-carriers. But perhaps his meaning is that he quaffs Rhenish in other people's kitchens in Strasburg, and Rhonish in his own attic at Lyons. B.A.H.

Dulled and darkened is mine 'Inward Light;'
  (Soular light or solar—Doctor Kerner
States that one's the other,* and he's right.)
  I grow stupider, or sterner—
Sneerers think the former—slobs the last.   65
  Wasn't something similar said of Swift, eh?
Ah! had but his lot and mine been cast
  In the Spring of Eighteen Hundred Fifty!
What rare trumps were Hogarth, he, and I,
Meeting not to η β π,†   70
But to talk and joke, and mystify!
  Dazzlingly should flash Time's now so slow wing,
    As a firefly's in the Torrid Zone.
  Hark! again the rueful winds are blowing,
    And, alas! I stand alone!   75

Yet I dream, too, when at whiles my mind
  Slips, like some galled hack, its work-day harness.
Leaving Strasburg's pipes and swipes behind,
  Then I soar into the death-bright Farness.
There the temple of Celestial Fame   80
  Shines from heights divinely steep and clifty.‡
What d'ye lay I *don't* inscribe my name
  On its walls in Eighteen Hundred Fifty?
Feelings noon-dazed Reason can't recal,
Thrill my spirit, glad me and appal,   85
While I wander through that Phantomhall,
  Where the Fates are nightly busy throwing
    Dice for Philip's lath-and-plaster throne.§
  Hark! again the rueful winds are blowing,
    And, alas! I live alone!   90

---

* Not exactly. Dr. Kerner merely states that the light within us is that of *a* sun. Of course he is not
such an ass as to confound spiritual things with natural. B.A.H.
† Hogarth it seems occasionally invited his friends to η β π (eat a bit o' pie) with him at his rooms. The
Greek letters are plain enough; but what is the meaning of the Chinese within the parenthesis? B.A.H.
‡ *Celestial* fame, observe, not earthly. Selber's toploftical disdain of human applause is the only
great thing about him, except his cloak. It is refreshing to meet with a man whose esteem you can
gain only by touching him with a crowbar. B.A.H.
§ Twaddle, mere twaddle. What are the fourteen Bastiles for? The old codger himself, I admit, is
not very stout on his pins; but De Joinville sports a fine military pair of whiskers, and is my parti-
cular friend besides. I have therefore no apprehension. B.A.H.

Golden Year when Earth shall rise agen,
   Like the Phœnix, from her own red ashes,
Mayest thou last an age! Meantime, young men,
   Let no razor mar your French moustaches!
France will yet be Europe.* I shan't add   95
More. But watch her, if you twig my drift. He
Who nods once will wake like Nourjahad,
   Somewhere *after* Eighteen Hundred Fifty!
Work. Pray. Meditate. Keep out of debt.
Flee Temptation. Bib no heavy wet;   100
And be sure you never play Roulette.
   That's the source to which *my* woes are owing;
    That's what gives my song its dolorous tone.
   Hark! again the rueful winds are blowing,
     And, alas! I want A Loan!   105

The Ruby Mug
AN ANECDOTE

A voice of wailing rang through Bagdad!
   The Khalif's Ruby Mug was lost,
   That splendid heirloom which had cost
Seven sacks of sequins—which, 'twas bragged, had
Been in his family since the Flight   5
   And out of which he had largely swigged
    Small beer. Some swore it had been smash-èd
     By the jolly ugly hookah in his hand,
While others hit upon the bright
   Idea that it had been prigged.   10
Meanwhile the Kahlif noon and night
   Wept like a spout. 'I'll give,' quoth he,
'My daughter's hand by way of boon
   To him who shows my Mug to me,
Even though the journals dub me Spoon!'   15
    So spake the stout Haroun-al-Rashèd,
     With his jolly ugly hookah in his hand.

---

* *Qu:* France will yet be Your Hope? I don't know why it is that Strasburghers are so fond of being Frenchmen. But as Africa is fast becoming France, it is not impossible that France may be Europe yet. I get my own hair, whiskers, teeth, legs and shoulders from Paris already. B.A.H.

Time went ahead, but brought no answer.
 The year waxed venerably old.
 Ten moons were wasted, when, behold!   20
A nice young man, a necromancer,
One day knocked at the palace gate,
 And asked to see 'the stout Haroun,
  That fine old fellow, black moustach-èd,
   With his jolly ugly hookah in his hand!'   25
Guards showed him up. In silver state
 Upon a sofa sat Haroun.
 'Well,' cried the youth, 'well, Silver Spoon!
I bring you tidings of your Mug!'—
 'You don't?'—'I do'—'Where is it?'—'Snug   30
 In Tigris, fifty fathom deep.
 That's where it is. So cease to weep!'
  'Bosh!' said the stout Haroun-al-Rashèd,
  With his jolly ugly hookah in his hand.

'Nay, hear me out, long-headed Khalif!   35
 Your Grand Wézeer or Court Buffoon
 Can fish it up!' 'Then,' cried Haroun,
'By Djing (that's Djinghiz Khan), they shall, if
I have the power to make them dive!
 Hey, Djaffer! what d'ye say, my boy?'   40
  'Sire!' groaned the Grand One, much abash-èd
  With his jolly ugly hookah in his hand,
'I never *should* come up alive!
 Indeed, you let this Loss annoy
You overmuch. Our Prophet————' 'Stuff! 45
 Profit and Loss,' exclaimed the Stout.
'I hate such huckster slang. Enough
 Of that! But what are you about,
Young man? Accept a pinch of snuff!'
  Exclaimed the stout Haroun-al-Rashèd, 50
  With his jolly ugly hookah in his hand.

'From whom, pray, did you learn your magic?'
 'From Shuckabac of Koordistán.'
 'Ah! so? That *was* a matchless man!'
'Yes, but his end was rather tragic,   55
And owing to his matchlessness.'

'Indeed?' 'Fact. Once a twelvemonth he
   (Being first half-staved and well self-thrash-éd)
     With a jolly ugly hookah in his hand,
And fourscore matches, more or less,   60
     For lighting lamps below the sea,
     Sought out a cave in deep Tasmeer
     To study in. His plunging plan
Did famously, till, one fine year,
     The poor old mooncalf of a man   65
Forgot his match-box clean and clear.
     What followed you may easily guess.
     He couldn't navigate in the dark
     His wet way back to Koordistán,
     And perished. So his fate, you mark,   70
Was owing to his matchlessness!'
     'Fudge!' said the stout Haroun-al-Rashèd,
       With his jolly ugly hookah in his hand.

'Come, Djaffer, my fat friend, the Bathos,
     Or Art of Sinking, is your forte.   75
     Confess it!' 'I have risen at court,'
Replied the Grand, with pride and pathos.
'Besides, you see, I have a bill,
     (An eight-and-forty pounder) which
      I'm just now going to get cash-èd,   80
       With my jolly ugly hookah in my hand.
And jobs increase on me, and will,
     In divers ways.' 'Well, that is rich,'
Sneered stout Haroun. 'Yes, Djaff, your joys
And jobberies are by no means few.   85
I don't know any man who fobs
     The public revenues like you.
     In *divers'* ways? That's comic too;
Yet you *won't* dive, you sire of slobs!
     Shame!' cried the stout Haroun-al-Rashèd,   90
       With his jolly ugly hookah in his hand.

'What name d'ye bear, young man?'—'Bham-Bhooz-eel,'
     Replied the stranger, with a bow
     That very nearly brought his brow
Down to the level of his shoe's-heel,   95

Which rose, however, pretty high,
  Because, as he remarked himself,
    A gentleman 'salaamed' and 'Pasha-èd,'
    With a jolly ugly hookah in his hand.
High-souled and low-heeled, looked so shy!   100
  And, soon or late, was shown that shelf
Where souls and heels too oft lie by.
'Bham-Bhooz-eel?' cried the Khalif. 'Humph!—
  I guess you count me glossy green,
A simpleton, a soap-soft sumph!—   105
    You swindling scoundrel, what d'ye mean?'
    Vociferated stout Al-Rashèd,
      With his jolly ugly hookah in his hand.

'Commander of the True Believers,'
  Returned the youth, 'I really think   110
  You must have taken too much drink.
I am none of those profane deceivers
Who trade upon the faith and fears
  And prayers and pockets of the crowd,
    Those fleecers of the Great Unwash-èd—   115
      With their jolly ugly hookahs in their hands.
  That is, if I may speak it loud,
Your juggling Moolahs and Wezeers.
So, don't begin to chide and chafe,
  Like some old fish-fag or dragoon.   120
I tell you that your Mug is safe.
  Call in your Principal Buffoon!'—
  The Khalif blew a small bassoon.
    'Now!' said the stout Haroun-al-Rashèd,
      With his jolly ugly hookah in his hand.   125

In trundled the Buffoon, Ghooz-Ghabbi.
  'Here!' cried the Khalif. '*Now* and *here?*'
  Ghooz-Ghabbi answered—'Those, I'm clear,
Are *Nowhere!*' 'Miserably shabby!'
Observed Haroun. 'But, mark me now!   130
  My Mug lies low in Tigris' bed,
    All wave-besprent and slime-besplash-èd.
    By this jolly ugly hookah in my hand,

And that's a somewhat serious vow,
   You, therefore, must descend like lead   135
And grope it out. I can't swig beer
   From any other mug or cup,
And none but you or my Wezeer,
   I understand, can bowl it up,
But *he* will *not*. There, now! To hear   140
   Is to obey!' So spake Al-Rashèd,
      With his jolly ugly hookah in his hand.

Ghooz-Ghabbi, while Haroun thus twaddled,
   Stood grinning like a cask of nails.
    'O! Prince!' he cried, 'my stomach fails,   145
My syntax halts, my brains are addled—
   And—if you please—I won't go down,
    I'd be so long a-getting dried!'
    'What, wretch!—you *won't*, d'ye tell me?' roared
     The Khalif, and his dark eyes flash-èd,   150
      And the jolly ugly hookah in his hand
Shook, and he frowned a tempest-frown.
    '*Begone*, then!' 'So I will,' replied
    The Jester, 'for I'm sadly bored;
    But first I'll *beg-one* glass of rum!'—   155
   'No! Go!'—the Khalif cried, 'you grow
Intolerably wearisome!'
'Ay,' said Ghooz-Ghabbi, with his thumb
   Beside his nose, 'it *is* No Go!'
    'Bah!' said the stout Haroun-al-Rashèd,   160
     With his jolly ugly hookah in his hand.

The Khalif now got in the tea-things,
   And hid a thimbleful of tea
   And bit of biscuit. 'Bham,' said he,
'I love to watch those vapoury wreathings   165
   O'er yonder tea-urn, as they rise
   Like incense from some triple-shrine.
    Here, crownless and un-sabretach-èd,
     With a jolly ugly hookah in my hand,
I dream of purer worlds and skies   170
   And soar from Earthly to Divine.
Come: improvise an Ode on Tea!'

'Excuse me,' said the youth; ''twould be
 Both ode-ious and tea-dious,
 Besides, I'm going to discuss   175
A thimbleful myself. Let *me*
 Hear *you* sing rather.' 'Well, then, thus
  I tune my pipe,' returned Al-Rashèd,
   With his jolly ugly hookah in his hand.

THE KHALIF'S SONG

'Bak-ey-Boul the Hakem has completely smashed my Teapot. 180
What a blow to China! I could crawl to bed and weep hot
Tears to think how stupidly my Winters will pass off! He
 Hasn't even left entire the spout for me to sneak up.
 Were he here I'd soon give *him* his Howqua in a—Teacup.
If I wouldn't may I never pound an ounce of coffee!   185
     Lalla-lalla-lalla, lalla-lá!

Woe to Man! His life is but a vast expanse of Tea-tray,
Over which the gleamy Teapot sheds a bright but fleet ray.
Nature gives him health and wealth, yet one by one he *sees* boon
 After boon forsake him: Time, the thief, is ever busy 190
 Mulcting him of brains and breath; and what at fifty is he?
Nothing but a porter-cask, a milk-sop, or a Tea-'spoon.'
     Lalla-lalla-lalla, lalla-lá!

Tea-plers are not tipplers; yet, Philosophy, thou preachest
Vainly unto all who take to tippling or the tea-chest;   195
Wonder-worker truly wert thou couldst thou but achieve a
 Change in our Tea-totalites, who sit and count their siller;
 Or in our Teetotumites, who reel from post to pillar,
Staggered by strong arguments of Xeres or Geneva!
     Lalla-lalla-lalla, lalla-lá!   200

I had forty battered friends, whom I to that degree bored,
That the tagrag scamps at last levanted from my Tea-board.
Tearless, though not tealess, I had nightly seen them tea-zèd,
 So they went to broil themselves in hotbaths near the Kaaba,
 Like those other Forty Thieves you've met in Ali Bába, 205
Whom Mordjana fried alive in oil—at least so *she* said.
     Lalla-lalla-lalla, lalla-lá!

O! the Arabian Nights when I could feast on Tea and Tea-cake,
Fearless that a cup too much would make my head a week ache!
Then my heart could hail the Dawn, and bless the Noon, and feel Eve's   210
  Gentleness and beauty as the dahlia feels the dew-drops.
  Now I can but mope at home, and, while I sip a few drops
Of thin laudanum-gruel, weep my withered hopes and Tea-leaves.
                Lalla-lalla-lalla, lalla-lá!

Friend Bham-Bhooz, you seem a quiz, and I, believe me, *am* one;   215
Yet, by wisdom, not by quizdom, is the Eternal Palm won.
Cherish, while you have them yet, the spirit's better breathings,
  And keep clear of Hell's decoys, among the which I rank wet
  Poison-stuffs: then may you look to share a nobler banquet
When Death comes at nine P.M. to take away the Tea-things.   220
                Lalla-lalla-lalla, lalla-lá!

'Bravo!' cried Bham. 'You've got some brandy?'
   'No!' sighed Haroun. 'I'll order in,
    In lieu thereof, a jug of gin.'
It came, with lots of sugarcandy,   225
Of which the Khalif ate some lumps.
   'Now, Bham,' quoth he, 'shake off your gyves!
    May I be signally squabash-èd,
     With my jolly ugly hookah in my hand,
If We, the King and Knave of Trumps,   230
   Don't get as blind as tinkers' wives!
But come! About my Ruby Mug?
   Can anybody shew me it?'—
   'One only,' answered Bham, 'to-wit
Myself. But please to push that jug   235
   Across. D'ye tremble?'—'Not a bit!'
    Replied the stout Haroun-al-Rashèd,
     With his jolly ugly hookah in his hand.

'Then, slock your goggles!' quoth Bham-Bhooz-eel,
   'Eh?—shut my eyes?'—'Yes.'—'There, then.'—'Good!   240
   I thought I *should* be understood.
I'll now go through the task with *true* zeal.'
So saying, he raised the jug, and—dashed
   Its burden in the Khalif's phiz!—
    'Wretch!' roared Al-Rashèd, gin-besplash-èd,   245

With his jolly ugly hookah in his hand.
'Wretch! what means this?' 'It means, and is,'
   Returned the youth, quite unabashed,
'A nice be-*gin*ning. Just survey
    Your frontispiece in yonder glass,   250
     And if you don't behold therein
Your long-lost *Ruby Mug*, you may
    Write *me* down a conspicuous ass.'
'Humph!' growled Haroun. 'You've won the day—
    Ay, laugh away! They laugh that win.'   255
     So spake the stout Haroun-al-Rashèd,
      With his jolly ugly hookah in his hand.

'The joke,' said Bham, 'is worth a hogshead
    Of gin, I think, much more a jug.'
    'Oh!' sighed Haroun, 'my Mug! my Mug!—   260
WHO are you, pray?'—'A Prince incog.,' said
Bham-Bhooz-eel. 'I have come from Bheer,
    (Of which I'm Khan, being of the line
     Of those old cut-throat Shahs of Djash-èd,
      With their jolly ugly hookahs in their hands,)   265
To wed your daughter. Let me see her!'—
    'Ah!' said Haroun, '*she* takes the shine
Off bread-and-butter!'—'Then, I'll pay
My addresses, Sire!—though, by the way,'
    Observed the youth, 'it *may* seem queer   270
That she should on her wedding-day
    Get nothing but a Khan of Bheer!'
     'Ha! ha!' guffawed Haroun-al-Rashèd,
      With his jolly ugly hookah in his hand.

MORAL OF THE PRECEDING ANECDOTE

               What   275
Though the fist of Destiny should fall upon your Mug, leer
    Not upon its ruins long with overflowing eye, for
     If the matter wore an ugly face before
    'Tis Bohemia to a barn, sextillions to a cypher,
              That   280
Blubbering will but make it (and yourself too) wear an uglier.
              [Unsigned, *DUM*, January 1845]

from *Stray Leaflets from the German Oak—Sixth Drift*

Where's my Money?
FRANZ FREIHERR GAUDY

Ay! where's my money? That's a puzzling query.
  It vanishes. Yet neither in my purse
Nor pocket are there any holes. 'Tis very
  Incomprehensible. I don't disburse
For superfluities. I wear plain clothes.   5
  I seldom buy jam tarts, preserves, or honey;
And no one overlooks what debts he owes
  More steadily than I. Where *is* my money?

I never tipple. Folks don't see me staggering,
  Sans cane and castor, in the public street.   10
I sport no ornaments—not even a *bague* (ring).
  I have a notion that my own two feet
Are much superior to a horse's four,
  So never call a jarvey. It is funny.
The longer I investigate, the more   15
  Astoundedly I ask, *Where* is my money?

My money, mind you! Other people's dollars
  Cohere together nobly. Only mine
Cut one another. There's that pink of scholars
  Von Doppeldronk, he spends as much on wine   20
As I on—every thing. Yet *he* seems rich,
  He laughs, and waxes plumper than a tunny,
While I grow slim as a divining-switch,
  And search for gold as vainly. Where's my money?

I can't complain that editors don't pay me;   25
  I get for every sheet One Pound Sixteen;
And well I may! My articles are flamy
  Enough to blow up *any* Magazine.
What's queerest in the affair though is, that at
  The same time I miss nothing but the *one*. He   30
That watches me will find I don't lose hat,
  Gloves, fogle, stick, or cloak. 'Tis always money!

Were I a rake I'd say so. Where one roysters
  Beyond the rules, of course his cash must go.
'Tis true I regularly sup on oysters,   35
  Cheese, brandy, and all that. But even so?
What signifies a ducat of a night?
  'The barmaids,' you may fancy. No. The sunny
Loadstar that draws *my* tin is not the light
  From *their* eyes anyhow. Where then's my money?   40

However, *àpropos* of eyes and maidens,
  I own I *do* make presents to the Sex—
Books, watches, trinkets, music too (not Haydn's),
  Combs, shawls, veils, bonnets—things that might perplex
A man to count. But still I gain by what   45
  I lose in this way. 'Tis experience won—eh?
I think so. My acquaintances think *not*.
  No matter. I grow tedious. Where's my money?

The Bewildered Vintner

HEINRICH AUGUST HOFFMAN (VON FALLERSLEBEN)

'What, host! a *glass?* That's not the thing
  For any man that ever *drank* hard.
Levant, you jolly dog, and bring
  Me in at least a gallon-tankard!'
The crookèd-and-hookèd-nosed host   5
  Looks blind as a partridge,
  Looks blank as a cartridge,
Looks owlish and muzzy: 'tis plain as a post
He has had some schnapps to-day with his krout.
He stoops, he stumbles, he staggers about,   10
He toddles in and he toddles out,
    For—he can't lay his hands on the key!

Covering the sanded floor, long bands
  Of guests throng tap-wards, thicker, quicker.
—'Amid those barren burning sands   15
  We faint,' they cry, 'for lack of liquor!

O, host with the hooky beak,
  Thou stoopest and staggerest,
  And puffest and swaggerest,
And lookest most owlish! What bothers thee? Speak!'—   20
The host, however, is mute as a trout.
He stares at them all from lord to lout.
He turns his pockets inside-out.
He reels, he wheels, he wriggles about.
The case is beyond any measure of doubt—   25
    He—can't lay his hand on the key!

Two hundred men besiege the bar
  For cider, hock, and eau-de-Dantzic,
And gin*ger*-beer for such as *are*
  And gin-*and*-beer for such as *a'n't* sick.   30
Tremendous excitement exists
  In kitchen and tap-room,
  In smoke-room and schnapp-room;
And porter-tables and porters' fists
Come into collision. Meantime, the lout   35
Of a host keeps trundling in and out.
He stares at the groups within and without,
Burschen and burghers and rabble-rout.
He jumps and skips and capers about.
The fact is beyond a shadow of doubt   40
That he isn't a martyr to palsy or gout:
    But—he can't lay his hand on the key!

—'O, host! thou scamperest out and in,
  While we, thy guests, fry here like rashers.
Thy lips are thin, thy nose and chin   45
  Meet like a pair of nut-squabashers.
Small man of the nutcracking phiz,
  Who twistest and wheelest,
  And wrigglest and reelest,
We warn thee, bring drink, ere our dander be riz!'—   50
The host in silence hears them shout,
He knows they are dying of horrible drought,
He hears them roaring for 'cold without'
'Tumblers of brandy,' and 'beakers of stout,'

While the only *tumblers* and *beakers* about   55
The house are himself and his hooky snout.
He peers around, above, about.
He stalks to-and-fro like a turkey-pout.
His wits, it is clear, are up the spout,
  For—he can't lay his hand on the key!   60

The guests, thus turned to 'waiters,' grow,
  Some sad, some sulky, some outrageous;
But, as their threats are found 'no go,'
  The wrath ere long becomes contagious.
They seize on the poker and tongs,   65
  The shovel and fender;
  And every contender
For justice and brandy harangues on his wrongs.
They swear, they stamp, they storm, they shout,
They bellow like Muscovites under the knout.   70
They call for 'soda,' 'perry,' and 'stout,'
'Hollands' and 'hock' and 'cold without,'
And other swash for a drinking-bout.
Meanwhile the landlord runs about,
And speers and spies like a Prussian scout   75
Inspecting the strength of a Russian redoubt,
Till at length and at last, like a gasping trout,
He opens his mouth, and his words dribble out
Like tea from a choked-up teapot-spout.—

    '𝔍—can't—lay my—hand on—the key!'   80

(Upon which the customers, in a general chorus of amazement, repeat—)

    '𝕳e can't lay his hand on the key!'
                      [Unsigned, *DUM*, February 1845]

from *Spanish Romances and Songs–No. I*

Song: The Mariner's Bride
(FROM THE POEMS OF LUIS DE CAMOENS)

'Irme quiero, madre,
A aquella galera,
Con el marinero
A ser marinera.'

Look, mother! the mariner's rowing
  His galley adown the tide;
I'll go where the mariner's going,
  And be the mariner's bride!

I saw him one day through the wicket,   5
  I opened the gate, and we met.
  As a bird in the fowler's net
Was I caught in my own green thicket.
Oh, mother, my tears are flowing,
  They've quenched my maidenly pride—   10
I'll go if the mariner's going,
  And be the mariner's bride!

This Love, the tyrant, evinces
  Alas! an omnipotent might.
  He darkens the mind like Night,   15
He treads on the necks of princes!
Oh, mother, my bosom is glowing,
  I'll go, whatever betide,
I'll go, since the mariner's going,
  And be the mariner's bride!   20

Yes, mother! the Spoiler has reft me
  Of reason and self-control;
  Gone, gone is my wretched soul,
And only my body is left me!
The winds, oh, mother, are blowing,   25
  The ocean is bright and wide;
I'll go where the mariner's going,
  And be the mariner's bride!

              [J. C. M., *DUM*, May 1845]

from Stray Leaflets from the German Oak–Seventh Drift

The Wayfaring Tree
SELBER

We
Old bachelor bards, having none to mind us,
    Are seized at seasons with such a heart-aking
That, leaving home and its wants behind us,
    We hie elsewhither, the spirit's car taking   5
Us east and west, and aloft and nether,
    And thus I, also, both night and day faring
From Hartz to Hellas, pass weeks together
    (𝔍𝔫 𝔳𝔦𝔰𝔦𝔬𝔫) 𝔲𝔫𝔡𝔢𝔯 𝔪𝔦𝔫𝔢 𝔬𝔩𝔡 𝔚𝔞𝔶𝔣𝔞𝔯𝔦𝔫𝔤
              𝔗𝔯𝔢𝔢,   10
    𝔐𝔶 𝔠𝔥𝔦𝔩𝔡𝔥𝔬𝔬𝔡'𝔰 𝔡𝔢𝔞𝔯𝔩𝔶 𝔟𝔢𝔩𝔬𝔳𝔢𝔡 𝔚𝔞𝔶𝔣𝔞𝔯𝔦𝔫𝔤
              𝔗𝔯𝔢𝔢!

Free
Of pinion then, like the lonely pewet,
    I watch through Autumn its golden leaves dropping,   15
And list the sighs of the winds that woo it—
    A somewhat silly but sinless eavesdropping!—
And sadly ponder those rosy dream-hours
  When Boyhood's fancies went first a-May-Fairing.
Ah! we may smile, but the joys that *seem* ours   20
    𝔖𝔬𝔬𝔫 𝔩𝔢𝔞𝔳𝔢 𝔲𝔰 𝔪𝔬𝔲𝔯𝔫𝔢𝔯𝔰 𝔟𝔢𝔫𝔢𝔞𝔱𝔥 𝔬𝔲𝔯 𝔚𝔞𝔶𝔣𝔞𝔯𝔦𝔫𝔤
              𝔗𝔯𝔢𝔢!
    𝔍𝔫𝔰𝔬𝔩𝔳𝔢𝔫𝔱 𝔪𝔬𝔲𝔯𝔫𝔢𝔯𝔰 𝔟𝔢𝔫𝔢𝔞𝔱𝔥 𝔬𝔲𝔯 𝔚𝔞𝔶𝔣𝔞𝔯𝔦𝔫𝔤
              𝔗𝔯𝔢𝔢!

Me   25
No Muse amuses or flatters longer,
    No couplet cozens, no trashy trope bubbles,
Yet, though my judgment grows daily stronger,
    I love this blowing of psychic soap-bubbles.
The soul tends always in one direction,   30
    Its course is *homeward*; and, like a fay faring
Through airy space, even each deflection

𝕭ut brings it nearer its destined 𝖂ayfaring
   𝕿ree.
𝕴ts way is short to its final 𝖂ayfaring   35
   𝕿ree.

    See,
Oh, see to your ways then, my mad young masters,
 Blind pleasure-chasers and headstrong highfliers,
Nor tempt your fate for those dark disasters   40
 Which make, alas! the best hopes of Life liars.
And you, ye grubbers of dirt and dollars,
 Whose dungeoned hearts fear a fresh and safe airing,
Think how Experience plants all her scholars
 𝕬lone at last under 𝕬ge's 𝖂ayfaring   45
   𝕿ree!
𝕬lone at 𝕹ight under 𝕬ge's 𝖂ayfaring
   𝕿ree!
      [J. C. M., *DUM*, August 1845]

Khidder

I
 Thus said or sung
 Khidder, the ever young.
Journeying, I passed an ancient town—
Of lindens green its battlements bore a crown,
And at its turreted gates, on either hand,   5
Did fountains stand,
In marble white of rarest chiselling,
The which on high did fling
Water, that then like rain went twinkling down
With a rainbow glancing in the spray   10
As it wreathed in the sunny ray.
I marked where, 'neath the frown
Of the dark rampart, smiled a garden fair;
And an old man was there,
That gathered fruit. 'Good father,' I began,   15
'Since when, I pray you standeth here

This goodly city with its fountains clear?'
To which that agèd man
Made answer—'Ever stood
The city where it stands to-day,   20
And as it stands so shall it stand for aye,
Come evil days or good.'

II
Him gathering fruit I left, and journeyed on;
But when a thousand years were come and gone
Again I passed that way, and lo!   25
There was no city, there were no
Fountains of chiseling rare,
No garden fair;
Only
A lonely   30
Shepherd was piping there,
Whose little flock seemed less
In that wide pasture of the wilderness.

III
'Good friend,' quoth I,
'How long hath the fair city passed away,   35
That stood with gates so high,
With fountains bright, and gardens gay,
Where now these sheep do stray?'
And he replied, 'What withers makes but room
For what springs up in verdurous bloom—   40
Sheep have grazed ever here, and here will graze for aye.'

IV
Him piping there I left, and journeyed on—
But when a thousand years were come and gone,
Again I passed
That way, and see! there was a lake   45
That darkened in the blast,
And waves that brake
With a melancholy roar
Along that lonely shore.
And on a shingly point that ran   50

Far out into the lake, a fisherman
Was hauling in his net. To him I said,
'Good friend,
I fain would know
Since when it is that here these waters flow.'   55
Whereat he shook his head,
And answer made, 'Heaven lend
Thee better wit, good brother! Ever here
These waters flowed, and so
Will ever flow;   60
And aye in this dark rolling mere
Men fished, and still fish,
And ever will fish,
Until fish
No more in water swim.'   65
Him
Hauling his net I left, and journeyed on,
But when a thousand years were come and gone,
Again I passed that way, and lo! there stood,
Where waves had rolled, a green and flourishing wood—   70
Flourishing in youth it seemed, and yet was old,
And there it stood where deep blue waves had rolled.

V
A place of pleasant shade!
A wandering wind among the branches played,
And birds were now where fish had been;   75
And through the depth of green,
In many a gush the golden sunshine streamed;
And small flowers gleamed
About the brown and mossy
Roots of the ancient trees,   80
And the cushioned sward so glossy,
That compassed these.

VI
Here, as I passed, there met
Me, on the border of that forest wide,
One with an axe, whom when I spied,   85
Quoth I, 'Good neighbour, let

Me ask, I pray you, *how* long hath the wood
Stood,
Spreading its covert, broad and green,
Here, where mine eyes have seen   90
A royal city stand, whose battlements
Were like the ancient rocks;
And then a place for shepherds' tents,
And pasturage of flocks;
And then,   95
Roughening beneath the blast,
A vast
Dark mere—a haunt of fishermen?'

VII
There was a cold surprise
In the man's eyes   100
While thus I spake, and, as I made an end,
This was his dry
Reply—
'Facetious friend,
This wood   105
Hath ever stood
Even where it stands to-day;
And as it stands, so shall it stand for aye.
And here men catch no fish—here tend
No sheep—to no town-markets wend;   110
But aye in these
Green shades men felled, and still fell,
And ever will fell
Trees.'

VIII
Him with his axe I left, and journeyed on,   115
But when a thousand years were come and gone,
Again I passed
That way, and lo! a town—
And spires, and domes, and towers looked proudly down
Upon a vast   120
And sounding tide of life,
That flowed through many a street, and surged

In many a market-place, and urged
Its way in many a wheeling current, hither
And thither.   125
How rose the strife
Of sounds! the ceaseless beat
Of feet!
The noise of carts, of whips—the roll
Of chariots, coaches, cabs, *gigs*—all   130
Who keep the last-named vehicle we call
Respectable—horse-trampings, and the toll
Of bells; the whirl, the clash, the hubbub-mingling
Of voices, deep and shrill; the clattering, jingling,
The indescribable, indefinable roar;   135
The grating, creaking, booming, clanking, thumping,
And bumping;
The stumping
Of folks with wooden legs; the gabbling,
And babbling,   140
And many more
Quite nameless helpings
To the general effect; dog-yelpings,
Laughter, and shout, and cry; all sounds of gladness,
Of sadness,   145
And madness—
For there were people marrying,
And others carrying
The dead they would have died for, to the grave—
(Sadly the church bell tolled   150
When the young were burying the old,
More sadly spake that bodeful tongue
When the old were burying the young.)
Thus did the tumult rave
Through that fair city—nor were wanting there   155
Or dancing dogs or bear,
Or needy knife-
Grinder, or man with dismal wife,
That sang deplorably of '*purling groves*
And verdant streams, all where young Damon roves   160
With tender Phillida, the nymph he loves,
And softly breathe

The balmy moonbeam's wreathe,
And amorous turtle-doves,'
Or other doleful men, that blew   165
The melancholiest tunes—the which they only knew—
On flutes, and other instruments of wind;
Or small dark imp, with hurdy-
Gurdy,
And marmoset, that grinned   170
For nuts, and might have been his brother,
They were so like each other;
Or man,
That danced like the god Pan,
Twitching   175
A spasmy face
From side to side with a grace
Bewitching,
The while he whistled
In sorted pipes, all at his chin that bristled;   180
Or fiddler, fiddling much
For little profit, and a many such
Street musics most forlorn,
In that too pitiless rout quite overborne.

IX
Now, when as I beheld   185
The stir, and heard the din of life once more
Swell, as it swelled
In that same place four thousand years before,
I asked of them that passed me in the throng,
How long   190
The city thereabouts had stood,
And what was gone with pasture, lake, and wood.
But at such questions most men did but stare,
And so pass on; and some did laugh and shake
Their heads, me deeming mad; but none would spare   195
The time, or take
The pains to answer me, for there
All were in haste—all busy—bent to make
The most of every minute,
And do, an if they might, an hour's work in it.   200

X
Yet as I gave not o'er, but pertinaciously
Plied with my question every passer-by,
A dozen voices did at length reply
Ungraciously—
'What ravest thou   205
Of pasture, lake, and wood? As it is now,
So was it always here, and so will be for aye.'
Them, hurrying there, I left, and journeyed on—
But when a thousand years are come and gone,
Again I'll pass that way.*   210
                    [Unsigned, *DUM*, August 1845]

from *Loose Leaves from an Odd Volume–No. I*
Translations from Friedrich Rueckert

Counsel of a Cosmopolitan

Give smiles and sighs alike to all,
  Serve all, but love not any;
Love's dangerous and delicious thrall
  Hath been the tomb of many.

The sweetest wine-thoughts of the heart   5
  Are turned ere long to bitter;
Sad memories loom when joys depart,
  And Gloom comes after Glitter.

Why pawn thy soul for one lone flower,
  And slight the whole bright garland?   10
Clarissa's eyes, Lucinda's bower,
  Will fail thee in a far land!

* Khidder is, I believe, the prophet Elias, whom the Persians or the Arabs, or both for what I know,
believe to revisit the earth from time to time, and journey about in various directions, for the
purpose of ascertaining whether mankind have filled up the measure of their sins, or whether the
judgment of the world can yet be postponed a little longer.

Love GOD and Virtue! Love the sun,
  The stars, the trees, the mountains!
The only Living Streams that run   15
  Flow from Eternal Fountains!

[The night is falling]

The night is falling in chill December,
  The frost is mantling the silent stream,
    Dark mists are shrouding the mountain's brow;
    My soul is weary: I now
                    Remember   5
  The days of roses but as a dream.

The icy hand of the Old Benumber,
  The hand of Winter, is on my brain;
    I try to smile, while I inly grieve;
    I dare not hope, or believe,   10
                    That Summer
  Will ever brighten the earth again.

So, gazing gravewards, albeit immortal,
  Man cannot pierce through the girdling Night
    That sunders Time from Eternity,   15
    Nor feel this Death-vale to be
                    The portal
To realms of Glory and Living Light.

Rest only in the Grave

I rode till I reached the house of Wealth—
'Twas filled with Riot and blighted health.

I rode till I reached the House of Love—
'Twas vocal with sighs beneath and above!

I rode till I reached the House of Sin—   5
There were shrieks and curses without and within.

I rode till I reached the House of Toil—
Its inmates had nothing to bake or boil.

I rode in search of the House of Content,
But never could reach it, far as I went!   10

The House of Quiet, for Strong and Weak,
And Poor and Rich, I have still to seek.

This House is narrow, and dark, and small,
But the only Peaceful House of all.

    [James Clarence Mangan, *Irish Monthly Magazine*, October 1845]

from *Specimens of the Early Native Poetry of Ireland*

[. . .] In the latter part of the sixth, and the course of the seventh, century, the academies of Ireland had attained such a reputation as to draw students not only from England, but from many of the continental states. With respect to the former we have the authority of Bede, Camden, and Lord Lyttleton—some of the very highest authorities with regard to early English affairs. Lyttleton even assures us that the Anglo-Saxon students brought from thence the first knowledge of letter possessed by their countrymen, in which opinion Dr Johnson also coincides. Indeed, that the Saxons brought no alphabet with them to England, appears a matter of almost absolute certainty.

    Among the Anglo-Saxon students thus resorting to Ireland, we find Prince Aldfrid, afterwards king of the Northumbrian Saxons. This event, which occurred about A.D. 684, is corroborated by Bede in his 'Life of St. Cuthbert.' Aldfrid appears to have spent several years in Ireland, and there is still extant in the Irish language a poem attributed to this prince, descriptive of the various provinces and cities of the kingdom, of which the public are here presented, for the first time, with the only metrical version that has appeared.

Prince Aldfrid's Itinerary Through Ireland

I
I found in Inisfail* the fair,
In Ireland, while in exile there,
Women of worth, both grave and gay men,
Many clerics and many laymen.

II
I travelled its fruitful provinces round,   5
And in every one of five† I found,
Alike in church and in palace hall,
Abundant apparel and food for all.

III
Gold and silver I found, and money,
Plenty of wheat and plenty of honey;   10
I found God's people rich in pity,
Found many a feast and many a city.

IV
I also found in Armagh, the splendid,
Meekness, wisdom, and prudence blended,
Fasting, as Christ hath recommended,   15
And noble councillors untranscended.

V
I found in each great church moreo'er,
Whether on island or on shore,
Piety, learning, fond affection,
Holy welcome and kind protection.   20

VI
I found the good lay monks and brothers
Ever beseeching help for others,

* Inisfail—one of the ancient titles of Ireland—signified the island of Destiny, from the *Lial Fail*,
or Stone of Destiny, on which the monarchs were crowned.
† Three of the provinces have undergone little change except in name. Their ancient titles were
Ulad or Ultonia, Ulster; Momonia, Munster; Connacia, Connaught; Lagenia, Leinster; but the
two Meaths then formed a fifth, now merged into the latter province.

And in keeping the holy word
Pure as it came from Jesus the Lord.*

VII
I found in Munster unfettered of any,   25
Kings, and queens, and poets a many—
Poets well skilled in music and measure,
Prosperous doings, mirth and pleasure.

VIII
I found in Connaught the just, redundance
Of riches, milk in lavish abundance;   30
Hospitality, vigour, fame,
In Cruachan's† land of heroic name.

IX
I found in the country of Connall‡ the glorious,
Bravest heroes, ever victorious;
Fair-complexioned men and warlike,   35
Ireland's lights, the high, the starlike!

X
I found in Ulster, from hill to glen,
Hardy warriors, resolute men;
Beauty that bloomed when youth was gone,
And strength transmitted from sire to son.   40

XI
I found in the noble district of Boyle
         (MS. here illegible)
Brehons, Erenachs,§ weapons bright,
And horsemen bold and sudden in fight.

---

* Some fine specimens of the skill and ingenuity expended by the early Irish Christians upon their copies of the sacred writings and theological works are still extant. The beautiful illuminated copy of the Four Gospels, attributed to St. Columba, now preserved in the library of Dublin University, is worthy of particular admiration.

† Cruachan, or Croghan, was the name of the royal palace of Connaught.

‡ Tyrconnell, the present Donegal.

§ The Brehons were the judges and promulgators of the law. The signification of *Erenach* is not distinctly known, except that it was a ruler of some kind, and has sometimes been interpreted as synonimous [*sic*] with the office of archdeacon.

XII

I found in Leinster the smooth and sleek,   45
From Dublin to Slewmargy's* peak;
Flourishing pastures, valour, health,
Long-living worthies, commerce,† wealth.

XIII

I found, besides, from Ara to Glea,
In the broad rich country of Ossorie,   50
Sweet fruits, good laws for all and each,
Great chess-players,‡ men of truthful speech.

XIV

I found in Meath's fair principality,
Virtue, vigour, and hospitality;
Candour, joyfulness, bravery, purity,   55
Ireland's bulwark and security.§

XV

I found strict morals in age and youth,
I found historians recording truth;
The things I sing of in verse unsmooth,
I found them all—I have written sooth.   60

To the Ruins of Donegal Castle

I

O, mournful, O, forsaken pile,
    What desolation dost thou dree!
How tarnished is the beauty that was thine ere while,
    Thou mansion of chaste melody!

---

* Ath-Claith was the ancient name of Dublin. Slewmargy, a mountain in Queen's County, near the river Barrow.

† Tacitus, in his life of Agricola, states that the harbours of Ireland were better known by means of commercial navigators than those of Britain. (Melius aditus portusque, per commercia et nego-ciatores, cogniti.)

‡ There are frequent allusions to the game of chess in most of the Irish poems.

§ The allusion here is to the palace of Temur or Tara, the residence of the supreme monarch.

II
Demolished lie thy towers and halls;　　　　　　　5
  A dark, unsightly, earthen mound
Defaces the pure whiteness of thy shining walls,
  And solitude doth gird thee round.

III
Fair fort! thine hour has come at length,
  Thine older glory has gone by.　　　　　　　　10
Lo! far beyond thy noble battlements of strength,
  Thy corner-stones all scattered lie!

IV
Where now, O rival of the gold
  Emania, be thy wine-cups all?
Alas! for these thou now hast nothing but the cold,　　15
  Cold stream that from the heavens doth fall!

V
Thy clay-choked gateways none can trace,
  Thou fortress of the once bright doors!
The limestones of thy summit now bestrew thy base,
  Bestrew the outside of thy floors.　　　　　　　20

VI
Above thy shattered window-sills
  The music that to-day breaks forth
Is but the music of the wild winds from the hills,
  The wild winds of the stormy North!

VII
What spell o'ercame thee, mighty fort,　　　　　　25
  What fatal fit of slumber strange,
O palace of the wine!—O many-gated court!
  That thou shouldst undergo this change?

VIII
Thou wert, O, bright-walled, beaming one,
  Thou cradle of high deeds and bold,　　　　　　30
The Tara of Assemblies to the sons of Con,
  Clan-Connell's Council-hall of old!

IX

Thou wert a new Emania, thou!
　A northern Cruachan in thy might—
A dome like that which stands by Boyne's broad water now,　　　35
　Thou Erin's Rome of all delight!

X

In thee were Ulster's tributes stored,
　And lavished like the flowers in May;
And into thee were Connaught's thousand treasures poured,
　Deserted though thou art to-day!　　　40

XI

How often from thy turrets high,
　Thy purple turrets, have we seen
Long lines of glittering ships, when summer time drew nigh,
　With masts and sails of snow-white sheen!

XII

How often seen, when gazing round,　　　45
　From thy tall towers, the hunting-trains,
The blood-enlivening chase, the horseman and the hound,
　Thou fastness of a hundred plains!

XIII

How often to thy banquets bright
　We have seen the strong-armed Gaels repair,　　　50
And when the feast was over, once again unite
　For battle, in thy bass-court fair!

XIV

Alas, for thee, thou fort forlorn!
　Alas, for thy low, lost estate!
It is my woe of woes, this melancholy morn,　　　55
　To see thee left thus desolate!

XV

O! there hath come of Connell's race
　A many and many a gallant chief,
Who, if he saw thee now, thou of the once glad face!
　Could not dissemble his deep grief.　　　60

XVI

Could Manus of the lofty soul
  Behold thee as this day thou art,
Thou of the regal towers! what bitter, bitter dole,
  What agony would rend his heart!

XVII

Could Hugh Mac Hugh's imaginings   65
  Pourtray for him thy rueful plight
What anguish, O, thou palace of the northern kings,
  Were his through many a sleepless night!

XVIII

Could even the mighty Prince whose choice
  It was to o'erthrow thee—could Hugh Roe   70
But view thee now, methinks he would not much rejoice
  That he had laid thy turrets low!

XIX

Oh! who could dream that one like him,
  One sprung of such a line as his,
Thou of the embellished walls, would be the man to dim   75
  Thy glories by a deed like this!

XX

From Hugh O'Donnell, thine own brave
  And far-flamed sovereign, came the blow!
By him, thou lonesome castle o'er the Esky's wave,
  By him was wrought thine overthrow!   80

XXI

Yet not because he wished thee ill
  Left he thee thus bereaven and void;
The prince of the victorious tribe of Dalach still
  Loved thee, yea, thee whom he destroyed!

XXII

He brought upon thee all this woe,   85
  Thou of the fair-proportioned walls,
Lest thou shouldst ever yield a shelter to the foe,
  Should'st house the black, ferocious Galls!*

* 'Foreigners.'

XXIII

Should'st yet become in saddest truth
   A *Dun-na-Gall**—the strangers own.   90
For this cause only, stronghold of the Gaelic youth,
   Lie thy majestic towers o'erthrown.

XXIV

It is a drear, a dismal sight,
   This of thy ruin and decay,
Now that our kings, and bards, and men of mark and might,   95
   Are nameless exiles far away!

XXV

Yet, better thou shouldst fall, meseems,
   By thine own King of many thrones,
Than that the truculent Galls should rear around thy streams
   Dry mounds and circles of great stones.   100

XXVI

As doth in many a desperate case
   The surgeon by the malady,
So hath, O shield and bulwark of great Coffey's race,
   Thy royal master done by thee!

XXVII

The surgeon, if he be but wise,   105
   Examines till he learns and sees
Where lies the fountain of his patient's health, where lies
   The germ and root of his disease;

XXVIII

Then cuts away the gangrened part,
   That so the sounder may be freed   110
Ere the disease hath power to reach the sufferer's heart,
   And so bring death without remead.

XXIX

Now, thou hast held the patient's place,
   And thy disease hath been the foe;
So he, thy surgeon, O proud house of Dalach's race,   115
   Who should he be if not Hugh Roe?

* 'Fort of the foreigner.'

XXX
But he, thus fated to destroy
  Thy shining walls, will yet restore
And raise thee up anew in beauty and in joy,
  So that thou shalt not sorrow more.   120

XXXI
By GOD's help, he who wrought thy fall
  Will reinstate thee yet in pride;
Thy variegated halls shall be rebuilded all,
  Thy lofty courts, thy chambers wide.

XXXII
Yes! thou shalt live again, and see   125
  Thine youth renewed! Thou shalt outshine
Thy former self by far, and Hugh shall reign in thee,
  The Tirconnellians' king and thine!

[. . .] O'HUSSEY, the last hereditary bard of the great sept of Maguire, of
Fermanagh, who flourished about 1630, possessed a fine genius. [. . .] The noble
ode which O'Hussey addressed to Hugh Maguire, when that chief had gone on a
dangerous expedition, in the depth of an unusually severe winter, is as interesting
an example of the devoted affection of the bard to his chief, and as vivid a picture
of intense desolation, as could be well conceived. The present version, which is
the only metrical one that has appeared, is now published for the first time:—

O'Hussey's Ode to the Maguire*

I
Where is my Chief, my Master, this bleak night, *movrone?*
O, cold, cold, miserably cold is this bleak night for Hugh,
Its showery, arrowy, speary sleet pierceth one through and through,
Pierceth one to the very bone!

---

* Mr. Ferguson, in a fine piece of criticism on this poem, remarks: 'There is a vivid vigour in these
descriptions, and a savage power in the antithetical climax, which claim a character almost approach-
ing to sublimity. Nothing can be more graphic, yet more diversified, than his images of unmitigated
horror—nothing more grandly startling than his heroic conception of the glow of glory triumphant
over frozen toil. We have never read this poem without recurring, and that by no unworthy asso-
ciation, to Napoleon in his Russian campaign. Yet, perhaps O'Hussey has conjured up a picture of
more inclement desolation, in his rude idea of northern horrors, than could be legitimately employed
by a poet of the present day, when the romance of geographical obscurity no longer permits us to
imagine the Phlegrean regions of endless storm, where the snows of Hæmus fall mingled with the
lightnings of Etna, amid Bistonian wilds or Hyrcanian forests.'—*Dublin University Magazine*, vol. iv.

II
Rolls real thunder? Or, was that red livid light   5
Only a meteor? I scarce know; but, through the midnight dim
The pitiless ice-wind streams. Except the hate that persecutes *him*,
Nothing hath crueller venomy might.

III
An awful, a tremendous night is this, me-seems!
The floodgates of the rivers of heaven, I think, have been burst wide—   10
Down from the overcharged clouds, like unto headlong ocean's tide,
Descends grey rain in roaring streams.

IV
Though he were even a wolf ranging the round green woods,
Though he were even a pleasant salmon in the unchainable sea,
Though he were a wild mountain eagle, he could scarce bear he,   15
This sharp sore sleet, these howling floods.

V
O, mournful is my soul this night for Hugh Maguire!
Darkly, as in a dream, he strays! Before him and behind
Triumphs the tyrannous anger of the wounding wind,
The wounding wind, that burns as fire!   20

VI
It is my bitter grief—it cuts me to the heart—
That in the country of Clan Darry this should be his fate!
Oh, woe is me, where is he? Wandering, houseless, desolate,
Alone, without or guide or chart!

VII
Medreams I see just now his face, the strawberry-bright,   25
Uplifted to the blackened heavens, while the tempestuous winds
Blow fiercely over and round him, and the smiting sleet-shower blinds
The hero of Galang to-night!

VIII
Large, large affliction unto me and mine it is,
That one of his majestic bearing, his fair, stately form,   30

Should thus be tortured and o'erborne—that this unsparing storm
Should wreak its wrath on head like his!

IX

That his great hand, so oft the avenger of the oppressed,
Should this chill, churlish night, perchance, be paralysed by frost—
While through some icicle-hung thicket—as one lorn and lost—   35
He walks and wanders without rest.

X

The tempest-driven torrent deluges the mead,
It overflows the low banks of the rivulets and ponds—
The lawns and pasture-grounds lie locked in icy bonds,
So that the cattle cannot feed.   40

XI

The pale bright margins of the streams are seen by none.
Rushes and sweeps along the untameable flood on every side—
It penetrates and fills the cottagers' dwellings far and wide—
Water and land are blent in one.

XII

Through some dark woods, 'mid bones of monsters, Hugh now strays,   45
As he confronts the storm with anguished heart, but manly brow—
Oh! what a sword-wound to that tender heart of his were now
A backward glance at peaceful days!

XIII

But other thoughts are his—thoughts that can still inspire
With joy and an onward-bounding hope the bosom of Mac Nee—   50
Thoughts of his warriors charging like bright billows of the sea,
Borne on the wind's wings, flashing fire!

XIV

And though frost glaze to-night the clear dew of his eyes,
And white ice-gauntlets glove his noble fine fair fingers o'er,
A warm dress is to him that lightning-garb he ever wore,   55
The lightning of the soul, not skies.

XV

AVRAN*

Hugh marched forth to the fight—I grieved to see him so depart;
And lo! to-night he wanders frozen, rain-drenched, sad, betrayed—
But the memory of the limewhite mansions his right hand hath laid
In ashes warms the hero's heart!   60

[James Clarence Mangan, *Specimens of the Early Native Poetry of Ireland,* 1846]

from *Literæ Orientales–No. VI*
Ottoman Poetry

[...] We shall [in our next article] probably enter into the consideration of the
various extraordinary metres peculiar to Oriental poetry, and the rules—some of
which are fantastical—laid down by authority for the better guidance of the poet
in his arduous labours. One rule is that, in some poems, 'whatsoever word begins
a verse, the same word, or a part therof, written reversely, must terminate the
same verse.' With specimen of this description of rhyming we shall conclude for
the present.

Advice

*Tra*verse not the globe for lore! The sternest
   But the surest teacher is the heart.
Studying that and that alone, thou learnest
   Best and soonest whence and what thou *art.*

Time, not travel, 'tis which gives us ready   5
   Speech, experience, prudence, tact, and wit.
Far more light the lamp that bideth steady
   Than the wandering lantern doth *emit.*

Moor, Chinese, Egyptian, Russian, Roman,
   Tread one common downhill path of doom: 10
Everywhere the names are Man and Woman,
   Everywhere the old sad sins find *room.*

* A concluding stanza, generally intended as a recapitulation of the entire poem.

Evil angels tempt us in all places.
  What but sands or snows hath Earth to give?
Dream not, friend, of deserts and oäses,   15
  But look inwards, and begin to *live*.
                    [Unsigned, *DUM*, January 1846]

The Warning Voice

*'Il me semble que nous sommes à la veille d'une grand bataille humaine. Les forces sont là; mais
je n'y vois pas de général.'*   BALZAC: *Livre Mystique*

I
  Ye Faithful!—ye Noble!
    A day is at hand
  Of trial and trouble,
    And woe in the land!
  O'er a once greenest path,   5
    Now blasted and sterile,
      Its dusk shadows loom—
  It cometh with Wrath,
    With Conflict and Peril,
      With Judgment and Doom!   10

  False bands shall be broken,
    Dead systems shall crumble,
      And the Haughty shall hear
  Truths yet never spoken,
      Though smouldering like flame   15
    Through many a lost year
  In the hearts of the Humble;
  For, Hope will expire
  As the Terror draws nigher,
      And, with it, the Shame   20
  Which so long overawed
    Men's minds by its might—
  And the Powers abroad
    Will be Panic and Blight,
  And phrenetic Sorrow—   25
    Black Pest all the night,
  And Death on the morrow!

Now, therefore, ye True,
  Gird your loins up anew!
  By the good you have wrought!   30
  By all you have thought,
    And suffered, and done!
      By your souls! I implore you,
        Be leal to your mission—
      Remembering that *one*   35
        Of the *two* paths before you
          Slopes down to Perdition!
  To you have been given,
    Not granaries and gold,
  But the Love that lives long,   40
    And waxes not cold;
  And the Zeal that has striven
    Against Error and Wrong,
  And in fragments hath riven
    The chains of the Strong!   45
  Bide now, by your sternest
  Conceptions of earnest
  Endurance for others,
  Your weaker-souled brothers!
  Your true faith and worth   50
    Will be History soon,
  And their stature stand forth
    In the unsparing Noon!

II
  You have dreamed of an era
    Of Knowledge, and Truth,   55
      And Peace—the *true* glory!
  Was this a chimera?
    Not so!—but the childhood and youth
      Of our days will grow hoary
Before such a marvel shall burst on their sight!   60
    On *you* its beams glow not—
    For *you* its flowers blow not!
  You cannot rejoice in its light,
    But in darkness and suffering instead
    You go down to the place of the Dead!   65

To *this* generation
The sore tribulation,
The stormy commotion,
And foam of the Popular Ocean,
  The struggle of class against class;   70
The Dearth and the Sadness,
  The Sword and the War-vest;
To the *next*, the Repose and the Gladness,
  'The sea of clear glass,'*
  And the rich Golden Harvest!   75

III
  Know, then, your true lot,
    Ye Faithful, though Few!
      Understand your position,
      Remember your mission,
And vacillate not,   80
  Whatsoever ensue!
Alter not! Falter not!
  Palter not now with your own living souls,
    When each moment that rolls
      May see Death lay his hand   85
On some new victim's brow!
Oh! let not your vow
  Have been written in sand!
  Leave cold calculations
Of Danger and Plague   90
  To the slaves and the traitors
Who cannot dissemble
  The dastard sensations
That now make them tremble
  With phantasies vague!—   95
The men without ruth—
  The hypocrite haters
Of Goodness and Truth,
Who at heart curse the race
  Of the sun through the skies;   100
And would look in God's face

* Apoc., iv. 6.

With a lie in their eyes!
To the last do your duty,
    Still mindful of this—
That Virtue is Beauty,   105
    And Wisdom, and Bliss;
So, howe'er, as frail men, you have erred on
    Your way along Life's throngèd road,
Shall your consciences prove a sure guerdon
        And tower of defence,   110
        Until Destiny summon you hence
    To the Better Abode!
              [J. C. M., *Nation*, 21 February 1846]

The Rye Mill

There is an old mill in the Valley of the Rye, near Leixlip, which many of our city readers must know. The true poet who uttered in thunder, a 'Warning Voice' in the last NATION—(the most impressive poem, perhaps, we ever published)—has thought fit to celebrate it in this strange style. [...]

I
'Twas a wet summer eve; there had been such heat
    All the day!—the rain-drops *fell* huge
And heavily to earth, as though they would repeat
    The old-world drama of the Deluge—
'Twas, I say, such an eve, when I first caught sight   5
    Of a roof that through years of crime, ill,
And sorrow, I still remember with delight—
    The roof of the once merry Rye Mill!

II
The drab-coloured river rushed on at full speed—
    The Rye, that noblest of trout-streams—   10
The coppices around looked very dim indeed,
    As dim as the dimmest of Doubt's dreams.
To the north rose a hill o'er a field—or a fen—
    But, albeit, I felt able to *climb* hill
And cliff like a goat—I didn't see it then—   15
    I saw but the picturesque Rye Mill!

III

And winged, as with light, were the weeks of my stay
　In its neighbourhood! We all know *how* slips
The long day away with a boy while at play,
　With a girl while gathering cowslips;   20
But mine was but a moment from morn unto eve,
　Though in truth I was part of the time ill
With a cold in my throat, which I caught, I believe,
　Through a hole in the wall of the Rye Mill.

IV

Adam Smith's philosophics had superseded Burke's   25
　Just then; and Mill and Ricárd were
The bores of the day; I have never read their works,
　Which treat of cotton, corn, and hardware;
But I *do* feel some pity for ruralist distress,
　A weakness I cheerfully deny Mill,   30
Macculloch, and Ricardo, though their theories, I guess,
　Have played the very deuce with the Rye Mill.

V

Yet, opposed as I am to free trade, if it mean
　Revolution among hoppers and haggards,
Let nobody imagine I am base enough to lean   35
　To the side of those vagabond blackguards,
The absentee rackrenters! These, to their graves,
　Have ever been Hibernia's prime ill;
And, by Jove, as they *so* relish grinding—their slaves,
　I'd send them to grind—in the Rye Mill!   40

VI

Perhaps *that*, however, mightn't ruffle them at all—
　For myself, I confess I would rather
Be a miller—not a bruiser,* save of grain—than call
　Even Curry-powder Norfolk my father.
What's the Chancellor himself? A mummy in a wig.   45
　What's his office? At best a sublime ill.
Take the woolsack, O Brougham! but let *me* sit and swig
　Adam's ale on a meal-sack in Rye Mill!

---

* I deem it necessary to make this distinction, forasmuch as *milling*, taken *Anglice*, means bruising
or 'hitting with the fist,' as Pierce Egan observeth.

VII

'Tis decaying, that mill; yet still, as a bard,
  I will say—and I needn't go farther—   50
That, were Leixlip a heaven, I should certainly regard
  Its mill as the brilliantest star there!
Oh, my fellow-Eblanians!—and I end with a French rhyme—
  (For the French, though they *write* well, *rhyme* ill)—
March westwards, I beg of you, in double-quick time,   55
  And visit the venerable Rye Mill!

                        [J. C. M., *Nation*, 28 February 1846]

To the Pens of The Nation

'Sing a song of sixpence.'—NURSERY RHYME

Pens of all THE NATION's bards,
  Up and do your duty!
Sing—not valour's meet rewards
  In the smile of beauty:
Sing—not landlordism laid low   5
  In down-trampled ricks, Pens!
Sing of British overthrow—
  SING A SONG OF SIKHS, PENS!

                [Unsigned, *Nation*, 28 March 1846]

The Domiciliary Visit
(A scene in the Faubourg St. Antoine, Paris)

As we are shortly likely to know something of 'domiciliary visits' under the
'Coercion Act,' we give this translation, by a friend, of a scene in Paris, under
Louis Philippe:—

DRAMATIS PERSONÆ
An Officer of the Gend'armerie and a Citizen.

OFF.   *De par le Roi!* You are Pierre Coulisse!
CIT.   I am.
OFF.   I thought so! Scan date,
        Address, and signature of this!
                    (Gives him a paper.)
CIT. *(reads)* 'Arrest . . . . *by Royal Mandate* . . .'
        Why, what's my crime? *J'ignore*—
OFF.   Poh! Poh!   5
            Of course, young man, you ignore it—
        Your name is in the Black Book, though,
            With two red marks before it!
        Whence came you by those four cane-swords?
CIT.   Cane-swords! Which?
OFF.   Yonder sham-rods!   10
CIT. They are mere tobacco-pipes.
OFF.   No words!—
        (Writes) 'Two poniards and two ramrods.'
CIT. Heavens! You don't mean—
OFF.   A Frenchman means
        The thing he does. Your press-keys!
                    (Opens a drawer.)
        What make you with those tools?
CIT.   Machines.   15
OFF.   Ay, such machines as Fieschi's!*
        Pray, what's that carbine-like affair
        Behind the window-shutter?
CIT. A walking stick. *Il en a l'air.*
OFF.   Speak up, sir! What d'ye mutter?   20
CIT. A stick.
OFF.   Don't shout! A lie's no truth
        Because 'tis bellowed louder.
        A gun you mean? A stick, forsooth!
        Why, one can smell the powder!
                    (Takes up a book.)
        Ha!—Treatise on the *Poles.*

* I need not remind the reader that Fieschi is regarded as the inventor of the most terrific 'infernal machine' of modern times.

Cɪᴛ.   The South   25
      And North Poles only.
Oғғ.   Rebel!
      How dare you ope your *gamin* mouth?
         Your explanations treble
      Your guilt. South Pole and North! To what
         Owes Earth its *revolutions*,   30
      If not to these, you leveller-flat
         Of thrones and institutions?
      Give up that letter! Ha!—what's here?
                    (Reads.)
         'Dear Claude, I could not borrow
         One hour to-day; but never fear!   35
         I'll do the job to-morrow.'
      So, ho! *The* job? Oh, yes!—we hit
         The meaning of such letters—
      You'll do *the King's* job—eh? That's it!
         Come, Jean, put on his fetters!
                    (Ex.omn.)
            [Unsigned, *Nation*, 4 April 1846]

Siberia

In Siberia's wastes
   The Ice-wind's breath
Woundeth like the toothèd steel.
Lost Siberia doth reveal
   Only blight and death.   5

Blight and death alone.
   No Summer shines.
Night is interblent with Day.
In Siberia's wastes alway
   The blood blackens, the heart pines.   10

In Siberia's wastes
　　No tears are shed,
For they freeze within the brain.
Nought is felt but dullest pain,
　　Pain acute, yet dead;   15

Pain as in a dream,
　　When years go by
Funeral-paced, yet fugitive,
When man lives, and doth not live,
　　Doth not live—nor die.   20

In Siberia's wastes
　　Are sands and rocks.
Nothing blooms of green or soft,
But the snowpeaks rise aloft
　　And the gaunt ice-blocks.   25

And the exile there
　　Is one with those;
They are part, and he is part,
For the sands are in his heart,
　　And the killing snows.   30

Therefore, in those wastes
　　None curse the Czar.
Each man's tongue is cloven by
The North Blast, who heweth nigh
　　With sharp scymitar.   35

And such doom each drees,
　　Till, hunger-gnawn,
And cold-slain, he at length sinks there,
Yet scarce more a corpse than ere
　　His last breath was drawn.   40
　　　　[Clarence Mangan, *Nation*, 18 April 1846]

To the Ingleezee Khafir, Calling Himself Djaun Bool Djenkinzun

(A learned friend—by which we don't mean a lawyer, but a scholar—sends us
this translation of 'a particularly genuine Persian poem,' addressed to a distin-
guished Foreign traveller in Persia, (whom we would call John Bull Jenkinson,)
who appears to have excited the bile of the Oriental poet.)

I
Thus writeth Meer Djafrit (1)—
  I hate thee, Djaun Bool,
Worse than Márid or Afrit (2),
  Or corpse-eating Ghool.
I hate thee like Sin,   5
  For thy mop-head of hair,
Thy snub nose and bald chin,
  And thy turkeycock air.
Thou vile Ferindjee! (3)
  That thou thus shouldst disturb an   10
Old Moslim like me,
  With my Khizzilbash (4) turban!
Old fogy like me,
  With my Khizzilbash turban!

II
I spit on thy clothing,   15
  That garb for baboons!
I eye with deep loathing
  Thy tight pantaloons!
I curse the cravat
  That encircles thy throat,   20
And thy cooking-pot hat, (5)
  And thy swallowed-tail coat!
Go, hide thy thick sconce
  In some hovel suburban;
Or else don at once   25
  The red Moosleman turban.
Thou dog, (6) don at once
  The grand Khizzilbash turban!

III
Thou vagabond varlet!
   Thou swiller of sack!   30
If our heads be all scarlet
   Thy heart is all black! (7)
Go on to revile
   IRAN's (8) nation and race,
In thy fish-faggish style!   35
   He who knows with what face
Thou can'st curse and traduce
   Thine own Mufti, Pope Urban, (9)
May scorn thine abuse
   Of the Khizzilbash turban—   40
Scorn all thine abuse
   Of the Khizzilbash turban!
                    [Unsigned, *Nation*, 18 April 1846]

(1) The Oriental poets up to the 17th century, as the Irish up to the 10th, almost always introduced their own names into their poems.
(2) Evil Djins of a very powerful order.
(3) European.
(4) Literally, *Scarlet head*, the Persians wearing exclusively red turbans, while the other oriental nations commonly affect white.
(5) Major Skinner informs us that, during his travels in the East, his hat procured for him the title of 'The Father of a Cooking-pot.'
(6) *Ei Gaour!* (the Irish, *A Gadar*.)
(7) The original is remarkably pointed:—

            Ei, gurraku galagh,
               Ei, rakiha bara
            Hu bash Khizzel mava
               Il dil a dah kara!

(8) Iran, as our readers may be aware, is the ancient name of Persia. The Turks and Arabs, however, commonly call it *Djemistan*, or the Land of *Djem*, the oldest Persian monarch on record.
(9) From this line it is clear that these verses cannot be older than the earlier part of the 17th century, as Pope Urban VIII (the last of the name) deceased in 1644.

The Peal of Another Trumpet

'Irlande, Irlande, rejouis-toi! Pour toi l'heure de vengeance est sonnee. Ton tribun prepare ta deliverance.'—From the 'Derniers Mots' of Mdlle. Lenormand, the celebrated French Pythoness.

I
Youths of Ireland, patriots, friends!
  Know ye what shall be your course
When the storm that now impends
  Shall come down in all its force?
Glance around you! You behold   5
  How the horizon of the Time
    Hourly wears a duskier hue,
From all else await we bold
  Bearing, and Resolve sublime—
    Youths of Ireland, what from you?   10

II
Will you bide irresolute?
  Will you stand with folded arms,
Purposeless, disheartened, mute,
    As men hopeless of escape,
  Till the wildest, worst alarms   15
    Of your souls take giant shape?
Are you dastards? Are you dolts?
  Irishmen! shall *you* be seen
  With white lips and faltering mien,
    When all on earth—when heaven above,   20
Torn by thousand thunderbolts,
  Rocks and reels which way you move?

III
Oh, no! no!—forfend it Heaven!
  Such debasement cannot be!
  Pillaged of your liberty,   25
You are not as yet bereaven
Of that heritage of bravery
    Which descends to you through ages,
And ennobles all—save Slavery.

Yours, thank God, are Manhood still,   30
  And the inborn Strength of Soul,
  Which nought outward can control,
And the headlong chariot-Will,
Ever-bounding, never-bending,
    Which, alike with Sword or Song,   35
  As befits the season, wages
    Unrelenting war with Wrong—
Unrelenting and unending.

IV
Gentler gifts are yours, no less,
  Tolerance of the faults of others,   40
  Love of mankind as your brothers,
Generous Pity, Tenderness,
Soulfelt sympathy with Grief:
  The warm heart, the wingèd hand,
Whereso Suffering craves relief.   45
Through all regions hath your fame
  For such virtues long gone forth.
  The swart slave of Kaffirland,
  The frore denizen of the North,
The dusk Indian Mingo chief   50
  In his lone savannahs green,
  The wild, wandering Beddaween
'Mid his wastes of sand and flame,
All have heard how, unsubdued
  By long centuries of sorrow,   55
    You still cherish in your bosoms
      The deep Love no wrongs can slay,
      And the Hopes which, crushed to-day,
Rear their crests afresh, renewed
  In immortal youth, to-morrow,   60
    Like the Spring's rejoicing blossoms.

V
And 'tis well you thus can blend
  Softest moods of mind with sternest—
  Well you thus can temper earnest
Might with more than Feminine Meekness—   65

Thus can soar and thus descend;
  For even now the wail of Want,
The despairful cry of Weakness,
    Rings throughout a stricken land,
    And blood-blackening Plague and gaunt   70
      Famine roam it hand-in-hand!
To you, now, the millions turn
With glazed eyes and lips that burn—
To you lies their last appeal,
  To your hearts—your feelings—reason!—   75
  Oh, stretch forth your hands in season!
Soothe and solace—help and heal!
Rich in blessings, bright with beauty,
  Shine their names throughout all æons,
    Their's who nobly consecrate   80
To self-sacrificing Duty
  Their best years—the new St. Leons,
    Who thus conquer Time and Fate!*

VI
But, for more, far more, than this,
  Youths of Ireland, stand prepared!   85
Revolution's red abyss
  Burns beneath us, all-but bared—
And on high the fire-charged Cloud
  Blackens in the Firmament,
And afar we list the loud   90
  Sea-voice of the Unknown Event.
  Youths of Ireland, stand prepared!
For all woes the Meek have dreed,
  For all risks the Brave have dared,
As for Suffering, so for Deed,   95
    Stand prepared!
For Contumely and Coercion,
For dark Treachery and Desertion
In the ranks of your own host,
In the friends you prize the most,   100
    Stand prepared!

* 'For me the laws of nature are suspended, the eternal wheels of the universe roll backward; I am destined to be triumphant over Fate and Time.'—GODWIN'S ST. LEON.—Vol. II.

For the Pestilence that striketh
Where it listeth, whom it liketh,
For the Blight whose deadly might
Desolateth day and night—   105
For a Sword that never spared
    Stand prepared!
Though that gory Sword be bared
    Be not scared!
  Do not blench and dare not falter!   110
  For the axe and for the halter
    Stand prepared!
  And give God the glory
  If, whene'er the WREATH OF STORY
Swathe your names, the men whose hands   115
    Brightly twine it,
    May enshrine it
In one temple with your land's!
            [J. C. M., *Nation*, 2 May 1846]

The Dream of John Mac Donnell
(TRANSLATED FROM THE IRISH)

(John Mac Donnell, usually called Mac Donnell *Claragh*, from his family resi-
dence, was a native of the county of Cork, and may be classed among the first of
the purely Irish poets of the last century. He was born in 1691, and died in 1754.
His poems are remarkable for their energy, their piety of tone, and the patriotic
spirit they everywhere manifest. The following is one of them, and deserves to
be regarded as a very curious topographical 'Jacobite relic.')

I
I lay in unrest—old thoughts of pain,
  That I struggled in vain to smother,
Like midnight spectres haunted my brain—
  Dark fantasies chased each other;
When, lo! a Figure—who might it be?—   5
  A tall fair figure stood near me!
Who might it be? An unreal Banshee?
  Or an angel sent to cheer me?

II
Though years have rolled since then, yet now
  My memory thrillingly lingers   10
On her awful charms, her waxen brow,
  Her pale, translucent fingers,
Her eyes that mirrored a wonder-world,
  Her mien of unearthly mildness,
And her waving raven tresses that curled   15
  To the ground in beautiful wildness.

III
'Whence comest thou, Spirit?' I asked, methought,
  'Thou art not one of the Banished!'
Alas, for me! she answered nought,
  But rose aloft and evanished;   20
And a radiance, like to a glory, beamed
  In the light she left behind her.
Long time I wept, and at last medreamed
  I left my shieling to find her.

IV
And first I turned to the thunderous North,   25
  To Gruagach's mansion kingly;
Untouching the earth, I then sped forth
  To Inver-lough, and the shingly
And shining strand of the fishful Erne,
  And thence to Cruachan the golden,   30
Of whose resplendent palace ye learn
  So many a marvel olden!

V
I saw the Mourna's billows flow—
  I passed the walls of Shenady,
And stood in the hero-thronged Ardroe,   35
  Embosked amid greenwoods shady;
And visited that proud pile that stands
  Above the Boyne's broad waters,
Where Ængus dwells with his warrior-bands
  And the fairest of Ulster's daughters.   40

VI

To the halls of Mac Lir, to Creevroe's height,
  To Tara, the glory of Erin,
To the fairy palace that glances bright
  On the peak of the blue Cnocfeerin,
I vainly hied. I went west and east—   45
  I travelled seaward and shoreward—
But thus was I greeted in field and at feast—
  'Thy way lies onward and forward!'

VII

At last I reached, I wist not how,
  The royal towers of Ival,   50
Which, under the cliff's gigantic brow,
  Still rise without a rival;
And here were Thomond's chieftains all,
  With armour, and swords, and lances,
And here sweet music filled the hall,   55
  And damsels charmed with dances.

VIII

And here, at length, on a silvery throne,
  Half seated, half reclining,
With forehead white as the marble stone,
  And garments so starrily shining,   60
And features beyond the poet's pen—
  The sweetest, saddest features—
Appeared before me once agen,
  The fairest of Living Creatures!

IX

'Draw near, O, mortal!' she said, with a sigh,   65
  'And hear my mournful story!
The Guardian-Spirit of ERIN am I,
  But dimmed is mine ancient glory.
My priests are banished, my warriors wear
  No longer Victory's garland;   70
And my Child,* my Son, my beloved Heir,
  Is an exile in a far land!'

* Charles Stuart.

X
I heard no more—I saw no more—
  The bands of slumber were broken;
And palace and hero, and river and shore,   75
  Had vanished, and left no token.
Dissolved was the spell that had bound my will,
  And my fancy thus for a season;
But a sorrow therefore hangs over me still,
  Despite of the teachings of Reason!   80
                    [J. C. M., *Nation*, 16 May 1846]

Dark Rosaleen
(TRANSLATED FROM THE IRISH)

(This impassioned song, entitled, in the original, *Roisin Duh*, or The Black Little
Rose, was written in the reign of Elizabeth by one of the poets of the celebrated
Tirconnellian chieftain, Hugh the Red O'Donnell. It purports to be an allegorical
address from Hugh to Ireland on the subject of his love and struggles for her, and
his resolve to raise her again to the glorious position she held as a nation before
the irruption of the Saxon and Norman spoilers. The true character and mean-
ing of the figurative allusions with which it abounds, and to two only of which I
need refer here—*viz.*, the 'Roman wine' and 'Spanish ale' mentioned in the first
stanza—the intelligent reader will, of course, find no difficulty in understanding.)

I
O, my Dark Rosaleen,
  Do not sigh, do not weep!
The priests are on the ocean green,
  They march along the Deep.
There's wine . . . . from the royal Pope,   5
  Upon the ocean green;
And Spanish ale shall give you hope,
  My Dark Rosaleen!
  My own Rosaleen!
Shall glad your heart, shall give you hope,   10
Shall give you health, and help, and hope,
  My Dark Rosaleen!

II
Over hills, and through dales,
  Have I roamed for your sake;
All yesterday I sailed with sails   15
  On river and on lake.
The Erne, . . . at its highest flood,
  I dashed across unseen,
For there was lightning in my blood,
  My Dark Rosaleen!   20
  My own Rosaleen!
Oh! there was lightning in my blood,
Red lightning lightened through my blood,
  My Dark Rosaleen!

III
All day long, in unrest,   25
  To and fro, do I move.
The very soul within my breast
  Is wasted for you, love!
The heart . . . . in my bosom faints
  To think of you, my Queen,   30
My life of life, my saint of saints,
  My Dark Rosaleen!
  My own Rosaleen!
To hear your sweet and sad complaints,
My life, my love, my saint of saints,   35
  My Dark Rosaleen!

IV
Woe and pain, pain and woe,
  Are my lot, night and noon,
To see your bright face clouded so,
  Like to the mournful moon.   40
But yet . . . . will I rear your throne
  Again in golden sheen;
'Tis you shall reign, shall reign alone,
  My Dark Rosaleen!
  My own Rosaleen!   45
'Tis you shall have the golden throne,
'Tis you shall reign, and reign alone,
  My Dark Rosaleen!

V

Over dews, over sands,
   Will I fly, for your weal: 50
Your holy delicate white hands
   Shall girdle me with steel.
At home . . . . in your emerald bowers,
   From morning's dawn till e'en,
You'll pray for me, my flower of flowers,   55
   My Dark Rosaleen!
   My fond Rosaleen!
You'll think of me through Daylight's hours,
My virgin flower, my flower of flowers,
   My dark Rosaleen!   60

VI

I could scale the blue air,
   I could plough the high hills,
Oh, I could kneel all night in prayer,
   To heal your many ills!
And one . . . . beamy smile from you   65
   Would float like light between
My toils and me, my own, my true,
   My Dark Rosaleen!
   My fond Rosaleen!
Would give me life and soul anew,   70
A second life, a soul anew,
   My Dark Rosaleen!

VII

O! the Erne shall run red
   With redundance of blood,
The earth shall rock beneath our tread,   75
   And flames wrap hill and wood,
And gun-peal, and slogan cry,
   Wake many a glen serene,
Ere you shall fade, ere you shall die,
   My Dark Rosaleen!   80
   My own Rosaleen!
The Judgment Hour must first be nigh,
Ere you can fade, ere you can die,
   My Dark Rosaleen!

           [J. C. M., *Nation*, 30 May 1846]

Cean-Salla

(THE LAST WORDS OF RED HUGH O'DONNELL ON
HIS DEPARTURE FROM IRELAND FOR SPAIN)

'After this defeat at Cean-Salla (Kinsale) it was remarked that the Irish became a totally changed
people, for they now exchanged their valour for timidity, their energy and vigour for indolence, and
their hopes for bitter despondency.'—Annals of the Four Masters, A.D. 1602.

I

Weep not the brave Dead!
  Weep rather the Living—
    On them lies the curse
    Of a Doom unforgiving!
Each dark hour that rolls,   5
    Shall the memories they nurse,
Like molten hot lead,
Burn into their souls
  A remorse long and sore!
    They have helped to enthral a   10
  Great land evermore,
    They who fled from Cean-Salla!

II

Alas, for thee, slayer
  Of the kings of the Norsemen!
    Thou land of sharp swords,   15
And strong kerns and swift horsemen!
  Land ringing with song!
    Land, whose abbots and lords,
  Whose Heroic and Fair,
    Through centuries long   20
Made each palace of thine
    A new western Walhalla—
Thus to die without sign
    On the field of Cean-Salla!

III

My ship cleaves the wave—   25
  I depart for Iberia—
    But, oh! with what grief,

With how heavy and dreary a
  Sensation of ill!
I could welcome a grave: 30
  My career has been brief,
But I bow to God's will!
Not if now all forlorn,
  In my green years, I fall, a
Long exile, I mourn—   35
  But I mourn for Cean-Salla!
      [Monos, *Nation*, 4 July 1846]

An Invitation

I
Friends to Freedom! is't not time
  That your course were shaped at length?
    Wherefore stand ye loitering here?
Seek some healthier, holier clime,
  Where your souls may grow in strength,   5
    And whence Love hath exiled Fear!

II
Europe,—Southron, Saxon, Celt—
  Sits alone, in tattered robe.
    In our days she burns with none
Of the lightning-life she felt   10
  When Rome shook the troubled globe
    Twenty centuries agone.

III
Deutschland sleeps: her star hath waned.
  France, the Thundress whilome, now
    Singeth small, with bated breath.   15
Spain is bleeding, Poland chained;
  Italy can but groan and bow.
    England lieth sick to death.*

* 'England leidet von einer todtlichen Krankheit, ohne Hoffnung wie ohne Heilung.' England labours under a deadly sickness without hope and without remedy.—NIEBUHR.

IV
Cross with me the Atlantic's foam,
  And your genuine goal is won.   20
    Purely Freedom's breezes blow,
Merrily Freedom's children roam,
  By the dædal Amazon,
    And the glorious Ohio!

V
Thither take not gems and gold.   25
  Nought from Europe's robber-hoards
    Must profane the Western Zones.
Thither take ye spirits bold,
  Thither take ye ploughs and swords,
    And your fathers' buried bones!   30

VI
Come!—if Liberty's true fires
  Burn within your bosoms, come!
    If ye would that in your graves
Your free sons would bless their sires
    Make the Far Green West your home,   35
    Cross with me the Atlantic's waves!
                [A Yankee, *Nation*, 4 July 1846]

A Vision of Connaught in the Thirteenth Century

'Et moi, j'ai ete aussi en Arcadie.'—*And I, I, too, have been a dreamer.*—Inscription on a
Painting by Poussin.

I
  I walked entranced
    Through a land of Morn;
The sun, with wondrous excess of light,
  Shone down and glanced
    Over seas of corn   5
And lustrous gardens aleft and right.

Even in the clime
   Of resplendent Spain,
Beams no such sun upon such a land;
   But it was the time,   10
    'Twas in the reign,
Of Cáhal Mór of the Wine-red Hand.*

II
   Anon stood nigh
    By my side a man
Of princely aspect and port sublime.   15
   Him queried I,
    'O, my Lord and Khan,†
What clime is this, and what golden time?'
   When he—'The clime
    Is a clime to praise,   20
The clime is Erin's, the green and bland;
   And it is the time,
    These be the days,
Of Cáhal Mór of the Wine-red Hand!'

III
   Then saw I thrones,   25
    And circling fires,
And a Dome rose near me, as by a spell,
   Whence flowed the tones
    Of silver lyres
And many voices in wreathèd swell;   30
   And their thrilling chime
    Fell on mine ears
As the heavenly hymn of an angel-band—
   'It is now the time,
    These be the years,   35
Of Cáhal Mór of the Wine-red Hand!'

* The Irish and Oriental poets both agree in attributing favorable or unfavorable weather and
abundant or deficient harvests to the good or bad qualities of the reigning monarch. What the
character of Cahal was will be seen below.
† Identical with the Irish *Ceann*, Head, or Chief; but I the rather gave him the Oriental title, as
really fancying myself in one of the regions of Araby the Blest.

IV

    I sought the hall,
      And, behold! . . . a change
From light to darkness, from joy to woe!
    King, nobles, all,   40
      Looked aghast and strange;
The minstrel-groupe sate in dumbest show!
    Had some great crime
      Wrought this dread amaze,
This terror? None seemed to understand!   45
    'Twas then the time,
      We were in the days,
Of Cáhal Mór of the Wine-red Hand.

V

    I again walked forth;
      But lo! the sky   50
Showed fleckt with blood, and an alien sun
    Glared from the north,
      And there stood on high,
Amid his shorn beams, A SKELETON!*
    It was by the stream   55
      Of the castled Maine,
One Autumn eve, in the Teuton's land,
    That I dreamed this dream
      Of the time and reign
Of Cáhal Mór of the Wine-red Hand!   60
      [Clarence Mangan, *Nation*, 11 July 1846]

---

* 'It was but natural that these portentous appearances should thus be exhibited on this occasion, for they were the heralds of a very great calamity that befel the Connacians in this year—namely, the death of Cathal of the Red Hand, son of Torlogh Mor of the Wine, and King of Connaught, a prince of most amiable qualities, and into whose heart GOD had infused more piety and goodness than into the hearts of any of his cotemporaries.'—*Annals of the Four Masters*, A.D. 1224.

The Lovely Land
*(On a Landscape, painted by M******)*

I
Glorious birth of Mind and Colour!
  Gazing on thy radiant face
  The most lorn of Adam's race
Might forget all dolor!

II
What divinest light is beaming   5
  Over mountain, mead, and grove!
  That blue noontide sky above
Seems asleep and dreaming.

III
Rich Italia's wild-birds warble
  In the foliage of those trees,   10
  I can trace thee, Veronese,
In these rocks of marble!

IV
Yet no! Mark I not where quiver
  The sun's rays on yonder stream?
  Only a Poussin could dream   15
Such a sun and river!

V
What bold imaging! Stony valley
  And fair bower of eglantine!
  Here I see the black ravine,
There the lilied alley!   20

VI
This is some rare clime so olden,
  Peopled, not by men, but fays;
  Some lone land of genii days,
Storyful and golden!

VII

Oh, for magic power to wander   25
  One bright year through such a land!
  Might I even one hour stand
On the blest hills yonder!

VIII

But—what spy I? . . . O, by noonlight!
  'Tis the same!—the pillar-tower   30
  I have oft passed thrice an hour,
Twilight, sunlight, moonlight!

IX

Shame to me, my own, my sire-land,
  Not to know thy soil and skies!
  Shame, that through Maclise's eyes   35
I first see thee, IRELAND!

X

No! no land doth rank above thee
  Or for loveliness or worth!
  So shall I, from this day forth,
Ever sing and love thee!   40
                [Lageniensis, *Nation*, 18 July 1846]

Lament over the Ruins of the Abbey of Teach Mologa*
(TRANSLATED FROM THE ORIGINAL IRISH OF JOHN O'CULLEN,
A NATIVE OF CORK, WHO DIED IN THE YEAR 1816)

'*Oidche dhámh go doilg, dúbhach.*'

I

    I wandered forth at night alone,
Along the dreary, shingly, billow-beaten shore.
Sadness that night was in my bosom's core.
    My soul and strength lay prone.

---

* Literally 'The House of (St.) Molaga', and now called Timoleague. Our readers will find its
position on the Map of Munster.

II

   The thin wan moon, half overveiled   5
By clouds, shed her funereal beams upon the scene;
While in low tones, with many a pause between,
   The mournful night-wind wailed.

III

   Musing of Life, and Death, and Fate,
I slowly paced along, heedless of aught around,   10
Till on the hill, now, alas! ruin-crowned,
   Lo! the old Abbey-gate!

IV

   Dim in the pallid moonlight stood,
Crumbling to slow decay, the remnant of that pile
Within which dwelt so many saints erewhile   15
   In loving brotherhood!

V

   The memory of the men who slept
Under those desolate walls—the solitude—the hour—
Mine own lorn mood of mind—all joined to o'erpower
   My spirit—and I wept!   20

VI

   In yonder Goshen once—I thought—
Reigned Piety and Peace: Virtue and Truth were there.—
With Charity and the blessed spirit of Prayer
   Was each fleet moment fraught!

VII

   There, unity of Work and Will   25
Blent hundreds into one: no jealousies or jars
Troubled their placid lives: their fortunate stars
   Had triumphed o'er all Ill!

VIII

   There, knolled each morn and even
The Bell for Matin and Vesper: Mass was said or sung.—   30
From the bright silver censer, as it swung,
   Rose balsamy clouds to Heaven.

IX
   Through the round cloistered corridors
A many a midnight hour, bareheaded and unshod,
Walked the Grey Friars, beseeching from their GOD   35
   Peace for these western shores!

X
   The weary pilgrim, bowed by Age,
Oft found asylum there—found welcome, and found wine.
Oft rested in its hall the Paladine,
   The Poet and the Sage!   40

XI
   Alas! alas! how dark the change!
Now round its mouldering walls, over its pillars low,
The grass grows rank, the yellow gowans blow,
   Looking so sad and strange!

XII
   Unsightly stones choke up its wells;   45
The owl hoots all night long under the altar-stairs;
The fox and badger make their darksome lairs
   In its deserted cells!

XIII
   Tempest and Time—the drifting sands—
The lightning and the rains—the seas that sweep around   50
These hills in winter-nights, have awfully crowned
   The work of impious hands!

XIV
   The sheltering, smooth-stoned, massive wall—
The noble figured roof—the glossy marble piers—
The monumental shapes of elder years—   55
   Where are they? Vanished all!

XV
   Rite, incense, chant, prayer, mass, have ceased—
All, all have ceased! Only the whitening bones half sunk
In the earth now tell that ever here dwelt monk,
   Friar, acolyte, or priest.   60

XVI
  Oh! woe, that Wrong should triumph thus!
Woe that the olden right, the rule and the renown
Of the Pure-souled and Meek should thus go down
    Before the Tyrannous!

XVII
  Where wert thou, Justice, in that hour?   65
Where was thy smiting sword? What had those good men done,
That thou shouldst tamely see them trampled on
    By brutal England's Power?

XVIII
  Alas, I rave! . . . If Change is here,
Is it not o'er the land?—Is it not too in me?   70
Yes! I am changed even more than what I see.
    Now is my last goal near!

XIX
  My worn limbs fail—my blood moves cold—
Dimness is on mine eyes—I have seen my children die.
They lie where I too in brief space shall lie—   75
    Under the grassy mould!

*   *   *   *

  I turned away, as toward my grave,
And, all my dark way homeward by the Atlantic's verge,
Resounded in mine ears like to a dirge
    The roaring of the wave.   80
            [Clarence Mangan, *Nation*, 8 August 1846]

*A Lamentation for the Death of Sir Maurice Fitzgerald, Knight of Kerry**
(AN ABRIDGED TRANSLATION FROM THE IRISH OF PIERCE FERRITER)

I
There was lifted up one voice of woe,
  One lament of more than mortal grief
Through the wide South to and fro
  For a fallen Chief.
In the dead of night that cry thrilled through me,
  I looked out upon the midnight air; 5
Mine own soul was all as gloomy,
  And I knelt in prayer.

II
O'er Loch Gur, that night, once—twice—yea, thrice—
  Passed a wail of anguish for the Brave
That half curdled into ice 10
  Its moon-mirroring wave.
Then uprose a many-toned wild hymn in
  Choral swell from Ogra's dark ravine,
And Mogeely's Phantom Women†
  Mourned the Geraldine! 15

III
Far on Carah Mona's emerald plains
  Shrieks and sighs were blended many hours,
And Fermoy in fitful strains
  Answered from her towers.
Youghal, Keenalmeaky, Eemokilly 20
  Mourned in concert, and their piercing *keen*
Woke to wondering life the stilly
  Glens of Inchiqueen.

* Who was killed in Flanders in 1642.
† Banshees.

IV
From Loughmoe to yellow Dunanore   25
  There was fear: the traders of Tralee
Gathered up their golden store,
  And prepared to flee;
For, in ship and hall, from night till morning
  Showed the first faint beamings of the sun,   30
All the foreigners heard the warning
  Of the Dreaded One!

V
'This,' they spake, 'portendeth death to *us*,
  If we fly not swiftly from our fate!'
Self-conceited idiots! thus   35
  Ravingly to prate!
Not for base-born higgling Saxon trucksters
  Ring laments like those by shore and sea;
Not for churls with souls of hucksters
  Waileth our Banshee!   40

VI
For the high Milesian race alone
  Ever flows the music of her woe;
For slain heir to bygone throne,
  And for Chief laid low!
Hark! . . . . . . Again, methinks, I hear her weeping   45
  Yonder! Is she near me now, as then?
Or was but the night-wind sweeping
  Down the hollow glen?
              [J. C. M., *Nation*, 29 August 1846]

Counsel to the Worldly-Wise

I
Go A-FOOT, and go a-head!
  That's the way to prosper.
Whoso must be carriage-led
  Suffereth serious loss per
Day in health as well as wealth   5

By that laziness with which
  Walkers have from birth warred;
And ere long grim Death by stealth
  Mounts the tilbury, and the rich
    Loller tumbleth earthward!   10

II
Also keep your conscience pure.—
  NEITHER LIE NOR BORROW;
He who starves to-day, be sure,
  Always carves to-morrow.
March in front; don't sculk behind;   15
  DARE TO LIVE, though sneering groupes
    Dub you *rara avis*—
'Serve your country—love your kind,'
  And whene'er your spirit droops
    Think of THOMAS DAVIS!   20
        [J. C. M., *Nation*, 3 October 1846]

from *Anthologia Hibernica–No. I*

Courteous Reader,

IN the course of our wanderings through the Gardens of Northern Literature, wherein, among much that is fragrant and blooming beyond aught to be met with elsewhere,

  'The hemlock, and hembane, and darnel rank,'

are too often suffered to flourish in unchecked luxuriance, it has occasionally occurred to us that we might perhaps be as gracefully, if not as profitably, employed in 'looking at home,' and culling the simple Poetical Wild-flowers of our own dear Mother-land.

The idea came over us from time to time rather as an impression than as a thought. By degrees, however, it assumed, if we may so speak, form and symmetry. It grew to be an opinion, and in a short time afterwards deepened and settled down into a conviction.

In confessing so much, it might appear to thee, Reader, as though we had acted the part of a waiter on Apollo, who takes rank, we presume, as the Providence of Poets. But in so judging thou wouldst be mistaken. We copy no man. We follow

in the track of none. Our labours—inferior as we cheerfully admit them to be—
are altogether peculiar to ourself and our own tastes. At the same time we will
not deny that the great and general impulse given to the Irish mind of late has
exercised its legitimate influence over us. Slender as our talents are, we have
become exceedingly desirous to dedicate them henceforth exclusively to the
service of our country. For that country—and we now express ourselves merely
in reference to its literature—we see a new era approaching. Ireland has been

'for a certain term doomed to walk the night'

of tribulation and ignorance. But that 'night is far spent,' and 'the day is at hand.'
The better time is coming—approaching with chariot-like speed. The dawning
of a new era is heralded by many a rising star and gilded cloud. And hereafter,
Courteous Reader, when Ireland shall have re-assumed her place among the
nations, it surely cannot fail to be a peace-offering both to thy manes and ours,
that we, both of us in our day, in some sort contributed towards the glorious
event of her regeneration.

As the result, therefore, of our speculations and meditations, we have ven-
tured to commence a series of articles on our native Gaelic poets. [. . .]

Andrew M'Grath was, in one word, a scamp. A man of more graceless habits,
perhaps, never dipped pen in inkstand. He was a native of Clare, or, as some
affirm, Limerick, and flourished, or rather decayed, about the middle of the last
century. His 'profession' was nominally that of a hedge-schoolmaster; but as his
vacations were somewhat numerous, it happened that he was less frequently to
be found behind his hedge than behind a pedlar's box, chiefly stocked with soft
goods for the softer sex, with which he was accustomed to traverse the counties
of the south. A rover's life is not always exactly the most moral; and M'Grath's
was, in every sense of the word, that of a thorough-paced vagabond. [. . .]

We look in vain through his pages for any of those vigorous and indignant
outbursts of spirit so often to be met with in the majority of our native poets.
How, in truth, could we expect to find them? He had burdened his better Muse
with his conscience, and no wonder that she sank under the oppressiveness of
the load. That, however, he by no means lacked poetical power, is certain. [. . .]
But, in general, he wanted enthusiasm, and that true tranquil perception of the
Beautiful which a life led according to the rules of Divine Law alone can confer
on Man. The poems we transcribe here are examples in point; and while we
cannot but admire their harmony and freedom from the ordinary trammels of
versification, it still appears to us as if even their best passages were but maudlin
and puling attempts to supply, by an affectation of piety, the absence of that
heroic tone, that elevation of spirit, without which Poetry is but a name, and its
life nothing better than mere artificiality and appearance.

Neither One Thing nor T'other

I

  Oh, my love, see and pity
    My desolate plight!
    I am on the *shughraun*,*—and the move,—day and night.
  I am hunted from country and city,
  The Church, my own mother,   5
Opines I must go to Old Nick for a home,
For she vows that I'm neither for England nor Rome,
    Neither One thing nor T'other.

II

  The Parson looks knowing,
    And talks about 'rogues,'   10
    And of 'sculkers that foot it in *all* people's brogues,
  To get share of what spoil may be going.'
  'There's Luther—and Gother'
Quoth he, 'but, if *your* creed be worth an old song,
Shame the devil—speak truth—say to *which* you belong,   15
    And be One thing or T'other.'

III

  Or he threatens—preferring
    Such bluster to blar-
    ney—to have me hauled up some fine day to the bar,
  As I'm neither fish, flesh, nor red herring.   20
  And then, waxing wrother,
He bids me beware of the gallows-tree cord,
Since I 'chuse to be neither for Baal nor the Lord,
    Neither One thing nor T'other.'

---

* *Seachrán* is a phrase of a nature peculiar to the Irish language. A man who is on the *seachrán* is rather shabby than positively poor. He sneaks through by-lanes in an elbowless coat, and breakfasts at an uncertain hour and place in the afternoon, on a pennyworth of bread, a red herring, and a tumbler of porter.

IV

'Tis the same with the Priest; he   25
  Too wishes me '*hung*,'
    For he says I bewitch the *colleens* with my tongue,
  Though my talk is all 'windy and yeasty,'
  And myself 'a mere frother,
A rhymester, a gamester, a hangabone thief—   30
With a double-faced phiz, and a hybrid belief,
  Neither One thing nor T'other.'

V

In vain do I reason
  That no love of Truth
    Should lead one of his cloth to assault a pour youth,   35
  That even wrong thoughts are no treason,
  And more—that a brother
Of Mankind should hardly be left in the lurch,
On the ground that he kneels both in chapel and church,
  And is This, That and T'other.   40

VI

His knock-me-down answer
  Is always the same—
    That I've long been a knave, *without* conduct or shame,
  And *with* conscience corrupt as cancer.
  So he bids me not bother   45
His ears with my balderdash triplets and tropes,
Since I'll neither enlist under Harries* nor Popes,
  Nor be One thing nor T'other.

VII

I yield to my betters—
  Of course I am wrong;   50
    Yet, think of King David!—and Paul, who so long
  Went about, putting Christians in fetters.
  Why folk should be lother
To-day to absolve a poor mortal from crime
Than of old I can't guess—though I *do* grant that I'm   55
  Neither Paul nor—the Other.

*The allusion here is to Henry VIII., the first English monarch, as our readers are aware, who
contested the Pope's supremacy.

VIII

  Is any course left me?
   I sadly fear not!
   The choice of a faith for myself is a lot
  Of which Fate and my faults have bereft me.   60
  I'm like to no other!
I must seek for some sect whose adherents don't care
A potato what garb one's religion may wear,
  Whether This, That, or T'other.

IX

  'Twont do to join Calvin,   65
   Or Arius's crew,
   For each damns the other. I think I'll turn Jew,
  And perhaps I may then find a salve in
  The doubts I now smother.
Alas! tis ill jesting with such a grave theme,   70
For, certes, one ought to be, or, at least, *seem*
  Either One thing or T'other.

X

THE SUMMING UP

  O, GOD! Thou who savest
   All much-loving souls!
   Look down on a wretch with whom no one condoles!   75
  Aforetime Thou freely forgavest
   A recreant brother,
Saint Peter, his backsliding, when he became
A penitent—now forgive *me* for the same,
  For, Lord! I am another.   80

[...] Let us now try our hand on a love-song. It has often been remarked, that to express in words of the simplest pathos, feelings of the deepest grief, one must have recourse to the Irish language: and certainly the touching melody and tenderness of this little piece would seem to bear out the truth of the assertion. We have not been able to discover the name of its author:—

Love-Song

I

Lonely from my home I come,
  To cast myself upon your tomb,
    And to weep.
Lonely from my lonesome home,
  My lonesome house of grief and gloom,   5
    Where I keep
Vigil often all night long,
  For your dear, dear sake,
Praying many a prayer so wrong
  That my heart would break!   10

II

Gladly, O my blighted flower,
  Sweet Apple of my bosom's Tree,
    Would I now
Stretch me in your dark death-bower
  Beside your corpse, and lovingly   15
    Kiss your brow.
But we'll meet ere many a day,
  Never more to part,
For ev'n now I feel the clay
  Gathering round my heart.   20

III

In my soul doth darkness dwell,
  And through its dreary winding caves
    Ever flows,
Ever flows with moaning swell,
  One ebbless Flood of many Waves,   25
    Which are Woes.
Death, love, has me in his lures,
  But that grieves not me,
So my ghost may meet with yours
  On yon moon-loved lea.   30

IV
When the neighbours near my cot
  Believe me sunk in slumber deep,
     I arise—
For, oh! 'tis a weary lot,
  This watching aye, and wooing sleep   35
     With hot eyes—
I arise, and seek your grave,
  And pour forth my tears,
While the winds that nightly rave,
  Whistle in mine ears.   40

V
Often turns my memory back
  To that dear evening in the dell,
     When we twain,
Sheltered by the sloe-bush black,
  Sat, laughed, and talked, while thick sleet fell,   45
     And cold rain.
Thanks to GOD! no guilty leaven
  Dashed our childish mirth.
You rejoice for this in Heaven,
  I not less on Earth!   50

VI
Love! the priests feel wroth with me,
  To find I shrine your image still
     In my breast,
Since you are gone eternally,
  And your fair frame lies in the chill   55
     Grave at rest;
But true Love outlives the shroud,
  Knows not check nor change,
And beyond Time's World of Cloud
  Still must reign and range.   60

VII
Well may now your kindred mourn
  The threats, the wiles, the cruel arts,
     They long tried
On the child they left forlorn!

They broke the tenderest heart of hearts,   65
   And she died.
Curse upon the love of Show!
  Curse on Pride and Greed!
They would wed you 'high'—and woe!
  Here behold their meed!   70
           [J. C. M., *DUM*, February 1847]

The Hymn 'Stabat Mater Dolorosa'
RENDERED INTO ENGLISH

I
LONG she stood, the Mourning Mother,
  Long by Calvary's Cross she stood,
    Pierced as with a hundred spears;
While the grief she could not smother
  Bathed her pale face in a flood   5
    Of exhaustless tears.

II
Who shall paint her heart's affliction,
  Who depict her soul's dismay,
    In that ghastliest hour of hours,
The dark hour of Crucifixion,   10
  When Hell triumphed in the sway
    Of the Evil Powers?

III
When she saw her Son, the glorious
  God of Mercy, Love and Light,
    Tortured by a ruffian horde—   15
Then, alas! awhile victorious
  O'er the world-controlling might
    Of that Son and Lord?

IV
And what pen, what power of painter,
  May describe how sharp a sword   20
    Rent her anguished Virgin breast

When, each moment waxing fainter,
  Her Beloved, her Son and Lord,
    Sank at length to rest?

V
Oh! thou holiest, fondest, meekest   25
  Mother of the Holiest Son,
    Let me weep His woes and thine!
So may I even, though the weakest
  Child of Clay, when Life is done,
    Soar to realms divine!   30
    [Unsigned, *Duffy's Irish Catholic Magazine*, April 1847]

from *Anthologia Hibernica–No. II*

[...] The ditty entitled, *A raibh tu ag an-g-Carraig?* and of which the reader will meet with a neat translation, but somewhat different from ours, in Mr Walsh's volume of 'Irish Popular Songs,'* is one which we intended to have supplied in our opening article, but were compelled to omit, for want of space. Although very popular in Munster, it is an anonymous production, but we would say, judging from its tone of sentiment, and style of expression, that the authorship of it cannot be referred to a very remote period.

The Lass of Carrick

I
'O, have you been in Carrick . . . and have you met her?
  You know my love, all beauty and all grace!
Forth from her eyes come flowing
      Bright threads that fetter
  The hearts of all who gaze upon her face!   5
    The fairest, rarest flower is she
      In Banba's bloomful gardens blowing;
    The wondrous Living Apple-tree,
      Whose golden fruit keeps ever glowing.
  O, tell me, tell me, have you met her,   10
  And does my long, long tarrying fret her?'

* Dublin: J. McGlashan, 1847.

II

'Yes, I have been in Carrick, and there have met her;
  I know the maid, all beauty and all grace,
From whose dark eyes come flowing
        Bright threads that fetter   15
  The hearts of all that gaze upon her face;
      The fairest, rarest flower to see
        In Banba's bloomful gardens blowing,
      The wondrous Living Apple-tree,
        Whose golden fruit keeps ever glowing.   20
  Yes! I have seen her, I have met her,
  And your long tarrying does not fret her!'

III

'And yet I love her dearly! Methinks that now I
  Behold her tripping o'er the morning dew!
Sure, that's *her* step of lightness!   25
        Her sunny brow, eye,
  And smile are beaming through my soul anew!
      I see her hair that sweeps the ground
        In clusters of a golden brightness,
      Her swan-like lily neck so round,   30
        Her teeth outshining pearl for whiteness,
  And through them all the soul informing,
  Illumining, enlivening, warming!

IV

'Were mine five hundred guineas, I'd feel them burning
  My heart and hands to keep them, had they power   35
To save those glorious tresses
        From ever turning
  From gold to silver in blank Age's hour.
      Yet there's a glory brighter far,—
        The light in which pure Virtue dresses   40
      The soul!—O, may it, as a star,
        Guide her ... and him her heart's love blesses!
  For Beauty's mask ere long must moulder
  Where *this* wanes faint, or waxes colder.

V

'In some lone glen a-lying ... all night, mine absent   45
  And mourning spirit seeks my darling's home,
While visions without number,
        Perchance by Mab sent,
  Perchance by some less kind *shee-og* or gnome,
    And all wild fantasies and dreams,   50
      Pursue me through my troubled slumber,
    Until, with Morning's first red beams,
      Again the body's cold clay cumber
Returns, and I upwake,—to sorrow
And labour through another morrow.   55

VI

'Till Easter's holy season shall fall in August,
  And Patrick's Festival nigh Christmas tide,
Till ice and snow appear in
        July, and raw gust
And sleet and snow extinguish Summer's pride—   60
    Till, in a word, above my tomb
      Your own fair hand at last shall rear in
    The silent night, to bud and bloom,
      The whitest rose in gardened Erin,
My love shall know nor change nor chillness,   65
Burn though it must in gloom and stillness.'
                        [Unsigned, *DUM*, May 1847]

The Death and Burial of Red Hugh O'Donnell
(A.D. 1602)

I

The dark day of Kinsale was over,
  And Ireland lay again in thrall;
No hope seemed left her to recover
  From this her fatal, final fall.
Her goal was lost, her strength departed;   5
  The Saxon hosts had scattered far
Those bright prestiges her High-hearted
  Had shed around her arms in war.

Her glory bode a burnt-out star,
  A voice of wailing and lamenting,   10
  A cry of late and vain repenting
Rose from the centre to the sea,
   Throughout the once-glad, songful isle;
   And ruffian Force and treacherous Wile
Rode rampant o'er the Brave and Free.   15
  A Night without a Morrow,
  An ever-wounding Sorrow,
  A death-trance that might borrow
   No ray from Hope to gild its gloom,
  A wild, vague thirst unsated   20
For vengeance on the Hated—
  A bondage fixed and fated,
   Such seemed the trampled Nation's doom!

II
And He, the Chieftain of the North,
   The Red O'Donnell,   25
Who led her banded legions forth,
   In green Tirconnell,
O'er fortressed height and battle-plain,
  So many a day to Death or Danger,
  He, tended by the hireling stranger,   30
He droops—he sinks—he dies in pain—
He breathes his last in far-off Spain,
Alone, alas! in far-off Spain,
  Mourn ye the Brave!
Mourn him with tears,   35
  He goes down to his grave
   In his youth, in his bloom!
  On Iberia's dusk shore,
In the flowers of his years
Is his life's lamp outquenched;   40
  It bides dark evermore
   In the gloom of the tomb!
He who never once blenched
  Before falchions or foemen
Lies low, like a tree   45
  Laid in ashes by lightning.

Alas! for the omen,
  Sad Erin, to thee,
When thy fate appeared brightening!
  Mourn we the Brave!   50
Mourn him with tears:
  For he goes to his grave
In the flower of his years!

III
Behold yon pile, that rises lone
  Within Zimanca's* cloistered walls,   55
On whose dark arabesques of stone
  Scarce even the noon-day sunbeam falls—
An ancient fabric! reared, I ween,
  What time the Moors were here the masters,
As telleth well the sombre sheen   60
  Of its carved arches and pilasters.
We enter, passing court by court,
And long-deserted hall and fort,
And blank alcoves and corridors,
And rooms whose tesselated floors,   65
And faded sandal-roofs appear
  To shadow forth, in many a token,
The gloom and splendour blended here
  Before the Arab arm was broken.
Now, up yonder winding stairs,   70
Which Time day by day impairs,
  We wearily clamber,
  And lo! a long chamber,
  Dim-lighted and cold,
  Like a King's mausoléum of old.   75

* Zimancas is a small, but by no means insignificant, town, in the province of Old Castile. The
historical associations connected with it (among which Irishmen, we hope, may be allowed to class
those belonging to our melancholy story) are peculiarly interesting. In point of antiquity it stands,
if not alone, at least on a parallel with the most ancient cities of Spain, and on this account was
chosen by the Spanish monarchs of the sixteenth and seventeenth centuries as the National Depôt
for the chronicles of the kingdom. It was besieged and taken by storm by the Moors in the year 967,
after a gallant resistance on the part of its inefficient garrison, but regained its independence (in
common with most of the cities and provinces of Spain) long before the final victories of King
Ferdinand, in the fifteenth century. Of late but little has been heard of it; but it has nevertheless (as
we have reason to know) taken an active and decided part in the unfortunately over-numerous
revolutions, for which the Spanish Peninsula has been disastrously distinguished in modern times.

Therein sleeps the boldest of Erin's best Bold!
There sleepeth, laid low
  Not by musquet or spear in
The field, but by Sickness and Wo,
  The last Prince that may battle for Erin!   80
The winds, as in pity, sweep sighing
  Around the pale-canopied bed
Where the corpse of the Hero is lying;
  One brief hour ago
They wailed o'er the Dying,   85
  They now pour their dirge for the Dead!
Two tall figures kneel beside him,
  These received his parting breath;
These alone stood by to guide him
  Through the Gates of Death.   90
Their sacred robes, their prayerful mien,
  At once reveal those holy priests
At home, abroad, far oftener seen
  At poor men's graves than at rich man's feasts.
O! blest and honoured be the names   95
  Of O'Mulconry and Dunleavy;
Who, though themselves of worn-out frames,
  Yet, when the thought of Erin's woes,
And future fate lay dark and heavy
  On their Prince's bleeding bosom,   100
Nobly cheered him to the close
  Of this his bitterest hour of hours!
May their memories ever blossom,
  Fresh and bright in Time's meridian bowers!

IV
The moon is dawning, the West is darkening;   105
  A sighing sound haunts the bodeful air;
The forest-pines appear hushed and hearkening,
  Like living forms, for the Vesper prayer.
Their leaves are sparkling, but not in gladness—
  Who readeth well what their sheen bespeaks   110
Will deem those pearly-pale dews of sadness
  Most like the tear-drops on weepers' cheeks.
The knelling fall of the Douro's waters

Floats down the dells like the saddest song,
As though the flood's fabled Fairy Daughters   115
   Bewailed some victim or deed of Wrong.
And, as the gold of the sunset slowly
   Decays and darkens, till all hath fled,
Those tones appear to unite in holy
   And choral swell for the Lost or Dead.   120
Is this illusion?—a poet's dreaming?
   An airy legend from Peristán?*
Or are the Thoughtful more wise in deeming
   That Nature sometimes may mourn with Man?

V
   'What, ho! my lords and lieges all!   125
      I call a Golden Revel!'
The King commands; the trumpets peal;
And all ranks known in Old Castile
   Meet in the royal palace-hall—
      Meet on one joyous level!   130
And Pleasure takes the reins from Power,
And Mirth unbounded rules the hour!

———

The festival—the song—the dance—
   The brilliant lights and gay attire
Recalled those days of Old Romance,   135
   And gallant knightly Chivalrie,
Even then but known through lay or lyre;
   A goodly sight it was to see!
Here, some illustrious Caballero
   Bent low before an aguadara,†   140
And there, a noteless calesero‡
   Led out the blood of Alcantara.
While many Hidalgos, who, for years,
   Had proudly stood aloof and single,
Almost from even their very peers,   145
   Cast off their state, and stooped to mingle
      With all who thronged around—unasked.
      And, what though every face was masqued?

* Fairy-land.   † Female water-carrier.   ‡ Itinerant merchant.

Condemn not this! for men have made
  Of Life a darker Masquerade,   150
Where nought is genuine more—save Guile.
  His wrinkles mock the Conqueror's wreath;
And, where the false lips fain would smile
  The veiled heart often bleeds beneath.
Enough!—but if thou wilt win pleasure   155
  From pondering how the things that seem
The stablest—Beauty, Pomp, and Treasure,
  May vanish like a morning dream,
Or turn to dolorous memories after;
  If thou wilt fondly mark how soon   160
Sighs may resound where late rang Laughter,
  Glance round thee through this wide saloon—
The lights are quenched, the guests are gone,
A few stray menials glide alone,
Like spectres, o'er the matted floor.   165
  It is the gloomiest hall in Spain,
For always ten-fold Wo must reign
  Where Gaiety was King before!

VI
And wherefore such a change? Oh, Spain! unto thee
  Be the tribute of those tears, that fill mine eyes unbid!   170
Thy Sovereign sought to make my country great and free!

The gay lamps are darkened, and the wine-cups are hid,
  Because the cold corpse of the young Irish Chief,
The Red Hugh O'Donnell, is in Valladolid!

Yes! He whose career was so bright, but so brief,   175
  He lieth on his bier in the palace-chapel aisle;
And Spain shares the glory and gloom of Erin's grief!

Yet a few fleeting hours, and a train shall defile
  From hence through the city to the Place of the Dead
Such as never until now left this venerable pile!   180

Oh, Philip, king of Spain, be blessings on thy head!
  Thou honoredst O'Donnell for his nobleness and worth;
Thou lovest, too, the land for whose weal he fought and bled!

But this thou guessest not—that the House that gave him birth
  Is matchless even in Spain for its ancientness of line—   185
Perchance is truly royaller than any on the earth!

Yet, thou givest him a tomb—thou yieldest him a shrine
  Among the highest lords—the magnates of thy land!
The greater meed of praise, O King, is therefore thine!

VII
  Hark! the Cathedral bell!   190
    One deep knoll,
    And no more!
  How it thrills to the core
  Of the heart and the soul,
    That knell!   195
  Hark! yet another and deeper knoll!
    A long hour hath passed
    Since the last.
Now torch-lights are flitting to and fro
  Around the high palace-wall,   200
  And a Hearse, with coffin and pall,
Standeth anear in plumèd woe.
  Another hour—and a final knoll!
    For the night weareth late.
  The signal is given and obeyed,   205
  And slowly the Funeral Cavalcade
    Moves from the chapel-gate
  On its way to its last dark goal!

VIII
  The Bannermen lead the van,
Their black flags flapping high in the wind—   210
  Singly they move, man after man;
    After them pass
The Guards and Senórs of the Bascalier class,
  Two and two, in a long, long train behind;
The Torch-bearers march afoot by their side;   215
    The chief Caballeros ride
On crape-covered steeds in front of the Hearse,
  With its coffin and pall.

The Serge-bearers march afoot by their side.
   In silence march all—   220
  No sound ariseth to pierce
The ear of Night save the moanful toll
   Of the far Esgueva;
And so they wind through the Puerta del Sól.*

   The Bannermen lead the van,   225
Their black flags flapping again and again:
   Singly they ride, man after man.
    Behind them appears
The line of the Guardsman and Bass-cavaliers,
Two and two, in a long, long sable train—   230
  The Torch-bearers march on foot by their side.
  The King and his Nobles ride
In the rear of the Hearse:—and hark! anon
   A slow musical strain,
Funereal and sad, resounds from the wide   235
   Ravines† to the plain,
And the notes fall, one after one,
Off the muffled drum, and blend with the swell
   Of the rolling Esgueva,
Till the Cavalcade winds through the Puert' d'Isabel.‡   240

   The Bannermen ride in the van;
Then follow the Guards, Knights, Nobles and King;
   Slowly move all, as when they began.
    The mists of the night
Dull the red glare of the torches' light;   245
And the Hearse, with its plumes of black heron-wing,
  And its formless look in the dusk, damp air,
  Seemeth like an Embodied Despair!
While the horn and the bass-bugle mingle their tones
   In funereal strains,   250
That sound like the wailings of Dolorous Prayer
   From a soul in her pains,

* Gate of the Sun.
† The city of Valladolid lies in a hollow, and is surrounded by cliffs.
‡ Isabella, the Queen of Ferdinand the Victorious.

And seem sadder at whiles from the groans
Of the muffled drum, and the mournful flow
  Of the rolling Esgueva,   255
As the Cavalcade winds through the Portal of Woe.*

IX
But lo! the Gate, with its Gothic arch,
 The Convent, with its mitred wall!
 The lurid rays of the torches fall
 Aslant on Saint Francis' Convent-wall.   260
Enough! here halts the processional March.

X
 With measured and solemn tread
The buriers all, the King the while
 Advancing at their head,
Move to the end of the lamp-lighted aisle,   265
 And there lay down their Dead.
 The Mass is chanted for the Dead,
 Before the altar of the Lord!
The Brethren of Saint Francis raise
  Aloft,   270
 With one accord,
The voice of prayer, the hymn of praise,
 To Him, the All-wise GOD and LORD,
 The only Ever-blest,
  Who oft   275
Works out by chastening and mysterious ways
 Salvation for the souls He loveth best!
And, as the midnight bell tolls forth its warning
That Night is nearing Morning,
 The corpse is lowered into its bed of rest. 280

XI
 It is done! All is over!
 The too fond-hearted lover
Of his Motherland is lying in his crypt of marble stone.

* *Puerta de la Péna*, the Gate of Sorrow, or Punishment.

   May a blessèd resurrection
     Be the meed of that affection   285
That burned in his bosom for Her, and Her alone!
   Many, since, have shared his doom,
     Of our Noble-souled and True—
For, wo is me, the brightest of the laurels Erin gathers
   Still bestow their barren bloom   290
     But on those, who, like to Hugh,
Lay their bones far away from the valleys of their fathers!
     [J. C. M., *Duffy's Irish Catholic Magazine*, May 1847]

The Dawning of the Day

(The following song, which I have translated from the Irish of O'Doran, refers to a singular atmospheric phenomenon said to be sometimes observed at Blackrock, near Dundalk, at daybreak, by the fishermen of that locality. Many similar narratives are to be met with in the poetry of almost all countries; but O'Doran has endeavoured to give the legend a political colouring, of which, I apprehend, readers in general will hardly deem it susceptible.)

'Maidin chiuin dham chois bruach na tragha.'

I
'Twas a balmy summer morning
   Warm and early,
  Such as only June bestows;
Everywhere the earth adorning,
   Dews lay pearly   5
  In the lily-bell and rose.
Up from each green-leafy bosk and hollow
  Rose the blackbird's pleasant lay,
And the soft cuckoo was sure to follow.
  'Twas the Dawning of the Day!   10

II
Through the perfumed air the golden
   Bees flew round me;
  Bright fish dazzled from the sea,
'Till medreamt some fairy olden-

World-spell bound me   15
   In a trance of witcherie.
Steeds pranced round anon with stateliest housings,
   Bearing riders prankt in rich array,
Like flushed revellers after wine-carousings—
   'Twas the Dawning of the Day!   20

III
Then a strain of song was chanted,
   And the lightly-
  Floating sea-nymphs drew anear.
Then again the shore seemed haunted   24
   By hosts brightly
  Clad, and wielding shield and spear!
Then came battle-shouts—an onward rushing—
  Swords, and chariots, and a phantom-fray.
Then all vanish'd; the warm skies were blushing
  In the Dawning of the Day!   30

IV
Cities girt with glorious gardens,
   Whose immortal
  Habitants in robes of light
Stood, methought, as angel-wardens
   Nigh each portal,   35
  Now arose to daze my sight.
Eden spread around, revived and blooming;
  When . . . . . . lo! as I gazed, all passed away—
. . . . I saw but black rocks and billows looming
  In the dim chill Dawn of Day!   40
               [J. C. M., *Nation*, 12 June 1847]

Song of the Albanian
(1826)

I
Why, from the dawn till Day declines,
  Why hear we cries aloft and under
    Upon Albania's crested hills
And through her long ravines?
  Flood, War, destroy not now:—no thunder,   5
    No lightning, strikes and kills.

II
No! Fire and Flood appal not now!
  The dominant Moslem need not war on
    This down-trod land of ours again.
Storm sleeps on Góvra's brow,   10
  But Charon comes—the ghastly Charon,
    He comes with all his train!

III
Gaunt Famine rideth in the van,
  And Pestilence, with myriad arrows,
    Followeth in fiery guise: they spare   15
Nor Woman, Child nor Man!
  The stricken Dead lie without barrows
    By roadsides, black and bare!

IV
Down on the burnt-up cottage roofs
  The sick sun all the long day flashes.   20
    In vain the old men seek the wood.
'Neath Charon's hot horse-hoofs
  At every step a fresh corpse plashes
    Into a pool of blood!

V
Yet is there food—but, take and eat,   25
  And still thou diest:—the sharp sword slaughters
    Thee, daring robber! So, by fount
And field,—on path, in street,
  Amid the Blessed Living Waters,
    Souls perish without count!   30

VI

Oh, GOD! it is a fearful sign,
  This fierce, mad, wasting dragon Hunger!
    Were there a land that cold at most
But sink and peak and pine,
  Infant-like, when such Agony wrung her,   35
    That land indeed were lost!

VII

Were there a land whose people could
  Lie down beneath Heaven's blue pavilions
    And gasp, and perish, famished slaves!—
While the ripe golden food   40
  That might and should have fed their millions
    Rotted above their graves—

VIII

That land were doomed! .. But, glorious Greece,
  Not such art thou! Even now thou risest
    Reborn from that drugged Sleep of Death   45
And soul-embruting Peace
  Which all-too-long thy Bravest, Wisest,
    And Best lay sunk aneath!

IX

Upon thy hills methinks I see,
  Flashing like light and fire, the *khandjers*   50
    Worn by our godlike sires of old!—
I hear that shout of jubilee
  Which tells that neither Death nor Dangers
    Avail to daunt the Bold!

X

Come, Charon, then, and crown thy work!   55
  The few heroic souls thou leavest
    Surviving still are strong to wrest
Their birthright from the Turk!
  Slay on! Perchance the task thou achievest
    Is one Heaven's Powers have blessed!   60
                [J. C. M., *Nation*, 15 August 1847]

* Curved daggers.

from *Lays of Many Lands*

Owen Reilly: a Keen
(FROM THE IRISH)

I
Oh! lay aside the flax, and put away the wheel,
  And sing with me, but not in gladness—
The heart that's in my breast is like to break with sadness—
  GOD, GOD alone knows what I feel!

II
There's a lone, a vacant place beside the cheerless hearth,   5
  A spot my eyes are straining after—
Oh! never more from thence will ring my boy's light laughter,
  The outgushing of his young heart's mirth!

III
No more will his hands clasp the cross before the shrine
  Of Christ's immaculate Virgin Mother!   10
Never, oh! never more will he pour forth another
  Prayer for himself, or me, or mine!

IV
The young men on the mountain sides will miss—miss long,
  The fleetest hurler of their number.
Powerless, alas! to-night in Death's unbroken slumber,   15
  Lies he, the Lithe of Limb, the Strong!

V
Oh! raise the keen, young women, o'er my darling's grave—
  Oh! kneel in prayer o'er his low dwelling;
At break of day this morn there knelt his mother, telling
  Her beads for him she could not save!   20

VI
Oh! plant, young men, the shamrock near my darling's head,
  And raise the hardy fir-tree over
The spot: the strange wayfarer then will know they cover
  My Oweneen's dark burial-bed!

VII

Heard ye not, yestereven, the Banshee deplore 25
  His death on heath-clad Killenvallen?
'Ul-ullalu!' she cried, 'a green young oak is fallen,
  For Owen Reilly lives no more!'

VIII

There stands a lone grey hazel-tree in Glen-na-ree,
  Whose green leaves but bud forth, and wither. 30
I sigh and groan as often as I wander thither,
  For I am like that lone grey tree!

IX

My four belovèd sons, where are they? Have they not
  Left me a wreck here all as lonely?
They withered and they died! I, their old mother, only 35
  Remain to weep and wail my lot!

X

But I will follow them now soon; for oft amid
  The storm I hear their voices calling,
'Come home!'—and in my dreams I see the cold clay falling
  Heavily on my coffin-lid! 40

XI

When the dark night films o'er my eyes, oh! let me be
  Laid out by Aileen Bawn Devany;
And let the lights around me at my wake be as many
  As the white hairs yet left to me!

XII

See that the tall white slender gowans blow and bloom 45
  In the grass round my head-stone brightly;
I would not have the little orphan daisy nightly
  Mourning in solitude and gloom!

XIII

Let there be shrieking on the hill and in the glen,
  Throughout the length and breadth of Galway's 50
Green land! Kathleen Dubh Reilly has herself been always
  The Queen of Keeners: mourn her then!

XIV

Lights will be seen to dance along Carn Corra's height,
  And through the burial-field; but follow
Them not, young men and women! for, o'er hill and hollow,   55
  They will but lure to Death and Night!

XV

But come ye to my grave when, in the days of May,
  The gladsome sun and skies grow warmer,
And say, 'Here sleeps Kathleen, where tempest cannot harm her,
  Soft be her narrow bed of clay!'   60

XVI

And count your beads, and pray, 'Rest her poor soul, oh, GOD!
  She willed no ill to breathing mortal—
Grant her, then, Thou, a place within Heaven's blessèd portal,
  Now that her bones lie in the sod!'

                              [J. C. M., *DUM*, September 1847]

from *Lays of Many Lands–No. II*

Moreen: a Love-Lament
(FROM THE IRISH OF CHARLES BOY MAC QUILLAN)

I

My lone, and once my own, Moreen,
  I know you sigh, I know you mourn,
    But ask me not to meet you more.
This heart of mine, once gay and green,
  Now, woe-the-day! is grey and worn,   5
    And feels, as 'twere, one cancered sore!
      I walk alone in trouble,
        Revolving thoughts of gloom.
      Each passing day doth but redouble
        The miseries of my doom!   10

II
In trouble? Oh! how weak a word!
  In woe, in horror, let me say—
    In wretchedness without a name.
The wrath of God, the avenging Sword
  Of Heaven burns in my bones alway,   15
    With ever-freshly torturing flame;
      And Desolateness and Terror
        Have made me their dark mate,
      The ghastly brood of Sin and Error
        Repented all-too-late!   20

III
Moreen, my veins run gall, not blood;
  A poison-plant flowers in my soul
    Whose deadly rankness never fades.
My thoughts, dark as a midnight flood,
  Burst forth beyond mine own control,   25
    And take all hideous shapes and shades.
      Unbreakable chains have bound me
        Prisoned within Hell's pale;
      The accursèd fiends and forms around me
        Hold me in hopeless bale.   30

IV
I see black dragons mount the sky;
  I see Earth yawn aneath my feet;
    I feel within the Asp, the Worm,
That will not sleep and cannot die,
  Fair though may show my winding sheet!   35
    I hear all night, as through a storm,
      Hoarse voices calling, calling
        My name upon the wind—
      All omens monstrous and appalling
        Affright my guilty mind!   40

V
I exult alone in one wild hour,
  That hour in which the red cup drowns
    The horrors it anon renews

In ghastlier guise, in fiercer power;—
  Then Glory brings me golden crowns,   45
    And visions of all brilliant hues
     Lap my lost soul in gladness,
      Until I awake again,
    And the dark lava fires of Madness
     Once more sweep through my brain.   50

VI

Yet, oh, Moreen! my woe of woes,
  The sharpest shaft I am pierced withal,
   Is Memory's ever-festering barb.
This tells me that of all my foes
  The falsest was Moreen Mulhall,   55
   The traitress under Friendship's garb!
    'Twere meet if one I had slighted
     Had wrought me Wrong and Dole,
    But, oh! to find my best hopes blighted
     By you—this rends my soul!   60

VII

'Tis anguish far beyond what they
  Who dree Life's workday toils and pains
   Even in intense excess, can know,
To feel a false Love's dagger slay
  The joyous lifeblood in the veins,   65
   And turn to ice its bounding flow!
    'Tis agony to remember
     How soon Love waxeth cold—
    How soon the frosts of its December
     Follow its June of gold!   70

VIII

For, oh, Moreen! there was a time,
  A happy time, when you appeared
   The Moon amid the starry host.
No levity, no approach to Crime,
  As yet had made you less endeared   75
   To those who sought and loved you most.

My bright dreams made you peerless,
  Till Truth bade all depart;—
And an awakening hour more cheerless
  Ne'er broke a lover's heart!   80

IX

And now you fain would win me back
  By promises, and prayers, and tears—
    In vain, in vain, my poor Moreen!
The Gone is gone! Man cannot track
  Afresh his course of blasted years,   85
    Or bid flowers bloom where fires have been!
      Our goals,—for you, Contrition,
        For me, Despair,—are set.
      My path lies onwards to Perdition:
        Your tears may save you yet!   90

X

In those resplendent years of Youth
  When Virtue seems the true Romance,
    And nought else lures the generous mind,
I might, even had I strayed from Truth,
  Have yet retrieved my road perchance,   95
    And left mine errors far behind.
      But, return *now*—Oh, never!
        Never and nevermore!
      Truth's holy fire is quenched for ever
        Within my bosom's core!   100

XI

The Past belongs to Eternity,
  And we once more shall meet it there,
    And reap from thence our fitting meed.
Let me not curse you, therefore:—He
  Before whose ken all hearts are bare   105
    Alone is Judge of Thought and Deed.
      We see, we purblind mortals,
        But the Unveiled and Nigh;
      The view beyond Life's Inner Portals
        Is for the Omniscient Eye.   110

XII

But Thought, even here, will brook no bonds;
  And Memory's pictures burn with hues
    Which neither Time nor Will may blot.
The wretch who, like myself, desponds,
  Is free to ponder and peruse   115
    The history of his lost life's lot:—
      And if I o'er-severely
      Judge you, Moreen, believe
    That still I love you not less dearly
      Than ere you bade me grieve!   120

THE SUMMING-UP

No more! Farewell! My fate is fixed!
  What yours may be I guess not well;
    But, for myself, I nightly die;
And the two worlds I stand betwixt,
  The Outward and the Inward Hell,   125
    Appear outrolled before mine eye.
      May sights far different meet you
      Beyond this Vale of Woes—
    And may your attendant spirits greet you
      In cheerier words than those!   130
              [J. C. M., *DUM*, October 1847]

The Testament of Cathaeir Mor

(One of the most interesting archaeological relics connected with Irish literature
is unquestionably the Testament of Cathaeir Mor, King of Ireland in the second
century. It is a document whose general authenticity is established beyond
question, though some doubt exists as to whether it was originally penned in the
precise form in which it has come down to modern times. Mention of it is made
by many writers on Irish history, and among others, by O'Flaherty in his *Ogygia*—
(Part III.c.59.) But in the LEABHAIR NA G-CEART, or, the Book of Rights,
now for the first time edited, with Translation, and Notes, by Mr. O'Donovan,
for the CELTIC SOCIETY, we have it entire. The learned editor—to whose
genius and exertions Irish literature is so deeply indebted—is of the opinion that
'it was drawn up in its present form some centuries after the death of Cathaeir

Mor, when the race of his more illustrious sons had definite territories in Leinster.'
Be the fact as it may, the document is certainly one of those characteristics remains
of an earlier age which most markedly bear the stamp of the peculiarities that
distinguish native Irish literary productions. I have thought therefore that a
rhymed and yet faithful translation of it might possibly find favour with some of
our readers.)

Introduction

HERE IS THE WILL OF CATHAEIR MÓR,
    GOD REST HIM!
  Among his heirs he divided his store,
   His treasures and lands,
   And, first, laying hands   5
On his son Ross Faly, he blessed him.

———

I

'MY SOVEREIGN POWER, my nobleness,
My wealth, my strength to curse and bless,
My royal privilege of protection
I leave to the son of my best affection,   10
ROSS FALY, Ross of the Rings,
Worthy descendant of Ireland's Kings!
To serve as memorials of succession
For all who yet shall claim their possession
   In after-ages.   15
Clement and noble and bold
   Is Ross, my son.
Then, let him not hoard up silver and gold,
  But give unto all fair measure of wages.
Victorious in battle he ever hath been;   20
  He therefore shall yield the green
And glorious plains of Tara to none,
   No, not to his brothers!
   Yet these shall he aid
   When attacked or betrayed.   25
This blessing of mine shall outlast the tomb,
  And live till the Day of Doom,
   Telling and telling daily,
And a prosperous man beyond all others
   Shall prove Ross Faly!'   30

THEN he gave him ten shields, and ten rings, and ten swords,
And ten drinking-horns; and he spake him those words.
    'Brightly shall shine the glory,
      O, Ross, of thy sons and heirs,
    Never shall flourish in story   35
      Such heroes as they and theirs!'

II

THEN, laying his royal hand on the head
Of his good son, DARRY, he blessed him and said:—
  'My Valor, my daring, my martial courage,
    My skill in the field I leave to DARRY,   40
    That he be a guiding Torch and starry
Light and Lamp to the hosts of *our* age.
A hero to sway, to lead and command,
Shall be every son of his tribes in the land!
O, Darry, with boldness and power   45
  Sit thou on the frontier of Tuath Lann,[*]
And ravage the lands of Deas Ghower.[†]
    Accept no gifts for thy protection
      From woman or man.
    So shall Heaven assuredly bless   50
    Thy many daughters with fruitfulness,
      And none shall stand above thee,
    For I, thy sire, who love thee
      With deep and warm affection,
    I prophesy unto thee all success   55
      Over the green battalions
      Of the redoubtable Galions.'[‡]

AND he gave him, thereon, as memorials and meeds,
Eight bondsmen, eight handmaids, eight cups, and eight steeds.

* *Tuath Laighean*, viz., North Leinster.
† *Deas Ghabhair*, viz., South Leinster.
‡ *Gailians*, an ancient designation, according to O'Donovan, of the Laighnigh, or Leinstermen.

III

T H E noble Monarch of Erin's men   60
Spake thus to the young Prince Brassal, then,—
 '𝕸𝖞 𝕾𝖊𝖆, with all its wealth of streams,
I leave to my sweetly-speaking B R A S S A L,
To serve and to succour him as a vassal—
 And the lands whereon the bright sun beams   65
Around the waves of Amergin's Bay*
As parcelled out in the ancient day.
By free men through a long long time
 Shall this thy heritage be enjoyed—
 But the chieftaincy shall at last be destroyed   70
Because of a Prince's crime.
And though others again shall regain it
 Yet Heaven shall not bless it,
 For Power shall oppress it,
And Weakness and Baseness shall stain it!'   75

A N D he gave him six ships, and six steeds, and six shields,
 Six mantles and six coats of steel—
And the six royal oxen that wrought in his fields,
 These gave he to Brassal the Prince for his weal.

IV

T H E N to Catach he spake,   80
 '𝕸𝖞 𝖇𝖔𝖗𝖉𝖊𝖗 𝖑𝖆𝖓𝖉𝖘
Thou, CATHACH, shalt take,
 But ere long they shall pass from thy hands,
  And by thee shall none
  Be ever begotten, daughter or son!'   85

V

 𝕮𝖔 𝕱𝖊𝖆𝖗𝖌𝖍𝖚𝖘 𝕷𝖚𝖆𝖘𝖈𝖆𝖓 spake he thus—
'Thou FEARGHUS, also, art one of us,
 But over-simple in all thy ways
 And babblest much of thy childish days.

* *Inbhear Aimherghin*, originally the estuary of the Blackwater, and so called from Aimherghin, one
of the sons of Milesius, to whom it was apportioned by lot.

For thee have I nought, but if lands may be bought   90
  Or won hereafter by sword or lance
    Of those, perchance,
  I may leave thee a part,
    All simple babbler and boy as thou art!'

VI

Young Fearghus, therefore, was left bereaven,   95
And thus the Monarch spake to Creeven.

'To my boyish Hero, my gentle CREEVEN,
Who loveth in Summer, at morn and even,
  To snare the songful birds of the field,
  But shunneth to look on spear and shield,   100
I have little to give of all that I share.
His fame shall fail, his battles be rare.
And of all the Kings that shall wear his crown
But one alone shall win renown.'*

AND he gave him six cloaks, and six cups, and seven steeds,   105
And six harnessed oxen, all fresh from the meads.

VII

But on Aenghus Nic, a younger child,
  Begotten in crime and born in wo,
The father frowned, as on one defiled,
  And with louring brow he spake him so:—   110

'To Nic, my son, that base-born youth,
  Shall nought be given of land or gold;
  He may be great and good and bold,
  But his birth is an agony all untold,
Which gnaweth him like a serpent's tooth.   115
    I am no donor
      To him or his race—
    His birth was dishonor;
      His life is disgrace!'†

* The text adds: *i.e. Colam mac Criomhthainn*; but O'Donovan conjectures, and, in our opinion,
correctly, that this is a mere *scholium* of some scribe.
† The reader may, perhaps, here be reminded of the line [*sic*] in Byron's *Parisina*, addressed by
Hugo to his father, Count Azo:—
    'And, with thy very crime, my birth
      Thou tauntedst me as little worth
        A match ignoble for thy throne!'

VIII

   AND thus he spake to EOCHY TIMIN,   120
   Deeming him fit but to herd with women.

'𝔚𝔢𝔞𝔨 𝔰𝔬𝔫 𝔬𝔣 𝔪𝔦𝔫𝔢, thou shalt not gain
Waste or water, valley or plain.
From thee shall none descend save cravens,
   Sons of sluggish sires and mothers,   125
     Who shall live and die,
But give no corpses to the ravens!
     Mine ill thought and mine evil eye*
   On thee beyond thy brothers
     Shall ever, ever lie!'   130

IX

   And to Oilioll Cadach his words were those:—
    '𝔒, 𝔒𝔦𝔩𝔦𝔬𝔩𝔩, great in coming years
   Shall be thy fame among friends and foes
    As the first of *Brughaidhs*† and Hospitaliers!
     But neither noble nor warlike   135
       Shall show thy renownless dwelling;
       Nevertheless
       Thou shalt dazzle at chess,
     Therein supremely excelling
   And shining like something starlike!'   140

AND his chess-board, therefore, and chessmen eke,
He gave to Oilioll Cadach the Meek.

X

   Now Fiacha,—youngest son was he,—
    Stood up by the bed . . . of his father, who said,
     The while, caressing   145
      Him tenderly—
    'My son! I have only for thee my blessing,
     And nought beside—
     Hadst best abide
With thy brothers a time, as thine years are green.'   150

---

* In the original—'*Mo faindi, mo eascaine*'—literally, 'My weakness, my curse.'
† Public victuallers.

THEN Fiacha wept, with a sorrowful mien;
 So, Cathaeir spake, to encourage him, gaily,
  With cheerful speech—
 'Abide one month with thy brethren each,
And seven years long with my son, Ross Faly.   155
  Do this, and thy sire, in sincerity,
  Prophesies unto thee fame and prosperity.'

—————

AND further he spake, as one inspired:—
'A Chieftain flourishing, feared, and admired,
  Shall Fiacha prove!   160
The gifted Man from the boiling Berve*
Him shall his brothers' clansmen serve.
His forts shall be Aillin and proud Almain,
 He shall reign in Carman and Allen;†
The highest renown shall his palaces gain   165
 When others have crumbled and fallen.
His power shall broaden and lengthen,
 And never know damage or loss;
The impregnable Naas he shall strengthen,
 And govern Ailbhe and Arriged Ross.   170
Yes! O, Fiacha, Foe of strangers,
 This shall be *thy* lot!
 And thou shalt pilot
Ladhrann and Leeven‡ with steady and even
Heart and arm through storm and dangers!   175
 Overthrown by thy mighty hand
  Shall the Lords of Tara lie;
 And Taillte's§ fair, the first in the land,
  Thou, son, shalt magnify,
And many a country thou yet shalt bring   180
To own thy rule as Ceann and King.

* *Bearbha*, viz., the river Barrow.
† The localities mentioned here were chiefly residences of the ancient kings of Leinster.
‡ Forts upon the eastern coasts of Ireland.
§ Taillte, now Teltown, a village between Kells and Navan, in Meath.

The blessing I give thee shall rest
  On thee and thy seed
    While Time shall endure,
Thou grandson of Fiacha the Blest!   185
  It is barely thy meed,
    For thy soul is childlike and pure!'

Here ends the Will of Cathaeir Mor, who was king of Ireland. Fiacha abode with his brothers, as Cathaeir had ordered. And he stayed for seven years with Ross Faly; and it was from Ross Faly that he learned the use of arms; and it has since been obligatory upon every man of his descendants who aspires at excellence in martial exercises to receive his first arms from some descendant of Ross Faly.

As for Cathaeir himself, be it known to all that he lived in good health for a season after making this Will, but that when some years had elapsed, he went to Taillte, and there fought a battle, and was killed there by the *Fian* of Luaighne. To commemorate his death this quatrain was written by that complete poet, Lughair:

A world-famed, illustrious, honorable man,
  The pride of his tribe in his day,
King Cathaeir, the glory and prop of each clan,
  Was killed by the Fian, in Magh Breagh!
             [J. C. M., *Nation*, 13 November 1847]

Rights of Property

(There's something so easy and audacious in the style of 'Terrae Filius,' that we must give a specimen:—)

'It is impossible to trench on the rights of Property.'—Morning Herald

Bah, scribe! 'tis a lie!—and a lie that lies
  At the root of much of our pauperty.
'Tis the Rich Man ever who descries and decries
  The sin of intermeddling with property.
The Poor Man groaneth and grovelleth prone,   5
  Like the Hindoo wretch in the Brahmin's truck;*

---

* 'Hour after hour we saw the victims of the cholera pass us in the trucks of the Brahmins.'— *Sketches of India.*

For the hearts of his 'betters' have grown to stone,
  And he dies despairing and famine-struck.
'One ha'penny, your honor!'—'You lazy young wench,
  Begone!—I'll not give a copper t'ye!   10
You slut! how dare you attempt to trench
  On the rights of pockets and property?
Trot home to your mother!'—'She's lying on the moor!'—
  'To your the father!'—'He's dying of the fever, and'—
'To the devil, then!'—'God! the lot of the Poor   15
  Is alone in Thy Retriever-hand!'

                       [Terrae Filius, *Nation*, 1 January 1848]

A Voice of Encouragement
A New Year's Lay

[I]

𝖄ouths! Compatriots! Friends! Men for the time that is nearing!
Spirits appointed by Heaven to front the storm and the trouble!
You, who in seasons of peril unfaltering still and unfearing
Calmly have held on your course, the course of the Just and the Noble!
𝖄ou, young men, would a man unworthy to rank in your number,   5
Yet with a heart that bleeds for his country's wrongs and affliction,
Fain raise a Voice to in Song, albeit his music and diction
Rather be fitted, alas! to lull to, than startle from, slumber.

II

𝖋riends! the gloom in the land, in our once bright land, grows deeper.
Suffering, even to Death in its horriblest form, aboundeth,   10
Through our black harvestless fields the peasant's faint wail resoundeth.
Hark to it even now! . . . The nightmare-oppressed sleeper
Gasping and struggling for life beneath his hideous bestrider,
Seeth not, dreeth not, sight or terror more fearful or ghastly
Than that poor paralysed slave! Want—Houselessness,—
    Famine, and lastly   15
Death in a thousand-corpsed grave, that momently waxeth wider.

III

𝔚𝔬𝔯𝔰𝔢! The great heart of the country is chilled, and throbbeth but faintly!
Apathy palsieth *here*—and *there* a panic misgiving:
Even the Trustful and Firm, even the Sage and the Saintly,
Seem to believe that the Dead but foreshow the doom of the Living.   20
Men of the faithfulest souls all but brokenhearted
On the dishonored tombs of the glorious Dreams that have perished—
Dreams that almost outshone Realities while they were cherished,
All, they exclaim, is gone! The Vision and Hope have departed!

IV

𝔚𝔬𝔯𝔰𝔱 𝔞𝔫𝔡 𝔰𝔞𝔡𝔡𝔢𝔰𝔱! As under Milton's lowermost Tophet   25
Yawned another yet lower*, so for the mourning Million
Still is there deeper woe! Patriot, Orator, Prophet,
Some who a few years agone stood proudly in the Pavilion
Of their land's rights and liberties, gazing abroad through its casement
On the fair Future they fondly deemed at hand for their nation,   30
Now not alone succumb to the Change and the Degradation,
But have ceased even to feel them! God! *this* indeed is abasement!

V

𝔦𝔰 the last hope, then, gone? Must we lie down, despairing?
No! there is always hope for all who will dare and suffer;
Hope for all who will mount the Hill of Exertion, uncaring   35
Whether their path be brighter or darker, smoother or rougher;
No! there is always hope for those who, relying with earnest
Souls on God and themselves, take for their motto, 'Labour.'
Such see the rainbow's glory where Heaven looms darkest and sternest;
Such in the storm-wind hear but the music of pipe and tabor.   40

VI

𝔉𝔬𝔩𝔩𝔬𝔴 your destiny up! Work! Write! Preach to arouse and
Warn and warm and encourage! Dangers, no doubt, surround you—
But, for Ten threatening you now, you will soon be appalled by a Thousand
If you forsake the course to which Virtue and Honor have bound you!
O, persevere!—persevere! Falter not!—faint not!—shrink not!   45
Hate and Hostility serve but as spurs to the will of the Zealous—
Though your foes flourish awhile, and you *seem* to decline, be not jealous!
Help from 'the Son of Man cometh in such an hour as you think not!'

---

* 'And in the lowest deep a lower deep
        . . . . opens wide.'

VII
𝔖lavery debases the soul, yea reverses its primal nature.
Long were our fathers bowed to the earth by fetters of iron—   50
And, alas! wE inherit the failings and ills that environ
Slaves like a dungeon-wall, and dwarf their original stature.
Look on your countrymen's failings with less of anger than pity—
Even with the faults of the Evil deal in a manner half-tender,
And, like an army encamped before a beleaguered city   55
Earlier or later you *must* compel your foes to surrender!

[VIII]
𝔏o, a 𝔑ew 𝔜ear! a year, into whose bosom Time gathers
All the past lessons of ages—a mournful but truth-teaching muster.
All the rich thoughts, and deeds, and the marvellous lore of our fathers,
All the sun-light experience that makes men wiser and juster.   60
Hail it with steadfast resolve—thankfully if it befriend you—
Guardedly lest it betray—without either Despair or Elation,
Panoplied inly against the sharpest ills it may send you,
But with a high hope still for yourselves and the RISE OF YOUR NATION.

[IX]
𝔒men -full, arched with gloom, and laden with many a presage,   65
Many a portent of woe, looms the Impending Era.
Not, as of old, by Comet-sword,* Gorgon, or ghastly Chimera,
Scarcely by Lightning and Thunder, Heaven to-day sends its message.
Into the secret heart—down through the caves of the spirit,
Pierces the silent Shaft—sinks the invisible Token—   70
Cloaked in the Hall the Envoy stands, his mission unspoken,
While the pale banquetless guests await in trembling to hear it.

                                        [J. C. M., *Nation*, 1 January 1848]

---

* 'At this time there was plainly seen in the sky a comet or star, shaped like a sword.'—(DEFOE)
Plague of 1666.

Hush-a-By Baby
A LULLABY, FROM THE IRISH OF OWEN ROE O'SULLIVAN,
AS SUNG BY HIM TO HIS CHILD

I
O, hush-a-by Baby! Why weepest thou?
The diadem yet shall adorn thy brow—
And the jewels thy sires had long agone
In the regal ages of Eoghan and Conn
 Shall all be thine!   5
 O, hush-a-by, hush-a-by, child of mine!
 My sorrow, my woe, to see thy tears
 Pierce into my heart like spears!

II
I'll give thee that glorious Apple of Gold
The three fair Goddesses sought of old—   10
I'll give thee the diamond Sceptre of Pan,
And the Rod with which Moses, that holiest man,
 Wrought marvels divine!
 O, hush-a-by, hush-a-by, child of mine!

III
I'll give thee that Courser, fleet on the plains, 15
That Courser with golden saddle and reins
Which Falvey rode, the Mariner-lord,
When the blood of the Danes at Cashel-na-n-Ord*
 Flowed like to dark wine,
 O, hush-a-by, hush-a-by, child of mine! 20

IV
I'll give thee the dazzling Sword was worn
By Brian on Cluan-tarava's† morn,
And the Bow of Murrogh, whose shaft shot gleams
That lightened as when the arrowy beams
 Of the Noon-Sun shine,   25
 O, hush-a-by, hush-a-by, child of mine!

* Viz. Cashel of the Orders, or Friars.
† *Cluan-tarabh, i.e.* Clontarf.

V
And the Hound that was wont to speed amain
From Cashel's Rock to Bunratty's plain,
And the Eagle from gloomy Aherlow,
And the Hawk of Skellig—all these I'll bestow   30
    On thee and thy line,
    O, hush-a-by, hush-a-by, child of mine!

VI
And the Golden Fleece that Jason bore
To Hellas's hero-peopled shore,
And the Steed that Cuchullin bought of yore,   35
With matals* and torques† and golden store,
    And meadows and kine,
    O, hush-a-by, hush-a-by, child of mine!

VII
And Connal's unpierceable Shirt of Mail,
And the Shield of Nish, the Prince of the Gael,   40
These twain for thee, my babe, shall I win,
With the flashing Spears of Achilles and Finn,
    Each high as a pine—
    O, hush-a-by, hush-a-by, child of mine!

VIII
And the Swords of Diarmid and fierce Fingal,   45
The slayers on heath, and—alas! in hall—
And the charmed Helmet Osgar wore
When he left Mac Treóin to welter in gore,
    Subdued and supine—
    O, hush-a-by, hush-a-by, child of mine!   50

IX
And the Jewel wherewith Queen Eefa proved
The valor and faith of the hero she loved
The magic Jewel that nerved his arm
To work his enemies deadly harm
    On plain and on brine!   55
    O, hush-a-by, hush-a-by, child of mine!

* Cloaks   † Neck ornaments.

X
And the wondrous Cloak, renowned in Song,
The enchanted Cloak of the dark Dubh-long,
By whose powerful aid he battled amid
The thick of his foes, unseen and hid. 60
    This, too, shall be thine—
    O, hush-a-by, hush-a-by, child of mine!

XI
The last, not least, of thy weapons, my Son,
Shall be the glittering Glaive of O'Dunn;
The gift from Aonghus's powerful hands, 65
The hewer-down of the Fenian bands,
    With edge so fine!
    O, hush-a-by, hush-a-by, child of mine!

XII
And a Princess, too, transcending all
Who have held the hearts of men in thrall— 70
Transcending Helen of Historie—
Thy bride in thy palmier years shall be;
    Thy bride and thy heroine,
    O, hush-a-by, hush-a-by, child of mine!

XIII
Even Hebe, who fills the nectar up 75
For Jove, in his luminous crystal cup,
Shall pour thee out a Wine in thy dreams
As bright as thy poet-father's themes,
    When inspired by the Nine.
    O, hush-a-by, hush-a-by, child of mine! 80

XIV
And silken robes and sweet soft cakes,
Shalt thou wear and eat beyond thy mates.
Ha, see!—here comes thy mother, Moreen—
She, too, has the soul of an Irish Queen—
    She scorns to repine! 85
    Then, hush-a-by, hush-a-by, child of mine—
    My sorrow, my woe, to see thy tears,
    Pierce into my heart like spears!
            [J. C. M., *DUM*, February 1848]

St Patrick's Hymn before Tarah
(FROM THE ORIGINAL IRISH)

THE original Irish of this hymn was published eight years ago, by Dr Petrie, in vol. xviii, 'Transactions of the Royal Irish Academy.' It is in the Bearla Feine, the most ancient dialect of the Irish, the same in which the Brehon laws were written. It was printed from the 'Liber Hymnorum,' preserved in the Library of Trinity College, Dublin, a manuscript, which, as Dr. Petrie proves by the authority of Usher and others, must be nearly 1250 years old. [. . .] The translation now presented to the public, is rigidly, wonderfully literal, the best substitute that can be had for the original, since it is not yet in our power to effect what ought to be one of the great objects of an IRISH CATHOLIC MAGAZINE—the publication, in their native dress, of every fragment of religious literature that ever made the heart swell with the glories of the olden times, or scorn the threats of the tyrant in later ages.

The original is exclusively Irish, except the closing words, which are in Latin, namely, '*Domini est salus, Domini est salus. Christi est salus, salus tua Domine sit semper nobiscum.*'

In the old 'Liber Hymnorum' the hymn is prefaced by the following prose statement in Irish, which we give in the words of the learned translator:

'St Patrick composed this hymn. In the time of Leogaire, the son of Nial, it was composed. The cause of its composition was to protect himself with his monks against the enemies unto death, who were in ambush against the clergy. And this is a religious armour to protect the body and soul against demons and men and vices. Every person who sings it every day with all his attention on God, shall not have demons appearing to his face. It will be a protection to him against every poison and envy. It will be a safeguard to him against sudden death. It will be an armour to his soul after death. Patrick sang this at the time that the snares were set for him by Leogaire, that he might not come to propagate the faith at Temur (Tarah).'—ED. of *Duffy's Irish Catholic Magazine*

I
AT TARAH TO-DAY, in this awful hour,
  I call on the Holy Trinity!
Glory to Him who reigneth in power,
The GOD of the elements, Father, and Son,
And Paraclete Spirit, which Three are the One,   5
  The ever-existing Divinity!

II

AT TARAH TO-DAY I call on the Lord,
On Christ, the Omnipotent Word,
Who came to redeem from Death and Sin
 Our fallen race;   10
 And I put and I place
The virtue that lieth and liveth in
 His Incarnation lowly,
 His Baptism pure and holy,
His life of toil, and tears, and affliction,   15
His dolorous Death—his Crucifixion,
His Burial, sacred and sad and lone,
 His Resurrection to life again,
His glorious Ascension to Heaven's high Throne,
And, lastly, his future dread   20
 And terrible coming to judge all men—
Both the Living and Dead . . . . .

III

AT TARAH TO-DAY I put and I place
 The virtue that dwells in the Seraphim's love,
And the virtue and grace   25
 That are in the obedience
 And unshaken allegiance
 Of all the Archangels and angels above,
And in the hope of the Resurrection
To everlasting reward and election,   30
And in the prayers of the Fathers of old,
And in the truths the Prophets foretold,
And in the Apostles' manifold preachings,
And in the Confessors' faith and teachings,
And in the purity ever dwelling   35
 Within the immaculate virgins' breast,
And in the actions bright and excelling
 Of all good men, the just and the blest . . . . .

IV

AT TARAH TO-DAY, in this fateful hour,
I place all Heaven with its power,   40
And the sun with its brightness,

And the snow with its whiteness,
And fire with all the strength it hath,
And lightning with its rapid wrath,
And the winds with their swiftness along their path,   45
And the Sea with its deepness,
And the rocks with their steepness,
And the earth with its starkness,*
    All these I place,
    By GOD's almighty help and grace,   50
Between myself and the Powers of Darkness.†

V
    AT TARAH TO-DAY
    May GOD be my stay!
May the strength of GOD now nerve me!
May the power of GOD preserve me!   55
May GOD the Almighty be near me!
  May GOD the Almighty espy me!
May GOD the Almighty hear me!
  May GOD give me eloquent speech!
May the arm of GOD protect me!   60
May the wisdom of GOD direct me!
  May GOD give me power to teach and to preach!
May the shield of GOD defend me!

* Properly, 'strength,' 'firmness,' from the Anglo-Saxon, *stark*, 'strong,' 'stiff'.
† 'Powers of Darkness.'— It has been conjectured, we perceive, that this hymn would not be considered orthodox in the 17th century, and that no other reason can be assigned why Colgan, who certainly must have had a copy in his possession, did not publish or take farther notice of it. The conjecture we believe is groundless. There is nothing in the hymn inconsistent with sound doctrine, nothing that requires even an explanation, except, perhaps the introduction of the 'whiteness of the snow, the force of fire, the swiftness of the wind,' &c. &c. in this verse, and the allusion to the spells of 'woman, smiths, and Druids' in line thirteen, of strophe vi. The appeal to the elements of nature appears to us to be only a repetition, at least in spirit, of the words of the Psalmist, 'Praise ye Him, O sun and moon; praise Him, all ye stars and light—praise the Lord from the earth—fire, hail, snow, ice, stormy winds, which fulfil his word.'—*Ps.* 148. [. . .] As to the prayer against the spells of Druids, &c. &c., it is sufficient to say that there has been always an order of exorcists in the Church—the 'women' may have been the 'bean-draoid' or sorceress: that one smith, at least, was reputed a magician, see note 126, p.40.—*Antiquities of Tarah Hill.*—ED.

May the host of GOD attend me,
  And ward me,   65
  And guard me,
Against the wiles of demons and devils,
Against the temptations of vices and evils,
Against the bad passions and wrathful will
  Of the reckless mind and the wicked heart   70
Against every man who designs me ill,
  Whether leagued with others or plotting apart!

VI

  IN THIS HOUR OF HOURS
  I place all those powers
Between myself and every foe,   75
  Who threaten my body and soul
  With danger or dole,
To protect me against the evils that flow
From lying soothsayers' incantations,
From the gloomy laws of the Gentile nations,   80
From Heresy's hateful innovations,
From Idolatry's rites and invocations.
  Be those my defenders,
  My guards against every ban,
And spells of smiths, and Druids, and women;   85
In fine, against every knowledge that renders
The light Heaven sends us dim in
The spirit and soul of Man!

VII

  MAY CHRIST, I PRAY,
  Protect me to-day   90
  Against poison and fire,
Against drowning and wounding,
That so, in His grace abounding,
  I may earn the Preacher's hire!

VIII

  CHRIST, as a light,
  Illumine and guide me!   95
CHRIST, as a shield, o'ershadow and cover me!

CHRIST be under me! CHRIST be over me!
　　CHRIST be beside me
　　On left-hand and right!　　　　　　　　　　　　　　　　　100
CHRIST be before me, behind me, about me!
CHRIST this day be within and without me!

IX
CHRIST, the lowly and meek,
　CHRIST, the All-Powerful, be
In the heart of each to whom I speak,　　　　　　　　　　　　105
　In the mouth of each who speaks to me!
　　In all who draw near me,
　　　Or see or hear me!

X
AT TARA TO-DAY, in this awful hour,
　I call on the Holy Trinity!　　　　　　　　　　　　　　　　110
Glory to Him who reigneth in power,
The GOD of the Elements, Father, and Son,
And Paraclete Spirit, which Three are the One,
　The ever-existing Divinity!

XI
Salvation dwells with the Lord,　　　　　　　　　　　　　　115
With CHRIST, the Omnipotent Word.
From generation to generation
Grant us, O Lord, thy grace and salvation!
　　[J. C. M., *Duffy's Irish Catholic Magazine*, February 1848]

A Vision
A.D. 1848

I
In the vastness of Night,
　In the Valley of Dream,
　When our thoughts, like a stream
That in vain seeks the light,
Yet rolls onward in might,　　　　　　　　　　　　　　　　5

Sweep in legions along
   The lone paths of the soul,
Dark, chainless, and strong,
A chariot-like throng,
   That mock our control!—   10
In that spectralest hour,
   In that Valley of Gloom,
    Fell a Voice on mine ear,
Like a wail from the tomb,
   Or that dread cry which Fear   15
Gives our Angels of Doom,*
But of world-waking power.
   What it spake ye shall hear.

II

THE ANOINTING

1839–1842

'Thus the Oracle saith:
   The land long had lain bound   20
As in fetters of Death.
In the soul-killing cup
   Her despairing sons drowned
Half the sense of their woe,
   Half the life of their shame,   25
Till the Great GOD rose up,
And sent a Man forth,
   Who enkindled a flame
Of celestialest glow
   East and west, south and north.   30
At the Man's high command,
There woke life through the land,
   As God had forespoken,
And the red bowl was broken,
   And the chain fell asunder   35
Which—worst bondage of all!—
Had held Mind in its thrall
   Through long ages. This wonder,
Of heaven's own appointing,
Was IRELAND's Anointing.   40

---

* The Banshees.

III

THE MUSTER
1842–1845

'𝕿𝖍𝖚𝖘 𝖙𝖍𝖊 𝕺𝖗𝖆𝖈𝖑𝖊 𝖘𝖆𝖎𝖙𝖍:
  The Great GOD once again
Cast a glance down beneath,
And, behold! there uprose
  A Man among men,   45
With a soul stern and warm,
And a voice like the storm
When through midnight it blows.
And the people by millions
  At the Man's call assembled,   50
Under Heaven's blue pavilions,
And they heard from him words
That pierced them like swords,
For the Man spake with might
Of Strength, Freedom, and Right,   55
And the Powers in high places
Looked on; and some trembled,
And more hid their faces.
This marvel of story—
This sunburst of glory—   60
Unmatched for its lustre,—
Was Ireland's 𝕲𝖗𝖆𝖓𝖉 𝕸𝖚𝖘𝖙𝖊𝖗.

IV

THE FAMINE
1845–1848

'𝕿𝖍𝖚𝖘 𝖙𝖍𝖊 𝕺𝖗𝖆𝖈𝖑𝖊 𝖘𝖆𝖎𝖙𝖍:
  The 𝕬𝖓𝖔𝖎𝖓𝖙𝖊𝖉 must fall—
The Weak Ones must yield   65
Up in silence their breath
  Ere the Last Scene of all.
For that scene must behold
But stern spirits and bold,
  When the Lord takes the field.   70

Therefore Famine first came
And then Pestilence came,
  And careered through the land
Like twin giants of Flame—
And men's hearts were updried,   75
  And a seventh of that Band,
Who are still to be tried,
Fell in death, mute, unmanned,
And with names writ in sand.
There fell One for each Seven—   80
  Pray thou peace for their souls
In the homesteads of Heaven!
  Hark! *another* Bell knolls
  Than for *their* vanished souls.
It sounds from afar   85
With an omenful peal—
With a clangor most like
That ye hear when men strike
With sharp steel upon steel.
  'Tis the Tocsin of War!'   90

V

THE END
1848–185*

So the Oracle spake,
  And was silent once more.
  Then medreamt I turned round,
For I felt the earth quake,
And I saw in the West   95
  A cloud lurid as gore,
Looming shoreward and seaward,
And nearing to me-ward;
And I heard, as I guessed,
  The far-echoing sound   100
Of a trumpet, with tones,
  And lightnings and thunders,
As ye read of in John's
  Revelation of Wonders.
What meant they? I trow not.   105

What might next befal?
And how ended All?
This, too, friends, I know not—
For here were my cords
  Of Sleep suddenly broken,   110
    The bell booming Three;
But there seemed in mine ears,
  As I started up, woken,
A noise like fierce cheers,
Blent with clashings of swords,   115
  And the roar of the sea!
   [J. C. M., *United Irishman*, 26 February 1848]

Sacred Irish Poetry

['Holy are the Works of Mary's Blessed Son']

THE original Irish of the following poem, by John Murphy, is the property of
Mr. John Daly, Assistant Secretary of the Celtic Society. The author was born in
the year 1700, at Rathaoineach, parish of Whitechurch, county of Cork. At the
early age of 26, he had finished a copy of Dr. Keating's History of Ireland; and if
we can judge from the large folio and other volumes in his handwriting, in
possession of Mr. Daly, his life must have been devoted exclusively to the liter-
ature of his country. Some of the pieces are original, but far the greater portion
are transcripts on all subjects interesting to the Irishmen of his time, especially
several pieces on the sufferings of Ireland in 1641 and 1689, from contemporary
poets, the contention of the bards which worked the genius of Irish poetry and
prognoscity at the commencement of the seventeenth century, and a very mis-
cellaneous and interesting collection of the ancient religious and bardic history
of Ireland:

Naomhtha ceáirda mhic Mhuire

Holy are the Works of Mary's Blessed Son.
Holy are His Mercies unto every one.
Holy is the Sun that lighteth Heaven.
Holy is the Weather, morn and even.

Holy is the Wind, that woos the flowers.   5
Holy are the gentle April Showers.
Holy is the Summer's cheering Glow.
Holy is the Rain GOD sends below.
Holy are all in His Abodes of Love.
Holy is every Heaven of His above.   10
Holy is the Sun and every Star.
Holy is He who sends their light afar.
Holy are the Winds that fall and rise.
Holy are the Water and the Skies.
Holy is all outspread beneath His eye.   15
Holy are the Birds He formed to fly.
Holy are the Hazel woodlands green.
Holy are the Vineyards in their sheen.
Holy are the Fruits they bear and bring.
Holy is the Earth from which they spring.   20
Holy is the ever-circling Heaven.
Holy is every thought to JESUS given.
Holy is all that He hath made and sees.
Holy are all His ways and His decrees.
Holy are the Oceans, Strands, and Floods.   25
Holy are the dark umbrageous Woods.
Holy are the Herbs and Plants and Flowers.
Holy is all Creation, with its powers.
Holy are the Earth's four corner-bosoms.
Holy are the mossy Rocks and Blossoms.   30
Holy is Fire, that giveth light and cheer.
Holy is all that I have written here.
Holy is the Sea's Voice, calm or hoarse.
Holy are the Streamlets in their course.
Holy are the Heathy Moorlands bare.   35
Holy are the Fishes, and the Air.
Holy are the Counsel and the Will.
Holy are GOD's Works, and pure from ill.
Holy are His Laws, His Faith and Troth.
Holy are his Wrath and Patience both.   40
Holy is Heaven, with its Nine Orders bright.
Holy is JESUS, its Great Lord and Light.
Holy is Heaven above all Holiness.
Holy is the King the Angels bless.

Holy are the Saints in Heaven that be. 45
Holy is the Adorable Trinity.
Holy are all High Heaven's works and words.
Holy is Love, the Saints' Love, and the Lord's.
 [J. C. M., *Duffy's Irish Catholic Magazine*, March 1848]

Irish National Hymn

I

 O! Ireland! Ancient Ireland!
  Ancient! yet for ever young!
 Thou our mother, home and sireland—
  Thou at length hast found a tongue—
   Proudly thou, at length, 5
   Resistest in triumphant strength.
Thy flag of freedom floats unfurled;
 And, as that Mighty God existeth,
 Who giveth victory when and where He listeth,
Thou yet shall wake and shake the nations of the world. 10

II

 For this dull world still slumbers,
  Weetless of its wants or loves,
 Though, like Galileo, numbers
  Cry aloud, 'It moves! it moves!'
   In a midnight dream, 15
   Drifts it down Time's wreckful stream—
All march, but few descry the goal,
 O! Ireland! be it thy high duty
 To teach the world the might of Moral Beauty,
And stamp God's image truly on the struggling soul. 20

III

 Strong in thy self-reliance,
  Not in idle threat or boast,
 Hast thou hurled thy fierce defiance
  At the haughty Saxon host—
   Thou hast claimed, in sight 25
   Of high Heaven, thy long-lost right.

Upon thy hills—along thy plains—
  In the green bosom of thy valleys,
  The new-born soul of holy freedom rallies,
And calls on thee to trample down in dust thy chains! 30

IV

    Deep, saith the Eastern story,
      Burns in Iran's mines a gem,
    For its dazzling hues and glory
      Worth a Sultan's diadem.
        But from human eyes 35
        Hidden there it ever lies!
The aye-travailing Gnomes alone,
  Who toil to form the mountain's treasure,
  May gaze and gloat with pleasure without measure
Upon the lustrous beauty of that wonder-stone. 40

V

    So is it with a nation
      Which would win for its rich dower
    That bright pearl, Self-Liberation—
      It must labour hour by hour.
        Strangers, who travail 45
        To lay bare the gem, shall fail:
Within itself must grow, must glow—
  Within the depths of its own bosom
  Must flower in living might, must broadly blossom,
The hopes that shall be born ere Freedom's Tree can blow. 50

VI

    Go on, then, all-rejoiceful!
      March on thy career unbowed!
    IRELAND! let thy noble, voiceful
      Spirit cry to God aloud!
        Man will bid thee speed— 55
        God will aid thee in thy need—
The Time, the Hour, the Power are near—
  Be sure thou soon shalt form the vanguard
  Of that illustrious band whom Heaven and Man guard:—
And these words come from *one whom some have called a Seer*. 60
        [James Clarence Mangan, *United Irishman*, 13 May 1848]

The Tribune's Hymn for Pentecost

I
Pure Spirit of the Alway-Faithful GOD!
   Kindler of Heaven's true light within the soul!
From the lorn Land our sainted fathers trod,
   Ascends to Thee our cry of Hope and Dole!
      Thee, Thee, we praise!   5
      To Thee we raise
Our choral Hymn in these awakening days!
   O! send us down anew that fire
   Which of old lived in David's and Isaiah's Lyre!

II
Centuries had rolled, and Earth lay tomb'd in sleep,   10
   The nightmare sleep of Nations beneath Kings;
And far abroad o'er Liberty's Great Deep
   Death's Angel waved his black and stilling wings.
      Then struck Thine Hour!
      Thou, in Thy Power,   15
But breathedst, and the Free stood up, a Tower;
   And Tyranny's thrones and strongholds fell,
   And men made jubilee for an abolished Hell.

III
And she, our Mother-home, the Famed, the Fair,
   The Golden House of Light and Intellect,   20
Must she still groan in her intense despair?
   Shall she lie prone while Europe stands erect?
      Forfend this, Thou
      To whom we vow
Souls even our giant wrongs shall never bow!   25
   Thou wilt not leave our Green Flag furled,
   Or bear that we abide the by-word of the world!

IV
Like the lost lamp that burned in Tullia's tomb
   Through ages vainly with unwaning ray,
Our star of Hope lights but a path of gloom,   30
Whose false track leads us round and round alway.

But Thou canst ope
A gate from Hope
To Victory: Thou canst nerve our arms to cope
  With looming Storm and Danger still,   35
  And lend a Thunder-voice to the land's Lightning-will!

V
Descend, then, Spirit of the Eternal King!
  To Thee, to Him, to His Avenging Son,
The Triune GOD, in boundless trust we cling.
  His help once ours, our nationhood is won.   40
    We watch the Time,
    Till that sublime
Event shall thrill the Free of every clime.
  Speed, Mighty Spirit, speed its march,
  And thus complete for earth Mankind's Triumphal Arch! 45
              [James Clarence Mangan, *Irish Tribune*, 17 June 1848]

An Ode of Hafiz

I can't but think you much in the wrong, Prophet,
  When you cursed the swine and the wine-grape's juice.
Trust me, this is the short and long of it,
  Every thing pleasant has its use.
This is as true as is the Koran—   5
  I will maintain it against a host.
The sage of Mecca, with all his lore, ran
  Here his wise head against a post.
Great, undoubtedly, was Mohammed—
  Great in all his divine affairs;   10
But the man who banished good wine and ham, said
  More, believe me, than his prayers.
Both suit most tastes—I could hardly take on
  Myself to say which is most to mine;
But I almost think, to save my bacon,   15
  I'd 'go the whole hog,' and give up the wine!
              [Unsigned, *DUM*, November 1848]

from *Lays of Many Lands–No. VI*

Elleen A-Ruin
(FROM THE IRISH OF CARROL O'DALY)

I
For ever, for ever, you have my heart,
     O, Elleen a-Ruin!
'Tis rueful, 'tis woeful, when lovers part,
     O, Elleen a-Ruin!
Mayo would I travel from morn to night,   5
For one sweet smile from your face of light,
For one soft kiss from your red lips bright,
     My Elleen a-Ruin!

II
O! how shall I woo you—how make you mine—
     Fair Elleen a-Ruin!   10
Can warm words win you?—can gold?—can wine?
     Sweet Elleen a-Ruin?
I would walk the wide world from east to west,
Inspired by love, if I could but rest
One heavenly hour on your beauteous breast,   15
     O, Elleen a-Ruin!

III
Come with me, come with me, then, darling one!
     Come, Elleen a-Ruin!
The moments are precious—O, let us be gone,
     My Elleen a-Ruin!   20
To the uttermost bounds of the world I'll go
With you, my belovèd, come weal or woe;
You, you are my Heaven on Earth below,
     O, Elleen a-Ruin!

IV
And all my glad kindred shall welcome you,   25
     My Elleen a-Ruin!
With a hundred thousand welcomes true,
     Sweet Elleen a-Ruin!

And Love and rich Plenty shall bless our home,
As though 'twere a royallest palace-dome;   30
We both will be happy till Death shall come,
    O, Elleen a-Ruin!
            [J. C. M., *DUM*, November 1848]

from *Lays of Many Lands—No. VII*

The Irish Language
(FROM THE DAN MHOLADH NA GAOIDHEILGHE
OF PHILIP FITZGIBBON, A KILKENNY POET)

I
The language of Erin is brilliant as gold;
It shines with a lustre unrivalled of old.
Even glanced at by strangers to whom 'tis unknown,
It dazzles their eyes with a light all its own!

II
It is music, the sweetest of music, to hear;   5
No lyre ever like it enchanted your ear.
Not the lute, or the flute, or the quaint clarionet,
For deep richness of tone could compete with it yet!

III
It is fire to the mind—it is wine to the heart—
It is melting and bold—it is Nature and Art!   10
Name one other language, renowned though it be,
That so wakes up the soul, as the storm the deep sea!

IV
For its bards,—there are none in cell, cottage, or hall,
In the climes of the haughty Iberian and Gaul,
Who despair not to match them—their marvelful tones   15
Might have won down the gods of old Greece from their thrones!

V
Then it bears back your spirit on History's wings
To the glories of Erin's high heroes and kings,
When the proud name of Gael swelled from ocean to shore,
Ere the days of the Saxon and Northman of yore.   20

VI

Is the heart of the land of this tongue undecayed?
Shall the Sceptre and Sword sway again as they swayed?
Shall our Kings ride in triumph o'er war-fields again,
Till the sun veils his face from the hosts of the slain?

VII

O, then shall our halls with the Gaelic resound,   25
In the notes of the harp and the *claoirseach** half-drowned,
And the banquet be spread, and the chess-board all night
Test the skill of our Chiefs, and their power for the fight.

VIII

Then our silken-robed minstrels, a silver-haired band,
Shall rewake the young slumbering blood of the land,   30
And our bards no more plaintive on Banba's dark wrongs,
Shall then fill *two* worlds† with the fame of their songs.

IX

And the gates of our *Brughaidhs*‡ again shall stand wide,
And their *cead mile failte* woo all withinside,
And the travel-tired wayfarer find by the hearth   35
Cheery Plenty where now, alas! all is black Dearth.

X

The down-trodden Poor shall meet kindness and care,
And the Rich be so happy to spare and to share!
And the Mighty shall rule unassailed in their might,
And all voices be blent in one choir of delight!   40

XI

The bright Golden Era that poets have sung
Shall revive, and be chaunted anew in our tongue;
The skies shall rain Love on the land's breadth and length,
And the grain rise like armies battalioned in strength.

---

* Bagpipes.
† Viz., America and Europe.
‡ Public Victuallers.

XII

The priest and the noble, the serf and his lord,   45
Shall sustain one another with word and with sword—
The Learned shall gain more than gold by their lore,
And all Fate took away she shall trebly restore.

XIII

Like rays round a centre, like stars round the moon,
Like Ocean round Earth, when it heaves in the noon,   50
Shall our chiefs, a resplendent and panoplied ring,
In invincible valour encircle their King.

XIV

And thou, O, Grand Language, please Heaven, shalt win
Proud release from the tomb thou art sepulchred in.
In palace, in shieling, on highway, on hill,   55
Shalt thou roll as a river, or glide as a rill!

XV

The history of Eiré shall shine forth in thee;
Thou shalt sound as a horn from the lips of the Free;
And our priests in their forefathers' temples once more
Shall through Thee call on men to rejoice and adore!   60
                         [J. C. M., *DUM*, January 1849]

The Vision of Egan O'Reilly

(For the original of the following poem, now translated for the first time, I am
indebted to my friend, Mr. O'Daly, publisher, of Bedford-row. Its author,
Eghan O'Rahilly, was a native of Cork, and flourished in the earlier half of the
eighteenth century.)

I

    The loveliest of the Lovely
I met upon my path, with honeysuckle rich bestrewn,
    And million daisies all as bright
As the rayed stars that round the moon
     'Mid Heaven's blue wells of light   5
      Above lie.

II
　　　Than purest crystals clearer
Were her translucent eyes, like fairy mirrors to behold
　　　Much marvelling, I, who had but read
Of such bright orbs in tales of old,   10
　　　　With blent amaze and dread
　　　　　　Drew near her.

III
　　　I saw her hair so golden,
Her more than mortal brow, her beautiful and delicate nose,
　　　Her cheeks, like Heaven on gilded eves,   15
Or like the blushing virgin rose
　　　　When Summer sees its crimson leaves
　　　　　　Unfolden.

IV
　　　In accents like the Spanish
She warbled me a tale, a tale of hope in him who stood   20
　　　With myriad armed hosts, prepared
For fight,—that youth of regal blood
　　　　Whom Saxon power had dared
　　　　　　To banish.

V
　　　Another tale thereafter   25
She also sang to me, a tale of mournfulness and ill,
　　　And days whose annals Time should blot—
When Erin's every glen and hill
　　　　Should ring aloud, but not
　　　　　　With laughter.   30

VI
　　　What shame it seemed, what pity,
In one so vile as I to stand before a Queen like her!
　　　I felt a thrill of agony;
I feared myself her worshipper,
　　　　So inly moved it me   35
　　　　　　Her ditty!

VII

    'O! holy Virgin Mother!'
I groaned within my heart, 'protect from evil wiles and spells
      Thy now so lone and helpless child!
O! for one peal from Patrick's bells!*   40
      For thus was ne'er beguiled
          Another!'

VIII

    As water from a fountain
Gushed forth my burning tears; and, with a faint, unearthly cry,
      The fair enchantress fled away.   45
I followed, till I reached the high
      Brow of Sliev Cruachra's grey
          Old mountain.

IX

    There stood a glorious mansion,
All bright and lighted up with lamps that shone like starry spheres,   50
      A dwelling never reared by Dole!
A house to banish cares and fears,
      And give the endungeoned soul
          Expansion!

X

    So dreamt I in my folly!   55
Alas! how sadly soon my brilliant dream dissolved to nought!
      For this was Cror, that far-famed pile
Upreared by arts the Druid taught,
      And dark with every wile
          Unholy!   60

XI

    Ere long came round me thronging,
In multicolored shapes, a weird and wild and wizard band.
      I shrieked, and feared my soul was lost.
O! once again secure to stand
      In Daltry then was most   65
          My longing!

---

*The hand-bells which St. Patrick carried about him were popularly supposed to possess the power of charming away evil spirits. The largest of those bells—a genuine relic—is at present in the possession of my worthy friend, Dr Petrie.

XII

    And now—a sight to blast me!
I saw my bright unknown dragged forward by a troop of churls,
      Who buffeted her beauteous face,
And tossed and tore her golden curls,   70
        Till all, in whirlwind race,
           Swept past me!

XIII

    Anon the scene was shifted—
She stood before me anew, the loveliest nymph below the skies,
      With graces past the power of Art;   75
I gazed into her diamond eyes,
      And felt my sunken heart
         Uplifted.

XIV

    But worlds of sorrow deeper
It sank down, down again, as, pointing to her waist she shewed   80
      Me underneath her jewelled cloak
A zone, whereon those dark words glowed—
      'The Wearer of the Yoke,
        And Weeper.'

XV

    'Depart,' she said, 'O, mortal!   85
Me to my midnight lot, me in my bondage must thou leave!
      But I shall yet be born anew!
Meanwhile, I may but groan and grieve—
      The path to Life lies through
         Death's portal!'   90

XVI

    And lo! a thunderous tremor
Shook all the enchanted pile: I saw before me spread the green
      And thickly honeysuckled plains;
But trace of Cror no more was seen
      Than at this day remains   95
         Of Temor!

THE SUMMING UP

     Alas, for us, the Darkened!
We dream our years away; we mingle False and True in one.
     Pain chides us now; now Pleasure chains;—
But we are taught by nought and none—   100
       God's voice itself remains
          Unhearkened!

              [J. C. M., *Irishman*, 27 January 1849]

Duhallow

(FROM THE IRISH OF CHARLES BOY M'QUILLAN)

I

Far away from my friends,
  On the chill hills of Galway,
My heart droops and bends,
  And my spirit pines alway—
'Tis as not when I roved   5
  With the wild rakes of Mallow—
All is here unbeloved,
  And I sigh for Duhallow.

II

My sweetheart was cold,
  Or in sooth I'd have wept her—   10
Ah! that Love should grow old
  And decline from his sceptre!
While the heart's feelings yet
  Seem so tender and callow!
But I deeplier regret   15
  My lost home in Duhallow!

III

My steed is no more,
  And my hounds roam unyelling;
Grass waves at the door
  Of my dark-windowed dwelling.   20

Through sunshine and storm
  Corrach's acres lie fallow;
Would Heaven I were warm
  Once again in Duhallow!

IV
In the blackness of night,   25
  In the depths of disaster,
My heart were more light
  Could I call myself master
Of Corrach once more
  Than if here I might wallow   30
In gold thick as gore
  Far away from Duhallow!

V
I loved Italy's show
  In the years of my greenness,
Till I saw the deep woe,   35
  The debasement, the meanness,
That rot that bright land!
  I have since grown less shallow,
And would now rather stand
  In a bog in Duhallow!   40

VI
This place I'm in here,
  On the grey hills of Galway,
I likc for its cheer
  Well enough in a small way;
But the men are all short,   45
  And the women all sallow;
Give M'Quillan his quart
  Of brown ale in Duhallow!

VII
My sporting days o'er,
  And my love-days gone after,   50
Not earth could restore
  Me my old life and laughter.

Burns now my breast's flame
  Like a dim wick of tallow,
Yet I love thee the same   55
  As at twenty, Duhallow!

VIII
But my hopes, like my rhymes,
  Are ex(s)pelled and expended;
What's the use of old times
  When *our* time is nigh ended?   60
Drop the talk! Death will come
  For the debt that we all owe,
And the grave is a home
  Quite as old as Duhallow!
    [J. C. M., *Irishman*, 24 February 1849]

EPIGRAM
The Richest Caliph

I
'O, Caliph!' 'twas said to the great Haroun,
'On us thou hast showered many a boon,
  For which we gratefully *pour* tears.
Never will Caliph again exist
Who will put so much gold in any man's fist,   5
  As thou in the fists of thy courtiers.'

II
'Your flattery, dodges and dogs! is no go,'
The Caliph replied—'I'd have you to know,
  And, you rascally robbers! I warn ye a
Day will arrive when a Caliph shall give   10
More gold in a day than I while I live,
  And his name will be Caliph-ornia.'
    [Unsigned, *Irishman*, 3 March 1849]

March Forth, Eighteen Forty-nine!

I

Nightly must I make my choice
  Between ill dreams and restless pillows,
But once in sleep I heard a voice,
  Commingling with the roll of billows;
And, in accents deep, it gave   5
  Utterance to this mystic line—
March Fourth, Eighteen Forty-nine!—
  Then sank silent as the grave—
March Fourth, Eighteen Forty-nine,
Or, perchance, as I opine,   10
March forth, Eighteen Forty-nine!

II

March Fourth, Eighteen Forty-nine—
  The day has come, nor yet departed,
But it revokes my thraldom's ban;
  And I, the faint, the feeble-hearted,   15
Shell and shadow of a man,
  Arise, like one refreshed with wine.
A treasure of more golden worth
  Than California's Mine, is mine,
From this fourth day—from this day forth—   20
  This fourth March, Eighteen Forty-nine!

III

March Fourth, Eighteen Forty-nine.
  O, would that, standing up myself,
I could but see my country stand too!
  Would Heaven that now the Irish Guelph   25
Would sink the Past, and stretch the hand to
  The wronged and suffering Ghibelline!*
That North and South—that West and East,
  Would this bright day at last combine!
But I will still cry out at least—   30
  'March forth, Eighteen Forty-nine!'

* My readers are, of course, familiar with the melancholy history of those rival Italian factions, the Guelphs and Ghibellines.

IV

March forth, Eighteen Forty-nine!
  Yet, not as marched thy predecessor,
With flashing glaive and cannon-peel.
  Of no law, human or divine,   35
Shalt thou be, even in thought, transgressor.
  Strike with amaze—but not with steel!
Blood enough has flowed, Heaven knows,
  Even at Freedom's holy shrine.
Not by blowings-up, or blows,   40
  Shall conquer Eighteen Forty-nine!

V

March forth, Eighteen Forty-nine—
  Achieve thy grand and glorious mission,
Illumining minds and softening hearts,
  And cheering all who droop and pine,   45
And rescuing from the last perdition
  Slaves worse than those of Barbary's marts!
March forth, undeterred by sneers
  From spectators asinine—
Europe tracks thy way with cheers,   50
  March forth, Eighteen Forty-nine!

VI

March forth, Eighteen Forty-nine!
  Myself will march with thee, GOD willing,
Through thorniest paths of toil and pain,
  So stern Resolve no more decline   55
From its high throne, or sloth come chilling
  My spirit back to Death again!
March, then, sustained by Heaven above,
  And blessed by Man—the power is thine
To wake the world's repentant love,   60
  March—March forth, Eighteen Forty-nine!

March 4th, 1849.
                    [J. C. M., *Irishman*, 10 March 1849]

The Funerals

I

  It was a vision of the night,
    Ten years ago—
A vision of dim FUNERALS that passed
  In troubled sleep before my sight,
With dirges and deep wails of woe,   5
  That never died upon the blast!

II

  Swiftly,—not as with march that marks
    The earthly hearse,
Each FUNERAL swept onward to its goal—
  But, oh! no horror overdarks   10
The stanzas of my gloomsome verse
  Like that which then weighed down my soul!

III

  It was as though my Life were gone
    With what I saw!
Here were the Funerals of my thoughts as well!   15
  The Dead and I at last were One!
An ecstasy of chilling awe
  Mastered my spirit as a spell!

IV

  On, on, still on and on they swept,
    Silently, save   20
When the long FUNERAL chant rose up to Heaven,
  Or some wild mourner shrieked and wept—
Earth had become one groanful grave—
  The isles and lands were left bereaven!

V

  And on each hearse there sat enthroned   25
    A skeleton!
The FUNERALS showed him by a lurid gleam,
  And round each stood, as 'twere, enzoned,
Others, the like, so many a one
  They might have peopled worlds of Dream!   30

VI

  And towards the West at first they marched,
     Then towards the South—
Those endless FUNERALS, till the sky o'erhead,
  As one vast pall, seemed overarched
With blackness, and methought the mouth   35
  Of Hades had cast up its Dead!

VII

  And one night passed, and there was day—
     So dreamt I there!
The FUNERALS, then, had been but phantoms all—
  How cheats Imagination's play!   40
Give her illusions, thou, no care,
  O, Man! but hearken Reason's call!

VIII

  But night fell dark on Earth once more,
     And many a night,
And still the FUNERALS knew nor pause nor change;   45
  And ever nightly, as before,
I again felt dead to mark a sight
  So terrible, so dread, so strange!

IX

  What was this mystery? Years would seem
     To have rolled away,   50
Before those FUNERALS halted on their path—
  Were they but mockeries of a dream?
Or did the vision darkly say,
  That here were signs of looming wrath?

X

  I know not! but within the soul   55
     I know there lives
A deep, a marvellous, a prophetic power,
  Far beyond even its own control—
And why? Perchance, because it gives
  Dread witness of a JUDGMENT HOUR!   60
          [J.C.M, *Irishman*, 31 March 1849]

Gasparo Bandollo
An Anecdote of the South of Italy
(1820)

I

Once—twice—the stunning musquetry
    Peals echoing down the dark ravine.
    Sevrini's blood wells forth like wine.
Weak—footsore—faint as faint may be,
And powerless to resist or flee,   5
He drags him to a peasant's hovel.
'Ha! Giambattista!—thou, good boy?
One short hour's shelter! I can grovel
Unseen beneath yon scattered sheaves.
So!—there! Departing Daylight leaves   10
This nook dark; and, methinks, the spot
Is safe if thou betray me not.
Let me but baffle those base hounds!
If *mine* plead not, Italia's wounds
    May—that Italia *they* destroy!'   15
—He speaks, and crouches down, and gathers
    Around his limbs the light loose litter,
    With one deep groan, O, GOD, how bitter!
Given to the lost land of his fathers.

II

Hark! his pursuers follow after.   20
    On by the bloody track they follow.
Rings their fierce yell of demon laughter
    Upon the winds, adown the hollow.
Rings loud exulting yell on yell.
—'By Heaven!—See!—here the miscreant fell   25
And rose again!—and, if these black
Leaves mock us not, here fails the track!
Ha, so!—a hut! The hunted rebel
Hath earthed him here! Now, comrades, treble
Your care! A thousand gold Zecchini   30
    Are on the head, alive or dead,
Of the outlaw, Vascoló Sevrini!'

III
Half loth alike to leave or linger,
    In burst the slaves of Alien Law.—
        O! ruefullest of sights to see!   35
Mute stands yon trembler, but his finger
    Points to the blood-bedabbled straw,
        That blushes for his perfidy.
        Ill-starred Sevrini, woe for thee!
God be thy stay, thou Doomed One, thou!   40
Strong hands and many are on thee now;
Through the long gorge of that steep valley
They drag thee up Mount Bruno's brow,
And thy best bravery little skills!
O! stood'st thou on Calabria's hills,   45
With nought beside thine own good sword,
    With nothing save the soul that slumbers
Within thee now, to quell this horde!—
    But, bleeding—bound—o'erborne by numbers,
Thy day is by to strike and rally!   50
Thou fallest by the hands of cravens
    Rock-hardened against all remorse;
And Morn's red rays shall see the ravens
    Fleshing their foul beaks in thy corse!

IV
But Heaven and Earth are hushed once more.   55
    Young Giambattista's eyes are bent
In fearful glances on the floor.
But little weeneth he or weeteth
Of the deep cry his land repeateth
    In million tones of one lament.   60
Nought pondereth he of wars of yore,
Of battling Ghibelline and Guelph,
    And bootless fights and trampled lands,
    And Gallic swords and Teuton chains,
    His eye but marks yon dark-red stains.   65
Those red stains now burn on himself,
    And in his heart, and on his hands!

V

But sky and sea once more are still.
   The duskier shades of Eventide
Are gathering round Mount Bruno's hill.   70
The boy starts up, as from a dream;
   He hears a low, quick sound outside.
Was it the running valley-stream?
No! 'twas his father's foot that trod.
   Alas, poor nerveless youth! denied   75
      The kindling blood that fires thy race,
Dost thou not weep, and pray thy GOD
    That Earth might ope its depths, and hide
      Thee from that outraged father's face?

VI

The eye is dark, the cheek is hollow,   80
To-night of Gasparó Bandollo,
And his high brow shews worn and pale.
Slight signs all of the inward strife!
   Of the soul's lightning, swift to strike
    And sure to slay, but flashing never!   85
   For Man and Earth and Heaven alike
Seem for him voiceful of a tale
    That robs him of all rest for ever,
    And leaves his own right hand to sever
The last link binding him to Life!   90
Calm even to marble, stern and sad,
   He eyes the spots of tell-tale hue,
Then, turning to the cowering lad,
   With stirless lips but asks him, '*Who?*'

VII

'Oh, father!' cried the boy,—then, wild   95
   With terror of some dreadful doom,
He gasped for breath.—'Speak, wretched child!
Who sought my asylum, and from *whom?*
—'O, GOD! Sevrini!'—'From?————' 'The Sbirri.'—
'The fugitive was wounded, weary?'————   100
—'O, father! I—this dreary room————'

—'And thou betrayedst him?'—'O, Heaven!'—
—'And thou betrayedst him?'—'I—only———'
—'And thou betrayedst him?' 'O! hear me,
My father! I watch here so lonely   105
All day, and feel, oh! so bereaven,
   With not a sight or sound to cheer me!
My mind—my—But, I only pointed—
I spake not!'———And, with such disjointed
And feeble phrases, the poor youth,   110
Powerless to gloss the ghastly truth,
Sank on his knees with shrieks and tears
Before the author of his years.
—And *he?* What throes his breast might stifle
   Were hidden as beneath a pall.   115
   He merely turned him to the wall,
And, with closed eyes, took down his rifle.

VIII

'Go forth, boy!'—'Father! father!—spare'—
—'Go forth, boy! So! Now kneel in prayer!'
—'My GOD!—my father!'—'Ay, boy, right!   120
Hast now none other!'—There is light
Enough still for a deed of blood.
Stern man, whose sense of nationhood
So vanquishes thy love paternal,
And wilt thou, then, pollute this vernal   125
And virgin sod with gore even now,
And a son's gore? What answerest thou?
—'Kneel down!' Ay! he will kneel—and fall,
   Will kneel, and fall to rise no more,
    But not by thee shall thus be sped   130
The spirit of yon trembling thrall!
   Didst thou dream nought of this before?
    FATE slayeth him. Thy child is dead.

IX

The child is dead of old Bandollo,
And he, the sire, hath scarce to follow   135
His offspring to the last dark barrow,

So much hath Grief's long-rankling arrow
Forestalled for him that doom of Death
Which takes from Suffering nought save breath—
A grief that speaks, albeit untold,   140
And lives, where all seems dead and cold,
And finds no refuge in the Past,
And sees the Future overcast
With broader gloom than even the Present.
Better that thou, unhappy peasant,   145
Hadst died in youth and made no sign,
    Nor dreamt Life's Day must have an Even.
Better thy child's lot had been thine—
    The best lot after all! for Heaven
Most careth for such weakling souls.—   150
Onwards in power the wide flood rolls
Whose thunder-waves wake evermore
The caverned soul of each far shore,
But when the midnight storm-wind sweeps
In wrath above its broken deeps,   155
What heart but ponders darkly over
The myriad wrecks those waters cover!
It is the lowly brook alone
That winds its way with Music's tone
    By orange bower and lily-blossom,   160
And sinks into the Parent Wave,
Not as worn Age into its grave,
But as pure Childhood on God's bosom.
                    [J. C. M., *DUM*, May 1849]

Bear Up!

I
Time rolleth on; and, with our years,
  Our sorrows grow and multiply—
      Our visions fade;
With late remorse and withering fears
  We look for Light to days gone by,   5
      But all is Shade.

Our dear fond friends have long been gone;
  No moon is up in Heaven above;
    The chill winds blow;
The dolorous Night of Age comes on;   10
  The current of our Life and Love
    Moves low and slow.

II
Yet Earth hath still a twofold dower:
  On desert sands the palm-trees rise
    In greenest bloom: 15
The dawn breaks at the darkest hour;
  Stars brightliest shine when Midnight skies
    Are palled in gloom;
The Deep hath treasures unrevealed
  Of gold and gems and argosies,   20
    And gallant ships:
The sword strikes hurtless on the shield,
  And from the once plague-laden breeze
    Health greets thy lips!

III
Thou, therefore, Man, shalt never droop,   25
  Shalt never doubt, shalt always trust
    The power of GOD!
Thou art not Heaven's or Nature's dupe;
  This fleshly hull shall rot in dust,
    A trodden clod;   30
But shalt thou cower, though Death draw nigh?
  The mouldering frame, the eternal soul,
    Which, say, is best?
Thou canst not live unless thou die;
  Thou must march far to reach thy goal   35
    Of endless rest!

IV
Bear up! even though thou be, like me,
  Stretched on a couch of torturing pain
    This weary day,
Though Heaven and Earth seem dark to thee,   40

And thine eyes glance around in vain
    For one Hope-ray!
Though overborne by Wrong and Ill—
   Though thou hast drained, even to its lees,
     Life's bitter cup—   45
Though Death and Hell be round thee, still
   Place faith in GOD! He hears! He sees!
    Bear up! Bear up!
            [J. C. M., *Irishman*, 12 May 1849]

Ghazel
(FROM THE ARABIC OF MOHIR-IBN-MOHIR-IBN-KHALAKAN)

All that hath existence is eternal;
Therefore Bliss and Glory are eternal.
All that hath existence must remain;
Therefore Pain and Darkness are eternal.
All that hath existence must be twofold;   5
Wouldst thou have this proved? Behold the proof old
As the days of Abel and of Cain,
As the day when Abel perished, slain
By his murderous anti-brother Cain.
Love, and *therefore* Hate,—Good, *therefore* Evil,—   10
GOD, and *therefore* Man,—Man, *therefore* Devil.
Life, with all its well-known ways, and *therefore*
Death, with all its mysteries. 'But wherefore
Doth not GOD abolish Hell and Pain?'
Friend! He cannot. He can *not*. The twain   15
Have their being in a source eternal.
Action and Reaction. Here behold
The One Law by none to be controlled!
Leaven *with* Lump, or *neither* Lump nor Leaven.—
Heaven *and* Hell, or *neither* Hell nor Heaven—   20
Such is Nature, seen through Truth eternal.
GOD created Man first in His own
Image—but an image gives again
Back to thee the thing *reversed*—though fain
Would I, too, deny this truth eternal.   25

See this. Sift this. Test it. Know it. Plain
As the world it lives a truth eternal.
Have I spoken from a mind insane?
Am I cruel, or unkind, or vain?
Ah, friend! thou wilt know, when GOD's eternal   30
World of all worlds only shall remain,
That my tears were poured like wintry rain,
Even for him* whose doom the Prophet Issa†
Wailed for, too, in words that rest eternal.
More I say not now. The worst abyss a   35
Poet falleth down is tedious length.
Briefness is essential unto strength—
So, we part:—yet, take those words from me:
Blame not any. Love. Believe. And see
That thou keep thy conscience pure from stain.   40
Conscience also hath a life eternal.

[J. C. M., Irishman, 19 May 1849]

A Word in Reply to Joseph Brenan

(*Note.*—The Poets have fallen in love with each other—they like themselves much
better than their readers like them.—*Printer's Devil.*)

I
Friend and brother, and yet more than brother,
    Thou endowed with all of Shelley's soul!
Thou whose heart so burneth for thy Mother,‡
That, like *his*,§ it may defy all other
    Flames while time shall roll!   5

II
Thou of language bland and manner meekest,
    Gentle bearing, yet unswerving will—
Gladly, gladly, list I when thou speakest,
Honored highly is the man thou seekest
    To redeem from ill!   10

---

* Judas.   † Jesus.
‡ Ireland. Shelly's [*sic*] heart could not be burned.   § The allusion here.

III

Truly shewest thou me the One thing Needful!
  Thou art not, nor is the world, yet blind.
Truly have I been long years unheedful
Of the thorns and tares that choked the weedful
    Garden of my mind!   15

IV

Thorns and tares which rose in rank profusion
  Round my scanty fruitage and my flowers,
Till I almost deemed it self-delusion,
Any attempt or glance at their extrusion
    From their midnight bowers.   20

V

Dream and Waking Life have now been blended
  Longtime in the caverns of my soul—
Oft in daylight have my steps descended
Down to that Dusk Realm where all is ended,
    Save remeadless dole!   25

VI

Oft, with tears, I have groaned to GOD for pity—
  Oft gone wandering till my way grew dim—
Oft sung unto Him a prayerful ditty—
Oft, all lonely in this throngful city
    Raised my soul to Him!   30

VII

And from path to path His mercy tracked me—
  From a many a peril snatched He me,
When false friends, pursued, betrayed, attacked me,
When gloom overdarked, and Sickness racked me
    He was by to save and free!   35

VIII

Friend! thou warnest me in truly noble
  Thoughts and phrases! I will heed thee well—
Well will I obey thy mystic double
Counsel, through all scenes of woe and trouble
    As a magic spell!   40

IX

Yes! to live a bard in Thought and Feeling!
  Yes! to act my rhyme by self-restraint
This is Truth's, is Reason's deep revealing
Unto me from thee, as GOD's to a kneeling
    And entranced Saint!   45

X

Fare thee well! We now know each the other,
  Each has struck the other's inmost chords—
Fare thee well, my friend and more than brother,
And may Scorn pursue me if I smother
    In my soul thy words!   50

               [J. C. M., *Irishman*, 2 June 1849]

The Famine

I

It was a time when thoughts and violets bloomed—
  When skies were bright, and air was bland and warm,
And Pleasure every fleeting hour assumed
  A new and strange Cameleon hue and form.
When, suddenly, that hand-cloud, once beheld   5
From Carmel by the Tishbite seer of Eld—
  Appeared, and foresayed coming storm.

II

All minds were called away. The slumberers who
  Had slept through years of Idleness awoke—
All felt a consciousness of somewhat new,   10
  The lightning prelude to the thunder-stroke.
GOD struck on every heart, and men grew pale—
Their bliss was metamorphosed into bale.
  There was no Power they dared evoke!

III

Even as the dread Simoon of Araby   15
   Sweeps o'er the desert through the pathless air,
So came, 'mid Ireland's joy and revelry,
   That cloud of gloom above her visions fair.
The thoughtless wondered, and the thoughtful wept.
And those who through long years had dreamt and slept   20
   Arose—too many to Despair!

IV

Despair? Yes! For a blight fell on the land—
   The soil, heaven-blasted, yielded food no more—
The Irish serf became a Being banned—
   Life-exiled as none ever was before.   25
The old man died beside his hovel's hearth,
The young man stretched himself along the earth,
   And perished, stricken to the core!

V

O, GOD! Great GOD! Thou knowest, seest, Thou!
   All-blessed be Thy name! This work is Thine—   30
To Thy decrees, Thy law, Thy will, we bow—
   We are but worms, and Thou art THE DIVINE!
But Thou wilt yet in Thine own day redeem
Thy Faithful; and this land's bright sun shall beam
   To Earth a Pharos and a Sign!   35

VI

Ye True, ye Noble, who unblenching stand
   Amid the storms and ills of this dark Day,
Still hold your ground! Yourselves, your Fatherland,
   Have in the Powers above a surest stay!
Though Famine, Pest, Want, Sickness of the Heart,   40
Be now your lot—all these shall soon depart—
   And Heaven be yet at your command!

           [J. C. M., *Irishman*, 9 June 1849]

Still a Nation

(The following verses were written by our lamented friend a few weeks before his death.—ED. *Irishman*)

I
Yes! *we* stand a Nation still:
  Yes! we scorn the Saxon's threat:
Yes! the Celt hath yet a will—
  Hath a power and purpose yet.
The dark, stern resolve of soul,   5
  And the tenderness that melts
Earth, Heaven, Nature, in one whole—
  These are all the Celt's!

II
What makes Man immortal? *Love!*
  Steam-gun, power-loom, telegraph,   10
All in a brief few years will prove
  England's tombstone's epitaph!
In the breast, not in the brain,
  Burns the true Promethean fire;
Prostrate though thou long hast lain—   15
  Ireland, sound thy lyre!

III
Suffering, Patience, Faith, and Love,
  Such lot Heaven appointed thee;
Never country stronglier strove
  For the Crown of Liberty.   20
But thy mission rather seems
  This—to abide the Nation's thrall—
And, when *they* have dreamt their dreams,
  Then to awake them all!

IV
And, albeit I hasten home,—   25
  I, a nameless child of thine,
To the last, the lampless dome—
  Though I die, and make no sign,

My last thoughts shall be of thee—
    My rejoicings, my regret;   30
And even now I prophesy
    THY GRAND TRIUMPH YET!
        [James Clarence Mangan, *Irishman*, 8 September 1849]

The Expedition and Death of King Dathy
(FROM THE IRISH OF OWEN JOHN O'HENNESSY)

I
King Dathy assembled his Druids and Sages,
    And thus he spake them—'Druids and Sages!
        What of King Dathy?
What is revealed in Destiny's pages
    Of him or his? Hath he   5
Aught for the Future to dread or to dree?
Good to rejoice in, or Evil to flee?
    Is he a foe of the Gall*—
Fitted to conquer, or fated to fall?'

II
And Beirdra, the Druid, made answer as thus—   10
    A priest of a hundred years was he—
'Dathy! thy fate is not hidden from us!
    Hear it through me!
Thou shalt work thine own will!
    Thou shalt slay—thou shalt prey—   15
And be Conqueror still!
    Thee the Earth shall not harm!
    Thee we charter and charm
    From all evil and ill!
    Thee the laurel shall crown!   20
    Thee the wave shall not drown!
    Thee the chain shall not bind!

---

* Foreigner.

Thee the spear shall not find!
Thee the sword shall not slay!
Thee the shaft shall not pierce!   25
Thou, therefore, be fearless and fierce,
And sail with thy warriors away
  To the lands of the Gall,
  There to slaughter and sway,
  And be Victor o'er all!'   30

III
So Dathy he sailed away, away,
  Over the deep resounding sea;
Sailed with his hosts in armour grey
  Over the deep resounding sea,
Many a night and many a day,   35
  And many an islet conquered he—
He and his hosts in armour grey.
  And the billow drowned him not,
  And a fetter bound him not,
  And the blue spear found him not,   40
  And the red sword slew him not,
  And the swift shaft knew him not,
  And the foe o'erthrew him not.

IV
Till, one bright morn, at the base
  Of the Alps, in rich Ausonia's regions,   45
His men stood marshalled face to face
  With the mighty Roman legions.
    Noble foes!
Christian and Heathen stood there among those,
Resolute all to overcome,   50
Or die for the Eagles of Ancient Rome!

V
When, behold! from a temple anear
  Came forth an aged priestlike man,
Of a countenance meek and clear,
  Who, turning to Eire's Ceann,   55
Spake him as thus, 'King Dathy! hear!

Thee would I warn!
Retreat! retire! Repent in time
  The invader's crime,
Or better for thee thou hadst never been born!'   60

VI
But Dathy replied, 'False Nazarene!
  Dost thou, then, menace Dathy, thou?
  And dreamest thou that he will bow
To one unknown, to one so mean,
So powerless as a priest must be?   65
He scorns alike thy threats and thee!
On! on, my men, to victory!'

VII
And, with loud shouts for Eire's King,
  The Irish rush to meet the foe,
And falchions clash and bucklers ring,—   70
    When, lo!
Lo! a mighty earthquake's shock!
And the cleft plains reel and rock;
Clouds of darkness pall the skies;
    Thunder crashes,   75
    Lightning flashes,
And, in an instant Dathy lies
On the earth, a mass of blackened ashes!

VIII
Then, mournfully and dolefully,
  The Irish warriors sailed away   80
  Over the deep resounding sea,
Till, wearily and mournfully,
They anchored in Eblana's Bay.
Thus the Seanachies and Sages
Tell this tale of long-gone ages.   85

    ['Unpublished Poems of James Clarence Mangan', *Irishman*, 15 September 1849]

The Nameless One

THE following pictures, with vivid power and intensity of feeling, the soul-harassing consciousness that tortured our friend in his reflective moments:—

I

Roll forth, my song, like the rushing river
  That sweeps along to the mighty sea;
GOD will inspire me while I deliver
      My soul of thee!

II

Tell thou the world, when my bones lie whitening   5
  Amid the last homes of youth and eld,
That there was once one whose veins ran lightning
      No eye beheld.

III

Tell how his boyhood was one drear night-hour,
  How shone for *him*, through his griefs and gloom,   10
No star of all Heaven sends to light our
      Path to the tomb.

IV

Roll on, my song, and to after-ages
  Tell how, disdaining all earth can give,
He would have taught Men, from Wisdom's pages,   15
      The way to live.

V

And tell how, trampled, derided, hated,
  And worn by Weakness, Disease, and Wrong,
He fled for shelter to GOD, who mated
      His soul with song—   20

VI

With song which alway, sublime or vapid,
  Flowed like a rill in the morning-beam,
Perchance not deep, but intense and rapid—
      A mountain-stream.

VII

Tell how this Nameless, condemned for years long   25
   To herd with demons from Hell beneath,
Saw things that made him, with groans and tears, long
      For even Death.

VIII

Go on to tell how, with genius wasted,
   Betrayed in Friendship, befooled in Love,   30
With spirit shipwrecked, and young hopes blasted,
      He still, still strove—

IX

Till, spent with Toil, dreeing Death for others,
   And some whose hands should have wrought for *him*
(If children live not for sires and mothers),   35
      His mind grew dim;

X

And he fell far through that pit abysmal
   The gulf and grave of Maginn and Burns,
And pawned his soul for the Devil's dismal
      Stock of returns—   40

XI

But yet redeemed it in days of darkness,
   And shapes and signs of the Final Wrath,
When Death, in hideous and ghastly starkness,
      Stood on his path.

XII

And tell how now, amid Wreck and Sorrow,   45
   And Want, and Sickness, and houseless nights,
He bides in calmness the Silent Morrow
      That no ray lights.

XIII

And lives he still, then? Yes! Old and hoary
   At thirty-nine, from Despair and Woe,   50
He lives, enduring what future Story
      Will never know.

XIV

Him grant a grave to, ye pitying Noble,
  Deep in your bosoms! There let him dwell!
He, too, had tears for all souls in trouble,   55
      Here and in Hell.

['Unpublished Poems of James Clarence Mangan', *Irishman*, 27 October 1849]

from *The Poets and Poetry of Munster*

The Fair Hills of Eire O!
BY DONOGH MAC CON-MARA (THE RED)

AIR:—*'Uileacan Dubh O!'*

WE have no means of tracing the antiquity of the air to which these beautiful
words are written; but it may with probability be ascribed to the early part of the
seventeenth century. *'Uileacan Dubh O!'* literally means *a black-haired head of
round shape, or form;* and we have frequently heard it applied so by the Munster
peasantry, with whom it is a favourite phrase, when speaking of the head, par-
ticularly that of a female. Some writers are of opinion that *'Uileacan Dubh O!'*
allegorically means Ireland; but we cannot concur in this opinion, for it is
evidently a love expression. [...]

Take a blessing from my heart to the land of my birth,
    And the fair Hills of Eire, O!
And to all that yet survive of Eibhear's tribe on earth,
    On the fair Hills of Eire, O!
In that land so delightful the wild thrush's lay   5
Seems to pour a lament forth for Eire's decay—
Alas, alas! why pine I a thousand miles away
    From the fair Hills of Eire, O!

The soil is rich and soft—the air is mild and bland,
    Of the fair Hills of Eire, O!   10
Her barest rock is greener to Me than this rude land—
    O! the fair Hills of Eire, O!
Her woods are tall and straight, grove rising over grove;
Trees flourish in her glens below, and on her heights above,
O, in heart and in soul, I shall ever, ever love   15
    The fair Hills of Eire, O!

A noble tribe, moreover, are the now hapless Gael,
    On the fair Hills of Eire, O!
A tribe in Battle's hour unused to shrink or fail
    On the fair Hills of Eire, O!   20
For this is my lament in bitterness outpoured,
To see them slain or scattered by the Saxon sword.
Oh, woe of woes, to see a foreign spoiler horde
    On the fair Hills of Eire, O!

Broad and tall rise the *Cruachs* in the golden morning's glow   25
    On the fair Hills of Eirc, O!
O'er her smooth grass for ever sweet cream and honey flow
    On the fair Hills of Eire, O!
O, I long, I am pining, again to behold
The land that belongs to the brave Gael of old;   30
Far dearer to my heart than a gift of gems or gold
    Are the fair Hills of Eire, O!

The dew-drops lie bright 'mid the grass and yellow corn
    On the fair Hills of Eire, O!
The sweet-scented apples blush redly in the morn   35
    On the fair Hills of Eire, O!

The water-cress and sorrel fill the vales below;
The streamlets are hushed, till the evening breezes blow;
While the waves of the Suir, noble river! ever flow
 Near the fair Hills of Eire, O! 40

A fruitful clime is Eire's, through valley, meadow, plain
 And the fair land of Eire, O!
The very 'Bread of Life' is in the yellow grain
 On the fair Hills of Eire, O!
Far dearer unto me than the tones music yields, 45
Is the lowing of the kine and the calves in her fields,
And the sunlight that shone long ago on the shields
 Of the Gaels, on the fair Hills of Eire, O!

O'Tuomy's Drinking Song

AIR:—*'The Growling Old Woman'*

THE song which we lay before our readers was written by O'Tuomy amid those festive scenes for which his house was remarkable; and a reply to it, by the witty *Mangaire Sugach*, will be found on the next page.

Moderate time

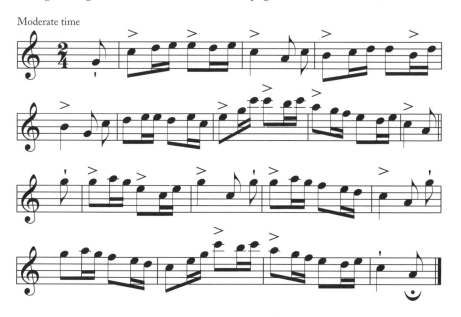

This pleasing air, though quite common in Munster, has, we believe, escaped the notice of Bunting. Like Moirin Ni Chuillionain, the poets made it a general theme for their effusions, some of which are in our collection, and rank highly among the Jacobite class peculiar to the middle of the last century. [...]

I sell the best brandy and sherry,
To make my good customers merry;
  But, at times their finances
  Run short, as it chances,
And then I feel very sad, very!   5

Here's brandy! Come, fill up your tumbler,
Or ale, if your liking be humbler,
  And, while you've a shilling,
  Keep filling and swilling,
A fig for the growls of the grumbler!   10

I like, when I'm quite at my leisure,
Mirth, music, and all sorts of pleasure.
  When Margery's bringing
  The glass, I like singing
With bards—if they drink within measure.   15

Libation I pour on libation,
I sing the past fame of our nation,
  For valor-won glory,
  For song and for story,
This, this is my grand recreation!   20

Andrew Magrath's Reply to John O'Tuomy

AIR:—*'The Growling Old Woman'*

O, Tuomy! you boast yourself handy
At selling good ale and bright brandy,
  But the fact is your liquor
  Makes everyone sicker,
I tell you that, I, your friend Andy.   5

Again, you affect to be witty,
And your customers—more is the pity—
  Give in to your folly,
  While you, when you're jolly,
Troll forth some ridiculous ditty.   10

But your poems and pints, by your favour,
Are alike wholly wanting in flavour;
  Because it's your pleasure,
  You give us short measure,
And your ale has a ditch-water savour!   15

Vile swash do you sell us for porter,
And you draw the cask shorter and shorter;
  Your guests, then, disdaining
  To think of complaining,
Go tipple in some other quarter.   20

Very oft in your scant overfrothing,
Tin quarts we found little or nothing;
  They could very ill follow
  The road, who would swallow
Such stuff for their inner man's clothing!   25

You sit gaily enough at the table,
But in spite of your mirth you are able
  To chalk down each tankard,
  And if a man drank hard
On tick—oh! we'd have such a Babel!   30

You bow to the floor's very level,
When customers enter to revel,
  But if one in shy raiment
  Takes drink without payment,
You score it against the poor devil.   35

When quitting your house rather heady,
They'll get nought without more of 'the ready.'
  You leave them to stumble
  And stagger, and tumble
Into dykes, as folk will when unsteady.   40

Two vintners late went about Killing
Men's fame by their vile Jack-and-Gilling;
  Now, Tuomy, I tell you
  I know very well you
Would, too, sell us all for a shilling. 45

The Old Bards never vainly shall woo me,
But your tricks and your capers, O'Tuomy,
  Have nought in them winning—
  You jest and keep grinning,
But your thoughts are all guileful and gloomy! 50

The Geraldine's Daughter*
BY EGAN O'RAHILLY

AIR:—'*Sea and Shore*'†

A Beauty all stainless, a pearl of a maiden,
  Has plunged me in trouble, and wounded my heart.
With sorrow and gloom is my soul overladen;
  An anguish is there, that will never depart.
I could voyage to Egypt across the deep water, 5
  Nor care about bidding dear Eire farewell,
So I only might gaze on the Geraldine's Daughter,
  And sit by her side in some pleasant green dell.

Her curling locks wave round her figure of lightness,
  All dazzling and long, like the purest of gold; 10
Her blue eyes resemble twin stars in their brightness,
  And her brow is like marble or wax to behold!
The radiance of Heaven illumines her features,
  Where the Snows and the Rose have erected their throne;
It would seem that the sun had forgotten all creatures 15
  To shine on the Geraldine's Daughter alone!

* Such of our readers as wish to become acquainted with the history of the Geraldines need only consult a work bearing that title, edited by the Rev. C.P. Meehan, for 'Duffy's Library of Ireland.'
† We have no recollection of ever having met this air; but such of our readers as have, will oblige by giving us some information about it.

Her bosom is swan-white, her waist smooth and slender,
  Her speech is like music, so sweet and so free;
The feelings that glow in her noble heart lend her
  A mien and a majesty lovely to see.   20
Her lips, red as berries, but riper than any,
  Would kiss away even a sorrow like mine.
No wonder such heroes and noblemen many
  Should cross the blue ocean to kneel at her shrine!

She is sprung from the Geraldine race—the great Grecians,   25
  Niece of Mileadh's sons of the Valorous Bands,
Those heroes, the sons of the olden Phenicians,
  Though now trodden down, without fame, without lands!
Of her ancestors flourished the Barrys and Powers,*
  To the Lords of Bunratty she too is allied;   30
And not a proud noble near Cashel's high towers
  But is kin to this maiden—the Geraldine's Pride!

Of Saxon and Gael there are none to excel in
  Her wisdom, her features, her figure, this fair;
In all she surpasses the far-famed Helen,   35
  Whose beauty drove thousands to death and despair.
Whoe'er could but gaze on her aspect so noble
  Would feel from thenceforward all anguish depart,
Yet for me 'tis, alas! my worst woe and my trouble,
  That her image will always abide in my heart!   40

---

* *Paoraig agus Barraig*, Powers and Barrys, two ancient and respectable families in the county of Cork.
  The Powers are descended from Robert le Paure, or Poer, Marshal to Henry II., from whom, in 1177, he obtained a grant of Waterford, the city itself and the cantred of the Ostmen alone excepted. So early as the fifteenth century the descendants of Le Poer renounced the English legislature, and embraced the Brehon law and Irish customs.
  The male race of the Powers, Viscounts Decies and Earls of Tyrone, became extinct by the death of Earl James in 1704. His only daughter, Lady Catherine Poer, married Sir Marcus Beresford, Bart., who was created Lord Viscount Tyrone by George II.
  The Barrys are descended from Robert Barry, who came over in 1169 with Fitz-Stephen.

Conor O'Riordan's Vision

Air:—'The Mower'

Conor O'Riordan, author of this song, was a native of West Muskerry (Muscraidhe), in the county of Cork, and flourished a.d. 1760. He followed the occupation of parish schoolmaster in his native district, whence he obtained the appellation of 'Conchubhair Maister' (Conor Master), by which he is better known at this day, and from which many if his compositions, current among the peasantry of Cork, take their name. He had a son named Peter, who 'lisped in numbers,' but not with that inspiration which fired the father's poetic muse. He followed the profession of his father, and went by the name of *Peadair Maister* (Peter Master), but we cannot tell when, or where, either of the Riordans closed his earthly career. [...]

Moderately slow

Once I strayed from Charleville,
 As careless as could be;
I wandered over plain and hill,
 Until I reached the Lee—
And there I found a flowery dell   5
Of a beauty rare to tell,
With woods around as rich in swell
 As eye shall ever see.

Wild birds warbled in their bower
  Songs passing soft and sweet;   10
And brilliant hues adorned each flower
  That bloomed beneath my feet.
All sickness, feebleness, and pain,
The wounded heart and tortured brain
Would vanish, ne'er to come again,   15
  In that serene retreat!

Lying in my lonely lair,
  In sleep medreamt I saw
A damsel wonderfully fair,
  Whose beauty waked my awe.   20
Her eyes were lustrous to behold,
Her tresses shone like flowing gold.
And nigh her stood that urchin bold—
  Young Love, who gives Earth law!

The Boy drew near me, smiled and laughed,   25
  And from his quiver drew
A delicately pointed shaft
  Whose mission I well knew;
But that bright maiden raised her hand,
And in a tone of high command   30
Exclaimed, 'Forbear! put up your brand,
  He hath not come to woo!'

'Damsel of the queenly brow,'
  I spake, 'my life, my love,
What name, I pray thee, bearest thou   35
  Here or in Heaven above?'
—'Banba and Eire am I called,
And Heber's kingdom, now enthralled,
I mourn my heroes fetter-galled,
  While all alone I rove!'   40

Together then in that sweet place
  In saddest mood we spoke,
Lamenting much the valiant race
  Who wear the exile's yoke,*

---

* Here the poet laments the persecutions suffered by his brethren of the bardic profession at this period; because of the exposure which they made of the delinquencies of state officials and men in authority, they were looked upon as the greatest evil the supreme power had to contend with.

And never hear aught glad or blithe,   45
Nought but the sound of spade and scythe;
And see nought but the willow withe,
   Or gloomy grove of oak.

'But hear! I have a tale to tell,'
   She said—'a cheering tale;   50
The Lord of Heaven, I know full well,
   Will soon set free the Gael.
A band of warriors, great and brave,
Are coming o'er the ocean-wave;
And you shall hold the lands GOD gave   55
   Your sires, both hill and vale.

'A woeful day, a dismal fate,
   Will overtake your foes,
Grey hairs, the curses of deep hate,
   And sickness and all woes,   60
Death will bestride them in the night—
Their every hope will meet with blight,
And GOD will put to utter flight
   Their long-enjoyed repose!

'My curse be on the Saxon tongue,   65
   And on the Saxon race!
Those foreign churls are proud and strong,
   And venomous and base.
Absorbed in greed, and love of self,
They scorn the poor:—slaves of the Guelph,   70
They have no soul except for pelf.
   God give them sore disgrace!'

The Coolun

THE Coolun, or *Cul fionn*, literally means *The maiden of the fair flowing locks*. In Hardiman's 'Irish Minstrelsy,' Vol. i., p. 251, will be found another version of this song in six stanzas, with a translation by Thomas Furlong, the original of which has been attributed to Maurice O'Dugan (*Muiris Ua Duagain*), an Irish bard who lived near Benburb, in the county of Tyrone, about the middle of the seventeenth century, but is probably of much greater antiquity.

The air of this song is by many esteemed the finest in the whole circle of Irish music, and to it Moore has adapted his beautiful melody, 'Though the last glimpse of Erin with sorrow I see.'

The three stanzas here given are all that we have been able to procure of this song, after a diligent search in Munster, where our version is in the hands of every peasant who has any pretensions to being a good songster.

Moderately slow

Have you e'er seen the Coolun when daylight's declining,
With sweet fairy features, and shoes brightly shining?
Though many's the youth her blue eyes have left pining,
She slights them, for all their soft sighing and whining.

Have you e'er on a summer's day, wandering over   5
The hills, O, young man, met my beautiful rover?
Sun-bright is the neck that her golden locks cover—
Yet each paltry creature thinks *she* is his lover!

Have you e'er seen my Fair, on the strand, in her bower,
With gold-ringed hands, culling flower after flower?   10
O! nobly he said it, brave Admiral Power,
That her hand was worth more than all Erin for dower.

Caitilin Ni Uallachain

BY WILLIAM HEFFERNAN (THE BLIND)

SEVERAL imperfect versions of this song are already before the public, and were we not anxious to preserve the best copy, we might pass it over in silence. *Caitilin Ni Uallachain* (Catharine Holahan) is another of those allegorical names by which Ireland is known in Irish song; and for an account of the author, *Uilliam Dall O'Hearnain* (William Heffernan, the Blind), we have only to refer our readers to p. 92 of our 'Reliques of Irish Jacobite Poetry.' With respect to the prefix '*Ni*,' used before surnames in the feminine gender, we may close these observations with an extract from Conor Mac Sweeny's 'Songs of the Irish, No. VI.,' where he says 'It is proper here to warn Irish ladies that they commit a blunder in writing their names with *O* or *Mac* instead of *Ni*. [. . . A] lady who writes *O* or *Mac* to her name calls herself son, instead of daughter. What should we say of a Hebrew lady who should write herself 'Esther *Son* of Judah?' and yet we do not notice the absurdity in ourselves. I therefore advise every Irish lady to substitute *Ni*, pronounced *Nee*, for *O* or *Mac*. Julia Ni Connell, Catharine Ni Donnell, Ellen Ni Neill, will at first sound strange, but they are not a whit less euphonious than the others, and use will make them agreeable. In Irish we never use O or Mac with a woman's name, and why must it be done in English?' [. . .]

In vain, in vain we turn to Spain—she heeds us not.
Yet may we still, by strength of will, amend our lot.
O, yes! our foe shall yet lie low—our swords are drawn!
For her, our Queen, our *Caitilin Ni Uallachain!*

Yield not to fear! The time is near—with sword in hand   5
We soon shall chase the Saxon race far from our land.
What glory then to stand as men on field and bawn,
And see all sheen our *Caitilin Ni Uallachain!*

How tossed, how lost, with hopes all crossed, we long have been!
Our gold is gone; gear have we none, as all have seen.   10
But ships shall brave the Ocean's wave, and morn shall dawn
On Eire green, on *Caitilin Ni Uallachain!*

Let none believe this lovely Eve outworn or old—
Fair is her form; her blood is warm, her heart is bold.
Though strangers long have wrought her wrong, she will not fawn—   15
Will not prove mean, our *Caitilin Ni Uallachain!*

Her stately air, her flowing hair—her eyes that far
Pierce through the gloom of Banba's doom, each like a star,
Her songful voice that makes rejoice hearts Grief hath gnawn,
Prove her our Queen, our *Caitilin Ni Uallachain!*   20

We will not bear the chains we wear, not bear them long.
We seem bereaven, but mighty Heaven will make us strong.
The God who led through Ocean Red all Israel on
Will aid our Queen, our *Caitilin Ni Uallachain!*

O, Virgin pure! our true and sure defence thou art!   25
Pray thou thy Son to help us on in hand and heart!
Our Prince, our Light, shall banish night—then beameth Dawn—
Then shall be seen our *Caitilin Ni Uallachain!*

SUMMING-UP
[*by* O'Daly]
Phoebus shines brightly with his rays so pure,
The moon and stars their course do run;   30
The sky is shining brightly without cloud or mist,
To greet the true king with his troops o'er the sea.

Our priests are as one man imploring Christ,
Our bards are songful, and their gloom is dispelled;
The poor Gaels of Inis-Eilge are in calm repose,   35
Expecting James,* the son of James, and the Duke† to land.

Donall na Greine

OF Donall na Greine, the hero of this song, little is known. We find the following allusion to him in a Jacobite ballad by the Rev. Patrick O'Brian [. . .]

> 'Beidh hata maith beabhair,
>   Air *Dhomhnall na Greine,*
> Da chathadh is na speartha le mor-chroidhe.'

> *Donal na Greine*
>   Shall have a fine beaver,
> Which he will toss to the skies with delight.

Our own opinion is, that *Donall* was a fellow who loitered his time idly basking in the sun, as his cognomen *na Greine* (of the sun) would indicate, and consequently became a fitting subject for the poets to display their wit upon.

On this air the Scotch have founded their 'Bucky Highlander,' which was by some wag burlesqued in an Anglo-Irish rhyme beginning thus:—

> Praties and butter would make a good supper
>   For Bucky Highlander,
>   For Bucky Highlander.

Of Arthur Wallace we know little; but we have seen some records of a family of that name living in Cork about a century ago—patrons of poets and poetry—and it is probable that 'Arthur' was a distinguished member of this family.

We forgot placing the following stanza in the hands of our poetical translator:—

> Bion Domhnall air meisge 's a bhean ag ol uisge,
>   'S a phaisdighe a beice—'s a phaisdighe a beice

---

* The Chevalier de St. George.
† James, second Duke of Ormond.

Olfach se a d-tuillean se, 's da m-beidheach a thuille 'ge,
   Donall na Greine—Donall na Greine.

Donall is drunk, and his wife drinking water,
   And the children screaming, and the children screaming.

He'd drink what he earns, and more if he got it,
   Donall na Greine! Donall na Greine!

Wild Donall na Greine!—his frolics would please ye,
   Yet Wallace, confound him,
   Came trickishly round him!
He'd sit, without winking, in alehouses drinking
   For days without number,   5
   Nor care about slumber!

O! jovial and funny—a spender of money—
   A prince at his Table,
   Was Donall the Able!
The Soul of Good-breeding, in fashions his leading   10
   Was copied and stuck to
   By tradesman and buck too!

Old crones, of diseases, of coughings, and sneezes,
    He'd cure without catch-up,
    And quarrels he'd patch up.   15
With flattery and coaxing, with humbug and hoaxing,
    And song-singing daily,
    He'd pass the time gaily.

O! he was the spalpeen* to flourish an alpeen!†
    He'd whack half a hundred,   20
    And nobody wondered!
He'd have taught a right new way to Long-handed Lughaidh,
    Or Great Alexander,
    That famous Commander.

On water and land he was equally handy,   25
    He'd swim without fear in
    A storm o'er Lough Erin!
Not a man born of woman could beat him at *coman*,‡
    Or at leaping could peer him,
    Or even come near him!   30

Every artisan's tool he would handle so coolly—
    From the plough to the thimble,
    Bright Donall the Nimble!
A blacksmith and tailor, a tinker and nailer,
    And weaver of cambrick,   35
    Was also the same brick!

He made stout shoes for winter—he shone as a printer,
    He'd shape a wheelbarrow,
    A plough and a harrow!
His genius for glazing was really amazing,   40
    And how in Cork city
    He'd harp to each ditty!

---

* *Spalpeen* (*rectius*, spailpin), a person following the spade—a spade-officer.

† *Alpeen* (*rectius*, ailpin), a wattle. Used at country fairs in faction fights.

‡ Hurling.

In a week's time, or shorter, with stones and with mortar,
    He'd rear a high stronghold,
    And a bridge that would long hold.   45
With wood from the valley he's build a gay galley,
    To cleave the deep waters
    To Greece of the Slaughters!

He reigned a musician without competition,
    And coursed like a jockey,   50
    O'er ground the most rocky.
'Twas he that was able to make bed and table—
    And breeches to match you,
    Of sheepskin he'd patch you.

No churl and no grumbler, he'd toss off his tumbler,   55
    And chat with a croney,
    In speech sweet as honey.
For the Fair and the Richer he'd shape a neat pitcher
    For gin or for sherry
    To make the heart merry.   60

With married and single he'd oftentimes mingle,
    And many's the maiden
    He left sorrow-laden.
A wig for a noble he'd make without trouble,
    Hat, saddle, and bridle—   65
    He couldn't be idle!

All airs, pure or garbled, that ever were warbled
    By harpers or singers,
    He had on his fingers!
Greek, Erse, English, Latin, all these he was pat in,   70
    And what you might term an
    O'erwhelmer in German!

Long, long, they'll regret him, and never forget him,
    The girls of Cork city,
    And more is the pity!   75
What more? By his courage he topped all in our age—
    To him, then, be glory!
    And so ends my story.

Black-haired Fair Rose*

Slow time

Since last night's star, afar, afar, Heaven saw my speed;
I seem'd to fly o'er mountains high, on magic steed,
I dashed though Erne:—the world may learn the cause from *Love*;
For, light or sun shone on me none, but *Roisin Dubh!*

My friends! my prayers for marts and fairs are these alone—   5
That buyers haste home ere evening come, and sun be gone;
For, doors, bolts all, will yield and fall, where picklocks move—
And faith the Clerk may seize i'the dark, my *Roisin Dubh!*

O, Roisin mine! droop not nor pine, look not so dull!
The Pope from Rome hath send thee home a pardon full!   10
The priests are near: O! never fear! from Heaven above
They come to thee—they come to free my *Roisin Dubh!*

* We present the reader with two different settings of this air, for from their extraordinary beauty
we could not justly omit either. *Rois Gheal Dubh* (Black-haired Fair Rose), sometimes written
Roisin Dubh (Dark-haired little Rose), sometimes written *Roisin Dubh* (Dark-haired little Rose),
is supposed to be one of these names by which Ireland is known in the language of allegory.

Thee have I loved—for thee have roved o'er land and sea:
My heart was sore;—it evermore beat but for thee.
I could but weep—I could not sleep—I could not move; 15
For, night and day, I dreamed alway of *Roisin Dubh!*

Through Munster's lands, by shores and strands, far could I roam,
If I might get my loved one yet, and bring her home.
O, sweetest flower, that blooms in bower, or dell, or grove,
Thou lovest me, and I love thee, my *Roisin Dubh!* 20

The sea shall burn, the earth shall mourn—the skies rain blood—
The world shall rise in dread surprise and warful mood—
And hill and lake in Eire shake, and hawk turn dove—
Ere you shall pine, ere you decline, my *Roisin Dubh!*

Little Black-haired Rose*

O, bitter woe, that we must go, across the sea!
O, grief of griefs, that Lords and Chiefs, their homes must flee!
A tyrant-band o'erruns the land, this land so green,
And, though we grieve, we still must leave our Dark *Roisin!*

My darling Dove, my Life, my Love, to me so dear, 5
Once torn apart from you, my heart will break, I fear,
O, golden Flower of Beauty's bower! O, radiant Queen!
I mourn in bonds; my soul desponds; my Dark *Roisin!*

In hope and joy, while yet a boy, I wooed my bride;
I sought not pelf; I sought herself, and nought beside, 10
But health is flown, 'tis old I'm grown; and, though I ween
My heart will break, I must forsake my Dark *Roisin!*

---

* This song was sent us as the composition of a Munster bard; but upon examination we found it deficient of that smooth and graceful flow peculiar to Munster poetry. The merit of the translation, however, entitle [*sic*] it to a place in the present collection.

The original song of *Roisin Dubh* is supposed to have been composed in the reign of Elizabeth for the celebrated *Aodh Ua Domnaill*, Prince of *Tir Chonaill* (Tirconnell). The allegorical allusions to Ireland under the name of *Roisin* have long been forgotten, and it is now sung by the peasantry merely as a love song.

The fairest Fair you ever were; the peerless Maid;
For bards and priests your daily feasts were richly laid.
Amid my dole, on you my soul still loves to lean,   15
Though I must brave the stormy wave, my Dark *Roisin!*

In years gone by, how you and I seemed glad and blest!
My wedded wife, you cheered my life, you warmed my breast!
The fairest one the living sun e'er decked with sheen,
The brightest rose that buds or blows, is Dark *Roisin!*   20

My guiding Star of Hope you are, all glow and grace,
My blooming Love, my Spouse above all Adam's race;
In deed or thought you cherish nought of low or mean;
The base alone can hate my own—my Dark *Roisin!*

O, never mourn s one forlorn, but bide your hour;   25
Your friends ere long, combined and strong, will prove their power.
From distant Spain will sail a train to change the scene
That makes you sad, for one more glad, my Dark *Roisin!*

Till then, adieu! my Fond and True! adieu, till then!
Though now you grieve, still, still believe we'll meet again;   30
I'll yet return, with hopes that burn, and broad-sword keen;
Fear not, nor think you e'er can sink, my Dark *Roisin!*

Edmund of the Hill

Edmund O'Ryan, better known as *Eamonn an Chnoic* (Edmund, or Ned of the
Hill), was born at Shanbohy, in the parish of Temple-beg, in the upper half
barony of Kilnemanagh, in Tipperary, previous to the wars of 1691. His father,
who being possessed of a considerable amount of property after the confis-
cations and plunders of 1641, was descended from the valiant and warlike race of
the O'Ryans, of Kilnelongurty, many of whom lost their lives and properties in
the obstinate, but ineffectual struggle for independence, by the Earl of
Desmond, in the reign of Elizabeth. His mother was of the ancient family of the
O'Dwyers, lords of Kilnemanagh. Edmund was intended for the priesthood; but
by an occurrence in which he took a prominent part after his return from the
Continent, where he had studied for the clerical profession, he had to relinquish

that idea. After many strange vicissitudes in life, his body now lies interred on the lands of Curraheen, near Faill an Chluig, in the parish of Toem, in the upper half barony of Kilnemanagh, near the Hollyford copper mine, and the precise spot is marked on sheet 45 of the Ordnance Survey of Tipperary, as the grave of *Eamonn an Chnoic.*

We have received a long sketch of him from a distinguished literary member of the family, but are obliged to reserve it for another volume.

Moderately slow

'You, with voice shrill and sharp,
Like the high tones of a harp,
Why knock you at my door like a warning?'
'I am Ned of the Hill,
I am wet, cold, and chill,   5
Toiling o'er hill and vale since morning'—
'Ah, my love, is it you?
What on earth can I do?
My gown cannot yield you a corner.
Ah! they'll soon find you out—   10
They'll shoot you, never doubt,
And it's I that will then be a mourner!'

'Long I'm wandering in woe,
  In frost and in snow,
No house can I enter boldly;   15
  My ploughs lie unyoked—
  My fields weeds have choked—
And my friends they look on me coldly!
  Forsaken of all,
  My heart is in thrall: 20
All-withered lies my life's garland,
  I must look afar
  For a brighter star,
Must seek my home in a far land!

'O! thou of neck fair,   25
  And curling hair,
With blue eyes flashing and sparkling!
  For a year and more
  Has my heart been sore,
And my soul for thee been darkling.   30
  O, could we but both,—
  You nothing loth,—
Escape to the wood and forest,
  What Light and Calm,
  What healing balm,   35
Should I have for my sorrows sorest!

'My fond one and dear,
  The greenwood is near,
And the lake where the trout is springing—
  You will see the doe,   40
  The deer and the roe,
And will hear the sweet birds singing,
  The blackbird and thrush
  In the hawthorn bush,
And the lone cuckoo from his high nest,   45
  And you never need fear,
  That Death would be near,
In this bright scenery divinest!'

O! could the sweet dove,
  The maiden of my love,   50
But know how fettered is her lover!
  The snows all night
  Fell in valley and on height,*
Through our fated island over,
  But ere the sun's rays   55
  Glance over seven days,
She and I, as I hope, will renew love;
  And rather would I be
  Deep drowned in the sea,
Than be faithless to her, my true love!   60

     [James Clarence Mangan, *Poets and Poetry of Munster*, November 1849]

from *The Tribes of Ireland: A Satire, by Angus O'Daly*

I

I BEGIN WITH THE MAC MAHON

I'd travel the island of Banba all o'er,
  From the sea to the centre,
  Before I would enter
That niggard Mac Mahon his damnable door!
  He'll give you the ghost of a dinner
That leaves you, by jing, rather hungrier and thinner!

III

WHAT I THINK OF THE FEENAGHTYS

They are blackguards the whole of the Feenaghty tribe,
  They are swindlers and schemers,
  And awful blasphemers.
They are worse, in good sooth, than I care to describe
  Moreo'er, if you sit at their table
You'll soon think the Barmecide's banquet no fable!

---

* From this and the preceding line it would appear that the song was composed in the year of the great frost, 1739.

IV

HOW THEY DINED ON SHROVE TUESDAY

I called on them once on Shrove Tuesday at night,
  But the devil a pancake,
  Flour, oatmeal, or brancake
In parlour or kitchen saluted my sight,
  I walked off. I'd have starved ere I'd pray to
One thief of the gang for a single potato!

VI

THE O'BYRNES

I got some roast meat in house of O'Byrne
  Though I can't tell you whether
  'Twas goat's flesh or leather,
But for drink I plumbed vainly jug, pitcher, and churn
  And a tallish tin tankard with delf nose
What swash they *do* tipple is more than myself knows!

VII

OF THE PIG-JOBBERS OF GRANARD

The sooty-faced swineherds of Granard I hate,
  They are shabby and seedy
  In garb, and though greedy
As cormorants over the pot and the plate,
  Yet, O Heavens! only think! in their utter
Abasement, they really—eat bread without butter!

IX

AS TO CLONTOBRED

Should you visit that hungriest town in the land,
  Famed for nothing but *no* bread,
  Which men call Clontobred,
You had best, my gay spark, make your will beforehand
  Far from getting an oaten or wheaten
Cake in it to eat, you yourself may be eaten!

XI

MY NOTION OF THOMOND

Bread, fish, flesh, or fowl, you are safe to see none
  In the districts of Thomond,
  But lots of our *beau monde*,
Who deluge your inside with wine from the tun—
  Ale, uιsce beaċa, cider, and sherry,
In fine, all potations that make the heart merry.

XII

I PUT MY BAN ON DROM SNEACHTA

My curse on Drom Sneachta!—that beggarly hole!
  Without meat-stall or fish-shop,
  Priest, vicar, or bishop!
I saw in *their* temple—and oh my sick soul!
  A profound Irish feeling of shame stirs
Thy depths at the thought, playing hookey, two gamesters!

XIII

THE MAC CAHANS

Do you know the Mac Cahans? Be thankful you don't,
  For you hardly could bear them,
  I've sworn not to spare them,
But, merciful still, as is mostly my wont
  I but point my poetical spear in
Their dull eyes, and dub them—the snorers of Erin!

XXI

WITH GRIEF I SATIRIZE THE O'CONOR

By my oath,* my friend Charley, you're covered with shame,
  And a cloud of dishonor,
  The name of O'Conor!
You stint your poor children, you starve your fair dame!
  They are all such *squelettes* as a man shall
See once. For Heaven's love give them something substantial!

---

* A common aduration throughout Ireland.

XXIV

MY JUDGMENT OF THE CLAN RICKARD

The Clan Rickard I brand as a vagabond crew,
  Who are speeding to wreck fast,
  Ask *them* for a breakfast!
They march to Mass duly on Sundays, 'tis true
  But within their house-portal
For a morsel was ne'er yet admitted a mortal.

XXV

WHO ARE REALLY NOTHING BUT STACKS (OF STRAW)

From the plains of Kilcorban to Burren, and back,
  Not a townland or bally
  From hill-peak to valley
But knows that their true name is nothing but—Stack,
  Though, tell them as much, and they'll kick hard,
Against you, and swear that they *are* the Clan-Rickard.

XXVI

THE HOGGISH JOHNSONS

All the Johnsons feed hogs, and *are* hogs too, I think
  Such deaf-and-blind mopers,
  Such ditch-water topers
That is, when they *can* have ditch-water to drink,
  Haven't cumbered the land since the time of
Magh Guaire, when poets had battles to rhyme of.

XXVII

HOW I FARED WITH THEM

In the house of this black-muzzled tribe I once passed
  A whole day without meeting
  One bit fit for eating.
Heaven bless them!—they do teach a sinner to fast!
  I never yet found near or far a
More niggardly people than curse Inis-cara!

XXIX

A PLEASANT DAY WITH THE ROCHES

One day feeling footsore and faintish, I made
  By tardy approaches
  My way to the Roches
It relieved me at least to creep into the shade
  I got bread, but my landlady shut her
Old rat-haunted cupboard at once on the butter!

XXX

WHAT I HAVE TO SAY OF THE O'FLYNNS

The O'Flynns, as a Clan, have been always obscure,
  Both in Albion and Erin,
  And if I did sneer in
My own pleasant way at their doings,* I am sure
  They should thank me; for, what notoriety
Would they have gained but for me, in society?

XXXI

WITH WHOSE BREAD AND BUTTER I HAVE TO QUARREL

I found in their district bread, butter and dirt,
  And the very last plenty,
  But hungry as twenty,
I asked for a morsel. 'Twas black as my shirt,
  What they gave me (my shirt is my jerkin)
The butter was scooped from a grimy horn-firkin.

XLII

WHY I LEFT BANTRY

Three reasons there were why I lately withdrew
  In a hurry from Bantry.
  Its want of a pantry
Was one; and the dirt of it people was two.
  Good Heavens! how they daub and bespatter
Their duds! I forget the third reason. No matter.

---

* This is an allusion to a former satire.

XLIII

A SLY STIRRING-UP OF THE MAC DERMOD

Mac Dermod of Muskerry, *you* have a way
  Which at least I must term odd.
  You gave me, Mac Dermod
One hot summer noon half a wine-glass of whey!
  Before I could reach Ballincollick
I swallowed six bushels of dust through your frolic!

XLV

THE HUM-DRUM-HUMBUG MAC AULIFFES

The McAuliffes I loathe, for I never could yet
  Take to humbugs and humdrums
  Slow coaches and dumb drums,
They're a lazy, yet saucy and cock-nosish set
  They sleep upon beds of green heather,
And eat all that falls in their way,—lamb or leather.

XLVI

OF THE MAC DONOGH, WHO CONFOUNDS TIMES AND SEASONS

Last Easter I spent with Mac Donogh, a stiff
  Kind of person, yet silly,
  So gloomy and chilly
His whole house appeared that it *did* seem as if
  Easter-Sunday, that holy and high day,
Had fallen by some fatal mistake on Good Friday.

XLVII

DEPLORABLE CONDITION OF THE O'KEEFE'S WARDROBE

The poor tattered O'Keefe! How he shivers and shakes!
  The sad ragamuffin!
  He hasn't got stuff in
His carcass to battle with agues and akes—
  But I spare him. He's drooping, the luckless
Poor devil! The Cloakless are always the Pluckless!

LXIV

O'DOHERTY'S HOUSE OF HUNGER

'Tis a hungry house that of O'Doherty of Inch.
For a meal you can get in it *of* meal just a pinch,
And when you look round you for drink there's a churnfull
Of milk, dust, and flies, Oh! his Christmas is mournfull.

LXV

O'REILLY'S GHASTLY FEASTS

O'Reilly, the feeble, the palsied, the old,
The most wretched of wretches the earth can behold
Dines along with his dumb sons, whose glazed eyes and lank wet
Chin and cheeks make each dinner a sort of Death's Banquet!

LXVI

THE SKINFLINT O'CARROLLS

The O'Carrolls, who so love the sound of the quern,
Have got only one cow and one sheep, as I learn;
After starving some while in the house of these skinflints,
My hands became hard, black and meagre, like thin flints.

LXIX

THE UGLY BARRONS

The badger-faced Barrons, who sculk through Cloneen,
Are the ugliest blackguards I think I have seen;
They know not, the hounds, what veal, mutton and beef are,
But sneak to and fro with a roost-robbing thief air.

LXX

THE CHIEF BARRON

In the darkest back room of his house you may see
The Chief Barron himself, with a cup on his knee,
What is in it? Thick milk! That's the whole of his supper—
No bread, not a bite, neither crust, nor yet upper.

LXXVI

HOW I FARED AT CAPPA

They are talkers at Cappa,—no more; if inclined,
You may swallow, as diet, the east or west wind,
For you'll get little else; just imagine or map a
Black briary desert out—that's cursed Cappa!

LXXVII

Yes! they gave me some bread, a small mouldy old crust,
With cold water, for which I was thankful, I trust;
Were the bread weighed against a small wafer 'twere safer
To bet for best weight on the side of the wafer.

LXXXIII

THE GOOD PEOPLE (NOT THE FAIRIES) OF ARA

The good people of Ara are four feet in height;
They are heroes, and really stand stoutly in fight;
But they don't sacrifice overmuch to the Graces,
And Hunger stares forth from their fly-bitten faces.

LXXXIV

There is one waste, wide, bleak, blank, cold old pile,
On the highway: its length is one third of a mile
Whose it is I don't know, but you hear the rats gnawing
Its timbers inside, while its owner keeps sawing.

LXXXV

OF THE BARNACLE-DESTROYER, MAC TAVISH

Ard-Uladh, vile sink! has been time out of mind
But a region for owls; 'mid its dens you will find,
Slaying barnacle-snails with a mallet, that knavish
Old-hang-dog-faced, hangabone, hangman, Mac Tavish.

LXXXVI

HOSPITALITY OF O'HANLON OF THE RAGS

O'Hanlon the Tattered I saw in the Glen
Getting ready a dinner for Orrery's men.
He was roasting it brown on two bars of a narrow
Old gridiron there: 'twas the leg of a sparrow.

LXXXVIII

THE SCYTHES, FORKS, AND—RAKES OF MALLOW

In Mallow you meet many pitchforks and Rakes
But for aught besides these I account it no shakes,
'Twere a glorious old country if straw, grass and hay meant
The same things precisely as rations and raiment.

XCI

THE GRAVES OF DUHALLOW

In Duhallow, that region of Hunger and Storms
The Sick die of want by the roadsides in swarms.
If you fancy a grave where broad meadows lie fallow
And blighted, you'll find one in dreary Duhallow.

XCII

KYAN O'CARROLL AND HIS LADY

Cross Kyan O'Carroll dwells there, with his rib,
In a hovel the size of a basket or crib.
A withered and weazened old couple, forgetful
Of GOD and the Devil,—sick, snappish and fretful.

XCIII

Knocked down by a pig, I fell into their den
Such an upset I hadn't got Munster knows when,
I looked round quite bewildered, and heard Kyan squall out—
'Fall out again, friend, or perhaps we'll *both* fall out!'

XCIV

THE RED MAC MAHONS

The pinch-bowel clan of Mac Mahon, the Red,
Give you just in your dish the bare shadow of bread
An ant, put in harness, I think, would be able
To drag their best cake and their biggest from table.

XCVI

A MARVEL OF A STANZA

In the house of O'Brien (that's Donogh) I spent
A Christmas that lasted till long after Lent,
We had bread, butter, bacon and beef in abundance,
And oft round the board made the bottle, our sun, dance.

C

I (PROMISE TO) LAUD THE MACANS

You'll allow that I haven't much flattered the clans,
But there's one that I *will* praise—the doughty Macans,
For, if *I* didn't *who* would? I guess, not a man on
Earth's face—at least no one this side of the Shannon.

CIV

THE POET'S UNLUCKY APOSTROPHE TO O'MEAGHER WHICH AT ONCE
BROUGHT HIS LAMPOON AND LIFE TO AN ABRUPT TERMINATION

Last, O'Meagher, for yourself—last, though, certes, not least—
You're a prince, and are partial to Mirth and the Feast—
Huge cauldrons, vast fires, with fat sheep, calves and cows, and
Harp-music distinguish your house 'mid a thousand.*

[unpublished manuscript]

Consolation and Counsel

I

Is all, then, gone, for ever lost and gone?
And have our brilliant hopes been quenched in tears?
Doth Darkness veil the suns that lately shone
   The beacons of a thousand years?
Have we—We grown the byword of the earth—   5
Our own reproach—our country's shame—the scorn
And proverb of all Time to come—the mirth
   Of names and nations yet unborn?

II

In sheer despair, and dreariness of soul,
I sometimes yield me to such thoughts of gloom: 10
I sigh lest Inisfail have reached her goal,
   And be, indeed, the Isle of Doom!†
Her glories wane and darken, star by star;
Her highest hopes turn out but swindling dreams;
Her Lamp of Freedom, seen through clouds afar,   15
   Shines but by cold phosphoric gleams!

---

* The following lines which I give in the rude metre of the original, are those that the dying poet is
said to have addressed to his murderer.

   Many are the bitter satires that I acknowledge, alas! to have written
   On the nobles and clans of Munster—but none ever requited me with a blow
   'Till O'Meagher gave me a murdering wound! I perish, down smitten
   By a Chieftain whom I eulogised—this is my lamentation and my woe!

† As most readers are aware, Inisfail signifies 'Island of Destiny.'

III

Alas! we have vaunted all-too-much our Past,
Or fondly hearkened those who vaunted us!
We have scarcely deigned to mark how Creed and Caste
  Divide us wide as Pole and Russ.   20
Drinking, like wine, the flattery of that Chief
Who rarely scourged us but with bulrush rods,
We have waxed o'erwanton, till our own belief,
  If sane, would make us demigods!

IV

My countrymen! you have much to learn and see;   25
You have yet to know yourselves, and what you are,
And what you are *not*, and cannot hope to be,
  Till Fate shall break the severing bar
That insulates you now from Europe's Mind
And leaves you what you have been too truly named,   30
Une nation d'enfants—but you are still not blind—
  Why let your views of Life be shamed?

V

Eye not arch, pillar, hall alone; but glance
At MANKIND's mighty Temple, roof to base;
The Clootzes, Dantons, Lafayettes of France   35
  Were Orators of the Human Race,*
Not Celtic only. Praise be theirs!
Not seldom golden. They had words for even the foes
They drew their steel on. Is't not somewhat sad
  The niggard show WE make of those?   40

VI

Yet, courage! Still bear up! Who beareth *up*
At last bears *down* all obstacles, be sure!
What, though you have deeply quaffed Affliction's Cup,
  It may have left your hearts more pure.
Invoke the help that comes from Heaven above;   45
Make Him who sits on Heaven's high Throne your Friend.
And doubt it not, as his best name is Love,
  Your groans and woes ere long shall end!

* We believe our contributor is not exactly correct. The only one of the three who took the title of
'Orator of the Human Race' was Baron Clootz; and he was a madman.—ED.

VII
Curst be Revenge! O! teach—and learn—to think.
Be all your aims and objects just and high.   50
GOD gave you hearts that must not shrink or sink:
    He gave you souls that cannot die.
Knowledge is Power, not Powder. That man strikes
A blow for Ireland worth a hundred guns
Who trains one reasoner. Smash your heads of Pikes,   55
    And form the heads of Men, my sons!

VIII
And with their heads their hearts—for, if you shut
The gates on Feeling, what's your Man? A horse!
(Or ass, more likely.) Mind *sans* soul is but
    A Plato's vizard on a corse!   60
Form Soul and Mind alike, and then your Man
Walks forth like Howard or Haughton, and can give
The best example of the noblest plan
    For teaching how to dare to live!
        ['Unpublished Poems by James Clarence Mangan', *Irishman*, 5 January 1850]

When Hearts were Trumps!

THE following singularly beautiful poem, unequalled in felicity of thought or
language, and perhaps among the most exquisite of poor Mangan's lyrics, was
written in the days of his deepest destitution, and the distress of his country.

I
O! the days when HEARTS were Trumps!
    Then the soul made *great* way—
With slight leaven and largest lumps,*
    Man marched forward straightway.———
GOD revealed His Lightning-face   5
    That time unto Moses—
O, my life on't! Adam's race
    Slept not then on roses!

* 'A little leaven leaveneth the whole lump.'—*Holy Writ.*

II
Praise the days when HEARTS were Trumps,
　Ere yet Heads were talked of—　　　　　　　　　　　　　10
Ere yet Gall's and Spurzheim's bumps
　Were mapped out and chalked off!
When men yet could laugh and quaff,
　When Hope's Tree bore blossoms,
And the Electric Telegraph　　　　　　　　　　　　　　15
　Spoke from living bosoms!

III
CLUBS were Trumps in 'Ninety-three—
　With the gaunt Parisians,—
And with Us too, while yet we
　Had our dazzling visions.　　　　　　　　　　　　　　20
Our CLUBS—all remembered these:—
　Wide and well we held them,
Till the Castle-Hercules
　Raised *his* club, and felled them!

IV
SPADES are *now* Trumps: far and near　　　　　　　　　25
　All seek out the sexton,
What with Cholera, Famine, Fear,
　Men ask what comes next on.
No more marryings, no more cheer;
　All is dark and lonely;　　　　　　　　　　　　　　　30
Town and country both appear
　One wide churchyard only.

V
Praise the days when HEARTS were Trumps!
　Though *couleur-de-rose* days,
Brummell's gloves and D'Orsay's pumps　　　　　　　　35
　Made no MAN in those days!
Then the Heart, as Nature's bark,
　Both with oar and sail rowed—
Science then but lost her mark
　On fresh *Feeling's* rail-road!　　　　　　　　　　　40

VI

But, will HEARTS be Trumps again?
  That they will, I fancy!
Love will yet abolish Pain,
  As by necromancy;
And, friends, trust me! your—(not *my*)—   45
  Offspring will have wondered
Much at myriad changes—by
  Anno Nineteen-hundred!

    ['Unpublished Poems by James Clarence Mangan', *Irishman*, 26 January 1850]

PROSE

An Extraordinary Adventure in the Shades

The day of the week was Sunday; of the month the first—the month itself was April, the year, 1832. Sunday, first of April, 1832!—*de mortuis nil nisi bonum,*[1] but I really must say that thou wert, in very truth, a beautiful, a bland, and a balmy day. I remember thee particularly well. Ah! which of the days that the departed year gave birth to, do I not remember? The history of each and of all is chronicled in the volume of my brain—written into it as with a pen of iron, in letters of ineffaceable fire! It is pretty generally admitted by the learned, that an attempt to recall the past, is labour in vain, else should I, for one, purchase back the bygone year with diadems and thrones—(supposing that I had the diadems and thrones to barter.) Under present circumstances my only feasible proceeding is to march onward rectilineally, cheek-by-jowl, with the spirit of the age—to abandon the bowers of Fancy, for the broad beaten pathway of Reason—renounce Byron for Bentham,[2] and resign the brilliant and burning imagery of the past, for the frozen realities of the present and the future. Be it so. Whatever may become of me, my lips are sealed—a padlocked article. *Tout est perdu, mes amis:*[3] and when the case stands thus, the unfortunate victim had much better keep his breath to cool his porridge withal, for he may stake his last cigar upon it, that anything more supremely ridiculous than his efforts to soliloquise his friends into a sympathetic feeling, will never come under cognizance of the public.

The foregoing paragraph is exclusively 'personal to myself.' I am now going to relate what will be generally interesting.

For the evening of the 1st of April, '32, I had an appointment with an acquaintance whom I had almost begun to look upon as a friend. The place of rendezvous was in College-green, at the Shades Tavern[4]—a classic spot, known to a few select persons about town. At half-past six o'clock I accordingly repaired thither. As yet, my acquaintance, whom I had almost begun to regard as a friend, had not made his appearance. Taking possession of a vacant box, I ordered the waiter to bring a bottle of port and two glasses. He obeyed. Mechanically I began to sip the wine, awaiting, with some anxiety, the arrival of my acquaintance, whom I had almost, &c. But half an hour elapsed, and he came not. Now I grew fidgetty and thoughtful and began to form a variety of conjectures. At length, for very weariness, I gave this up. Suddenly I heard someone cough slightly. I raised my head, and looked forth at the door. Seated at an opposite table, I beheld a gentleman of tall stature and commanding aspect, striking, indeed to a degree, in his physiognomy. He was reading a newspaper, and was apparently deeply absorbed in its contents. How was it that I had hitherto neglected to notice this man? I could not forbear wondering. I was unable to account for the circumstance, except by referring to my previous abstraction, the pre-occupied nature of my thoughts, and the agitation which the anticipation of the meeting with my acquaintance, whom I had almost begun, &c., had necessarily tended to produce, in a person of my delicately nervous temperament. Now, however, I was resolved to compensate for my previous absence of mind. I examined the stranger opposite me minutely. I criticised him, without saying a syllable, from hat-crown (he wore his beaver[5]) to shoe-tie (he sported pumps). His cravat, waistcoat, frock, unutterables, all underwent a rigid analysis by my searching eye. I scrutinised all, first collectively and afterwards consecutively; and I owe it truth and justice to protest, that, upon my honour, the result was decidedly satisfactory. All was perfect, lofty, gentlemanlike. Viewed as a whole, his countenance was, as I have remarked, peculiarly particular. I was, however, determined to institute an examination into it *stückweise*,[6] as they say at Vienna, and I reviewed every feature distinctively and apart. Had I been a *Quarterly Reviewer*,[7] or Professor Wilson himself,[8] I could not have discovered the slenderest groundwork to erect a super-structure of censure on. Had similar perfection ever until that hour been encountered by any? Never and nowhere. I knew not what to imagine; my faculties were bewildered. The thing was too miraculous, it was over-magnificent, extra-odd, super-inexplicable. Who was this man? I had always been a considerable peripatetic, but I could not recollect that in town or country he had ever until now encountered my inspection. Such a figure and such a face I could not, had I but once beheld them, possibly forget; they would have been enrolled among the archives of my memory, as treasures to be drawn lavishly and largely upon, on some future night, when the current of my ideas should run darkly and low, among underwood and over brambly places, and the warehouse of my imagination be ransacked in vain for a fresh assortment of imagery, and the punchless jug should stand solitarily upon the dimly-lighted table, and not a human voice be heard to set that table in a roar. I had never before seen this man: of course, then, it was obvious that I now saw him for the first time. As this reflection, which I conceived to be a strictly logical one, occurred, I filled a glass a fifth time, and sipped as usual. The stranger continued to peruse his newspaper. His attitude was partially recumbent and wholly motionless. It was a reasonable inference from this, that he must be an individual of steady habits and unchangeable principles, whom it might be exceedingly difficult to detach from a favourite pursuit, or draw aside from the path of prudence and duty. Rectitude of conduct is a quality that commands my esteem: if I had before admired the stranger, this consideration annexed to my admiration by a feeling of respect. Yes! he was evidently a cautious and force-thoughtful character—perhaps he was a little too inflexible in his determinations; but, then, has not inflexibility ever been the invariable concomitant of vast powers? Whether, however, this interrogatory were answered negatively or affirmatively, it was

certain that adequate testimony of the positive inflexibility of this man's dispo-
sition was as yet wanting; and I should perpetrate an enormous act of injustice in
condemning him, unless I had been antecedently placed in possession of every
fact and circumstance exercising the remotest influence upon the question. It is
essential to the passing of an upright sentence, that crude and precipitate
opinions be discarded; and should I, by over-hastily following the dictates of a
rash judgement, irrevocably commit myself in the eyes of philosophy, and
eternally damn my own character as an impartial observer of the human family
at large, would it be reasonable?—would it be even politic? Should I not, in fact,
deserve to be hooted down wherever I exhibited myself, and driven, like
Ahesuerus the wanderer,[9] from post to pillar; seeking refuge now in a cavern, and
now in a pot-house, and finding rest nowhere—a houseless wretch—a spectacle
to society, and a melancholy memorial to after ages of the ruinous results of that
self-conceit which prompts to the headstrong perseverance in opinions of a ridi-
culous order? What a doom! I shuddered as I silently contemplated the abstract
possibility of such a contingency; and then, filling a sixth glass, went on sipping.
Still my acquaintance, who was not yet a friend, had not blessed me with the
light of his countenance; and my only resource was to watch, with an attentive
eye, the proceedings, if any should take place, of the being at the opposite table.
I felt my interest in the destiny of the unknown augment moment by moment.
Questionlessly, thought I, the Platonical theory[10] is not wholly visionary—not
altogether a bam. I must have known this man in some pre-adamite world; and
the extraordinary sensations I experience in his presence, are explicable only by
reference to an antenatal state of existence. He and I have been ancient com-
panions—fraternized members of the aboriginal *Tugendbund*[11]—the Orestes
and Pylades[12] of a purer and loftier sphere. Perhaps I died on the block for him!
Who shall expound me the enigma of the sympathetical feelings reciprocated
between master-minds, when upon earth each meets the other for the first time,
unless by pointing to the electrical chain which runs dimly back through the
long gallery of time, ascending from generation to generation, until it has
reached the known beginning of all things, and then stretches out anew, far, far
beyond that, wide away into the measureless deep of primary creation—the
unknown, unimaginable infinite! There is nothing incredible if we believe life to
be a reality; for, to a psychologist, the very consciousness that he exists at all, is a
mystery unfathomable in this world. An ass will attempt to illuminate us on the
subject, and may produce, with an air of consequential cognoscity, a schedule of
what he is pleased to call reasons; but it is all hollow humbug. So stands a leaden-
visaged geologist, up to his knees in the centre of a quagmire, and silently and
sedulously pokes at the mud with his walking stick, fancying himself, the while,
a second Cuvier;[13] though the half-dozen clowns who officiate as spectators, and

whom he takes for assembled Europe, perceive that the poor creature does nothing but turn up sludge eternally. As to the illuminating ass, only suffer him to proceed, and he will undertake to probe infinity with a bodkin, and measure the universe with a yard of pack thread. There are two distinguished plans for the extinction of such an annoyance;—first, to cough him down—second, to empty a pot of porter against his countenance. I have tried both experiments, and can vouch that the most successful results will follow.

The stranger, as I continued to gaze, elevated his hand to his head, and slightly varied the position of his hat. Here was a remarkable event—a landmark in the desert—an epoch in the history of the evening, affording scope for an unbounded conjecture. I resolved, however, by no means to allow imagination to obtain the start of judgement on this occasion. The unknown had altered the position of his hat. What was the inference spontaneously deducible from the occurrence of such a circumstance? Firstly that anterior to the motion which preceded the change, the unknown had conceived, that his hat did not sit properly on his head: secondly, that he must be gifted with the organ of order in a high degree. Individuals in whom that organ is prominently developed are rarely, if ever, imaginative or poetical: hence it was to be inferred, that the energies of the unknown were exclusively devoted to the advancement of prosaical interests. But here again rose cause to bewilder and embarass. I could see by a glance, that the unknown was conning a column of poetry, and that his expressive countenance, as he went on, became palely illumined by a quenchless lamp from the sanctuary within; how did this harmonise with my former conclusion? I surmounted the difficulty, however, by reflecting that it is, after all, possible for a man to be, at once illimitably imaginative, and profoundly philosophical, as we find, said I mentally, in the instance of Dr. Bowring.[14] *Bowring? Ah stupidity!* thy name is Clarence. That, until this moment, the truth should never have struck thee! That, only now shouldst thou have been made aware that Bowring himself was before thee! A thrill of joy pervaded my frame, as I reclined my brow on my hand, and internally exclaimed: yes! it is, indeed, Bowring! It must be he, because it can be no other!

CLARENCE.

(To be concluded in our next.)

[*Comet*, 20 January 1833]

(CONCLUDED)

As I had always been ardently desirous of an introduction to that illustrious man, whom I justly regard as one of the leading genii of modern Europe, I shall leave the public to imagine the overpowering nature of my feelings upon discovering that the golden opportunity had at length been vouchsafed, and that I was now free to enter into oral communication with a master-spirit of the age. I paused to deliberate upon the description of address I should put forth, as well as the tone of voice which it would be most appropriate to assume; whether aristocratical or sentimental, free-and-easy or brokenhearted; and also upon the style of expression properest for my adoption, and best calculated to impress the mind of Bowring with a conviction that, whatever my defects might prove to be in detail, I was—take me all in all—a young man of magnificent intellect and dazzling originality, and possessed a comprehensiveness of capacity discoverable in nobody else within the bills of mortality. Whether I should compress my sentiments within two bulky sentences, or subdivide them into fifteen little ones, was likewise a matter of serious importance. So acute an observer of mankind and syntax as Bowring is, will infallibly, said I, detect the slenderest inaccuracy in my phraseology. To betray any philological inability would be a short method of getting myself damned in his eyes; and I should go down to the latest posterity as a bungler and a bumpkin. Mannerism is a grand thing. Let me, therefore, review this question minutely and microscopically, under all the various lights and shades in which it can be presented to the mind, before I pass the Rubicon[15] irremeably.

Mannerism is a grand thing, pursued I, following the current of my reflections. It is the real, heavy bullion, the genuine ore, the ingot itself; every other thing is jelly and soap-suds. You shall tramp the earth in vain for a more pitiable object than a man of genius, with nothing else to back it with. He was born to amalgamate with the mud we walk upon, and will, whenever he appears in public, be trodden over like that. Transfuse into this man a due portion of mannerism: the metamorphosis is marvellous. Erect he stands, and blows his trumpet, the sounds whereof echo unto the uttermost confines of our magnificent world. Senates listen,—empires tremble,—thrones tumble down before him! He possesses the wand of Prospero,[16]—the lamp of Aladdin,[17]—the violin of Paganini,[18]—the assurance of the devil! What has conferred all these advantages upon him? *Mannerism!*—destitute of which, we are,—so to speak,—walking humbugs,—destitute of which the long odds are, that the very best individual among us, after a life spent upon the tread-mill system, dies dismally in a sack.

For myself, concluded I, I laugh at Charlatanism in all its branches; but it is, nevertheless, essential that I show off with Bowring. I am nothing, if not striking. It is imperative on me, therefore, to strike.

Six hours of unremitting study a few weeks previously had enabled me to concoct a very superior joke about the *March* of Intellect's becoming a *Dead* March on the *first of April*.[19] This had never appeared. Should I suffer the diamond to sparkle? It was a debatable question whether Doctor B. would not internally condemn me as an unprincipled ruffian for sneering at my own party. I know not, said I:—I am buried in Egyptian darkness on this point; but, *primâ facie*, I should be inclined to suppose Bowring a moral cosmopolite, who could indifferently floor friends and enemies, *con amore*.[20] To humbug the whole world in the gross is certainly a herculean achievement; but the conquest of impossibilities is the glory of genius. Both Bowring and I are living in a miraculous era,—the second quarter of nineteeth century,—and shall *I* deny to *him* the capability of appreciating one of the loftiest efforts of the human mind? Perish the notion!

I had nearly arrived at a permanent decision, when the progress of my meditations was abruptly arrested by the intervention of a new and startling consideration. Bowring was a universal linguist, a master of dead and living languages to any extent. Admirably well did he know,—none better,—the intrinsic nothingness of the English tongue. Its periods and phrases were, in truth, very small beer to him. Suppose that I were to accost him in the majestical cadences of the Spanish. A passage from Calderon[21] might form a felicitous introduction. Or in the French? I could draw upon Corneille,[22] Malherbe,[23] Voltaire,[24] &c. to any amount. Or in the German? Here again I was at home. To spout Opitz,[25] Canitz,[26] Uz,[27] Wieland,[28]—and oh! above all, Richter—*meines Herzens Richter*— *(ach! wenn ich ein Herz habe)*[29] was as easy as to mix a fifth tumbler. Of Latin and Greek I made no account; Timbuctooese I was slightly deficient in. As to the Hungarian and Polish, they were not hastily to be sneezed at. The Unknown Tongues merited some attention, on account of the coal-black locks of the Reverend Ned Irving.[30] In short the satisfactory adjustment of this point was to be sedulously looked to. After some further deliberation I at length concluded upon doing nothing hurriedly. First ideas, said I, should be allowed time to cool into shape. A grammatical error would play the devil with me. The great Utilitarian[31] would dub me quack, and the forthcoming number of the *Westminster*[32] would nail me to the wall as a hollow-sculled pretender to encyclopediacal knowledge, a character which I am much more anxious that Oliver Yorke[33] should fasten upon Lardner[34] than Rowland Bowring upon *me*.

As, however, I languidly sipped my ninth glass, a heart-chilling and soul-sinking reminiscence came over me. I remembered to have somewhere read that Bowring was a Cassius-like[35] looking philosopher. Now the stranger before me was rather plump than spare;—certainly more *enbonpoint*[36] than corresponded with the portrait given of the Doctor. Thus was my basket of glass instantaneously shattered to fragments, while I,—like another Alnascher,[37]—stood weeping over the brittle ruin. This, then, was *not* Bowring! The tide of life ran coldly to my heart; and I felt myself at that moment a Conscious Non-entity!

What was to be done? Hastily to discuss[38] the remainder of my wine, to order a fresh bottle, and to drink six or eight glasses in rapid succession, was the operation of a few minutes. And oh! what a change! Cleverly indeed had I calculated upon a glorious reaction. Words have I none to reveal the quiescence of spirit that succeeded, the interior balminess that steeped every faculty in blessed sweetness. I felt renovated, created anew: I had undergone an apotheosis; I wore the cumbrous habiliments of flesh and blood no longer; the shell, hitherto the circumscriber of my soul, was shivered; I stood out, in front of the universe, a visible and tangible Intellect, and held, with giant grasp, the key that had power to unlock the deep prison which enclosed the secrets of antiquity and futurity!

The solitary thing that excited my surprise and embarrassment was the anomalous appearance which the nose of the stranger had assumed. But a few brief minutes before, and it had exhibited a symmetry the most perfect, and dimensions of an every-day character: now it might have formed a respectable rival to the tower of Lebanon.[39] As I concentrated the hitherto scattered energies of my mind, and brought them soberly to bear upon the examination of this enormous feature, I learned, from an intimate perception, of too incommunicable a nature to admit of developement, that the stranger was no other than a revivification of MAUGRABY,[40] the celebrated oriental necromancer, whose dreaded name the romances of my childhood had rendered familar to me, and who had lately arrived in Dublin for the purpose of consummating some hell-born deed of darkness, of the particulars of which I was, in all probability, destined to remain eternally ignorant. That there is, as some German metaphysicians maintain, an idiosyncracy in some individuals, endowing them with the possession of a *sixth* sense, or faculty, to which nomenclature has as yet affixed no distinct idea, (for our ideas are in fewer instances derivable from things than from names) is a position which I will never suffer any man, woman, or child to contest. Had I myself ever at any former period been disturbed by the intrusion of doubts upon the subject, here was evidence more than sufficient to dissipate them all. Here was evidence too weighty to be kicked down stairs in a fine *de haut en bas*[41] fashion; for although I had never, until the present evening come into contact with MAUGRABY, this sixth faculty, this fine, vague, spiritual, unintelligible lightning-like instinct had sufficed to assure me of his presence and proximity. It was even so. Certainty is the sepulchre of scepticism: scepticism is the executioner of certainty. As the believer, when he begins to doubt, ceases to believe, so the doubter, when he begins to believe, ceases to doubt. These may be entitled eternal moral axioms, philosophical aphorisms, infinitely superior to the aphorisms of Sir Morgan O'Doherty[42] touching the relative merits of soap and bear's grease, black puddings, *manches à gigot*,[43] cravats, cold fish, and similar bagatelles;—and I may as well take this opportunity of observing that Sir M. O'D. has by such discussions, inflicted incalculable injury upon the cause of philosophy, which mankind should be perpetually instructed to look up to as the very soul of seriousness, and centre of gravity.

That he whom I surveyed was, identically and *bonâ fide*, MAUGRABY, it would have betrayed symptoms of extravagent lunacy in me to deny; because the capability of producing so remarkable an effect as the preternatural growth of nose which I witnessed, was one which,—as far as my lucubrations enabled me to judge,—had always been exclusively monopolized by MAUGRABY. It was by no manner of means material whether what came under my inspection were a tangible reality or an optical illusion: that was MAUGRABY's business,—not mine; and if he had juggled my senses into a persuasion of the fidelity of that appearance which confounded me, when in point of fact the entire thing, if uncurtained to the world, would turn out to be a lie,—a shabby piece of '*Lock-und-Gaukel-Werk*,'[44]—a naked bamboozlement;—if he had done this, upon his own head be the deep guilt, the odium, the infamy attachable to the transaction. It would be hard if I were compelled to incur any responsibility for the iniquitous vagaries of an East-Indian sorcerer. To the day of my death I would protest against such injustice. The impression transmitted along the cord of the visual nerve to the external chambers of the brain, and thence conveyed, by easy stages, into the inner domicile of the soul, is all, quoth I, that I have to do with. Of such an impression I am the life-long slave. Whether there be other physical objects upon the surface of this globe as well as myself,—whether there be the *materiel*[45] of a globe at all,—whether matter be an entity or an abstraction,—whether it have a *substratum* or not,—and whether there be anything anywhere having any existence of any description, are problems for Berkeleyans;[46] but if there be reasoning essences here below, independent of myself, in circumstances parallel with my own, their opinions will corroborate mine; our feelings will be found to coalesce; our decisions to coincide. In any event, however, no argument arising from the metaphysics of the question can annihilate the identity of MAUGRABY.

Were I to have been hanged for it, in the course of the evening, at the first convenient lamp-post, I could not suppress a sentiment of envy at the superiority over his fellow-creatures which characterised the Indian juggler. Elevate me, said I, to the uppermost step of the ladder,—establish me on the apex of the mountain,—and what, after all, is my preëminence? Low is the highest! contemptibly dwarfish the loftiest altitude! Admit my powers to be multifarious and *unique:* yet am I, by comparison with this intelligence, sunk 'deeper than ever plummet sounded.'[47] Lord of this earth is MAUGRABY:—his breath exhales pestilence,—his hand lavishes treasures! he possesses invisibility, ubiquity, tact, genius, wealth exhaustless, power undreamed of! Such is MAUGRABY: such is he on whom I gaze. He is worthy to be champion of England, or to write the leading articles for the Thunderer![48]

Gradually the current of my thoughts took another course, and my mind yielded to suggestions and speculations that were anything but tanquillizing and agreeable. I am not prone to be lightly affected: legerdemain[49] and playhouse thunder move me never;—it might be even found a task to brain me with a lady's fan; and hence, the mere size of MAUGRABY's nose, though I admitted it to be a novelty of the season, was insufficient to excite any emotion of terror within me. Viewed in the abstract, it was unquestionably no more than an oddity,—a bugbear to the uninitiated of the suburbs,—a staggering deviation from the appearances that everyday life presents us with;—and if this were the Alpha and Omega of the affair, MAUGRABY was a bottle of smoke. But this was *not* all: it was to be recollected that the nose encreased each moment in latitude and longitude: here was the rub. The magnitude of a man's nose is not, *per se*, and object of public solicitude: the Balance of Power[50] is not interfered with by it, and its effects upon the social system are comparatively slight; but if a progressive increase in that magnitude be discernible, such an increase becomes the subject of intense interest to the community with whom the owner of the nose associates, and will, in course of time, absorb the undivided attention of mankind. (See *Slawkenbergius*, vol. xi, chap, xxxii, p. 658, art. *Nosology*.)[51] It was apparent that in MAUGRABY's case dismal damage would accrue to the proprietor of the Shades. His (MAUGRABY's) nose would speedily become too vast for the area of the apartment; it would soon constitute a barricade; it would offer a formidable obstacle to the ingress of visitors; eventually the entrance to the tavern would be blocked up; all intercourse would thus be impracticable; business would come to a dead stand-still; and an evil whose ramifications no penetration could reach would thus be generated.

But experience alone could testify to the absolute amount of injury that would be inflicted through the agency of this mountainous feature. Extending itself from College Green through Dame-street, Westmoreland-street, and Grafton-street, it would, by regular degrees, occupy every square foot of vacant space in this mighty metropolis. Then would ensue the prostration of commerce, the reign of universal terror, the precipitate departure of the citizens of all ranks into the interior,—and Dublin would, in its melancholy destiny, be assimilated by the historian of a future age, with Persepolis, Palmyra, and Nineveh! As the phantasmagoria of all this ruin arose in shadowy horror upon my anticipations, is it wonderful that I shook, as if affected with palsy, and that my heart sank in my bosom to a depth of several inches? I fell at once into a train of soliloquy.

Too intimately, MAUGRABY, am I acquainted with thine iron character to doubt for an instant thy rocky immovability of purpose. What thou willest, that executest thou. Expostulation and remonstrance, oratory and poetry are to thee so much rigmarole; even my tears will be thy laughing-stock. I have not the ghost of a chance against thee.

MAUGRABY! thou damned incubus! what liberty is this that thou hast dared to take with me? Supposest thou that I will perish, as perishes the culprit at the gallows, bandaged, night-capped, hoodwinked, humbugged? Is thy horn, after all, so soft? I am, it is true, weaponless, unless we consider this glass decanter in my fist a weapon; but all the talons with which nature has endowed me shall be exercised against thee. Still, and at the best, 'my final hope is flat despair.'[52] I stand alone: like Anacharsis Clootz,[53] I am deserted by the human race:—I am driven into a box, three feet square; there I am cooped up;—a beggarly bottle of wine is allotted to me; *pour toute compagnie*,[54] I am placed in juxtapostion with a hell-hound, and then I am left to perish ignobly.

That I should at this moment have neither poker, pike, pitchfork, nor pickaxe, will be viewed in the light of a metropolitan calamity by the future annalist of Dublin, when he shall have occasion to chronicle the circumstance. The absence of a vat of tallow from this establishment is of the greatest detriment to me, for in such a vat it might be practicable to suffocate this demidæmon. There being no such vat, it becomes obvious he can never be suffocated in it. How then, good heavens! can any man be so senseless, betray so much of the Hottentot, shew himself so far sunk in stupidity, as to expect that I should find one at my elbow? How deplorably he needs the Schoolmaster! How requisite it is that some friend to human perfectibility should advance him one halfpenny each Saturday wherewith to procure a Halfpenny Magazine! He is, this night, the concentrated extract of absurdity: the force of assery can no further go. I protest, with all the solemnity that belongs to my awful position, that if there be a chandler's vat under this roof the fact is the most extraordinary that history records. Its existence is not to be accounted for on any commercial principle. No man can tell how it was conveyed hither, or at whose expense it was established. An impenetrable veil of mystery shrouds the proceeding. The whole thing is dark—it is an enigma, a phenomenon of great importance. I had better leave it where I found it.

My regards were now painfully fascinated by the great magician of the Dom-Daniel.[55] To look in any direction but the one, I felt to be totally impracticable. He had spell-bound me, doubtlessly; his accursed jugglery had been at work while I, with the innocent unsuspiciousness which forms my distinguishing characteristic, had been occupied in draining the decanter. Was ever an inhabitant of any city in Europe so horribly predicamented? It was manifest that he had already singled me out as his first victim. I foreknew the destiny whereunto I was reserved. I saw the black marble dome, the interminable suites of chambers, the wizard scrolls, the shaft and quiver, and in dim but dreadful perspective the bloody cage, in which incarcerated under the figure of a bat I should be doomed to flap my leathern wings dolefully through the sunless day.

Mere human fortitude was inadequate to the longer endurance of such agonising emotions as accompanied the pourtrayal of these horrors upon my intellectual retina. Nature was for once victor over Necromancy. I started up, I shrieked, I shouted, I rushed forward headlong. I remember tumbling down in a state of frenzy, but nothing beyond.

> The morn was up again, the dewy morn
>> With breath all incense, and cheek all bloom,
> Laughing the clouds away with playful scorn,
>> And living as if earth contained no tomb.[56]

But I could not enjoy it, for I was in bed, and my temples throbbed violently. I understood that I had been conveyed from the Shades in a carriage. Dr. Stokes[57] was at my bedside: I enquiried of him whether he had seen Maugraby hovering in the vicinity of the house. As the only reply to this was a shake of the head, I at once and briefly gave him a narration of my adventure.

Well said he, I can satisfy you of the individuality of your unknown. He is neither MAUGRABY nor Bowring, but BRASSPEN,[58] of the COMET Club. I saw him there last night myself.

Tout est mystere dans ce monde-ci, thought I; *je ne sais trop qu'en croire.*[59]

CLARENCE.

[*Comet*, 27 January 1833]

A Treatise on a Pair of Tongs

Sure such a pair was never seen.
So justly formed.[1]—THE DUENNA.

Why, man, it doth bestride the narrow world
Like a Colossus.[2]—JULIUS CAESAR.

𝔍 introduce my subject stylishly.

There is nowhere to be met with in this world, a more interesting spectacle than a pair of tongs. Throughout Japan and the provinces of Tartary,—from boundary to boundary of the Celestial Empire,[3]—among the Moguls, even, not to speak of Van Dieman's [*sic*] land,—in Piccadilly, Philadelphia, Stamboul, Timbuctoo and Bilboa,—I see nothing that I admit to be worthy of standing up by the side of a pair of tongs. It suggests a prolific universe of reflections, each the parent of an additional universe. Contemplate the subject as you will,—handle it as you may, you are certain to discover, day after day, some new quality to blow your trumpet concerning. Small wonder:—it is everlasting as the March of Eternity,— inexhaustible as the depths of Infinity. Only consider, Public, what a pair of tongs really is. Its shape and figure,—the attitudes it unconsciously assumes,— the *materiel* of which it is constructed,—the purposes to which it is destined,— are all topics of the loftiest nature. To discuss any one of these topics apart, should be the work of a succession of generations; to dilate upon the entire conjunctively we know to be a dead impracticability. The bare attempt in any man to do it in 3 vols. post octavo,[5] sickens our stomachs;—it is entirely too revolting,—monstrous beyond measure. Any proposal, emanating from New Burlington Street,[6] and addressed to me, insinuating that I should undertake the business, would prove to us all how slenderly the great European publisher has profited by the intellectual treasures piled behind his counter by Bulwer and D'Israeli.[7] Colburn's lunacy[8] would be at once established as a melancholy fact; and his solitary resource would be to plant himself solas on the pinnacle of the Temple of Humbug, and continue there to all eternity, occupying a position too deplorably conspicuous for human imagination, unaided by the Spirit of the *Age*,[9] to be capable of conceiving.

𝔍 proceed now to point out to observers, what a blessed thing it is for mankind that there is nothing like a pair of tongs.

A pair of tongs is a unique object. There is nothing exactly resembling it upon the surphiz[10] of the earth. It is alone: a phoenix: a study for the amateurs of the singular. This is fortunate. If there were any other object from the North Pole to the South, preferably analogous in form to the tongs, the individuality of the tongs would be at an end: it would, in fact, be merged in the other object. Hence would result a startling question: By what process shall the learned societies of Europe be enabled to distinguish between the identity of the tongs and the identity of the other object? No discovery in physics hitherto accomplished could assist us in framing a satisfactory reply to this question. It is worse than a Chinese puzzle.

𝔍 enter into a mysterious question, to wit, when and by whom the first pair of tongs was built: 𝔑obody can tell me, and thus the thing goes to the devil.

The origin of tongs is involved in obscurity. The period of their introduction into Europe in particular, and among civilized nations in general, has never been clearly ascertained. It is to be deeply regretted that antiquarian research has in few instances been directed to the development of the mystery that hangs over the invention of tongs. This indifference is not merely culpable—it is atrocious:—it inculcates however, a splendid moral lesson, by pointing out the melancholy consequences of neglect, and by establishing the necessity of diligence and perseverance with regard even to what may be too toploftically termed the *minutiæ* of life. Perhaps a conjecture of my own may be hazarded without presumption. I should imagine that tongs first came into use as soon as they began to be wanted. Any theory which assumes that they existed antecedent to the discovery of fire by Prometheus, in Kilkenny, 5600 years ago, must be baseless,—unless, Public, you and I take it for granted that they might have been applied to widely different purposes,—*par exemple*, to the taking up of little pebbles of lump sugar and dropping them into the mouth of the punch-jug.* And considering that the average length and dimensions of tongs altogether unfit for such an office, the hypothesis must be rejected as the reverie of a drunken dreamer.

𝕴 come down with heavy fist upon the spare-tongs niggard.

Tongs are more frequently handled in the depth of winter, than during the sweltering sultriness of the dog-days—oftener in requisition where there is fire, than where there happens to be none. The reason of this is obvious: it is because there is a greater occasion for them. Tongs, however, are by no means invariably made use of even in a chamber where the occasion requires their exercise; and this circumstance is generally attributable either to inability or disinclination in the proprietor of the chamber. Possibly he has no tongs:—possibly, though he may have them, he declines using them. Putting case the first as true, he is destitute of the ability to produce a pair; in case the second, he is, though possessed of a pair, evidently unwilling to devote them to the ends to which they were primarily appropriated. Both transactions are of the shabby and beggarly order; but moral jurisprudence will for ever erect a distinction between the pauper and the niggard; and a rational man will be always found ready to give the pauper more halfpence than kicks, and the niggard more kicks than halfpence.

𝕴 wax fearfully erudite, in descanting upon the guilty doings of Cartesius[11] and his clique: Because they have Burked[12] the existence of tongs, therefore 𝕴 make an example of them.

Why should I blink it? The existence of tongs involves the destruction of a certain antiquated metaphysical dogma. Ascertainable by a reference to the writings of Schelling,[13] Gassendi,[14] Reid,[15] Mallebranche,[16] Wolfe,[17] Descartes, Leibnitz,[18]

---

* Punch was formerly made in a jug. The practice, even to-day, has some disciples in the suburbs.

and many more, is the fact, that with the hypothetical exception of the Berkleyans, all philosophers have agreed in the truth of the theory which maintains that there are *in esse vel posse*[19] but two things, i.e. body and spirit. This theory is a fallacy. What manner of thing is a pair of tongs? Clearly, it is neither body nor yet spirit. It is all head, neck and legs: it possesses therefore no body. It is inert and lifeless; therefore it has no spirit. Hence it is not body—it is not spirit;—and not being body, and not being spirit, the inference follows that it is neither. How frequently have I, during the slowly-rolling winter nights, from midnight till day-dawn, in the solitude of my lamp-illumined apartment, how frequently have I perused the works of those illustrious labourers whom I have named, and of others whom I might have named, if I had chosen to name them, but whom I have not chosen to name, and therefore have not named,—and as I have perused the works of those illustrious labourers whom I have named, and of others whom I might have named, if I had chosen to name them, but whom I have not chosen to name, and therefore have not named,—and as I have perused them, how have I been para-lysed with astonishment to observe the total omission of any allusion in those works to a pair of tongs! I have ransacked Reid's Powers,[20] Mill's Phenomen,[21] and Brown's Philosophy,[22] in vain. Give me—I have exclaimed, while fathoming, muddler in hand,[23] the depth of my eleventh tumbler,—give me the remotest allusion—the faintest reference to the existence of tongs. I shall be satisfied with the shadowyest semblance of an acknowledgement. In vain, Public. No tongs—no allusion,—nothing whatever. Damning evidence this, of something!—such has been my emphatical exclamation, while fathoming with a muddler the abyss of my fifteenth tumbler. The thing, Philander,[24] was hollow. Any admission of the exis-tence of a pair of tongs would have been death to the systems of philosophy palmed upon us all. Good herrings! How afflicting it is to see men of extensive intellectual resources stooping to such dirty paltriness. The iniquity of suppression is more heinous than the iniquity of misquotation, because the misquoter merely garbles, whereas the suppressor suppresses. He who garbles a fact merely submits it to us in a garbled state, but he who suppresses it entirely, omits it, in fact, altogether.

𝕴 𝖘𝖍𝖊𝖜 𝖜𝖍𝖆𝖙 𝕳𝖔𝖜𝖉𝖞𝖉𝖔𝖜𝖉𝖞 𝖙𝖍𝖔𝖚𝖌𝖍𝖙 𝖔𝖋 𝖆𝖑𝖑 𝖘𝖚𝖈𝖍 𝖘𝖈𝖆𝖒𝖕𝖘 𝖆𝖘 𝖘𝖓𝖚𝖋𝖋 𝖈𝖆𝖓𝖉𝖑𝖊𝖘 𝖜𝖎𝖙𝖍 𝖙𝖔𝖓𝖌𝖘. 𝕱𝖔𝖑𝖑𝖔𝖜𝖘 𝖆 𝖑𝖆𝖒𝖊𝖓𝖙𝖆𝖇𝖑𝖊 𝖍𝖔𝖜𝖑 𝖋𝖔𝖗 𝕳𝖔𝖜𝖉𝖞𝖉𝖔𝖜𝖉𝖞.

A select friend of my own, the late Doctor Howdydowdy, an Englishman of infinite research and surpassing powers of genius, of whose acquaintance, Philander, you would have been vainglorious, never ceased expressing the highest veneration for tongs. To have listened to the indignant eloquence of that man upon the profanation undergone by a pair of tongs, when converted, by hand of vulgarian, into a pair of snuffers! I was accustomed deferentially to hazard a few remarks by way of palliating the enormity. It's all gammon, he would reply, after having heard me out with that lofty patience that characterises elevated minds;—it's all gammon 'at 'ere fudgification of yours!—Darn it!—if a man ha'n'nt got fingers clean enough to trim a glimmer, let him cadge a pair of snuffers and be darned to un!—It is a pity that Howdydowdy should have died as he did, in a ditch. For six months previous to his death he had been subsisting exclusively upon whiskey, a practice that should never be recommended to persons of a delicate constitution. He rests in Bully's Acre.[25]

I argue the merits of the case as between tongs and poker. In what way the poker-champions are to be dealt with.

Claims have been authoritatively advanced by plodders and dowdlers in favor of the poker; and the superiority of the poker over the tongs has been warmly contended for by nincompoops and drivellers. The mode of treating these bores and boobies consists in tripping them up and treading them joyously in the gutter. What is a poker?—A bare unit,—a figure of 1,—a Brobdignagian[26] pin,—striking implement, it is true, in the gripe of a savage; but left to itself, abandoned to its own private resources,—seen reclining in its ordinary attitude by the mantel-piece, *nihil*, nothing. What stupid humbuggers there are alive this day! Let no man henceforth syllable poker and tongs in the one sentence.

I dilate celestially upon the effects produced on me by a glimpse of a superb pair of tongs. I prove that nobody has a right to call me a robber.

The preservation of tongs in a state of purity and brilliancy constitutes one of the noblest objects to which human attention can be directed. If a bachelor be so unfortunate as to have neither cook nor housemaid, the concentrated energies of his own mind should be lavished upon the task of burnishing his tongs. When I stalk into a drawing-room, and perceive a magnificent brace of tongs genteelly lounging by the fire-side, I experience a glow of spirit and a flow of thought bordering on the archangelical. Standers-by are instantaneously stricken lifeless with astonishment at the golden tide of poetry which in myriads of sunny streams and glittering rivulets, issues from my lips; poetry as far beyond what you, Public, are accustomed to get from me, as ambrosia is beyond hogwash. With modest effrontery I take a chair; and if my quick eye detect the presence of any thing in the shape of wine or punch on the table, I cheerfully abolish its existence. Impelled as I am, on such occasions, by an irresistible impulse, all apology is superfluous; but to speak the truth, the mingled grace and gravity that accompany my performance of the manœuvre afford superabundant compensation to the company for the disappearance of the drinkables. I may add that I re-establish the spiritless bottle upon the table, instead of putting it into my pocket as a robber would do, or shattering it into shivers upon the hearth-flag as a ruffian would do. Why is this? Because, Public, I, Clarence, am neither a ruffian nor a robber.

Herein J develope the rueful consequences of lazily suffering a tongs to get rusty. My romance conquers me, and J display sentimentalism of a heavenly order.

De l'autre coté,[27] whenever a pair of tongs covered with a cloak of ignominious rust strikes the eye of me, the heart-withering spectre paralyses the majority of my faculties in the twinkling of a bed-post. Darkest pictures arise melancholically and flit in lugubrious guise before my fancy. So pines, ejaculate I, a neglected genius in obscurity,—his prospects shaded,—his powers running to waste,— destitute of a fair field for his talents,—and looking forward to a dreary death and dismal burial in the vicinity of some dunghill! I see Trenck in Magdeburgh,[28] Tasso in Ferrara,[29] Galileo in Florence,[30] and you, Philander, in Kilmainham.[31] (Yet you, Philander, are not rusted, albeit you have quitted one rusty city for another rusticity. You rather remind me just now of a parboiled egg than of a rusty pair of tongs. Why? Because you are under Dunn.[32]) Then flow my tears like rain in winter. The immediate application of *eau-de-Cologne* or *sal volatile*[33] to my temples becomes a matter of pressing necessity; and while this charitable duty is in progress of performance by thee, my own beloved *Eglantine*,[34] I,— totally mastered by the romance interwoven with my nature, unconsciously kiss the fair hand that is thus employed, and bedew it again and again with passionate tears, which gush less from the eyes than from the heart. I am, indeed, a being of incredible susceptibility. I wonder very much that it is not generally known among my acquaintance. But half the world seems to be battishly blind.

(*I shall take up the tongs again, Public, in the next number of the* COMET.)

CLARENCE.
[*Comet*, 17 February 1833]

(CONTINUED.)

J start a poser that would have sorely puzzled Zeno.[35] When J have got pretty deeply into it, J am unfortunately called off to a bowl of brandy and gruel.

I now approach the analysis of an argument of intense interest. It is taken for granted that a pair of tongs has lost one of its grippers. A question to be mooted then results: whether the remnant be a pair of tongs or not? A presumption in favor of an affirmative conclusion is started from the fact, that although a man (whether a native of the Cannibal Islands, a Chinese, or a Tipperary man) may have lost a toe, he is not the less a man on account of the loss of his toe. But to this it may be objected, that the reasoning is not of universal application; inasmuch as if you,—to purchase a pennyworth of buttermilk for your breakfast,— deduct a penny from twenty pounds, the residue is no longer twenty pounds. Let me conceive the hypothesis that I have a pot of porter on the table before me. I abstract a spoonful of porter from the pot. *Quere*: Is the unabstracted *residuum* of porter left in the quart, a potful of porter or not? It will not be denied by the most determined doubter, that the aggregation of a specific number of spoonfuls of porter is requisite to constitute a total pot of porter. Two spoonfuls will not do. Three are a failure. Four spoonfuls are a decided bam.[36] Five are no go. No man in town will make me a potful out of six. Seven are a beggarly humbug. *Quere*, again, then: Is what remains in the pot a potful of porter or not? If it still be a potful of porter, antecedent to the abstraction of the spoonful of porter. If it be not a potful of porter, what is it? Is it a potful of froth,—a bubble,—a juggle on touch, taste, and sight? Here we are left to speculate in the dark. Doubt and obscurity surround us on every point of our starless pathway. At every step we make, we sink half a foot deeplier into the bog. We are bewildered, labyrinthed, lost! I am free to admit, however, that, taken in the abstract, scarcely any perceptible analogy subsists between a pot of porter and a pair of tongs. The tongs are of steel or brass; the pot is of pewter. You swallow the porter; no man swallows tongs. The solitary link of brotherhood between porter and tongs is this,—that tongs have a head, and that porter has a head. Still I am satisfied with the general tone of my logic. I perceive that I have shed a wide illumination upon the subject. I have pick-axically pioneered my way to the original question, that of the grippers. It is not, therefore, Public! deplorable,—must it not be considered dismal,—is it not an awful circumstance that I should feel at present too dozy and drowsy to push along any farther? My visage is buried in a basin of brandy and gruel: as soon as I shall have cleared the basin, off I toddle to bed.

𝕭𝖊𝖎𝖓𝖌 𝖓𝖔𝖜 𝖆𝖌𝖆𝖎𝖓 𝖔𝖓 𝖒𝖞 𝖕𝖎𝖓𝖘, 𝖆𝖓𝖉 𝖋𝖊𝖊𝖑𝖎𝖓𝖌 𝖗𝖊𝖋𝖗𝖊𝖘𝖍𝖊𝖉, 𝖑𝖎𝖐𝖊 𝖆 𝖌𝖎𝖆𝖓𝖙 𝖆𝖋𝖙𝖊𝖗 𝖆 𝖑𝖔𝖓𝖌 𝖉𝖗𝖎𝖓𝖐 𝖔𝖋 𝖜𝖍𝖎𝖘𝖐𝖊𝖞, 𝕴 𝖌𝖔 𝖔𝖓 𝖎𝖓 𝖙𝖍𝖎𝖘 𝖜𝖆𝖞.

The miraculous resemblance between the shape of man and the shape of tongs cannot fail to make a profound impression upon the soporiferous observer. To the moral philosopher it is a source of never-dying interest; the zoologist contemplates it in the light of a singular phenomenon; but above all, it appeals with irresistible power to the sympathies of the philanthropist. It has oftener than once occurred to me that Robert Owen[37] might, with great advantage and propriety, commit the superintendence of his parallelograms to a pair of tongs. The Trades' Union might occasionally, in the absence of their president, show their independence of all precedents, by moving, 'That until Tom Steele[38] do arrive, the chair be taken by Steel Tongs.' Tongs for ever! Tongs will yet triumph. At some future period, when Reason shall reign *solus*,[39]—when illuminism shall really prevail among men,—when Brougham's Useless Knowledge-books[40] shall be carted, waggon-load after waggon-load, into the mud of Father Thames,— when the human race shall have become rational,—when monarchies shall have tumbled, and kings become nobodies,—and—spiral climax!—when persons like myself, with intellect of the superhuman sort, shall drop in for an equitable proportion of such snacks as may be going;—than,—at that time,—in that day,— about that period, shall Governments and Unions award a tardy tribute of veneration to tongs. Some better Bowring,[41] yet unswathed, will arise to celebrate the glories of tongs in all languages!—senators will legislate with tongs in their hands!—duels will be decided by appeals to tongs!—tongs will, as Warton superfinely expresses it, 'be slowly swung with sweepy sway'[42] from side to side by right arm of pedestrian,—fair presumption for his dextrality!—and poets will magnify tongs in all measures and out of all measure,—anapæstic, pyrrhic, trochaic, dactyle, alexandrine, iambic, and even hexameter,—which that illustrious member of societies and industrious member of society, Dr. Southey,[43] has, in his latter days, with miserable want of gumption, endeavoured to see whether he could have any chance in trying to make a barbarous attempt at. But I lament to add that in those distant times none of us nineteenth-century men shall be alive,—because we shall all be dead. I speak of the year 7000.

Growing desperate and terrible as I proceed, I attack William Godwin,[44] and threaten to slaughter him.

I guess it is Helvetius,[45] who in his trumpery book, *De l'Esprit*, observes that a man vegetates like a tree, and that he (Helvetius) would as willingly be a tree as a man. Helvetius has totally omitted to inform us how much he would take to become a pair of tongs. The only mode left to us of accounting for this culpable oversight, is by presuming that Helvetius was as drunk as a piper while he was writing his book. Godwin, in his preface to St. Leon, categorically tells me that 'it is better to be a human being than a stock or a stone.'[46] Upon my honor, I cannot away with such an implied condemnation of tongs. William Godwin! I contest it with you. Strip, Sir! I will do battle with you on that article. How dare you, W. G. erect yourself into a dogmatist on men, stocks, and stones? Come, Godwin,—come, my man,—whence is your experience? What is the extent of your dabblings in the stocks? Were you ever in the *stock*ing trade,—and if so, how much was your *stock in trade* worth? Have you ever devoured a stockfish? Do you sport a black stock?[47] Come, never shrink from my *attacks, man*, as if I were a *tax man*; but answer me: How often do you play at jackstones? How far can you see into a millstone? Did you ever sell even a single stone of potatoes? I am a-*stone*-ished at your *stock* of assurance. You cub, what do you mean? Explain yourself, you varlet! Do you know, you sumph,[48] to whom it is that you stand opposed? Why, you greenhorn of a month's growth, is it possible that you forget that the knotted club of Clarence is already lifted up to prostrate you in your mother-mud, and that you are destined to kiss the bosom of your father-land incontinent? Godwin, I venerate your forty-quill[49] power as an author; and therefore, Godwin, I challenge you to a public disputation in my native city, Dublin, upon this subject; allowing you, as Crichton[50] allowed the University of Paris, the choice of thirty languages, and six and thirty various kinds of verse. There, now;—*c'est là une affaire finie*; so you may take your change out of that, and small blame to you, my gay fellow, for doing so.

(To be concluded in our next.)

[Unsigned, *Comet*, 10 March 1833]

(CONCLUDED.)

𝔚𝔥𝔶 𝔞𝔰 𝔪𝔞𝔫 𝔬𝔲𝔤𝔥𝔱 𝔫𝔬𝔱 𝔱𝔬 𝔟𝔢 𝔱𝔴𝔢𝔞𝔨𝔢𝔡 𝔟𝔶 𝔱𝔥𝔢 𝔫𝔬𝔰𝔢 𝔴𝔦𝔱𝔥 𝔞 𝔭𝔞𝔦𝔯 𝔬𝔣 𝔱𝔬𝔫𝔤𝔰, 𝔪𝔢𝔯𝔢𝔩𝔶 𝔬𝔫 𝔞𝔠𝔠𝔬𝔲𝔫𝔱 𝔬𝔣 𝔥𝔦𝔰 𝔭𝔬𝔩𝔦𝔱𝔦𝔠𝔰.

Listen to me now, reader. If you have invited a gentleman to dinner, it is a piece of suburban vulgarianism to tweak him by the beak with a pair of tongs, merely because his political opinions are not in harmony with yours. Truth compels me to add, that it betrays devilish impertinence in you; and affords a strong proof that neither your morals nor your manners were properly cultivated when you were a gaffer. Your guest may play the devil; but that is no reason why you should presume to play Saint Dunstan.[52] Your criminality assumes a deeper dye, if you have taken no pains to ascertain whether or not his beak had been soaped before he came into the room; for whenever the beak has not been soaped, and that well, the tweaking is an expressibly painful operation to the tweaked party. In conclusion, I must observe that I have never seen the act done; that I have never heard that any man did it; and that I do not believe any man to be capable of doing it; any man, at least, who reflects that the beak is the leading article of a gentleman's countenance.

P.S. Beak-tweaking is, indeed, very much out of fashion in general. Every one *nose* that it is *beak*ause of the Reform *Bill*.[53]

𝕴 ask whether any man supposes that 𝕴 am to write to all eternity upon tongs, and never get a drop of punch.

I want to put one question. I demand an answer in the face of congregated Europe—of the COMET CLUB[54]—of the Allied Powers[55]—and of the Black*- bearded, Grey-headed,[57] and Blue-devilled[58] Ministry of England. Is there, then, on the *Globe*, under the *Sun*,[59] or in the COMET, a man, with the *pia mater*[60] of an ass's foal, who will tell me that I ought to go on writing upon a pair of tongs to all eternity, without once slipping down to the nearest public-house to moisten my whistler? Why, what a hoggish stupidity such a fellow must have inherited! How muzzy he feels at all times! The world would,—(as Shelley says)—'laugh with a vast and inextinguishable laughter'[61] to see him slowly trailed through some sludgy puddle of interminable longitude, while I, standing alone, aloof from all, would look tearfully on, compassionating the sufferings of the unfortunate man from the depths of my soul,—and swilling (from time to time) as I looked on, protracted draughts from a pitcher of punch, to invigorate my nerves, and preserve me from hysterics. Let me reflect. It is now two, A.M. Taverns are closed. Not a minum of rum under my roof. I am waterless, sugarless, and spir—no, not spiritless! I go forth, Public, in terrible might, amid flashing rain and howling tempest, to storm the city for a beaker, though but of small beer! This is the most eventful morning of my life; and the adventures that I shall meet with before the sun gets up, are to form the subject of a future paper in the COMET.

𝕴 dive into the ocean of wit for a stray pearl, and fetch up a casket of gems.

We are now to consider what species of scene socialised life would exhibit, in case tongs were a nullity,—that is, if the space they fill presented a blank to the eye of the gazer,—that is, if there were no tongs. Imagine then, Philander,— think, Public, to what extremities we should be reduced! Stars and garters! Public, figure to yourself Francis Blackburne,[62] Esq., Grey's Attorney-General for Ireland, poking with his fingers among the cinders and semicalcined coals, and dropping them into the fire! Picture to yourself William Coyngham Plunket,[63] Lord High Chancellor of Ireland, descending to such a degradation as this is! *Raking* in his old days! Getting *smutty* in our eyes! Lowering himself to the level of the *Bar!* Disturbing the ashes of the *Grate!* Shaking hands with the most brazen *offenders!* Shewing that he is a *good* warrant at 'posting the *coal*,'[64] and a better on the *Turf!*[65] Instead of hasting away to Coke on Littleton,[66] wasting away his *little ton* of *coke!* In place of poring over Blackstone's Commentaries,[67]

---

* Any allusion to the Editor of the *Morning Chronicle?* PHIL.[56]

fingering coals, which are merely *black stones* (*Common tories*, Phil!) And possibly bringing a *Black burn*[68] on his hands! (No joke, Phil.) The blood, as he stoops, gushes cataract-like to his *cranium*, turning topsy-turvy the mighty kingdom of ideas in brain of Plunket, and sending the king himself adrift, Heaven knows whither, like the Dey of Algiers,[69] or the ex-Rex Charles X.[70] Look at his forehead and suppress your tears! It has come bump into contact with that smutty bar, now a trifle the brighter for the loss of the smut. Did you ever lay your eyes on such a dark-browed Chancellor? Only conceive what sums must, in consequence, be disbursed by Plunket, for cleansing lotions, for *Pommade divine*,[71] for ambrosial soap, otto of rose soap, soap of almonds, cocoa-nut oil soap, &c. &c. &c. &c. &c. &c. And yet his is but one instance in many—but *ex uno disce omnes*.[72] Let us therefore, Public, who possess tongs, who enjoy the unlimited use of them, who have received the capability of turning them to account as often as we like,—let us, I say, be careful how we undervalue so distinguished a blessing.

I adduce testimony on behalf of the antiquity of tongs.

Since I commenced this essay, my excellent friend Moses Cohen,[73] of Dame-street, a philosophical Hebrew (whose cigars I warmly recommend to the 'lip-homage' of all devout cloud-blowers) has directed my attention to the following passage in the fifth book of the Jewish Ethics, compiled by Levi:—

> Ten things were created on the eve of the Sabbath in the twilight; and these are they: the Mouth of the Sabbath, the Mouth of the Ass (of Balaam), and the Mouth of the Spring; the Rainbow, Manna, the rod of Moses, the Shameer, Characters, Writing, and the Tables. And some say, also the Dæmons, and the grave of our legislator Moses, and the ram of our father Abraham, and also THE PREPARED INSTRUMENT OF A TONGS.[74]

A passage worth the whole of the Talmud! I shall leave it to speak for itself.

Public and I have a tussle.

If we dispassionately investigate the nature of our conceptions with regard to the abstract idea of a pair of tongs, we shall discover that it is by no means what the Aristotelians denominate an *ens rationis*,[75] but rather—

PUBLIC *(with outrageous impatience.)* O! curse you and your tongs, and your *ens rationis* to boot! Is there no end to this trumpery? You bore me to death's door! But, bless my soul! Is it possible? He is positively dead asleep! *(approaches and shakes me.)*

I. *(yawning and rubbing my orbs.)* You have disturbed me, old woman, in the enjoyment of as hazily-beautiful a doldrum as ever soul of poet revelled in. You have cruelly broken my talisman. For which I feel cruelly disposed to break your neck. My occupation's gone:[76]—asleep, I wrought wonders: awake, my brain-case is a base-built pumpkin.

SHE. But, what, in the name of all that is odd, induced you to select such a subject?

I. Why, old woman,—if I am an original genius,—if nature has gifted me with certain toploftical powers,—

SHE *(interrupting me in an unmannerly manner.) Toploftical!* Pah! Do you think that I will tolerate such rebel English?—Like your prohibition, forsooth, against '*syllabling* poker and tongs in one day.'

I. What! antiquated dame,—have you, then, never heard of Shakespeare's

———Airy *tongs* that *syllable* men's names
In desert wildernesses?[77]

It is clear that you have never been to the Tonga Islands, or eaten (and drunk, too,) your share of a *hog's head* in company with King Tongataboo.[78]

SHE. Well, Sir, *pour couper court*[79]—if you wish me to patronise—I mean *matronise* you, will you desist from a subject only calculated for the meridian of an ironmonger's shop. I lay my injunction on you.

I—*(with an air).*—An injunction that the Chancellor shall never dissolve. I yield to the fair—though it is hard. With Schiller I exclaim,—

Das Jahrhundert
Ist meinem Ideal nicht reif—Ich lebe
Ein Bürger derer welche kommen werden.* [80]

Adieu! respectable old creature.
SHE. Adieu! my son.

CLARENCE.

P.S.—Every one remembers Lord Anglesey's modest and quiet *entrée* into Dublin some time back, and Marcus Costello's pair of tongs and pair of black stockings.[81] Costello's conduct on that occasion was looked on, at the time, as a symbolical hint to such of the Marquis's friends as were determined to keep up

---

* This age is not ripe for my theories. I live a denizen of the centuries that are to come.

the *game* 'at all *hazards*,' that thus would all *blacklegs* be ultimately caught and suspended. For my part I always, from the bottom of my *sole*, considered it a mark of respect from the noble Marcus to the noble Marquiz for the *heeling measures* set on *foot* by the latter, which I am *shoe-r* it would be *bootless* to enumerate. The Marquis himself says he *under-stand*s it in that light, and vows he will take *steps* to put down *White feet*[82] every where. Whiggery, it is said, has got beyond *standing:* if so, Angelsey's first proclamation will make a capital *l-e-g*[83] for it.

[*Comet*, 17 March 1833]

My Bugle, and How I Blow It
BY THE MAN IN THE CLOAK*

Ein Alphorn hor ich schallen,	A Mystical Bugle calls o'er
Das mich von hinnen ruft.	The Earth to me everywhere—
Tont es aus wald'gen Hallen	Peals it from forest halls or
Tont es aus blauer Luft	The crypts of the azure air?
Tont es von Bergeshohen	From the snow-enrobed mountains yonder?
Aus blumenreichen Thal	From the flower-strewn vales below?
Wo ich nur steh'und gehe,	O! whithersoever I wander
Hor ich's in suszer Qual.	I hear it with sweetest woe!
Bei Speil und frohen Reigen,	Alone in the wood, or present
Einsam mit mir allein,	Where mingle the song and the dance,
Tont's ohne je zu schweigen	That summoning sound incessant
Tont tief in's Herz hinein.	Is piercing my heart like a lance.
Noch nie hab'ich gefunden	Till now hath my search been ceaseless,
Den Ort, woher es schallt	And its place I have nowhere found;
Und nimmer wird gesunden	But my spirit must ever be peaceless
Diesz Herz bis e3 verhallt.	Till that bugle shall cease to sound!

If the German poet[2] speak truth in the last two lines, he had better set sail for England without delay, and assassinate ME, for I am the Bugle-player! I plunge at once, like an Epic versifier, in *medias* res,[3] you perceive, reader, and 'give my

* We are prepared to find that some of our readers will not relish this admirable extravaganza; but the 'inextingushable laughter' which it will create in all who are familiar with the German metaphysics and mysticism that it quizzes, must be our excuse to the uninitiated for gladly giving it a place in our columns. It was written for the *Vindicator* by one of the most able, popular, and learned contributors of the *University Magazine.*—ED. VIN.[1]

worst of thoughts the worst of words.'⁴—Yes! *I* am the Bugle-blower; and like
Sam Slick's cloud-blower, I am willing to blow away and 'take the responsi-
bility.'⁵ And who, you ask, is the poet? That will I tell you instanter. The original
grubber-up of the gem that I have set in gold, silver or pewter, as the metal may
turn out to the touchstone, is, be it known to you, Justinus Kerner, man of many
accomplishments, poet, physician, metaphysician, hobgoblin-hunter, widower
and weeper. He is by birth a Swabian,⁶ or perhaps I should say a Swab; just as we
call a native of Poland a Pole: the word 'Swab,' moreover, has the advantage of
'Swabian' in being shorter by three letters; and I have seen three letters take up
six newspaper columns. Little did Kerner imagine the first evening the Bugle
smote his ears that the Man in the Cloak, whom he saw climbing the hill to the
right, was his electrifier! Up went his dexter ogler along the rocks, and there
encountered—a goat: him the poet did not for a moment suspect of practising
on either of his own Horns; and so down went his sinister peeper to the flood
below, where, however, it was at once rebuked by a corpulent codfish, whose
interrogative eye appeared fixed on 'the first demonologist in Europe,'⁷ with a
library of wondering questions in the pupil thereof. I, my Cloak and my Bugle,
meantime had vanished for the night. Pretty considerably bewildered, my Swab
toddled homeward to his attic, and over a second tankard of heavy wet
composed the stanzas I have quoted.

I confess, nevertheless, it has always appeared to me singular—I would say
shameful—that neither during the concert of that nor of any subsequent evening
did Kerner seem to recognise Me as the musician. True it is that I wore a Cloak
a quarter of a hundred weight, with expansive wings at the sides, and a hood
that hung down from the head, obscuring the light of my countenance;⁸ and
bugle-players are generally less cumbrously clad, but still it is difficult for me to
acquit him of most hoggish stupidity if I suppose that his suspicions were not at
intervals directed towards me. Indeed the very circumstance of a man's walking
about perspiring under such a peculiar Cloak ought alone to have been suffi-
cient to convince him (the Swab) that there was a mystery of some sort
connected with the perspirer; and had he only trundled up to me and put the
interrogatory,—Man in the Cloak, art thou He? I would have responded to his
sagacity by nobly and without all disguise flapping my side-wings in his
physiognomy, and treating him to a blast that would have shaken him to the
centre of his system.

I was one day—very recently indeed—recounting this adventure, with slight
additions, to my friend the King of the Sicilies,⁹ when an Englishman near me,
who had just been admitted to the horrors of an audience, turned round, *à la
Jacques Corveau*,¹⁰ and stares at my Cloak from hood to hem in the rudest man-
ner through his *lorgnette*.¹¹

'Pray, Sir,' he asked, 'are you celebrated for anything besides wearing a Cloak?' Every hair in my moustache quivered at the ruffianism of the fellow, but on account of the King's proximity I restrained myself from sneering, or even sneezing.

'Yes, Sir,' I replied, 'for playing on my bugle: have you not heard my anecdote, you sumph[12] of the muddiest water?'

'Come, come,' interposed the King, 'no personalities—this gentleman is a Corn-law Repealer.'[13] (This he said, evidently not knowing the signification of his words.)

'Ay,' cried the Englishman, 'I *am* a Corn-law Repealer!'

'And I,' cried I, flapping my pinions, 'I—I am a Unicorn-law Repealer!'

'A Unicorn-law Repealer!'—and the Manchesterian grinned—'what may that be?'

'A Repealer in virtue of that Law of my being which compels me to play on One Horn,' said I, holding up my Bugle.

'How a Repealer?' he asked.

'Thus,' quoth I: 'a Pealer, when I peal: a Re-pealer, when I peal again. Do you understand trapp?'[14]

'Pardon me,' said the Englisher, waving his hand, 'I do not carry a flash vocabulary about me.' Here the King should thrust himself in—'What does he mean by a flash vocabulary?'[15] said he to me in an under voice. 'A horn of sulphur, your Majesty,' I answered, in the same tone; 'I take it as a direct insult to you, your recent political squabble with Great Britain considered.' Up flared the King, like a rocket from Mount Vesuvius. 'Who talks of Sulphur at this time of day?' he cried. 'What on earth is he after?' asked the Corn-law Repealer of me, *sotto voce*. 'He wants your opinion of the Sulphur Question,'[16] whispered I. 'I shall be happy to give it,' said the Englishman: 'the Sulphur Monopoly, your Majesty, I conceive to be totally————' 'I wish the devil had the Sulphur Monopoly from the beginning!' roared the King. 'I think the devil *has* had the Sulphur Monopoly from the beginning,' observed the Corn-law Proser—'I was just about to remark that he is the legitimate monopolist of the article.' 'You were, were you?' cried the King—then turning to me—'did any man ever see such a silly fellow?' 'I fancy,' said I, folding my Cloak about me like an Emperor, 'that your Majesty's subjects are pretty much in the habit of seeing fellows quite as silly.' 'Indeed! Why so?' 'Because,' said I, 'you are the King of the See-sillies.' This tickled the Monarch so home that his good humour returned like fine weather on an April day, and he ordered in coffee, cigars, and a steaming bowl of bishop,[17] in return for my share of which executed an unapproachable solo on my Bugle, which dissolved the entire Court in an extacy of tears, and made the King, strong as his nerves were, instantaneously mix an additional tumbler to save himself from fainting.

Then I was at Naples—now I am in London. From sulphur to coal-gas—out of the frying-pan into the fryer—'a bitter change, severer to severe,'[18] as the poet Young, now alas! grown Old in dusty obscurity, sings. I have imported myself hither, free of duty—free of all duties at least save one, that of blowing my Bugle; and here I am, in 'the great Metropolis,'[19] though I have got no *Grant* (either from Government or otherwise) to place me there;—my Bugle on the table of mine inn, and my Cloak, 'fold over fold, inveterately convolved,'[20] around my majestic person. A thousand troubles menace me. *Cælum non animam mutant qui trans mare currunt*[21]—; yet I care not. Come what may, my Cloak will stick to me, my Bugle depend from my baldric. My Cloak and my Bugle I must always retain, until My Last Hour shall see the one rended into shreds and the other divested of its identity, melted into air, transmuted into an ethereality as viewless and intangible as one of its own melodies.

Here, however, and before I advance a sentence further, I know that some noodles will be disposed to take me very short. 'Bah!' the jackasses will bray, 'you over-rate your pretensions to notice. How are you a greater man than Plato, Brougham or Bombastes Paracelsus?[22] You have a Bugle and you wear a Cloak:—well, and what of all that? In what way can those extraneous appendages of the man confer intellectual pre-eminence on the mind?' Were I for answering those greenhorns seriously, I should certainly drub them till they dropped. Do the twaddlers not know that the whole thing is æsthetical? That it involves the abstrusest metaphysical views at all? That Philosophy beholds an admirable harmony in the connection between the interior and exterior of Man, not only in the abstract but in the individual, and moreover recognises the eternal truth, not to be controverted by scepticism, not to be shaken by twaddle, that Every Individual is Himself, and that He cannot become Another as long as He remains Himself, for the simple reason that if He were to become Another He would cease to be Himself? No, the ganders, they don't, because they know nothing upon any subject connected with anything that has ever at all existed anywhere whatever. Let the dunderheads for once show themselves tractable and attend to what I am going to spout. Public! do you also listen—you are also elevated to the high honour of being my confidante. I am about to confer an incredible mark of my favour on you, Public.

Know, then, the following things:—

Firstly: That I am not *a* Man in *a* Cloak, but *the* Man in *the* Cloak. My personal identity is here at stake, and I cannot consent to sacrifice it. Let me sacrifice it, and what becomes of Me? 'The earth hath bubbles as the water hath,'[23] and I am thenceforth one of them: I lose my Cloak and my Consciousness both in the twinkling of a pair of tongs: I become what the Philosophy of Kant (in opposition to the Cant of Philosophy) denominates a *Nicht-ich*, a Not-I, a Non-

Ego. Pardon me, my Public, if I calmly but firmly express my determination to shed the last drop of my ink before I concede the possibility of such a paltry, sneaking, shabby, swindling, strip-and-pillage-me species of contingency.

Secondly: That I am the *Man* in the Cloak. Viz.: I am not an 'Old Woman,' as Mrs. Trollope[24] complains that the Yankees *would* call her, despite of her best bonnets, satin frocks and flounces, and corsets *à l'enfant*.[25] Neither am I a lump of moonshine, all out. Stigmatise me if you will as a Hottentot, as a Troglodyte, as a hang-a-bone jailbird; still you cannot put your hand on your heart and assert that I am a make-believe, a bag of feathers, a *non-ens*,[26] a bull-beggar, a hobgoblin, a humbug, a lath-and-pulley get-up, like Punch. Not at all. I do not say that you *dare* not, but I clap my wings like a bantam on a barn-roof, and I crow aloud in triumph that you *cannot*, Public. It is outside the sphere of your power, my Public! I am the MAN in the Cloak. *Mettez cela dans votre pipe, et fumez-le, mon public!*[27]

Thirdly: That I am the Man *in* the Cloak. In other words, I am by no manner of means the Man *of* the Cloak, or the Man *under* the Cloak. The Germans call me, Der Mensch *mit* dem Mantel, the Man *with* the Cloak. This is a deplorable error in the nomenclature of that otherwise intelligent people, and I am speechless with astonishment that they should have fallen into it. Why? Because my Cloak is not part and parcel of Myself.—The Cloak is outside and the Man is inside, as Goldsmith said of the World[28] and the Prisoner; but each is a distinct entity: of that I am satisfied; on that point I, as the Persians would say, tighten the girdle of assurance round the waist of my understanding, though perhaps there is no waste of my understanding whatever. I admit that you may say, 'The Man with the Greasy Countenance,' or 'The Chap with the Swivel Eye:' thus also Slawkenbergius[29] (vide *Tristram Shandy*) calls his hero 'The Stranger with the Nose,' and reasonably enough, for although it was at one period conjectured that the Nose in question might extend to five hundred and seventy-five geometrical feet longitude, not even the most incredulous among the Faculty of Strasburg were found to advance an opinion that the Nose was not an integral portion of the Individual. With Me the case is a horse of another colour. I do not put my Cloak on and off, I grant, but I can do so when I please by a mere exercise of volition and muscle; and therefore it is obvious to the meanest capacity (I like the original *tours de phrase*[30]) that I am just the Man *in* the Cloak, and no mistake. If any cavillers feel inclined to dispute the proposition with me further they may await my arrival in Dublin at the Fifteen Acres.[31]

Finally: That I am in the Man in the *Cloak*. Other men tabernacle their corporeality in broad cloth, Petershams, Redingotes, Surtouts, Mackintoshes, Overalls, Wraprascals, Kangaroos, Traceys, Dreadnoughts. Every blunderer to his fancy or the fashion. I quarrel with no booby for his taste or want of taste. I do not approach any mooncalf in the public street with an uplifted crowbar,

poker, pitchfork or pick-ax in my grasp, because his toggery is of a different order
from my own. I could not do so: independent of my intuitive benevolence of
disposition I have what Harriet Martineau would call 'a powerful preventive
check'[32] in my sense of what is due to the *bienséances*[33] of society. On the other
hand, however, I yield up not a whit of my own liberty. I am aware that in Africa
and Asia people wear 'cotton, muslin and other stuffs with which I won't stay
puzzling'[34]—that in parts of America the run is upon blankets—that in the West
Indies nankeens are all the go—that in Egypt the men sometimes carry their
duds under their arms. But am I therefore to ape their example—to become an
African, an American, a West-Indian, an Egyptian? I see not the decillionth part
of a reason for doing so. I call Europe to witness that I shall N E V E R do so as long
as I have my Cloak. In a cause like this I laugh at coercion and despise the
prospect of torture.—What did I buy my Cloak for? Why did I pay fifteen
shillings and six pence, besides boot, for it to a Jew hawker of Old Rags but that
I might don it and never doff it, I should be glad to know?

After all, I am the most rational of mankind, including Robert Owen[35]
himself, and I will show that I am. Notwithstanding all I have so eloquently said
there may still remain some persons reluctant to concede my qualifications for
amusing or illuminating them because I carry a Bugle and wear a Cloak. Suppose,
then, that in compassion to the hidebound prejudices of these poor creatures I
gallantly wave all ground of superiority derivable from my Bugle and my Cloak!
What if I cast away, as far as I possibly can,—much further than they could cast
a bull by *his* Horns—both the one and the other? Will my magnanimity be
appreciated? Surely it may, can, might, could, would or should be—only really
the world is such a settled dolt! Let me not be misunderstood.—I cannot avoid
blowing my Bugle and showing my Cloak. What I mean to state is, that I shall
refrain from claiming any especial merit in possessing either. I shall not glorify
myself because I split the ears of groundlings,[36] nor shall I give myself any extra-
mundanc airs, though my wings *do* occasionally flap like winking in the eyes of
the lieges, children of dust,—dusts themselves—as they are. In the very fulness
and churchflower of my triumph I shall talk 'with bated breath and whispering
humbleness'[37] of what I have done, am doing, and mean to do; so that spectators
shall say of me, as I said t'other day of my friend Barney Higgins the vintner, while
he was trying to coax the Bench into (or out of) a renewal of his spirit-license—

'How like a fawning Publican he looks!'[38]

With which specimen of my 'Wit and Wisdom' (N.B.—I am not the father of
all the jests in the book that goes by that title[39]), good reader, I bid you farewell
for the present.

There is much talk here of 'embarking capital.' I wish the talkers could embark *the* Capital itself, for never did city need an aquatory excursion so much—'all the town's a fog, and all the men and women merely fograms.'[40] I shall steam over to the Green Isle shortly; and, once there, I mean to apply to some *Vindicator* of Talent in my own behalf and that of my Cloak and Bugle, and supplicate his patronage for six weeks. Beyond that period, alas! I may not remain an abider within any town. Your surprise, reader, is doubtless excited—ah! you know not what a Vagabond I am!—Perhaps I may communicate my history to the Irish People, and if I should I have no hesitation in assuring them that they will pronounce it without a parallel in the Annals of the Marvellous and Mournful. Only see the result!—for me there is no stopping place in the city or county. An unrelenting doom condemns me to the incessant exercise of my pedestrian capabilities. It is an awful thing to behold me at each completion of my term scampering off like Van Woedenblock[41] of the Magic Leg—galloping along roads—clearing ditches—dispersing the affrighted poultry in farm-yards as effectually as a forty-eight pounder could. Other men sojourn for life in the country of their choice; there is a prospect of ultimate repose for most things; even the March of Intellect must one day halt; already we see that pens, ink, and paper are—stationary. But for me there is no hope: at home or abroad I tarry not. Like Schubart's Wandering Jew,[42] I am 'scourged by Unrest through many climes.' Like Coleridge's Ancient Mariner, 'I pass, like Night, from land to land.'[43] No matter who or what becomes paralytic and refuses to budge, I must progress. 'Tramp, tramp, along the land; splash, splash, across the sea,'[44] is my maledictory motto. A fearful voice, to all but me inaudible, for ever thunders in mine ear, 'Pack up thy duds!—push along!—keep moving!' I see no prospect before me but an eternity of peripateticalism.

'The race of Life becomes a hopeless flight
To those that walk in darkness—on the sea
The boldest steer but where their ports invite,
But there are wanderers o'er Eternity
Whose bark drives on and on, and anchored ne'er shall be!'[45]

Once again, reader, farewell, but forget not

THE MAN IN THE CLOAK.
[*Vindicator*, 27 March 1841]

Critical Writings

from *'Anthologia Germanica'* series

[1]

[...] For though there be those who would cry shame upon us for the confession, we do confess that to our ear no language sounds as pleasing as that of England; and we would not exchange our own mother tongue, with all its harshness, and with all its imperfections, (harshness, it is true, that has never grated upon our ear, and imperfections that we never have detected,) for all the languages that either modern ages or antiquity can boast. No, not for the rich and sonorous melody of the Greeks—not for the terse and racy conciseness of the Latins, nor for the almost boundless vocabulary of the German, nor yet for the soft and melting flow of the Italian. And why should we? Is it not the language of our homes? Is it not that in which we remember the voices of our parents, and of the friends of our youth? Is it not that in which we first heard the words of tender endearment, in which we first listened to the teachings of religion? Is it not thus twined, as it were, in hallowed association with all our recollections of this world, and all our hopes of the next? and where is the linguist, we care not how ardent his devotion to other tongues, who will not return, with all the fervour of first love, to his own? Ay, and as the thoughts of first love will arise unbidden, we know not why, at a moment when we did not wish for them—is not the language of England that in which we spoke the words of young and ardent, and generous, affection to one who—but no matter, we must not become sentimental, and surely to our readers we will need far less excuse than we have already made, for loving the English above all other languages.

And yet we love the language of Germany, and we admire her poetry, and, therefore, it is that we would pay to that poetry the highest compliment we can, that of translating it into the language that we honour most; wishing at the same time that our strains were worthier to do justice to its merits. [...]

If we were asked what it is that constitutes the leading characteristic of German Poetry, we should be disposed to answer—Too adventurous an attempt to assimilate the creations of the ideal with the forms of the actual world. Throughout that poetry we can trace a remarkable effort to render vivid and tangible and permanent those phantasmagoria of the mind which by the statutes of our nature are condemned to exhibit an aspect of perpetual vagueness and fluctuation. And as this is the prominent characteristic, so it is the darkest blemish of German Poetry. Let no absurd admirer of the style that approximates to the unintelligible tell us that we censure as an imperfection what we should, if we properly entered into the spirit of the writer, applaud as an excellence. Advocates for the highest possible degree of perspicuity in poetry we are and shall always continue to be, because we are persuaded that it is the want of that perspicuity which, more than any other want, has contributed to the growth of the popular indifference at present so prevalent with regard to poetry, and has made the eldest-born of Heaven, even in the eyes of her own worshippers, an object rather of wonder than of love. Remote from us be the narrowness of soul that would under-estimate or contest the capabilities of genius. Imagination may in many great poets have its own wondrous forms, and seem to produce its own strange creations, without any restraint, save that of which the ancient critic speaks—

'εισ νομοσ το δοξαν ποητη'[1]

But even this latitude, wide as it is, is not infinite. The 'το δοξαν' was always a barrier, however distant it might appear, if all was left to the poet's discretion— the existence of discretion was presumed, and we hold it to be all but an axiom that if, while Imagination operated, it had not, after all, limited its operations to a sphere whose boundaries were prescribed and sentinelled with jealous vigilance by Reason and Precedent, we should at this day possess but a scanty show indeed of poetical monuments to boast of. We would venture to say, that we should scarcely be able to produce one that would be accounted worthy of more than the momentary gaze of admiration we bestow upon the shifting colours of the air-bubble or the kaleidoscope. [...]

[from 'Anthologia Germanica No. IV', unsigned, *DUM*, October 1835]

[2]

Faust[2] may, in one respect, be looked upon as the *chef d'œuvre* of Goethe. It is the most remarkable by far of all of his productions. [...] It is, and to latest ages must remain, the most imperishable of all the monuments of the marvellous genius of its marvellous author.

Yet not because of its intrinsic importance; certainly not because we should pronounce it a work which the spirit of Utility, or even of Utilitarianism,[3] would care to patronise. For any high moral purpose it may be deposited on the shelf as valueless. It inculcates nothing either consolatory or ennobling. It possesses no tendency to elevate him who reads and studies it above his fate or his fellows. There is no lesson conveyed by a single page of it, the perusal of which tempts a man to exclaim, This is indeed a legacy!—this is worthy of being treasured up in the memory for ever! It communicates no restorative, no freshening impetus to the soul of him who, having set out in quest of Truth, droops by the way-side when storms begin to muster, and clouds first overcast the prospect. It is a specimen of mere but magnificent Power. This is the attribute which we have always regarded as constituting the distinguishing excellence of Goethe as a writer. But there are in *Faust* more of the elements that go to the composition of this attribute than in all the other great works of Goethe together. [...]

We care but little for the man Faustus; little for him in poetry, less in the world. Divest him, indeed, of the robe which Goethe has embroidered for him, and you leave him slight title to more notice than falls to the lot of any other inheritor of the penalty of Adam. You discern nothing but a human being, somewhat unhappier, it is true, than his fellows, but scarcely differing from them in any particular of a more prominent nature than his unhappiness. How many of the more cultivated order of minds should we not presume that there are, whose progress through this mysterious existence is characterised by the same suffering, the same scepticism, the same vague ambition, the same vicissitudes of enthusiasm and lassitude that make miserable the days and nights of Faustus! Are there in reality such in the world? Assuredly. We do not, it is true, meet with them. Why do we *not* meet with them? *Because they are in the world.* Being *in* the world they appear as *of* the world; the thick veil of worldly error and worldly illusion interposes betwixt us and them, and the naturally strong outlines of their individuality grow dim and undefined to the eye. Besides, the heavy moral atmosphere their souls breathe without intermission presses upon themselves. Even they, confused in their perceptions and disorganised in their faculties, are not always conscious that they suffer more than others. *No one among them is capable of seeing himself in the same point of view in which he regards the Faustus of the drama.* 'The world is too much with them'[4]—though it is still more with those who would scrutinize and understand them. Hence the utility and lofty moral excellence of the poet. He disperses, by his wizard art, the mists which envelope the shapes of Actual Life, and marshals those shapes before us, apparelled, perhaps, in more gorgeous vesture than the philosopher might require to see them arrayed in, but preserving, withal, their indestructible identity, and all those distinctive peculiarities of aspect and proportion which render it impossible that any one of them shall be confounded with any other of them. Goethe has done so much for Faustus, and if he has failed in awakening our deeper sympathies in behalf of the child of his creation, not to any defect in his art is the failure attributable, but to the essentially common-place character of the being the record of whose struggles against the constitution of Nature and the universe he has rendered imperishable. [...]

[from 'Anthologia Germanica No. V', unsigned, *DUM*, March 1836]

[3]

[. . .] We cannot object to the employment of prose-language in poetry, where it is in character, or may be essential to the integrity of the poem. All that we insist upon is, that we have a right to repudiate it where the poet, in the plenitude of his emptyheadedness, tries to pass it off upon us as the most felicitous of all modes for the development of poetical conceptions. And is not the imposture now rather too common in Germany? Is it or is it not true, true to the letter, that more than a moiety of all the productions of all the German poets are beneath criticism—that they are a stigma upon the national taste—that they bear about the same resemblance to poetry which a collection of visages chiselled out of a timber-log by some bungling booby, less accustomed to the chisel than to the pick-axe, might bear to the 'human face divine'[5] of Greece or Asia? With great confidence we assert that it is; and we challenge contradiction from any literary authority in existence. We allude not now to those outrageous violations of the Arisotelian canon—the standing reproach of German literature—which every-body had heard of and nobody palliates. These are diagnostics peculiar to diseased intellect, and nothing besides; and a reflecting mind will no more find fault with them than with the ravings of lunacy. They are attempts to illustrate whatever is most senseless in theory, or least tangible in principle, and, of course, to be uniform, *must* be absurd. We speak merely of the comparative dryness and insipidity of German poetry generally. And how dry, how insipid this is, let those tell who have studied it *au fond*,[6] are best qualified to pass judgment on it. Common-places that the ear grows intolerant of in conversation,—driftless paradoxes—clumsy descriptions—lack-a-daisiacal lamentations—rhodomon-tade[7]—puerility—nonsense—these are the stock in trade of the German poet; and if any one wonder that his business should ever be a flourishing one, let it be borne in mind that he, the same poet, is the exception to this rule that 'a prophet hath no honor in his own country,'[8] and this not, of course, because of his own deserts, but because of his *lieber Deutchsland's*[9] immemorial proneness to patronize all sorts of common-places, driftless paradoxes, lack-a-daisiacal lamentations, rhodomontade, puerility and nonsense. Were it otherwise, where were the six-compound-epithetted Tiedge,[10] with his baffling nouns, about as tangible as shadows; or Hölty,[11] who, whenever we indulge in a rural stroll with him, grows enthusiastic upon horseponds and haystacks? How had it fared with Klopstock,[12] whose feeble phraseology is only the more pitiable for its feebleness, because for a space it dupes ear and eye with a semblance of force? Or with Bürger[13] the celebrated, whose platitude, save in two or three of his ballads and lyrical pieces, is alas! unendurable? Or what had become of those twin-giants, Werner[14] and Schubart;[15] seeing that neither of them knows what to do with his club, unless he sit down upon the highway and split pebbles with it? Or of Tieck,[16] who, rich and imaginative beyond all praise as his prose is, was the first writer whose poems ever helped us to a perfect conception of the meaning of the word *twaddle?* Or of Novalis[17]—but no—erroneous as the views of Novalis were with regard to the nature of poetry, we cannot doubt that if he had lived, his comprehensive understanding would have corrected them. Time will yet gather the ashes of Novalis in an urn apart: in the meantime let not common hands presume to weigh them. [. . .]

In contrasting the condition of the German poet with that of the English we must acknowledge that the genuine and sterling advantage abides with the English. The German poet is hugged and fondled out of his proper independence. He is beslavered with the slime of popular adulation, until he becomes a spectacle for the pity of the rational. The English poet is left to himself. He is cast upon his own resources. He is compelled to make head against all obstacles; and his power to annihilate those obstacles is made, and fitly made, the test of his genius. The consequence is that he either attains eminence and celebrity, or is thrown down, trampled on and forgotten, as Nature intended. It is all (among us) just as it ought to be. There is no error more decided than that of supposing that a mind of a great and original tone requires what is called encouragement or patronage. On the contrary, such a mind should voluntarily erect an impassable barrier between its own operations and any support that others might be inclined to tender it. All support of the kind, like that which the ivy affords to the oak, would, in fact, have a latent tendency to impair its vigorousness. Popular favour too frequently bereaves its idol of that freedom of thought without which it is impossible for any man to calculate upon the ability of accomplishing an enduring benefit for his fellow-men. It is like the Magnetic Mountain[18] in the Persian Tale, which mariners hailed at a distance with delight, but which, as they approached more and more within the sphere of its influence, drew out from their ship all its nails and clench-bolts, and thus left it to drift or founder. And if the pinnace of the German poet, after living its hour in the sunshine, goes down and is seen no more, where lies the wonder? We know where the blame lies.

It may be inferred from what we have said that we are dissatisfied with ourselves for having undertaken these Anthologia.[19] But we have always considered any deprecation of censure for our own attempts to be quite out of the question. The entire weight of the blame rests upon the authors from whom we versify. We cannot, like the experimentalist in Gulliver,[20] undertake to extract a greater number of sunbeams from a cucumber than it is in the habit of yielding. Beyond the mere ability to classify, the discernment necessary for selecting and rejecting, there is neither labour nor knowledge that we will submit to be tasked for. Still we uniformly do the best we can both for ourselves and our originals. [. . .]

[from 'Anthologia Germanica No. VII', unsigned, *DUM*, August 1836]

[4]

Ludwig Tieck,[21] man-milliner to the Muses, poet, metaphysician, dramatist, novelist, moralist, wanderer, weeper and wooer, a gentleman of extensive and varied endowments, is, notwithstanding, in one respect, a sad quack. Such rubbish, such trumpery, such a farrago of self-condemned senilities, so many mouthy nothings, altogether so much snoring stupidity, so much drowsiness, dreariness, drizzle, froth and fog as we have got in this his last importation from Cloudland, surely no one of woman born before ourself was ever doomed to deal with. We now, for the first time in our life, stumble on the discovery that there may be less creditable methods of recruiting one's finances than even those which are recorded with reprobation in the columns of the Newgate Calendar. [...][22]

All that we can gather is that he is delectably miserable. He maintains almost from first to last one monotonous wail, as mournful and nearly as unvarying as the night-lament of the Whip-Poor-Will in the forests of South America. He simpers and whimpers; and yet, one cannot tell whether he would fain be thought glad or sad. [...] Trifles and things of nothing also exercise prodigious power over him. It is easy to see that, if tempted to 'make his quietus,'[23] it will be with nothing savager than 'a bare bodkin,' and that a yard or two of packthread will be quite sufficient to aid his efforts at exhibiting a case of suspended animation in his own person. Hotspur complains of being 'pestered by a popinjay,'[24] but Tieck's patience, like that of Tristram Shandy's uncle,[25] is put to the test by a blue-bottle fly. He is knocked down by a bulrush every half-minute in the day, and reverently kisses the face of his fatherland fourteen hundred and forty times in twelve hours. A dead leaf throws him into convulsions, and at the twittering of a swallow the heart of the poor man batters his ribs with such galvanic violence of percussion that at three yards' distance you suspect the existence of hypertrophy, and are half-disposed to summon a surgeon. Like Gulliver in the hands of the Lilliputians,[26] he is the victim of a million of tiny tormentors, who slay him piecemeal, the ten-thousandth part of an inch at a time. The minuter his calamity, too, the more he suffers. He may exclaim, with the lover in Dryden's play, 'My wound is great, because it is so small!'[27] The colossal evils of life he passes over *sous silence*,[28] as unworthy the notice of a sentimentalist. Like the bronze figure of Atlas,[29] he can stand immoveable with a World of Woes upon his shoulders; but a single disaster, particularly if it be very slight, is too tremendous for his equanimity. The last feather, it is said, breaks the horse's back; but Tieck's back is broken by one feather. He is ready to oppose, as our friend Fergusson would say, an 'ironbound front,'[30] to the overwhelming allurements of an entire parterre,[31] while a simple *bouquet* brings on an attack of *delirium tremens*. He can lounge through a flower-garden half-a-mile long, his hands in his pockets, a Peripatetic in appearance and a Stoic at heart; but 'dies of *one* rose in aromatic pain.'[32]

Under such circumstances one should suppose that he was much to pity. The case is the contrary. His sufferings are the sole source of his pleasures. Reversing the saying of the frogs in the fable,[33] what seems death to you is sport to him. Every emotion that tenants his heart must pay a rack-rent,[34] or the income of his happiness is so far deficient. Like Sindbad in the Valley of Diamonds,[35] the lower the gulf he descends into, the wealthier he becomes. If he be found in tears, it is a proof that he is lost in extacy. He not only agrees with the author of Hudibras,[36] that 'Pain is the foil of pleasure and delight, and sets them off to a more noble height,'[37] but goes further, and, like Zeno,[38] makes pain and pleasure identical. To help him to an annoyance or two, therefore, is to confer a favour on him that awakens his most lugubrious gratitude. He is like Brother Jack in the *Tale of a Tub*,[39] whose felicity consisted in planting himself at the corners of streets, and beseeching the passengers, for the love of Heaven, to give him a good drubbing. Or he reminds us of Zobeide's porter[40] in the *Arabian Nights*, who, as each successive load was laid upon his aching shoulders, burst forth with the exclamation: 'O fortunate day! O, day of good luck!' But why waste our ink in these vain illustrations? There is no saying what he resembles, or what he is or what he does, except that he doubts and groans, and allows his latitudinarianism in the one volume to carry on the war so soporifically against his valetudinarianism in the other, that not Mercury himself, if he took either in hand, could avoid catching the lethargic infection, and dropping dead asleep over the page. [...]

[from 'Anthologia Germanica No. X', unsigned, *DUM*, March 1837]

from *Literæ Orientales* series

[1]

[...] Warm and bright climes are preferable to chilly and cloudy. Poussin[1] thought it essential to the effective development of his Arcadia to represent the sunset as illumining the looks of his shepherds. We even bury our dead with their faces towards the Orient. The Greater and Lesser Lights of Dante's Paradiso[2] were never borrowed from Northern skies. 'The savage loves his native shore;'[3] so at least saith the ballad; but nationality is not always rationality, and taste is confessedly questionable where its canons cannot be made answerable. Some difference may be presumed to exist between Italy and Iceland. No soil not classic is consecrated ground; we may believe the contrary when we are satisfied to refer the question to the arbitration of the Houzouana[4] or the Troglodyte, for a tedious and excellent account of whom, consult, inquisitive reader, the pages of that respectable traveller, La Vaillant.[5]

The mind, to be sure, properly to speak, is without a home on the earth. Ancestral glories, genealogical charts, and the like imprescriptible indescriptibles are favorite subjects with the composite being Man, who also goes now and then the length of dying in idea for his fatherland—but for Mind—it is restless, rebellious—a vagrant whose barren tracts are by no means confined to the space between Dan and Beersheba.[6] It lives rather out of the world. As the stranger said at the sermon, when asked why he did not weep with the rest of the congregation, it 'belongs to another parish.' It is apt, when in quest of its origin, to remount quite as far as the Welshman who across the middle of his pedigree wrote, *About this time the earth was created.* It is a Cain that may build cities, but can abide in none of them. It repudiates every country on the map; it must do so; it should; it would not be Mind if it did otherwise. But, all this notwithstanding, matters as they regard the general truth advocated by Segur[7] and ourself remain where they were. No private principle worth preserving is interfered with by reason of the dominance of a certain great catholic feeling in the human spirit. Abstract in its nature, such a feeling is ever compatible with the co-existence of particular and temporary preferences and prejudices. We do confess that the Mind, with all its indifferentism, looks rather Eastward than Northward; do acknowledge, are proud to acknowledge, that, whatever the human sympathies it has, they are with the East, or with its conceptions of the East. That shadowy species of affinity which the Mind in its complacent moods delights to assume as subsisting between the Orient and its own images of Genii-land possesses rich and irresistible charms for human contemplation. Imagination feels averse to surrender the paramount jewel in the diadem of its perogatives—a faith, to wit, in the practicability of at some time or another realizing the Unreal. If the East is already accessible, so may be at last—the reverse who dares prophesy?— 'the unreached Paradise of our despair;'[8] and so long as the Wonderful Lamp, the dazzler of our boyhood, can be dreamed of as still lying *perdu*[9] in some corner of the Land of Wonders, so long must we continue captives to the hope that a lovelier light than any now diffused over the dusky pathway of our existence will yet be borne to us across the blue Mediterranean. Alas! wanting that which we have not, cannot have, never shall have, we mould that which we really have into an ill-defined counterfeit of that which we want; and then, casting a veil over it, we contemplate the creature of our own fancy with much the same sort of emotion that may be supposed to have dilated the breast of Mareses,[10] the artist of Sais, when he first surveyed the outlines of the gigantic statue himself had curtained from human view. Yet it is on the whole fortunate that Speculation can fall back upon such resources. Slender and shifting though they seem, they serve as barriers against Insanity. From amid the lumber of the actual world prize is made of a safety-valve which carries off from the surface of our reveries the redundant smoke and vapour that, suffered to continue pent up within us, would suffocate every healthier volition and energy of the spirit.

When we speak of Mind, readers must understand us to mean Mind *par excellence* Mind. Visions of lovers and poets and lonely *reveurs*,[11] who have read no metaphysics, and are therefore best qualified to become original metaphysicians, subtlest of the subtle, flit before us as the word assumes shape under our quill. Of mathematicians one perhaps in a thousand comes, but even that one hardly lingers. Few ploughmen dazzle us, and no *millionaires*. But the absence of these last is of small import, nor are we now quarrelling for the assertion of any principle. Power and Beauty best vindicate themselves. Multiform and omnipresent in their manifestations have they ever been; and he who passes ninety-nine altars without worshipping must perforce kneel before the hundredth. There is a reverence independent and apart which neither poet nor man of the world can well refuse to the East. The universal consent of nations assigns to Asia a character it assigns to no other portion of the globe. The title of Rome herself to any celebrity beyond that derivable from her military triumphs must be shared with Asia, the 'mother of science, and the house of gods.'[12] Asia was the cradle of the human race, was man's primeval world. We look to it from childhood as 'the land of the sun;' our young ideas of glory, antiquity and enchantment are associated with it. The coldest of cosmopolites must feel that it is the Great Caravanserai at which he is oftenest disposed to put up in the resting pauses of his pilgrimage. To trace with effect the revolutions of centuries to their source he must turn to Asia. If he would know how empires were founded, how society was formed, how civilization originated, Asia must be his book of reference. If he be desirous of an acquaintance with the history of the establishment of governments and legislatures, with the history of the earliest discoveries, with the history of the first wars and the first conquest, he must seek them in Asia. Picture to yourselves, you who think but travel not,—behold, you who travel and think not, those monumental miracles of ancient conception, those stupendous relics of the Past, which seem to have been bequeathed to the Present as much in defiance of the comparative labours of all succeeding generations as in a sublime despair of rivalling Deity. Look upon these as they are; reflect on what these were; and wonder, if you can, that the traveller of old, treading the earth of the East for the first time, should have fancied himself half-restored to Eden, and that even the sword of the seraph over the Prohibited Walls[13] should have appeared to gleam from afar less in menace than in invitation. Where flourished gardens then, it is true, we stray in wildernesses now; where palaces rose we find roofless walls and broken columns. But the justness of the trite remark, that Greatness though in decay is Greatness still, is nowhere more fully exemplified than in the East. Amid the ruins of Palmyra, and Balbec, and Babylon, and above all of Persepolis,* the wanderer becomes deeplier convinced than ever of its truth. Tabor[15] is to-day the holiest of mounts. The name of Galilee remains eternal. In the shrouded and tabular inscriptions of Egypt we meet still those mysterious hieroglyphs, of whose less unfamilar counterparts, 'the *Mythi* of the breast,'[16] we are suffered to gain glimpses when the lightning of Inspiration and Genius plays over their surface. Our conclusion, then, is not an idle one. Poet, artist, archaeologist, philosopher, philanthropist, warrior, mystic, religionist—all may meet in Asia, as on ground common to all. Each will be acquitted of all supererogatory enthusiasm, even if, as he looks around him and exclaims, 'This is my own, my native land!'[17] every responsive chord in his heart vibrates to the utterance of the sentiment. [. . .]

[from 'Literæ Orientales No. I', unsigned, *DUM*, September 1837]

[2]

[. . .] Indeed, if we were to succinctly describe the difference between this [Oriental] poetry and our own we should say that the latter depends chiefly upon *Ex*pression, but the former chiefly upon *Im*pression. It is true that Expression always proposes Impression as its end, and that Impression is producible only through the agency of Expression; but what we mean to assert is that whereas in the West strict attention to the modes and accidents of Expression is indispensible to the production of Impression, in the East it seems almost wholly superfluous. How the Mohammedan poet treats his theme is a matter of slight consequence. The only thing likely to puzzle his readers would be mystification; and that he cannot employ, because he knows nothing about it: in his darkest opacities his good faith and single-mindedness are still transparent: he may be sometimes silly; he is always serious; and, being so, it is wonderful to what an extent his very *niaiseries*[18] will tell in his favor. He sonnetizes his mistress's face and of course compares it to the sun: so far well, but the sun probably suggests, as it did to Hamlet, the image of a dead dog; and without more ado we have 'the

---

* 'Les ruines de Tchéhel-minar,' writes Le Blonde, (Chelminar, the Forty Pillars, is the native name of Persepolis,) 'présentent aujourd'hui les débris de plus de deux cents colonnes et de treize cents figures d'hommes ou d'animaux. Deux siècles auront-ils suffi pour exécuter des travaux aussi multipliés? On ne trouve dans le monde connu que les pyramides d'Egypte qui puissent être comparées a la majesté de ces ruines. En se rappellant cependant que les Egyptians n'ent eu pour construire les pyramides qu'à employer une multitude d'ouvriers peu instruits, et que ces vastes amas de pierres n'offrent aucun relief, aucune figure, hésitera t-on à les placer au-dessous des monumens de Tchéhel-minar?'[14]

god kissing the carrion.'[19] Among us, with whom coherence and consistency of thought and diction are fast growing into a positive nuisance, this incongruous combination would be at once ascribed to mental imbecility; but the Turk well knows that the philosophy of *his* readers will help them to a far more liberal conclusion—and so it does: they look on the passage as mystical—it was perhaps designed to serve as a type of the alliance often subsisting where least suspected between Genius and Idiotcy—or else there may be real poetical beauty in the specimen of bathos before them—or possibly thay cannot fathom the drift of the poet—or finally all is right and as it ought to be, whatever they may think or feel to the contrary. The truth is that the Mooslem has more *faith*, humanly speaking, than an Englishman. It is an easier task to satisfy him. He reverences with deeper emotion, cherishes sympathies more comprehensive, has a roomier capacity for the reception of mysteries of all sorts. He does not start objections, and moot evidences, and balance probabilities, and wrangle and 'cavil on the ninth part of a hair.'[20] Not he: of such huxtering and shabbiness his soul has an intuitive contempt. He takes higher ground. [...]

[from 'Literæ Orientales No. IV', unsigned, *DUM*, March 1840]

[3]

[...] 'Every religious man,' observes Shelley, 'is a poet.'[21] This we take to be the truth. But it is not intellectual religion that constitutes the religious man. True religion must strike its roots in the soil of the spiritual nature. And it must begin by the development of a feeling which some would consider rather more kindred to irreligion. In the religious man, hate must precede love. Such a man must first hate the spirit of the world. He must hate with immitigable hatred all that the world loves—Pleasure—Glory—Riches, 'Yea, and his own life also.'[22] When his hatred is perfect, his love is born from it as its legitimate antithesis. This is Holy Love, commencing for the Highest Being, and terminating for the lowest but not at all including the lover himself. It is then that his spirit becomes susceptible of all celestial influences. Poetry, divinest of all, springs up within him as a fountain; and he pours it forth upon the world in ever-flowing streams. By a process like to this it was that the many—not all—of the oriental recluses were first converted into poets. And not only were they poets in thought, in word, but their lives themselves, were poems. [...]

[from 'Literæ Orientales No. VI', unsigned, *DUM*, January 1846]

from introduction to *Poets and Poetry of Munster*

[...] The first peculiarity [of Irish song] likely to strike an English reader is the remarkable sameness that prevails in the pieces that assume a narrative form. The poet usually wanders forth of a Summer evening over moor and mountain, mournfully meditating on the wrongs and sufferings of his native land, until at length, sad and weary, he lies down to repose in some flowery vale, or on the slope of some green and lonely hill-side. He sleeps, and, in a dream, beholds a young female of more than mortal beauty, who approaches and accosts him. She is always represented as appearing in naked loveliness,—a fancy evidently borrowed from ancient Greece, for the Irish, renowned though they have always been for their inventive faculties, do not seem, at least until of late years, to have exhibited themselves any original genius for the arts of sculpture or painting. Her person is described with a minuteness of detail that borders upon tedious-ness, her hands, for instance, being said to be such as would execute the most complicated and delicate kinds of sampler-work,—a sort of compliment which might, perhaps, with some propriety be addressed to an actual living woman, but which, when predicated of a being of the imagination, is certainy an absurdity. The enraptured poet enquires whether she be one of the heroines of ancient story, Semiramis, Helen or Medea[1]—or, if his mind be more familiar with the illustrious women of his own country,—Deirdre, Blahmuid, or Cearnuit[2]—or some Banshee, like Aoibhill, Chria, or Aine[3];—and the answer he receives is that she is none of those eminent personages, but *Eire*, once a queen, and now a slave,—of old in the enjoyment of all honor and dignity, but today in thrall to the foe and the stranger. Yet, wretched as her condition is, she does not despair, and encourages her afflicted child to hope, prophecying that speedy relief will shortly reach him from some quarter or other—France, perhaps, or Spain—a melancholy illustration, by the way, of the fact that the oppressed Irish never appear to have had sufficient moral strength to rely on themselves. The song then concludes, though in some instances the poet appends a few consolatory reflections of his own, by way of winding up his poetical clock gracefully.

Another characteristic of the Irish song is the frequent, indeed almost the continual introduction into it, of the heroes and heroines, the gods and god-desses, of the Heathen Mythology. But the Englishman who has ever, in the course of his travels, chanced to come into proximity with an Irish 'Hedge-school,'[4] will be at no loss to conjecture the origin of these allusions. They are to be traced, we may say, exclusively to that intimate acquaintance with the Classics which the Munster peasant never failed to acquire from the instructions of the road-side pedagogue. The Kerry rustic, it is known, speaks, or at least used to speak, Latin, like an old Roman of the Romans, and has frequently, though ignorant of a syllable of English, conversed in the language of Cicero and Virgil with some of the most learned and intellectual of English tourists. Alas! that the acuteness of intellect and extensive capacity for the reception of instruction, for which the Irish peasant is remarkable, should not have afforded a hint to our rulers amid their many and fruitless attempts at what they call conciliation! Would it not have been a policy equally worthy of their judgment, and deserving of praise in itself, to establish schools for the Irish in which they might be taught at least the elementary principles of education through the medium of their native tongue?

A third, and the last, peculiarity that we shall notice, is one of a rather singular order. It is the frequent and almost perpetual employment by the Irish poet of the word ᵹan, *without*. With him it is always ᵹan—, without pleasure, ᵹan—, without hope, ᵹan soʟas, without light, ᵹan—, without friends. We are more struck by this peculiarity, because our translator, a German scholar, has informed us that the favorite Saxon phrase is—in contradistinction to the Irish—mit, with:, as when they write, *mit* Gott, *with* (the help of) GOD, *mit* Muth, *with* courage, *mit* unseren guten Schwerten,—*with* our own good swords. But as the contrast between the Celtic and the Saxon character in this respect, might, if we pursued this topic further, be brought out into a relief too humiliating to our countrymen to contemplate, we forbear from any metaphysical speculation with respect either to the origin of the anomaly, of the causes that may have contributed to its growth and progress. [...]

[unpublished manuscript]

from 'Sketches and Reminiscences of Irish Writers' series

[Charles Maturin] [1]

'Maturin! Maturin! what an odd hat you're in!' My friend Dr. Anster,[2] in this extempore exclamation of his, addressed to the author of 'Bertram,'[3] little dreamt that he was cutting with a two-edged blade. Maturin, morally to speak, *was* always in 'an odd hat.' He was one of those three-corned men[4] whom society insists upon infixing into circular cavities. An inhabitant of one of the stars, dropped upon our planet, could hardly feel more bewildered than Maturin habitually felt in his consociation with the beings around him. He had no friend— companion—brother; he, and the 'Lonely Man of Shiraz' might have shaken hands, and then—parted. He—in his own dark way—understood many people; but nobody understood him in *any* way. And therefore it was that he, this man of

highest genius, Charles Robert Maturin, lived unappreciated—and died unsym-
pathised with, uncared for, unenquired after—and only *not* forgotten, because he
had never been thought about.

'Man, being reasonable, must get drunk,'⁵ observes Byron. It is an ugly line;
but one that embodies a volume of philosophy—especially if we read it in juxta-
position with that other line, by Boileau, 'Souvent de tous nos maux la raison est
le pire.'⁶ The world points her finger of scorn at the intellectual intemperate
man—not reflecting—not caring to reflect—that it is his very superiority to the
world that drives him to habits of intemperance. His nature is 'averse from life'*⁷—
he has an impatience of existence. From such an impatience Charles Lamb⁸
rushed forward, and forced the Gates of Death; and actuated by a similar feeling,
Maturin trod in his footsteps, though only trippingly. Lamb found his Lethe in
the quart—Maturin sought his in the quadrille. One drank, the other danced.
They were the two Kings of Brentford 'smelling at one nosegay,'⁹ only each
experienced the sensation of a different odour from the flowers.

I saw Maturin but on three occasions, and on all three within two months of
his death. I was then a mere boy; and when I assure the reader that I was strongly
imbued with a belief in those doctrines of my Church which seem (and only
seem) to savour of what is theologically called 'exclusiveness,' he will appreciate
the force of the impulse which urged me one morning to follow the author of
'Melmoth' into the porch of St Peter's Church, in Aungier-street, and hear him
read the burial service. Maturin, however, did not read—he simple repeated; but
with a grandeur of emphasis, and an impressive power of manner, that chained
me to the spot. His eyes, while he spoke, continually wandered from side to side,
and at length rested on me, who reddened up to the roots of my hair at being
even for a moment noticed by a man that ranked far higher in my estimation
than Napoleon Bonaparte. I observed that, after having concluded the service,
he whispered somewhat to the clerk at his side, and then again looked steadfastly
at me. If I had been the master of sceptres—of worlds—I would have given them
all at that moment to have been put in possession of his remark!

The second time that I saw Maturin he had been just officiating, as on the
former occasion, at a funeral. He stalked along York-street, with an abstracted,
or rather distracted air; the white scarf and hat-band which he had received
remaining still wreathed around his beautifuly-shaped person, and exhibiting to
the gaze of the amused and amazed pedestrians whom he almost literally
encountered in his path, a boot upon one foot and a shoe on the other! His long,
pale, melancholy, Don-Quixottish, out-of-the-world face, would have inclined
you to believe that Dante, Bajazet,¹⁰ and the Cid,¹¹ had risen together from their

* BYRON—*Manfred.*

sepulchres, and clubbed their features for the production of an effect. But Maturin's mind was only fractionally pourtrayed, so to speak, in his countenance. The great Irishman, like Hamlet, had that within him which passed show,[12] and escaped far and away beyond the possibility of expression by the clay lineament. He bore 'the thunder-scars'[13] about him; but they were graven, not on his brow, but on his heart.

The third and last time that I beheld this marvellous man I remember well. It was somewhere about a fortnight before his death, on a balmy autumn evening, in 1824. He slowly descended the steps of his own house, which perhaps some future Transatlantic biographer may thank me for informing him was at No. 42, in York-street, and took his way in the direction of Whitefriar-street. Thence he passed into Bride-street, proceeded up through Werburgh-street, into Castle-street, and passed the Royal Exchange into Dame-street, every second person staring at him and the extraordinary double-belted and treble-caped rug of an old garment, neither coat nor cloak, which enveloped his person. But here it was that I, who had tracked the footsteps of the man as his shadow, discovered that the feeling to which some individuals, rather oversharp and shrewd, had been pleased to ascribe this 'affectation of singularity'[14] had no existence in Maturin. For, instead of passing along Dame-street, where he would have been 'the observed of all observers,'[15] he wended his way along the dark and forlorn locality of Dame-lane, and having reached the end of this not very classical thoroughfare, crossed over to Angelsea-street, where I lost sight of him. Perhaps he went into one of those bibliopolitan establishments wherewith that Paternoster-row[16] of Dublin abounds. I never saw him afterwards!

Maturin wrote, besides his tragedies, three works of unsurpassable interest and power—'Montorio,'[17] 'The Milesian Chief,'[18] and 'Woman.'[19] They are all truly wonderful: you see the mind of the author rising up from every sentence in them 'like a volcano from the sea.'*[20] Of the three, 'Montorio' is that which, without being very well understood by the multitude, yet nearliest reaches their understandings through the broad highway of their feelings. The characters of Annibal and Ippolito Montorio are finely contrasted; and although the idea upon which the romance was founded had been long before apparently exhausted by Young in his 'Zanga,'[21] Maturin has contrived to invest it with a new and overpowering interest. The story of 'Woman,' in which even the 'small numskull of Jeffrey'†[22] found matter for praise, is best epitomised by its own concluding sentence—one that at once characterises the author and the hero. When great talent is combined with calamity, their union forms the 'tenth wave'‡[23] of human misery: grief becomes immortal from the inexhaustible fertility of genius; and the serpents that devour us are generated out of our own vitals.[24]

* D'Israeli.   † Maginn.   ‡ An allusion to the well-known line of Horace.

But 'The Milesian Chief,' although it has remained comparatively unnoticed, was, in my opinion, the grandest of all Maturin's productions. I have never met anything that surpasses the artistic and graphic power of description in particular displayed in this work; while the characters—the hero and heroine especially—are pourtayed with admirable fidelity to nature. That 'The Milesian Chief' should never have reached a second edition, while 'Montorio' has been repeatedly reprinted in various forms by the bibliophiles of London—but of course these worthies must cater for the public taste, which, in the matter of novel-reading, is admittedly a trifle depraved in our days.

Maturin's other tale of 'Melmoth,'[25] ranks next to 'The Milesian' in point of energetic writing and magnificent description; but the idea upon which the narrative is founded, is at once hackneyed and monstrous, and the impossibility of feeling a genuine human interest in the characters, damns the book, despite of its many beauties. Melmoth himself, in particular, is a bore of the first magnitude, who is always talking grandiloquent fustian, and folding his cloak about him.

The other romances of our author—'The Wild Irish Boy,'[26] and 'The Albigenses,'[27] scarcely merit any notice apart. In the first, the grouping is altogether overdone; and the attempt to marry history to fiction, in the second, turns out a decided failure. Maturin did not shine in the gossipry of chronicle. His power as he truly avers of himself, 'lay in darkening the gloomy and deepening the sad, and depicting those scenes and situations of life in which Passion trembles on the verge of the unlawful and unhallowed.'*

'If there be any writer of the present day,' said the author of 'Caleb Williams,'[28] 'to whose burial-place I should wish to make a pilgrimage, that writer is Maturin.' I could almost echo that sentiment; but where the remains of my distinguished countryman repose, I confess I know not. Maturin was killed off in a mistake and buried in a hurry. He died of an apothecary's blunder.

[James Clarence Mangan, *Irishman*, 24 March 1849]

[George Petrie][29]

[. . .] As an artist and an antiquary, Dr. Petrie, it is superfluous to remark, is without a rival in this country. He has successfully introduced several of the Italian styles of painting into his pictures, which are all characterised as much by their chaste faithfulness to Nature, as by a certain warmth of imagination that

---

* Preface to 'The Milesian.'

diffuses itself throughout them like a poetical atmosphere—a something rather to be felt than distinctly perceived. It marks the just appreciation of what a painter owes to his own art. It is, in fact, the perfection of correct judgement—the same intuitive species of good sense which appears to have guided the worthy Doctor in the prosecution of most of his antiquarian researches also.

With very great diffidence I here presume to set a limit to the past exercise of this faculty on the part of Dr. Petrie in such researches. It is confessedly by those who are intimately familar with archæological evidences and illustrations that the Doctor should be judged as an antiquary, and not at all familiar with them after any fashion [*sic*]. But my mode of forming an opinion suiteth myself, and scandaliseth nobody. I take a few facts, not caring to be overwhelming by too many proofs that they *are* facts: with these I mix up a dash of the marvellous—perhaps an old wife's tale—perhaps a half-remembered dream or mesmeric experience of my own—and the business is done. My conclusion is reached, and shelved, and must not, thenceforward, be disturbed. I would as soon think at any time afterwards of questioning its truth, as of doubting the veritable existence of the Barber's five brothers[30] in the 'Arabian Nights,' or the power of Zeyn Alasnam, King of the Genii.[31] There it is; and an opponent may battle with me anent it, if he please; I manage to hold my ground by the help of digressions and analogies.

The reader will, therefore, understand why it is that I am dissident—as I happen to be—from Dr. Petrie's theory of the origin and uses of the Irish Pillar Towers.[32] That they are of Chadean construction, and were intended by their architects to promote the objects of astrological science, are points upon which I have satisfied myself. From the fact, upon which so much stress has been laid, that they are usually found in the vicinity of churches, the inference is a reasonable fair one, that when their applicabilty to certain Christian uses first became apparent to the monks and priests, those monks and priests built churches in *their* vicinity. If their erection was subsequent to that of the churches, how comes it to pass that the annalists, who frequently record the minutest particulars in reference to the latter, are totally silent with respect to the former? The Towers were surely not quite such every-day structures as that any notice of them would have seemed a piece of impertinence. They were peculiar to this country; for, though I believe that similar monuments existed anciently in Asia, the complete desolation which, besom-like,[33] had so often swept over that portion of the world, had, doubtless, destroyed all vestiges of them long before the introduction of Christianity into Ireland. Another fact greatly relied on is the apparently modern architecture of the Irish towers. But, though apparently modern, it may not be really so. Art and science move in a perpetual circle. The sculpture of Phidias[34] was not essentially different from that of Canova.[35] In the nineteenth century we come round again to the magical rites and mysteries of ancient

Egypt.[36] This argument of apparent modernness goes, in my opinion, for nothing. And so of all the other arguments. None of them weigh with me. I look with suspicion at every one of them. I am determined not to yield an iota of belief to any of them. I fortify the ears of my conscience with gun-cotton against them all. [...]

[James Clarence Mangan, *Irishman*, 7 April 1849]

[John Anster][37]

[...] Dr. Anster has understood the heart, mind, and soul of Goethe better than any man of our time. Carleton,[38] in his own dry and expressive way, told me that he believed that God had created Shelley for the sole purpose of translating 'Faust' into English. But my friend misunderstood the tenor and character of the German poem. He mistook the 'May-day Night Scene'[39] for the whole of the work, whereas it is really a digression, a deviation, a departure from that work. It is a compound of moonshine and lollypop—you see nothing clearly in it, and neither taste nor feel anything very sensibly. Dr. Anster perceived this at a first glance— and hence the masterly manner in which he has discriminated between the two. Shelley's balloon floated through the ether of the poem—Anster's firm foot stood upon the solid ground of it. Shelley never could have given a *true* translation of 'Faust.' If he had attempted such a labour, his essay would have sunk 'deeper than ever plummet sounded'[40] below even the abortion of Blackie,[41] who, nevertheless, has really 'done into English' by far the faithfulest version of the poem that has appeared. It was reserved for our illustrious townsman to achieve the task, and praiseworthily, and nobly, and wonderfully has he succeeded in his great effort.

Dr. Anster has not merely translated 'Faust:' he has done much more—he has translated Goethe—or, rather, he has translated that part of the mind of Goethe which was unknown to Goethe himself. The great German, as I have already hinted, continually limped and staggered; but Anster furnishes him with a pair of crutches. He sheds light upon the dark places that he meets; he fills up every vacuum, and reduces to a common level all inequalities. He is a hundred times more Goethian than Goethe himself. He sees through his author, as through glass, but corrects all the distortions produced by the refraction of the substance through which he looks. In a few words, he has actually made of Goethe the man which his German worshippers proclaim him to be—he has created a soul under the ribs of that Death which they had revered as a Jupiter—he is, in short, *the real author of* 'Faust.' [...]

[James Clarence Mangan, *Irishman*, 21 April 1849]

[Maria Edgeworth][42]

Who is there that is not familiar with the name of Miss Edgeworth? What reader but must have perused her numerous writings with pleasure and profit? It was the good fortune of Miss Edgeworth to commence her literary career at a period when the public had become thoroughly disgusted with the sickly sentimental twaddle of the Laura Matildas[43] and Charlotte Smiths[44] of the day, and were all on the *qui vivre*[45] for the appearance among them of some woman of real intellectual power. [. . .]

Miss Edgeworth dashed off in quick succession with a rapid yet steady hand the novels of 'Belinda,' 'Patronage,' 'Manœvering,' 'Ennui,'[46] and half a score more besides. Of these, 'Belinda'—a name dear to readers from its associations with one of the most fanciful of Pope's poems[47]—is, if not essentially the best, at least the best managed in point of incident. The high intellectual, yet impassioned and tender character of Clarence Hervey is also delineated with a masterly—I beg pardon, a mistressly—hand. [. . .]

The work of Miss Edgeworth which most charmed my boyhood was her 'Popular Tales.'[48] They are a series of stories of many lands—France, Italy, Ireland, Turkey, and, for aught that I now remember to the contrary, perhaps the Cannibal Islands also. By two of those stories in particular was I delighted; one, 'Roseanna,' an Irish tale, illustrating the evil effects of that spirit of procrastination and improvidence, which, alas! too generally inheres in our national character; the other 'Murad the Unlucky,'—a poor devil who was always stumbling over some stone or other upon the highway of life, for no purpose that I can perceive except to enable Miss Edgeworth to show that the stones should not have been on the highway, not that the 'Unlucky' One should *not* have stumbled over them. Of course she does not affirm this—rather the contrary; she leaves—that is, she fancies she leaves—it to be inferred that all the fault lay in the stumbler. [. . .]

Since the preceding paper was written, I have learned, with deep regret, that Miss Edgeworth is no more—[49] [. . .] A melancholy feeling oppresses me at the present moment—for I had hoped that I should have lived to look on her lineaments, and exchange a few words with her—and this feeling will be my apology with the reader for saying no more of her now. But my inability to pen her eulogy is of no consequence. All that need ever be said of her is, that she was an Irishwoman, a woman of genius, and, withal, a woman of strong common sense. Her works were distributed among society for the benefit of mankind. If they did not tend towards the intellectual and physical improvement of all those around her, *I* must be a strange sort of person, for they sunk deep into my mind, and have peculiarly influenced my character. [. . .]

[James Clarence Mangan, *Irishman*, 26 May 1849]

[William Maginn][50]

[...] Maginn wrote alike without labour and without limit. He had, properly speaking, no style, or rather, he was master of all styles, though he cared for none. His thoughts literally gushed from his brain in overflowing abundance. He flung them away, as he flung himself away, in the riotous exuberance of his heart and spirit. He cast the rich bread of his intellect upon the waters, but he did not find it again after many days, or if he did, it came back to him in the shape and with the properties of poison. [...]

For all intents and purposes of posthumous renown he has lived in vain. His name, like that of Keats, has been 'written in water;'[51] or, more properly speaking, in gin-in-water. [...]

[James Clarence Mangan, *Irishman*, 28 July 1849]

[James Clarence Mangan]

(The following sketch of Mangan was written by himself about six weeks before his death. He had previously contributed nine 'Sketches of Modern Irish Writers' to the *Irishman*; and, in an eccentric mood, under a fictitious signature, thus described himself. The *Sketch* is, in our opinion, rather over-drawn, but few will fail to recognise its truthfulness in many parts, particularly where he accuses himself of 'fathering upon other writers the offspring of his own brain.' On this subject his friend Joseph Brenan[52] tells an anecdote most characteristic of Mangan. Dr. Anster once having exposulated with him on the impropriety of ascribing to Hafiz[53] a poem which certainly bore little or no resemblance to the original, 'Ah!' said Mangan, 'it is only *Half-his.*'

'Poor Mangan!' light be the turf upon your grave.)

PART I

The somewhat impolite intrusion of this sketch into the society of the other sketches of eminent Irishmen who have appeared in this Journal, will, perhaps, be pardoned, when I state that I happen to be intimately acquainted with Mr. Mangan, and that I have his entire sanction for giving it to the public. Poor Mangan! he dies uncared for,—he dies unknown—but, as he has said himself, 'uncomplaining.' How far he has contributed to his own premature death is a question the solution of which must, perhaps, be referred to eternity. Many voices have been raised against him; but, to my knowledge, they are those of persons who have never seen him, and do not understand him. I am not a believer in what is popularly called predestination;—but I think that there does appear to be a destiny about Mangan.

He was born amid scenes of blasphemy and riot. If the sins of the fathers be still visited on the children,[54] here, assuredly, is a case quite in point. His childhood was neglected, just as now is his death-bed. He had no companions. A hair-brained girl, who lodged in his father's house, sent him out one day to buy a ballad: he had no covering on his head, and there was a tremendous shower of rain; but she told him that the rain would make him *grow*. He believed her—went out—strayed through many streets, and by-places, now abolished—found, at length, his way homeward—and for eight years afterwards—from his fifth year to his thirteenth—remained almost blind. In the twilight alone could he attempt to open his eyes and then he—read. He never mingled in the amusements of other boys. His childhood was dark and joyless. Of a strongly-marked nervous temperament by nature, his nerves, even then, were irretrievably shattered.

His father had embarked in an unholy business—one too common and patent in every city—and he was robbed by those around him. Upon poor Clarence, at the age of fifteen, devolved the task of supporting him and his mother, even while they were yet in the prime of life. With ruined health and a wandering mind, that knew not where to find a goal, he undertook the accomplishment of what he considered to be a duty. Eleven other years passed away, during which he was compelled to be the daily associate of some of the most infernally heartless ruffians on this side of Hell. Yet he, somehow, battled against what seemed Destiny itself. Very despair lent him an energy. All day at an attorney's desk, amid thick smoke, sulphur, blasphemies, and obscenities worse than blasphemies; half the night *reading*, and almost all the other half sleepless; so passed poor Mangan his years at this period. His father and mother never spoke to him, nor could he exchange ideas with them. He had gold and they had copper.

About this time, as I believe, he became acquainted with the Editors of the *Comet*, a journal which, some fifteen years back, earned and enjoyed a high degree of notoriety through Ireland. They tried to corrupt him, and failed. He wrote for them gratuitously; but when he attended at their drinking bouts, always sat at the table with a glass of water before him. They, and their hangers-on—most of whom have gone to the———Angel—at length laughed him to scorn; voted him a 'spoon,'[55] and would have no more to do with him. ''Tis a mad world, my masters!'[56]

Mangan then took to writing for the *University Magazine*. I have never seen any of his contributions to that world-renowned periodical; but I have read innumerable critiques upon them, and scarcely in one instance have I seen a disparaging word from the critic. It has been said that he has translated from fourteen languages; but he himself has assured me that he understands only eight. Like the man who, some years back, published an enormous volume in Germany, and fathered it upon Sanconiatho[57]—(pity he did not add 'Manetho, Berosus, and Ocellus Lucanus'[58])—my poor friend Clarence has perpetrated a great many singular literary sins, which, taken together, as a quaint and sententious friend of mine remarks, would appear to be 'the antithesis of plagiarism.' It is a strange fault, no doubt, and one that I cannot understand, that Mangan should entertain a deep diffidence of his own capacity to amuse or attract others, by anything emanating from himself. But it is the fact. I do not comprehend it; but he has mentioned it to me times without number.

I conclude the first part of this sketch for the present with a most solemn statement:—that Mangan is *not* an opium-eater. He never swallowed a grain of opium in his life, and only on one occasion took—and then as a medicine— laudanum. The report with respect to his supposed opium-eating propensities, originated from the lips of William Carleton, who for some or no purpose thought proper to spread it.

PART II

My professional avocations as a medical man have made me acquainted with many singular neuralgic cases, but I have never met anybody of such a strongly-marked nervous temperament as Mangan. He is in this respect quite a pheno-menon: he is literally all nerves and no muscles. In accordance with such a temperament Providence has endowed him with marvellous tenacity of life. He has survived casualties that would have killed thousands—casualities of all kinds— illnesses, falls, wounds, bruises, wet clothes, no clothes at all, and nights at the round table. His misfortunes have been very great; and he ascribes them all to his power of writing, facetiously deriving *calamity* from *calamus*, a quill. People have called him a singular man, but he is rather a plural one—a Proteus,[59] as the *Dublin Review* designates him. I confess that I cannot make him out; and I incline strongly to suspect that there must be a somewhat, that is dark and troubled in his mind—perhaps a something very sore and very heavy on his conscience.

Mangan understands eight languages, and has translated from many besides that he does not understand. He has been also overmuch addicted to a practice akin to this, that of fathering upon other writers the offspring of his own brain. This is what a friend of mine pointedly calls 'the antithesis of plagiarism.' I cannot commend it. A man may have a right to offer his property to others, but nothing can justify him in forcing it upon them. I once asked Mangan why he did not prefix his own name to his anti-plagiaristic productions, and his reply was characteristic of the man: 'That would be no go; nohow you fixed it: I *must* write in a variety of styles; and it wouldn't do for me to don the turban, and open

my poem with a *Bismillah*;[60] when I write a poem to the Arab Mohir-Ibn-
Mohir—Ibn Khalakan[61] is the man from whom it should come; and to him I
give it.' 'And do you really sympathise with your subject?' I demanded. 'Yes,
always, always,' was his answer: 'When I write as a Persian, I feel as a Persian, and
am transported back to the days of Diemsheed and the Genii;[62] when I write as
a Spaniard, I forget, for the moment, everything but the Cid, the Moors, and the
Alhambra; when I translate from the Irish, my heart has no pulses except for the
wrongs and sorrows of my own stricken land.' I asked him for his opinion of
German humour: 'Why,' said he, 'you have, doubtless, heard of the author who
began and ended a work 'On the Rats of Iceland,' with the words, 'There are no
Rats in Iceland.' So, my opinion of German humour is, that there is no such
thing as German humour. If there be any exception to this remark, it is in the
quaint story of Peter Schlemihl,[63] the man who sold his shadow. Peter, you know,
applies to a painter to paint a shadow for him, and the painter gravely enquires
how his own shadow came to be lost. Peter, ashamed to acknowledge that he had
sold it, answers, that on one very frosty day it stuck so hard to the ground that he
was forced to walk away without it. The painter listens to this statement with
solemn gravity; and, after a considerable pause of deep thoughtfulness, closes the
conversation with the words, 'I am afraid that such a shadow as I might paint
you, not being naturally your own, would be apt to give you the slip on the first
opportunity, and return to me, its maker;—and then, my dear sir, matters would
be worse than before for while you would still be shadowless, I should be
burdened with two shadows; and, something strange concerning me might go
abroad.' This is certainly droll enough; but perhaps it is not genuine Teuton after
all; the name of the author, Chamisso, has a suspicious Italian twang; and he, or
his father before him, may have gone down the Rialto in a gondola.' Mangan has
an odd manner of expressing himself, or perhaps I should say *had*, for, alas! he is
fast losing that firm hold of life of which I have written. He lies upon a bed of
sickness, forsaken and uncared for, steeped in the slough of poverty to his lips,
and sunk to the lowest depths of suffering and sorrow. His deplorable condition,
I sincerely commiserate. I would I could do more.

From habits of prayer and fasting, and the study of the Lives of the Saints,
Mangan was at one period of his mysterious life drawn away, and enticed into
the snare of Love and was even within an aim's ace of becoming a Benedict.[64] But
certain strange circumstances—the occurrence of which he has described to me
as having been foreshadowed to him in a dream—interposed their ungallant
proportions between the lady and him; and so he abode a Maledict,[65] and Hymen[66]
despatched Cupid and Plutus to look for somebody else. Mangan had a queer
opinion concerning dreams; but it is not worth explaining. He believes in a
particular Providence, as every Christian should believe; but he also avers that he

has often been in the invisible world, and has converse with ghosts. 'Such tricks hath strong imagination!'[67] But, if contradicted on this point, he never argues it: he is silent—a fact which would seem to indicate the possession of more good sense on his part than his belief in the nonsense to which he give credit would warrant me in attributing to him.

I have said that Mangan is neglected and forsaken; but I had forgotten. There is one friend of his, who has known him only in adversity, but who occasionally visits him, and of late has been exerting himself for the relief of the poet's exigencies, though hitherto, I believe, without success; I mean Mr. Mooney,[68] the portrait painter, and himself a poet also of no mean order. If it be not to late, possibly Mangan may yet be rescued and restored to society; but when a fly is rapidly sinking in a glass of water, and not a soul in the house besides himself, it is difficult for him to forbear conjecturing that he must go to the bottom.

['E.W.'[69] *Irishman*, 17 August 1850]

Autobiography

Chap. I.

... ... A heavy shadow lay
On that boy's spirit: he was not of his fathers. MASSINGER.[1]

At a very early period of my life I became impressed by the conviction that it is the imperative duty of every man who has deeply sinned and deeply suffered to place upon record some memorial of his wretched experiences for the benefit of his fellow-creatures, and by way of a beacon to them to avoid, in their voyage of existence, the rocks and shoals upon which his own peace of soul has undergone shipwreck. This conviction continually gained strength within me, until it assumed all the importance of a paramount idea in my mind. It was in its nature, alas! a sort of dark anticipation, a species of melancholy foreboding of the task which Providence and my own disastrous destiny would one day call upon myself to undertake.

In my boyhood I was haunted by an indescribable feeling of something terrible. It was as though I stood in the vicinity of some tremendous danger, to which my apprehensions could give neither form nor outline. What it was I knew not, but it seemed to include many kinds of pain and bitterness—baffled hopes—and memories full of remorse. It rose on my imagination like one of those dreadful ideas which are said by some German writers of romance to infest the soul of a man apparently foredoomed to the commission of murder. I say apparently, for I may here, in the outset, state that I have no faith in the theory of predestination, and that I believe every individual to be the architect of his own happiness or misery; but I did feel that a period would arrive when I should look back upon the Past with horror, and should say to myself, Now the Great Tree of my Existence is blasted, and will never more put forth fruit or blossom. And it was, if I may so speak, one of the nightmare loads lying most heavily on my spirit, that I could not reconcile my feeling of impending calamity with the dictates of that Reason which told me that nothing can irreparably destroy a man except his proper criminality, and that the verdict of Conscience on our own actions, if favourable, should always be sufficient to secure to us an amount of contentment beyond the power of Accident to affect. Like Bonnet,[2] whose life was embittered by the strange notion that he saw *an honest man* continually robbing his house, I suffered as much from my inability to harmonise my thoughts and feelings as from the very evil itself that I dreaded. Such was my condition from my sixth to my sixteenth year.

But let me not anticipate my mournful narrative. The few observations that I make in this preliminary chapter I throw out without order or forethought, and they are not intended to appear as the commencement of a history. In hazarding them I perhaps rather seek to unburden my own heart than to enlist the sympathies of my readers. Those few, however, who will thoroughly understand me need not be informed why I appear to philosophise before I begin to narrate.

I give my Confessions to the world without disguise or palliation. From the first my nature was always averse, even almost to a fault; the second, if it be possible in my case, I resign to that Eternity which is rapidly coming alike upon me, my friends, and my enemies. These latter I also have, and from my heart I say, May G O D bless them, here and hereafter! Meantime they, as well as those excellent individuals whose kindness towards me through the period of my probation I have experienced to an extent scarcely credible, may in these pages read the simple and undecorated truth with regard to all that has so long appeared worst in my character and conduct. To all I owe a debt, and that debt I shall endeavour to repay to the uttermost.

There have been some men who may be said to have published their autobiographies without directly revealing themselves in these, as there have been others who have avowedly laid bare to the eyes of mankind their own delinquencies without cloak or equivocation. Among the former we may class Godwin[3] and Byron;[4] the latter will comprehend St. Augustine,[5] Rousseau,[6] Charles Lamb,[7] and perhaps a few besides. It is neither my wish nor my ambition to take any one of these as my model in sentiment or expression. I cannot do so if I would, and I know that I would not if I could.[8] My desire is to leave after me a work that may not merely inform but instruct— that may be adapted to all capacities and grades of intellect—and that, while it seeks to develope for the thinking the more hidden springs of human frailty, shall also operate, simply in virtue of its statements, as a warning to the uneducated votary of Vice. And let me not be esteemed presumptuous if I add that it will be one which, with G O D's blessing, shall achieve both objects.

For myself, individually, I crave nothing. I have forfeited all claim upon human generosity. The kindness that during my life and amid all my errors, I have endeavoured to exercise towards others, will doubtless be denied to me; but I complain not. May my unhappy memoirs serve in some degree to benefit my fellow-beings! May G O D's justice be vindicated in me and them! May no human creature ever arise from their perusal without, if a good man, feeling his virtuous resolutions confirmed, and if a bad, without experiencing some portion of that salutary remorse which indicates the first dawning of that reformation. These I would wish and ambition—but no more than these.

Chap. II.

(Epigraph)—These things are but the beginning of sorrows.[9]—JESUS CHRIST.

I share with an illustrious townsman of my own* the honor, or the disreputability,—as it may be considered,—of having been born the son of a grocer. My father,[10] however, unlike his, never exhibited any of the qualities of a guardian towards his children. His temper was not merely quick and irascible, but it also embodied much of that calm concentrated spirit of Milesian fierceness a picture of which I have endeavoured to paint in my Italian story of 'Gasparo Bandollo.'†[11] His nature was truly noble: to quote a phrase of my friend O'Donovan, he 'never knew what it was to refuse the countenance of living man'‡[12] —but, in neglecting his own interests—and not the most selfish of misanthropes could accuse him of attending too closely to those—he unfortunately forgot the injuries that he inflicted upon the interests of others. He was of an ardent and forward-bounding disposition, and, though deeply religious by nature he hated the restraints of social life, and seemed to think that all feelings with regard to family connections, and the obligations imposed by them, were totally beneath his notice. Me, my two brothers, and my sister,[13] he treated habitually as a huntsman would treat refractory hounds. It was his boast, uttered in pure glee of heart, that we 'would run into a mouse-hole' to shun him. While my mother[14] lived he made her miserable—he led my only sister such a life that she was obliged to leave our house—he kept up a succession of continual hostilities with my brothers—and if he spared me more than others it was perhaps because I displayed a greater contempt of life and every thing connected with it than he thought was shown by the other members of his family. If any one can imagine such an idea as a human boa-constrictor *without his alimentive propensities,* he will be able to form some notion of the character of my father. May GOD assoil[15] his great and mistaken soul and grant him eternal peace and forgiveness!—but I have an inward feeling that to him I owe all my misfortunes.

My father's grand worldly fault was—*improvidence.* To any one who applied to him for money he uniformly gave double or treble the sum requested of him. He parted with his money—he gave away the best part of his worldly property—and in the end he even suffered his own judgment and disposition to become the spoil of strangers. In plainer words, he permitted cold-blooded and crafty men to persuade him that he was wasting his energies by following the

---

* Moore.

† See *Dubl. Univ. Mag.* for Dec. 1848. N°. CXCII.

‡ *Annals of the Four Masters.* Anno

grocery business, and that by re-commencing life as a vintner, he would soon be able not only to retrieve all his losses but to realise an ample fortune. And thus it happened, reader, that I, James Clarence Mangan, came into the world surrounded, if I may so express myself, by an atmosphere of curses and intemperance, of cruelty, infidelity, and blasphemy—and of both secret and open hatred towards the moral government of GOD—such as few infants, on opening their eyes to the first light of day had ever known before.

From the fatal hour which saw my father enter upon his new business the hand of a retributive Providence*[16] was visibly manifested in the change that ensued in his affairs. Year by year his property melted away. Debts accumulated on him; and his creditors, knowing the sort of man they had to deal with, always proved merciless. Step by step he sank, until, as he himself expressed it, only 'the desert of perdition' lay before him. Disasters of all kinds thickened around him: disappointment and calamity were sown broadcast in his path. Nothing that he undertook prospered. No man whom he trusted proved faithful to him. 'The stars in their courses fought against Sisera.'[17] And his family? They were neglected, forgotten,— left to themselves. For me, I sought refuge in books and solitude; and days would pass during which my father seemed neither to know nor care whether I were living or dead. My brothers and sister fared better: they indulged in habits of active exercise, and strengthened their constitutions morally and physically to a degree that even enabled them to present a successful front of opposition to the tyranny exercised over them. But I shut myself up in a close room: I isolated myself in such a manner from my own nearest relatives that with one voice they all proclaimed me 'mad.' Perhaps I was: this much at least is certain, that it was precisely at that period—from my tenth to my fourteenth year—that the seeds of that moral insanity were developed within me which afterwards grew up into a tree of giant altitude.

My schooling during those early days stood me in some stead. Yet I attended little to the mere technical instruction given to me in school. I rather tried to derive information from general study than from dry rules and special statements. One anecdote I may be permitted to give here, which will somewhat illustrate the peculiar condition of my moral and intellectual being at this period. I had been sent to Mr. Courtney's Academy[18] in Derby Square. It was the first evening of my entrance, in 1820, when I had completed my eleventh year. Twenty boys were arranged in a class; and to me, as the latest comer, was allotted the

---

*   My reader will pardon the frequent allusions to GOD and Providence which occur in the course of these Memoirs. But as Mallebranche saw all things in GOD, so I see GOD in all things. GOD is *the* idea of my mind. ~~The psychological meaning of Mallebranche's expression I may mention en passant, I know (May my knowledge of it not~~

lowest place—a place with which I was perfectly contented. The question propounded by the schoolmaster was—'What is a parenthesis?' But in vain did he test the philological capacities of his pupils: one alone attempted some blundering explanation from the grammar; and finally to me, as the forlorn hope that might possibly save the credit of the school, was the query referred. 'Sir,' said I, 'I have only come into the school to-day, and have not had time to look into the grammar; but I should suppose a parenthesis to be something included in a sentence—but which might be omitted from the sentence without injury to the meaning of the sentence.'—'Go up, Sir,' exclaimed the master, 'to the head of the class!' With an emotion of boyish pride I assumed the place allotted me, but the next minute found me once more in my original position. 'Why do you go down again, Sir?' asked the worthy pedagogue. 'Because, Sir,' cried I, boldly, 'I have not deserved the head-place: give it to this boy'—and I pointed to the lad who had all but succeeded—'he merits it better, because at least he has tried to study his task.' The schoolmaster smiled: he and the usher whispered together; and I was remanded to a seat apart. On the following day no fewer than three Roman Catholic clergymen, who visited the Academy, condescended to enter into conversation with me; and I very well recollect that one of them, after having heard me read 'Blair on the Death of Christ'[19] from 'Scott's Lessons'—clapped me on the back with the exclamation—'You will be a rattling fellow, my boy— but see and take care of yourself!'

~~From my eleventh to my fifteenth year I read, read, read incessantly; and, though singular, it is true, that not only the general matter~~ In connection with this anecdote I may be permitted to mention a singular fact—namely, that in my earlier years I was passionately fond of declaiming—not for my auditory but for myself. I loved to indulge in solitary rhapsodies—and if intruded on upon those occasions I was made very unhappy. Yet I had none of the ordinary shyness of boyhood. I merely felt or fancied that between me and those who approached me no species of sympathy could exist; and I shrank from communion with them as from somewhat alien from my nature. This feeling continued to acquire strength daily, until in after years it became one of the grand and terrible miseries of my existence. ~~Is it, as I have sometimes asked myself, a genuine and proper product of misanthropy, or~~ It was a morbid product of the pride and presumption which, almost hidden from myself, constituted even from my childhood, governing traits in my character, and have so often contributed to render me repulsive in the eyes of others.

But a severe check was in preparation for these faults. My father's circumstances at length grew desperate: within the lapse of a very limited period he had failed in eight successive establishments in different parts of Dublin, until, finally, nothing remained for him to do but to sit down and fold his arms in despair. Ruin and beggary stared him in the face; his spirit was broken; and as a last resource he looked to the wretched members of his family for that help which he should have rather been able to extend to them. I was fifteen years old: could I not even then begin to exert myself for the behoof of my kindred? If my excellent mother thought so she said nothing, but my father undertook the solution of the question; and I was apprenticed to a scrivener.[20] Taken from my books—obliged to relinquish my solitary rambles and musings—and compelled for the miserable pittance of a few shillings weekly, to herd with the coarsest of associates and suffer at their hands every sort of rudeness and indignity which their uncultivated and semi-savage natures prompted them to inflict on me! 'Thus bad began, but worse remained behind.'[21]

Chap. III.

At this time we—that is, my father and mother, my brothers, my sister and myself—tenanted one of the dismallest domiciles perhaps to be met with in the most forlorn recesses of any city in Europe. It consisted of two wretched rooms, or rather holes, at the rear of a tottering old fragment of a house, or, if the reader please, hovel, in Chancery Lane. These dens, one of which was over the other, were mutually connected by means of a steep and almost perpendicular ladder, down which it was my fortune to receive many a tumble from time to time upon the sloppy earthen floor beneath. Door or window there was none to the lower chamber—the place of the latter in particular being supplied, not very elegantly, by a huge chasm in the bare and broken brick wall. In the upper apartment which served as our sleeping-room, the spiders and beetles had established an almost undisputed right of occupancy; while the winds and rains blew in on all sides, and whistled and howled through the winter nights like the voices of unquiet spirits. It was to this dreary abode, without, I believe, a parallel for desolateness, that I was accustomed to return from my employer's office each night between eleven and twelve through three long years. I scarcely regarded my own sufferings when I reflected on those of my relatives, my mother espe-cially, whose fortitude was admirable—and yet I did suffer and dreadfully. I was a slave of the most miserable order. Coerced to remain for the most part bound to one spot from early morning till near midnight—tied down to 'the dull drudgery of the desk's dead wood'*[22] unceasingly—without sympathy or companionship,— my heart felt as if it were gradually growing into the inanimate material I wrote on. I scarcely seemed like a thing of life; and yet at intervals the spirit within me

---

* Lamb.

would struggle to vindicate itself; and the more poetical part of my disposition would seek to burst into imperfect existence. Some lines which I produced about this time may serve to give my readers a notion of the sentiments which even amid want and pain and bitter loneliness of soul may sometimes agitate the breast of a boy of sixteen[23]: —

Genius.

O, Genius! Genius! all thou dost endure
First from thyself, and finally from those,
The Earth-bound and the Blind, who cannot feel
That there be souls with purposes as pure
And lofty as the mountain-snows, and zeal   5
All quenchless as the spirit whence it flows!—
In whom that fire, struck but like spark from steel
In other bosoms, ever lives and glows!
Of such, thrice-blest are they whom, ere mature
Life generate woes which GOD alone can heal   10
His mercy calls to a loftier sphere than this—
For the mind's conflicts are the worst of woes,
And fathomless and fearful yawns the Abyss
Of Darkness thenceforth under all who inherit
That melancholy, changeless hue of heart   15
Which flings its pale gloom o'er the years of Youth—
Those most—or least—illumined by the spirit
Of the Eternal Archetype of Truth.—
For such as these there is no peace within
Either in Action or in Contemplation,   20
From first to last,—but, even as they begin,
They close, the dim night of their tribulation,
Worn by the torture of the untiring breast,
Which, scorning all, and shunned of all, by turns,
Upheld in solitary strength begot   25
By its own unshared shroudedness of lot,
Through years and years of crushed hopes throbs and burns,
And burns and throbs, and will not be at rest,
Searching a desolate Earth for that it findeth not!

My physical and moral torments—my endurances from cold, heat, hunger and fatigue—and that isolation of mind which was perhaps worse than all, in the end flung me into a fever, and I was transmitted to an hospital. This incident I should hardly deem worthy of chronicling if it had not proved the occasion of introducing into my blood the seeds of a more virulent disease than any I had yet known,—an incurable hypochondriasis. There was a poor child in the convalescent ward of the institution, who was afflicted from head to foot with an actual leprosy; and there being no vacant bed to be had, I was compelled to share that of this miserable being, which, such was my ignorance of the nature of contagion, I did without the slightest suspicion of the inevitable result. But in a few days after my dismissal from the hospital this result but too plainly shewed itself on my person in the form of a malady nearly as hideous and loathsome as that of the wretched boy himself; and though all external traces of it have long since disappeared, its moral effects remain incorporated with my mental constitution to this hour, and will probably continue with me through life. It was woe on woe, and 'within the lowest deep a lower deep.'[24] Yet, will it be credited? my kindred scarcely seemed to take notice of this new and terrible mark so set on me. Privation and despair had rendered them almost indifferent to every thing; and for me, sullen, self-inwrapt, diseased within and without, I cared not to call their attention to it: 'My heart had grown hard, and I hurt my hand when I struck it.'[*25]

Very slowly, and only when a kind acquaintance—for I was not yet utterly deserted—came forward to rescue me from the grave by his medical skill—did I in some degree conquer the malignity of this ghastly complaint. Another disease, however, and another, succeeded, until all who knew me began to regard me as one appointed to a lingering living martyrdom. And, for myself, I scarcely knew what to think of my own condition, though I have since learned to consider it as the mode and instrument which an All-wise Providence made use of to curb the outbreakings of that rebellious and gloomy spirit that smouldered like a volcano within me. My dominant passion, though I guessed it not, was Pride; and this was to be overcome by pain of every description and the continual sense of self-helplessness. Humiliation was what I required; and that bitterest moral drug was dealt out to me in lavish abundance. Nay, as if Pelion were to be piled on Ossa[26] for the purpose of contributing to my mortification, I was compelled to perform my very penances—those enjoined me by my spiritual director—in darkness and subterranean places—wheresoever I could bury myself from the face of living man. And they were all merciful dispensations, these, to lift me out of the hell of my own nature, compared with those which the Almighty afterwards adopted for my deliverance.

My apprenticeship terminated[27]—but so did nothing else in my unhappy position. The burden of an entire family lay on me, and the down-dragging

* Shsp.

weight on my spirit grew heavier from day to day. I was now obliged to seek employment wheresoever I could find it—and thankful was I whenever my father and mother were enabled to reap the fruits of my labor. But my exasperated mind (made half mad through long disease) would frequently enquire—though I scarcely acknowledged the enquiry to myself—how or why it was that I should be called on to sacrifice the Immortal for the Mortal—to give away irrevocably the Promethean fire within me for the cooking of a beefsteak—to destroy and damn my own soul that I might preserve for a few miserable months or years the bodies of others. Often would I wander out into the fields, and groan to GOD for help. 'De profundis clamo!'[28] was my continual cry. And, in truth, although my narrative scarcely appears at a glance to justify me, my circumstances taken altogether were amply sufficient to warrant the exclamation. A ruined soul in a wasted frame:—the very *ideal* and perfection of moral and physical evil combined in one individual: let the reader imagine these and—draw his conclusion.

After a short while matters appeared to brighten with me, or rather to assume a less dusky aspect. I was advised by a worthy medical friend of mine, Mr. Graham[29] of Thomas St.—a man of considerable knowledge and skill, though but an apothecary—to try what such kinds of exercise as fencing or ball-playing might accomplish for me. 'The mind, my dear young friend,' observed this intelligent man to me— 'is the key to the health—a somewhat rusty key to persons of coarser constitutions—but an oiled key to all of nervous temperaments and susceptible apprehensions. You have taken long walks: they have done you no good—why? Because you felt no interest in them—*because while your limbs walked one way your mind walked another.* Try the foil or the racket, and you will be a new being at the end of a fortnight.' I took my friend's advice and soon was in a condition to bear testimony to the truth of his vaticination. Never, perhaps, was such a change witnessed in the health and spirits of a human being as that which supervened in mine after the lapse of a week. The almost miraculously recuperative power which has since been frequently observed to exist in me enjoyed full and fair play. I arose, as it were, out of myself. I had for a long time subsisted upon nothing but bread and tea, or milk, with my heart only for animal food—'bitter diet,'[30]—as Byron remarks—giving the grosser aliments they required to my relatives—but I now felt as though I could feast upon air and thought alone. The great overcurtaining gloom which had become to me a sort of natural atmosphere—a fifth element—still in a degree surrounded me; but my experience of existence at this time was that of a comparative Paradise. Alas! it could not endure—and it did not. Another book in the Iliad of my woes was to be opened, and black and appalling was the page that it presented to my view.

Chap. IV.

'Farewell the tranquil mind!—farewell content!'[32]

Amid the glow of soul which I experienced through the change in my situation from absolute bondage to comparative liberty I could not forget the links that bound me to those who still depended on me for the very breath of life. That they appeared as indifferent to my powers of endurance as the storms are to those of the rock they assault was nothing to me. That they were in health, and in the prime of life, while I was in a state of chronical illness, and old in soul though young in years, touched me little or nothing. They were still my parents, and only as such could I regard them. I willingly overlooked the maxim of St. Paul, that the elder should lay up for the younger portion of the family, and not the younger for the elder. Within about nine months after the termination of my apprenticeship a situation was offered me in a solicitor's office,[34] the salary derivable from which, though humble enough, was sufficient to elevate us in some degree above the depths of our former poverty; and this situation I accepted,— not gladly—for a foreboding of what was to come haunted me now with more intense force than ever—but resignedly, and in the full belief that I was merely fulfilling a destiny which I could not oppose, and which I had no right to arraign.

I weary the reader by calling on him for ever to listen to a tale of unmitigated calamity. But as I am bound to adhere to strict truth in this autobiography, he will kindly forgive as well the monotony of general reflection as of particular detail which he here encounters. By-and-by I may invite his attention to more cheerful and consolatory matter. At present the scroll which I am compelled to unroll before him is, like that of the Prophet, 'written within and without with mourning and lamentation and woe.'[35] And perhaps those who are more desirous of understanding the motives than of listening to a cold recital of the actions of another may find some interest in perusing a record which, I willingly admit, embodies hardly a sentence upon which the mere worldling or witling would care to expend a moment's reflection.

I had not been long installed in my new situation before all the old maladies under which I had laboured returned with double force. The total want of exercise to which I was subjected was in itself sufficient to tell with ruinous effect upon a frame whose long continued state of exhaustion had only received a temporary relief from the few months' change of life to which I have adverted. But other agencies also combined to overwhelm and prostrate me. The coarse ribaldry, the vile and vulgar oaths, and the brutal indifference to all that is true and good and beautiful in the universe, of my office-companions affected me in a manner difficult to conceive. My nervous and hypochondriacal feelings almost verged upon insanity. I seemed to myself to be shut up in a cavern with serpents and scorpions and all hideous and monstrous things, which writhed and hissed around me, and discharged their slime and venom over my person. These hallucinations were considerably aided and aggravated by the pestiferous atmosphere of the office, the chimney of which smoked continually, and for some hours before the close of the day emitted a sulphurous exhalation that at times literally caused me to gasp for breath. In a word I felt utterly and thoroughly miserable. The wretched depression of my spirits could not escape the notice of my mother, but she passed no remark on it,—and left me in the evenings altogether to myself and my books; for, unfortunately, instead of endeavouring somewhat to fortify my constitution by appropriating my spare hours to exercise I consumed these in unhealthy reading. My morbid sensibilities thus daily encreasing and gaining ground, while my bodily powers declined in the same proportion, the result was just as might have been anticipated. For the second time in my life nature succumbed under the intolerable burden imposed upon her; and an acute attack of illness removed me for a season from the sphere of my irksome and melancholy duties. My place in the office was assumed by my younger brother John, a stout and healthy lad of nineteen,[36] who had already acquired some slight experience in the mysteries of scrivenery and attorneyship; and I returned home.

My confinement to bed on this occasion was not of long duration; but, though after the lapse of a few days able to crawl about once more, I was far indeed from being recovered. A settled melancholy took possession of my being. A sort of torpor and weariness of life succeeded to my former over-excited sensibilities. Books no longer interested me as before; and my own unshared thoughts were a burden and a torment unto me. Again I essayed the effect of active exercise, but was soon compelled to give over, from sheer weakness and want of animal spirits. I indulged, however, occasionally in long walks into the country around Dublin; and the sight of hills, fields and streams, to which I had been long unaccustomed, produced in me a certain placidity of mind, with which, had I understood my own true interests for time and eternity, I ought to have remained contented. But contented I did not and would not remain. I desired to be aroused, excited,— shocked even. My grand moral malady—for physical ailments I also had, and singular of their kind,—was—an impatience of life and its commonplace pursuits. I wanted to penetrate the great enigma of human destiny and my own—to know 'the be-all and the end-all'[37]—the worst that could happen here or hereafter— the final *dénouement* of a drama that so strangely united the two extremes of broad farce and thrilling tragedy, and wherein mankind played at once the parts of actors and spectators.

If I perused any books with a feeling of pleasure they were such as treated of the wonderful and terrible in art, nature and society. Descriptions of battles and histories of revolutions; accounts of earthquakes, inundations and tempests; and narratives of 'moving accidents by flood and field,'[38] possessed a charm for me which I could neither resist nor explain. It was some time before this feeling merged altogether into another—the sentiment of religion and its ineffable mysteries. To the religious duties enjoined by my church I had always been attentive, but I now became deeply devotional, addicted myself to ascetic practices, and studied the lives of the saints with the profoundest admiration of their grand and extraordinary virtues. If my mind had been of a larger and sterner order all this had been well enough, and I should doubtless have reaped nothing but unmixed advantage from my labours. But, constituted as I was, the effect of those upon me was rather injurious than beneficial. I gradually became disquieted by doubts, not of the great truths of faith, for these I never questioned, but of my own capacity, so to speak, for Salvation. Taking a retrospective view of all the events of my foregone years—reflecting on what I had been and then was,—and meditating on what it was probable that I should live to be, I began to think, with Buffon,[39] that it is not impossible that some beings may have been created expressly for unhappiness; and I knew that Cowper[40] had lived, and perhaps died, in the dreadful belief that he himself was a cast-away, and a 'vessel of wrath, fitted for destruction.'[41] Scruples of conscience also multiplied upon me in such numbers in the interval between each of my confessions that my mind became a chaos of horrors, and all the fires of Pandemonium[42] seemed to burn in my brain. I consulted several clergymen with regard to what I should do in this extremity. Most recommended me to mix in cheerful and gay society; one alone, I remember, counselled me to pray. And pray I did, for I had so held myself aloof from the companionship of others that I knew of no society with which I could mix. But I derived no consolation from prayer. I felt none of that confidence in GOD then, which, thanks to His Almighty power and grace, I have since so frequently known. The gates of Heaven seemed barred against me: its floor and walls, of brass and triple adamant, repelled my cries; and I appeared to myself to be sending a voice of agony into some interminable chasm. This deplorable interior state, one which worlds and diadems should not bribe me into experiencing again, continued for about a twelvemonth, after which it gradually disappeared, not through progress of time, not through any process of reasoning or indeed any effort of my own, but, remarkably enough, precisely through the agency of the very remedy recommended me by my spiritual advisers.

Chap. V.

'Farewell the tranquil mind! Farewell content!' —SHAKSP.[43]

On the south side of the city of Dublin, and about half-way down an avenue which breaks the continuity of that part of the Circular Road extending from Harold's Cross to Dolphin's Barn, stands a house,[44] plain in appearance, and without any peculiarity of external structure to attract the passenger's notice. Adjoining the house is a garden, with a sort of turret-lodge at the extreme end, which looks forth on the high road. The situation is lone and unpicturesque; and he who should pause to dwell on it must be actuated by other and deeper and possibly sadder feelings than any that such a scene would be likely to excite in the breast of the poet or the artist.

Perhaps he should be under the influence of such emotions as I recently experienced in passing the spot after an absence from it of seventeen years. Seventeen years!—let me rather call them seventeen centuries. For, life upon life has followed and been multiplied on and within me during that long, long era of passion, trouble and sin. The Pompeii and Herculaneum[45] of my soul have been dug up from their ancient sepulchres. The few broken columns and solitary arches which form the present ruins of what was once Palmyra[46] present not a fainter or more imperfect picture of that great city as it flourished in the days of its youth and glory than I, as I am now, of what I was before I entered on the career to which I was introduced by my first acquaintance with that lone house in 1831. Years of so much mingled pleasure and sorrow! whither have you departed, or rather, why were you allotted me? You delivered me from sufferings which, at least, were of a guiltless order, and would shortly in a better world have been exchanged for joys, to give me up to others, the bitter fruits of late repentance, and which await no recompense, and know no change, save change from severe to severer. But, alas! thus it was, is, and must be. My plaint is chorussed by millions. Generation preaches to generation in vain. It is ever and everywhere the same old immemorial tale. From the days of Adam in Eden to our own we purchase Knowledge at the price of Innocence. Like Aladdin in the Enchanted Subterranean Garden,[47] we are permitted to heap together and gather up as much hard bright gold and diamonds as we will—but we are for ever therefore entombed from the fresh natural green pastures and the healthful daylight.

In the course of my desultory rambles about the suburbs of the city it would sometimes happen that I should feel obliged to stop and rest, even though nothing better than a hedge-side or a field-hillock afforded me the means of a few moments' repose. The reader will, therefore, imagine me reclining, rather than seated, on a long knoll of grass by a stream-side beyond Rathfarnham, and closely adjacent to Roundtown,[48] while the sun is setting, on an evening in June; I held in my hand a book, with the covers turned down; it was *Les Pensées de Pascal*.[49] As I lay revolving in my mind some of the sublime truths contained in this celebrated work, I was somewhat suddenly approached and accosted by a fashionably dressed and intelligent looking young man, whom I had twice or thrice before observed sauntering about this neighbourhood.

'May I ask,' he enquired, 'the nature of your studies'?'

I placed the book in his hand: he looked at it for a moment, and then returned it to me without speaking.

'You don't read French?' said I, interrogatively.

'Oh, yes, I do,' he replied. 'Who does not now-a-days? But that is a very unhealthy work.'

I perceived at once that there was a great gulf between us; and as I had even then learned enough of the nature of the human mind to know that disputation hardly ever converts or convinces, I contented myself with remarking, in an indifferent manner:—

'Everything in this world is unhealthy.'

The stranger smiled. 'And yet,' said he, 'you feel pleasure, I am sure, in the contemplation of this beautiful scenery; and you admire the glory of the setting sun.'

'I have pleasure in nothing, and I admire nothing,' answered I. 'I hate scenery and suns. I see nothing in Creation but what is fallen and ruined.'

My companion made no immediate remark upon this, but, after a pause, took the book out of my hand, and turning over the leaves, read aloud that passage in which Pascal compares the world to a dungeon, and its inhabitants to condemned criminals, awaiting the hour that shall summon them to execution.[*50]

'Can you believe, my friend?' the stranger asked, 'for, short as our acquaintance has been, I venture to call you such—can you believe this to be true?'

'Why not?' I replied. 'My own experiences, feelings, life, sufferings, all testify to my soul of its truth. But before I add anything further, will you allow me to ask what religion you profess?'

---

* Upon which, by the way, Voltaire has nothing better to say than this:—'*Regarder le monde comme un cachot, et les hommes comme des criminels qu'on va executer, c'est là la pensée d'un fanatique.*' Strange that a man of such an analytical mind as the philosopher of Ferney should not have perceived that Fanaticism, so called, is but another name for Enthusiasm: the spirit that has always governed and to eternity will govern the Universe. Its proper name is Activity. It

'———makes the madmen who have made men mad
By their contagion,—conquerors and Kings,
Founders of sects and systems.'—Byron.

But with the vast amount of Evil which it has unquestionably generated is intermingled a still vaster amount of Good,—and if 'a little leaven leaventh the whole lump,' what may we not anticipate from an abundance of it?

'A good one, I hope,' he answered; 'I have been reared a Catholic Christian.'

'Then,' said I, 'you know that it is the belief of the holiest and most learned theologians of your church that the majority of mankind will be irrevocably consigned to eternal misery?'

'Really I know no such thing,' he replied.

'Have you never read Massillon,'[51] I asked, 'on "The Small Number of the Saved"?'

'I take the judgment of no one individual even in my own church,' he answered, 'as my guide. The goodness—the justice of GOD————'

I interrupted him. 'Stop,' said I. 'What do you

[*The manuscript ends here*]

[unpublished manuscript]

Letters

[To Tynan, mid-1832]

My dear Tynan,[1]
I offer you, according to the usual form, an extensive variety of apologies for my apparent neglect. Having always been as Byron says 'a mortal of the careless kind',[2] I of course, mislaid your letter, and being at a loss for your address, to send you an *answer* was out of the *question*. A few days since however I found your letter again and I shall now attempt to say something or nothing to the purpose by way of reply. You will please to give me considerable credit in your books for modesty: modesty has always been the greatest of my littlenesses, and the most strongly-marked of my weaknesses. And yet, sooth to say, my letters are generally good, for whenever they are not good for something they are good for nothing. You will swear by Madam de Sevigne's[3] 'epîtres,' that they are not short at all events, but I am slightly acquainted with Burgersdicius,[4] and will prove that they are, for all things that are not, are, because they are the things that are not. You may call this logic strange, and even odd:—if you do I will prosecute you before the High Court of Reason for turning a promulger of paradoxes, for nothing is even and odd together. A propos des bottes;[5] talking of reason; can you tell me, pray, why that which is *hight reason* when uttered by A. B. becomes *high treason* when uttered by Y. Z? As Brutus[6] says, I pause for a reply.—

You know, now, well, that I know very well that you know remarkably well that I know nothing whatever about Politics. It is a saying of Talleyrand's,[7] that speech was given to man that he might conceal his thoughts, and the principal utility of governments appears to me to be to shew that governments are unnecessary things. 'So, my son' said the Eastern sage to his pupil, 'go and see what a little quality of wisdom sufficeth to rule the world'. His observation was good. I am quite of opinion with Washington Irving[8] that there are and have ever been but two distinct political parties in the world, the one being the predominant party, and the other wanting to become the predominant party. The first party are always for killing the second. Thus *L'apostolique*[9] recommended the killing of La Fayette[10] and the Duke of Newcastle[11] recommended the killing of O'Connell.[12] On the other hand, the second party are always for deposing the first party, as every body knows. But beyond the mere merits of the killing and deposing systems respectively, neither party N° 1 nor party N° 2 exhibit any particularity of a particularly particular nature. With respect to the people, le peuple souverain[13] &c. &c. there is very little wisdom among *them* either, in any town or country in the geography, but there is proportionally as much ambition & thirst of

domination on a smaller scale and within a pettier sphere, as any one can meet
with at Court. The difference between the people that are at court, and those
that are not at court, I think to be this: the first attend levees, dress magnificently,
pocket pensions, and do nothing, the second are desirous of being able to attend
levees, dress magnificently, pocket pensions, and do nothing. The first are the
INS, the last the OUTS. There is some truth in the remark of Jefferson, that all
the feeble-minded and unhealthy are tories by nature, and that all the lion-
hearted and healthy are whigs by nature,[14]—but I still think that all classes, sick
and sound, have a leaning towards aristocracy of one kind or another. Exceptions
there are, beyond all doubt, but they come immediately under the inspection of
nobody that any one knows. Of old, there used to be sublime characters who
tried to become statues: these were great saints; and there was one man (Helvetius)[15]
in the last century, who was no saint whatever; and this man concocted a book
called 'De L'Esprit' (a dry-looking quarto) and in this book he states that a man
vegetates like a tree, and that he (Helvetius) would have no objection to become
a tree. But he got none to echo him, for as that other great man, Godwin[16] (author
of a drama 'so middling, bad were better,'[17] so heavy that it appears, not Miltonic,
but Mill-stone-ic) profoundly observes in his preface to St Leon 'It is better to
be a human being than a stock or a stone.' Even the writer of the Arabian Tales
makes his metamorphosed Prince in the Black Palace,[18] half-marble, half man,
marble only from the middle downwards, leaving him the free exercise of his
brains, such as they are, and there are really not bad, considering that he was son
of a king. These are my notions,—perhaps they betray a plentiful lack of political
wisdom; but some persons are wise, and others are otherwise, though not all-so.
N'importe:[19] 'I'm a philosopher: confound them all!' quoth Byron,[20] and so say I.
When the Millennium shall arrive it will be very well for us all. In the meantime,
let us not wrangle about the wool of a goat.

  You talk about newspapers and their venality. The venality of newspapers is a
matter of course. It is the fifth element of those who edit them. The idea of
venality is about as essentially connected with the idea of a newspaper as the idea
of heat is connected with the idea of fire. He who thinks otherwise has his folly
for his pains; he is asleep and dreaming. My impression is this; that the
Periodical Press is a dead weight upon the vitality of society, a drag upon the
intellect of mankind, an incubus over us all. It is, I rather think, 1stly, a curse, 2ndly a
scourge, 3rdly a bore, 4thly an evil, 5thly an eyesore, 6thly a bugbear, 7thly, an ugliness, 8thly
an horror, 9thly a woe, & 10thly an abomination, not that spoken of by Daniel[21] the
prophet, but as bad. I say this quietly, for I pique myself on being cool when I
ought to be redhot with wrath. I am neither Job nor Epictetus,[22] but I bear the
P.P. with the patience of both. I would not exclaim with the former, 'Oh! That
mine enemy had written a book!'[23] for I think, with Diogenes,[24] the Caliph

Omar,[25] & Mygasarus[26] that books are too numerous. A proposal was made some time ago in the N.M.M.[27] for setting fire to Paternoster Row,[28] but nobody chose to hang the bell about the cat's neck, and the affair dropped. I sustained the disappointment with equanimity, for it is my way on these occasions to reflect on what the wise man said to the daughter of King Cophetua when her lover was married, or buried, (I forgot which) namely, that when a thing is, it is, and there is an end of the matter.[29] Affording, as I can, to laugh at many things and several people, I conceive I should have been one of the Pococurante[30] School; I would have made a docile disciple. By the way, now, I ought to be ashamed of egotizing after this manner, and so I really am, for you know that after all I am not one who delighteth in thrusting the private I into the public eye. The truth is that my practice, like that of Pascal and the Port Royalists,[31] is to sink the first personal pronoun altogether, and if I ever happen to make use of it, it is only when I do not adhere to that practice.

Retournons à nos moutons.[32] In paragraph the last you have my opinion on the P.P.—in what I say there, I include the whole P.P. even the Cherokee Tribe Gazette[33] which has lately been taken into hand, and the Almanac of Van Dæmon's Land[34] which has been lately set on foot. (By the way, I believe I should have written, Van *Diemen's* Land;—I must learn how to spell) What my reasons are for paying the P.P. so many lofty compliments, we shall not now discuss, because I am not writing a treatise for the public but a letter to a friend. Thinking about these nothings is throwing away thought, and writing on the same subject is merely filling page by page of waste paper. I would rather go and count the tiles on my neighbour's roof, as Moses Mendelsohn used to do when bored to Death's door by his geometrical problems.[35] A newspaper itself,—the Times even, 'drap de lit'[36] as it is (you may use it for a table cloth any day) would not contain the preface to what I could (not *should*) write on the subject of the P.P. But I consent that a veil be drawn over the topic now and for ever, Amen.

I must say, with regard to (but without any regard *for*) Cobbett,[37] that he is a tremendous weight when he has any body or any system to tumble down upon;—deprive him, through, of these, and he looks as Hercules at the distaff did;[38] he becomes the flattest, deadest, spiritlessest proser at all. [You must not quarrel with my grammar je suis trop paresseux pour parler Vaugelas.[39]] He (not Vaugelas, but Cobbett) says a few new things, & a few true things, but the true are not new, and the new are not true.[40] He is a good farmer, not a bad lawyer, a passable historian, and if not an Alcides[41] in politics, he is at least an All-sides, which he thinks better. Moreover and above, his knowledge of the world (I don't mean le savoir vivre[42]) is perfect, but as Huygens[43] and Herschel[44] acquaint us, there are spots on the sun, and nobody can be an admirable Creichton[45] A.D.1832. Such characters could only exist in the dark ages, as the real Aurora Borealis is visible only in the gloom of the North. Lucus a non lucendo,[46] said the Poet of yore. Hazlitt's character of Cobbett[47] is the best I have seen; I recommend it to you.

'Religion, love—the ceaseless themes bestow—How can we reason but from what we know'[48]—So sang Pope in writing of the Spanish ladies, but between us two for 'love' read politics. Religion and politics are grave things to analyse, but it strikes me that they are more intimately connected each with each than it is the fashion to imagine. The laws of any land being just, two things are clear. I: that the monarch who violates any of them acts irreligiously, II: that no truly religious man violates any of them. Suppose that on some beautiful evening in the merry month of June next when Ennui and Listlessness are clubbing together to kill me piecemeal, I waylay an old woman on the road to Bray; suppose that I transfer her loose cash to my pocket. As might be expected a mob is collected; I, looking dejected, am quickly suspected: in short I'm detected; my capture's effected; my prayers are rejected, my pockets inspected, my person protected, and its owner directed to march forward towards Newgate.[49] Then the chaplain corrects me for my want of piety, the hangman projects me from the Drop, to take a 'New View of Society',[50] and the surgeon dissects me: all this is matter of notoriety. But will the Court of Rome canonize me? Not for some time, nor through all eternity. Pour couper court,[51] the best statesmen the world ever saw have been religious men; witness Ximenes,[52] and vice versa, witness Richelieu.[53]

Your ideas on society are probably juster that mine are, but they do not appear to me to be so. My conception is (observe, I do not dogmatise) that every body is an unit, an 'ego' as Kant has it,[54]—a figure of 1, a personal pronoun of the singular number. Society I take to be by no means one vast whole integer, but simply a perceptibly divisible aggregate of all these little units. (I beg the cyphers' pardon for omitting them; they are an important class; 2 dozen generally and of each 24) If you pour a thousand million drops of water into an immense tub, drop by drop, you will, upon mounting a ladder, and looking into the immense tub, see an immense tub—full, not of drops of water, but of water. But take the 1000,000,000 people on the globe to day and I will wager ten to one (ten guineas to one cockle-shell) that if you were possessed of all the skill that Paracelsus[55] had when he attempted to create a man in a bottle, you would be at a dead loss how to begin building up the 1000,000000 into a single human Colossus. I wonder whether Bentham in his Book of Fallacies[56] has noticed this fallacy about Society: it is one that should be exposed and exploded at once. People are really prone to talk about the human race as though it were one body animated by one soul, just as Kircher[57] supposed the Earth to be a living animal, and Spinoza[58] believed the universe to be God. Even Tom Moore says that the bondage that *Venice* groans under at present is a chastisement for *her* wickedness 200 years ago!—'Desolate *Venice*! when I track *thy* course of crime in ages back'[59] &c. &c.

But the absurdity of this is clearly pointed out by Dr Bowring in the Westminster Review. 'Certain persons, Venetians, (says the Dr) committed great atrocities in the year 1620; therefore certain other persons, Venetians, are to suffer the punishment of this in 1823.'[60] Leave such views of Society, my dear Tynan, to those who carry the nursery along, with them to old age. Nobody is bound to any other person. Links and chains and bodies and members are very well in declamation and poetry, and nowhere else. The Romans manacled every prisoner to an incubus of a soldier, and Mezentius[61] tied a dead and living body together, it is true, but these were punishments. I can do what I will with myself and my own, provided I do not contravene conscience. Property, liberty, life, and so forth, I can surrender each and all when circumstances require the surrender,—everybody beside can do as I do:—where no circumstances require the surrender, I can stay as I am;—every one else can do the same; 'the rest is all but leather and prunella'.[62] You are to swallow all this, however, with a grain or two of salt, because as I have already said, I don't wish to dogmatise.

Revolutions, and Constitutions, and Charts, and Diplomacy, and Père Enfantin[63] and his chimæras, and St Simon and his organic periods,[64] and Robert Owen[65] and his New Structure of Society, his Grand Plan for the abolition of Evil, his parallelograms and his Science of Circumstances, all these things and beings were at first very wonderful to me and are now very weariful to me; I have small sympathy with any of them; I have tired of all of them. I am a lover of liberty, such liberty as is to be had in this world, just as I am a lover of fresh air, good health, idleness, gay society, solitude, &c. &c. but I claim no merit for being so. I do no think that a man is a jot the more deserving of praise because he had the good fortune to be born in New York. Liberty is not a virtue, an attribute, or a quality: it is a possession; you have it just as you have an acre of land or a pair of boots. And the truth is, my dear fellow, that I think the man who labours to earn the price of a pair of boots for himself proportionably entitled to as many encomiums as the man who kills other people that he may procure freedom for himself. Depend upon it that Self is at the bottom of every struggle. Sift what I say thoroughly and I will thank you, for I really feel inclined rather to be right than to be wrong. I will put an extreme case: I like to be fair. A. and B. are guardian and ward. A. one morning discovers B. reading a newspaper. This is simple, and a common case, but A. in his wisdom or silliness knows or fancies he knows that there are matters in the paper not well calculated to serve his pupil's morals. Quoth he, therefore—'My child, I command you by my authority as your guardian to read no more of that.' Quoth B, 'You old tyrant, do you think we are in Algiers?[66] I will read every newspaper in the world.' Quoth A. 'I must be under the necessity of taking that newspaper from you, unless you quietly give it up.' 'Indeed!' quoth B. 'why then I must do something. If I allow you to deprive me of my newspaper I shall be unable to read what it contains, so I will tell you what I have determined to do: I have determined to bespatter the walls of this room with your blood and brains.' A. undismayed, attempts to take the paper (La Revolution,[67] or La France Nouvelle[68]) by force, upon which B. draws a pistol from a pocket and blows out the brains of A. He then sits down to breakfast and finishes his perusal. If you do not feel disposed to be enthusiastic on behalf of B in a case of this kind, yet pause ere you condemn him; consider that the reasons thus: 'If I allow my guardian to control me I shall be under the control of my guardian: if I suffer him to take this newspaper away I shall not have the pleasure of reading it. It is clear that my only way to retain the paper is blowing out his brains. He does not want to blow out my brains: all he wants is the Gazette: he will be satisfied by that: that—if it come to the tug, he must have, but that he shall not have. I appeal to Heaven and to man whether I have any mode left of retaining this little article but by slaughtering my guardian. He is unreasonable: it is better therefore that I should be savage. He is a fool, therefore I must become a ruffian and a cutthroat.' Consider I say that he reasoned thus, and you may learn to excuse him. As to the application of the case, if there be one you will discover it.

There being but two methods of viewing a given subject, the correct and the incorrect, it is sometimes amusing and sometimes amazing to observe with what an invariable pertinacity of irrationality, with what a steady regularity of wrong-headedness, most men will adopt the incorrect method.

Whether the Parisians during the days of 'la petite semaine'[69] were inspired by an angel or driven by a devil each, to do what they did, I shall forbear to enquire, because nobody can tell me. But that the transaction first and last would turn out a glorious blunder was foreseen by every one who possessed any more sagacity than characterizes butterflies generally. I am not the apologist of kings, I take Divine Right to be an unintelligibility of the muddiest pattern; Louis XI[70] (but he was not the founder of kingcraft in France; he merely stepped into the illustrious pantoufles[71] of his father Charles VII[72]) and his iron cages, daggers, and damnable ideas are honored by my selectest aversion; but yet,—but yet I am unable to feel as you do with regard to equal rights, liberty &c. &c. I have said that I am a lover of this world's liberty, and so I am, but I have never loved it passionately, because it is not the creature of my imagination, the beau-ideal[73] of my aspirations. I am occasionally metaphysical, (it is a slight misfortune which nobody can help;) and having meditated twice or thrice upon thy question, my conclusion is this; that political liberty is not worth a bag of chaff. Take notice that I speak for myself only. If I were tomorrow to enter into possession of all the advantages that the best of good governments have ever been able to bestow, I would feel precisely as an individual would, who, suffering under a complication of maladies, gout, palsy, stone, phthisis, scrofula, cancer, dropsy, cholic, catarrh, epilepsy, erysipelas &c. &c. should find himself one morning freed from a little wen upon his thumb. This I declare to you most solemnly. I protest that the age ought to be strait-waistcoated; its reasonings are the most pompous of senilities. Soame Jenyns has shewn to the perfect satisfaction of himself and me that no man can ever attain any liberty worth speaking of beyond the liberty of mere Volition.[74] His liberty is in point of fact infringed upon in his very birth, for he comes into existence independent of his own consent,—as he goes out of it against his will. But what the world would really be at I know no more than an elephant. It (the world I mean) is growing hoary in quackish theories. But the March of Intellect is growing a Dead March latterly and will be apt to terminate (as March ought) on some First of April,[75] and an appropriate day it will be. Sans rire[76] (as you say yourself) the inhabitants of the earth appear to me to be every day making an advance de plus[77] in foolishness. But the lunatic said of mankind that they were mad and had clapped him the only sane man alive, into prison, and you perhaps imagine that my own idiotism is the cause of all the idiotism I fancy I see in 'the nobility, gentry, my friends and the public at large', as the advertisements have it. A question with myself is, whether I am not intolerably stupid? and such is the depth of my stupidity that I really feel at a loss to decide whether I am or am not stupid. I will give up mooting the point this very day, for the mystery is one that human intelligence is baffled by, and it is better in cases like this to yield to despair without loss of time, than to go on poking a quagmire with a walking stick and turning up sludge, with a crowd of people spectatorising the while. It mattereth not —

> When men behold cold mould rolled cold around my mound of ground, all crowned with grass, alas! Mankind, though blind, will find my mind was kind, resigned, refined, but 'shrined like gas in glass.[78]

And these are two lines that I have a right to pique myself on, for the whole compass of English poetry exhibits nothing like them.

Retournons à nos moutons a second time. What do you mean, pray, by the hair's line breadth of distinction you have placed between abstract principle and universal principle? What I stand up for is correct principle, which is always abstract, and ought to be always universal. Perhaps you intend to put abstract principle on the one side, and convenient principle on the other; if you do, I understand you, but I do not admire what I understand. Peresse l'univers plutot qu'un principe!,[79] said the philosopher, and he was not very far wrong. Every thing can be reduced to principle; if there be an exception to cases that illustrate a principle, it is easy to make the exception a part of the principle. The pathway of duty is plain enough before us, the light that directs us along it is never under eclipse. One of your principles is that an aristocracy are a gang of robbers, and you think that they ought to cease robbing. Every one who is a robber ought, no doubt, to cease robbing, and if the aristocracy be robbers, they ought to cease to be so, and they will cease to be so when the shark and the pike and the crocodile become honest and abstemious members of Marine Society. These animals all and each, are accustomed to pounce upon and devour such other animals as are less powerful than themselves, and as the shark fastens his death-grip on his prey, and the pike lodges a gudgeon on the inside of his mouth, and the crocodile fixes his hooky gripe on the passenger, so the aristocrat plunders and slays, has plundered and slayed, and will plunder and slay till the end of the Chapter. You appear rather surprised that the tax-eaters and old usurers should have gained the whiphand again in France,[80] but when you are thirty years older, you will feel no surprise whatever at events of this nature. By this time too, you will see full-grown aristocracy in America, but even this will awaken no wonder within you, because you will see that it was the inevitable result of natural and artificial causes. Just wait until then. In the meanwhile keep cool.—

P.S. Nothing occurs in Ireland. No prospect of a Revolution. A year and a half ago[81] several persons in Dublin, 'waiters-of-inns who shone as inn-ov-ators, and slaters wanting to be legislators,'[82] workmen with no work to do, and tradeless tradesmen, were growing rapidly insane on the Repeal-of-the-Union question. 'That which had made them drunk had made me thoughtful'[83]—and I then acquainted all my acquaintance that they would see no change in Ireland but one for worse—de mal en pis, mes amis,[84] said I—no Repeal, no revolution bloody or bloodless. They who then sneered are now sighing. I should myself like a revolution better than you think, especially if it produced a general transfer of property and I had any prospect of robbing somebody, for my finances are too low for my ideas, which are of the princeliest. A revolution, besides, creates an extensive hubbub, a thing I am occasionally partial to, and exceedingly so whenever I see any likelihood of making anything by it. The principle objection I have to revolutions (particularly French) is that they now and then elevate persons from the lower ranks of society to the highest dignities, and Blackwood's Magazine has proved that elevations of this kind are preposterous. Its argument is profound and unanswerable 'The lower orders never can be properly qualified to legislate for a country, because they are composed of persons drawn from the lowest ranks.' An aristocracy besides is necessary for the sake of variety: were we all democrats there would be no variety, and variety is one of the charms of life. I could produce some other reasons in favor of our aristocracy, but as the foregoing is my best I omit the remainder. On the other hand however it will be asserted that I have overlooked another advantage produced by Revolutions, & that this may be placed in balance against the advantage of variety in ranks, I mean the change of a brown banner for a buff one, or vice versa. I admit the charge. When Charles X-King was Charles Rex (King) the French had merely a flag of one color; they have now a flag of three colors. It is allowed by all that this important change is the greatest benefit that the Revolution has conferred on France. It is generally the foremost of all the advantages that the prosers and poets of the Revolution enumerate. 'O'er Notre Dame[85] renowned in Story, the trinal banner proudly waves, and France resumes her march of Glory, her gallant sons no longer slaves', says one—'The pale white banner shrinks from sight'— says Bowring.[86] 'Sous le tri-colore, nous,'[87] etc., etc. rhapsodises a third. You may call this enthusiasm but for my part whenever I am unable to understand any thing well, I call it a mystery, and I think this therefore to be a mysterious matter which it was never intended by Destiny that man should comprehend. Thus, dangling a red rag before the eyes of a bull arouses him to madness, and nobody knows why. All that is left to us is to admire the influence of rags and colors, banners, garters, heraldry, humbug, and trumpery of all calibres and countries.

If I could by any means divest myself of a horrible species of laziness which constantly seizes me whenever I attempt to probe a political question I should be glad to enter into an analysis of the arguments for and against Republicanism. In the meantime my dear fellow, I am a despot in soul, and regard Abstract Despotism with such a degree of reverence that if the organ of Veneration on my head be not as immeasurable as the base of respectability-sized mountain, I will add Spurzheim[88] to the other quacks on my list and do my best to have his theory hooted out of creation. There is a je ne sais quoi[89] about Despotism which is really affecting: Despotism is a poetical government: there is a romance in the very idea; all the fairy tales are filled with kings and queens who did what they liked, and what is there so beautiful as the associations connected with a fairy tale! I prefer them even to the Catholic Association,[90] and the Association 'Aide-toi, le ciel l'aidera,'[91] which I translate thus, 'Help yourself,—God help you!'—I am unwilling to break off thus abruptly and I therefore intend to cross this letter with red ink: I hope you will be able to read the entire of my last—a silly remark by the bye, as you are not at my elbow to tell me.

[To Charles Gavan Duffy,[1] 1840 or 1841]

My hAnDy young MAN.

    I owed you no ode!—no one ode!—no one ode you an ode—any one ode!— no one knowed that any one owed you any one ode—or if any one knowed that anyone owed you any one ode, I am not that one—*o-de*-ar, not I!—Hear me for my caws,[2] as the rook said—I look on odes as ode-ious compositions—adulatory stuff—flattery of the flattest sort, worthy to be paid for, not in the glorious renown which all honest, honorable, high souled and high heeled men seek—but—out of the purse—one pound one a line—not a camae[3] less! Now you know I spit upon this sort of thing—I never *take* money for what I write—it is always given me—pressed on me—sent to me—flung in my phiz—and I, for sake of a quiet life, pocket the Affront.

But mark me, my friend, as the sheep said to the boy that carried the tar—I must tell you once again that the gift of song hath departed from me—henceforth look for poetry in a politician—a Peel[4]—a placeman—a pig in a poke—a pump—a ppair of ppumpps—a post paid parcel—a paint pot—a publican—a pint of porter—-a puncheon of perry—a pottle of purl—a pseudo-patriot—a poultice of putty—a pickpocket—a pyramid of potatoes—a penn'orth of pork—a pitcher of punch—a plum pudding—a pan of pastry—a peck of pink eyes—a periwig-pated pendant—a policeman—a protuberant paunch—a prig—a platter of porridge—a porringer of pottage—a potbellied poulterer—a pamphlet on poorlaws—a pedlar—a Palmerston[5]—a pot of prog—a poker—The Poker[6]—a pitchfork—a proser—in anything or anybody in short—but in the Man in the Cloak.

Don't think that I care either—the loss is a gain to me—it was a gain before—six or eight years agone—when I first took to prosing—it was a gain then, and it will be a *gain again*—it's strange if it don't, and I'd say it was *even odd*—but that would be parrydocksickle. Only fancy a sensible man domiciled all his life long in a garret—with his thumbs half a foot deep in ink and his feet in a tub of suds—a yard of pipe-clay in one daddle—as Westmeath[7] says of Bulwer[8]—and the stump of an intractable calamus in t'other—a head full of rhymes against reason and of reasons against rhyme on his shoulders—and such a night cap on the head!—imagine such a man—is there such a man? O, as Pope says—

Who would not weep if such a man there be?
Who would not grin if Atticus were he?[9]

And yet Attic-us must be he—and why? D'ye give it up?—Because he is a garreteer—and suffers woefully from room-attic complaints.

All that I had to say on this page is eggs-hausted—I (& you) must turn to page 3.—-I fill up the remainder of the blank thus—

Ring—tang—tong—tol—ol—oddy—hum—hew—poh—nogs. China—Egypt— India—

A. BRac, ADAB ra!!!

On looking back to the last two lines of my letter I find that they contain the substance of the next leading article in the Morning Herald[10]—quite an exadental co-inside-dance I assure you—great wits jump you know—Pray give me a paragraph in your Vindicator[11] setting me right with Posterity in this matter.

So you'll take no tales from me—your motto is 'Lex non talis'[12]—viz: 'the Law is—no tales!' What were you dreaming about when you came to such a verrrrrrrrry strrrrrrrrrange deterrrrrrrrrrrrrmination? Eh?—What?—Answer me—will you?

Apropos of dreams—I dreamt t'other night something out of the common—that the world was somehow altered—nobody knew how or why—that we had all been asleep or dead or tranced or something of that sort—and were—we could not say, wide awake—but silent, staring and puzzled—that nobody knew anybody—that Chronology had ceased counting the years and Almanacks were at a premium—but not to be had—that men were looking equally backward and forward into the abyss of Time, only to be mystified both ways—that the newspapers had ceased, Registers[13] having nothing to record, Spectators[14] being tired looking on at nothing, and Vindicators finding nothing that *could* be vindicated—in fine that Nature, Art & the Universe were all about to give up the ghost—You laugh! Take care, my fine fellow, than that the next time I dream such a dream I don't clap you into it!—how dare you put me into such a passion?—'Mens tuus ego'—i.e. Mind your eye![15]

['The Man in the Cloak']

[To Charles Gavan Duffy, 21 July 1847]

Kiltale, Summerhill,
Meath
21st. July, '47.

My dear Duffy,

I write to you from a lonely farm house in the heart of a wilderness. There is not a house within two miles of it—not a post-town nearer than five miles.

My brother had unfortunately a quarrel with me (I had none with him—and indeed never any with anyone) and he drove me out of our wretched lodgings with buffetings and blows (which, thank God, I did not return.) For some days and nights I wandered about the streets, dependent on chance and charity and thinking of poor Richard Savage.[1] I knew nobody to whom I could apply—perhaps I should rather say to whom I *would* apply—for my spirit seemed to rise in inverse proportion to the depth of my destitution. I had a melancholy consolation in thinking that I should be found dead of hunger somewhere about the suburbs of the city. And found at length I was, nearly in truth at the point of death, by one who did not know me, but who kindly assisted my fainting steps to a place to which I had just recollection enough to direct him—the classical locality of Copper Alley. There Mr. Plunket, the factor of my cousin Michl Smyth,[2] gave me a bed (A rug upon straw) in a barrel-loft, for two or three nights, and sent me up a cup of tea at intervals. God bless him! I then waited on my cousin himself—he who now owns the house that ought to be mine—and just said, 'Michael, I am going down to your father's—your family have often solicited me to pay them a visit—I will now test their sincerity.' He coldly told me that I would be welcome—and I set off—and paid my last maravedi[3] for a seat in the Caravan. And so, here I am—with the fresh breezes of Heaven blowing about me—with rivers of the purest spring water to drink—but with nothing, positively nothing to eat, excepting eggs, which I direct to be boiled very hard, to compensate for the absence of bread—though, if you consider that the bread itself here, (mill-stone griddle bread) is a thousand times harder than the eggs can be made, you may regard my assertion as more paradoxical than beseemeth.

My health is, after all, improving—but my mind is destroying me. What with the clear spring water and fresh air on one hand—and the absence of stimulants on the other—I find myself in a hybrid state which I shall not attempt to describe. I left my poor brother without a shilling for himself—and I retained but two or three shillings in my own pocket. Had I come down hither with a full purse the effect on my health would have been very different. But no matter. This cannot be helped.

In my despondency I almost hope that you may refuse my request—that I might have the selfish satisfaction of working for you from week to week without any further prospect of remuneration—but my heart is bowed and my spirit humbled—and I would be *rather* more grateful for a favorable reply. J.C.M.

[To Charles Gavan Duffy, 1847 or 1848]

[My dear Duffy]

I am utterly prostrated. I am in a state of absolute desolation of spirit.

For the pity of God, come to me. I have ten words to say to you. I implore you, come. Do not suffer me to believe that I am abandoned by Heaven and Man.

I cannot stir out—cannot look any one in the face.

[Regard this as my last request, and comply with it as if you supposed me dying.]

I am hardly able to hold the pen, but I will not and dare not take any stimulus to enable me to do so. Too long and fatally already have I been playing that game with my shattered nerves.

Enough. God ever bless you. Oh, come!

Ever your's
  J. C. Mangan

Mr. Mangan
To the Editor of the United Irishman[1]

MY DEAR MITCHEL,—There is a rumor in circulation, that the government intend to commence a prosecution against you. Insignificant an individual as I am, and unimportant to society as my opinions may be, I, nevertheless, owe it, not merely to the kindness you have shown me, but to the cause of my country, to assure you that I thoroughly sympathize with your sentiments, that I identify my views of public affairs with yours, and that I am prepared to go all lengths with you and your intrepid friend, Devin Reilly,[2] for the achievement of our national independence.

I mean to write to you, in a few days, a long letter, explanatory of the course which I think it becomes the duty of every Irish patriot to pursue, at the present eventful epoch. Meanwhile you are at liberty to make what use you please of this preliminary communication.

Yours, in life and death,
  JAS. CLARENCE MANGAN

[published in *United Irishman*, 25 March 1848]

[To James Hardiman,¹ 17 December 1848]

151, Abbey St. Dublin,
7ᵗʰ Decʳ. 1848.

Dear and Worthy Sir,

May GOD bless you! The half-note (N° 31669) has reached me safely. If this attain its destination by to-morrow (Friday) I suppose I might have the other half by Saturday.

The times are indeed dreadful. I myself have been for some time living, or rather half-living, upon two pence a day, or thereabouts. But it appears to me that something more awful than poverty and bankruptcy is impending. A new and strange storm seems gathering in the heavens. All the political changes that have convulsed Europe of late would appear to be but the precursors of some tremendous moral earthquake of which men entertain at present only a vague and dim presentiment. The pulpits of this city have rung with warnings to the people on this subject. May GOD arm and prepare us for it, whatever may be its nature!

O'Connell, like Burke, was as great a prophet as a politican. He said, years ago, that if the Poor-laws² were introduced into this country the estates of the gentry would soon pass into the hands of others. Time is verifying his prediction.

No tidings of the Pope³ as yet. Is not his disappearance a very mysterious affair? Can England have kidnapped him? I think of St. Jerome,⁴ and his lamentations over the downfal of the Roman Empire. But what was the Roman Empire in comparison with the Roman Papacy.

We shall see strange things, if we live, in 1849 and 1850. Meantime let us all pray, work, and humble ourselves before GOD. He is our only trust and stay.

Believe me, dear Sir,

Your's gratefully & faithfully
J. C. Mangan

Explanatory Notes

The following abbreviations are used in the notes:

AG   Anthologia Germanica
Chuto   Jacques Chuto, *James Clarence Mangan: A Bibliography* (Dublin and
                Portland, Or.: Irish Academic Press, 1999)
CW   *The Collected Works of James Clarence Mangan*, ed. J. Chuto, R.P. Holzapfel,
                P. Mac Mahon, A. Martin, P. Ó Snodaigh, E. Shannon-Mangan, P. Van
                de Kamp, 6 vols (Dublin and Portland, Or.: Irish Academic Press,
                1996–2002)
d'Herbelot   Barthélemy d'Herbelot, *Bibliothèque orientale*, 2 vols (The Hague: Neaulme
                & Van Daalen, 1777–79)
DPJ   *Dublin Penny Journal*
DUM   *Dublin University Magazine*
Hammer-Purgstall Joseph von Hammer-Purgstall, *Geschichte der osmanischen Dichtkunst*,
                4 vols (Pesth: Hartlebens Verlag, 1836–38)
Hardiman   James Hardiman, ed. *Irish Minstrelsy, or, The Bardic Remains of Ireland*,
                2 vols (London: Joseph Robins, 1831)
IPJ   *Irish Penny Journal*
IPS   *Irish Popular Songs*, ed. Edward Walsh (Dublin: McGlashan, 1847)
McCall   John M'Call, *Life of James Clarence Mangan* (Dublin: T. D. Sullivan, [1883])
Montgomery   Henry R. Montgomery, ed., *Specimens of the Early Native Poetry of Ireland*
                (Dublin: McGlashan, 1846)
MS 138   MS 138 (James Clarence Mangan manuscripts), National Library of Ireland
NLI   National Library of Ireland
O'Donoghue   D. J. O'Donoghue, *The Life and Writings of James Clarence Mangan*
                (Edinburgh: Geddes; Dublin: Gill, 1897)
PPM   *Poets and Poetry of Munster*, ed. John O'Daly (Dublin: Duffy, 1849)
RIA   Royal Irish Academy
Shannon-Mangan Ellen Shannon-Mangan, *James Clarence Mangan: A Biography* (Dublin
                and Portland, Or.: Irish Academic Press, 1996)
Tribes   *The Tribes of Ireland: A Satire, by Aenghus O'Daly*, ed. John O'Donovan
                (Dublin: O'Daly, 1852)

Unless otherwise noted below, copy-texts are the versions identified in brackets at the end of
each work.

Poetical Works

Lines, written at 17
Copy-text in MS 138. Possibly written in 1820, but because Mangan habitually omitted six years when stating his age (see Shannon-Mangan, 12), the poem may actually date from 1826.

Enigma [The Enchanted Earl of Kildare]
Copy-text is John McCall's transcription in MS 7953 (NLI). An 'enigma' was a type of puzzle-poem; in contrast to a rebus, the clues do not follow strict rules. Here the solution is 'The Enchanted Earl of Kildare' according to McCall. In Irish folklore, the enchanted earl of Kildare rides by night on a white stallion shod with silver shoes; when the shoes wear down, the earl will return. The 8th and 9th earls of Kildare, Gearóid Mór and Gearóid Óg Fitzgerald, were prominent in the struggle against Tudor power in Ireland in the early sixteenth century.
epigraph the opening lines of Goethe's 'Erlkönig', as translated by Matthew Lewis (1775–1818). Goethe's poem was later translated by Mangan himself as 'The Alder-King' (see pp. 43–5, above).

Enigma [A Vampire]
An alternative version exists in MS 138, entitled 'The Vampire, written at 17'. The solution to the enigma is 'A Vampire'.

Rebus [Emmet]
The rebus is solved by taking the initial letters of five words that answer the clues in the first stanza: 'Erin', 'Monarchy' 'Monarch', 'England' and 'Tyranny'. Robert Emmet (1778–1803) was captured and executed after the failure of his rebellion in Dublin in July 1803.
6   **Ierna** Ireland.

Enigma—To The Memory of the Late Lamented Mr. John Kenchinow, Butcher, of Patrick Street
The solution to the enigma is 'Fortitude'. McCall (9) explains that Mangan wrote the poem in response to a wager that in the space of a day he would write an elegy on the deceased butcher, 'of *twelve* stanzas of *five lines* each, every line of which should rhyme with either 'Kenchinow' or his 'stall."
4   **Dia's hall** 'Dia' was the name of the supposed Muse of the 'Diarians'; that is, the contributors to the Almanacs ('diaries') of the day.

The Young Parson's Dream
Based upon a prose tale ('Die Neujahrsnacht eines Unglücklichen') by Jean Paul Richter (1763–1825) that Mangan had earlier translated as 'The New-Year's Night of an Unhappy Man' (*Friend*, February 1830), and would translate twice again as poetry and once as prose. Here Mangan transforms Richter's 'old man' and 'young man' into Bishop and Parson to suit the politics of the *Parson's Horn Book*, a miscellany published by the 'Comet Club'. The *Horn Book* satirised clerical greed and corruption, mainly in the (Protestant) established church, as part of its campaign against the compulsory payment of tithes.

To My Native Land
An earlier version was published as an untitled enigma in *New Ladies' Almanack* in 1825, with the solution 'Ireland'. It is similar in tone and sentiment to Byron's 'The Irish Avatar' (1821), which criticises Ireland's craven condition in the wake of King George IV's visit to Dublin.

The Dying Enthusiast To His Friend
An earlier version of this poem, without the epigraph, had been published in the *Comet* in August 1832.
epigraph   Shelley, 'Adonais', ll. 462–64.

Elegiac Verses on the Early Death of a Beloved Friend
This poem memorialises Catherine Hayes, sister of Mangan's friend William Hayes, who probably died in October 1832. Mangan had tutored her in German and perhaps French. A later version, entitled 'Lines on the Death of **** **** ****', was published as a purported translation from Irish in the *DUM*, April 1839.
49   **Tullia's tomb**   when the tomb of Cicero's daughter Tullia (d. 45 BC) was discovered in Rome in the fifteenth century, it was said to contain a lamp that was still burning after 1500 years.

'Life is the Desert and the Solitude'
A re-written version of this poem was later published in the *DUM* as 'Stanzas which ought not to have been written in Midsummer' (June 1839).
title   Adapted from *The Revenge* (1721) by Edward Young:

> This vast and solid Earth, that blazing Sun,
> Those Skies thro' which it rolls, must all have End.
> What then is Man? the smallest part of Nothing.
> Day buries Day, Month Month, and Year the Year,
> Our Life is but a Chain of many Deaths;
> Can then Death self be fear'd? Our Life much rather:
> Life is the Desert, Life the Solitude,
> Death joins us to the great Majority.
> (IV, i)

The Philosopher and the Child
Mangan's last contribution to the *Comet*. The *Comet*'s editor, John Sheehan, may have written the commentary; John McCall apparently believed that Sheehan also authored the final 8 lines of the poem (see Shannon-Mangan, 134).
17   **Socrates**   Socrates, when sentenced to death for impiety and corruption of youth by the Athenian authorities, drank the customary hemlock rather than seek mitigation of his sentence, or avail of the escape plans organised by his friends.
27   **sky de copper** 'to play at pitch and toss' (O'Donoghue, 55).
30   **cropper** 'a half-glass of whiskey' (O'Donoghue, 55).
Note on commentary following the poem:
Sir Arthur Clarke 'a well-known Dublin physician, brother in law to Lady Morgan' (O'Donoghue, 55).

Curiosity
'Sensucht' by Johann Christophe Friedrich von Schiller (1759–1805). Mangan translated one of Schiller's verse dramas and more than seventy of his poems.

The Unrealities
Schiller, 'Die Ideale'.
17n **Pygmalion** a mythical king of Cyprus who fell in love with a statue; the goddess Aphrodite brought it to life.

A Railway of Rhyme
epigraph Alexander Pope, 'Essay on Man' (IV, 49).
8 **Ispahan** Isfahan; a major Persian city.
14 **Mendez Pinto** Fernão Mendez Pinto (?1509–83), Portuguese traveller and author of the fantastical travel account, *Peregrination* (1614).
18 **Alcoran** the Koran.
22 **COHEN's neat Cigar Divan** a smoking-room and shop located in Dame St, Dublin, mentioned also in Mangan's 'A Treatise on a Pair of Tongs'.
24 **Xantippe** the reputedly shrewish wife of Socrates.

Mignon's Song
'Kennst du das Land...' from Book III of *Wilhelm Meisters Lehrjahre* (1795) by Johann Wolfgang von Goethe (1749–1832). Mignon is a young girl who dies of unrequited love and yearning for her Italian home. Mangan published two earlier versions of the song in 1830 and 1834.

The Alder-King
Goethe, 'Erlkönig'. Scott's version is entitled 'The Erl-King'. Mangan was also aware of Matthew Lewis's translation; see note to 'Enigma [The Enchanted Earl of Kildare]', above.

A Song from the Coptic
Goethe, 'Kophtisches Lied'. Goethe's 'Coptic Songs' are not actually translations, but original poems. The Coptic language largely disappeared from Egypt after the fifteenth century.
Notes on commentary preceding the poem:
tableaux vivans correctly, *vivants*; a depiction of a scene by silent and motionless costumed participants.
Weimar Goethe's home for most of his mature life.
Wonderful Lamp refers to the tale of Aladdin from the *Arabian Nights*.
Note on poem
4 **una voce** Italian: 'with one voice'.

Another Song, from the Same Coptic
Goethe, 'Ein Andres'. See preceding note.

Ichabod! The Glory Hath Departed
'Nachtreise' by Ludwig Uhland (1787–1862). The title refers to 1 Samuel 4:21: 'And she named the child Ichabod, saying, "The glory has departed from Israel!"' The speaker is a dying Israelite mother whose husband has been killed in battle by the Philistines. In the same battle the Israelites lost the ark of the Covenant.

The King of Thule
Goethe, 'Der König in Thule'. An earlier version was published in November 1834. 'Thule' was the name applied to a country in the far north (perhaps Iceland) by the fourth-century-BC Greek explorer Pytheas, and by 8th-century Irish hermits.

Notes on commentary following the poem:
It is the speaker's . . . me remark recorded by Leigh Hunt in *Lord Byron and Some of his Contemporaries* (1828).
Comes o'er . . . odour slightly misremembered from *Twelfth Night* (I.i.5–7), as found in Alexander Pope's edition of Shakespeare (1725). Pope had notoriously emended the Folio's reading 'sound' to 'South'.
Dr. South religious polemicist Robert South (1634–1716).
Horne Tooke (1736–1812), a radical politician and linguist; in *The Diversions of Purley* (2 vols, 1786) he commented on the difficulty of determining the etymology for the words 'much', 'more' and 'most' (I, 467–72).
Death *mort* in French.
The torch . . . worthier slightly misquoted from Byron, *Childe Harold* (IV, clxxxiv).
Kerner Justinus Kerner (1786–1862) was a poet and physician with a particular interest in spiritualism.
Dogberry a character in *Much Ado about Nothing*; the quotation is from III.iii.15–16.
he lisps . . . come adapted from Alexander Pope, 'Epistle to Dr Arbuthnot' (1735), l. 128.
a weary chase . . . hour from Byron, *The Giaour*, l. 393.
many Priors and few Popes puns on the names of poets Matthew Prior (1664–1721) and Alexander Pope (1688–1744).

My Adieu to the Muse
Almost certainly an original poem; no corresponding original by Kerner has been traced.

from *Literæ Orientales—No. I—Persian and Turkish Poetry*
Mangan based most of his oriental translations (that is, those that he did not entirely invent) on German and French translations found in two collections: Joseph von Hammer-Purgstall, *Geschichte der osmanischen Dichtkunst*, 4 vols (Pesth, 1836–38) and Barthélemy d'Herbelot, *Bibliothèque orientale*, 2 vols (The Hague, 1777–79).
Notes on commentary:
Noureddin in the tale 'Noureddin' is a recurrent name in collections such as the *Arabian Nights*; this particular tale has not been traced.
Alexis Ruganoff unidentified.

Epigram—To A Friend Who had Invited the Author to Supper
Original unidentified, though a similar epigram by a different poet is found in d'Herbelot (see *CW*, I, 417).

Epigram—To Yusuf ben Ali ben Yacoob
Original unidentified.

A Triplet, on the Reign of the Great Sultan
From Hammer-Purgstall (I, 169).
Notes on commentary following the poem:
make a solitude . . . peace Byron, *Bride of Abydos* (II, xx).
Bajazet Ottoman sultan Bayezid II, the Just (1448–1512), noted patron of scholars and poets.

To Miriam, on her Hair
From Hammer-Purgstall (I, 65). The original poet is Elwan, not Selman.
Note on commentary following the poem:
Shelley's couplet in fact a misremembered passage from 'The Romance of the Lily' (1823) by Thomas Lovell Beddoes: 'It [the lily] is no earthly common flower / For man to pull, and maidens wear / On the wreathed midnight of their hair.'

Ghazel, from the Poems of Ahmedi
From Hammer-Purgstall (I, 90).
Notes on commentary following the poem:
Scaliger probably Julius Caesar Scaliger (1484–1558), Italian scholar, famous for two virulent critiques of the *Ciceronianus* of Erasmus.
Fichtean Johann Gottlieb Fichte (1762–1814), German philosopher, who viewed the ego as the ground of all human knowledge.
Baconian profundity Francis Bacon (1561–1626), English scientist and philosopher.
out of humanity's . . . alone from 'Verses Supposed to be Written by Alexander Selkirk' (1782) by William Cowper: 'I am out of humanity's reach / I must finish my journey alone' (ll. 9–10).
Abbé Sieyès (1748–1836), French politician; author of the influential revolutionary tract *Qu'est-ce que le tiers état?* (1789; trans. 'What is the Third Estate?').

The Time of the Roses
From Hammer-Purgstall (I, 299–301).
64n   from 'The Fire-Worshippers' in Thomas Moore's *Lalla Rookh* (1817). The 'date-season' is one of celebration.
75   **Soliman** Suleiman I the Magnificent (1494–1566), Ottoman emperor.
81n   This alleged calligraphical feature of Nasmi's manuscript seems to have been Mangan's invention (see *CW*, II, 418).

Fragment of Another [Drinking Song]
This poem is a re-writing of the final lines of Mangan's earlier 'Song' (*Dublin Satirist*, 26 October 1833), which was to be sung to the air of Moore's 'Oh! Ever thus from my childhood's hour' from 'The Fire-Worshippers' in *Lalla Rookh* (1817).
Note on commentary preceding the poem:
Drechsler a pseudonym for Mangan himself; it means '(wood-) turner' in German.
Note on poem:
14   **frows** from German *frau* ('woman')

To Mihrí
Original unidentified, in spite of Mangan's attribution to Rahiki.

Genuine Ethereality
Original unidentified.

Double Trouble
From Hammer-Purgstall (I, 214). The original poet is Tadschi, not Thalib.

[My heart is a monk]
Original unidentified.

Song For Coffee-Drinkers
Original unidentified; a poet by the name of Jakini does appear in Hammer-Purgstall, however.
5n   **arrack** an Asian alcoholic drink, similar to rum.   **Sir William Jones** (1746–1794), British orientalist, translator and jurist.
27   **Chian** wine from Chios, in the Aegean Sea.
40n **He was . . . mahogany** Byron, *Beppo*, LXX.
45n **de Sacy** Antoine Isaac Silvestre de Sacy (1758–1838) French orientalist. The quotation, the original of which has not been identified, may be translated: 'The Turks call Constantinople *Islambol* by an affected corruption, in place of *Istambol*, a word itself formed by a corruption of the Greek words εἰς τὴυ πόλιν. The word *Islambol* provides the Turk with the idea of a city where *Islam* is flourishing; from *Islam*, the Muslim religion, and *bol*, abundant.'
46n **Sofis** a *Sufi* is a Muslim mystic.

Lament, by Mulheed
From Hammer-Purgstall (II, 468).
10   **Tree of Liberty** an anachronistic addition by Mangan, since liberty trees were eighteenth-century republican symbols associated with radicalism in France, America and Ireland.
12n **Marmontel** Jean-Francois Marmontel (1723–99), French poet and dramatist.

Relic, of Prince Bayazeed
From Hammer-Purgstall (II, 443). Bayazid and Selim were sons of Suleiman the Magnificent, Ottoman sultan from 1520 to 1566. Selim prevailed in the conflict between them over the succession to the throne, and had Bayazid executed.
Notes on commentary following the poem:
march of mind a common nineteenth-century catchphrase for describing the supposedly inexorable moral and intellectual progress of Western culture.
Hoogly an arm of the Ganges which connects Calcutta to the Bay of Bengal. The source for Mangan's comments about Hindu sacrifice is uncertain.

Philosophy and Philosophers
Schiller, 'Die Weltweisen'.
25   **Descartes** René Descartes (1596–1650), French philosopher. Descartes argued that the physical universe is a plenum of matter in a state of constant collision and separation, a motion initiated by God.
45   **Vattel** Emerich de Vattel (1714–67), Swiss jurist and author of the influential *Le Droit des gens* (trans. *The Law of Nations*, 1758).

The Hundred-leafed Rose
From Hammer-Purgstall (II, 40–1). In fact Lamii's original is not part of the long poem *The Martyrdom of Houssain*.
Notes on commentary preceding the poem:
Brusa one-time Ottoman capital city, in northwestern Turkey.
Kinalizade 16th-century Ottoman biographer and compiler of Turkish poetry.

What is Love?
Original unidentified.

Volto Sciolto e Pensieri Stretti
Original unidentified. The title means 'Face open and thoughts held close'.

Haroun Al-Rashid and the Dust
Original unidentified, though *CW* (II, 376) suggests it may be loosely based on a quatrain in Hammer-Purgstall (I, 117). Haroun (AD 766–809) was the caliph of the Abbasid empire at its height. He is memorialized in the *Arabian Nights*.

Description of Morning
Original unidentified.

A New Moon
Original unidentified.
4n **D'Herbelot, and Moore's Lalla Rookh** see d'Herbelot (II, 184) and 'The Veiled Prophet of Khorassan' in *Lalla Rookh* (1817).

Lamii's Apology for his Nonsense
Original unidentified.

The Ghost and the Poet
'Der Gespenst' by Christian Fürchtegott Gellert (1715–69), German poet and novelist. Mangan gives his source as *C.F. Gellert's sämmtliche Fabeln und Erzählungen, in drei Büchern* (Leipzig, 1838).
subtitle the name of the inn (*Die Katze im Sack*) is Mangan's invention.
5 **Coromandel** in southern India.
19 **Boniface** an innkeeper, from a character in Farquhar's *The Beaux' Stratagem* (1707).
31 **Castle called Otranto's** from Horace Walpole's novel *The Castle of Otranto* (1765).
35 **Cato** Cato the Younger (95–46 BC) was a Roman statesman who opposed the policies of Julius Caesar.
45n **Paradise Lost** from Book II, ll. 672–3.

[When men behold old mould rolled cold]
These lines, with slight variations, also occur in Mangan's unpublished letter to 'Tynan' (1832; see p. 437, above) and again in the poem 'Verses to a Friend' (*Comet*, 27 January 1833).

The Dying Father
Gellert, 'Der sterbende Vater'. Mangan had published two previous translations of this poem (*Dublin Satirist*, 5 April 1834 and *DUM*, January 1835).
Notes on commentary following the poem:
Like Psaphon's . . . fame Thomas Moore, *Rhymes on the Road* (1819), 'Extract VII', ll. 13–14. Moore's own note to the lines reads: 'Psaphon, in order to attract the attention of the world, taught multitudes of birds to speak his name and then let them fly away in various directions . . .' Moore is using the tale to allegorise the fame of Byron's poems.
toises an old unit of measurement, equal to nearly two metres.

My Home
'Sehnsucht' by Friedrich Gottlob Wetzel (1779–1819). Mangan's gives his source as *F. C. Wetzel's gesammelte Gedichte und Nachlasz* (Leipzig, 1839).

Notes on commentary following the poem:
plunge his years ... penitence from Byron, *Childe Harold* (III, lxx).
mauvais sujet 'bad character'.
sleeps ... thunder *Macbeth* (IV.i.86).
more sinned against than sinning *King Lear* (III.ii.60).
writes daggers from *Hamlet* (III.ii.387): 'I'll speak daggers to her, but use none'.
Jacob Bœhmen German mystic (1575–1624).
His thoughts ... 'em adapted from Byron, *Don Juan* (I, xiii), where the lines refer to Don Juan's mother.

The Howling-Song of Al-Mohara
Seemingly an original poem. The source of the supposed Arabic quotation in the subtitle is untraced.

The Time of the Barmecides
An original poem, perhaps partly inspired by a Persian poem found in d'Herbelot, or by the opening of Goethe's *West-östlicher Divan* (see *CW*, II, 394). The source of the supposed Arabic transliteration of the subtitle is untraced. An earlier version of the poem was published in *DUM* in April 1839.
title the priestly family of the Barmecides were in fact Persian rather than Arabian. They served as advisers to the Abbasid caliphate in Baghdad at the height of its power in the eighth and ninth centuries.
23   **Karamanian** from Karaman, in southern Turkey.
36n   **Though sluggards ... chair** Byron, *Childe Harold* (I, xxx).

To Sultan Murad II
Original unidentified.

[Where art thou, Soul of Per-Version?]
Notes on commentary preceding the poem:
Vallencey Charles Vallencey (1721–1812), Irish antiquarian, who argued controversially and enthusiastically that the Irish language was related to Phoenician, Persian and Chinese.
Bowring Sir John Bowring (1792–1872), English translator of east European literature, and friend and advocate of the utilitarian theorist Jeremy Bentham.
Anster John Anster (1793–1867), poet and translator, and friend of Mangan, whose translation of Part 1 of Goethe's *Faust* in 1835 was much-acclaimed. Mangan published an appreciative article on Anster in 1849 (see p. 409, above).
Notes on poem:
5   **EGERTON** Lord Francis Egerton (1800–57), English poet and politician, translator of *Faust*.
6   **BLACKIES and GILLIESES** John Stuart Blackie (1809–95), translator of *Faust*; Robert Pearse Gillies (1788–1858), translator of German poetry.
7   **VON BROCKHAUS** noted German publishing house, founded in 1808.
7n   **Baron Mac Guckin is bringing out Ibn Kallahan** Baron MacGuckin de Slane published a 4–volume translation of *Ibn Khallikan's Biographical Dictionary* between 1842 and 1871. Abbas Ahmad ibn Khallikan (1211–82) served as a judge in Egypt and Syria.

The Erl-King's Daughter, a Danish Ballad
'Erlkönigs Tochter' by Johann Gottfried von Herder (1744–1803). According to *CW* (II, 396) Herder had mistranslated the original Danish title (*'Ellerkonge'*, meaning 'elven-king'). The word 'Erlkönig' signifies a wicked forest-spirit.

Twenty Golden Years Ago
'Selber' is a pseudonym, from the phrase *ich selber* ('I myself').
30   *en haut* literally, though not idiomatically, meaning 'on high'.
39   **dun duns** plays on two meanings for 'dun:' that is', dull', and 'a creditor'.
44   **Kerner** Justinus Kerner (1786–1862), German poet; Mangan is perhaps alluding to a Kerner poem he translates as 'The Garden that fades not' in *DUM*, August 1836: 'But on the mountains wither / All flowers thou takest thither'.
54   **Rousseau** Jean-Jacques Rousseau (1712–1778), Swiss-born French philosopher.

Alexander and the Tree
'Die wahrsagenden Bäume' by Friedrich Baron de La Motte Fouqué (1777–1843), German playwright and novelist.
epigraph   Alexander (365–323), king of Macedonia; the Apocryphal History referred to is perhaps the famous 'Romance of Alexander the Great' which dates back to the third century A D

The Editor's Room—Second Conclave
A MS version also exists (RIA MS 3/C/6). Mangan contributed three of these 'Conclaves' to the Belfast *Vindicator* while Charles Gavan Duffy was editor.
epigraph   from *Don Juan* (XV, xciii).
Notes on linking commentary:
Henry MacManus (?1810–78); painter and friend of Gavan Duffy; he was an associate member of the Royal Hibernian Academy.
Brown Thomas Brown (1778–1820), Scottish philosopher of the 'common-sense' school.
Gray Thomas Gray (1716–71), English poet, author of 'An Elegy Written in a Country Church Yard'.
Sir William Hamilton noted Irish astronomer and mathematician (1805–65), who published an influential essay 'Theory on Systems of Rays' in 1827.
toggery clothing.
Twiddle a character who appears in the 'Third Conclave' (*Vindicator*, 8 August 1840).
Quid rides Horace, *Satires* (I.i.69): 'Why do you laugh?'
Dear as . . . **eyes** Thomas Gray, 'The Bard', l. 40.
Hail, holy light! *Paradise Lost* (III, 1).
Shades *CW* (VI, 292) suggests that this refers to the Royal Tavern at 12–13 Grafton Street.
sesquipedalian multi-syllabled.
M'Nish's tale 'The Metempsychosis', a story published in *Blackwood's* in 1825 by Scottish poet Robert Macnish (1802–37)
Far-away-down-in-the-South Gazette this may be a reference to the Dublin-based *Comet*, in which Mangan had previously published a version of the poem 'Asses' that follows.

Asses
Mangan published two other versions of this poem, with names altered to suit the differing contexts, in the *Comet* ('The *Ass*embly', 23 December 1832) and in the *Nation* ('New Natural Philosophy', 11 February 1843).

epigraph from 'Memoirs of Martinus Scriblerus' (1741) by Alexander Pope and John Arbuthnot.

1 **Buffon** Georges-Louis Leclerc, comte de Buffon (1707–88), French naturalist.

9 **Brougham and Vaux** Henry Peter Lord Brougham and Vaux (1778–1868); pro-reform Whig politician, a frequent critic of Melbourne's second administration.

10 **Melbourne** William Lamb, Viscount Melbourne (1779–1848); conservative Whig politician, served as chief secretary for Ireland 1827–8 and then as British prime minister in 1834 and from 1835–41.

14 **Londonderry** Charles William Stewart, marquis of Londonderry (1778–1854); outspoken Tory politician.

17 **O'Connell** Daniel O'Connell (1775–1847) led the successful campaign for Catholic emancipation in the 1820s and, from April 1840, the campaign for the Repeal of the Union between Britain and Ireland.

21 **Ned Bulwer** Edward Bulwer-Lytton (1803–73), British politician, poet, critic, and prolific novelist.

23 **Bowring** Sir John Bowring (1792–1872), admired by Mangan as a poet and translator, edited Jeremy Bentham's *Deontology, or Science of Morality* in 1834.

25 **Trash Gregg** Rev. Tresham Dames Gregg (1799–1881), a well-known Protestant controversialist in Dublin in the 1830s and 1840s.

27 **Orange ruffian** the sectarian loyalist Orange Order (founded in 1795) had been proscribed by the British government in 1825.

[Let England's Old Womanhood tremble no more]

epigraph 'Punch' refers to the comic character from the Punch and Judy puppet-show.

2 **Peelites** Sir Robert Peel (1788–1850) was leader of the Conservative party from 1834 until 1846. O'Connell supported the opposing Whig party throughout the 1830s.

10 **Mother Bunch** an English storytelling figure, dating to the sixteenth century.

13 **(our Lower'd Mayor)** puns on the title 'Lord Mayor'. The allusion is uncertain.

15 **Guilds** the Municipal Corporations Act of 1840 put an end to guild involvement in municipal government.

Notes on commentary following the poem:

Planxty Kelly . . . Thady, you gander traditional Irish airs.

Lundy Foot's Royal a brand of snuff.

The Woman of Three Cows

The Irish text that accompanies this translation is entitled 'Bean na ttrí mbó' and is printed immediately after the headnote. Mangan worked from a literal translation provided by Eugene O'Curry, and the poem's headnote is signed 'P.' (= George Petrie).

1 **agragh** term of endearment, from *a ghrá* ('love').

9 **Momonia** Munster. **Owen More** Eógan Mór, legendary founder of the Eoghanacht dynasties of Munster.

13 **sons of the Lord of Clare** the two sons of the third Viscount Clare, Daniel and Charles O'Brien, were forced into exile after the Treaty of Limerick in 1691. Charles was the commander of the famous Clare's Dragoons that fought in the service of France.

14 **Movrone** from *mo bhrón* ('my sorrow').

17 **Donnell** Donal O'Sullivan Beare (1560–1618) an ally of Hugh O'Neill during the Nine Years' War. O'Sullivan Beare led a famous march from his home in Dunboy in Co. Cork to the

Leitrim stronghold of Brian O'Rourke in the winter of 1602–3, during which nearly a thousand of his followers died. He was assassinated in Spain by a servant.

21   **O'Ruark, Maguire** The Maguire and O'Rourke clans were also allies during the Nine Years' War (see 'O'Hussey's Ode to the Maguire').

25   **O'Carrolls** the O'Carroll clan of Ely, in present-day Co. Offaly.

An Elegy on the Tironian and Tirconnellian Princes Buried at Rome
The Irish original is by Eoghan Ruadh Mac an Bháird (d. ?1630). Eugene O'Curry provided the literal translation from which Mangan worked, but Mangan has made several alterations to placenames, often for rhyming effects. In a letter to Charles Gavan Duffy on 15 September 1840, Mangan described the poem as 'a *transmagnificanbandancial* elegy of mine (a perversion from the Irish), on the O'Neills and O'Donnells of Ulster, which is admired by myself and some other *impartial* judges' (letter published by C. P. Meehan in his preface to the 1883 edition of *Poets and Poetry of Munster*). The phrase may be the source of Joyce's neologism 'contransmagnificandjewbangtantiality' in *Ulysses* (see *CW*, VI, 364). The poem's narrative context is the aftermath of the 'Flight of the Earls' in 1607, when the families and retainers of Hugh O'Neill, Earl of Tyrone and Rory (or Roderick) O'Donnell, Earl of Tirconnell left Ulster for permanent exile on the continent. The poem is addressed to Rory O'Donnell's sister Nuala, and concerns the deaths of Rory O'Donnell and his brother Cathbarr in Rome in 1608, and the death of her nephew, Hugh O'Neill (son of the famous Hugh, Earl of Tyrone) in 1609. The headnote is probably by George Petrie.

8   **Tirconnell** part of present-day Donegal.

10   **Beann-Boirche** the Irish name of the Mourne mountains in Co. Down; the original Irish text actually signifies the 'host of Boirche', who was a mythical local figure.

14   **Dromore** in Co. Down.

15   **Killilee** perhaps Killileagh in Co. Armagh.

17   **Assaroe** a waterfall on the Erne river near Ballyshannon, Co. Donegal.

19   **Drumclieff** Drumcliff, in Co. Sligo.

26   **Dunluce** on the north coast of Co. Antrim.

27   **Lissadill** Lissadell, in Co. Sligo.

29   **Cruachan** Rathcroghan, the ancient royal seat of Connaught.

31   **Barrow-side** the river Barrow forms the border between counties Kilkenny and Carlow.

34   **Banna** the river Bann.

38   **Mount** Montorio, the supposed site of the martyrdom of St Peter in Rome.

49   **Conn** Conn 'of the Hundred Battles', legendary ancestor of both the O'Neills and the O'Donnells.

51   **O'Donnell Roe** neither of the O'Donnell brothers in question had the epithet 'Roe' (*ruadh*, 'red-haired'); it was in fact applied to their famous brother Hugh Roe O'Donnell who died in 1602 and was buried in Valladolid, Spain.

62   **Hugh** 'Black' Hugh O'Donnell, father of Nuala, Rory and Cathbarr.

76   **Dunnasava** *Dún ós sáimh* in the original, perhaps in Donegal.

86   **Lord of Mourne** title of the young Hugh O'Neill who has died.

91   **Criffan's plain** sobriquet for Ireland; from the name of the legendary king Criomhthann.

103   **Athboy** in Armagh; site of the Battle of the Yellow Ford (*áth buidhe*), Hugh O'Neill's famous defeat of the English in 1598.

104   **Ulidian** 'of Ulster'.

109   **Ballach-myre** the strategic Moyry Pass, scene of a battle between O'Neill and the English in 1600.

114   **Niall the Great** 'Niall of the Nine Hostages', fifth-century ancestor of the O'Neill clan.

117   **Mullach-brack** near Markethill in Co. Armagh.

121–4   **Day of Hostages . . . Mac-Nee's** the lines here may refer to campaigns in Munster by either the O'Donnells or the O'Neills; MacNee was a Munster chieftain.

127   **Ballach-boy** in the Curlew Mountains, Co. Roscommon; site of an O'Donnell victory over the English in 1599.

139   **Lifford's day** in 1600, the O'Donnell stronghold at Lifford, Co. Donegal was taken by Niall Garbh O'Donnell, who had sided with the English. Niall Garbh had been married to Nuala, the addressee of the poem.

157–8   **Dalcassian . . . Fergus' banks** the Dalcassians were the royal sept of Thomond in Munster; the river Fergus is in Co. Clare.

163   **Murbach** Murvagh, near Ballyshannon; the reference is to the battle alluded to in line 127.

170   **Sligo's field** refers to the capture of O'Conor Sligo's castle in 1595; as the Irish text indicates, it was Cathbar who led the O'Donnell side in this battle, not Roderick.

175   **Leith-Cuinn** signifying the northern half of Ireland; 'Cuinn' means 'of Conn'.

Lamentation of Mac Liag for Kincora

Eugene O'Curry probably provided the literal translation from which Mangan worked. Mangan may also have been familiar with a translation by John D'Alton that had appeared in Hardiman (II, 196–201).

8   **Dalcassians** a major dynasty of Munster, to which Brian Boru belonged.

11   **Murogh** Brian's eldest son, Murchadh, who was killed in the battle of Clontarf.

16   **Donogh** Donnchadh, Brian's son and successor.

17   **Conaing** nephew of Brian, killed at Clontarf.

18   **Kian** son of Maolmhuaidh (Molloy), son-in-law of Brian, killed in battle shortly after Clontarf.   **Corc** perhaps the legendary Corc, founder of the Eoghanacht kingship of Cashel.

22   **son of Evin the Brave** Domhnall, described by Hardiman as 'the great steward of Alba', and later in Mac Liag's poem as 'Prince of the Scots' (l. 32); he was killed at Clontarf.

23   **King of Onaght** Scannlán, Eoghanacht king, killed at Clontarf.

24   **hosts of Baskinn** Brian's allies from southwest Co. Clare.

26   **Duvlann** Dúbhlainn in the original; perhaps Dúnlang, who fought for the Danes at Clontarf and was killed.

28   **King Lonergan** the name in the original is 'Conn', perhaps cognate with Conaing, above.

Kathaleen Ny-Houlahan

'Is fada milte dhá gcartadh síos agus suas ar fan' by Uilliam Ó hAnnracháin (not to be confused with the poem entitled 'Caitilín Ní Uallacháin' by Ó hIfearnáin, which Mangan translated in 1849 for *Poets and Poetry of Munster* (see p. 336 above). The MS version from which Eugene O'Curry made his literal translation for Mangan is still extant (see *CW*, II, 404). Headnote is probably by George Petrie.

headnote   support for the Jacobite cause, that is, for the claim of the Stuarts-in-exile to the British and Irish thrones, was widespread among Irish Catholics in the early eighteenth century.

title   one of several women's names used to signify Ireland in 17th- and 18th-century poetry.

14   *Saxoneen* from Irish *Saxoinín*, 'little Englishman'.

16   **Young Deliverer** Charles Edward Stuart (1720–88), grandson of James II, also known as the 'Young Pretender'. His attempt to reclaim the British throne for the Stuarts ended in defeat at Culloden in 1746.

The Ride Round the Parapet
'Die Begrüßung auf dem Kynast' by Friedrich Rückert (1788–1866). Mangan translated nearly thirty of Rückert's poems. Mangan's version of this poem alters the names of the characters and extends the poem considerably.

50 **Ritter** knight.

78 **merlonwise** merlons are the solid intervals between the crenellations of a battlement.

O, Maria, Regina Misercordiæ
'Das Ave Maria' by Karl Joseph Simrock (1802–76).

33 **Pommerland** Pomerania.

69n **Luke x.** 42 Jesus is contrasting Martha's well-meant but misguided concern with hospitality to Mary's utter absorption in Jesus' teaching: 'one thing is needful. Mary has chosen the better part, which shall not be taken away from her.'

Gone in the Wind
Rückert, 'Hingegangen in den Wind'. Rückert was a self-taught reader of Oriental languages and published many translations; he does not give a source for this poem.

15 **Firmans** edicts.

35 **Abul-Namez** this name is an invention of Mangan's.

Our First Number
Reprinted, with slight variations, in the anthology *Spirit of the Nation* (1843, 1845), with the title 'The Nation's First Number', and the suggestion that it might be sung to the air of 'Rory O'More'. Mangan wrote the poem for the first issue of the *Nation*, the newspaper founded by Thomas Davis, Charles Gavan Duffy and John Blake Dillon in October 1842.

10 **couching** a method of treating cataracts of the eye.

25–6 *Nul n'a de l'esprit … amis* from Molière, *Les Femmes savants* (1672), III.ii: 'No one has wit, except our good friends.'

29 **reading like Parr's** Samuel Parr (1747–1825), English clergyman, was noted for his vast library.

35 **Mother Bunch** see note to l. 10 of 'Let England's Old Womanhood tremble no more', above.

36 **Punch** the English satiric magazine *Punch* had been founded in 1841.

44 **sneak up the spout** the phrase 'up the spout' means 'to be ruined'.

47 **Suir … Tweed … Boyne … Humber** the Suir and Boyne are Irish rivers; the Tweed and Humber are British. In the 1843 and 1845 *Spirit of the Nation* versions of the poem, 'Tweed' is changed to 'Rhine'.

Epigram ['Well, Pat, my boy']
2 **ground landlord** an owner of land which is leased.

Rayther Inconsistant
2 **Chartist mobs** Chartism was a working-class reform movement active in Britain from 1838 to 1848, led by Irishman Feargus O'Connor.

Pleasant Prospects for the Land-Eaters
2 **castor** a hat, especially one made of beaver-skin; the phrase 'all round my hat' meant 'nonsense'.

from *The Three Half-Crowns*
Mangan gives his source as 'I Tre Giulj; o Sieno Sonetti di Nicesti Abideno, P.A., sopra
l'Importunita d'un Creditor di Tre Giulj. In Roma; 1762.' The author, Giovanni Battista Casti
(1724–1803), was an Italian-born author of satiric poetry and comic libretti.
all that's bright must fade title and first line of one of Thomas Moore's *National Airs*, written
to an 'Indian air'.
pearl richer than all his tribe *Othello* (V.ii.345–6).
spent a gloomy time . . . alleys from Leigh Hunt, *Lord Byron and Some of His Contemporaries*
(Paris, 1828); following Shelley's death, Hunt says 'I passed a melancholy time at Albaro,
walking about the stony alleys and thinking of Mr. Shelley.'
Montfiascone a wine from a region north of Rome; Casti in fact was a seminarian there.
rencontre a hostile meeting.
head and front of his offending *Othello* (I.ii.80).
the proud . . . days see Byron's *Mazeppa* (X, 19).

(The poet bewaileth his ill luck in having contracted the debt of Tre Giulii)
title note according to Daniel 5, the Babyonian king Belshazzar held a last great feast at
which he saw a hand writing on a wall; the prophet Daniel interpreted the handwriting as
God's judgment on the king.
1 **Dun** a persistent creditor.
Notes on commentary following the poem:
Cobbett William Cobbett (1763–1835), English journalist and political campaigner.
Dædalus or Icarus Dedalus was a mythical inventor who built wings of wax; his son Icarus
flew too close to the sun with them and fell to his death.

(He is of the opinion that his Creditor would pursue him unto the Isle Of Sky)
title plays on the 'Isle of Skye', one of the Hebridean isles.
9n in Ariosto's fantasy *Orlando Furioso* (1532), Astolfo is a character who encounters a
hippogriff, which is half griffin, half horse.

(He proposes a plan of mutual accommodation to his Creditor)
8 *de l'autre côté* 'on the other hand'.
13 **Pilgarlic** a person to be humorously mocked.
Notes on linking commentary:
quand la Reine Berthe filait 'when Queen Berthe span;' a French and Italian folkloric phrase
signifying 'in the distant past'.

(He thinks his Creditor ought to admire even a refusal, if given in proper Spartan fashion)
Note on commentary preceding the poem:
Lacedemoniacs Spartans.
Notes on poem:
3 *tranchant* sharp.
8 *Pour toute reponse* 'Their only reply was . . .'
9n the Italian may be translated: 'Philip of Macedon having asked the Byzantines for
passage through their state, they responded with a single negative particle—"No".'

(He says that his Creditor is a more terrible sight than a comet, because his movements cannot be calculated on before-hand)

7   *Abord* manner.

(He threatens finally to escape into some desert, turn jack-ass, and live on thistles)
Note on commentary preceding the poem:
traduttore translator, with perhaps an allusion to the phrase *traduttore traditore* ('a translator is a betrayer').
Notes on poem:
1   *mentis vanitas* 'vain imaginings'; phrase appears in Augustine, *De Baptismo contra Donatistas* (IV, 15).
3   **Paracelsus . . . Plato . . . Bacon . . . Boyle** all scientists and philosophers, including Paracelsus (d. 1541), Swiss alchemist; Francis Bacon (1561–1626), English philosopher and scientist; Robert Boyle (1627–91), Irish chemist.
4   **το Παν** 'the All'.
5   **from Bershebah to Dan** a Biblical phrase, signifying the entire territory of Israel.

Grabbe
'Bei Grabbes Tod' by Ferdinand Freiligrath (1810–76), radical German poet. The poem eulogises Christian Dietrich Grabbe (1801–36), German nationalist poet and dramatist, author of several innovative historical plays. Grabbe died as a consequence of alcoholism and tuberculosis. Mangan is reviewing the volume *Gedichte von Ferdinand Freiligrath* (Stutgard and Tübingen, 1840).
17   **Hecate** Greek goddess of the Moon.
22   *Tzako ab!* 'shakos (headgear) off!'
29   **Fredericks-d'or** gold coins.
30   *a qui mieux mieux* 'vying with'.
31   *Who sets?* 'who is betting?'
34   **Yagers** riflemen.
38   *Qui en veut* 'who wants it?'
45   *Rouge et Noir* a game of cards.
52   **The Hundred Days** Grabbe's most famous play is *Napoleon oder die hundert Tage* ('Napoleon or the Hundred Days') (1831).
59   **Uhlan** Prussian cavalry.
74   **Hohenstauffen . . . Italy's shrines . . . Greece's hallowed streams** Grabbe wrote two plays about Hohenstaufen monarchs: *Kaiser Friedrich Barbarossa* (1829) and *Kaiser Heinrich VI* (1830). His other plays include *Marius and Sulla* (1827), *Don Juan und Faust* (1829), *Hannibal* (1835) and *Alexander* (1835).

Schnapps
'Selber' is a pseudonym, from the phrase *ich selber* ('I myself').
5   **Sancho Panza** Don Quixote's squire in Cervantes' novel (1605–15).
16   **Horace** Roman poet (65–8 BC); quoting a common pronoun is of course a joke.
18   **raps** worth less than a farthing.
Note to marginalia after l. 24:
Magnus hiatus, lugubre deflendus 'a great gap, sadly deplored'.

The Coming Event
'Selber' is a pseudonym, as in the previous poem. This poem was republished with slight variations by Gavan Duffy in the *Nation* in September 1849, and reprinted subsequently with the title 'Irish Temperance Hymn'.
12   **blue devils** low spirits.

from *Literæ Orientales—No. V—Ottoman Poetry*
Most of the historical and bibliographical information in this article is derived from Hammer-Purgstall.
Persian poetry ... turned Mangan's translation of a statement in Hammer-Purgstall (I, 51).

Stanza [See how the worlds that roll afar]
From Hammer-Purgstall (I, 63).

Good Counsel
From Hammer-Purgstall (I, 66).

The Caramanian Exile
The alleged author of this poem, the Karamanian poet Fahareyeh, is named 'Fachari' in Hammer-Purgstall (I, 122), but no poem of his resembling this has been traced. Karaman, in the Taurus mountains of south central Turkey, was finally subdued by the Ottomans in the mid-15th century. Mangan's inconsistency in spelling the name of the country may be due to the fact that 18th- and 19th-century English writers tended to use the name 'Caramania', while Hammer-Purgstall spells it 'Karaman'.
Note on commentary preceding the poem:
land of the mountain and the flood Sir Walter Scott, *Lay of the Last Minstrel* (VI, ii): 'O Caledonia! stern and wild, / Meet nurse for a poetic child! / Land of brown heath and shaggy wood; / Land of the mountain and the flood!'
Dr. Wilde Sir William Wilde (1815–76), noted surgeon and antiquarian, husband of poet 'Speranza' and father of Oscar Wilde. According to James Price, it was Dr Wilde who discovered Mangan dying in a hovel in June 1849 ('Gallery of Contemporary Writers No. 2: James Clarence Mangan', *Evening Packet*, 22 September 1849).
Notes on poem:
27   **Erzerome** Erzurum, ancient city in eastern Turkey, capital of the Seljuq dynasty in the middle ages; it came under Ottoman control in 1515.
30   **Ukhbar** reference untraced.
61   **Spahi** cavalry.
66   **Kaf's blasted plains** in a note to an earlier poem ('Ghazzel', *DUM*, April 1840), Mangan had described 'Kaf' somewhat differently as: 'the mountain which surrounds the earth and contains the treasures of the Pre-Adamite Sultans.'
95   **Murád** 'Murad' was the name of four Ottoman rulers between the fifteenth and seventeenth centuries. See 'To Sultan Murad II' (p. 87).

The Wail and the Warning of the Three Khalenders
Although there is a 'Story of Three Calendars' in the *Arabian Nights*, Mangan's poem is not related to it, and appears to be original.
9   **Bosphorus** the strait between Turkey and the European mainland.

Love and Madness
Original unidentified.
10   **Medjnûns** in a footnote to an earlier poem ('Opium and Wine', *DUM*, September 1838), Mangan identifies 'Medjnoon' as the 'hero of a celebrated romance by the Persian poet Nizami, and of many other romances by Turkish imitators: he is said to have stood so long rooted to the spot where he first beheld his beloved (Leila) that the birds came and nestled on his head. *Medjnoun* signifies *Love-crazed*.'
28   **bulk** stall.
32n   see 'Genuine Ethereality', p. 63.
36   **sumphs** fools.

Heaven first of all within Ourselves
Original unidentified.
2   **Bir-ból** unidentified.

The Thugs' Ditty
Probably an original poem. The Thugs were professional assassins who travelled in gangs throughout India, strangling and robbing their victims. They were largely eliminated in the 1830s after a systematic campaign against them by the British regime in India.
1   **neck-or-nought scamps** this '*equivoque*' (= wordplay) puns on the phrase's usual meaning of 'reckless', and on the fact that the Thugs normally strangled their victims.
5   **Marzawán** unidentified.
13   **Moolahs** honorific title for noble persons or religious leaders.
19   **toggery** clothing.

The Soffees' Ditty
Probably an original poem. 'Soffee' is from *Sufi*, meaning a Muslim mystic.
Bismillah! in the name of God!
14n   Mangan provided a longer note on Ben Manser with the earlier poem 'The Hundred-Leafed Rose'; see p. 70.
headnote to VI   Suleymán-Ben-Daood biblical Solomon, son of David; the allusion is to Ecclesiastes 7:3.

'Der Freiheit eine Gasse'—A Lane For Freedom
The German original, by the radical poet Georg Herwegh (1817–95), appeared in the volume *Gedichte eines Lebendigen* (1841). Mangan's translation was re-titled 'A Highway for Freedom' in subsequent printings, such as *Spirit of the Nation* (1845). The headnote is probably by Gavan Duffy.
3   **Winkelreid** Arnold Winkelried, Swiss patriot who sacrificed his own life to ensure a Swiss victory over the Habsburgs at the battle of Sempach in 1386.

from *Anthologia Germanica – No. XIX – Miscellaneous Poems*
Ferdinand Freiligrath German poet (1810–76), whose early poetry earned him a pension from the Prussian king Frederick William IV and enabled him to abandon his job as an accountant. In 1844, however, he renounced the pension and published a collection of radical political poems under the title *Glaubensbekenntniß* ('Statement of Conscience'). In 1848 he was arrested for subversion, and later became an associate of Karl Marx. Mangan had reviewed and translated

poems from Freiligrath's first collection (*Gedichte*, 1840) in the *DUM* in January 1843. Many of these poems contained exotic situations and locations.

Anthropophagi . . . shoulders *Othello* (I.i.144–5).

Thoughts . . . sneers from Wordsworth, 'Intimations of Immortality', l. 207; 'Thoughts that do often lie too deep for tears.'

catching . . . Tartars an expression frequently used for punning purposes by Mangan; it meant 'dealing with a troublesome person or situation'.

caco-magnetism evil charm or force of attraction.

His soul . . . apart adapted from l. 9 of Wordsworth's 'London, 1802', where it refers to Milton.

He had once . . . chalks compare line 52 of Mangan's poem 'Twenty Golden Years Ago'.

Don Diego Leon a general who supported a rebellion against the Spanish regent Espartero. In a note to his translation of Freiligrath's 'The Execution of Don Diego Leon' (*DUM*, September 1845), Mangan described him as 'the brave but unfortunate Carlist, Don Diego Leon, who was shot by order (we believe) of Espartero, on the 15th of October, 1841'. The 'Carlists' had supported the claim of the former king's brother Don Carlos to the Spanish throne, and thus opposed the rule of his daughter, the infant Isabella, for whom Espartero acted as regent.

['He was the tool of tyrants.' Be it so!]
The ninth stanza of Freiligrath's 'Aus Spanien'. Mangan translated the entire poem as 'The Execution of Don Diego Leon' for *DUM* in September 1845.

5 **Bourbon d'Enghien** the Duc d'Enghien, son of the Duc de Bourbon, a refugee from the French Revolution, was kidnapped by Napoleon's agents in 1804, brought back to France, and executed for conspiracy. The case became notorious throughout Europe, as the duke was widely believed to have been innocent.

5n **Er beugt . . . Todesschrei** 'He bends his knee to the hero Bonaparte, / And hears with anger D'Enghien's death-cry.'

[Be my goal, or not, a vain chimera]
This is the final stanza of Freiligrath's poem 'Guten Morgen!' Mangan did not translate the entire poem.
Note on commentary following the poem:
ground Young *Junges Deutschland* ('Young Germany') was a social reform and literary movement that lasted from 1830 to 1850. Georg Herwegh and Henrich Heine, both of whom were translated by Mangan, were Young Germanists.

The White Lady
Freiligrath, 'Die weiße Frau'.
headnote Professor Stilling Johann Heinrich Jung-Stilling (1740–1817), German writer and academic; Mangan cites his volume on the theory of ghosts in 'Chapters on Ghostcraft' (*DUM*, January 1842). **Dr. Kerner** Justinus Kerner (1786–1862); in 'Chapters on Ghostcraft', Mangan also discusses Kerner's *Blätter aus Prevorst* (1831–39) a serial work concerning reports and theories of spiritualism.

The Last Words of Al-Hassan
'Hassan' by Friedrich August von Heyden (1789–1851). Mangan found the poem in O. L. B. Wolff's *Poetischer Hausschatz des deutschen Volkes* (Leipzig, 1839).

12   **Ali** fourth caliph, or successor to Muhammad (reigned 656–661); those Muslims who supported the claim of his descendents to be the true caliphs became known as Shiites, as opposed to the majority Sunnite Muslims.

14   **Kaaba's Venerable Stone** the Kaaba is the highly-revered shrine in the centre of the Great Mosque at Mecca which contains the Black Stone, supposedly given to Adam after his expulsion from Eden.

15   **Wahabee** Wahhabi, a reformist puritan sect of Sunnite Islam who occupied Mecca in the late eighteenth century.

54   **firmàn** a decree.

Fuimus!
'Erinnerung an den Bundestag' by August Lamey (1772–1861). The German quotation in Mangan's headnote corresponds to the final six lines of the poem.

title Latin: 'we were!'

The Death of Hofer
'Sandwirth Hofer' by Julius Mosen. Andreas Hofer (1767–1810) was a Tirolese patriot who fought to keep Tyrol under Catholic Austrian rule after it had been ceded to Bavaria (1805) and to Napoleon (1809). Hofer was captured and executed at Mantua on Napoleon's orders.

16   **Sandwirth** Hofer's nickname, from *Wirt* ('innkeeper') and '*Sandhof*', the name of the inn which Hofer ran.

43   **Francis** Francis I (1768–1838), Austrian emperor.

Ein Wort Neander's. A saying of Neander
Rückert, 'Ein Wort Neanders'.

Notes on commentary preceding the poem:

Rückert Friedrich Rückert (1788–1866).

the common growth … Earth from Wordsworth, *Peter Bell*, l. 133.

Neander Johann Neander (1789–1850), German theologian.

Note on poem:

epigraph   The German quotation is Neander's original text. It may be translated: 'The creator, whose spirit governs his time, how can you explain him by his time? Explain his time by him!'

Notes on commentary following the poem:

Hegel G. W. F. Hegel (1770–1831), German idealist philosopher.

visée 'aimed at'.

Memnon and Mammon
Rückert, 'Memnon und Mammon'.

Note on commentary preceding the poem:

jeu d'esprit a witty trifle.

title 'Memnon' refers to one of the colossal statues of Amenhotep III near Thebes, which reputedly gave forth musical sounds at dawn. 'Mammon' was the biblical personification of greed.

5   **Ludovic Huss** not in original.

11   **Xerxes** king of Persia (486–465 BC); according to Herodotus he invaded Greece with over two million men.

And Then No More
Rückert, 'Und dahn nicht mehr'.
20 **Peri-land** from *peri*, Persian word for 'fairy'.

Eighteen Hundred Fifty
Notes on commentary preceding the poem:
Selber see note to 'Twenty Golden Years Ago' above, p. 91.
young Germanist a social reform and literary movement that lasted from 1830 to 1850.
Oh! life … corns! adapted from Thomas Moore's 'Oh! think not my spirits are always as light',
ll. 5–8:
> No:—life is a waste of wearisome hours,
>> Which seldom the rose of enjoyment adorns;
> And the heart that is soonest awake to the flowers,
>> Is always the first to be touch'd by the thorns.

A life … mankind adapted from Byron, *Childe Harold* (III, xii).
Jacobi Friedrich Heinrich Jacobi (1743–1819), German philosopher.
Ich bin … Andrer this is a translation of the first line of Mangan's poem.
Dr. Berri Abel Hummer Mangan's punning invention.
Notes on poem:
12 **De Quincey** Thomas De Quincey (1785–1859), author of *Confessions of an English Opium Eater* (1822).
13 **Kant** Immanuel Kant (1724–1804), German philosopher.
17 **the last of Cato's** Cato the Younger (95–46 BC), Roman politician and opponent of Julius Caesar, committed suicide after a military defeat.
22 **foul *is* fair** *Macbeth* (I.i.11).
32 **Arabian glassman** in the tale of the Barber's Fifth Brother in the *Arabian Nights*, a glass merchant mistakenly kicks over a basket full of glassware in which he has invested his inheritance, and destroys his shop.
40 **rixdollars** a form of silver coin.
43 **Dee's delightful stone** a reference to the Elizabethan alchemist and astrologer John Dee (1527–1608). He claimed to have found the legendary alchemical 'philosopher's stone' hidden in the ruins of Glastonbury Abbey.
49 **Tantalusian glory** in Greek myth, Tantalus was tormented by being placed just out of reach of food and water.
56 **Helicon** fountain associated with the Muses.
62 **Doctor Kerner** Justinus Kerner; see notes to 'The White Lady', p. 463, above.
66 **Swift** Jonathan Swift (1667–1745); the allusion is untraced.
69 **Hogarth** William Hogarth (1667–1764) English artist and satirist.
70 **η β π** the names of these Greek letters transliterate as: 'eta, beta, pi'.
88 **Philip's lath-and-plaster throne** Louis-Philippe, French king (1830–48) was the subject of several assassination attempts and rebellions, and abdicated after the 1848 insurrection in Paris.
88n **De Joinville** (1818–1900), son of Louis-Philippe, a naval officer and writer on military matters.
97 **Nourjahad** hero of Frances Sheridan's *The History of Nourjahad* (1767), who is granted immortality on condition that he should fall into lengthy sleep every time he commits a sin.

The Ruby Mug
5   **the Flight** the *hegira*, or flight, of Muhammed from Mecca to Medina which took place in AD 622; it is the traditional starting point of Islamic history.
10   **prigged** stolen.
15   **Spoon** a fool.
16   **Haroun-al-Rashèd** (763–809), caliph of Baghdad, made famous by the *Arabian Nights*.
40   **Djaffer** also 'Giafar', Haroun's grand vizier.
53   **Shuckabac** Schacabac is a name found in the *Arabian Nights*.
74–75 **Bathos / Or Art of Sinking** from Alexander Pope's satiric *Peri Bathouse, or the Art of Sinking* (1728), in which *bathos* refers to the comic descent from the elevated to the ordinary.
98   **Pasha-èd** a neologism; *pasha* is Turkish word for a man of high rank.
105   **sumph** a fool.
109   **Commander of the True Believers** honorific title for caliphs.
168   **un-sabretach-èd** a sabretach is a leather case suspended from a cavalryman's saddle.
175   **discuss** consume.
180   **Hakem** doctor.
183   **spout for me to sneak up** from a phrase meaning 'get away'.
184   **Howqua** a high-quality tea.
191   **Mulcting** depriving.
197   **siller** silver.
198   **Teetotumites** a teetotum is a top.
199   **Xeres** sherry.   **Geneva** a juniper-flavoured spirit.
204   **Kaaba** the holy sanctuary in Mecca.
206   **Mordjana** Ali Baba's slave, from the *Arabian Nights*, who poured boiling oil into the jars in which the thieves were concealed.
253   **Write me down a conspicuous ass** see *Much Ado about Nothing* (IV.ii.73): 'O that he were here to write me down an ass!'

Where's my Money?
'Wo bleibt's?' by Franz von Gaudy (1800–40), Prussian poet.
10   **castor** a hat.

The Bewildered Vintner
'Erläuterung zum 13. Artikel der Bundesacte' by August Heinrich Hoffman von Fallersleben (1798–1874), German nationalist poet, author of 'Deutschland, Deutschland über alles' (1841).
38   **Burschen** students.
50   **riz** risen.
53   **cold without** spirits with cold water and without sugar.
58   **turkey-pout** a young turkey.
59   **up the spout** ruined.
70   **knout** a Russian whip.
71   **perry** a drink made from pears.
72   **Hollands** a type of gin.

The Mariner's Bride
'Irme quiero, madre' by Luís de Camões (Camoens) (?1525–80), Portuguese poet and traveller.

The Wayfaring Tree
On 'Selber', see note to 'Twenty Golden Years Ago' above, p. 454.
title a 'wayfaring tree' is a tall shrub that grows often in hedgerows.

Khidder
Loosely based on Friedrich Rückert's 'Chidher', which Mangan had translated more faithfully as 'The World's Changes' (*Irish Penny Journal*, July 1840).
160–1 Damon . . . Phillida stock lovers' names from the pastoral tradition; see, for example, William Cowper's 'On the green margin of the brook'.

Counsel of a Cosmopolitan
Rückert, 'Losmachung'.

['The night is falling']
Rückert, 'Das Undenkbare'.

Rest Only in the Grave
Rückert, 'Vor den Türen'.

Prince Aldfrid's Itinerary
The Irish original of this poem was first printed in Hardiman as 'Ro dheat an inis Finn Fáil' (II, 372–5). Copy-text is Montgomery (111–15), the first publication of Mangan's translation. John O'Donovan had published an unrhymed translation in the *DPJ* (15 September 1832). The introductory comments, and probably the footnotes to the poem, are by Montgomery. The poem was reprinted with the title 'Ireland under Irish Rule' by the Irish-American newspaper *An Gaodhal—The Gael* in 1887.
Notes on commentary preceding the poem:
Bede (672–735), Anglo-Saxon theologian, historian, and chronologist.
Camden William Camden (1551–1623), English antiquary and historian.
Lord Lyttleton George Lyttleton (1709–73), English author and statesman.
Prince Aldfrid also Aldfrith, king of Northumbria (685–704), a noted patron of literature.
Note on poem:
49 Ara to Glea these locations have not been identified.

To the Ruins of Donegal Castle
'A dhúin thíos atá it éanar' by Malmurray Ward (Maolmuire Mac an Bháird), bard to the O'Donnells. Copy-text is Montgomery (123–9), the first publication of Mangan's translation. George Petrie had published an unrhymed translation in the *IPJ* (12 December 1840).
title the castle in Donegal town which had been the ancestral stronghold of the O'Donnells was burnt in the 1590s by Red Hugh O'Donnell in order to prevent it being garrisoned by the English. O'Donnell left Ireland for Spain in 1602 after the defeat at Kinsale, and died shortly afterwards.
14 Emania the ancient seat of the kings of Ulster.
31 Con Conn of the Hundred Battles, legendary ancestor of the O'Donnells.
34 Cruachan ancient seat of the kings of Connaught.
35 dome . . . now probably the passage tomb and mound at Newgrange in Co. Meath, which was formerly identified with the mythical palace Brugh na Boinne.

61   **Manus** Manus O'Donnell (d. 1563), grandfather of Red Hugh.
65   **Hugh Mac Hugh** Hugh Dubh O'Donnell, great-grandfather of Red Hugh.
70   **Hugh Roe** Red Hugh (from *rua*, red).
79   **Esky** Donegal Castle is set beside the river Eske.
83   **Dalach** legendary name for the O'Donnell clan.
103   **Coffey's race** a byname for the Irish people.
128   **Tirconnellians' king** Tyrconnell approximates to modern Donegal.

O'Hussey's Ode to the Maguire
'Fuar leam an adhaighse d'Aodh' by Eochaidh Ó hEódhasa (?1560–1612). Copy-text is
Montgomery (137–41), the first publication of Mangan's translation. Mangan may have made
use of Samuel Ferguson's unrhymed translation, published in the *DUM* (October 1834).
Notes on commentary preceding the poem:
Maguire the Maguire clan ruled Fermanagh from the fourteenth to the seventeenth cen-
turies. Hugh Maguire was an ally of O'Neill and O'Donnell in the Nine Years' War, but was
killed in an ambush near Cork in 1600. His successor joined the 'Flight of the Earls' that left
Ireland in 1607.
Notes on poem:
1   *movrone* from *mo bhrón*, 'my sorrow'.
22   **Clan Darry** in west Munster.
28   **Galang** name of an ancient tribe from the Cavan and Meath area.
50   **the bosom of MacNee** Mangan follows Ferguson's mistranslation of the original Irish
here (*Chráoi Mhaicnaidh*, which signifies 'Munster'); see *CW* (III, 436).

Advice
An original poem.

The Warning Voice
O'Donoghue (164–5) gives the following anecdote concerning this poem: 'A certain distin-
guished Dublin physician informs me that he saw him [Mangan] one bitterly cold night,
insufficiently clad, steal into the *Nation* office, and hand into Mr. Fullam, the manager, a few
pages of manuscript, begging at the same time that some money should be given to him on
account. The manager told him that he was prohibited from doing so; he had received
peremptory orders not to advance money to any contributor. Mangan implored so earnestly
that at last he was given a small sum, and my informant tells me that one would have imagined
from his manner in receiving it that he had just been reprieved from a sentence of immediate
death. The sequel is pathetic. The manuscript handed in was the "Warning Voice".'
epigraph Honoré de Balzac (1799–1850) collected three of his philosophical novels into the
volume *Le Livre mystique* in 1835. The quotation may be translated: 'It seems to me that we are
on the eve of a great human battle. The forces are there; but I cannot see any general.'

The Rye Mill
This poem appeared in the 'Answers to Correspondents' column rather than the main body of
the paper. The headnote may be by John Mitchel, who was editor of the *Nation* in early 1846.
25   **Adam Smith's philosophics** Adam Smith (1723–90), Scottish political economist and
philosopher whose radical theories provided justification for free trade and laissez-faire eco-
nomic policies.   **Burke's** the economic and social theories of Edmund Burke (1729–97) were
based upon conservative ideas of custom and moral obligation.

26 **Mill and Ricárd** James Mill (1773–1836) and David Ricardo (1772–1823) were proponents of utilitarianism.

31 **Macculloch** John Ramsey McCulloch (1789–1864), Scottish political economist, an advocate of utilitarianism, who published annotated editions of Adam Smith and David Ricardo.

34 **hoppers and haggards** 'hoppers' are bins for holding grain; 'haggards' are farmyard enclosures for collecting sheaves of grain.

43n **Pierce Egan** (1772–1849), noted English boxing reporter, author of *Boxiana* (1818–24).

44 **Curry-powder Norfolk** the Duke of Norfolk (Henry Charles Howard, 1791–1856) proposed in November 1845 that curry-powder ought to be substituted for potatoes in the Irish diet in order to prevent famine (see C. Woodham-Smith, *The Great Hunger*, London, 1962).

45 **Chancellor** Henry Peter Lord Brougham and Vaux (1778–1868), reformist Whig politician and Lord Chancellor of Britain (1830–34), and an advocate of laissez-faire economics.

47 **woolsack** the cushion which is the traditional seat for the Lord Chancellor in the House of Lords.

48 **Adam's ale** water.

53 **Eblanians** Dubliners; from 'Eblana' which appears on Ptolomy's 2nd-century map as the name of a town or tribe on the east coast of Ireland. **French rhyme** rhyming pairs that sound the same but have different meanings; here 'rhyme ill' and 'Rye Mill'.

To the Pens of The Nation

8 **SIKHS** a religious and cultural group in northern India, noted for their military prowess. A campaign was fought between the Sikhs and the British in 1845–46 over control of the Punjab; the *Nation's* editorial line supported the Sikhs.

The Domiciliary Visit

Original, if any exists, has not been traced. Appeared in the 'Answers to Correspondents' section of the *Nation*, rather than the main body of the paper. John Mitchel may have written the headnote.

1 *De par le Roi!* 'by order of the King!'

5 *J'ignore* 'I don't know'.

12 *poniards* daggers.

16 **Fieschi** Giuseppe Fieschi (1790–1836) built an 'infernal machine' capable of firing twenty gun-barrels, with which he made an unsuccessful attempt to assassinate the French king Louis-Philippe in July 1835. Eighteen people were killed in the incident, and Fieschi was captured and guillotined.

19 *Il en a l'air* 'It looks like one'.

25 **Poles** Poland had been partitioned between Russia, Austria and Prussia in 1795; in 1846 an uprising in Krakow was put down by Austrian troops.

39 **do *the King's* job** the phrase 'do someone's job' meant to kill that person.

Siberia

Chuto (208) has identified the likely source for this poem as 'Sibirien' by German poet Ernst Ortlepp (1800–64), which concerns Polish revolutionaries exiled to Siberia after the 1830–31 revolution.

23 **Nothing . . . soft** Mangan uses a version of this line again in 'The Phantom Ship', *DUM* (September 1847).

36 **dree** endure.

To the Ingleezee Khafir, Calling Himself Djaun Bool Djenkinzun
An original poem. The headnote is probably by John Mitchel.
2 **Djaun Bool** John Bull, conventional literary personification of England.
21, note (5) refers to Col. James Skinner (1778–1841), military adventurer in India, of Indian and Scottish parentage.

The Peal of Another Trumpet
epigram from Marie Anne A. Lenormand (1772–1843), French soothsayer. It may be translated: 'Ireland, Ireland, rejoice! For you the hour of vengeance has struck. Your leader prepares your deliverance.' The spelling found in the copy-text (lacking diacritical marks) has been retained.
48 **Kaffirland** southern Africa.
50 **Mingo** the Mingo tribe, related to the Iroquois, inhabited present-day Ohio and West Virginia.
52 **bedaween** Bedouin.
82n **GODWIN'S ST. LEON** *St Leon* (1799), novel by English novelist and political thinker William Godwin (1756–1836), was frequently alluded to by Mangan. The aristocratic hero of the novel acquires immortality, with consequences that are variously positive and painful.

The Dream of John Mac Donnell
'Oidhche bhíos am luaighe im shuan' by Seán Clarach Mac Dónaill (1691–1754). Mangan may have used the unrhymed translation by John O'Donovan in the *DPJ* (22 December 1832). MS 138 includes a draft version of the latter, possibly in O'Donovan's hand.
7 **Banshee** literally, fairy-woman (from *bean sí*); the folkloric banshee was a harbinger of death.
24 **shieling** hut.
26 **Gruagach's mansion** in the original Irish this is not a placename, but *sidh na ngrugach*, which means fairy-palace of the ogre or wizard.
28 **Inver-lough** not identified; it is not in the original.
30 **Cruachan** ancient royal seat of Connaught.
33 **Mourna** the Mourne river in Co. Tyrone; not in the original.
34 **Shanady** not identified.
35 **Ardroe** *Eas' Ruaidh* in the original, meaning Assaroe, a waterfall on the river Erne.
37 **that proud pile** the passage-tomb and mound at Newgrange were thought to be the site of the palace of the mythical Aenghus.
41 **Mac Lir** Manannán Mac Lir, god of the sea. **Creevroe** palace of the Red Branch knights at Emain Macha in Co. Armagh.
44 **Cnocfeerin** hill in Co. Limerick associated with the fairies of Munster.
50 **Ival** Aoibheall, queen of the fairies of Munster.
71 **Charles Stuart** 'Bonnie Prince Charlie' (1720–88), grandson of James II and Catholic claimant to the British throne. He landed with a army in Scotland in 1745 but was defeated at Culloden in 1746, following which he escaped to France.

Dark Rosaleen
'Róisín Dubh', author unknown. Hardiman (I, 254–6) gives the original Irish, with a translation by Thomas Furlong. Mangan's headnote draws largely on Hardiman's commentary, but he makes free with the structure and sense of the poem. Samuel Ferguson, in his review of Hardiman's volumes (*DUM*, August 1834), provides a more literal translation than Furlong,

and disputes Hardman's interpretation, arguing that the poem was actually written by 'a priest in love who was expecting a [papal] dispensation for his paramour'. The original is distinct from the the two Munster poems also titled 'Róisín Dubh', which Mangan translated for *PPM*.

5   **wine from the royal Pope** the original has 'Tiocfaidh do phárdún ó'n b-Pápa' ('Your pardon will come from the Pope'). Furlong does not translate this. The wine in the original poem comes from Spain ('fíon Spáinneach').

Cean-Salla
Appeared in the *Nation*'s 'Answers to Correspondents' column, rather than the main body of the paper.
title Kinsale, Co. Cork was the site of the final defeat of the Irish alliance in the Nine Years' War. Spanish forces took the town in September 1601 but were besieged by the English. The Irish attempt to relieve the siege on 24 December 1601 ended in a rout. Shortly afterwards, Red Hugh O'Donnell departed for Spain in a new attempt to raise support, but died there in 1602.
epigraph Mangan helped improve the English in Owen Connellan's translation of the *Annals of the Four Masters* which appeared in instalments between 1845 and 1846. The exact quotation here is not found in Connellan's translation, though a similar passage occurs that describes the Irish despondency after the death of O'Donnell in 1602; see *Annals of Ireland*, trans. Owen Connellan (Dublin: Geraghty, 1846), 701.
13   **thee** Brian Boru, high-king of Ireland who defeated the Danes at the battle of Clontarf in 1014.
22   **Walhalla** in Norse mythology, the hall reserved after death for warriors who have died in battle.

An Invitation
The poem was published on 4 July, American Independence day.
18n   **NIEBUHR** Barthold Georg Niebuhr (1776–1831), German historian who wrote on English and Irish affairs.
23   **dædal** intricate and variegated.

A Vision of Connaught in the Thirteenth Century
epigraph In 'The Arcadian Shepherds' by French painter Nicolas Poussin (1593–1665), a group of shepherds are shown observing a tomb on which are carved the Latin words *Et in Arcadia ego* ('And in Arcadia, I [am]'), which is usually understood to signify death's presence, even in paradise. Mangan, on the other hand, seems to be deriving his epigraph from the common French mistranslation of Poussin's inscription, as found in Diderot, or in Dellile's 1782 version: 'Et moi aussi, je fus pasteur dans l'Arcadie' (see Erwin Panofsky, *Meaning in the Visual Arts*, 1955). Mangan's version of the inscription literally means 'And me, I have been also in Arcadia.'
13   **Cáhal Mór of the Wine-red Hand** Cathal Ó Conchobair (O'Connor) (1152–1224), king of Connaught. He was nicknamed *Crobderg* ('red hand').
54n   **It was ... cotemporaries** this quotation has not been traced to either of the published versions of the *Annals* with which Mangan was associated (see *CW*, III, 455–6).
56   **Maine** a tributary of the Rhine.

The Lovely Land
title the painter referred to in the subtitle is Daniel Maclise (1806–70), Cork-born painter noted for his portraits and historical paintings. No Maclise painting matching this description has been traced.

11   **Veronese** Paolo Veronese (1528–88) Italian painter who specialised in mythological and historical canvases.

15   **Poussin** Nicolas Poussin (1593–1665), French painter renowned for his idealised landscapes.

signature 'Lageniensis' means 'Leinsterman'.

Lament Over the Ruins of the Abbey of Teach Molaga
'Máctnadh an Duine Dhóilghíosaich' by Seághan Ó Coileáin (?1754–1816). The original Irish text was published in Hardiman (II, 234–42), with a translation by Thomas Furlong. Samuel Ferguson published two translations in the *DUM* (October and November 1834).

title the Franciscan friary in Timoleague, Co. Cork was founded in 1312 and burned by an English army in 1642.

21   **Goshen** a blessed place, after the name of the Israelites' home in Egypt.

35   **Grey Friars** Franciscans.

39   **Paladine** a 'paladin' is a courtly champion.

68   **brutal England's power** the original poem does not mention England, but Hardiman's annotation describes these and other Irish ruins as 'appalling monuments of the ravages committed by the first protestant reformers' (II, 409).

77–80 **I turned . . . wave** this stanza has no corresponding equivalent in the original.

A Lamentation for the Death of Sir Maurice Fitzgerald, Knight of Kerry
'Mo thraochadh is mo shaoth rem ló thú' by Piaras Feiritéar (?1600–53). Mangan adds several placenames to Feiritéar's original.

9   **Loch Gur** in Co. Limerick.

14   **Ogra** in Co. Limerick.

15   **Mogeely's Phantom Women** Moygalla in Co. Clare; the phantoms are banshees, whose wailing signified the imminent death of notable person.

16   **Geraldine** a member of the Fitzgerald family.

17   **Carah Mona** in Co. Cork.

21   **Keenalmeeky, Eemokilly** both in Co. Cork.

22   *keen caoine*, a woman's funeral wail.

24   **Inchiqueen** in Co. Clare.

25   **Loughmoe** in Co. Tipperary.   **Dunanore** in Co. Kerry.

41   **Milesian race** descendents of the mythical king Milesius of Spain whose sons led the Gaelic conquest of Ireland; the term thus signifies 'Gaels'.

Counsel to the Worldly-Wise
9   **tilbury** a light two-wheeled carriage.

17   **rara avis** 'a rare bird'.

20   **THOMAS DAVIS** (1814–45); poet, journalist and co-founder of the *Nation* newspaper, and inspirational leader of the 'Young Ireland' movement. Mangan seems not to have shared others' high opinion of Davis (see Shannon-Mangan, 272).

from *Anthologia Hibernica—No. I*
'**The hemlock . . . rank**' from Shelley, 'The Sensitive Plant': 'And thistles, and nettles, and darnels rank, / And the dock, and henbane, and hemlock dank.'

'**for a certain term . . . night**' *Hamlet* (I.v.10): 'Doom'd for a certain term to walk the night.'

'night is far spent . . . hand' Romans 13: 12.

manes venerated spirits of the dead.

Andrew M'Grath Aindrias Mac Craith (?1708–95), poet also known as the 'Mangaire Súgach' ('merry pedlar').

Neither One Thing Nor T'other

'A dhalta dhil an dainid leat mo chás anois.' Mangan's source was probably Edward Walsh's translation in *IPS*, which had just been published.

6   **Old Nick** the Devil.

13   **Luther** Martin Luther (1483–1546), German theologian, leader of Protestant Reformation **Gother** John Gother (d. 1704), English Catholic priest and controversialist.

23   **Baal** in the Bible, the deity worshipped by Canaanites; thus an idolatrous god.

39   **chapel and church** in Ireland, the former term referred to Catholic churches, the latter to Church of Ireland (Protestant) churches.

51   **King David** in 2 Samuel 11–12, David repents of and is forgiven the sins of adultery and murder.   **Paul** before his conversion, the apostle Paul was a persecutor of Christians.

65   **Calvin** Jean Calvin (1509–64), French reforming theologian whose radical ideas shaped Presbyterianism.

66   **Arius's crew** the doctrines of the fourth century Egyptian Arius on the finite nature of Christ were condemned as heretical.

71   **certes** certainly.

78   **Peter** the apostle Peter denied Christ three times (Luke 22).

Love-Song

'Atáim sínte air do thúamba', author unknown. Mangan's source was probably Edward Walsh's translation, beginning 'From the cold sod that's o'er you', in *IPS*.

70   **meed** reward.

The Hymn 'Stabat Mater Dolorosa'

The original Latin hymn *Stabat mater dolorosa* ('The sorrowful mother stood') was written by Italian poet Jacopone da Todi (d. 1306).

The Lass of Carrick

title Edward Walsh noted in his version of this poem that 'there are so many places of the name of Carrick such as Carrick-on-Shannon, Carrick-on-Suir, &c., &c., that I cannot fix its precise locality' (*IPS*, 72).

7   **Banba** a figurative name for Ireland.

48   **Mab** queen of the fairies.

49   *shee-og* from Irish *sí óg* (young fairy).

53   **cumber** a cumbrance.

The Death and Burial of Red Hugh O'Donnell

title Red Hugh O'Donnell (1571–1602) went to Spain seeking further support from King Philip III after the defeat of the Irish and Spanish forces at Kinsale in January 1602. He fell ill (perhaps through poison) and died at Simancas on 10 September, near the royal residence of Vallidolid. Mangan's account is based largely on the one found in the *Annals of the Four Masters*.

27   **Tirconnell** approximating to modern Donegal.

65   **tesselated** adorned with mosaics.

96   **O'Mulconry and Dunleavy** Flaithri O'Malconry was O'Donnell's confessor; Maurice Ulltach O'Donleavy was a Franciscan and a member of O'Donnell's household.

113   **Douro** a major river near Valladolid.

142   **Led out the blood of Alcantra** 'led out' is to lead out for a dance; Alcantra is a town on the Tagus river, south of Old Castile.

143   **Hidalgos** noblemen.

171   **Thy Sovereign** Philip III, who had sent Spanish troops to Kinsale to aid the Irish.

189   **meed** reward.

213   **Bascalier** probably from *bas cavalier*, meaning a lower order of knight, as in 'Bass-cavalier', l. 229, below.

219   **Serge-bearers** candle-bearers.

223   **Esgueva** a river near Valladolid.

229   **Bass-cavaliers** see note to line 213, above.

240n   **Isabella** the monarchs Isabella of Castile and Ferdinand of Aragon were married in Valladolid in 1469.

The Dawning of the Day

'Déalradh án lae', author unknown. O'Doran has not been identified, though *CW* (III, 471) suggests that Mangan may have believed the poem was by Peter O'Dornin (Peadar Ó Doirnín, d. 1769) since an original MS of the poem was interleaved among a collection of Ó Doirnín MSS to which Mangan had access.

Song of the Albanian

An original poem. Mangan seems to be conflating Albania and Greece, both of which were part of the Ottoman empire. The Greek war of independence of the 1820s involved slaughter and massacres on both sides; 1826 saw significant defeats for the Greeks at Missolonghi and Athens. Independence for Greece (but not Albania) came in 1830.

10   **Góvra's brow** a mountain near Missolonghi.

11   **Charon** not the ferryman of classical mythology but a harbinger of death from Greek folklore.

45   **thou risest** Greek nationalists rose in rebellion in 1821.

50   *khandjers* curved daggers.

Owen Reilly: A Keen

Original unidentified. Probably an original poem; none of the placenames mentioned in the poem have been identified.

25   **Banshee** fairy woman whose wailing is a harbinger of death.

52   **Queen of Keeners** a keen (*caoin*) is an Irish funeral wail.

Moreen: A Love-Lament

Chuto (53) believes this to be an original poem, noting that the name Charles Boy McQuillan may be Mangan's version of the Cathal Buidhe Mac Giolla Ghunna, an eighteenth-century poet and rake. No known poem by Mac Giolla Ghunna resembles this poem. A shorter version of Mangan's poem was published posthumously as 'The Groans of Despair' (*Nation*, 6 October 1849).

62   **dree** endure.

103   **meed** reward.

Testament of Cathaeir Mor
Original Irish text published with literal translation by John O'Donovan in *Leabhar n-gCeart, or The Book of Rights* (Dublin: Celtic Society, 1847). In a letter to James McGlashan in 1847, Mangan wrote: 'It strikes me a very telling thing might be made out of "The Will of Cathaeir Mor," in O'Donovan's Leabhar na g-Ceart. I would cast the translation in the same irregular metre as the original, only occasionally doubling the rhymes in a single line, which has a very good effect on an English ear. It would, if attractively rendered, appear one of the most characteristic and extraordinary of our archaeological literary relics' (quoted in James Price, 'Gallery of Contemporary Writers, No. 6', *Evening Packet*, 3 November 1849). A slightly altered version of Mangan's translation was published as a pamphlet by the Celtic Society in February 1848.
title Cathaeir Mor was a legendary king (perhaps ancestor-deity) of Leinster; reputedly the father of 33 sons.
Notes to headnote
O'Flaherty in his *Ogygia* the *Ogygia* of Roderick O'Flaherty (1629–1718), the Galway-born historian, was a syncretic compilation of Irish annals, published in 1685.
LEABHAR NA G-CEART a twelfth-century MS compilation, preserved in the Book of Lecan.
Note to poem:
119n   'And with … throne' a slight misquotation of ll. 257–59 from Byron's poem 'Parisina' (1816).

Rights of Property
Appeared in the *Nation*'s 'Answers to Correspondents' column, rather than the main body of the paper.
epigraph the quotation has not been traced; the *Morning Herald* was a conservative London daily.
6n   *Sketches of India* by Capt Moyle Sherer (1789–1869) went through several editions in the early nineteenth century.

A Voice of Encouragement
14   **dreeth** endures.
26n   from Milton, *Paradise Lost* (IV, 76–7).
48   'the Son … not!' from Matthew 24:44.
67   **Gorgon … Chimera** mythical monsters.
67n   the quotation derives from the opening of *A Journal of the Plague Year* (1722) by Daniel Defoe (1660–1731). The closest analogous passage reads: 'they saw a Flaming-Sword held in a hand, coming out of a cloud, with a point hanging directly over the city'.

Hush-a-By Baby
'Seó hó, a thoil, ná goil go fóill' by Eoghan Rua Ó Súilleabháin (1748–84). Mangan probably used the translation entitled 'The Lullaby' by Edward Walsh in *IPS*.
4   **Eoghan and Conn** mythical kings, founders of the Eóghanacht and Connacht dynasties.

9　**Apple of Gold** in Greek legend, Paris was chosen by Zeus to determine which of three goddesses—Hera, Athena or Aphrodite—was the most beautiful. The winner was to be awarded a golden apple.

11　**Pan** Greek god of shepherds.

12　**Rod . . . Moses** in Exodus, Aaron's (not Moses') rod is used to display the might of God to the pharaoh.

17　**Falvey** the king of Munster, Failbhe Fionn, fought the Danes at Cashel.

18n　**Cashel of the Orders** Cashel was the site of a Dominican friary.

22　**Brian on Cluan-tarava's morn** Brian Boru (941–1014) defeated the Danes and their allies at Clontarf in 1014.

23　**Murrogh** son of Brian Boru, who also fought at Clontarf.

27　**Hound** the king of Cashel was supposed to own a hound capable of running messages between Cashel and Bunratty, in Co. Clare.

29　**Aherlow** Glen of Aherlow, in Co. Tipperary.

30　**Skellig** the Skellig Islands lie off Co. Kerry.

33　**Jason** legendary Greek hero, led the Argonauts in search of the Golden Fleece.

35　**Cuchullin** legendary Ulster hero.

37　**kine** cattle.

39　**Connal's** Connall Cernach, legendary Ulster warrior.

40　**Nish** Naoise, Ulster prince, subject of the tragic story of Deirdre and Naoise.

42　**Achilles** Greek hero of the Trojan war.　**Finn** Fionn Mac Cumhaill, legendary leader of the warrior band called the 'Fianna'.

45　**Diarmid** one of the Fianna　**Fingal** Mangan here follows Walsh's mis-transcription of the Irish original's word 'Finn', meaning Fionn Mac Cumhaill.

47　**Osgar** grandson of Fionn, one of the Fianna.

48　**Mac Treóin** Talc Mac Treóin, chieftain who fought against the Fianna.

51　**Eefa** Aoife, married to Cuchullain.

58　**Dubh-long** one of the Fianna.

64　**O'Dunn . . . Aonghus's**　Diarmuid (l. 45) was son of Duibhne (Dunn); Aonghus was his foster father.

66　**Fenian** adjectival form of 'Fianna'.

71　**Helen** Helen of Troy; rivalry for her love between Paris and Menelaus led to the Trojan War.

75　**Hebe** Greek god of youth and cupbearer to the gods.

79　**the Nine** the nine Muses of Greek mythology.

St Patrick's Hymn Before Tarah

title the original Irish contains no reference to Tara, the seat of the high-kings of Ireland. Petrie erroneously translated the phrase 'Atom-riug' in the original (probably meaning 'I arise') as 'At Temur', another name for Tara. Mangan reproduces this error (*CW*, IV, 274).

headnote probably written by C.P. Meehan, editor of *Duffy's Irish Catholic Magazine*.

51n　**Antiquities of Tarah Hill** *On the History and Antiquities of Tara Hill* (1839) by George Petrie.

A Vision A.D. 1848

16n　**Banshees** female spirits whose wailing foretold death.

27　**a Man** Fr Theobald Mathew (1790–1856), who began his national campaign for total abstinence from alcohol in 1839; by the mid-1840s up to 5 million Irish people had taken the pledge.

45   **A Man among men** Daniel O'Connell (1775–1847), whose 'monster meetings' in favour of Repeal took place in 1842 and 1843.

71   **Famine first came** the potato blight that precipitated the Great Famine first appeared in the autumn of 1845.

80   **One for each Seven** the population before the Famine was about 8 million.

104   **Revelation of Wonders** the last book of the New Testament, called the 'Apocalypse' or 'Revelation' of St John, foretells the end of the world.

Holy Are the Works of Mary's Blessed Son
headnote   John Daly is John O'Daly (1800–78), scholar, editor and bookseller, who worked with Mangan on the collection *PPM* in 1848–49.

41   **Nine Orders** the nine orders of angels.

Irish National Hymn
13   **Galileo** Galileo Galilei (1564–1642), Italian astronomer. Found guilty of heretically advocating the Copernican theory that the earth revolves around the Sun, he signed the recantation of his work demanded by the Inquisition, but is reported to have muttered 'And yet it [the Earth] moves' after he did so.

The Tribune's Hymn for Pentecost
title the *Irish Tribune* newspaper was established by Kevin Izod O'Doherty and R.D. Williams in June 1848 after the arrest of John Mitchel and closure of his radical paper, *United Irishman*. Pentecost is the seventh Sunday after Easter, and commemorates the descent of the Holy Spirit on the apostles.

9   **David's and Isaiah's Lyre** David was the composer of the Psalms; Isaiah's prophecies are preserved in poetic form.

17   **thrones and strongholds fell** in 1848 there were republican revolutions in France, Germany, Italy and Austria.

28   **Tullia's tomb** when the tomb of Cicero's daughter Tullia (d. 45 BC) was discovered in Rome in the fifteenth century, it allegedly contained a lamp that was still burning after 1500 years.

An Ode of Hafiz
Hafiz (1325–89) was a noted Persian poet, but this is an original poem of Mangan's.

Elleen a-Ruin
'Eibhlín a Rúin', attributed to Cearbhall Ó Dálaigh (fl. 1620). Mangan's source was the version in Hardiman (I, 264–7).
title the Irish *a rúin* is a form of address meaning 'my secret'.

The Irish Language
Mangan's original was probably supplied to him by John O'Daly; O'Daly published a shorter version of the poem in *Reliques of Irish Jacobite Poetry* (Dublin: Machen, 1844).

26n   **Bagpipes** in fact *cláirseach* means a harp.

31   **Banba** mythical name for Ireland.

34   *cead mile failte céad mile fáilte*, 'a hundred thousand welcomes'.

55   **shieling** a hut or cottage.

The Vision of Egan O'Reilly
'Gile na Gile', by Aogán Ó Rathaille (?1675–1729). He was in fact from Sliabh Luachra in Co. Kerry, not Cork as Mangan's headnote states. Mangan's original was supplied by John O'Daly, and Mangan later published a more literal translation in *PPM* as 'The Brightest of the Bright.'
20   **him** from the date of the poem (before 1729), this is probably James Francis Edward Stuart, 'the Old Pretender' (1688–1766) rather than his son Charles, as *CW* suggests (see also note to *The Dream of John MacDonnell*, line 71, above).
47   **Sliev Cruachra** the original refers to Slieve Luachra, a mountainous area in east Kerry where Ó Rathaille lived.
57   **Cror** unidentified; placename not in original. Mangan may have been alluding to Cruachan, the ancient royal seat of Connacht.
65   **Daltry** unidentified, not in original.
82   **zone** a belt.
96   **Temor** Tara in Co. Meath, seat of the high-kings of Ireland.

Duhallow
Probably an original poem; regarding Charles Boy M'Quillan, see note to *Moreen: a Love-Lament*, p. 474, above.
title Duhallow is in Co. Cork.
6   **the rakes of Mallow** the title of a well-known traditional song.
22   **Corrach** unidentified.

Epigram—The Richest Caliph
1   **Haroun** Haroun al-Rashid (763–809), caliph of Baghdad, made famous by the *Arabian Nights*.
12   **Caliph-ornia** the California Gold Rush reached its height in 1849.

March Forth, Eighteen Forty-nine!
27n **Guelphs and Ghibellines** Italian political factions prominent in the Middle Ages; the Guelphs supported the papacy while the Ghibellines supported the Holy Roman Emperor.
47   **Barbary's marts** slaves markets on the north African coast.

Gasparo Bandollo
'Matteo Falcone, der Korse' by Adelbert von Chamisso (1781–1838), German poet. Mangan changes the names of the characters, and the relocates the poem from Corsica to southern Italy. There was a Sicilian separatist rebellion in 1820 which was brutally suppressed by the Neopolitan government, assisted by Austria.
30   **Zecchini** Italian coins.
62   **Ghibelline and Guelph** see note to line 27 in the previous poem.
99   **Sbirri** the police.

Ghazel
Probably an original poem. Abbas Ahmad ibn Khallikan (1211–82) was a Arabian biographer rather than a poet.
7   **Abel . . . Cain** see Genesis 4:8–15.

A Word in Reply to Joseph Brenan

Mangan's poem is a response to the following poem by Joseph Brenan, published in the *Irishman* on 26 May 1849:

A Word to James Clarence Mangan

Brother and Friend! your words are in mine ear,
　　As the faint toning of a hidden bell:
At one time distant—at another near—
　　Something between a joy-peal and a knell.
The hidden bell, the hidden meaning; thus thy mind
　　Accompanies the undertone of rhyme;
As sylvan stream o'er flower and leaf will wind
　　Towards its goal, its murmur-keeping time.
The brook-notes which the Ancient Marinere
　　Heard whispered in 'the leafy month of June,'*
Thy song is now; again it thrills the air
　　Like the low crooning of a magic rune.
Each word is ARIEL—at thy command
　　Soothing the Cast-aways on life's dark shore;
Thou art the PROSPERO, of resistless wand—
　　King by the 'right divine' of mystic lore.
Dreamer of dreams, now gloomy as *La Morgue*,
　　Through which, as through 'glass darkly' loom the Dead,
Now like the Angel-trance of SWEDENBORG,
　　When heavenly portals opened o'er his head.
Seer of Visions; Dweller on the Mount;
　　Reader of the signs upon the Future's sky;
Scholar of *Deuchland*; drinker at the fount
　　Of old Teutonic awe and mystery;—
HERR MANGAN, listen:—Live with CATHAL MORE,
　　Sojourning in the wondrous 'land of morn;'†
Or, an' thou will'st with KŒRNER, bow before
　　The air-born music of the 'marvellous horn;'‡
Laugh the quaint laugh, or weep the bitter tear,
　　Be gay or sad—be humorous or sublime:
One thing remains—but one—HERR MANGAN, hear!
　　To live thy poetry—to act thy rhyme.

* Vide Coleridge's wild and beautiful poem, 'The Ancient Marinere.'

† One of Mangan's most exquisite lyrics is a vision of Ireland in the 13th Century, when Cathal More 'Of the Wine-red Hand' was living. Ah! 'There were giants upon the earth in those days.'

‡ I refer to Kœrner's mystic 'Horn-Song,' translated by Mangan.

title Joseph Brenan (1828–57) was an admirer of John Mitchel, and a friend of Mangan in the last year of the poet's life. Brenan was imprisoned in 1848 for his part in the Young Ireland rebellion. On his release from prison in March 1849 he became editor of the *Irishman* newspaper. He fled to the U.S. in October 1849 after being implicated in an attack on a police barracks, and died in New Orleans.

The Famine

5–6   **that hand-cloud . . . Eld** see 1 Kings 18:44; at the summit of Mt Carmel, the prophet Elijah sees a hand-shaped cloud that brings relief from drought.

15   **Simoon** simoom, a dry desert wind.

35   **Pharos** a beacon.

Still a Nation

epigraph   the *Irishman* editor was Joseph Brenan.

The Expedition and Death of King Dathy

Probably an original poem: no poet named Owen John O'Hennessy has been traced. The legend of King Daithi had been treated in an earlier poem by Thomas Davis ('The Fate of King Dathi'), but Davis's poem bears little resemblance to Mangan's. Mangan may have used the account of Daithi in John O'Donovan's edition of *The Geneologies, Tribes and Customs of Hy Fiachrach* (1844).

6   **dree** endure.

10   **Beirdra** unidentified.

45   **Ausonia** literary name for Italy.

55   **Ceann** literally, 'head'.

83   **Eblana's bay** Dublin bay (see note to line 53 of 'The Rye Mill', above).

84   **Seanachies** storytellers.

The Nameless One

headnote   by the editor of the *Irishman*.

33   **dreeing** enduring.

38   **Maginn and Burns** William Maginn (1793–1842), Cork-born poet and journalist, founder of *Fraser's Magazine* (1830); Robert Burns (1759–96), Scottish poet. Both were heavy drinkers and died impoverished.

from The Poets and Poetry of Munster

Mangan contributed 55 translations to this collection edited by John O'Daly, which was published in November 1849. The volume prints Irish texts on the verso and Mangan's translations on the recto of each page. Most texts have musical accompaniment. The headnotes and probably all of the footnotes are by O'Daly. Part of Mangan's unpublished critical introduction to the volume is reprinted at pp. 403, above.

The Fair Hills of Eire O!

'Ban-Chnoic Eireann O!' by Donnchadh Mac Con-Mara (1715–1810). The poem was written in Hamburg, where Mac Conmara ran a school for a time.

3   **Eibhear's tribe** the Irish people; Eibhear (or Heber) was one of the mythical sons of Milesius who supposedly invaded Ireland in prehistoric times.

25   **Cruachs** from *cruach*, a mountain.

46   **kine** cattle.

O'Tuomy's Drinking Song

'Ol-dun Sheaghain ui Thuoma' by Seaghan Ó Tuama (1706–75).

Andrew Magrath's Reply to John O'Tuomy
'Freagradh Aindreas mhic Craith' by Aindrias Mac Craith (?1708–95), also known as the Mangaire Súgach ('merry pedlar'); see Mangan's prose commentary on 'Neither One Thing Nor T'Other', p. 238, above.
42   **Jack-and-Gilling** gossiping about sexual scandal.

The Geraldine's Daughter
'Inghion ui Ghearailt' by Aogán Ó Rathaille (?1675–1729).
title according to O'Daly, the poem is 'written as a tribute of praise to a poetess, a lady named Fitzgerald, who resided at Ballykenely, in the county of Cork, and who, from her extra-ordinary beauty, was a theme of unceasing eulogy among the bards of Munster' (*PPM*, 26). The term 'Geraldines' signifies the descendents of Maurice Fitzgerald, one of the original Norman invaders. The family became very powerful in Munster and Leinster, gaining the titles of earls of Desmond and earls of Kildare in the middle ages.
25   **Grecians … Mileadh's sons … Phenicians** the references here are derived from popular myths about the origins of the Gaelic Ireland. The sons of Míl (Milesius) supposedly invaded Ireland, establishing Gaelic civilisation. In the theories of Vallencey and other 18th and early 19th century antiquarians, the Milesians were thought to have come originally from the Mediterranean world, with links to the Scythian, Greek and Phoenician civilisations.
30   **Lords of Bunratty** the O'Briens of Thomond, descendents of Brian Boru.
31   **Cashel** also associated with the Thomond dynasty.
35   **Helen** Helen of Troy.

Conor O'Riordan's Vision
'Aisling Chonchubhair Ui Riordain'.
1   **Charleville** in Co. Cork.
4   **Lee** river in Co. Cork.
38   **Heber's kingdom** Heber (or Eibhear) was one of the mythical sons of Milesius who invaded Ireland.
70   **Guelph** the name of a German noble family; George I, the Hanoverian monarch who acceded to the British throne in 1714 was related to them.

The Coolun
'An Chuilfhionn', author uncertain.
11   **Admiral Power** unidentified.

Caitilin Ni Uallachain
'Caitlin Ni Uallachain' by Uilliam Dall Ua h-Earnáin (?1720–1803). This song is not related to the song by Ó hAnnracháin which Mangan translated as 'Kathaleen Ny-Houlahan' in 1841 (see p. 113, above). O'Daly's headnote refers to his *Reliques of Irish Jacobite Poetry* (Dublin, 1844).
23   **God who led … on** alludes to the parting of the Red Sea which allowed the Israelites to escape from Egypt; see Exodus 14: 21–2.
29   **Phoebus** the sun.
35   **Inis-Eilge** 'noble island;' a name for Ireland.
36   **James son of James** James Francis Edward Stuart (1688–1766), son of the deposed James II, and claimant to the British throne.   **the Duke** James Butler, 2nd Duke of Ormond (1665–1745) who in 1715 went to France to serve in the Jacobite cause.

Donall Na Greine
Author unknown.
19   **spalpeen** a farm labourer.
22   **Long-handed Lughaidh** mythical god-king of the Tuatha Dé Danann.
23   **Alexander** Alexander the Great (356–23 BC), king of Macedon who conquered much of
Asia Minor. The original refers to Hercules instead.
27   **Lough Erin** Lough Erne.
70   **Erse** the Irish language.

Black-haired Fair Rose
'Rois Gheal Dubh', author unknown. The original of this poem is distinct from the original
of the following poem, and from 'Dark Rosaleen', p. 222, above. *PPM* presents two different airs
as accompaniment (see footnote to title); only the second, more well-known air is printed here.
8   **Clerk** a cleric.

Little Black-haired Rose
'Roisin Dubh', author unknown.
10   **pelf** wealth.

Edmund of the Hill
'Eamonn an Chnoic', author unknown.

from *The Tribes of Ireland*
In 1852, John O'Daly published a volume entitled *The Tribes of Ireland: A Satire, by Aenghus
O'Daly*, edited by John O'Donovan 'with poetical translation by the late James Clarence
Mangan'. It consists of the original Irish text, with a parallel literal translation by O'Donovan,
followed by Mangan's version, which is described as 'a versified paraphrase, or imitation'
(*Tribes* 87). Mangan had worked on the translation during 1849, and a MS version of this
translation exists, though it is in O'Daly's hand (RIA MS 24/M/13). The published translation
of 1852 differs from this MS in several ways, which suggests that O'Donovan and O'Daly
made alterations to Mangan's version after his death. I have chosen to use the MS as copy-text
for the selected stanzas in this edition, on the basis that it is probably closest to what Mangan
actually wrote or dictated. Some of the notes below derive from O'Donovan's or O'Daly's
footnotes for the 1852 edition.
title   Aonghus Ruadh Ó Dálaigh (d. 1617) was reputedly hired by the Elizabethan adminis-
trators Lord Mountjoy and Sir George Carew to write a satire that would stir up enmity
among the principal Irish families.
I   **Mac Mahon** rulers of Oriel, in Co. Monaghan.   **Banba** mythical name for Ireland.
III   **Feenaghtys** from Co. Leitrim.   **Barmecide's banquet** an imaginary feast set by a
Barmicide prince in the tale of the Barber's Sixth Brother in the *Arabian Nights*.
IV   **potato** an irritated footnote to the 1852 text reads: 'There is no mention of potatoes in
the original. In Shakespeare's time potatoes were a luxury. The poet Mangan, who had a
horror of potatoes, is not very happy in his translation here' (*Tribes* 87).
VI   **O'Byrne** from Co. Wicklow.
VII   **Granard** in Co. Longford.
IX   **Clontobred** in Co. Monaghan.   **you yourself may be eaten!** this is footnoted in the
1852 edition as follows: 'The translator goes too far here, for Aenghus makes no allusion to

eating the living. He merely says that the cake was so thin, small, and light, that the fly might carry it off under her wing' (*Tribes* 92).

XI   **Thomond** in north Munster.   *beau monde* fashionable society.   *uisce beata* whiskey.

XII   **Drom Sneachta** in Co. Monaghan.

XIII **Mac Cahans** from Co. Derry.

XXI   **Charley** Cathal O'Conor of Ballintober, Co. Roscommon.   *squelettes* skeletons.

XXIV **Clan Rickard** a branch of the Burke family from Co. Galway.

XXV   **Stacks** there is pun here on 'stack' and 'rick', both of which are used to describe a gathering of straw. A note in the 1852 edition comments that 'Aenghus calls them *Stickards* or misers'.   **Kilcorban to Burren** the former is in Co. Galway, the latter in north Co. Clare.

XXVI **Johnsons** the 1852 edition reads 'Jennings', a Co. Galway family related to the Burkes. **Magh Guaire** an area near Kinvara in south Galway, site of an ancient battle.

XXVII **Inis-cara** Gort, in Co. Galway.

XXIX **Roches** from Fermoy in Co. Cork.

XXX   **O'Flynns** from Co. Roscommon.   **Albion** England.

XXXI **horn-firkin** a note in the 1852 edition comments: 'The Bard here seems to suggest that O'Flyn's butter was so scant, as that it was preserved in a horn …'

XLIII **Mac Dermod** family descended from Diarmuid Mor Mac Carthy of Muskerry, in Co. Cork.   **Ballincollick** Ballincollig, a town west of Cork city.

XLV   **Mac Auliffes** from Duhallow, Co. Cork, with a seat at Newmarket.

XLVI **Mac Donogh** also from Duhallow in Co. Cork, with a seat at Kanturk.

XLVII **O'Keefe** from near Millstreet in Duhallow, Co. Cork.

LXIV **O'Doherty** Sir Cahir O'Doherty (1587–1608) of Inishowen in Co. Donegal.

LXV   **O'Reilly** 'Edmond O'Reilly of Kilnacrott, who died at a very advanced age in the year 1601' (*Tribes* 50). The O'Reillys were prominent in East Breifni (present-day Co. Cavan).

LXVI **O'Carrolls** of Ely, in present-day Co. Offaly.

LXIX **Barrons** the Maguires of Fermanagh.   **Cloneen** near Lisnaskea in Co. Fermanagh.

LXX   **Chief Barron** Conor Maguire.

LXXVI **Cappa** a Mac Carthy house in Co. Cork.

LXXXIII **Ara** the O'Haras, from Crebilly, Co. Antrim.

LXXXIV **keeps sawing** the 1852 edition footnotes these words as follows: 'i.e., O Hara himself. The translator is here very wide of the meaning. Aenghus's words are much more satiric. Why did he build his house on the road side to induce travellers to look for hospitality in a house where nothing is to be found but poverty; Why did he not build a hut far in the recesses of the mountains, where travellers would not have access to his door?' (*Tribes* 95)

LXXXV **Ard-Uladh** in east Co. Down, home of the Savage family.   **barnacle-snails** sea-snails that cling to rocks on the shore   **MacTavish** emended in the 1852 edition to 'Savadge'.

LXXXVI **O'Hanlon** from Mullagh, in Co. Armagh.   **Orrery's men** Orrery is actually in north Co. Cork; the original reads 'Orier', which is in east Armagh.

LXXXVIII **Rakes of Mallow** the title of a popular song; Mallow is in Co. Cork.

XCI   **Duhallow** a barony in Co. Cork; the original actually refers to a townland in Co. Clare.

XCII **Kyan O'Carroll**   see stanza LXVI, above.   **his rib** his wife (according to Genesis, Eve was created from Adam's rib).

XCIII **Fall out again** the 1852 edition footnotes this phrase as follows: 'This is in the true style of the satirist and the best stanza in the whole of this translation' (*Tribes* 102).

XCIV **Mac Mahon, the Red** from southwest Co. Clare.

xcvi **O'Brien (that's Donogh)** this is tersely footnoted 'This is not in the Irish original' in the 1852 edition (*Tribes* 101); the comment is true of the entire stanza. The stanza is scored through in the MS, but was nevertheless retained in the 1852 edition.

c   **Macan** from Clanbrassil, Co. Armagh.

civ   **O'Meagher** from near Roscrea, Co. Tipperary. Having actually uttered a more satiric verse than Mangan's translation suggests, O'Daly was stabbed to death by a servant of O'Meagher (see *Tribes* 85).

Consolation and Counsel

11   **Inisfail** Ireland.

31   *Une nation d'enfants* 'a nation of children'; the source of this epithet is untraced.

35   **Clootzes, Dantons, Lafayettes** Jean Baptiste, Baron de Cloots (1755–94), also known as Anacharsis Cloots, a Prussian aristocrat who became an enthusiastic supporter of the French Revolution, advocating international revolution and styling himself '*orateur du genre humain*'. Robespierre had him guillotined in the Terror. Georges-Jacques Danton (1759–94) was a noted orator and a revolutionary leader; his disapproval of Reign of Terror led to his own death on the guillotine. The marquis de La Fayette (1757–1834) fought in the American and French Revolutions and served in the French chamber of deputies in the early nineteenth century.

60   **Plato's vizard** a mask; Plato's theories suggest that the empirical world is merely a shadowy representation of true reality.

62   **Howard or Haughton** John Howard (1726–90), English philanthropist; James Haughton (1795–1873), Irish philanthropist, and supporter of the Repeal and temperance movements. According to O'Donoghue, Mangan sought Haughton's financial help early in 1848 (see O'Donoghue 204).

When Hearts Were Trumps!

3n   from Galatians 5:9.

5–6   **GOD revealed … Moses** see Exodus 24: 15–17.

11   **Gall's and Spurzheim's bumps** Franz Joseph Gall (1758–1828) and Johan Christoph Spurzheim (1776–1829) were noted practitioners of phrenology, which purported to be able to analyse personality from an examination of the shape of the skull.

17   **CLUBS …' Ninety-three** a reference to the Jacobin clubs of the French revolution.

21 24   *Our* **CLUBS … them** the nationalist Confederate Clubs, which were set up by seceders from the Repeal Association in 1847. The Clubs were suppressed by the government ('Castle-Hercules' alludes to Dublin Castle) on 26 July 1848.

34   *couleur-de-rose* rosy-coloured.

35   **Brummell's gloves and D'Orsay's pumps** a reference to two famous London dandies: George Bryan ('Beau') Brummell (1778–1840) and Alfred Guillaume Gabriel, Count d'Orsay (1801–52).

Prose

An Extraordinary Adventure in the Shades

1   *de mortuis nil nisi bonum* 'only speak well of the dead'.

2   **Byron for Bentham** abandon Byronic romanticism for the rational utiltarianism of Jeremy Bentham (1748–1832).

3   *Tout est perdu, mes amis* 'All is lost, my friends'.

4   **Shades Tavern** the Royal Shades tavern in the Royal Arcade in College Green; it burned down in 1837.

5   **beaver** hat made of beaver-skin.

6   *stückweise* piecemeal.

7   *Quarterly Reviewer* the *Quarterly Review* was a conservative journal founded in 1809 to counter the liberal *Edinburgh Review*. Contributors such as John Wilson Croker were known for the severe character of their critical writings.

8   **Professor Wilson** John Wilson (1785–1854), professor of moral philosophy at Edinburgh University, and contributor to the conservative *Blackwood's Edinburgh Magazine*.

9   **Ahesuerus** the name of the legendary 'Wandering Jew' in the German version of the tale. He was condemned to live as an outcast until the end of the world because he taunted Jesus on the way to the Crucifixion. Mangan's translation of Schubart's poem on the subject was published in the *DUM* (December 1837).

10   **Platonical theory** in the *Phaedo*, Plato outlines a theory of the immortality of the soul, including the idea that souls have the power to recollect their antenatal freedom.

11   *Tugendbund* an early nineteenth-century secret organization, influenced by the ideas of Herder and Fichte, founded to resist Napoleon's domination of Prussia. Its principal aim was 'to educate the masses and stimulate patriotic sentiment'.

12   **Orestes and Pylades** the son and nephew of Agamemnon; they were close friends.

13   **Cuvier** Georges, Baron Cuvier (1769–1832), French naturalist.

14   **Dr. Bowring** Sir John Bowring (1792–1872), poet, translator, diplomat and advocate of the theories of Jeremy Bentham. Mangan expressed admiration for Bowring several times in his work.

15   **pass the Rubicon** to take an irrevocable action; the crossing of the Rubicon river by Julius Caesar's army was considered an act of war by the Senate.

16   **wand of Prospero** Prospero is the magician hero of Shakespeare's *The Tempest*.

17   **lamp of Aladdin** the story of Aladdin's magic lamp is found in the *Arabian Nights*.

18   **violin of Paganini** Niccolò Paganini (1782–1840), Italian virtuoso performer and composer, noted for his flamboyant life and performance style, to the point that it was rumoured he had made a pact with the devil.

19   *March* **of Intellect . . .** *April* the joke is given in full in Mangan's unpublished letter to Tynan (1832); see p. 437, above.

20   *con amore* with love.

21   **Calderon** Pedro Calderón de la Barca (1600–81), Spanish dramatist.

22   **Corneille** Pierre Corneille (1606–84), French dramatist.

23   **Malherbe** François de Malherbe (1555–1628), French poet.

24   **Voltaire** (1694–1778), French author and philosopher.

25   **Opitz** Martin Opitz von Boberfeld (1597–1639), German poet.

26   **Canitz** Freidrich Rudolf, Freiherr von Canitz (1654–99), German satirist.

27   **Uz** Johann Peter Uz (1720–96), German poet.

28   **Wieland** Christoph Martin Wieland (1733–1813), German poet and novelist.

29   **Richter . . . habe** Jean Paul Richter (1763–1825), German poet and humourist. The German phrase may be translated: 'Richter of my heart—(ah! if I have a heart).'

30   **Reverend Ned Irving** Edward Irving (1792–1834), noted Scottish fundamentalist minister who preached the imminence of the Second Coming, and who believed strongly in the phenomenon of 'speaking in tongues'.

31   **great Utilitarian** Bowring.

32   *Westminster* the radical *Westminster Review*, founded by Bentham and edited and managed by John Bowring.

33   **Oliver Yorke** pen-name of Francis Mahony, or Fr Prout (1804–66), poet and journalist, and frequent contributor to *Fraser's Magazine*.

34   **Lardner** Dionysius Lardner (1793–1859), Irish scientist, steam enthusiast and encyclopaedist, a target of Prout's satiric attacks.

35   **Cassius-like** cf. 'Cassius has a lean and hungry look', *Julius Caesar* (I.ii.193).

36   *enbonpoint* in good condition.

37   **Alnascher** see note to line 32 of 'Eighteen Hundred and Fifty', p. 465 above.

38   **discuss** to dispel (arch.).

39   **tower of Lebanon** from Song of Solomon 7: 4: 'thy nose is as the tower of Lebanon which looketh towards Damascus'.

40   MAUGRABY the magician who is subject of several tales in the *Continuation of the Arabian Nights* by Dom Chavis and Jacques Cazotte (first published in French between 1788–93).

41   *de haut en bas* 'from top to bottom'.

42   **Sir Morgan O'Doherty** pen-name of Irish satirist and journalist William Maginn (1793–1842), who contributed to *Blackwood's* and *Fraser's Magazines*.

43   *manches à gigot* leg-of-mutton sleeve.

44   *Lock-und-Gunkel-Werk* trickery.

45   *materiel* physical being.

46   **Berkeleyans** Irish philosopher George Berkeley (1685–1753), who argued our knowledge is based upon our perception of what is, rather than direct knowledge of objects external to the mind.

47   **deeper than ever plummet sounded** *Tempest* (V.i.56).

48   **Thunderer** *The Times* of London.

49   **legerdemain** slight of hand.

50   **Balance of Power** the phrase came into widespread use after the Napoleonic wars; it referred to political equilibrium among the major powers Russia, France, Prussia, Austria and Britain.

51   *Slawkenbergius . . . Nosology* Slawkenbergius is a character in *Tristram Shandy* by Laurence Sterne (1713–68); he is the supposed author of a treatise on noses. In fact 'nosology' means the classification of diseases (from Greek *nosos*, disease).

52   **my final . . . despair** from *Paradise Lost* (II, 142–3).

53   **Anacharsis Clootz** see note to line 35 of 'Consolation and Counsel', p. 484 above.

54   *pour toute compagnie* 'for my only company'.

55   **Dom-Daniel** Maugraby's immense hall where sorcerers and evil spirits gathered to pay homage to Satan.

56   **The morn . . . tomb** see Byron, *Childe Harold* (III, xcviii).

57   **Dr. Stokes** perhaps the noted Dublin scholar and physician Whitley Stokes (1763–1845), but more probably his physician son William (1804–78). The latter attended Mangan as he lay dying at the Meath hospital in 1849.

58   **BRASSPEN** pen-name of Joseph L'Estrange, one of the contributors to *The Comet* satirical newspaper, in which this story appeared.

59   *Tout est ... croire* 'All is mystery in this world; I don't know what to think of it.'

A Treatise on a Pair of Tongs

1   *Sure such ... formed* from Richard Brinsley Sheridan, *The Duenna* (1776; II.ii).

2   *Why, man ... Colossus Julius Caesar* (I.ii).

3   **Celestial Empire** China.

4   *materiel* physical matter.

5   **post octavo** a paper size for book-printing.

6   **New Burlington Street** London street address of publisher Henry Colburn.

7   **Bulwer and D'Israeli** Edward George Bulwer-Lytton (1803–73), English politician and prolific novelist, friend of Benjamin Disraeli (1804–81), English novelist and, after 1838, Tory politician. Both were published by Colburn.

8   **Colburn's lunacy** see preceding note.

9   **Spirit of the *Age*** puns on *The Age*, a London newspaper that was partly a model for the *Comet*.

10   **surphiz** puns on 'phiz', meaning 'face'.

11   **Cartesius** René Descartes (1596–1650), French rationalist philosopher.

12   **Burked** probably a pun on the word 'burke' (to smother, or suppress an inquiry), after the name of the nineteenth-century murderer William Burke.

13   **Schelling** Friedrich Wilhelm Joseph von Schelling (1775–1854), German romantic philosopher.

14   **Gassendi** Pierre Gassendi (1592–1655), French philosopher.

15   **Reid** Thomas Reid (1710–96), Scottish 'common-sense' philosopher.

16   **Mallebranche** Nicolas Malebranche (1638–1715), French theologian.

17   **Wolfe** perhaps Christian Wolff (1657–1754), German philosopher.

18   **Leibnitz** Gottfried Wilhelm Leibniz (1646–1716), German philosopher.

19   *in esse vel posse* 'in actuality or possibility'.

20   **Reid's Powers** *Essays on the Intellectual Powers of Man* (1785) by Thomas Reid.

21   **Mill's Phenomen** *Analysis of the Phenomena of the Human Mind* (1829) by English utilitarian James Mill (1773–1836).

22   **Brown's Philosophy** *Lectures on the Philosophy of the Human Mind* (1820) by Scottish philosopher Thomas Brown (1778–1820), an admirer of Thomas Reid.

23   **muddler** a mixing stick for drinks.

24   **Philander** pen-name of John Sheehan (1812–82), co-founder of the *Comet*.

25   **Bully's Acre** burial ground in Kilmainham used by the poor of Dublin.

26   **Brobdignagian** the land of Brobdingnag in Swift's *Gulliver's Travels* (1726) is populated by giants.

27   *De l'autre coté* 'on the other hand'.

28   **Trenck in Magdeburgh** Friedrich, Freiherr von der Trenck (1726–94); German writer who was imprisoned in the prison of Magdeburgh for ten years.

29   **Tasso in Ferrara** Torquato Tasso (1544–95), Italian poet who was incarcerated for seven years in an asylum by the Duke of Ferrara.

30   **Galileo in Florence** Galileo Galilei (1564–1642), Italian astronomer was under house arrest in Florence for the last eight years of his life.

31   **Philander, in Kilmainham** John Sheehan (see note to 'Philander', above) was imprisoned for libel in Kilmainham gaol for several weeks in 1833, based upon an anti-clerical article published in the *Comet*.

32   **under Dunn** George Dunn was the warden of Kilmainham gaol.

33   *sal volatile* smelling salts.

34   *Eglantine* Mangan addressed his sonnet 'Symptom of the Disease of the Heart' to 'Eglantine' (published in the *Comet*, 17 March 1833).

35   **Zeno** Greek philosopher (fl. 420 BC), famous for his paradoxes.

36   **bam** a hoax.

37   **Robert Owen** Welsh-born social reformer and utopian (1771–1858). His ideal communities were to live in large structures arranged in the form of a parallelogram or square.

38   **Tom Steele** (1788–1848), a ardent supporter of O'Connell, given the title of 'Head Pacificator' by the latter. He often took the chair at Repeal Association meetings.

39   *solus* alone.

40   **Brougham's Useless Knowledge-books** Henry Peter, Lord Brougham and Vaux (1778–1868), Lord Chancellor 1830–34. In the mid-1820s he helped found the Society for the Diffusion of Useful Knowledge, intended to make good books available at low prices to the working class.

41   **Bowring** Sir John Bowring (1792–1872) a translator, diplomat and political economist; he published translations form more than twenty languages. He also figures in 'An Extraordinary Adventure in the Shades'.

42   **be slowly . . . sway** adapted from l. 209 of 'The Pleasures of Melancholy' by Thomas Warton (1728–90).

43   **Dr. Southey** Robert Southey (1774–1843), poet laureate. Mangan had already criticised Southey in his 'Sonnets by an Aristocrat' (*Comet* 24 June 1833): 'Southey who strings / Hexameters for butts of sack'.

44   **William Godwin** English novelist and political theorist, (1756–1836), author of *St Leon* (1799).

45   **Helvetius** Claude-Adrien Helvétius (1715–71), French philosopher; his work *De l'esprit* (1758) was highly controversial for its attack on religious morality.

46   **it is better . . . stone** a slight misquotation.

47   **black stock** the necktie of a clergyman.

48   **sumph** fool.

49   **forty-quill** a quill is a pen.

50   **Crichton** James Crichton (1560–82), Scottish man of letters, known as 'the Admirable Crichton;' on his arrival in Paris he is said to have posted a challenge to dispute in verse or prose, on any subject, whether in Hebrew, Syriac, Arabic, Greek, Latin, Spanish, French, Italian, English, Dutch, Flemish or Slavonian.

51   *c'est là . . . finie* 'the matter is settled'.

52   **Saint Dunstan** archbishop of Canterbury (924–88), who was accused of practising black magic, and was said to have tweaked the nose of the devil with a pair of red-hot tongs.

53   **Reform Bill** puns on the Reform Bill passed by the British parliament in 1832.

54   **COMET CLUB** founded as an anti-tithe organisation in 1831 by John Sheehan, Samuel Lover, John Cornelius O'Callaghan and others. The Comet Club published two volumes of the popular satiric *Parson's Horn-Book* in 1831, and established the *Comet* newspaper on 1 May 1831. The motto of the *Comet* was 'Knowledge is Power'.

55 **Allied Powers** in the early nineteenth century, this generally meant the 'Five Powers' of Russia, Austria, Prussia, France and Britain.

56 **Any allusion . . . PHIL.** the editor of the London *Morning Chronicle* was John Black.

57 **Grey-headed** Charles, Lord Grey (1764–1845) was then prime minister.

58 **Blue-devilled** 'blue devils' were low spirits.

59 **on the *Globe*, under the *Sun*** English newspapers.

60 *pia mater* brain.

61 **laugh with . . . laughter** Shelley, *Prometheus Unbound* (IV, 334).

62 **Francis Blackburne** (1782–1867), attorney-general for Ireland (1831–35).

63 **William Coyngham Plunket** (1764–1854), lord chancellor of Ireland (1830–34, 1835–41).

64 **posting the *coal*** 'coal' was slang for money; the phrase means 'pay down the money'.

65 **a better on the *Turf*** puns on 'turf' in its meanings as 'fuel' and 'horse-racing'.

66 **Coke on Littleton** refers to the edition of Littleton's 15th-century *Treatise on Tenures* by Sir Edward Coke (1628).

67 **Blackstone's Commentaries** famous legal text, *Commentaries on the Laws of England* by Sir William Blackstone (published 1765–1769).

68 *Black burn* see note to 'Blackburne', above.

69 **Dey of Algiers** the last Dey of Algiers was deposed after a French invasion in 1830.

70 **Charles X** French king (1757–1836); he abdicated after the July Revolution of 1830.

71 *Pommade divine* 'pomade divine', a fragrant hair preparation.

72 *ex uno disce omnes* 'you may infer all from one instance'.

73 **Moses Cohen** proprietor of a cigar divan (smoking-room) and shop located in Dame St, Dublin, mentioned also in the poem 'A Railway of Rhyme' (1835).

74 **Ten things . . . TONGS** this passage is adapted from the fifth section of the Mishnah, the codification of Jewish oral law. Tongs do appear in the list. The 'Shameer' was a special engraving stone associated with the Tabernacle.

75 *ens rationis* a being that exists only in the mind.

76 **My occupation's gone** *Othello* (III.iii.360).

77 *Airy tongs . . . wildernesses* from Milton, *Comus* (III, 208–9): 'And airy tongues, that syllable men's names / On Sands, and Shores, and desert Wildernesses.'

78 **King Tongataboo** Tongatabu is the largest of the Tonga Islands in the south Pacific.

79 *pour couper court* 'to be brief'.

80 **Das Jahrhundert . . . werden** from Schiller, *Don Carlos* (1787; III.x).

81 **Every one . . . .. stockings** Henry William Paget, Marquess of Anglesey (1768–1854) arrived in Dublin for his second term as Lord Lieutenant in December 1830. Marcus Costello, an O'Connellite, stood in a window in College Green and held up a black stocking with a pair of tongs as Anglesey's procession passed by, thereby mocking Anglesey's loss of a leg at the battle of Waterloo. Mangan also plays on this for his puns immediately following: 'game' (meaning 'lame') and 'blacklegs'.

82 *White feet* the name of a secret agrarian movement in the 1830s.

83 *l-e-g* when the names of the letters are pronounced, sounds like 'elegy'.

My Bugle, and How I Blow It

1 **ED. VIN.** the footnote is by editor of the *Vindicator*, Charles Gavan Duffy. For the phrase 'inextinguishable laughter' see note 61 to *A Treatise on a Pair of Tongs*, above.

2   **German poet** the poem is 'Alphorn' by Justinus Kerner (1786–1862); Mangan published an earlier translation of the poem the *DUM* in August 1836.

3   **in *medias* res** from Horace, *Ars Poetica*; the classical epic conventionally opens 'in the middle of things'.

4   **give my . . . words** *Othello* (III.iii.136–7).

5   **Sam Slick . . . responsibility** a reference to the satiric *The Clockmaker, or the Sayings and Doings of Samuel Slick of Slickville* (3 vols, 1836–40) by Canadian Thomas Chandler Haliburton (1796–1865). The work is full of colloquial sayings that became commonplace. The 'cloud-blower' (pipe-smoker) is Nick Bradshaw, but he does not in fact use the catchphrase cited by Mangan.

6   **Swabian** in southwestern Germany.

7   **the first demonologist in Europe** Kerner published extensively on ghosts and spiritualism.

8   **light of my countenance** from Job 29: 24.

9   **King of the Sicilies** Ferdinand II (1810–59) became King of the Two Sicilies in 1830; he was viewed as a liberal reformer at the start of his reign.

10   *Jacques Corveau* 'Jim Crow', stereotyped figure from the American minstrel tradition, invented in 1828 by Thomas Dartmouth Rice. Rice performed a famous dance to a song which included the chorus: 'Wheel about, an' turn about, an' do jis so; / Eb'ry time I wheel about, I jump Jim Crow.' Rice performed at the Theatre Royal in Dublin in April and May 1839.

11   *lorgnette* eyeglasses with a handle.

12   **sumph** fool.

13   **Corn-Law Repealer** the campaign for repeal of the protectionist Corn Laws began in Manchester in 1839 and was eventually successful in 1846.

14   **understand trapp** to recognise one's own interests.

15   **flash vocabulary** 'slang'.

16   **the Sulphur Question** in 1838 Ferdinand granted the monopoly on the trade in Sicilian sulphur to France, precipitating a dispute with Britain which had previously had most favoured status in the trade. The monopoly was abolished in July 1840.

17   **bowl of bishop** mulled port wine.

18   **a bitter change . . . severe** from *Night Thoughts* by Edward Young (1683–1765): 'Though now restored, 'tis only change of pain, / (A bitter change!) severer for severe' (I, 14).

19   **the great Metropolis** title of a book about London by James Grant, published in 1836.

20   **fold over fold . . . convolved** a misremembering of Wordsworth's lines from 'Yew-trees', ll. 16–18: '. . . intertwisted fibres serpentine / Up-coiling, and inveterately convolved.'

21   *Cœlum non animam mutant qui trans mare currunt* from Horace, *Epistles*: 'They change the sky, not their character, [those] who rush across the sea.'

22   **Brougham or Bombastes Paracelsus** Lord Brougham and Vaux (see note 40, p. 488, above); Theophrastus Bombastus von Hohenheim, known as Paracelsus (1493–1541), Swiss alchemist.

23   **The earth . . . hath** *Macbeth* (I.iii.79).

24   **Mrs. Trollope** English novelist Frances Trollope (1780–1863); in her *Domestic Manners of the Americans* (1832) she complained that 'My general appellation amongst my neighbours was "the English old woman", but in mentioning each other they constantly employed the term "lady".'

25   *à l'enfant* in the fashion of a child.

26   *non-ens* non-being.

27   *Mettez cela . . . fumez-le* unidiomatic but literal translation of: 'put that in your pipe and smoke it'.

28   **Goldsmith said of the World** perhaps an allusion to a passage in *The Citizen of the World* (1762) by Oliver Goldsmith, in which the narrator speaks of his entry into a prison: 'I was now on one side of the door, and those who were confined were on the other; this was all the difference between us.'

29   **Slawkenbergius** see note 51 to 'An Extraordinary Adventure in the Shades', p. 486, above.

30   *tours de phrase* turns of phrase.

31   **the Fifteen Acres** a duelling place in the Phoenix Park, Dublin.

32   **a powerful preventative check** a phrase misquoted from *Illustrations of Political Economy* (1832–33) by Harriet Martineau (1802–76). Martineau, in popularizing the theories of Thomas Malthus, adapted his distinction between a voluntary 'preventive check' on population increase, such as anticipation of the difficulties of rearing a family, and a more severe 'positive check', such as actual poverty. Martineau writes of the timely use of the 'mild preventative check'.

33   *bienséances* proprieties.

34   **cotton, muslin . . . puzzling** Byron, *Don Juan* (I, xii).

35   **Robert Owen** Welsh-born social reformer and utopian (1771–1858).

36   **split the ears of the groundlings** *Hamlet* (III.ii.10–11).

37   **with bated . . . humbleness** *Merchant of Venice* (I.iii.119).

38   **How like . . . looks** *Merchant of Venice* (I.iii.36).

39   **the book that goes by that title** the joke book *Wit and Wisdom, or the World's Jest Book* (1826).

40   **all the town's . . . fogroms** adapted from *As You Like It* (II.vii.139–40): 'All the world's a stage, / and all the men and women merely players.' A fogram is an old-fashioned person, a 'fogy'.

41   **Van Woedenblock** folkloric figure from Rotterdam with a magical wooden leg; Mangan published a poem entitled 'Myhneer Van Woodenblock' in the *DUM* in August 1838.

42   **Schubart's Wandering Jew** see note 9 to 'An Extraordinary Adventure in the Shades', p. 485 above. The quotation is a translation of the third line of Schubart's poem.

43   **I pass . . . land** Coleridge, 'The Rime of the Ancient Mariner', l. 586.

44   **Tramp, tramp . . . sea** adapted from a refrain in Sir Walter Scott's 'William and Helen' (1796), in which a demonic horseman carries away a young lover to her death.

45   **The race . . . be** Byron, *Childe Harold* (III, lxx).

from *'Anthologia Germanica' series*
Mangan published 22 'Anthologia Germanica' articles in the *DUM* between 1835 and 1846.

1   **εισ νομοσ το δοξαν ποιητη** source untraced; may be translated as 'the only law for the poet is the poet's belief'.

2   *Faust* Goethe's drama, in two parts (1808, 1832). Mangan translated passages of Part I of *Faust* in the article from which this extract is taken (*DUM*, March 1836).

3   **Utilitarianism** in utilitarian theory, value is determined by the ability of an action to promote a desired end.

4   **The world . . . them** adapted from Wordsworth's sonnet, 'The world is to much with us; late and soon' (1807).

5   **human face divine** *Paradise Lost* (III, 44).

6   *au fond* fundamentally.

7   **rhodomontade** bragging speech.

8   **a prophet . . . country** John 4: 44.

9   *lieber Deutschland* 'dear Germany'.

10   **Tiedge** Christoph August Tiedge (1752–1841).

11   **Hölty** Ludwig Heinrich Christoph Hölty (1748–76).

12   **Klopstock** Friedrich Gottlieb Klopstock (1724–1803).

13   **Bürger** Gottfried August Bürger (1747–94).

14   **Werner** Friedrich Ludwig Zacharias Werner (1768–1823).

15   **Schubart** Christian Freidrich Daniel Schubart (1739–91).

16   **Tieck** Ludwig Tieck (1773–1853).

17   **Novalis** Friedrich Leopold, Freiherr von Herdenberg Novalis (1772–1801).

18   **Magnetic Mountain** in the 'Tale of the Third Calendar' in the Arabian Nights, the magnetic power of this mountain draws the nails and iron out of the hero's ship, causing it to break up.

19   **these Anthologia** Mangan published 22 'Anthologia Germanica' articles in the *DUM* between 1834 and 1846.

20   **the experimentalist in Gulliver** in Gulliver's voyage to Laputa in *Gulliver's Travels* (1726) he encounters the Legado Academy.

21   **Ludwig Tieck** (1773–1853), German poet and collector of folktales.

22   **Newgate Calendar** a biographical account of notorious inmates incarcerated in London's Newgate prison, published in the 1820s.

23   **make his quietus** see *Hamlet* (III.i.75–6).

24   **pestered by a popinjay** see *1 Henry IV* (I.iii.49).

25   **Tristram Shandy's uncle** uncle Toby, from Laurence Sterne's comic novel *Tristram Shandy* (1767).

26   **Gulliver . . . Lilliputians** in Jonathan Swift's *Gulliver's Travels* (1726), Gulliver is attacked by six-inch-tall Lilliputians.

27   **my wound . . . small** a line wrongly attributed to Dryden in a comic story that features in Joseph Spence's *Anecdotes* (1820).

28   *sous silence* in silence.

29   **Atlas** in Greek mythology, one of the Titans who was punished by having to hold aloft the heavens. Statues normally represented him as carrying a celestial globe.

30   **Fergusson . . . front** probably Robert Fergusson (1750–74), Scottish poet. The quotation is untraced.

31   **parterre** an ornamental garden.

32   **dies of one . . . pain** Alexander Pope, *Essay on Man* (I, 200): 'Dies of a rose in aromatic pain?'

33   **the frogs in the fable** from Aesop's fable of 'The Boys and the Frogs'.

34   **rack-rent** an Irish term for exhorbitant and unjust rent.

35   **Sindbad in the Valley of Diamonds** see Sindbad's second voyage in the *Arabian Nights*.

36   **author of Hudibras** Samuel Butler (1612–80).

37   **Pain is . . . height** from Butler's 'Repartees between Cat and Puss', ll. 57–8.

38   **Zeno** Greek philosopher (fl. fifth century BC).

39   **Brother Jack in** *Tale of a Tub* a character representing Calvinism in Swift's satire (1704).

40   **Zobeide's porter** from the 'Story of the Three Calendars, Sons of Kings, and of Five Ladies of Bagdad' in the *Arabian Nights*.

from *'Literæ Orientales' series*
Mangan published six of these articles in *DUM* betwen 1835 and 1846.

1   **Poussin** Nicolas Poussin (1593–1665), French painter. Mangan refers to Poussin's painting of 'The Arcadian Shepherds' in his epigraph to 'A Vision of Connaught in the Thirteenth Century' (1846).

2   **Greater and Lesser Lights of Dante's Paradiso** in the *Paradiso* of Dante Aligheri, the souls of the blessed appear as lights whose brightness derives from their virtue.

3   **The savage . . . shore** from 'The Irishman' by James Orr (1770–1816).

4   **Houzouana** Hottentots.

5   **La Vaillant** François Levaillant (1753–1824), French traveller, author of *Voyages dans l'intérieur de l'Afrique*.

6   **space between Dan and Beersheeba** a biblical phrase meaning all of Israel.

7   **Segur** Philippe-Paul, comte de Ségur (1780–1873), French general and historian, author of *Histoire de Napoléon* (1825).

8   **the unreached . . . despair** from *Childe Harold* (IV, cxxii).

9   *perdu* lost.

10   **Mareses** a reference to a legend concerning the veiled statue in the Egyptian city of Sais, which when observed directly caused madness or death. Mangan translated Schiller's poetic version of the tale as 'The Veiled Image at Saïs' (*DUM*, November 1847).

11   *reveurs* dreamers.

12   **mother of science . . . gods** quotation untraced.

13   **seraph over the Prohibited Walls** see Genesis 3:24.

14   [Mangan's footnote] The French may be translated: 'The ruins of Chelimnar display the remains of over two hundred pillars and one thousand three hundred figures of men or animals. Can two centuries have sufficed to produce so numerous pieces of work? In the known world only the Pyramids of Egypt can be compared to those majestic ruins. When we remember, however, that all the Egyptians had to do in order to build the pyramids was to employ crowds of unskilled workers and that those huge heaps of stones show no reliefs or figures, we cannot but place them below the Chelminar monuments.' The quote is from Gaspard Michel Leblond (1738–1809), French archaeologist.

15   **Tabor** Mt Tabor, scene of Christ's transfiguration.

16   **the Mythi of the breast** quotation untraced.

17   **This is . . . land** Walter Scott, *Lay of the Last Minstrel* (VI, i).

18   *niaiseries* inanities.

19   **the god kissing carrion** from *Hamlet* (II.ii.181–2).

20   **cavil on . . . hair** from *1 Henry IV* (III.i.139).

21   **Every religious . . . poet** in fact Shelley argues the reverse case in *A Defence of Poetry* (published 1840), remarking that great poets are 'philosophers of the very highest power'. He argues that poetry is a means by which religion is restored to its true source, but is critical of orthodox and institutionalised forms of religion.

22   **Yea, and . . . also** Luke 14:26.

from introduction to *Poets and Poetry of Munster*
Copy-text is MS 90 (Gilbert Collection) in the Dublin Public Library, Pearse Street. A revised version of Mangan's introduction was published posthumously in the first edition of *PPM* in November 1849, but did not include the extract represented here.

1   **Semiramus, Helen or Medea** Semiramus, legendary Assyrian queen celebrated by Greek historians Herotodus and Diodorus; Helen of Troy, immortalised by Homer's *Iliad*; and Medea, legendary enchantress who assisted Jason in capturing the Golden Fleece and who featured in works by Euripides and Ovid.

2   **Deirdre, Blahmuid, or Cearnuit** female figures from the Ulster cycle of mythic tales.

3   **Aoibhill, Chria, or Aine** goddesses from Munster folklore; 'banshee' means fairy-woman.

4   **Hedge-school** informal schools for the peasantry common in late 18th and early 19th-century Ireland; Mangan claimed his father was a hedge-school master before coming to Dublin in the 1790s.

from 'Sketches and Reminiscences of Irish Writers' series
Ten of these 'Sketches', including an autobiographical one attributed to 'E.W'. were published in *DUM* betwen 1835 and 1850.

1   **Charles Maturin** (1780–1824), novelist, dramatist and Church of Ireland clergyman.

2   **Dr. Anster** John Anster (1793–1867), noted translator of Goethe's *Faust* and friend of Mangan's.

3   **Bertram** the title of Maturin's highly successful play, first performed in London in 1816.

4   **three-corned** three-cornered.

5   **Man, being . . . drunk** Byron, *Don Juan* (II, clxxix).

6   **Souvent de tous . . . pire** 'Often, of all our ills, reason is the worst', from *Satire iv* by Nicolas Boileau (1636–1711).

7   **averse from life** from Byron's *Manfred* (III, i.138): 'Because my nature was averse from life'.

8   **Charles Lamb** (1775–1834), English writer.

9   **two Kings . . . nosegay** an allusion to the satiric play *The Rehearsal* (1671), by George Villiers, 2nd Duke of Buckingham; in the stage tradition, the two actors playing the 'kings of Brentford' entered in Act II, scene ii 'smelling at one nosegay'.

10   **Bajazet** probably the famous Ottoman sultan Bayezid II (1448–1512), to whom Mangan also refers in *A Triplet, on the Reign of the Great Sultan*, p. 55, above.

11   **the Cid** eleventh-century Castilian warrior, celebrated in the Spanish medieval epic 'Song of the Cid'.

12   **that within . . . show** adapted from *Hamlet* (I.ii.85).

13   **the thunder scars** Byron, *Manfred* (III.iv.76–77): 'Ah! he unveils his aspect: on his brow / The thunder-scars are graven.'

14   **affectation of singularity** a phrase used by Samuel Johnson in his preface to the *Plays of Shakespeare* (1765): Johnson argues that his divergences from current opinion of Shakespeare are not simply an 'affectation of singularity'.

15   **the observed of all observers** *Hamlet* (III.i.156).

16   **Paternoster-row** a London street noted for its booksellers and publishers.

17   **Montorio** Maturin's first novel (1807).

18   **The Milesian Chief** published in 1812.

19   **Woman** *Women; or, Pour et Contre* (1818).

20   **like a volcano from the sea** from chapter 2 of Part II of the novel *Contarini Fleming* (1832) by Benjamin Disraeli (1804–81): 'He rose up, as I spoke, like a volcano out of the sea.'

21   **Zanga** a character in Edward Young's play *The Revenge* (1721).

22   **small numskull of Jeffrey** Mangan attributes this remark to Irish journalist and poet William Maginn (1793–1842), who contributed to *Fraser's* and *Blackwood's* magazines; Francis Jeffrey (1773–1850) was the editor of the liberal *Edinburgh Review*. Jeffrey was a harsh critic of Wordsworth and Byron.

23   **tenth wave** Mangan's attribution is incorrect; the phrase is from Ovid, *Metamorphoses* (XI, 530).

24   **When great . . . vitals** The final sentence of *Women* actually reads: 'When great talents are combined with calamity, their union forms the *tenth wave* of human suffering—grief becomes

inexhaustible from the unhappy fertility of genius, and the serpents that devour us, are generated out of our own vitals.'

25 **Melmoth** *Melmoth the Wanderer* (1820).

26 **The Wild Irish Boy** published in 1808, a response to Lady Morgan's *The Wild Irish Girl* (1806).

27 **The Albigenses** Maturin's final novel (1824).

28 **the author of 'Caleb Williams'** William Godwin (1756–1836); the novel was published in 1794.

29 **George Petrie** (1790–1866), noted antiquarian, artist, editor and collector of music. Mangan was employed as a copyist under his direction in the Ordnance Survey office, 1838–41. Petrie also edited the *Dublin Penny Journal* (1832–33) and the *Irish Penny Journal* (1840–41), to both of which Mangan contributed.

30 **Barber's five brothers** in fact the Barber in the *Arabian Nights* has six brothers.

31 **Zeyn Alasnam, King of the Genii** in fact, in the *Arabian Nights* tale, 'Prince Zeyn Alasnam' and the 'King of the Genii' are separate characters.

32 **Irish Pillar Towers** Petrie's most famous antiqarian work was his *Essay on the Round Towers of Ireland* (1833), in which he argued that the round towers were of Christian monastic origin rather than pagan or Oriental.

33 **besom-like** broom-like.

34 **Phidias** Greek sculptor (fl. 5th century BC), directed the artistic work on the Parthenon.

35 **Canova** Antonio Canova (1757–1822), Italian neoclassical sculptor.

36 **rites and mysteries of ancient Egypt** scholarly and popular interest in ancient Egypt became fashionable following Napoleon's invasion of Egypt in 1798 and the recovery of the Rosetta stone, which enabled the decipherment of hieroglyphic texts and inscriptions.

37 **John Anster** (1793–1867) poet and translator, and friend of Mangan, who published an acclaimed translation of Part 1 of Goethe's *Faust* in 1835.

38 **Carleton** William Carleton (1794–1869), novelist and short-story writer, and frequent contributor to the *DUM*.

39 **May-day Night Scene** one of two scenes from *Faust* that Shelley translated.

40 **deeper than . . . sounded** *The Tempest* (V.i.56).

41 **Blackie** John Stuart Blackie (1809–95) published a translation of Part 1 of *Faust*.

42 **Maria Edgeworth** (1767–1849), Irish novelist.

43 **Laura Matildas** Mangan's composite of 'Laura Maria', pen-name of Mary Robinson (1758–1800) and 'Anna Matilda', pen-name of Hanna Cowley (1743–1809); both were popular writers of the late 18th century.

44 **Charlotte Smith** (1749–1806) English poet and novelist.

45 **on the *qui vivre*** 'on the lookout'.

46 **Belinda . . . Ennui** *Belinda* (1801), *Patronage* (1814), *Manoeuvring* (1809), *Ennui* (1809).

47 **Pope's poems** the heroine of *The Rape of the Lock* (1714) is named Belinda.

48 **Popular Tales** published 1804.

49 **is no more** Edgeworth died on 22 May 1849, four days before the publication of Mangan's article.

50 **William Maginn** (1793–1842), Cork-born poet and journalist who moved to England in 1823. He was a frequent contributor to *Fraser's* and *Blackwood's* magazines, for which he created the character of 'Sir Morgan O'Doherty'. His alcohol addiction contributed to his early death.

51 **written in water** John Keats (1795–1823) desired that the following words should be inscribed on his tomb: 'Here lies one whose name was writ in water.'

52   **Joseph Brenan** see note to 'A Word in Reply to Joseph Brenan', p. 479, above.

53   **Hafiz** (1325–89), Persian poet from Shiraz, in present-day Iran. Mangan in fact did not publish any translations from Hafiz; his 'Ode of Hafiz' (see p. 293 above) is entirely original. John Mitchel repeats this anecdote in his introduction to *Poems by James Clarence Mangan* (1859).

54   **sins . . . children** see Numbers 14:18.

55   **spoon** a simpleton.

56   **'Tis a mad world, my masters!** title of a comedy (1604) by Thomas Middleton.

57   **Sanconiatho** Sanchuniathon, priest of ancient Phoenicia whose lost works are citied as a source by the historian Philo of Byblos (1st century AD).

58   **Manetho, Berosus, and Ocellus Lucanus** ancient historians and philosophers; *CW* (VI, 343) points out that these three names, along with Sanconiatho, are mentioned together in chapter 14 of Oliver Goldsmith's *Vicar of Wakefield* (1766).

59   **a Proteus** an anonymous review of Mangan's *German Anthology* (1845) in the *Dublin Review* in December 1845 remarks that 'The writer is a complete literary Proteus.'

60   *Bismillah* an Arabic invocation: 'in the name of God.

61   **Ibn Khalakan** Abbas Ahmad ibn Khallikan (1211–82), an Arabian biographer. Mangan claimed to have translated a 'Ghazel' by him (see p. 314, above).

62   **Diemsheed and the Genii** untraced.

63   **Peter Schlemihl** a story by Adelbert von Chamisso (1781–1838), German poet.

64   **Benedict** a newly married man who has long been a bachelor (after the character in *Much Ado About Nothing*).

65   **Maledict** an accursed person.

66   **Hymen despatched Cupid and Plutus** Hymen was Greek goddess of marriage; Cupid the god of love and Plutus the god of wealth.

67   **Such tricks . . . imagination** *Midsummer Night's Dream* (V.i.18).

68   **Mr. Mooney** unidentified.

69   **'E.W.'** Mangan appears to have been responsible for the most, if not all, of the writing of this sketch; thus the identity alluded to by these initials remains a puzzle. It has been suggested that they stand for the poet 'Edward Walsh', though the writer of the sketch identifies himself at the beginning of Part II as 'a medical man' (see Shannon-Mangan, 270).

Autobiography
Copy-text is MS 12/P/18 (RIA). It seems to have been written in the autumn of 1848, while Mangan was living in Fishamble Street. C. P. Meehan published an edited version in the *Irish Monthly* in 1882, and again in the 1883 edition of *Poets and Poetry of Munster*. The MS is written in a music copy-book and ends in mid-sentence at the foot of the last page. No continuation of the text has ever been located. Passages marked for deletion in the MS have been here retained but scored through.

1   **A heavy . . . MASSINGER** this quotation has not been traced in the work of playwright Philip Massinger (1584–1639).

2   **Bonnet** Charles Bonnet (1720–93), Swiss naturalist. As he lay blind and dying from a painful illness, he is reported to have imagined that he saw his loyal servant stealing papers from his desk.

3   **Godwin** English novelist and political thinker William Godwin (1756–1836), his *Memoirs of the Author of 'A Vindication of the Rights of Woman'* (1798) contains some autobiographical elements.

4   **Byron** Lord Byron's MS memoirs were destroyed after his death by Thomas Moore and John Murray; however his letters and journals were edited and published by Moore in 1830.

5   **St. Augustine** (354–430) whose _Confessions_ tell of his conversion from a hedonistic and pagan life to Christianity.

6   **Rousseau** Jean-Jacques Rousseau (1712–78), whose _Confessions_ were published between 1782 and 1789.

7   **Charles Lamb** (1775–1834); his _Essays of Elia_ (1823, 1833) contained autobiographical elements.

8   **I cannot . . . could** from William Godwin's _St. Leon_ (1799), chapter 11: 'Know I would not if I could, and cannot if I would, repose the secrets that press upon me in more than a single bosom.'

9   **These things . . . sorrows** Matthew 24:8.

10   **My father** James Mangan (1765–1843); originally from Shanagolden, Co. Limerick, and perhaps a hedge-school teacher, he moved to Dublin and married Catherine Smith in 1798.

11   **Gasparo Bandollo** in fact the poem, based on an original by Chamisso, was not published until May 1849.

12   **O'Donovan, he . . . man** John O'Donovan (1801–61), scholar and friend of Mangan. Volumes 3, 4 and 5 of O'Donovan's seven-volume edition of the _Annals of the Four Masters_ were published in 1848. Mangan had assisted in copying for this work, and had also assisted with Owen Connellan's version of the _Annals_, published in 1846. The quotation is from O'Donovan's translation of the entry for the year 1342 (Mangan's footnote does not give the year): 'Matthew Mac Manus a general and wealthy Brughaidh _farmer_, who never rejected the countenance of man, whether mean or mighty, died' (III, 579.)

13   **my two brothers, and my sister** John Mangan (1804–35), who became a scrivener, and William Mangan (1808–?1850), who became a cabinet-maker and lived with James Clarence through the 1840s. No documentary record of the sister has been found.

14   **my mother** Catherine Smith (1771–1846), whose family came from Kiltale, Co. Meath and had property in the Fishamble St area of Dublin.

15   **assoil** absolve.

16   **retributive Providence** Mangan's footnote cites Nicolas Malebranche (1638–1715), Cartesian theologian. The doctrine that 'we see all things in God' ('nous voyons toutes choses en Dieu') is central to his metaphysics.

17   **The stars . . . Sisera** Judges 5:20.

18   **Mr. Courtney's Academy** a school run by Michael Courtney, who was also a contributor to the Dublin almanacs. Mangan habitually dropped six years from his age; in fact he first attended the school in 1814.

19   **Blair on the Death of Christ** a sermon by Scottish preacher Hugh Blair (1718–1800), anthologised in William Scott's popular nineteenth-century textbook _Lessons in Elocution_.

20   **apprenticed to a scriviner** Kenrick's at 6 York St., where Mangan began his apprenticeship in 1818.

21   **Thus bad . . . behind** _Hamlet_ (III.iv.181): 'Thus bad begins, and worse remains behind.'

22   **the dull . . . wood** from 'Work' by Charles Lamb (1775–1834), l. 6.

23   **Some lines . . . sixteen** A similar account accompanied the (posthumous) publication of this poem in the _Irishman_ on 23 June 1849: 'Some few of my readers, may, perhaps, take an interest in the following verses, from the fact that they were penned at the age of sixteen, and were the first I ever committed to paper. I had, indeed, forgotten their existence, and only happened to light on them while rummaging the contents of an old chest of mine, which for

twenty years had been consigned to a lumber-room.' Given Mangan's tendency to drop six years from his age, and the fact that the poem was first published as 'Genius—A Fragment' in the *Dublin and London Magazine* in 1826, it seems more likely that Mangan would have been about 22 when the poem was written (perhaps in 1825).

24   within the ... deep from Milton, *Paradise Lost* (IV, 76).

25   My heart ... it *Othello* (IV.i.178–9): 'No, my heart is turned to stone; I strike it, and it hurts my hand.'

26   Pelion ... Ossa the *Odyssey* refers to the tale of giants placing Mt Pelion on top of Mt Ossa in order to reach the heavens; hence the phrase means 'to increase the difficulty'.

27   my apprenticeship terminated Mangan left Kenrick's in 1825.

28   De profundis clamo! from Psalm 130: 'Out of the depths I cry.'

29   Mr Graham not identified.

30   bitter diet from vol. 1 of Byron's *Letters and Journals*, edited by Moore (1830): 'had I not done something at that time, I must have gone mad, by eating my own heart—bitter diet!'

31   the Iliad of woes originally from the second of Edmund Burke's *Three Letters Addressed to a Member of the Present Parliament on the Proposals for Peace, with the Regicide Directory of France* (1796–97): 'It opens another Iliad of woes to Europe.' *CW* (VI, 346) points out that Mangan may have encountered the phrase in Hazlitt or De Quincey.

32   Farewell the tranquil .. content! *Othello* (III.iii.354).

33   the elder ... elder adapted from 2 Corinthians 12:14.

34   a solicitor's office Matthew Frank's, at 28 Merrion Square.

35   written within ... woe Ezekiel 2:10: 'he spread it before me; and it was written within and without: and there was written therein lamentations, and mourning, and woe.'

36   nineteen in fact John was 25 at that point.

37   be-all and end-all *Macbeth* (I.vii.5).

38   moving accidents ... field *Othello* (I.iii.135).

39   Buffon Georges-Louis Leclerc, comte de Buffon (1707–88), French naturalist. The passage Mangan refers to has not been traced.

40   Cowper William Cowper (1731–1800), English poet. His poem 'The Castaway' is an expression of despair.

41   vessel of wrath ... destruction Romans 9:22.

42   Pandemonium the capital of Hell in Milton's *Paradise Lost*.

43   Farewell the tranquil ... Shaksp see note 32, above.

44   a house this house has not been identified with certainty, though Shannon-Mangan suggests two possibilities (107).

45   Pompeii and Herculaneum Roman cities destroyed by the eruption of Vesuvius in AD 79; the excavations of them began in the 18th century. Mangan published a poem on 'The Desolation of Pompeii' in *The Friend* (12 January 1830).

46   Palmyra ancient city in the Syrian desert.

47   Like Aladdin ... Garden from the tale of 'Aladdin and the Wonderful Lamp' in *Arabian Nights*.

48   Roundtown now called Terenure.

49   *Les Pensées de Pascal* famous work of Christian apologetics by Blaise Pascal, first published posthumously in 1670. Pascal took an innovative psychological approach to the problem of the human condition, acknowledging the experience of despair and doubt, and arguing that humanity is an 'incomprehensible monster, at once sovereign greatness and sovereign misery'.

50   **that passage ... execution** the passage is from Section III of the *Pensées*: 'Let us imagine a number of men in chains and all condemned to death, where some are killed each day in the sight of the others, and those who remain see their own fate in that of their fellows and wait their turn, looking at each other sorrowfully and without hope. It is an image of the condition of men' (Trotter translation). Mangan's footnote cites a passage from Voltaire's *Lettres philosophiques* (1734), which may be translated: 'To regard the world as a dungeon, and men as criminals awaiting execution, that is the idea of a fanatic.' The Byron quotation which follows this is from *Childe Harold* (III, xliii). The quotation about the leavening is from Galatians 5:9, and is also cited in Mangan's poem 'When Hearts Were Trumps'.

51   **Massillon** Jean-Baptiste Massillon (1663–1742), French bishop and writer. His sermons, published in 1745, include one entitled 'Sur le petit nombre des élus'.

[To Tynan, mid-1832]

Copy-text is MS 138. The letter was never sent, though a space is left for an address. The date is suggested by a reference to the Repeal agitation of January 1831, and by the use of phrases that also appear in Mangan's comic prose piece 'The Two Flats', published in the *Comet* on 3 June 1832. It has been suggested that the letter may be a literary exercise intended for publication rather than a personal letter (see Shannon-Mangan, 113).

1   **Tynan** probably James Tynan, who, like Mangan, published poems in the Dublin almanacs between 1819 and 1826, but whose identity remains obscure. John McCall believed that Mangan had himself occasionally used the name 'James Tynan' as a pseudonym in the almanancs (see Shannon-Mangan 44–6).

2   **a mortal ... kind** *Don Juan* (I, xix).

3   **Madame de Sevigne** Marie-de Rabutin-Chantal, marquise de Sévigné (1626–96); she wrote 1700 letters to her daughter over a seven-year period.

4   **Burgersdicius** Francis Burgerdyk (1590–1629), Dutch philosopher.

5   **A propros des bottes** 'to change the subject ...'

6   **Brutus** see *Julius Caesar* (III.ii.35).

7   **a saying of Talleyrand** the saying is attributed to Charles-Maurice de Talleyrand (1754–1838), French politician, among others.

8   **Washington Irving** (1783–1859); American prose writer. The quotation has not been traced.

9   **L'apostolique** a conservative and anti-revolutionary French paper which was published from 1829 to 1830.

10   **La Fayette** the marquis de La Fayette (1757–1834) had a long and varied political career, participating in the American and French Revolutions, and serving in the French chamber of deputies in the early nineteenth century. In July 1830 he commanded the national guard that helped overthrow French king Charles X and in favour of Louis-Philippe.

11   **Duke of Newcastle** Henry Pelham Clinton, 4th duke of Newcastle (1785–1851) was a stauch opponent of Catholic Emancipation; see *Letter of the Duke of Newcastle to Lord Kenyon on the Catholic Emancipation Question* (1828).

12   **O'Connell** Daniel O'Connell (1775–1847), whose campaign for Catholic emancipation was successful in 1829.

13   **le peuple souverain** 'the sovereign people'.

14   **Jefferson ... nature** Thomas Jefferson (1743–1826), 3rd president of the US; in a letter to the marquis de La Fayette in November 1823, he commented: 'The sickly, weakly, timid man, fears the people and is a tory by nature. The healthy, strong and bold, cherishes them, and is formed a whig by nature.'

15   **Helvetius** Claude-Adrien Helvétius (1715–71), French philosopher; his work *De l'esprit* (1758) was highly controversial for its attack on religious morality.

16   **Godwin** William Godwin (1756–1836); the drama is *Antonio* (1800).

17   **so middling . . . better** untraced.

18   **Prince in the Black Palace** see the 'Story of the Young King of the Black Isles' from the *Arabian Nights*.

19   **N'importe** 'it's no matter'.

20   **Byron** from *Beppo*, lxxiv.

21   **Daniel** see Daniel 11:31.

22   **Job nor Epitectus** the prophet Job, and the Greek stoic philosopher Epictetus (AD ?55–?135), both advocates of wise acceptance of divine will.

23   **Oh! That . . . book** adapted from Job 31: 35.

24   **Diogenes** Greek philosopher (fl. 300 BC), leading proponent of Cynic school of philosophy.

25   **Caliph Omar** Umar ibn al-Khattub (d. 644), second caliph (successor to Muhammad) had a reputation for asceticism.

26   **Mygasarus** reference untraced.

27   **the N.M.M.** the *New Monthly Magazine*, founded in London in 1821.

28   **Paternoster Row** a London street noted for its booksellers and publishers.

29   **what the wise . . . matter** from Essay VII in William Hazlitt's *Table-Talk*, vol. 2 (1822): 'Indeed, to be a great philosopher, in the practical and most important sense of the term, little more seems necessary than to be convinced of the truth of the maxim which the wise man repeated to the daughter of King Cophetua, *That if a thing is, it is,* and there is an end of it!'

30   **Pococurante** 'indifferent;' from the name of a character in Voltaire's satire *Candide* (1759).

31   **Pascal and the Port Royalists** the philosopher Blaise Pascal (1623–62) joined the Jansenist community at Port-Royal des Champs near Versailles in 1655.

32   **Retournons à nos moutons** 'to return to the subject'.

33   **Cherokee Tribe Gazette** no periodical with this title has been traced; however there was a weekly newspaper entitled *Cherokee Phoenix, and Indians' Advocate* published in New Echota, Georgia from 1829 to 1834. It is not known if Mangan had ever seen this paper.

34   **Almanac of Van Dæmon's Land** the *Van Diemen's Land Almanac* was published between 1831 and 1835.

35   **Moses Mendelsohn . . . problems** Moses Mendelssohn (1729–86), German Jewish philosopher. The first English biography was published in 1825 as *Memoirs of Moses Mendelsohn* [*sic*], and contained an anecdote which may have been Mangan's source: '[Mendelssohn] being once asked how he passed his time, answered that to drive away tedium, he counted the pantiles on the neighbouring houses.'

36   **drap de lit** a bedsheet.

37   **Cobbett** William Cobbett (1763–1835), English journalist and political campaigner.

38   **Hercules at the distaff** in punishment for killing his friend Iphitus, Hercules was condemned to become the slave of Queen Omphale for three years; he was forced to wear women's clothes and do women's work such as spinning, while Omphale wore his lion-skin and carried his club.

39   **[You must . . . Vaugelas]** the square brackets are in the original; the French may be translated: 'I am too lazy to speak correct grammar' (Vaugelas was a 17th-century French grammarian).

40   **true are not . . . true** from Essay XV in William Hazlitt's *Table-Talk*, vol. 1 (1821): 'Sheridan once said of some speech in his acute, sarcastic way, that "it contained a great deal

both of what was new and what was true: but that unfortunately what was new was not true, and what was true was not new".'

41   **Alcides** Hercules.

42   **le savoir vivre** 'good manners'.

43   **Huygens** Christiaan Huygens (1629–95), Dutch astronomer.

44   **Herschel** William Herschel (1738–1822) British astronomer.

45   **an admirable Creichton** see note 50 to *A Treatise on a Pair of Tongs*, p. 488 above.

46   **Lucus a non lucendo** a phrase meaning 'an etymological contradiction', from the fourth-century Roman grammarian Servius Honoratus Maurus. Hazlitt also uses it in his essay on Thomas Moore in *Political Essays, with Sketches of Public Characters* (1822).

47   **Hazlitt's character of Cobbett** see Essay VI of Hazlitt's *Table Talk*, vol. 1 (1821).

48   **Religion, love . . . know** from Alexander Pope's 'Essay on Man' (I, 17–18): 'Say first, of God above, or Man below, / What can we reason, but from what we know.'

49   **Newgate** name of a prison located at that time in Green Street, Dublin.

50   **a New View of Society** title of a pamphlet (1813) by utopian reformer Robert Owen (1771–1858).

51   **Pour couper court** 'to keep it short'.

52   **Ximenes** Francisco Jiménez de Cisneros (1436–1517), Spanish cardinal and politician.

53   **Richelieu** Armand Jean du Plessis de Richelieu (1585–1642), French cardinal and politician.

54   **an 'ego' as Kant has it**   the concept of the 'transcendental ego' as an a priori source of knowledge is central to the epistemology of Immanuel Kant (1724–1804); Mangan is not using the term in its true Kantian sense.

55   **Paracelsus** Theophrastus Bombastus von Hohenheim, known as Paracelsus (1493–1541), Swiss alchemist.

56   **Bentham in his Book of Fallacies** Utilitarian philosopher Jeremy Bentham (1748–1832) published his *Book of Fallacies* in 1824.

57   **Kircher** Athanasius Kircher (1601–1680), Jesuit scholar and scientist.

58   **Spinoza** Baruch Spinoza (1632–1677), Dutch philosopher.

59   **Tom Moore . . . ages back** see Moore, *Rhymes on the Road* (VI, 37–8): 'Desolate Venice, when I track / Thy haughty course through cent'ries back.'

60   **Dr Bowring . . . 1823** Sir John Bowring (1792–1872), English linguist and translator, and editor of the *Westminster Review* from its foundation in 1824. A review of Moore's *Rhymes on the Road* appeared in the *Westminster Review* in January 1824, containing an extended version of this passage, though it was not written by Bowring.

61   **Mezentius** see Vergil's *Aeneid*, Book VIII; Mezentius was king of the Etruscans.

62   **the rest . . . prunella** Alexander Pope, 'Essay on Man' (IV, 204).

63   **Père Enfantin** Barthélemy Prosper Enfantin (1796–1864), French reformer, a leading member of the St. Simonian movement.

64   **St Simon . . . periods** Claude Henri de Rouvroy, comte de Saint-Simon (1760–1825), influential theorist of Christian socialism. Saint-Simon suggested that the histories of societies could be divided into two alternating periods, the socially coherent 'organic', and the conflict-ridden 'critical'.

65   **Robert Owen** see note 37 to *A Treatise on a Pair of Tongs*, p. 488, above.

66   **Algiers** the main base of the Barbary pirates from the sixteenth century until it was captured by the French in 1830.

67   **La Revolution** name of a French newspaper (*La Révolution*) that ran from July 1830 to October 1832.

68   **La France Nouvelle** name of a French periodical that ran from June 1829 to June 1833.

69   **la petite semaine** refers to the three-day revolution (27–29 July 1830), as a result of which Louis-Philippe replaced Charles X on the French throne.

70   **Louis XI** king of France (1461–83).

71   **pantoufles** slippers.

72   **Charles VII** king of France (1429–61).

73   **beau-ideal** the perfect type.

74   **Soame Jenyns . . . Volition** see the essay 'On Government and Civil Liberty' in *Disquisitions on Several Subjects* (1782) by the English writer Soame Jenyns (1704–87).

75   **March of Intellect . . . April** this joke is also used in 'An Extraordinary Adventure in the Shades', p. 367, above.

76   **Sans rire** 'seriously'.

77   **de plus** 'more'.

78   **When men . . . glass** these lines (with the alteration of the first four words to 'When men behold old') were used as the final lines of Mangan's poem 'Verses to a Friend, on His Playing a Particular Melody which Excited the Author to Tears' (*Comet*, 27 January 1833) and used again in the *DUM* (January 1839); see p. 79, above.

79   **Peresse l'univers . . . principe!** 'may the world perish rather than a single principle!' This appears to combine two different quotations, one from Cyrano de Bergerac and the other from a declaration of the French Assembly in 1791; see *CW* (VI, 353).

80   **the tax-eaters . . . France** the July 1830 Revolution in France resulted in a retention of the monarchy.

81   **a year and a half ago** on 3 January 1831, there was a pro-Repeal meeting in Dublin attended by up to 5000 people. Mangan's name appears as a signatory to a press notice calling on Dublin Law Clerks to attend the meeting (*Morning Register*, 1 January 1831).

82   **waiters-of-inns . . . legislators** see 'The Monkey-Martyr, a Fable' by Thomas Hood (1799–1845): 'Waiters of inn sublimed to innovators, / And slaters dignified as legislators'.

83   **That which . . . thoughtful** see *Macbeth* (II.ii.1): 'That which hath made them drunk hath made me bold.'

84   **de mal . . . amis** 'from bad to worse, my friends'.

85   **O'er Notre Dame . . . slaves** quotation untraced.

86   **Bowring** in August 1830 John Bowring wrote an address from the citizens of London to the people of France congratulating them on the July Revolution.

87   **Sous le tri-colore, nous** quotation untraced.

88   **Spurzheim** Johan Christoph Spurzheim (1776–1829), a famous phrenologist.

89   **je ne sais quoi** 'I know not what'.

90   **Catholic Association** founded by Daniel O'Connell in 1823; it campaigned successfully for Catholic Emancipation, achieved in 1829.

91   **Aide-toi, le ciel l'aidera** the name of a French political society active in the July Revolution of 1830.

[To Charles Gavan Duffy, 1840 or 1841]

Copy-text is MS 138. The reference to the *Vindicator* newspaper suggests a date of 1840; Mangan published five contributions to the paper between May and September 1840 and one further one in March 1841.

1   **Charles Gavan Duffy** (1816–1903), Young Ireland leader, editor of the Belfast *Vindicator* (1839–42) and the *Nation* (1842–48) and friend of Mangan from the late 1830s.

2   **Hear me for my caws** see *Julius Caesa*r (III.i.13): 'Hear me for my cause.'

3   **camae** *CW* (VI, 356) suggests this may be a misspelling of the word *came*, a name for a half rupee used in parts of India in the 19th century.

4   **Peel** plays on the name of Robert Peel, British conservative politician who began his second term as prime minister in 1841.

5   **Palmerston** Henry John Temple, viscount Palmerston (1784–1865), British foreign secretary (1830–34, 1835–41).

6   **The Poker** a persona used by Mangan in his three 'Editor's Room' articles in the *Vindicator* in 1840.

7   **Westmeath** George Thomas John, marquess of Westmeath (1785–1871), M.P. The quotation is untraced.

8   **Bulwer** Edward Bulwer-Lytton (1803–73), British politician, poet, critic, and novelist.

9   **Who would . . . he?** Alexander Pope, 'Epistle to Dr Arbuthnot' (1735), ll. 213–14: 'Who but must laugh, if such a man there be? / Who would not weep, if Atticus were he!'

10   **Morning Herald** a conservative London daily.

11   **Vindicator** twice-weekly Belfast nationalist paper edited by Charles Gavan Duffy between 1839 and 1842.

12   **Lex non talis** 'the law is not thus'.

13   **Registers** plays on the *Morning Register*, a pro-O'Connellite Dublin daily paper that ran from 1824–42.

14   **Spectators** plays on the title of conservative English weekly review, founded in 1828.

15   **Mens tuus . . . Eye!** a pun based on a literal translation of the individual Latin words.

[To Charles Gavan Duffy, 21 July 1847]
Copy-text is MS 138. Mangan appears to have spent about six weeks with his mother's family who owned a farm in Kiltale, Co. Meath. The visit is the only documented journey Mangan ever made.

1   **Richard Savage** (?1697–1743), impecunious English poet and satirist who died in a debtor's prison. He was the subject of a famous biography by Samuel Johnson, *An Account of the Life of Mr Richard Savage* (1744).

2   **Michl Smyth** Mangan's cousin Michael Smith was a successful butcher in Copper Alley, near Mangan's birthplace in Fishamble St in Dublin.

3   **maravedi** Spanish name for a variety of Arab gold coin.

[To Charles Gavan Duffy, 1847 or 1848]
Copy-text is MS 138; the MS is torn and incomplete. O'Donoghue's published version of the letter (204–5) includes the salutation and the sentence beginning 'Regard this . . .', neither of which is part of the existing MS. *CW* gives a date of 'Summer? 1847' (VI, 362) while O'Donoghue dates the letter early 1848.

Mr. Mangan to the Editor of the United Irishman
1   **the Editor of the United Irishman** John Mitchel (1815–75) broke with Gavan Duffy and the *Nation* in early 1848 and established the more radical weekly *United Irishman*. Mangan too cut his ties with the *Nation* and published three poems in Mitchel's paper between February 1848 and its suppression in May 1848. Mitchel was sentenced in June 1848 to fourteen years transportation for 'treason-felony'. The promised 'long letter' to Mitchel appears never to have been written.

2　　**Devin Reilly** Thomas Devin Reilly (1824–54), co-editor of the *United Irishman*. Under threat of arrest, he escaped to the United States in autumn of 1848 and worked as a journalist there until his early death.

[To James Hardiman, 7 December 1848]
Copy-text is MS 12/N/20 (RIA). This is Mangan's last surviving letter.
1　　**James Hardiman** (1782–1855), scholar and collector, appointed first librarian of Queen's College Galway in 1848. His *Irish Minstrelsy* (1831) was an important resource for Mangan. Mangan had written to Hardiman on 4 December requesting a loan of £1 to enable him to pay the rent on his lodgings. Mangan's residence at 151 Abbey St seems to have been relatively brief (see Shannon-Mangan, 410).
2　　**Poor-laws** through the 1830s O'Connell opposed Poor Law legislation for Ireland on the basis that it would undermine the traditional forms of charity, and also threaten property values. In 1837 however he supported Peel's introduction of the Irish poor relief bill for political reasons.
3　　**the Pope** to escape the revolutionary political situation in Rome in November 1848, Pope Pius IX fled incognito to the kingdom of Naples. He did not return to Rome until April 1850.
4　　**St. Jerome** (?347–420); his letters lament the devastation of Rome before and after its sacking by Alaric in 410.

Emendations to Copy-Texts

Copy-text reading is given after the brackets.

The Philosopher and the Child
9   sire] tire

Mignon's Song
16   follows.] follows

Literæ Orientales—No. I
title   No. I] First Article
p. 57   alone.'] alone.

Literæ Orientales—No. II
title   No. II] Second Article
p. 67   new materials] no materials

Literæ Orientales—No. III
title   No. III] Third Article

Alexander and the Tree
72   lot.] lot.'
73   'In] In

The Editor's Room—Second Conclave
p. 96   Popangoön Tutchemupp] Popangoön, Tutchemupp
p. 96   My dear Klaapptraapp,] My dear Klaapptrapp

Literæ Orientales—No. V
title   No. V] Fifth Article

The Death of Hofer
38   Farewell] 'Farewell

Eighteen Hundred Fifty
p. 167   'He could] He could

The Ruby Mug
13   'My] My
41   'Sire!'] 'Sire!
52   magic'] magic
67   guess] guest
78   you see,] you, see,
178   Rashed] Kashed

Khidder
114   Trees.'] Trees.

['The night is falling']
3   mountain's] mountains

To the Ruins of Donegal Castle
128   Tirconnellians'] Tirconnelian's

To the Ingleezee Khafir, Calling Himself Djaun Bool Djenkinzun
27, note 6 *Gadar*] *Gadan*

An Invitation
23   dædal] dœdal

The Lass of Carrick
headnote   ours] our's
55   morrow.] morrow

Song of the Albanian
50   khanjder] khanjder* [*but no corresponding footnote for the asterisk is provided*]

Testament of Cathaeir Mor
title   Mor] Mor* [*but no corresponding footnote for the asterisk is provided*]

Rights of Property
headnote   (There ... specimen:—)] (there ... specimen:—
12   property?] property?'

A Voice of Encouragement
33   despairing?] despairing!
stanzas 8 and 9 are misnumbered in copy-text

from *Lays of Many Lands—No. VII*
title   VII] Copy-text is erroneously numbered VI

Vision of Egan O'Reilly
44   cry,] cry.
68   of] o

A Word in Reply to Joseph Brenan
44   Unto] Unto to

Andrew Magrath's Reply to John O'Tuomy
17   shorter;] shorter

The Geraldine's Daughter
3   is] are

Edmund of the Hill
37   'My] My

from *The Tribes of Ireland*
VII   butter!] butter
XXV   Clan-Rickard.] Clan-Rickard
XXXI   horn-firkin.] horn-firkin
XLV   leather.] leather
LXXXIV   sawing.] sawing
LXXXVIII   raiment.] raiment
XCII   out!'] out!

An Extraordinary Adventure in the Shades
p. 369   an idiosyncracy] and iiosyncracy
p. 372   humbugged?] humbugged

A Treatise on a Pair of Tongs
p. 379   *residuum*] *residnum*
p. 384   I. *(yawning*] I *(yawning*
p. 384   Ein] Erin

My Bugle and How I Blow It
p. 388   Bah!'] Bah!
p. 388   'you] you

from *'Sketches and Reminiscences of Irish Writers' series*
p. 414   shadowless] shawdowless
p. 414   abroad.'] abroad.

Autobiography
p. 423   deep.'] deep.
p. 430   'on] on
p. 430   Saved"?'] Saved'?

[To Tynan, mid-1832]
p. 434   II:] II
p. 436   'If] If

Index of Titles of Poems

Index of First Lines